D0579097

IN THE HOUSE OF MY FEAR

Also by Joel Agee

Twelve Years: An American Boyhood in East Germany

TRANSLATIONS

Twelve Years (into German)

Poff the Cat, by Hartmut von Hentig

The Ballad of Typhoid Mary, by J. F. Federspiel

Letters on Cézanne, by Rainer Maria Rilke

Essays on German Theater

Rilke and Benvenuta: An Intimate Correspondence

Essays of Gottfried Benn in *Gottfried Benn: Prose, Essays, Poems*

The Assignment, by Friedrich Dürrenmatt

7000 Days in Siberia, by Karlo Stajner

The Secret Heart of the Clock, by Elias Canetti

Burned Child Seeks the Fire, by Cordelia Edvardson

Penthesilea, by Heinrich von Kleist

The End: Hamburg 1943, by Hans Erich Nossack

IN THE HOUSE
OF MY FEAR

JOEL AGEE

SHOEMAKER & HOARD, *Publishers*

WASHINGTON, DC

This is a work of memory and imagination. It cannot be relied on as a record of
fact. The method is storytelling, not historiography; portraiture, not reportage.
Throughout, and in every sentence, I have aimed to be true in one special sense
only: that of an arrow that flies to its mark.

Portions of this book first appeared in *Harper's, Esquire, DoubleTake,* and
Archipelago.org.

Library of Congress Cataloging-in-Publication Data
Agee, Joel.
    In the house of my fear / Joel Agee.
        p. cm.
        1.Agee, Joel—Travel. 2. Americans—Foreign countries—Biography. 3. Spiritual
    biography—United States. 4. Mentally ill—United States—Biography. I. Title.
    ISBN 1-59376-045-0
    CT275.A444A3 2004
    909'.04130825'092—dc22
2004011913

Text design by Amy Evans McClure
Printed in the United States of America

 Shoemaker & Hoard, Publishers
www.shoemakerhoard.com
A Division of Avalon Publishing Group Inc.
Distributed by Publishers Group West

10   9   8   7   6   5   4   3   2   1

To Susan

Contents

IN THE HOUSE OF MY FEAR

PART 1

A man, a poet, is told in a dream: "To leave, you must build the gate you came through." An arduous task, but not beyond his capacity. Then he discovers that building the gate was just the beginning. He must create the monster who guards the threshold. Out of what? Out of fear. But how does one work such fugitive material into the denser substance of language? Fear does not speak: it drives the word back to its panic origins: the gasp, the scream; and at its most acute and eloquent pitch, it silences utterance altogether and forces the mind to spell out the secret signs of an irremediable and growing torment. Until grace comes and wipes the slate clean. In that crucial moment between the curse and the miracle, where is there room for a single word? Not even "I" can set foot there to hold up its halo. Its one small, clawed foot.

German Lessons

Wo gehen wir denn hin? Immer nach Hause.
Where are we going? Always homeward.
　　　　　　　　　　　　　　　　　—*Novalis*

There is a German word, a feminine noun, that denotes like no other the welcoming warmth and sheltering intimacy of an origin to which one can return: *Heimat.* Strangely, it has no English equivalent. "Home" comes close—its German cognate, *Heim,* actually forms the root of *Heimat*—but it is too narrow, it usually means an apartment or house. The "land" in "homeland" makes the image more ample, but too geographic. What the German word means is, simply, the place where one feels at home, and that home need not have political or even physical boundaries. When Elias Canetti, a Sephardic Jew who was born in Bulgaria, studied in Zurich, lived in London, and wrote in German, was asked what he considered his *Heimat,* his reply was: "The German language."

I want to take this word, this concept, *Heimat,* and hold it like a divining rod over the shifting terrain I happen to be traversing—my life at the moment, which includes the deepening strata of the past and the shrouded outlines of what will be, and the mists of what is only possible—and with this magical aid seek out what living waters there may be of evidence or memory concerning the secret, perhaps unnamable conditions, the climate, the language, if any, the laws, under which this human being comes to feel at home in the world, as well as those plain and patent conditions under which he knows himself to be exiled. And already I feel a tug, resolutely away from the present and back toward the past.

I was born in New York City in 1940. When I was a year old, my American mother left my American father and took me to Mexico. There she married a German expatriate who became, in every sense of the word but the biological, my father. We stayed in Mexico for seven years. In the course of that time, I learned to speak Spanish better than my parents, better than I spoke English.

I played with Mexican children in Mexican schools. A Mexican maid, Zita, loved and scolded me like a second mother. I thought of myself as Mexican. Nevertheless, I knew I was a foreigner. No one deliberately made me feel that, but I sensed it. I wanted to be like the others. I wanted to sing those proud Mexican songs as if they were about me: *"Soy Mexicano del Norte!"* It seemed to me that talking like a native should be enough to make you the same, but it wasn't. I asked—insisted—on having my hair shorn to make me resemble Mexican street children. It didn't work: The bald head made me a *pelón.* Why didn't they call bald Mexican children *pelónes?* Because a bald Mexican child is Mexican, but a bald gringo is ridiculous. I put on a big sombrero. That covered up the baldness, but it didn't make me Mexican.

When I was eight, my parents took me and my two-year-old brother to the part of Germany that a year later became the Deutsche Demokratische Republik, DDR for short. The German kids didn't call me a gringo. They called me an Ami. How to become German? Obviously, I had to learn the language, but would that be enough—since it hadn't been in Mexico? It was enough. *Zum Glück!*

Glück is another German word without an exact English equal. Sometimes it means "luck," sometimes "happiness," but there is a third meaning that combines the first two—outer good fortune, inner felicity—and for this plenary good we have no single word. Of course there may not exist in reality such a thing as *Glück* in the hermetic sense suggested by that fluting ü embowered among consonants; but it exists in the mind—vaguely where the world utters itself in English, and rather tangibly in German, where that old word, *Glück,* stands waiting like a cage for the soul that would lose itself in it and sing. Beautiful poems have been made of this word, sublime music from the painful joy it encloses.

But I was speaking of *Heimat,* which could be defined as the province of *Glück*—its source in memory, its goal in longing—and my happy discovery, as a newly arrived immigrant, that in Germany, unlike Mexico, I could be released from the exile of foreignness simply by learning the language.

It really was simple. A tutor apprenticed me in the fundamentals of syntax and vocabulary, and two or three boys in my village grade school offered themselves as guides to the subtler refinements of pronunciation. But the real teacher was the fluid, breathing, intelligent life of language itself, and the student so swiftly taking increasingly difficult degrees of initiation, all the way up to the heights of poetry, all the way in to the arcane wit of dialect, was not the boy trying to memorize his conjugation tables but a miraculously responsive nervous system alerted by day and by night to the challenge of optimal adaptation: How to fit in, how to be the same as the others, not myself the other, no longer different.

The State, of whose existence I could have no notion yet, had interests remarkably consonant with mine. Through my school I was offered a virtual certificate of sameness, a blue neckerchief, identical in cut and color with dozens of other blue neckerchiefs worn by children in the village. That was the insigne of the Young Pioneers. Learning to tie the knot was an initiation in itself. And with the honor of membership came a set of statutes that called us—Us! No more lonely I: Us!—to high moral duty: Young Pioneers are *examples* (of maturity, comportment, studiousness, etc.) to other children; Young Pioneers are *hilfsbereit,* ready to help where help is needed. Not *should be,* but *are.* Virtue conferred by the sacred act of induction (a vow? Probably, I don't remember), and repossessed anytime you desired by the magical act of knotting your blue neckerchief in front of a mirror.

It is no different with collective identity than with the personal ego: Sooner or later you meet with the other, the "We" that is not your own. There were children in the village—the majority, in those early years—who did not join the Young Pioneers. I don't remember any outright animosity, but a difference was noticeable, particularly in the matter of virtue. Young Pioneers don't crack jokes behind the teacher's back. Young Pioneers don't paint obscene symbols on walls. Young Pioneers don't shoot stones with a slingshot. Young Pioneers don't have a whole lot of fun. I realized that after a while.

Those were the infant days of the Cold War, when the borders were open and lightly patrolled. The solution was simple: Blur the boundary, have it both ways. Lend those tough kids from across the lake your *Pionierhalstuch* for a face mask in a game of cops and robbers; then wear it to school, feel the thrill of virtue as you salute the rising flag, thumb-tip to forehead, while the national anthem swells your chest beneath the neckerchief's long, slightly smudged, blue ears. How good to be part of a "We," any "We," how painful to be excluded from it. Let "We" span the village, the country, the world! Sometimes, listening to Mozart or Bach, or at Christmas, the idea of limitless, haptic communion with all living beings seemed not just possible but imminent, almost real. I remember coming out of a performance of *The Marriage of Figaro* in Berlin and sustaining the fantasy, for a half hour or so, that if people—all people—really sang their emotions like those characters on the stage, the result would be an enormous chorus in which even the cruelest conflicts would be resolved in harmony.

Once again the State saw eye to eye with my desire. It, too, had a vision of global communion, and this wasn't a dream, but a scientific prediction—so scientific it couldn't be doubted. Sometime in the not too distant future there would be a world without strangers, all mankind working together—yes, working, not playing—in peace and amity, united at last under the banner of communism. Until then, though, the world would be sternly divided, not by custom, as Schiller put it in his "Ode to Joy," but by grim necessity. All the socialist countries with their wise, humane leaders were threatened without and within. Invisible enemies lived in our midst—Nazis, imperialists, saboteurs and wreckers, spies, bearers of false tales—hired by the West and intent on destroying the hope of humanity, while outside our borders stood armies with rockets and atom bombs poised against us. Only the utmost vigilance could preserve the peace. Fortunately our soldiers and politicians took care of this tough job, leaving us children to the manageable task of being responsibly cheerful, decoratively young—a political function, if the newsreels were any indication—and eventually growing into self-sacrificing defenders of the cause.

With the passage from grade school to high school came another graduation: from the Young Pioneers to their adolescent counterpart, the Free German Youth. I am holding in my hand a document of my condition at that time, more telling than any memory. It is my *Personalausweis,* the identity book every East German citizen was obliged to carry on his person at all times. The first thing that strikes the eye as one opens the small, dark blue book is a personal message from the State to the bearer:

"Citizen of the German Democratic Republic:
this identity book is your most important document."

There follows a four-point list of instructions concerning its use and misuse. On the inside of the first page, in the upper left corner, is a photograph of my face taken in quarter profile a month after my fifteenth birthday. The two circular metal staples employed to clamp the picture to the page also punched round holes through the paper, like oversized bullets or small cannonballs, one through my right collarbone and another grazing my forehead. The upper rim of the seal of the Potsdam District Police raises the letters CHE VOLKS from my left shoulder, and another seal, or possibly the lower rim of the same, marks the back of my head with the characters 1S3, also in high relief. A rectangular stamp, violet, sidles up to the edge of my face to declare me "Valid for 10 years." My lips, near the sharp lower corner of the stamp, are set in a manner that an American friend generously interprets as "defiant": Actually I was pushing forward my lower jaw to counteract the effect of what I considered a weak chin. Defiance can be justly attributed only to a tuft of hair over my right ear that refused to be flattened down with water. The eyes are set on nothing at all, unless it's the opposite page, where my "surname at birth" is neatly spelled out in black ink: *Uhse*. Not true. Besides, my stepfather, Bodo Uhse, had never formally adopted me. And my nationality: *Deutsch*—also not true. By the letter of the law, I should have been registered as a foreigner and given a corresponding document, but my parents asked a highly placed friend to make a semilegal arrangement on my behalf—to spare me the pain of exclusion, to help me to feel at home.

Stamped on all sides with false legitimations, this face looks sad, guilty, obedient, and absent, a juvenile Adam expelled from the garden. How did it happen? He never even noticed the snake. And no Eve in sight. What was that taste in his mouth? A word, "we." All the new songs had that word in them, none of them had the word "I." He sang them for the love of singing, for the sake of belonging: *"Weil wir jung sind, ist die Welt so schön!"* Imagine singing a song like that, thirty or forty voices strong: "Because we are young, the world is so beautiful!" Because. We. He was lost.

Five years later, my parents divorced, and my mother obtained for me through the American embassy in West Berlin and with the help of an American lawyer a passport that identified me correctly by my true patronymic and my rightful nationality. This was a very nice ticket to have, it promised swift passage from a messy pattern of officially recorded failure in one *Heimat* (I was a terrible student) to a perfectly clean slate in another. Amazing privilege! This is what certain gangsters receive in exchange for their testimony against the mob: a little plastic surgery, a wrecked existence swapped for a fictive whole one, a move to some palm-fronded spot where no one knows you, in short, a new destiny and a new self. If only things were that simple.

Somewhere in the archives of the Stasi, the infamous East German secret police, there must still exist a record of the arrest and interrogation of a young man, sometime in the spring of '63, who presented himself to the border authorities at Checkpoint Charlie with two documents of identity, one made out in Potsdam to Joel Uhse, the other in New York to Joel Agee. The suspect's bizarre explanation, first to the guards at Checkpoint Charlie, then, after a grim silent car ride through darkening streets, to professional interrogators at Stasi headquarters—that he was not and had never been a citizen of the DDR, though his *Personalausweis* identified him as such; that the *Personalausweis* was in fact a fraudulent document produced for his convenience and comfort by the DDR government; that he was and had always been an American citizen and had left the DDR with its government's blessings; that he was a filmmaker on his way from New York to the Leipzig film festival; that his motive in showing the border authorities his spurious *Personalausweis* was simply fear of their finding it on him if he *didn't* show it; that his purpose in bringing it at all was to identify himself to DEFA, the East German film company, as the stepson of the recently deceased winner of the national prize for literature, Bodo Uhse, so that they would equip and finance a film he, the suspect, intended to make about carnival season in the Cuban province of Oriente—all these avowals and sincere protestations only served to heighten his captors' suspicion.

"What agency do you work for?"

"I'm not a spy. If you call Alexander Abusch, the former Minister of Culture, he'll vouch for me, he's known me since I was a child."

"Who sent you?"

"No one sent me. Why don't you call Alexander Abusch?"

"Because we're not stupid."

"Why would a spy show up at your border with two IDs?"

"That's what we're trying to find out."

Two men took turns stirring this thick little dialogue until there was neither spice nor substance left in it. They stared at me with the desperation of boredom and perhaps the first glimmers of hatred. As for me, I was full of goodwill toward them. I wasn't worried. We were all socialists here, sharers in a common truth. To pass the time, I observed them for future reference in my journal. There wasn't much to record. They smoked a lot. They wore gray suits. One of them was bald, the other wore two-toned shoes. Above them hung a picture of Walter Ulbricht with an omniscient smile. By the window stood a shelf bearing law books and volumes of Marx, Engels, and Lenin.

"Who are you?"

That question took me aback.

"You can't be both these people."

"I'm not. I'm one person. And these are, I mean . . . they're passports. One person, two passports."

I thought I was being helpful. They didn't think so. They looked angry. I pulled myself together, resolved to cooperate in every way.

■

I remember dreams from that period, nightmares in which I shuttled from one country and language to another, often in a train patrolled by suspicious soldiers. These dreams always ended in my being asked for my papers and not finding them or inadvertently showing the wrong one that made me guilty. Many years later I learned that this is the prototypical dream of exiles, immigrants, and prisoners, and not just prisoners but also released or escaped convicts. The dreamer's position, inside or outside the barrier, seems to make little difference to the psyche as long as the barrier is there. The psyche wants wholeness, not in- or outsideness, and that's why her notions of freedom are different from those of the ego. More particularly, though, my dream was the prototypical East German dream. Here is one example: An old school friend in East Berlin told me in the late seventies that he had a recurring nightmare in which he found himself strolling on Kurfürstendamm, gazing at shop windows and pretty girls, and suddenly realizing that he had to get back to the other side of the Wall within minutes, or else be found guilty of treason. He runs to the East, but there is the Wall, solid and gateless, the guards in their turrets have already spotted him, the minutes are advancing, he is trapped in the free world when the law, the law of the soul, of the whole dream, says: Get back to the place of your bondage or be exiled forever.

■

A couple of hours later, my stomach began to grumble, and the bald man introduced a startling new theme.

"Are you hungry?"

"Yes."

"Do you like blood sausage?"

"I've never tried it."

The bald man opened a sandwich tin and handed me half of his sandwich. I took a bite.

"Not here," the man with the two-toned shoes said sternly. "Out the door, turn left, sit down on the bench at the end of the corridor. Wait there till we call you."

Viewed from the bench where I sat with my sandwich, the corridor proclaimed all the laws of rectilinear perspective: two rows of receding and converging doors right and left, one row of receding and converging bright neon tubes on the ceiling. Viewed from the brightly lit hallway, on the other hand, my chewing self on the bench was shrouded in darkness, for the two ceiling lights nearest me didn't work. This position afforded me the unique point of view of an unseen observer at Stasi headquarters.

I cite from my notes of the following day:

> Telephones ringing, muffled voices, silence. A door opens, I stop chewing. A man in a green suit steps out, says something over his shoulder, closes the door, takes a few steps in my direction, stops, shakes his head, looks around surreptitiously, takes a notebook out of his breast pocket, scribbles something in it, puts the pen and notebook back in his breast pocket, walks on, stops in front of a room just ten meters away from me, puts his ear to the door, hesitates, knocks.
>
> *"Herein!"*
>
> The man in the green suit steps in, closes the door behind him.
>
> More ringing telephones, mumbling voices, silence. Echoing shouts and the tramping of feet in the stairwell at the far end of the corridor. Four soldiers appear, hustling along a young man whose hands are cuffed behind his back. They shove him into the last room on my right, lock the door, and go back downstairs, laughing.
>
> Quiet. Telephones, mumbling voices. A familiar door opens. It is the man in the green suit. He walks down the corridor with a jaunty stride, jangling a bunch of keys in his hand, opens the room where the prisoner is, closes the door behind him. A moment later, a short, piercing scream. The door opens, the man in the green suit reappears. He locks the door, puts the keys in his pocket, walks back in my direction, adjusts the fit of his jacket with an athlete's rolling shrug, scrolls the fingers of his right hand in the air, and returns to the office from which he emerged.

And now it is time to introduce another German word: *Schlüsselerlebnis.* "Key experience" is the best possible translation. It sounds dryly analytical, but in German, the compounding of the two words charges them with the potency of a seed, or a bomb. The idle heiress robbed of her purse, begging for carfare, and spurned by the hard-working poor; the devout Christian learning that some venerable relic was manufactured in Taiwan; the young child who sees his parents in a grunting, moaning heap on their bed—each of these has had a *Schlüsselerlebnis.*   •

■

(I hear my soul-critic's voice protesting, the familiar voice of a contentious reader who knows German as well as I do:

"A scream in the secret police headquarters—if this is a Schlüsselerlebnis, so is my ingrown toenail. It may be unpleasant, but surely not out of the ordinary."

You don't know what faith is, my quarrelsome friend. Faith and loyalty.

"To what? To whom?"

To the man in whose name I had lived for twelve years of my life, and whose grave I had come to visit, my stepfather, Bodo, who wanted his children to be among those who inherit the kingdom of heaven on earth.

"You didn't tell that to the border guards."

It was none of their business. That was between me and Bodo. As I said, I was loyal to him.

"To him and his folly."

His folly, yes. His foolish, generous faith in the perfectibility of man by political arrangement. And that was why I was shocked by the sound of a scream in an East German secret police station.)

■

I must have sat there for another half hour. I was scared. I had come home through the cellar door and discovered a foul-smelling basement I never knew existed. There were rats in there, snakes. But no animal behaves like this. What should I call them: fascists? Fascists don't read Marx and Lenin. Whatever they were, I no longer felt safe in their company.

At last the man with the two-toned shoes came out to conduct me to my next interrogator, a stocky young man with blond hair and an ironic, not unfriendly expression in his eyes. He asked me to sit down on a chair facing his desk. The man with the two-toned shoes handed him my passports and several typewritten sheets of paper and left the room. The blond man quickly perused the report, compared my face with the two passport pictures, reread the report, shook his head with a snort of derision—was it at me or his colleagues?—and raised his eyes.

"Herr Uhse, Mr. Agee—which should I call you?"

"Agee."

"Pleased to meet you. Geiring."

We shook hands across his desk.

"You want to make a film?"

"Yes. In Cuba."

"You want help from DEFA?"

"Yes, I need it."

"You think they will be interested?"

"I hope so."

"In Carnival?"

"In Cuba."

"Let's say we help you. What would you give us in return?"

"A good film."

"That's not enough."

"A good *socialist* film."

"Films are expensive. This isn't Hollywood, we're talking about a state budget. Money is needed to mend roads, build factories, train teachers. Socialism is not a carnival."

"I know."

"If you did something of genuine, material value for us, we might support your Cuban project. In fact, I can guarantee that."

"What are you thinking of?"

"A show of loyalty. We would ask you to live in West Germany for, say, a few months. You would make contact with certain people there—young, progressive people like yourself—and supply us with regular reports about their activities. We would pay you, naturally—quite well, I might add. You would have a nice apartment."

"That's very interesting," I said. "It's a generous offer. I will think about it. But right now . . . I can't make such a big decision just like that."

"I understand," he said.

"I need time to think, and I'm tired. I need some sleep."

"Of course."

"May I go now?"

"I'll take you to a hotel."

"I already have a hotel."

"Where?"

"On Kurfürstendamm."

He smiled: "No good. We're not finished yet."

"What's lacking?"

"An answer to my proposal, for one. Yes or no? It doesn't have to be now. You can sleep on it."

"Where?"

"I'll find you a room."

He was overestimating his power. Not even a Stasi officer could procure a vacant hotel room in East Berlin, not after midnight and not on the spur of the moment. After five or six tries, Geiring gave up and drove me to the home of an aunt in the country—a picture-book house behind a white lattice fence where a picture-book proletarian couple greeted me with smiles and bows as if a prince had come to honor their dwelling:

"From so far away—America! Can we offer you anything? I'm afraid we don't have much. . . ."

"No, thank you, I just need some sleep."

They guided me upstairs. Geiring waved an ironic bye-bye from below. The guest room: a fat feather blanket on a short bed, flying geese on the wall, lacy curtains, dried flowers in a bowl on the night table.

"Good night."

"Good night."

"If you need anything, just knock."

"Thank you very much."

"You're welcome."

A key turned in the lock.

The first thing I heard after falling asleep was the sound of that key turning in the door again, and a knock. It was Geiring: "Lunch is ready." A light rain was tapping on the tin windowsill. I felt angry, and the thought of my meekness the previous day made me madder. Yes, meekness, not patience—subservient, cowardly meekness. A real DDR-*Untertan* I'd been.[1] Today I would thump the table. Today I would demand my American passport back, yes indeed, and tell them where to deposit the other one.

Geiring, his aunt, and her husband were awaiting me at a festively set table: roast duck, mashed potatoes, sauerkraut, three kinds of vegetables, Soviet champagne.

"To a happy homecoming," Geiring said, lifting his glass. What was this? Flattery? Apology? Seduction? I sat down and joined in the toast. The old couple beamed at me with obsequious malice. The old man in particular sucked his champagne through fluted lips and drank me in with his eyes. Evidently Geiring had told them a few things about me. A familiar of Abusch, and a prisoner in their house! What a day, what a day!

"May I ask you a personal question?" Geiring asked.

"You mean yesterday's questions weren't personal?"

"They were analytical. This one is personal."

I gave him a nod for permission.

---

1. *Untertan:* "Subject," "vassal," "underling." But to catch the proper meaning, add to these English words a gesture of inward and outward stooping expressive of voluntary and even grateful subjection.

"You have lived here for twelve years," he said, "and three years in America. You were born there, but spent your formative years here. Which do you consider your home?"

"There's a saying," I said, "'*Heimat* is where I am needed.'"

"That sounds right," Geiring said.

"But for me," I continued, "*Heimat* is where I'm not made to feel like a stranger."

He nodded thoughtfully.

"So which country is it?"

"Not here," I said.

He didn't ask any further, and no one else spoke either. I watched him eating. He was severing the meat from his drumstick with a fork and knife, never once touching the bone with his fingers. His aunt started fidgeting with her napkin. The old man chewed rapidly with cracking jaws. Outside, birds were singing.

Geiring's aunt started clearing the table. I offered to help. "No, no," she protested, "stay seated, there's more."

"By the way," Geiring said, putting his hand in his breast pocket, "before I forget." And he handed me my passports—both of them.

If this was meant to disarm me, it worked. I took my newfound Yankee defiance and put it in my breast pocket along with the passports.

Geiring's aunt came back with dessert—plum pudding.

"May I ask *you* a personal question?" I asked Geiring.

He looked at me sideways and waited.

"If you were to choose a different line of work, which would it be?"

"Psychology," he said.

"As a therapist?" Now I was being ironic.

"No," he said, sincerely. "As an analyst."

After lunch, Geiring offered to drive me to the city.

"Where do you want to be taken?"

"To the *Dorotheenstädtischer Friedhof*. My stepfather's buried there."

When we reached the graveyard, he gave me a piece of paper with his name and phone number.

"You have three days to respond to my offer."

"And if I don't?"

He smiled ambiguously.

We shook hands in a spirit of frank mutual indifference. I thanked him for the ride.

"Good-bye."

"Good-bye."

I never saw him again.

A herd of glistening black umbrellas preceded me through the gate to the cemetery. Beneath them, uniforms—a delegation of railroad men come to take leave of a colleague. A gardener showed me the way: "Bodo Uhse? To the left, near Kant and Fichte, ten steps before Brecht."

There it was, a tall, narrow rectangle with his name in tall, narrow capitals. I immediately felt a hot proprietary wrath at whoever had designed the stone, because he, or she, or they, more likely, had known him well but not well enough: These shapes did signal something recognizably his, but it was an aspect of him I had never accepted and wasn't prepared to accept now, something rigid and narrow that wasn't alive but constricting, that throttled the life in him when he still lived. The life, I say, but I don't mean the raw vital urge, I mean something rarer, a vaporous poetic soul-substance that moved in slow, curving, tentative gestures, that veiled itself in cigarette smoke and made his voice trail off to near-inaudibility.

(Instead of these dimensionless capitals why didn't they chisel his signature? Because you cannot even recognize it as such, let alone read his name in it, because it looks like a polygraph or seismograph registering God knows what secret disturbances, because the public needs clarity and information, not riddles. But riddles can be deciphered, and if you read this scrawl in the symbolic language of forms, you can see, first of all, how he joined his given and his family name in a single burst of up- and downward pulsations, as if to belie the cut he made between his family and himself at the age of seventeen; how the first steep Gothic stab at heaven is followed by an immediate dive back to earth; a modest bourgeois elevation then, followed by another, notably shorter flight, and another vertical descent; the line stops a little above the median, as if to avoid touching earth so soon again, lifts itself feebly, sinks, picks itself up, relaxes briefly, and soars up once more, but lower than the second flight and less than half the height of the first; plunges down far beneath the median, down, down with a will, as far down as the line soared up in its first sweep, and forms a decisive, curiously angular loop at the bottom, as if to anchor its transcendence there since it cannot do so on top; flies upward again, a long, razor-straight line, up, up, but coming as it does from far below, it rises only a little beyond the median, violently drops again to the furthest bottom, leaps up a last time, just barely reaching the middle plane, bends, and expires in a soft downward curl with just the subtlest intimation of another ascent before vanishing altogether. As a graphic sign, it is elegant, beautifully balanced. How much more of his nervous, unhappy spirit it carries than those eight solemn letters.)[2]

> In front of the stone stood a rusty tin can half full of rainwater. I, too, just stood there getting wet, feeling the sorrow of Bodo's absence and thinking that this was something I had felt even when he was near me during his lifetime. And then memories started to rise up. I could see Bodo as I had seen him on this same path just four years before, walking slowly next to me, one hand holding the other behind his back, his face relaxed, almost smiling. He had come here often, and now he had brought me with him, either with didactic purpose or, more probably, to share with me his pleasure in silently communing with the illustrious dead. But I had just wanted to get away, his reverence irritated me, I would much rather read the poets and thinkers than muse on their tombstones. And now, with a blunt ache I remembered a moment when I was sitting alone in the back of our car, I was twelve or thirteen, Bodo was sitting in the front next to Jochen, our driver. It must have been on the tree-lined street that led in a two-and-a-half-hour detour alongside the border from our village to Berlin. The car had slowed down. It was drizzling, just as it was now in front of his grave. We were passing a crew of workers repairing a road. They had put down their tools and were on their way to a nearby barracks, maybe to get out of the rain. One of them was a boy a year or two older than I was, he was walking side by side with a man who had laid an arm around the boy's back and a hand on his shoulder. The man was old enough to be the boy's father, but they looked like friends. It went through my heart like a stab. As I said, my stepfather was absent much of the time, not just from me but from himself. And now that absence was stamped with the seal of eternity.

I walked on. When I came to Brecht's grave, I stopped. On the broad horizontal slab lay some fifty long-stemmed carnations in a heap—a disproportionate amount, it seemed to me, for a champion of the dispossessed. I took one of Brecht's carnations, went back to Bodo's grave, and put the flower in his rusty tin can.

---

2. A German critic described Bodo's literary style as "alternately cool and passionate, controlled and impetuous, simple-minded and sophisticated, sensitive and brutal, dry and sensual. Every sort of contradiction besets his work, polar tensions which, frequently, he can neither overcome nor elucidate. But there is one thing one always senses—the suffering of this man who [in his novel *Leutnant Bertram*] wrote: 'These days it is a curse to be German.'" Marcel Reich-Ranicki, *Deutsche Literatur in Ost und West,* p. 445, Munich, 1963.

Bodo. How lost he was, driven into exile in his own country. And his son, my half brother, Stefan, how lost to himself and to all who knew him, lost and irretrievable to the end.

I was lucky, I was my mother's son. Alma, who was always afraid of getting lost on a drive almost anywhere outside her own neighborhood, who frequently said "my mind is a maze," had an unfailing sense of direction in life that saw her through trials that might have deranged someone weaker or less surely guided by instinct. She was a dangerous but lucky driver. So was I in my younger days, reckless even, but something saw me through, an angel, a star. Yet I got lost as deeply as it is possible to get lost. It's almost unimaginable to me now.

Eros at Sea

The young man I was in 1963, the one with the two passports, had no inkling of the danger he was facing. All the danger he could imagine lay in the past. He was running away, and had been running for a while. If the Stasi, instead of suspecting him of being a spy and trying to hire him as one, had asked whether he considered himself a refugee, he might, in his sincerity, have nodded "yes," and then qualified that: "Not politically: I am an emotional refugee."

It would have been precisely the truth. I was fleeing from the protracted aftermath of a love affair that had run afoul of a false pregnancy or a miscarriage or a chemically induced abortion, I was never able to determine which, but in any case an unhappy mess for the girl, and painful for me, too, since her mother's grief (her father was dead) had elicited what all the inveiglements of her Father Confessor hadn't: penitence and a sincere vow of chastity. No crueler joke could be imagined, because for half a year of almost daily after-school trysts and occasional getaways to cheap hotels, we had spent more time in bed than she would kneel at confession for the rest of her life, I was sure of that. And now all of a sudden she was telling me in maddeningly "reasonable" tones that it was really best if we parted, at least for a while, and that she would feel that way even if nothing had happened, life couldn't just consist of sex, sex, sex, and besides, I was just too oppressively jealous. And as if that wasn't enough, she told me her cousin Vince in Albany was threatening to take me to court: She was a minor, I an adult. Talk about blind justice.

I went to the Scandinavian Shipping Office on West 42nd Street with the plan of putting an ocean between us. But first I would make love to her one more time. I climbed the fire escape outside her window, knocked, was let in. She still loved me, she said, but she wouldn't make love, not until she was at least sixteen, it would hurt her mother too much. I tried to seduce her. She did not melt. I whispered my latest suspicion at her: that her mother's new tenant, that music student who had moved into the upstairs bedroom, was screwing her, wasn't he, and all this pregnancy stuff was a put-on, just to get rid of me. I think we both knew that I believed only a fraction of what I was saying, but I could not allow such a banal, no, such a mature interloper as common sense to take her away from me, it was too humiliating. This drama had to be played out by the rules of passion. She denied my allegations, I returned to the window. She got out of bed, her face wet with tears, to prevent me from leaving in anger. She had only a T-shirt on. As a sign of her new chastity, she pulled the hem down with one stiff arm and hand while with the other she reached out imploringly: "Stay!" The sound of steps in the hallway—her mother? the tenant? her mother!—propelled me down the fire escape. A few days later, I boarded the *Seven Seas,* a Swedish merchant ship bound for Australia, taking with me the memory of Sylvia, that was her name, in that final, ambiguous, ravishing pose.

I had met Sylvia in 1960, when I was twenty, a virgin in every sense but the physical (thanks to a hasty transaction with a Mexican whore), and undergoing that awful experience of spiritual dislocation for which "culture shock" would be the right term if it wasn't commonly used to describe the discomfort of tourists. Now imagine a tall, clear-skinned, fair-haired girl with a sweet, solemn face stepping into that aching void. She is only fifteen years old but she looks like one of Botticelli's heralds of spring come to life, and there is a depth in her eyes into which I begin to fall the moment I see her. A beauty, you say, but beauty explains nothing. What spoke to me from that depth was the void itself, but it was ensouled now, it no longer threatened, it had become a well of pure invitation and endless longing. The difficulty—I can tell of it now, but I was too far fallen then to even consider it as something from which one can step back and say: This is the problem, what shall I do—the hellish difficulty in loving her was that she was too young to have any sure sense of what it was that made her so wrenchingly desirable to me. If I gazed into her eyes long enough, I could reflect it back to her. Invariably she was frightened and turned away. She tried to describe the feeling—a kind of vertigo. What is vertigo but a foretaste of falling? Sometimes the same fear welled up in her when we listened to certain pieces of music together.

But there was one plane on which we met without any barrier and on equal terms, and that was her bed. There we invented each other. She was a natural actress, her sensuality was of the imagination as much as of the body: "Let's be other people!" Her favorite situation was a couple meeting in some forbidden zone of exquisite guilt and enticement. Then, when passion took over and we were ourselves again, it was like meeting anew. *Those* depths she swam with all the assurance of genius. It was my love that bewildered her, because what I loved in her was asleep and protected by fear. And I was always luring her to that edge, I wanted her to take the irreversible step. She took refuge in brief occasional flings with boys her age, entirely appropriate under normal circumstances, but our circumstances were not normal, she was fifteen and the mistress of a twenty-one-year-old man who had the sixth sense of jealousy, which needs but a hint to set the wheels of torment rolling. And I had more than hints, she was perverse or careless enough to leave evidence in places where I would find it. That is how making love to her became the obsession of my days, and why, after losing her, I was pursued by her memory for so long.

Shortly before we reached Panama, the third mate, who spoke excellent English, watched me attempting to tidy up the officers' dining room and remarked that I was taking my job title, "messboy," rather literally. He had a point. The officers were entitled to service at mealtimes, and I was feeding them annoyance. Not a day passed when one of them didn't have to complain that there was no salt in the shaker, or that the beer I had brought him was not the one he had ordered. Halfway across the Pacific, they decided to fire me as soon as we reached Australia. The chief steward gave me their ultimatum. "You have one chance," he said. What was that? "No more mistakes." By the slant of his smile and the lift of his eyebrow I saw that he considered such a feat possible, but not likely. I tried. God knows I tried! At mealtimes, I observed in the eyes of my judges two opposing expressions: one distinctly malevolent, scowling look, as if waiting for the oversight that would release the catch on the guillotine; the other, a surprised and gratified look of pleasure at my unusual efficiency. Then the radio officer's wife (she had been hired to do the ship's laundry) told me that they were betting on me, a wager like Satan's with God over Job, to see if this servant was capable of perfection. I wanted badly to show them the measure of my contempt, some big gesture, like dumping the mashed potatoes on the tablecloth, but what good would that do me? On the other hand, what if they really did fire me? How would I get home without money? What would I do for work? Cut brush in the outback? Hunt kangaroos?

The day before the continent came into view, the *Seven Seas* was adorned with flags to celebrate the first anniversary of her launching. The crew ate cardamom-flavored *limpa* bread, which was ordinarily served to the officers, and the officers ate cake. The crew consumed hundreds of gallons of beer, the officers drank champagne. After lunch, a short, stern, bearded man in a white uniform with a white visored cap and white gloves came into the pantry, accompanied by the chief steward, who introduced us in English: "Captain, this is the officers' messboy. Kalle . . ." (that's the name messboys are given on Swedish ships, it means "Charlie") ". . . this is the captain." I was ready, the chief steward had forewarned me. No doubt he was betting on my success. On his prompting, I had washed each fork, knife, and spoon three times over, checked the sink for suds and the glasses for thumbprints, the tile floor was a mirror, I had even scrubbed the outside of the porthole, which wasn't my job. But the captain did not even glance at this splendor. He strode through the pantry and stopped in front of the swinging door to the dining room. Was it clean? Yes, it was. He reached up to the top of the lintel, a surface I had never taken into consideration, stroked it lightly with one white-gloved finger, and showed me: dirt . . . swung open the door, and walked on. The chief steward gulped audibly. I went off to my cabin to pack my duffel bag.

That night, a movie was shown outside, on the main deck. For about an hour it dispelled my worries about what would become of me. The moon was full, the sea was calm. Because of the long distance between the officers' lounge, where the projector was set up, and the crew's cabins, where the screen was suspended, the image was very large. Was the ship's engine shut down? It seems unlikely, but as I remember it, we floated in a wonderful stillness. Every soul on the ship was assembled, from the oilers and deckhands on up to the officers and the captain and the radio officer's French wife, Marianne, the only woman on board, whose presence I'm sure accounted for the delicacy of the films we were shown. After a countdown of squarish numbers ticking from nine to nothing, the screen lit up with a black-and-white view of a bedroom furnished in the style of the early fifties: next to the bed a kidney-shaped night table, and above a dresser, in the center of the screen, a mirror framed with pale neon tubes. The door opened, a woman came in, turned around, forbade entry to an obscure male escort in suit and tie, granted him a kiss, closed the door, locked it, put her pocketbook on the dresser, opened a closet, took off her coat, put the coat on a hanger, and proceeded, rather primly, to undress. A few catcalls and whistles rang out, but soon the crew fell silent, as if stunned. Not by any wanton display of carnality—on the contrary, she was impeccably proper. No captain would find any dust in her room. The whole purpose of her performance, it seemed, was to document the thrill of knowing herself to be perfectly neat while believing herself to be safely alone. The camera, aroused by the sight of her naked arms and thighs, began a slow zoom, as if wanting to smell her. Unperturbed, she took off her brassiere, pulled off her stockings, stepped out of her underpants, folding each garment and putting it where it belonged. Then she slipped into a flowered nightgown, pulled back the blanket, lay down, covered herself, switched off her bedside lamp, and, still visible to the camera, emitted a soundless, smiling sigh, and fell asleep. Another succession of numbers, and another woman took off her clothes, this time in a bathing hut by the beach. She, too, was neat. She put on an old-fashioned bathing suit, cupped her breasts in her hands to improve the fit, and scampered out for a swim. The most elaborate and mystifying performance was the third and last one. It began with a woman taking a shower with her hair gathered up in a plastic cap. She soaped herself with great thoroughness and no evident pleasure. Then she toweled herself off, went into her bedroom, took off the plastic cap, and, still naked, brushed her blond hair in front of a mirror, made the bed (which showed off her behind to advantage), got dressed, put on lipstick, strapped a pocketbook over her arm, and left, probably on her way to work.

I no longer remember the name of the port where we docked the next morning. Some artist or prankster had painted an enormous white question mark on the mountain that loomed over the shabby little harbor. It was so large that there probably wasn't a house in the town that hadn't a view of some part of it from at least one of its windows. How dubious could a man feel in a place that conducted its business under such a sign? I almost looked forward to getting fired here. But fate intervened in the person of the radio officer's wife. She pleaded with the captain on my behalf, and he relented. She repeated to me, word for word, what she had said to him, wringing her hands, all but kneeling before him, in her heavy French accent: "*Pleez* don't geev'eem ze *keeck!* He eez a *boy* steel! What *weel'eez* meuzer *say!*"

Slowly we worked our way through some ten or twelve Australian harbors and slowly wended our way back. The sailors spent all their free time with the sluttish whores who waited for us in the pubs. I wasn't interested. Briefly, in Panama, I had lain on a filthy cot with a young girl whose breasts reminded me of bruised fruit. I felt only pity for her, and the wish to know that she was loved by some boy or young man, not me. Then, instead of leaving her or else taking her as befitted our contract—a dollar slipped into her mother's palm outside the hot clapboard room where we lay under a tin roof—I kissed her, and in that kiss showed her the passion that I felt for Sylvia and no one else, and realized only then, by the startled hurt in her eyes, what a violation that was. I didn't want to repeat that scene or vary it in any way. In Sidney, I stayed away from the brothels whose praises I had been hearing ever since we left New York, and went to the history museum instead. But then a devouring sexual hunger took possession of me. At the poste restante in Brisbane, I had found letters from my mother, my brother, some friends—none from Sylvia. I hadn't written her, either. Her silence was crushing nonetheless. I had to forget her. Discard her, annul her. Dispel her memory with every thrust into whatever willing body would offer itself, the more faceless and nameless the better. Oh, I could hardly wait!

The whores of Brisbane were monuments of unpleasure. Each one had a porch for a pedestal. There, if they were not occupied, they sat in the white-hard glare of a naked bulb, staring, exhausted and brutal, through a square window, showing us what we had come for—limbs, lips, nipples, locks—and, one of them, her gaping cunt like a vertical sneer between fat, blue-veined thighs. Eight men stood in a queue in front of a shack with a curtain drawn over the window, shifting from foot to foot. My crewmates joined the queue, this was the only bitch worth fucking here, they said, they knew her, Marjorie was her name. The man at the front of the line kicked the door several times and threatened to kick out the teeth, whether of Marjorie or of a client who was taking his time with her I couldn't tell, but presently Marjorie threw open the door, a tall blond woman in a blue bathrobe, and started haranguing "the whole fookin lot" of us in a voice and with words that shriveled every remnant of desire I had left in me.

My abstinence—then and at future ports—earned me a reputation as an odd, possibly queer bird. My cabin-mate was an effeminate homosexual boy from a neighborhood in Brooklyn called Bay Ridge ("Gay Ridge," he called it) who had moved in with me because he could no longer abide the manners of his alcoholic bunk neighbor. We liked each other. This gave rise to rumors about us. And I had other unmanly foibles. I didn't drink like an able-bodied seaman, just a couple of slugs from a bottle now and then, never to the point of stupor. In an argument over a gambling debt, I absorbed an insult a normal sailor would have answered with blows. Out at sea, on the way to Jamaica, I could be seen on deck in my leisure hours reading a fat book and growing a beard. But I knew how to compensate. I had an ability that has always been prized by men at sea: I could tell stories. I told war stories and ghost stories, I retold novels by Jack London and episodes from Prescott's *The Conquest of Mexico*. William Beebe's deep-sea exploits in the "bathysphere" were especially popular. These sessions usually took place on deck, at night, with the kitchen staff and a couple of seamen, or, if the weather was bad, with a larger crowd in the crew's mess-room, over beer and crackers.

One night the cook asked me in an "out with it" sort of tone whether I really did have a woman waiting for me in New York, as I had claimed. I produced Sylvia's picture for proof, and added a fictitious story about how I had seduced her (it was the other way around), and a true one about a manual for hypno-tists that had done wonders in heightening Sylvia's already more than adequate sexual response. Of this ability my audience demanded an immediate demonstration: Could I hypnotize the cook? He was the biggest man on board. I could not refuse this challenge without irreversible loss of face. After about forty minutes I had the cook, all three hundred pounds of him, balancing on one foot and then on the other, and swinging his arms, convinced he was skating on a lake in Upsala. I gave him the posthypnotic command that he serve me a glass of the captain's wine—which he did, after a bewildered descent to the storage room. That won me the day and regained me my crewmates' acceptance. There was only one thing I wanted more: oblivion in sex or love, an end to the memory of Sylvia, which, far from fading, had rooted itself in the center of my chest as a dull, churning ache.

There was another "Kalle" on the ship, the crew's messboy, a good-natured, wide-hipped Dane who was always grinning as if in memory or anticipation of a joke. Whenever he talked about Kingston, Jamaica, he would wrap his arms around an invisible woman and set his pelvis swinging: "The best! Better than Rio!" Then he would raise a finger and clap a hand over his back pocket: "But careful! Everybody steals in Kingston!"

The whores of Kingston were many in number, and many were pretty, and some even seemed to enjoy their profession. Was this a foretaste of hell? The more tempting a smile or glance or touch, the more savory the sight of a pair of long legs or the swell of a nipple hardening between my fingers, the more sharply Sylvia rose up in revolt against any substitution. I knew what would happen if I went to bed with any of these women: nothing at all, and the crew would hear of it. O thirst of Tantalus! I drank enough rum to drown a whale, but Sylvia, Sylvia just danced in that sea like a buoy. With me clinging to her. What was wrong with me? Was I impotent? How to murder her in my heart? I walked. I must have walked for miles, turning corners at random, getting lost, coming back to familiar places again, the ache in my chest so deep and wide there were moments when it made me gasp.

The next morning, a crew of dockworkers came aboard. The chief steward told me I could feed them leftovers. One glance at the faces crowding the open pantry window, and I could see why. These men were hungry. They pointed at their mouths and held up metal and clay bowls. One of them handed me a tin can. I hesitated, the food was too good to be turned into slop. "Put it in, mahn, put it in," he said. He insisted I give him a little of everything: meat, vegetables, eggs, bread, butter, potatoes, cheese, sausage, gravy, and milk, up to the top.

The men had their own spoons. When my supplies ran out, the crew's mess-boy gave from his.

After washing the dishes, I went to my cabin and found an old man in rags—old by the standards of a twenty-one-year-old: he was probably in his fifties—standing next to my cot with a bundle of outdated magazines he wanted to sell me. I cast a glance around to see if he had stolen anything. He read my suspicion. From a blue zippered pocket sewn onto his dirty white shirt, he drew a plastic folder containing a stained piece of paper bearing the stamp of a Kingston police precinct, a typewritten attestation of his moral probity, a signature, and his photograph affixed with two staples. To get rid of him, I offered to buy his magazines.

"How much?"

"Notting."

"You're not selling them?"

"No, mun, you can tekkem."

He was hurt. What could I do? I thanked him for the gift and held open the door for him. But he didn't leave. He asked me if I had any currency I needed to change, he would like to take it to the bank for me. Looking into his eyes, I believed him. In view of his rags, the hungry men I had fed, the crew's mess-boy's warnings, I didn't trust him one bit. But I was already taking out my wallet, what did it matter, and made a perfunctory count of the bills, and handed them to him. Better to lose my money than insult him.

"Can you change these into dollars?" I asked.

"Yes, sir, tank you, sir," he said, a little hastily, and left, taking the magazines with him. Ten minutes later he knocked on my door.

"Please, sir, if I can leave de magazine? It's raining, I doan wan dem to get wet-up."

Later I learned that the old man had gone from cabin to cabin offering his banking service and using my trust as a reference, telling everyone I had given him forty dollars' worth of Swedish, Australian, and Panamanian bills. No one thought highly of this transaction. Down the drain went my slim account in that precious currency, respect. I was the joke of the ship.

That evening I made the rounds of the harbor again, my collar turned up against a steady drizzle. Then the sky turned an eerie dark orange shading into purple, a wind started sweeping boxes and baskets about, the clouds cracked open, the city stood drenched in a thunderous lashing downpour, I hunched my shoulders and tried to skip out of the way of an ankle-deep river of garbage coming my way, and stopped at the sight of a skinny old woman who stood laughing out loud at the sight of me.

"What's so funny?"

"White mahn afraid of de rain!"

And off she went again, howling with laughter and clapping her long hands together. That laugh was itself a force of nature, there was nothing to do but endure it. Strangely, it wasn't unpleasant, maybe because there was no malice in it. She just found me very, very funny.

I invited her to come drinking with me, in a whorehouse and bar where my crewmates hung out. She was from Haiti, she said. I could hear it in her accent, but the melody of her speech was Jamaican. She told me the stories of the harbor—the police raids, the murders: "Lahst week one Feeneesh mahn keel Jamaica girl." I can still see our cook stooping to look down at us on his way upstairs with one girl straddling him piggyback and another one pushing his enormous rump as if rolling a rock up a hill. He shakes his head in dismay.

The old woman was teaching me how to drum with my hands on the table, or, rather, trying to prove that white men have no rhythm.

Da-doom-da, da-doom.

I repeated it.

"No, no. Not like dis. Like dis!"

"Kalle, Kalle," the cook said, and moved on with his girls. The boy from Bay Ridge was asleep on my left, his arms folded into a pillow on the counter. Other men, other girls descended the steps. Smiles of satiety, gestures of amorous languor.

Da-doom-da, da-doom.

This was getting tedious. I rose to my feet and offered her a dollar. She didn't take it.

"Don't go by self," she said. "Many mahn fight you, cut you, steal you. Come, sit down, I teach you."

And she repeated her beat, which was so simple any child could perform it. Was she taking me for a fool? I sat down and looked into her eyes.

"Do it," she said.

I just kept looking into her eyes. She stared back. Her look was hard at first, then it softened. Her irises were the color of pooled oil, very deep and dark and flecked with small spots of gold. It is an adventure to sit silently face-to-face with a stranger, and one of the most direct ways I know to persuade oneself of the possibility that there is no such thing as an individual, that each of us is a multitude. My drinking companion's skin, for example, was very dark, but there was a moment when I saw peering through her the features of a ruddy-cheeked white man with twinkling blue eyes. Was this illusion or vision? She, too, seemed startled at moments by what she saw. A couple of times she laughed. After a while, a tear rolled down one of her cheeks. I reached out to dry her face with my hand. She tilted her head, cradling her cheek in my palm, and closed her eyes. We sat like that until my arm got tired. Then I held her hand for a while. She was falling asleep. Several members of the *Seven Seas* crew sat staring at us in complete disbelief. I woke up my cabin-mate, said good night to my friend, and left.

The next morning, I saw an adolescent boy in tight shorts leave the chief steward's cabin and walk down the gangplank with downcast eyes. Not only I saw him, half the crew did. To this day I don't understand why the chief steward was allowed to live down this incident—a few grinning remarks, and it was forgotten—while I had to endure repeated recitals of what had been perceived as my romance with a hag.

After lunch, the old man's face appeared in the pantry window. He had come back to report to me about my money. The banks did not trust him, he said, despite his police affidavit, the guards wouldn't even let him near the counter. Would I please write a note saying that he was my messenger and that I needed his services? I was touched and repentant for ever having doubted him. I wrote the note and felt vindicated before the crew. I would show them my dollars when he came back. And tonight I would follow the cook's example. No more uptight white man! So many women! So many styles of allure! I thought of one girl in particular, she had hitched up her dress with an innocent lewdness that made my heart skip. Why didn't I go for her?

I actually met her again in the evening. She rubbed up against me: "Mek love to Jamaica girl?" But when I looked into her eyes, I saw only exhaustion and want. Pity is not an aphrodisiac, and neither is charity. I drank more liquor than I could hold that night. Some large men threw me out of their bar for vomiting on the jukebox. The next thing I remember is finding myself in a fight with a stocky blond man while my cabin-mate screams for help. The man curses me in a language I don't understand. He punches me in the chest, I punch the air and fall backward into a puddle, life is a dream, I am on my feet again, his blows are connecting better than mine, a swarm of screaming girls surrounds us, they are pulling at him, "Stop! Stop!", he is flashing a knife—is this possible? is this me?—I am elated, I am amazed, again I fall, something tells me to accept defeat, I am laughing, I love the world.

I have no memory of how I got home, but my cabin-mate told me what happened. I must have passed out in the ditch. My enemy walked away with his wrath appeased. Five girls escorted us back to the ship. I told one of them that I could imagine falling in love with her. She took down my address.

I overslept the next morning. The chief steward was furious because, not for the first time, he had to do part of my job. He needled me about my famous bank messenger. "And where is the man with your money, Kalle? Are you still hoping?" I was. We were scheduled to cast off at three-thirty.

At twelve the old man came to tell me the banks had refused to deal with him even after he brought them my letter. He handed me my money in a plastic envelope.

"I'm sorry, captain," he said. "Please to tek my apology."

"*I'm* sorry," I said. "You went to so much trouble. Let me pay you for that."

"No, no!" He held up his hands.

"Please," I said, "you'll make me feel bad."

"I never do notting fe you, so I cahnt tek ye money."

"At least let me pay you for your magazines."

"No no, sir, are fe *you* magazine, I *giv* dem to you."

So he hadn't forgotten that.

"But you need the money."

He smiled. "Maybe I do some thing fe you den. I will buy you a good-good souvenir."

"Like what?"

"You will see. A beauty-full thing. Fe to remember Jamaica."

"How much does it cost?"

He rolled his eyes, calculating: "Twenty dollar?" All my suspicions came back.

"You doan mean to say, sir, you still doan trust me?"

"Oh yes, yes, I do. But twenty dollars is a lot of money."

"It could be less. I doan remember."

"But there's no time. We're leaving very soon."

"Doan worry, sir. I come back. You trust me now. What I will bring fe you is a beauty-full thing. Fe to give to you' modder, you' sweetheart." I gave him a twenty-dollar bill.

The worst part of this interaction was that it took place in front of the chief steward, who would not fail to pass it on to the kitchen staff. I gave myself the philosophical consolation that if this was a scam, it was almost a work of art and deserved a reward.

After lunch, I fed the dockworkers, as usual, through the porthole window, and went on with my cleaning. The cook and the crew's messboy stuck in their heads: "Did your man come yet?" Grin, grin.

"He'll be back," I said, with feigned confidence.

"Kalle, Kalle."

At two-thirty, the chief steward told me to move several hundred pounds of onions from one storage room to another. It was not my job and this was my lunch hour, but I was in no position to object. When I came back up, tired and sweaty, I found my cabin-mate reading on his bunk.

"Have you seen him?"

He shook his head. I had the impression that he pitied me.

"No one's betting on this one," he said.

I lay down on my cot. I was exhausted, but I kept myself awake reading the old man's magazines until three-thirty. Then I fell asleep. A knock on the door woke me up.

"Come in."

It was my man, out of breath, holding in his hand a many-colored glistening object.

"Please, sir, I'm sorry I'm late. But here is de souvenir."

"It's beautiful," I said.

It was perfectly hideous, a pink porcelain conch shell drooling what looked like porcelain water and doubling as a paradise island covered with porcelain fern and porcelain palms, a green porcelain dinosaur, and a miniature pink naked porcelain couple. But I was happy, very happy, that he had come back. Just in time, too. I could hear the clangor of steel plates dropped into place as the hold was being closed on the main deck.

"It was only eleven dollar," he said, handing me the change, "on account of I bargain de mahn down."

"Thank you," I said, "thank you very much. And now let me pay you for all your efforts."

"No, please, I doan want no money," he said, "but if you have a shirt or a trousers that maybe you doan want, I *will* take dat."

I gave him most of my clothes—pants, shirts, underwear, socks, a windbreaker, a pair of sneakers, a pair of shoes, a couple of sweaters. My cabin-mate added two T-shirts. We wrapped all these things into a sheet. I would pay for it if the chief steward objected. Let him see it. Let the crew see it. The old man wished me a happy homecoming and left with the bundle slung over his shoulder. I took a shower, changed, and went outside to watch the harbor receding as the ship went out to sea. It would be a while yet. The dockworkers were still on board, waiting for the third mate to approve some papers their foreman had handed him. Some of the men I had fed earlier smiled at me. One of them was wearing my City College T-shirt. Another one had on my paint-spattered jeans. A third one was wearing my sneakers. Another one my shoes. My red socks. My blue sweater. My windbreaker. He had given away all my clothes.

The next day, during my afternoon break, I was leaning on the railing by the bow with the wind in my ears, watching a school of dolphins tumbling alongside the ship, when an impulse came to me, a whim really, but with the weight and definiteness of a decision confirmed and long past any doubting. I took my wallet from my back pocket and pulled the picture of Sylvia out of its plastic sheath and put the wallet back in my pocket and looked at her for a while. I tried to send her my love. This good resolve met with resistance. I wished her one moment of horrible remorse on my account and a reasonably happy life thereafter. That was more like it. Then I opened my fingers and watched the picture flutter away and spiral down into the sea.

Here I am, writing about how I was running away, but in doing so I left that other, slightly older version of myself standing by my stepfather's grave as if rooted in sorrow. Sooner or later the running one will catch up with the one by the grave, and then they'll move on together as one. And there are other selves elsewhere in various conditions. One of them in particular concerns me, he is in a torment beyond all imagining. And of course there is this one right here and now, older than all the selves I remember, writing.

Mrs. Libido

Returned to New York, I moved from my mother's apartment to a furnished room on West Seventy-ninth Street. The landlady's perfectly counter-indicative name, believe it or not, was Mrs. Libido. She forbade me to bring home female company after ten p.m. Her explanation was straightforward: She lived right above me, she slept poorly, and sounds carried. Therefore: "No vomans in zis room." I told her there would be no problem because my fiancée had tragically died in a fire. This won me her heart and the room. Maybe her name was more apt than I am allowing. She took an interest in my health (I was too pale), snooped around my room when I was out, left little packages of cookies outside my door, reminded me from time to time that she could hear "every Ting," and eventually informed the FBI about my activities.

But I had bigger worries than Mrs. Libido. Sylvia, for one. No sooner had the wound begun to heal than a nasty bit of news came to tear off the scab. A girlfriend of Sylvia's was in my brother's sophomore class at Walden High School. She told him, and he told me, that Sylvia was having an affair with an Assistant District Attorney who was risking his career for the pleasure of her company. "Some chick!" Stefan said. My brother was no hipster, he was sixteen and shyer than I was. No, these were sincere words of tribute, in the lingo of the time. Some chick. I had to agree with him. If she had been a gangster and I a hoodlum given fair warning not to set foot on his turf, I could not have eschewed Greenwich Village more assiduously. I dreaded meeting her, alone or with her Assistant D.A.

Another worry—not as pressing as the first, but more dreadful, in a way, because there was no escaping it—was that at twenty-two years of age I was not succeeding at anything for which the world gave credit. My employment record was spotty: Brentano's Book Store, the Alligator Shoe Company, Polanski Messenger Service, Manpower Inc., most recently the *Seven Seas*. My alibi was that I was a writer, but my literary products consisted almost entirely of deletions. And I had dropped in and out of City College twice. I decided to enroll a third time, to grit my teeth and work hard at the obligatory science and mathematics courses, hire a tutor if need be. The impassable obstacle, it turned out, was my own pride in the face of an English professor who told me my paragraphs were too long. In the privacy of his office, so as not to embarrass him in front of his students, I advised him of the opinion of a higher authority, the English grammarian H. W. Fowler: "The paragraph is essentially a unit of thought, not of length." "Not in *my* class, it's not! *Your* paragraphs are to be *short, short, short!*" "How short is short?" "No more than six sentences." For my next homework assignment, I copied a five-sentence, three-page paragraph from Scott-Montcrieff's translation of *Swann's Way*. The professor held up to the class my shamefully unindented text as a cautionary horror: "Ree-diculous! But the paragraph isn't the worst of it—listen to this!" And off he went on triumphant flat feet right into the magnificent labyrinth of a Proustian sentence, where he promptly lost his way. But who was the trapped one, he or I? With an angry flourish he tossed my pages on his desk and delivered his verdict: "F!" I went to the Dean of Students: "This man is incompetent," I said. "If he had any sense, he would have failed me for plagiarism. I mean, who besides Proust would write like this?" The Dean of Students was a thoughtful man. "Mr. Agee," he said. "Please don't be insulted if I give you some advice. Old people hate to admit their ignorance, but so do the young. There are many things you can learn in college. How to deal with a character like Professor M. is one of them." "This class is called English 1," I said, "not 'How to Learn from an Idiot.'" "What do you want me to do," he replied, "have him fired?" "No, absolve me from having to attend his class, and give me the credit I deserve." "For plagiarizing Proust?" "Yes." He laughed, shrugged, and shook his head. I dropped out for the third and last time.

I had two friends, Victor and Carl, both of them five years older than I, both of them serious aspirants to a knowledge I would have given my right hand to learn: the art of charming an unknown woman into your bed, and not just one woman but many in succession, and on rare lucky nights two or even three at a time. Aspirants, I say: They did not consider themselves masters. That pride of place they willingly yielded to a man named Alfonso whom I only knew through their stories. Once Carl showed me a letter Alfonso had written him from Paris. It was typed on several sheets of onionskin paper, partly in black type and partly in red. He wrote about racing around Paris on a motorcycle with a mad genius poet who said he was in love with Alfonso because Alfonso was a genius and he, being a poet, could only love genius. But Alfonso, though he, too, loved genius, loved women more. Just now he was awaiting a visit from a beautiful student of philosophy. Making love to her was just one of the pleasures he anticipated. Another was to persuade her, by a well-timed, rhythmically cadenced argument simultaneously verbal and phallic, that there was more truth, love, and beauty in one heartfelt fuck than in all of Plato. Ah! All this was awaiting him, but he was sad, sad beyond healing, and longing to die, and no woman could take this voluptuous sadness from him unless she was that horrendous witch he sometimes dreamed of, the one who would eat him alive.

That was Alfonso, that was the master, and though I found his letter faintly absurd, it impressed me, and so did the stories Victor and Carl told me about his accomplishments. But their own modest skills were nothing to sneeze at either, several conquests a week sometimes, and then the exacting business of keeping these liaisons going for a while, in tandem, without any entanglement or jealousy. How did they do it? Victor, who knew Sylvia and sympathized with my predicament, offered to instruct me.

"First you decide what sort of chick you have in mind. Is she middle- or working-class, black or white, hip or square? That choice determines your setting. I noticed you liked the looks of that beatnik who served us at the Figaro, you know, the one with the mysterious eye makeup. A lot of those beat chicks are pretty stupid, but they generally know how to fuck, and they'd love *you*. You're a poet, you play the guitar, you speak German, you've worked on a ship. Believe me! There's a party next week, I'll get you invited, one of those bongo-thumping events, there'll be loads of them sitting on Japanese cushions, palpitating, waving their long hair. Or else, if you want someone really refined and well-bred—go to the Metropolitan Museum on a weekday morning, there are always five or six beautiful girls who go there supposedly to be alone with great art. The Baroque section is a good one, you've got all those meaty abductions and swooning martyrs—something to talk about. Or you could try Alfonso's way, I can't do it, I don't have it in me, but maybe you do. You see an exciting girl on the street, you follow her, match your stride to hers, talk to her softly, telling her how lovely she is, how *lyrical*—that's an important word—and if she seems offended, tell her how conscious you are of the imposition, the rudeness of telling her these things, but how could you live with yourself if you let her pass by as if she were just anyone, and so on and so on; and if she's with you still, if she smiles, tell her you want nothing more than to make her happy, to show her how very worthy she is of being loved like a queen, and so on. Then, if she wants to hear more . . . but if she wants more, the game's already won. The question is, what if she says no? If she says no, and more often than not she'll say that and mean it, don't waste your time and hers, apologize, retreat, review your performance, prepare for the next one. Half the trick is to learn how to swallow rejection."

I made exactly two attempts in the direction outlined by Victor. Both of them were strangled by shame at the outset. Fortunately! But I wish there were a way to undo the last one, to take back the insult I inflicted on a friendly and serious young woman whose escort by parental arrangement I was when she visited New York for a weekend, and on whose neck, at a moment when we were alone, I placed my hand, to her obvious and immediate, paralyzing discomfort, and whom I then tried to compensate with a gush of unsolicited candor involving an account of my affair with a girl of unstatutory age, crowning the whole sad performance with a ridiculously debonair remark about Sylvia's "ripeness."

It takes leisure to be a Don Juan, that thought consoled me for my poor showing. Victor and Carl could afford it, Victor was a painter living on family money, and Carl, Victor's roommate and a Ph.D. candidate at Columbia, was living off Victor. But I had to pay Mrs. Agnes Libido, and I was looking for work. I took night-jobs loading crates on the docks and day-jobs with wrecking crews on construction sites. That helped pay the bills, but you couldn't depend on it, sometimes you'd wait with thirty or forty guys until a fat man stepped out of a shack, selected ten or fifteen by a gauge of their shoulders and biceps, and sent the rest home. I circled ads in *The New York Times*. "Warehouse Manager's Asst. Typing a must." I could hunt and peck fairly fast with four fingers and a thumb, but not accurately enough, as the tests consistently proved. "Office clerk. HS grad, gd with figures a plus." I remember that one for its satisfying conclusion and also for its Gogolian setting: a large wood-paneled room furnished with ancient oak desks, behind each desk a bowed head and a pair of scribbling or typing hands, and elevated above them all, on top of a broad, three-tiered podium, a larger desk, behind which, above which, throned the minion who did the hiring and firing. He scanned my skimpy employment record and looked down at me over the top of his glasses.

"What do you do in your spare time? Of which you seem to have a lot."

"I write."

"Oh, really? What do you write?"

"Stories."

"How quaint. Have you published any 'stories'?"

"Not yet."

"So you're a failed writer."

"I'm not a failed writer and you're not a literary critic. You're just an asshole with a desk."

That one gave me a boost. But for the most part, looking for work was a draining, humiliating experience of learning to swallow rejection—a bitter parody of Alfonso's teaching.

In my room at Mrs. Libido's stood a wood-burning stove. I used it one day to burn several notebooks and journals I had kept when I was fifteen years old. I destroyed them because I could not bear to live with what I perceived as their mediocrity. In that ritual murder of my younger self I must have hoped for the miracle of a reprieve, the grace of a rebirth in the realm of genius. The pure land! Now I wish I could salvage those papers, especially the journals, or at least the moments I thought worth commemorating in them. I do remember one of those. I had told Bodo about a play I had seen on West German television. It was about a writer and about some angelic judges who determine his place in the temple of Memory. "We shall put him on this middle shelf between X and Y." I no longer remember who X and Y were, but their names had a cruel accuracy. The judgment was not unkind, it was just. The man's gifts were modest, his accomplishments would almost certainly be forgotten. Still, he had a place in that enormous library, and those two heavenly critic-librarians with their kind, superior smiles were pleased with their judgment. This play had impressed me—but more than that, it had touched a sensitive point. I was going to be a writer, I knew that already; and Bodo was a writer; and my father in America, who had recently died, he had been a writer too. Writers are judged, and judge themselves, as all artists are judged and judge themselves, against standards that condemn all but a few to failure. At least that's how I thought of my calling then, and in a deep unsobered place in my heart I still see it that way, and affirm it to be a just arrangement. I believe Bodo saw it that way too. In fact, I know he did. When I told him about the writer, his death, and the judges, his face became sad. He looked hurt. Did he think I was judging him? Maybe I was. And there was another memory I consigned to the flames, related to this one, in the same key, with a similar dramatic structure. I had been studying a song on the piano, a poem by Heine set to music by Hanns Eisler:

Zuweilen dünkt es mich, als trübe
Geheime Sehnsucht deinen Blick.
Ich kenn es wohl, dein Missgeschick:
Verfehltes Leben, verfehlte Liebe.

Du blickst so traurig, wiedergeben
Kann ich dir nicht die Jugendzeit.
Unheilbar ist dein Herzeleid:
Verfehltes Leben, verfehlte Liebe.

The tune is lovely, simple, lyrical. But the words, seemingly tender, are cruel:

At times it seems to me as if
a secret longing dimmed your eye.
I know what your affliction is:
a life that failed, a love that failed.

You look so wistful, I can not
give back to you the days of youth.
Your heart-ache is incurable:
a life that failed, a love that failed.

They are cruel because they could only wound the person to whom they are addressed. But I was not aware of that when I played and sang the song for Bodo, looking for his praise, and also wanting to share that poignant sadness with him. (Alma, my mother, spoke poor German and might not have understood the poem. And Stefan was too young.) I sang it, and there it was again, that hurt look, that surprise and retreat in his eyes. It was just a moment, but it revealed to me more about my stepfather—more sorrow, more failure—than I was prepared to know. And that I had tossed that dart of a song at him, as if knowing without knowing that he was the right target, the one that would show me the immediate effect of the power I was borrowing from Heine and Eisler: the power of art, the power to wound.

The notebooks burned well, but the journals produced an acrid smoke that drove me out of the house. When I came home, I found a note on my table:

Dear Mr. Eggee!
I trace smok in you room
whats wrong?

Something was definitely wrong. But I confessed it to no one. In my letters to Bodo, I affected a stylish intellectual ennui. With my friends, I talked about art and love and politics as if I felt at home in my skin and the world. The more I masked myself to others, the more naked I looked to myself in a mirror: a would-be, not even a has-been! A washout, pale, like a newt. A wrung-out soul, not the type to disturb the night peace of Mrs. Libido.

So he's running, running to catch up with his future self, the one I left standing in the rain by his stepfather's grave, standing and waiting, he's not sure for what, and imagining that the flower he put in the rusty tin can feels something like gratitude for the fresh water. He sees a worm drowning in a puddle and picks it up and puts it on the grass next to the grave. It occurs to him that there are people who speak to the dead. The thought frightens him. What if the dead were to answer? On the other hand, what if the dead are afraid of the living? What if we are like ghosts to the dead? He feels something in back of him drawing near, and I, the one who is writing this many years later, am anxious to speed up the pace of the running one, for the sake of the one who's waiting but also for the others who are standing like statues marking the various partings of the way, and especially for the one whose torment I've already mentioned, and who should not be made to wait. But the running one, unaware of the future, slows down and virtually stops. He finds himself in conversation with a girl in the poetry section of the Columbia University Bookstore.

Amy

She had asked for poems by Pablo Neruda and the salesman had recommended the translations of Ben Belitt. I couldn't allow her to walk off with this travesty.

"It's no good," I said, "he's too slick, and he's always adding some Anglo-American corn of his own. Look here . . ."

I opened the book at random and pointed at the left page, where the Spanish original stood: "*Tocas mi pecho mientras duermo.* That means: 'You touch my chest while I sleep.'"

"Mmm," she said.

"Now look what *he* does with it: 'Touching my heart while I sleep.'"

"I see what you mean," she said, "'Chest' is much more . . ."

We looked at each other as she gulped back the unspoken word, and I saw that she was pretty in that apologetic way that makes shy pretty girls with glasses suffer the pangs of invisibility, and that she found me appealing, and that I had chanced into what Victor and Carl would have called a pickup. I asked her if she would like to join me for a cup of coffee. She said she'd love to. I hailed a cab, we drove to the Café Figaro on the corner of MacDougall and Bleecker (an expensive ride), and there, deliberately, I steered us to the table where Sylvia and I had often sat. Maybe this girl could supplant her. We talked, I asked her about herself. Her name was Amy, she wrote poems but wasn't ready to show them, she was intelligent and timid and generous, and obviously flattered by my interest, and I liked her and thought she was pretty. (But would Victor and Carl approve of her? Would their seeing me with her make me proud? Probably not, she wasn't flashy enough—I would try to avoid them.) It turned out she lived in the Village. I walked her home. We exchanged phone numbers. A few days later, I called her, we made a date for a movie, I don't remember which, and after the movie, sitting in the grass in Central Park and then lying on our sides, face-to-face, with our heads propped up on our hands, I noticed—we both did—that there were moments when our conversation flagged, not awkwardly, but as if to make room for some unspoken meaning— a touch? a kiss? But we talked and fell silent and talked again until it was time to go home, and agreed to meet at the Gaslight Cafe on Saturday night, and parted with a handshake at the subway station.

The Gaslight Cafe was dimly lit, a freckled man played country music on a banjo, we ordered drinks, our knees were touching, we smiled at each other, I thought, yes, I could imagine wanting her, it would be different from sleeping with Sylvia, but it would be good. A kid with a corduroy cap on his head stepped onto the podium, he was holding a guitar and around his neck was a metal contraption with a harmonica mounted on it. He sang a song about this land being everyone's land which everyone except me had evidently heard many times and then he sang a witty sentimental song about a hobo which nobody had heard because he had just written it. Then the kid started strumming a new tune and brought his mouth close to the microphone and began singing, slowly and soulfully:

I'm a man of constant sorrow,
I've been wandering all my life . . .

and then I noticed heads turning and I too turned my head and saw a woman in a form-fitting cocktail dress wending her way through the tables whom at second glance I recognized as an astonishing version of Sylvia, her full lips painted scarlet, her blond hair dyed black and cut short and bobbed in the manner of Louise Brooks. She was coming toward me, squinting to adjust her near-sighted eyes, and she was being followed by an extremely handsome man in a black three-piece suit. They sat down at a table right next to ours, she was so close I could smell her perfume, her Assistant D.A.—it had to be him—was smiling to himself and examining the wine list, she turned her head slowly, saw me, and exclaimed: "Joel!", her voice almost inaudible beneath the music. She was happy to see me, I could tell. It was almost as if we were alone together, but of course we weren't, Narcissus had glanced up from his wine list, and no doubt Amy was watching us too, though I couldn't see her. I didn't care, a stream of emotion was pouring through me, so strong I was sure that Sylvia must feel it too—and maybe she did, because, still looking at me, she reached for her friend's hand and held it, whether for his support or her own was not clear, but I took it to be a sign of fealty to him and turned away.

The kid was still singing about constant sorrow. Amy's knee was no longer touching mine. I looked at her, she was looking at me with a wary, uncertain look. I wanted to stroke her hand and smile at her, do something to assure her of my friendship, but at the same time, that stream of desire kept pouring out of the center of my chest—my heart, I suppose—not to embrace Amy or the wide world, but unilaterally toward my left side and a little behind me, like an ectoplasmic extrusion, reaching for Sylvia. I desperately wanted to turn my head so I could see her again. With all the will at my disposal I stared at the singer. He was inspired, even his simple guitar-playing was inspired. After each stanza he blew a dolorous, wailing refrain on his harmonica. When he was done, there was a burst of vigorous applause from the audience, Amy and I too applauded. I looked at her, she was shutting me out of her sight. Several voices shouted "Bravo!" One of them, I was fairly sure, belonged to the Assistant D.A. "Amy," I said, touching her hand. She looked at me. She was trying to look indifferent, but I could see she was hurt. How to undo this? I leaned in toward her: "Amy, I'm so sorry. This is awful. Let's get out of here."

She nodded and picked up her purse and got up to leave. Sylvia's enigmatic face turned to follow us as we passed.

"Good-bye," I said to her.

"Good-bye," she said.

Outside, I suggested we go to the Figaro but Amy said she'd rather go home. On the way to her house, I tried to explain myself. She said I didn't have to apologize, none of this was my fault, I was in love with that girl and she, Amy, was something like a stand-in, even if I didn't mean it that way. I protested against the word "stand-in." She said: "Call it 'substitute,' call it anything, but don't deny that it's true." At her door, much too late, I asked her how she felt.

"Humiliated," she said.

"I'm so sorry."

"I know you're sorry. I'm sorry too."

And she went inside.

And off he goes, running again, which is good, since the others are waiting, but where is he going? If he could only write his way out! For he wants to be a writer. Wants to! It's almost an assignment: His father, whom he never knew, expects it from beyond the grave, and so does his stepfather, still living and writing in Berlin. But there is a critic looking over his shoulder, probably East German, probably a member of some supernal politburo, whose strictures grind like the screws of a torture machine. This formidable presence wants irony, erudition, sophistication, he wants Robert Musil and Thomas Mann, and on top of that, he wants political relevance: What about poverty, racism, social injustice? There is only one remedy: turn to concerns over which the critic has no jurisdiction. Write about your personal experience, your life, your love. The truth, in short. But the truth is that you are a failure, and that of course is unconfessable. He is running, but running in circles. Then, finally, he comes to one of those junctures where a seeming accident throws a switch and he finds himself shunted to an unfamiliar track.

A Double Life

Through a newspaper advertisement I found a job at the Berlitz School of Languages. My first assignment was to teach German to the test pilots of the Sikorsky Aircraft Company in Bridgeport, Connecticut. I was amazed that a factory producing war machines would allow a stranger, especially a stranger raised in the enemy's camp, to move about and look around without any security clearance. This would not have happened in East Germany. Evidently being a Berlitz teacher counted for something.

It seems to me now that while teaching German, I was given a series of gentle lessons in the nature of prejudice. I had misgivings, for instance, when I learned that my students would be teaching West German pilots how to fly Sikorsky helicopters. What if those machines were ever used to invade the DDR? To drop bombs on my friends, on Bodo? One day a young German air force officer was shown around the plant, I don't know for what purpose, maybe to close the deal. He dropped in on my class, and later we chatted a little. He was just a touch too spunky and proud in his uniform, there was a clipped precision in his speech that reminded me of old movies about the Wehrmacht. Surprisingly, though, our conversation turned to literature, and he declared himself a fan of Nabokov's *Lolita,* which I had not read yet. "Oh, you must, you must," he said, and proceeded to commentate the book in the manner of a literary scholar: "In the foreground it is the story of a grown man's obsessive love of a schoolgirl, but really it's the story of Europe seduced by this wonderful childish America. It is *hochinteressant!*"

I was similarly prejudiced against Mr. LeClerq, my French colleague at the Berlitz School in Bridgeport, who, I was told, had recently served as a paratrooper in Algeria. I had read *La Question,* a French communist's account of his horrible mistreatment at the hands of the "paras," and now, here was one of those monsters, guilty at least by association, a cologne-scented, good-natured man whose most violent imprecation was *"mille dieux de merde,"* who told me in secretive tones that he was a theosophist, and, when I asked him what that meant, drew me a picture of two straight lines called "time" and "space" that converged in a focal point marked "Ego" and fanned out again, reborn and renamed, as "eternity" and "infinity." I still have a book I forgot to return to him, and should he read these words, he is most welcome to reclaim it: Edmond Jaloux's essay on Rilke's friendship with Eloui Bey.

I remember also two of the capitalist technocrats at Sikorsky Aircraft: Mr. Brainard, a cheerful energetic middle-aged man with a white crew cut who seemed to be in charge of the place, and a melancholy engineer who drove me home in his car a few times and who assumes in my memory the appearance of Humphrey Bogart in a raincoat. I liked these men, they were friendly, thoughtful, cultivated. My students, the test pilots, weren't exactly cultivated—I remember them laughing for several days each time the word *"warum"* was uttered, because, they said, it resembled an elephant's fart—but I liked them, too, and felt warmly accepted by them. So these are American workers, I thought: I wonder what their politics are, whether they feel any attraction to socialism, in Cuba if not in Russia. I found out on the last, fearsome day of the Cuban missile crisis, the day when the world's peace hung in the balance of a game of nerves between two politicians (announced by a voice on my wake-up radio station in the manner of a carnival barker: *"Rondayvoo with destiny!"*). One of the pilots, a middle-aged family man, thought the U.S. should nuke Cuba off the face of the earth: "Who needs Cuba?" A younger man suggested a worldwide roundup of communists, "and then shoot the women and string up the men by the balls."

One Friday night, after work, I went to a bar in my neighborhood, got into a conversation with two women, and went home with one of them. Both of us were too drunk for more than a few minutes of numb copulation. We slept back to back and exchanged an awkward good-bye in the morning. That afternoon Mrs. Libido informed me that we had offended her sensitive ear, and that if it happened once more I would have to move out. I'm sure she expected me to apologize and promise to be good, but instead I got angry and said something foolish about basic human rights. She was shocked, maybe frightened, and told me to start looking for a new place or she would have me evicted.

I found a new room nearby, in a large slummy rooming house that called itself the "Student Living Center" and was subsidized by Columbia University. No more than a third of the people living there were students. At the same time, Berlitz transferred me from Bridgeport to New York, which saved me the daily train ride and introduced me to some real capitalists, three executives of the advertising firm of Doyle, Dane & Bernbach, famous for their VW "Lemon" ad.

I taught them the rudiments of German in their top-floor office on Madison Avenue. One of them, Mr. Bernbach, I remember chiefly for his failure to learn any German at all. He was nice enough to acknowledge that it was his inability, not mine. The other two have lost their names in my recollection—they were not Doyle or Dane—in fact one of them lost everything, he has become a pure shadow. But I remember his colleague. He had gray hair and a long, youthful face, laughed a lot, and liked to cross his long legs on top of his desk. He was proud of his company's achievements. In the past, he said, Americans thought Brazilian coffee was the only coffee there was. Now they thought Colombian coffee was the only coffee there was—all thanks to Doyle, Dane & Bernbach.

Every morning an elderly black man named Sam came to shine our shoes while we went over the previous day's lesson. When Sam was done—a moment he marked with a ceremonial snap of his rag—my student would flip a quarter over his thumb and watch the old man lunge for it from his kneeling position. "Sam, you'd make one hell of a shortstop," he said once. Sam always grinned and said "thank you, boss." After the second or third shoeshine I wanted to pay the man too, but my student forbade me: "It's on the house," he said, laughing.

After Doyle, Dane & Bernbach, I taught a motley collection of people: a Peruvian diplomat, a skier who competed a lot in Austria, an anti-Semitic teutonophile, two Japanese businessmen who smiled and nodded in unison, a fashion model who took off her long lashes in my class and put them on again when she left, a Haitian expert on Hugo Wolff, a singer of German lieder, a historian of World War II.

But I am talking only of work. Like most employees, I was leading a double life. Weekday mornings I'd rush off to the Berlitz School sprinkled with pomade and wearing a black or gray suit and a tie, only to spend my evenings and weekends in bohemian squalor at the Student Living Center.

I didn't realize it at the time, but that scam of a college dormitory was a most uncommon and enlightened institution, precisely by being no more and no less than a pragmatic arrangement for the mutual benefit of a crafty landlord and a fairly random assortment of young New Yorkers, some of them students and the rest willing and able to pass themselves off as such, white, black, and Hispanic, male and female, hetero- and homosexual, all of us sharing communal kitchens and bathrooms (one for each floor), all of us adhering, by tacit and common consent, to a few rules relating to considerations of hygiene, and for the rest granting each other a very wide berth of personal freedom to read, watch TV, gossip, paint, fornicate, marry, quarrel, go to work, collect welfare, pray to Jesus, chant to Allah, study Lenin, or join the perpetual debating society around the kitchen table.

One of the regulars of that society, its vital center really, was Luke Ronaldson, a black actor who compensated for his chronic unemployment with hilarious displays of histrionic brilliance. Luke and I became friends. We talked a lot: about books, love, religion, theatre, politics, but mainly about the very different lives we had led. I liked him, and I know he liked me, but I think he was irritated by my comfortable East German innocence of the American race problem, and confused by my lack of evident interest in women, so he tried to test me: first by proposing that we go to bed together, an invitation which, I frankly told him, I found alarming, and also flattering, but not really appealing, since basically I seemed to be heterosexual, and then by attempting to shock me with not always tasteful impersonations of this or that icon of Afro-American dignity or bizarre stories about black people whose behavior conformed to some racist cliché—like the one about a stylish friend whose picture he showed me, the handsome African profile set off against the bilateral symmetry of a garden in Versailles, in order then to inform me, with darkly bubbling malice in his eyes and voice, that this emblem of elegance was an evil little whore and the source of all of Luke's problems, that he made little wax dolls resembling Luke and stuck pins in them, that he sat every day at sunset naked on a Paris rooftop thumping a bongo and sending evil thoughts in the direction of the Student Living Center. Gradually, though, as I came to know Luke, he showed me, through stories and jokes and often by way of small, deftly pointed remarks, something of what it had been like to learn, as a growing boy, that a quirky imagination, superior intelligence, a homosexual disposition, and African ancestry could not combine in one person—not in America, at any rate—without threatening just about everybody, and how deeply that knowledge had torn him.

One day my supervisor at the Berlitz School told me some gentlemen had come to ask about me, and that they would be back at one. One o'clock was my lunch break. The gentlemen wore gray hats, gray suits, and gray trench coats. They were from the FBI. Could they have a few words with me, it wouldn't take long. Of course, I said, where shall we go? Later, friends told me I could have said no, it was my right. My right! Never would it have occurred to me to say no to a government official. They took me to a Horn & Hardart's cafeteria. They took off their hats and revealed blond crew cuts. They kept on their coats and did not reveal their tape recorder. They wanted to hear my views concerning the nature of citizenship in the U.S. and "under communism." What was the difference? "The difference," I said, "the difference . . . ," and this word, "difference," set so many conflicting thoughts into motion that I couldn't complete the sentence. Today I can say it: "The difference is that here there is room for difference." I couldn't think this then, let alone say it, but I acted as if I knew it. I told the FBI what I believed, and where I wasn't sure of my beliefs I adopted the sort of opinions my stepfather would have been proud of. Democracy? A good idea, but not realizable under capitalism. Dictatorship of the proletariat? A transitional phase on the way from socialism to communism (that was a new one to them). The Soviet invasion of Hungary? A good thing, suppressing a fascist coup. The Berlin Wall? A bulwark against American tanks and a seal on the East German labor pool which was being drained by the unfair recruiting strategies of West German companies. Would I wish to overthrow the American government? This question exceeded the bounds of my political education. "What do you mean?" "Just that," they said. "Are you in favor of overthrowing the United States government?" "That would depend on who does the overthrowing. If Jesus Christ came to denounce Mammon and proclaim the Kingdom of Heaven, I would be in favor of it." "In that case, can you tell us what you were burning on December 11, 1961, in your last apartment on West Seventy-ninth Street?" They had me there. Off went the mask of political savvy, out came a certain sheepish smile well-known to me from kamikaze snapshots taken at parties and a few awful moments with mirrors. "Personal stuff," I said, "diaries. Bad poems." "Why didn't you dispose of them in the garbage?" "Because I wanted them thoroughly destroyed." The more sincere I got, the more they believed the revolutionist mask and the less they believed me. We parted with a firm handshake. One of them warned me: "Mr. Agee, you are an intelligent man, and frankly, I like you. Please don't ruin your life by going up against our system of government. It is stronger than you are. Heed my words." Because of them, I missed lunch that day. Because of them, I was fired the next week, supposedly for being five minutes late to work.

The Turtle

A friend of my mother's introduced me to the folksinger and photographer John Cohen, who was planning to make a documentary film about Kentucky country musicians and needed an assistant. I said I wanted the job, he said "you got it." I said I had no experience with a movie camera, he said "I don't either." In fact he didn't have a camera.

We borrowed a 16 mm Arriflex from a friend of his. He showed us how to mount it on the tripod, load it, wind it, use it. We should give the machine a trial run, though, he said, just to make sure it was in working order. The trial run took place on top of a second friend's building. We were going to film the roofs of the Village, the sky, the pigeons, each other. But a third friend of John's dropped by, a folksinger named Bob Dylan who was all excited about some new songs he had written, and we ended up making a fifteen-minute film of him. I recognized him immediately: "I saw you at the Gaslight Cafe," I said.

"I saw you too," he said. "You walked out on me. You and your girl."

"It wasn't because of you," I said.

"I didn't think so," he said.

John Cohen was the filmmaker and I was the assistant. Throughout our work in Kentucky, he rarely let me use the camera. But on that roof, he let me do the shooting. After all, it was just a trial run.

Because we didn't have any sound equipment, Dylan could pretend to do virtuoso runs up and down the neck of his guitar. Then he sang one of his new songs, something involving a request for a pillow from the woman who had locked him out of her room.

"It's rock 'n roll!" John said.

"Yeh. Do you like it?"

"You've got something there. Keep it up."

"I will."

Memory is fickle, and maybe snobbish, and fame is a glue that makes time stick fast for a while. Why else would a relatively banal moment like this one continue to burn as clear as yesterday while the entire month I spent in Kentucky, in circumstances as strange to me and as interesting as any I have encountered since, lies largely submerged in oblivion, with just a few details rising through the mist like fragments of a dream? But as I jot down these fragments, I see others coming up with them: the tiny village of Daisy, some twenty wooden houses scattered in a valley among rugged hills, and the long, haggard face of one of its denizens, Roscoe Holcomb, looking old in his early sixties, with thin sad lips and creased cheeks, deep-set puzzled pale blue eyes shaded by a wide-brimmed hat, bony hands plucking the banjo strings, singing with a high reedy voice:

> *Uhcross the Rocky Maa-oon-taaaaaaaaaaains . . .*
> *Ah've traaaaaaaa-veled far'n'wide . . .*

An alien sound interferes, it's Chubby Checker on the radio, Roscoe's daughter is dancing the twist and maybe protesting against the folkways we're here to record. Roscoe quietly puts down the banjo and looks out over the hills, as he often does, sometimes for hours. There is time in those hills, he told us that: "Waaay back inna ole Pro-high-bishun days you could hear the sound of banjers comin down, clangity-clang, from all over dem hee-ills." And now I see the spirit moving like a whirlwind through a dark pinewood church, moving the women especially, "Jesus!" "Oh Jesus!", one of them driven up and off her bench so suddenly she drops her one-year-old—*clunk!*—on the wooden floor: *"waaaaa!"*, to be picked up by another woman, because the mother is hopping up and down with flat feet tight together raising her face and stretching her arms to heaven and letting out strangely sexual yelps and squeals and then dropping to her knees in a puddle of sunlight with her arms thrown out from her sides, her head thrown back, her long blond hair spread over her shoulders, and immediately several women swoop in to stroke her hair, stroke, stroke, urging her deeper into ecstasy, while in front of the altar one of the five musicians, the guitarist, goes into a different kind of seizure, he's strumming away with his eyes rolled up and his whole body vibrating vertically, very fast, so that his shoes rattle against the floor like a jackhammer, and then I notice he's slowly sliding across the platform until he's facing the altar and has his back turned on the congregation. I see Roscoe again, in his garden, stalking one of his chickens with a rifle and shooting it inexpertly in the side and then whacking its head on a rock a few times, while John Cohen and Roscoe's wife and a neighbor watch, laughing and clapping their hands. And now I realize why John urged me to read Isaac Babel's short stories and especially the one called "My First Goose," in which a bookish young Jew conscripted to a Red Army detachment of Cossacks proves his mettle by brutalizing a blind old woman and crushing a goose's head with his heel, and why John told me a couple of times that "we'll make a man of action out of you." That was his fantasy for himself, going South with a banjo and telling the folks there his name was Cone ("no definitely not Coon, no *sir*, it's Cone as in pinecone, yup") was as close an approximation as could be found, in American terms, to Isaac Babel's riding with the Cossacks, and if I flinched at the sight of our dinner still half alive, mangled and fluttering in the bushes, it was because I was still, like the young Babel, content to live with "winter in the heart," ignorant of the inseparable beauty and cruelty of life. Of course John didn't say this outright, but for several days after the chicken episode all our talk took place in the nimbus of some such meaning. For example, I had brought with me a book of poems by Yeats and read out loud to John one evening that tremendous poem, "The Second Coming." There was one phrase in particular that struck me: ". . . and everywhere / The ceremony of innocence is drowned." I said I imagined the image had come to Yeats from the common practice, among country people, of drowning kittens in a sack weighted with stones. John shrugged and said: "Maybe. But the poem isn't about pity. The point of view is cosmic, not human. It's the icy lake, not the kittens. And that's something country people know in their bones." It was the shrug that bothered me. I finally told him that I didn't believe in the virtue of blood and cathartic violence. I was quivering with anger, but I spoke with an air of philosophic dispassion. Consequently, the heat of our disagreement simmered on, unacknowledged and unabated, until it manifested itself, not as an argument but in a ghastly and, as it were, illustrative event.

We went to visit the Carsons, a family of musicians. Mr. Carson, a miner, was late coming home from work. We waited for him. John chatted with Mrs. Carson while she peeled potatoes. A five-year-old girl stood half hidden behind her, staring alternately at me and at John, the expression on her face constantly shifting from a look of wide-open astonishment to a faint and quickly suppressed tickle of amusement, which, I noticed, overcame her especially at moments when I spoke, I suppose because of my unfamiliar accent. Another daughter, approximately my age, sat shucking corn and partaking in her mother's conversation with smiles and nods of her head. A third girl, fourteen or fifteen years old, tall and slender, with carrot-red hair reaching down to her waist, appeared briefly at the edge of the kitchen from behind the doorpost and watched me as I loaded the camera. When I looked at her, she withdrew— slowly, as if to hide the very movement of her disappearance. After a while, half her body and face emerged again, and this time I avoided looking at her. With Mrs. Carson's permission, I took a few preliminary shots of the house and the garden, the chickens, the tethered goat with its legs splayed the better to tear up dry clumps of grass at the foot of the porch, and an old dog twisted in furious battle with the fleas at the root of his tail. Presently Mr. Carson could be heard roaring up the hill and with a bump through the creek we had stopped at on our drive up, and then we saw him in a battered Jeep, waving his hat as he pulled up. He was still in his work clothes and his face and hands were streaked with soot, he hadn't washed up too good, he said, so he couldn't shake hands just yet, but he'd be right out, and while he went into the kitchen his wife said, smiling, that sometimes her husband came home looking just like a nigger. Then, by the time he'd come out washed and combed wearing a clean cotton shirt and a fresh pair of frayed overalls and had shaken our hands and admired the camera and chatted with John and played on John's banjo and listened to John playing, the light had gotten too dark for shooting and John asked if we could come back, maybe Sunday after church, and make pictures of all of them singing, and Mr. Carson said that would be just fine, and for now, he hoped we could stay for dinner because he'd brought something special, a big surprise for the kids, but it would take some work to prepare it and then a good long time of cooking. John said he was sorry but we were expected for dinner at the Holcombs', but he'd sure like to see what the big surprise was. I started packing up the gear while Mr. Carson went down to his Jeep and lifted a pile of rags off the backseat and, with an effortful squatting heave, lifted a large object and turned and walked toward us with bent knees, pressing it against his waist, a giant snapping turtle, upside down, legs walking the air in slow motion, the gray serpentine head swiveling slowly from side to side. He put the turtle on its back on a table next to the porch and said to his youngest daughter, who was still hiding behind her mother, "Emily, go tell America to come on out." And while Emily went inside, he went into a shed in the back of the house and came out with a hammer and a handful of nails and laid them next to the turtle, which was still steadily moving its feet, and pulled out a jack-knife and opened it and put it next to the hammer and nails, and said, looking at John, that he hoped we didn't mind if he just got to work on the turtle, and John said that was no problem at all, we'd be leaving soon anyhow, and picked up his banjo, and started playing a cheerful, here-we-sit-on-the-porch sort of tune. Emily came out with her older sister. All I remember now of her appearance is that her skin was of that creamiest white that makes the lips look painted, and that her eyes were wide-set and of gentle expression and fero-ciously blue, but what I thought then was: I can see why she hides herself, she's dangerous to look at.

"Girl," Mr. Carson said, "it ain't polite, hidin back there when folks come and visit."

She bowed her head.

"You remember Mr. Cone?"

"I sure do," she said, smiling at John and nodding hello. John nodded and smiled back, still playing his tune. Then she came over to me, and as we shook hands, she made a slight dipping movement, a remnant or intimation of a curtsy, and in that moment I heard Mr. Carson pounding in his first nail. I pressed the girl's hand and held her eyes with mine, and then my chest began to ache as if some sharp thing was being driven into me, and there was no telling, later, when I thought back on it, whether it was the sight of her or the thought of the mute agony on the table that made me feel that way, or some unimaginable amalgam of these, but the frightening notion was there right away, that if I had to stay here another day, I would fall in love with this girl as hopelessly as I had with Sylvia. "Joel," I said, "my name's Joel." "My name's America," she said, and "pleased to meet you," she added, and began to blush. I released her hand, I'd held it much too long, and for a moment the only sounds were those of John's quiet playing and of the corn dropping softly into the pot between the oldest girl's feet, and of Mrs. Carson's knife carving the peel off the potatoes, but then came the pounding of the hammer again, and I decided to turn and look.

Emily was standing by the table, next to her father. The turtle was still upside down, its hind legs steadily walking—or, who knows, in a turtle's measure, maybe scampering, racing. Mr. Carson was pressing one hand against the gray under-shell and with the other pulling the turtle's left front leg out of its socket and over the rim of the shell and forcing it all the way down to the table. Then he set a nail against the foot and took the hammer and drove the nail through the foot into the table. The other front foot was already nailed down and grotesquely elongated. The neck, too, was pulled long and taut like a rubber rope and held fast by a nail just below the jaw, which was mouthing the air in a sideward scissoring motion. Mr. Carson picked up the knife and stepped around the table and bent over the turtle, blocking my sight. What I saw was the child, who was standing opposite. I looked at John, who was still plunking away at his ditty, and realized he couldn't see what Mr. Carson was doing, though he might well have imagined it, if he wished to. What he couldn't imagine, what I could not imagine either, though I was looking into her face, was what was happening to Emily. But it froze the blood in my veins to see the signs of it: her shoulders hunched almost up to her ears, her mouth open, the corners of her lips pulled way down, her arms cramped to her sides, her fingers splayed. She didn't look human. A demon? No. If I were to paint a soul at the gate of hell, that is how I would picture it: right on the threshold, looking down, with nothing to hold her. Ten feet away, her two sisters, her mother, and John, like the rustic extras in a Breughel landscape. But there is another figure in this tableau. Of course I can't see him. It's me. I am just looking. Everything in me has turned cold, and in that coldness, there is no pity, no pain, only the prayer for an end.

Here, had he stayed with the moment, he might have found himself standing in the ever-open door where all selves converge and from which all paths issue. But already he's back in his tiny room at the "Student Living Center," opening a package from Germany, it's a new book by his stepfather, *Im Rhythmus der Conga*, an account for the walled-in East Germans of what it's like to travel to a tropical island. The story opens with a description of Bodo's departure "in the glassy light of a cold morning in June," he is being driven past "the stony desolation of Strausberger Platz," past a building covered with scaffolding, a metal gridwork "like the bars of a prison." Is this a realistic description or political commentary, wonders the stepson in New York, and how did it slip past the censors? Meanwhile his future self in Berlin, still standing by Bodo's grave, feels again in his back the approach of something eerily familiar, turns, and sees nothing but rain and wet graves. "What is it?" he asks himself. "What am I trying to remember?" The question sends him into his body and through a labyrinth of nerves and synapses far back to another, much younger self, a child who is lying with his cheek and ear pressed against a stone floor in Mexico, hearing the silence of stone and feeling its hardness and coldness as something mysteriously pleasant and comforting. The child is content to be wooed by mystery, but the one by the grave wants to know: "What is it?" The one in New York, meanwhile, riffles the pages in his stepfather's book, he's impatient, he hopes for some message not meant for the conscience of generations but just for him. The later one in Berlin walks out through the cemetery gate onto the wet street, uncertain whether to drop in on his old school friend, Ralle, or return to his hotel near Kurfürstendamm. He stops in front of a bookstore and decides to ask for his stepfather's last book, the one about Cuba, which he left unread in New York: What better time to read it than now, after this belated visit? His earlier self in New York puts *Im Rhythmus der Conga* on a shelf and, in his half-somnolent way, moves on. He is not in a hurry. He should be, it will be disastrous for him if he comes to Berlin and finds himself missing.

Enter Stefan

Last night, before falling asleep, I performed a spiritual exercise of sorts, I don't know under what inner prompting. It felt vaguely Yogic, maybe a memory of some instruction I had read in a book. I imagined a white-gold globe of light descending over the top of my head and moving down slowly through the neck, torso, arms, pelvis, thighs, knees, calves, to the feet, where I intended to reverse the flow and move upward again in a different color, probably blue. But when I arrived at my feet, I saw clearly before me, unbidden, unexpected, my brother as he appeared at the time I am remembering here: tall, gaunt, his shirt collar too wide for his neck, his soft lips parted on the verge of either a snarl or a sob, his head turned to the side with the chin slightly raised, as if craning for a view, but he wasn't looking at anything. I saw him very clearly for a moment, and then he was gone. There was an awful expression in his eyes, something worse than sorrow, a despair that had abjured all protest or appeal as hopeless and meaningless. And now an old worry comes up in me, the fear of hurting him with my thoughts. Didn't he complain of this while he was still alive? Don't I remember a rhymed letter he sent from India, in which he asked us to please not think of him so hard, because he could feel our thoughts, and it was hard enough to fend off his own? And now, without the brittle shield of the body, would he not be even less defended against mental influence? Should I not therefore imagine him healthy and sane? These worries beset me, and then I remember that thirteen years after his death I saw him wholly restored and in perfect health. It was in a series of nocturnal visions—I call them that because they weren't normal dreams, they were preternaturally real in their texture and so strong that their message of miracle pulverized all doubt: *He is well, he is whole and sane, and strangest, most wondrous of all, he is alive.*

I won't retrace his path through the realms of pain. But I will have to tell about him.

I will be careful.

Where to begin among the enormous sheaves of his journals, poems, sketches, stories?

Maybe this: Here is what he wrote on a day when he couldn't bring himself to go to school (I am translating from his German):

Went to the Met to look at Cézanne again, after reading some Rilke letters. Stood around, "experienced" nothing, as was to be expected, but was far less distracted than usual by the giggling and talking around me and by my own scruples and random thoughts. I took note, as I walked around, of a few pictures which I wasn't able to "grasp" at the moment, but where I felt hopeful. For ten minutes I stared at six goddamned red and green apples and finally said to myself: patience, patience, patience. And though that was not an original piece of advice, it was good. Not till I reached an unfinished portrait of his wife was I surprised by a substance that was really there and not of my making: the "wholeness" of the form, and the immediately real, convincing, "engaging" quality, especially of the face, was "simple, good, right." But there is so much nauseating prattle around, you have to be awfully careful with your words, above all you mustn't praise the picture, the understanding has to take place without words, and you have to be modest—because art-historical panegyrics are noisy and immodest. I went to the Rembrandt for a few minutes (Pilate), noticed (without words) some similarities, went back, in passing skimmed some Modiglianis, which struck me as almost dandyish, and stared at another Cézanne. Tried to take the right stance, pull myself together, concentrate. No angel whispered in my ear. I sat down and watched a group of chattering art lovers standing in front of a huge picture and waving their hands. They were wearing drab, dreary street clothes. They moved like ghosts, but without a touch of the uncanny— amorphous, stupid, characterless. The portrait next to them: a strong expression, but not and never rigid, just "simple, right, good"—(the word "beautiful" is so beautifully superfluous!)—a picture, a thing—spreading a feeling of certainty and honesty—except it wasn't a "feeling"—which is something you can wait for till the end of time, because that's in the realm of the shapeless—no, there was no feeling being spread, it was just there, emotion had become a thing, and while you attended to your ears just in case an angel did come with a whisper, it was all right in front of you. The contrast between the noisy, anonymous people waffling and wavering like smoke, and the silent, absolute, self-evident certainty of the picture, is all. And so every painter is really a different kind of painter, and his pictures are absolutely individual, for things are substances, and forms are limits, and reified feelings form the limits of his subjectivity.

On the way home from the museum, alongside the park, a woman about 45 years old came toward me; thin, with the features of an older self in the lines of her face, bent forward and seemingly driven by the wind, but actually following the paths of a skipping, yanking little dog she was holding by a leash. Noticing that she was touching her eyes with a handkerchief and sniffing, I looked at her. She came toward me in a tentative slantward way, and her face showed that she had cried and was still crying. Sensing that she would look at me the next moment, I quickly and inadvertently closed my eyes, shuddered, and let out a soundless gasp. At that moment there was no doubt that I understood and she did too.

Which, written down, may sound contrived and "artistic." But on my walk it was just what it was.

He was sixteen years old when he wrote that.

Here is another, very different page, written in English. There's a lot more of the snarl than the sob in this one. It's about the people who impinged on his senses at the Walden High School:

N., thumb-nosed, a chin like a knee, always "interested" quasi-ethereal blue eyes, whistles almost constantly the same snatch from a Brandenburg Concerto, always eager to catch every word that escapes my mouth, bending forward as he listens, a seriousness that has its origin in the heavy chin. O., the smily pimply Artist with the massive roundeyed square face, good marks wax-haired belted fat but well-dressed (suit!). P., the well-read boring redhaired history teacher, Q. the tolerantly smiling social studies lady, R., the slickslimsmilethintongued extremely well-read napoleonhaired eloquent amusing statisticslecturing-at-NYU but only almost brilliant Frenchteacher, and there, approaching lazysteppedly sloppy-clothed, S., brown bovine eyes round empty lips rustic hair and chin, and T., the well-groomed curlyflaxhaired smallstepped thinsmiling poetryprize author, and U., bullet-skulled intelligent well-read and cheerful but incurably liberal and dull, and of course the 99.47% pure bourgeois well-adjusted girls, unutterably pleased with their pre-packaged selves, and millions in the narrow swarming corridor, eating, bumping into me, hair faces eyes brushing past, "HI!" and "HELLO!" and fluttering smiles all without seriousness or substance. And then the mirrors where I bump into a strangely familiar person, moi-même, looking back at me QUATSCH.

Terrifying thought: to meet the maker of all that hate. Better to bring down a word like an axe between himself and himself: QUATSCH! All that the word means is "nonsense," but wielded like this, it means murder, and worse than that, capital punishment. Not now, but eventually, ten years later. Until then, a gradual torture, of which his drawings give testimony: writhing supplicants, disemboweled amid flames and mechanical wreckage. Finally, the sentence: death by defenestration. And he has to do it himself—be the shivering victim and the hooded executioner, on a windowed tower above the multitude. Was it the same pedestal where he once stood enshrined as the Walden Private High School's undisputed genius, surrounded by the grotesque "millions" conjured out of a few dozen boys and girls and a couple of teachers who did their best to welcome the tall pale stranger in their midst, to include him in their entertainments, to teach him to dance, and even to love him? He bungled the first fall, producing nothing but broken bones and a temporary restoration of human appetite, human affection. The second and last execution was clean and final, headfirst from the sixth-floor window of his mother's apartment.

■

Ah, but I have my own selves to attend to. The older one in Berlin is back in his hotel on Kurfürstendamm reading in his stepfather's book about Carnival in Santiago de Cuba:

"Two wonderfully lithe and musical Negroes dance to the crowd's happy chant: 'I lost the key, I lost the key, I lost the key, I lost the key.'"

What would that be in Spanish? "Se me perdió la llave." He thinks of a likely tune and hums it:

Se me perdió la llave,

Se me perdió la llave.

The younger one in New York meanwhile (but he's just ten days younger now) boards a Dutch ship that will take him to Germany. He is in a very great hurry, running away, in fact, from several things:

a) the need to work for a living,

b) the pressure to "make something of himself,"

c) boredom and self-disgust,

d) Sylvia, who appears to have found "mature love" with Victor, of all people.

That is the last straw. Away! And besides, he wants to make a film about Carnival in Cuba, and has cooked up the idea of asking DEFA for help. The Statue of Liberty slides past, Manhattan recedes under a cloud of soot, the ship is full of teenagers dancing that new pelvic dance, the Twist, under the benign supervision of their social science teacher. Two hours before docking in Bremen, shivering on the windy deck, he finds himself sounding like Frantz Fanon as he debates the teacher in front of his class on the role of the intellectual in capitalist society: "We have to fight fire with fire," he says impressively, causing a boy with a round bespectacled face to nod in openmouthed admiration, which makes him ashamed of his imposture, but he can't change course without losing face, and besides it's pleasant to sound like a man of conviction. "You're so ruthless," the teacher says. That knocks all the pomp out of him. "I'm not ruthless," he'd like to say, "I'm lying," but he doesn't say that, he just stands there looking bitter. In his cabin, later, he is ashamed, and never again plays the intransigent revolutionist. Away! Faster, faster! The night train takes him to Berlin, he shares a compartment with a profoundly depressed Polish intellectual and his achingly timid ten-year-old daughter, the man's face is a map of the century's terrors and disillusionments, but he loves his daughter, his love and his heartache fill the compartment like deep old music, and for the first time since receiving the news of his stepfather's death a few months before, Joel feels orphaned and secretly weeps into his Mitropa pillow. But in the middle of his grief there's a strange sense of having been here before, in this same train compartment precisely, with this same ad for Stolichnaya Vodka overhead, and this same brooding Pole opposite, and this same little girl with the pale solemn face and white bony knees. He awakes at dawn to an East German border guard's charmless demand for identification. Why does everything feel so secondhand, so—remembered? A brief nap in West Berlin, he gets arrested at Checkpoint Charlie, spends the night in the house of a Stasi officer's aunt, arrives, dazed, at his stepfather's grave, is transported back to his childhood, facedown on a cool tile terrace in Cuernavaca, hears himself softly singing words in Spanish, his first language, the language of beautiful dark-skinned sweet-smelling Zita, the maid who once let him rest his face against her large cool naked breast after she had washed herself in the garden:

> Se me perdió la llave,
>> Se me perdió la llave,
> Se me perdió la llave,
>> Se me perdió la llave.

Flights

For three days now I've been sitting here stranded—"I" being the one who is writing this, "here" being my desk in Brooklyn—trying to find the right line, the right tone, the right key in which to continue. *Se me perdió la llave.* I could advance my two-selves-become-one through five bizarre weeks in Berlin as he waited for DEFA to respond to his proposal. I could show him standing like Janus with one face looking forward and the other looking back. I could sail him through the dream-time in which he has been traveling, right on to his destination in Cuba, bypassing minor stations and secondary selves along the way (they don't need help, they'll catch up on their own). Between these and other alternatives I dithered, filling my notebook with alternative beginnings. But this morning a dream came and showed me another route. In the dream, I had requested an airplane from the Cuban government, represented by a friendly woman in army fatigues who was seated behind a plain wooden table, outside, near a beach, surrounded by palms. Unlike DEFA, she met my request with a simple stroke of her pen—so matter-of-factly, I couldn't believe her "yes" had the weight of official sanction. I thought: I do have credentials to back me up: My stepfather fought in the Spanish Civil War. And I began to tell her how Bodo had saved the life of the great French writer and aviation pioneer Antoine de Saint-Exupéry. She was keenly interested.

What a helpful dream! With this airplane, I can survey the whole landscape of my travels through time, not just in Cuba but elsewhere. But before taking off, before leaving Bodo's grave and the walled-in city behind and below me, I shall tell the story of how Bodo saved Saint-Exupéry, and a second, loosely connected story about Bodo's escape to France in April 1933.

The first story is just the bare bones of an anecdote, the way he told it. I was reading *Wind, Sand, and Stars.* I asked Bodo if he had ever met Saint-Exupéry.

"As a matter of fact yes," he said. "In Spain."

"Was he in the International Brigades too?"

"No, he was his own private army. He would come flying in from France and drop bombs on the fascists and fly home. Until one day he was shot down. By us."

"Why?"

"By mistake. His plane had no colors to tell you what was what. No one knew who he was."

"Did he crash? Was he hurt?"

"No, he bailed out and came down with a parachute."

"Is that how you met him?"

"Yes. I was the commissar. The soldiers wanted to shoot him, they thought he was some kind of fascist adventurer. But then they turned him over to me, and of course the minute he told me his name, I knew who he was, because I had read his books and admired him very much."

That's it. Another man, another writer, would have made hay out of this. But if I hadn't asked him, he would never have told me about it, and as far as I know, he never wrote it down.

The story of his flight to France is precious to me, because it is one of the very few stories he ever told me about himself. And yet I'm not sure whether it is altogether factual. Not that he made it up, but it may have changed in my memory. When did he tell it to me? It may have been early in my life. That would account for the color and glow of certain details.

I have searched Bodo's books for corroboration. Nowhere does he describe how he left Germany. That's where my doubts come from. Why would a writer not use such a story? I know that he left illegally. The police were after him. He had been in hiding since the day the Nazis accused the communists of setting fire to the Reichstag building.

Last night I called Berlin to ask Günther Caspar, Bodo's former secretary and the editor of his collected works, if he could fill me in on some of the details of this adventure.

He said: "I've never heard of this. I believe it's a legend."

"If it's a legend," I said, "it's one he created, because I heard it from him."

"That's not inconceivable. You were a child. Parents sometimes tell their children tall tales."

"Do you know how he got out of Germany?" I asked.

"I think he got in a train and went to Paris."

But Bodo wouldn't have made up this story. Except for this one time, he never talked about his encounters with danger and war, out of a kind of modesty, I think. So why did he tell me this story in such detail? He must have thought it important.

He told me he took the train from Berlin to some town near the French border and walked off into the woods. He had hiking boots on and one of those little green hats German hikers wear, and a rucksack. In his breast pocket was a set of false identity papers and a map. The trees had sprouted tender new leaves, and there were little blue flowers in the moss. I'm suspicious of this detail, because the blue flower is an old German symbol of romantic transcendence, so I may very well have put it here in an unconscious reflex of associative memory. Or else Bodo invented the flowers, for the same sentimental reason. But it's just as likely that there really were blue flowers in that forest. When a symbol, even the most hackneyed symbol, presents itself at a time of danger, it is recharged with its original power and the mind is stirred to its depths. I can imagine that this is what happened to Bodo on that walk which could have been his last.

The reason for the hiker's disguise and for walking instead of taking the train across the border was that he couldn't risk the passport control—though again, I'm not sure of the details. Was it that he needed an exit visa and didn't have one? Or were his false papers too crudely made to pass careful inspection?

He followed the path drawn with ink by the friends who had helped plan his escape. Then he left the path and walked south with the help of a compass. And then he saw a man with a rifle, a German border guard, and the guard spotted him and ordered him to halt, approached, saluted him, demanded to know where he was going and where he came from. Bodo said he was from X and was staying in a hotel at Y, and that he had come here to see this wonderful forest in the spring. The guard asked for his papers. Bodo showed them to him. And there, inside the passport, was the train ticket showing his place of departure, not X but Berlin. How unimaginably careless! This was the most terrible moment of his life, because it was like receiving a death sentence which he had inexplicably passed on himself.

The guard told him to raise his hands and searched him. In his coat was the map with the inked paths and arrows pointing toward France, and in the rucksack were several sets of clothes.

"You are under arrest," the guard said. "Put your hands down. Walk in front of me. If you run, you will be shot."

They walked silently together for a while, until they came within sight of a ruined castle.

As they passed the castle, Bodo stopped. The guard ordered him to move on. Bodo just stood there. Now the guard pointed his gun at him and barked: "Move!" But Bodo just looked at him and said: "Please let me look out from that tower, just for a minute. Do me this one favor. I'll probably never see a sight like this again." The soldier considered this request, examined the top of the tower, shrugged, and said: *"Von mir aus"*—"It's all right with me"—and motioned Bodo to walk ahead, up the broad flight of stairs and into the castle, and followed him along a hallway, up to the entrance of the tower. As Bodo started going up the winding stairs, he noticed the man was not following him, and for a moment he thought: "Now he'll shoot me in the back." But the guard said: "I'll wait here. Don't try to escape, I'll shoot you." There was no way to escape in any case. A leap from the tower would have broken his legs.

I don't know what Bodo saw and felt on top of that tower. I don't know whether he thought of his parents or of Ellen Roy, the American woman he had lived with in Berlin, or of his comrades, or of his grandfather, a retired Prussian officer, whom he had loved and who used to cut lard sandwiches into neat little squares, or of his boyhood dream of flying a plane, or of the better world he wanted to build and would not live to see, or of the children he would never have. All of these thoughts are conceivable and even probable, but he didn't tell me anything except that he was up there for a while. Then he walked back down the winding stairs.

The guard wasn't there. What to do? The man was probably hiding, waiting for a move that could be interpreted as flight. So Bodo waited. There was no sound. He coughed. No response. He called: *"Hallo?"* Then, very cautiously, he took a step, and another step, and so on. Very slowly he entered a large roofless hall, which was full of shrubs and dead leaves and rustling lizards. Right in front of him was a spider in the middle of its web.

Now he knew the guard was outside. He went back to the corridor, stopped, and waited again; plucked up his courage and walked back to the main entrance. There, on the top of the stairs, lay his passport and the map. He picked them up, put them in his coat pocket. I think he stood there for a while. Then he took out the map again, oriented himself, and slowly set off again in the direction of France.

■　　■　　■

And now for my dream-plane. This is not an ordinary plane, I realize. It is one I have to imagine, but it is itself a vehicle for the imagination. It's not made for time-travel, after all. To raise myself up with it—up and above the flatlands of memory. So how do I imagine it?

It appears to be a small military plane, very primitive by contemporary supersonic standards. Maybe it's Saint-Exupéry's plane, even though it's a gift from the Cuban government. The cockpit is cramped, offering room for one person only, and it's dark, of a dark-leathery color. The springs of the seat creak metallically beneath my weight. Of course I'm wearing goggles and one of those leather helmets that cover the ears and are strapped below the chin and make the head look like a brown egg. Before me the crowded constellations of the instrument panel, and the joystick. Among the instruments is one that resembles a cat's eye, and I notice that as I pause to wonder at its possible use, it opens, and a word appears, not as it will on this page when I write it down, as three letters, and not as a sound either, but disembodied, as a complete thought and meaning, almost an impulse:

No, I'm not ready for that. The eye closes. I turn the key in the ignition. The motor kicks in, the propellers—one on either wing—start to heave, turn, whirl, the motor roars its readiness, but I must let it warm up for a few minutes. Pleasure of all this contained power and potentiality. And of my solitude. The plane is rolling now, righting itself on the runway. Am I steering it? No, it moves by itself. But in accord with my will. So far, anyway. Why did I say that? Perhaps it's my will to yield the controls to another, invisible pilot; I don't know. Perhaps it's his wish that I tune my will to his. Perhaps I'm imagining him along with the plane and myself in the plane. Perhaps he's imagining me. But in any case, the plane is now rising above Berlin, the sun is setting over Brandenburg, and without transition we are surrounded by an ocean of stars in black space, and below, far below, on the black earth, I see stars that are cities and towns, and a long, sinuous line, like a strand of silver hair, a river. I could rise higher, I realize—and no sooner does the thought enter my mind than I feel myself rising: higher, higher, leaving Europe behind me, Africa, the globe itself, higher and higher, beyond the stratosphere, past Mars and Jupiter, past Saturn, Uranus, past Pluto, who has transgressed Neptune's sphere to come nearer to the sun, as if to soak up some warmth before returning to the outer darkness—but this is later, much later, 1989 to be exact, when I was near fifty and Pluto in his perihelion presided over the collapse of communist rule in Europe. How did I get here, this is much too fast, I had no intention of skipping all those years! Neptune slides past with his moons, and after a span of darkness in the relentless drone of the motor, another large body floats past, and now the plane swerves—who is flying this thing, anyway?—and I see the sun and the planets shrink down to a shimmering oval bulge of light, a star, one among billions, lost, and now the personal pronoun reverts to me here at my desk in Brooklyn, for the one in space is no longer capable of saying the word "I" and feeling its meaning—his airplane, his precious shell, has dissolved, he is spread out in space without even the resistance of air to tell him the difference between inside and out, up and down, far and near, large and small. He knows he is lost, a speck in the infinite, all his yearning is toward this place where I am, but when he cries out for home, the word seems to swallow the whole immensity. HOME. He says it again, from the aspirant "h" through the huge round "o" to the final closing and sealing. Is he falling? Where would he be falling from, or to? Rising? To what eminence higher than his? This creature who once was the measure of all things has become boundless.

What happened? I thought I was going up for a wider view, for surveillance maybe, for reconnaissance—it was a military plane, after all. But it took off in the dark and went, literally, nowhere.

Which leaves me back where I started, with two widely separate selves to worry about, one of them in oblivion and the other one in Berlin. Not to mention the other ones further ahead. Including the one in hell whom I've already mentioned, and who, as I've said before, should not be made to wait. Nothing to do but continue on foot. And I notice with what relief I say that. I don't really want to get there in a hurry.

My first errand in East Berlin was to meet with the former Minister of Culture, Alexander Abusch, in his office at the Ministry of the Interior. He was not as friendly to me as I thought I had reason to expect. Like the Stasi, he scoffed at my film proposal.

"Carnival," he said with distaste. "This is not what we need. It may, of course, be excellent for Cuba. . . ."

He raised his hands forfendingly.

"Far be it from me to deny the Cuban people their cultural heritage. But for us . . ."

He pointed through the window at the Wall.

"We are beleaguered. Culturally as well as militarily."

He drummed his fingers on his desk. Everything he did looked like a bad actor's portrayal of statesmanship under duress.

"You know the kind of music our young people are attracted to."

"Yes."

"Hmmm . . ."

Some unspoken thought had caught his attention. He took his chin in his hand and nodded: "Hmmm . . . Maybe . . . Maybe . . ." And then, for the first time since I had formulated my proposal, he looked at me.

"Do you like American Negro music?"

"Um, yes, frankly I do."

"My question surprises you," he said, pleased with the effect. "What are you doing for money these days? I'm sure you could use a job."

"Well . . . the job I'm looking for is to make this film."

"I know, I know. I'll bring the matter up with DEFA. It may take some time before they respond. In the meantime, though, you have to make a living. Or not?"

"I suppose I do. But I don't have a work permit."

"Don't worry. I know just where you're needed."

"I was already offered a job."

"Oh?"

"By the *Staatssicherheitsdienst*. I turned it down."

"This one is different."

It *was* different. In East Berlin, where even the radio dial was subject to border patrols and listening to the wrong kind of music could land you in jail, there was a radio station, approved and financed by the stodgiest politburo on the planet, that risked the corruption of East German youth by broadcasting a daily fare of wonderful jazz and rhythm-and-blues, auditory bait for the souls of GIs stationed in the West, especially black GIs, the idea being to haul them in, once they were hooked, on some frankly political line. I very much doubt that any GI was ever converted to communism by this radio program, but the people running it—two black Americans, a couple of white compatriots, and some German technicians—were hopeful of success, and felt that a new American voice might add to their credibility.

My audition focused on the rendering of the following phrase, against a background of thumping drums:

> This
> is the heartbeat
> of the Negro people.
> Listen
> to the heartbeat.

The two black Americans tried to help me sound black: "Linger a little on the s's . . . speak more from your chest. . . ." I was hopeless as a Negro, but they used my voice anyway, because theirs were already overexposed. I proved more useful as an actor in their radio plays. Every week, they ran a play about some West German big shot with a past in the Waffen-SS or Gestapo. I was a natural for these parts because, not being German but speaking the language fluently, I could inject a snarling Hollywood-Nazi accent into my English lines, like a burst from a clogged machine-gun—something the German technicians could not bring themselves to do. On the other hand, their emotional delivery was better than mine. A Nazi, to them, was not a vicious man but a fiend incarnate, and they played him as such, shrieking with rage in his heyday, and later subdued but slimy behind a democratic mask, with an oily sort of menace. I always held back in the portrayal of evil. Not that I didn't believe in it, on the contrary; but it felt embarrassing, almost immodest, to put your heart into it.

One day when I came home from work—I don't remember to which of the several apartments where I stayed as the guest of friends and friends of friends—I found a letter waiting for me, from the United States Armed Forces Local Draft Board Number so-and-so, requesting my appearance for a physical examination at such and such a date, for the purpose of determining my fitness for service in the United States Army. The news hit me like a blow to the chest, and as I sat there, stunned, the whole absurdity of my situation revealed itself to me. Here I was, transfixed by Uncle Sam's finger, in East Berlin, of all places, with a U.S. passport in one pocket and a DDR passport in another, on my way to Cuba, where I was forbidden to go according to a recent State Department edict, waiting for the Stasi's own film company to help me imagine a marriage between Marxism and Carnival, working by day, within sight of the Wall, for a radio program designed to persuade Americans that their freedoms were a sham, and spending my evenings with communist friends who had still not gotten over the experience of waking up one gray morning to find themselves locked inside their own borders. But in this welter there was one thing I knew: I was no more prepared to kill for America than I was to spy for the Stasi. I called my mother in New York and asked her to tell the draft board that I was out of the country, and that my whereabouts were unknown. Then I telephoned Alexander Abusch, hoping he might expedite matters with DEFA; his secretary did not forward my call. I wrote to DEFA's program director and received no answer. There was nothing to do but wait.

A week or so passed, and Kennedy was assassinated. The "heartbeat" program's DJ, a sad middle-aged black hipster who had lost his country by deserting his army unit in West Germany, celebrated the event by getting drunk with the program director and singing the "Internationale" in German. I felt sorry for him.

My mother sent on to me a second letter from the draft board, with a new date for my induction, generously set two months ahead, and a curt notice that failure to appear at the time indicated would earn me the status of a "delinquent," with unspecified consequences. In a dream, I had an uncanny vision: a paradisial jungle scene, huge trees and a calmly flowing river. A man in camouflage holding a gun, kneeling by the water. Stillness, depth, then a single, sudden, clear report from a gun. The kneeling man falls forward. Silence, the trees, the calmly flowing river, the dead man with his head submerged in the green water. It could have been a scene from a movie, but I was convinced it showed me in a possible future, either as the victim or as the invisible killer.

I bought a ticket for a flight to New York. I had to take care of this.

■　■　■

There was a lot of yelling at the Army Induction Center at Whitehall Street. The uniformed men wanted the men who were not yet in uniform to feel the difference right away, and the difference evidently had to do with being yelled at. "This ain't the movies!" one of them yelled, very much like an officer in a movie. The recruits also yelled, in the undisciplined manner befitting recruits. So did the medical staff. Their shouts were functional instructions, devoid of ceremony: "Put your hands on your ass! Bend over! Spread your cheeks!" One or two men blessed with hemorrhoids were sent home. Every conceivable ethnic group was represented, but the majority were black and Hispanic. There were those who made jokes and those who were made jokes of, like the ones unable to pee into an ampule on command. I was one of them. Maybe, I thought, if I really can't pee, they'll dismiss me. But the intern in charge of urine knew what to do: "If you can't piss now, we'll give you a quart of water to drink and just wait." That did the trick. My hopes rose again with my blood pressure, which was exorbitant. The intern in charge of blood pressure told me to sit down and count backward, starting with a hundred, and loud enough for him to hear. I yelled: "One hundred! Ninety-nine!" "Not that loud," he said. As I counted, I put my hand on my breast pocket. There was my hope, my fate, a sealed letter from a pacifistically inclined psychiatrist who had encouraged me to persuade him, in two expensive sessions, that the army and I would have an unfortunate effect on each other. By the time I had counted down to thirty, the intern had tested several recruits and found them fit. My blood pressure was found to be normal. On to the psychologist.

The psychologist had a wrinkled, worried, intellectual face.

"Sit down," he said, pointing to a chair that stood in front of his desk. Mumbling, I handed him the letter.

He tore open the envelope, read the letter, looked at me.

"Please sit down."

I sat down, pressing my knees together like a girl in a short skirt, slumped, let my head hang. My hair obliged by falling into my face. With an effeminate gesture, I lifted the strand over my ear.

"Is it true, what this letter says?"

His voice was gentle. I suspected a trap.

"What does it say?"

"That you're afraid of sharing a barracks with men. With many men."

There was no trap. He was a good, gentle man, probably Austrian, to judge by his accent.

"It's true," I said.

He nodded, wrote something on a printed form, and handed it to me. "Show this to the soldier outside that door." I hesitated. "You may leave," he said. His smile was kind.

I don't recall whether that document in my hand was large or small, a file or a card, or whether I even looked at it, but I remember the effect it had on the soldier outside the door: none at all. He glanced at it and sent me on to the foot specialists (no luck with my high instep), and from there to the intelligence test. It was all over. I stared at the pictures in front of me: line drawings of machine parts without discernible function, each one a Chinese puzzle of tubes, planes, serrated edges, acute and oblique angles. Which of these fit together? I hadn't a clue. At five desks near me sat five men contemplating the same page. Their faces showed signs of comprehension. They had a future in the U.S. Army. My future was to die in a trench.

I arrived at the brightly lit room where the induction ceremony was to take place. I have a dim memory of a large flag, a picture of Lyndon Johnson, a room full of young men on chairs, lots of yelling. What I remember much more clearly are my thoughts. It was an important moment. Until then, all I knew was that I didn't want to serve in the army. Now I knew that I would refuse to, even if that meant going to jail. It was as simple as that. The only question was *when* to announce my refusal, now or after the ceremony. A soldier stopped me at the door, looked at the psychologist's note in my hand. "What the hell are *you* doing here? You're 4-F! Go home!" In a daze, I wandered back to the entrance, presented my papers there one last time, walked down several flights of stairs. I walked slowly, hiding my elation, as if the walls had eyes. The sun was shining when I stepped out onto the street. I didn't start running until I had turned the corner.

Unfortunately, I had no idea where to go with this precious freedom or what to do with it. I went home to the tepid conviviality of the Student Living Center (I had moved in there again), and to whatever temporary or part-time job was keeping me afloat, and to reading, writing, and tearing up what I had written. I went to the movies and I went to peace demonstrations. I had no friends, though I talked with Stefan, argued with Luke, philosophized with Carl, and avoided Victor, who was still sleeping with Sylvia. But she hardly mattered anymore. Nothing much mattered. Life was becoming dull. I slept inordinate lengths of time. I masturbated. I watched TV. When I looked in the mirror, I saw bleary eyes, sallow skin. I felt unattractive, and no doubt I was. Once in a while, I would find myself at a party, numb as a frozen foot, surrounded by dancers and laughter, wishing I were alone, and lacking the will to get up and leave. I remember in particular one horrible moment when someone peered in through the anesthetic haze in which I believed myself to be invisible and asked: "*Who* are *you*?" and I found myself unable to answer with even so much as a shrug.

■　　■　　■

One day, in a secondhand bookstore, I stopped in front of the section marked "Occult." My Marxist schooling had not predisposed me to take such works seriously, but I was charmed by the first pages of a young Englishman's account of his life and times outside the body. The author was no longer capable of flying in his astral form, remembrance was all he had left, so the book was elegiac in tone. Happy, happy days! Blessed freedom! I bought the book and took it home.

I don't think I have read another book in my adult life that moved me more profoundly. And having said that, I understand why. I did not read it as an adult, but as a child. Even now, as I contemplate the author's name—Oliver Fox—it takes me back to my earliest years, by the sideward-scissoring route of free-association which follows the lateral logic of dreams: When I was four years old, during a visit to New York with my mother, I developed a crush on a little boy in my kindergarten who had red hair and whose name was Robin. He got into trouble with the teacher because he was wild, meaning that he wasn't tame, but this wildness seemed to me unobjectionable, in fact beautiful, mainly because of the implications of his name and the color of his hair. I knew what a robin was from a nursery rhyme which my mother and an illustration in my *Golden Book of Songs and Rhymes* had infused with an atmosphere of mystery, beauty, and, I think, singularity—singular as Robin was with his fiery hair, which was surely as rare as the red-breasted bird singing in its tree. At least I had never seen red hair before, except in pictures. Something wonderful had happened: A feeling ordinarily encased between the covers of a book had taken wing and settled on a real little boy who liked to tip over other children's constructions. I don't think I ever played with him. I just adored him from afar. Now what does this have to do with Oliver Fox? Simple: A fox has red hair and lives free and wild in the olive groves (a place imbued with myth and poetry, probably having to do with Greece). But above all, Oliver Fox could once fly, unassisted by wings or a motor, and it takes a child's imagination, or a dreaming adult's, to believe that.

I searched for more books on astral projection, and found some that offered techniques, and that promised success if one applied himself diligently. There was nothing in the world I wanted more than to leave my body. The method I tried over and over, because it brought me closest to success, was called the "inflation" method. First you make yourself heavy by imagining that your limbs are made of lead—not a difficult task for me in my depression. Then you imagine an inner body separate from the leaden one being pumped full of a gas that is lighter than air. With each inhalation, this lightness and buoyancy increase until you start rising up—up through the ceiling, through the rooms above yours, through the roof. Once there, you can navigate pretty much at will, though there are astral currents that can sweep you to unexpected places, not all of them on this earth or synchronous with your body's time. But there is no need to worry about getting lost, you are attached to the body by a silver cord. And the body's own vital needs will retract you, its double, if you wander too far or too long.

I'm sorry to say I was never able to test the truth of these teachings by experience. My gas-filled inner body rose, as promised, out of the leaden physical frame, but not as one self-complete quivering man-shaped bubble or blimp, no, it was more like a piece of cloth being gradually lifted from one of its corners. It began in my feet: They rose. And as they rose higher, the lower legs followed, the knees and thighs. At this point I felt folded, because my torso refused to rise. But after much pumping of gas, the pelvis, belly, arms, chest, back, and shoulders and even the neck were free and only the head was still trapped in the skull. And there I remained, yearning and caught, like a tethered balloon, wavering slightly, with my feet pointing up at a forty-five-degree angle, and no amount of gas, no prayers and no curses, no effort of any kind, could dislodge my astral head from that firm clamp of bone.

I was too conscious—too self-conscious—that much was clear. I could hypnotize others but not myself. I needed help.

In the Yellow Pages I found under "Hypnotists" the name of a Dr. Psych. Emanuel Abarvanel-Krauss, Ph.D., in the West Eighties, near where I lived. I called him, made an appointment for the next day. He had a deep, old man's voice and a bizarre speech defect, or was it an accent? All his s's were pronounced as sh's.

I arrived early for my appointment. The button beneath his nameplate released a chime when I pressed it. The door opened after a minute and a bald, massive head appeared: "Pleash shit in zhe hall," he said sternly, "I heff a client."

There was a couch in the hall. I sat down on it. After a while, the door opened and the client emerged, a man with an overcoat, a hat, an umbrella, and an attaché case, as conventional an appearance as could be imagined. He said good-bye to the doctor and avoided my eyes as he passed me. The doctor welcomed me in the door. As we shook hands I noticed he lacked the middle finger of his right hand. He led me into a large, thickly carpeted room at the center of which stood a high, thronelike chair, on which he sat down, and a soft, green, and low leather armchair, on which he asked me to sit. Between two heavily curtained windows stood an ornate bookcase filled with books, in front of it a massive oak desk and a brass-studded chair. At the far end of the room, in the corner, stood a large black leather chaise longue. In the other far corner was a stand with a black and white spiral disc.

I told him I wanted to learn self-hypnosis.

"Vy?" he asked.

"To control my moods," I said.

He stared at me through heavy-lidded turtle eyes.

"Vich moodsh do you vish to control?"

The question interested me. I answered it truthfully. Why lie to him on this score? That would only be counterproductive. Quickly the doctor extracted from me the fundamental data of my existence: my half-hearted writing, my poverty, my avoidance of full-time and long-term work, my loneliness, my depression.

"You are a shaboteur," he said.

"Excuse me?"

"A shaboteur. You shabotash everyting. You shabotash your talent, your shexsh, your friendshipsh, your life."

He went on like this, droning, and while he spoke, he massaged his right thigh with firm steady strokes of his four-fingered hand.

Life was like a train, he said, but in my case the train was out of control. The saboteur in me had destroyed the brakes, and there was no stopping, except— here he held up his fascinating hand—except with the help of hypnosis. Five or six sessions would put to sleep the saboteur and awaken the dormant engineer, who alone could direct the train of my life to its proper destination: "Him ve vill teach shelf-hypnoshish."

We began our first session. I crossed the broad expanse of carpet and lay down on the reclining chair, while the doctor's squat imperial presence remained in his high chair, far away. Somewhere above and behind me, a metronome started to tick. I heard the doctor's deep voice: "Ash I count from ten to vun, you feel yourshelf shinking, deeper and deeper. . . ."

I knew too much about hypnosis. When he said: "You are no longer able to open your eyesh," I thought: "That would be true if I had given over to you my power of volition." When he said: "Your arm ish getting heffier," I thought: "I am making believe that my arm is getting heavier." When he said: "Your arm ish shtiff as a board now, you cannot bend it," I thought: "I have now tensed the muscles of my arm to make it fit the specifications of a 'board,' but not for a moment do I believe that I cannot bend it." When he started reciting a generic message of uplift and release and I heard the faint rattle of paper in his hands, my contempt knew no bounds, and I thought: "I could just get up and walk out of here, in fact I should do just that, I should give him his twenty-five dollars, tell him this isn't what I had in mind, go home, and get on with my astral projection." And then I thought: "I'm just pretending to be hypnotized but in fact I'm very calm and content to just lie here and listen." And so I lay, and after a while I stopped listening to the words with their suggestions of optimism and social ease and listened instead to the tick-tock machine, thought of Edgar Allan Poe, rats, white mice, mad scientists, the arms race, Vietnam, death and the afterlife, spirits, and astral projection, and the next moment I was being summoned back to my toes and fingertips ("viggle zhem"), then to my eyelids ("feel zhem flutterink"), and I was awake.

I came back four more times for this treatment. On that fifth and last day, I decided that, if he did not bring up the question of self-hypnosis, I would. I lay in my trance and listened to the familiar recital. There were no limits to what I could do, he said. I knew myself to be attractive and charming, able and talented, healthy and strong. I was open to all manner of new and wholesome experience. Open to meeting new people. Open and eager for the adventure of life. Ready and willing to inherit my birthright of joy and happiness and shuckshesh.

Then the phone rang. Dr. Abarvanel-Krauss told me that I would remain content and inert until he returned. He picked up the receiver.

"Hello? Shpeaking. Yesh. Yesh. No, you shouldn't heff dundat. Vy? You know vy. Datsh right, you can't trusht a Schvartze. No, not vit money. Don't talk to me about prejudish. Datsh right. Datsh right. You know better. Call me later. I heff a client."

I opened my eyes.

The doctor returned to his seat.

"I shee your transh ish broken. I am shorry. Closhe your eyesh. . . ."

"No, doctor, I think I prefer to be awake." I sat up.

"Do you really think Negroes can't be trusted with money?"

"You don't undershtand. I vash shpeaking of a shervant, a maid. You don't know me. Shome of my besht friendsh are Negrosh!"

He really said that. We argued for a while about prejudice and trust. He was upset with my perception of him. I, too, was upset. I left when my time was up, paid him, and never came back.

And so I never learned how to leave my body. But Dr. Abarvanel-Krauss's posthypnotic suggestions had an extraordinary effect on my life within it. A week after my last session with him, I was invited to a party, went without reluctance, and found myself enjoying the kind of small talk that usually made me long for solitude or else the company of my brother. At the buffet, I made the acquaintance of a short, nervous, balding Cuban composer named Hector Angulo who blinked a lot and was constantly throttling a wide smile by pursing his lips. Had I heard about Fidel Castro's invitation to American youth? We should come and see socialism in action—two months in Cuba, all expenses paid by the Cuban government! I couldn't have been more surprised if he had conveyed to me the kind regards of Alexander Abusch. I had almost forgotten my wish to go to Cuba. By what magic was it now being granted? Could it be that I had asked for this with such fervor that I had called it into being? Now all I needed was film equipment. Then I realized that in my heart I had never really wanted to make a film, that the goal of my desire hadn't been Cuba either, nor true socialism, nor even the Carnival feast of Santiago, but some bacchanalian replacement of my nights with Sylvia, so that I could forget her; and now that she was very nearly forgotten, I might be getting what I no longer wanted. Or did I? I did. When could I go and how could I apply?

"Before you decide," Hector said, and he lowered his voice to a whisper, "you must know that this trip is forbidden."

He explained: The State Department had issued a ban on travel to Cuba. Anyone breaking that law would end up in an FBI file, at the least. But there was strength in numbers: If enough people went and returned with a show of defiance, the government might be embarrassed into repealing the ban. Was I still interested? Of course I was. He took my phone number: He would introduce me to Milt Rosen, the leader of the Progressive Labor Party, the group that was organizing the trip. Was I free next Saturday evening? There was going to be an exciting event in some Lower East Side clubhouse—Milt Rosen and a Trotskyite would disagree in public about the nature of the Cuban revolution! (Trotskyists were always called "Trotskyites" by their Stalinist enemies.)

All I remember of the debate was the way Milt Rosen used a handkerchief as a rhetorical device. The Trotskyite, who was sitting next to him behind a table, made the mistake of depending on Milt Rosen for the sort of signs people normally exchange to support the frail enterprise of communication. Milt Rosen held out these little crutches—a nod, a hm-hm—, waited for his opponent to lean on them, and then pulled them away: He would yawn, sniff, rub the bristles on his cheek, roll his head to loosen his neck muscles, crack his knuckles, scrutinize the ceiling. The Trotskyite rambled on, looking discomfited. Who was he talking to, if not Milt Rosen? The audience consisted almost entirely of the speakers' friends. Now Milt Rosen reverted to proffering recognizable signs of attention, indeed he seemed interested. The Trotskyite caught fire, something like oratorical zeal animated his words and gestures. But then he faltered again, because Milt Rosen was no longer there, he was crossing the room to the coat stand where his jacket was hanging, searched the pockets, found what he had been looking for—a handkerchief—and returned to the table, where he proceeded to wipe his face and balding head with gestures expressive of the utmost weariness, like a traveler removing the silt and sweat of a weeklong trek through a desert. Years later I read a description of Lenin unsettling some scholarly Menshevik with the same tactics and the same props, including the handkerchief.

After the debate, I went with Hector and Milt Rosen and his comrades to a coffee shop. Hector had described the PL leadership as "wonderful, courageous people, true revolutionaries." They reminded me a lot of the more earnest cadres of the Free German Youth, except that, not having state power on their side, their ambition was still garbed in sincere idealism. They were deeply and sentimentally persuaded of the correctness and the humanity of their views, which, if their slogans were to be taken seriously, condemned large parts of the American population to death. They asked me why I wanted to go to Cuba. I told them I had grown up in East Germany and . . .

Their pupils widened: What a find! A native socialist!

"And?"

"And I'd like to see what Caribbean socialism is like. It must be different."

That did sound suspiciously apolitical, I could hear it myself. I added some notes of utopian assurance, of which I had credible reserves still in storage. Amid glances and smiles of consensus, I was inducted into the organizing committee. Not much was required. Secrecy, mainly. In three weeks, I would go to Chicago with another, as yet unappointed liaison, there to collect some eight fellow travelers arriving from various American cities, and report with them to the group leader.

It felt good to be trusted with such an important mission. It felt even better to be surrounded by people whose faces lit up when they saw me. I looked in the mirror. Where was that glum, sallow face? Even my hair looked healthier. Something was opening up, I could feel it. This was a time to cross thresholds. Some of those steps took me to unexpected rooms.

Luke Ronaldson, for example, gave me a marijuana joint and a set of exotic instructions. I lit the joint in the privacy of my room, sucked in as much smoke as I could, held my breath, ran down three flights of stairs and up again, sat down on my bed, exhaled, blacked out, and saw a small bright yellow lion standing upright and gesturing with his front paws in the manner of the British state emblem. I have asked myself many times what that vision meant and why I was shown it, and contented myself with this or that standard interpretation. Now, thirty years later, my heart leaps at the recognition: It was given to me as an initiatory emblem, a sign of valor: *in hoc signo vinces*. I had seen it before, of course—for the first time, I think, when I was twelve years old, in a book my American father sent to me in Germany. It was part of King Arthur's escutcheon in Howard Pyle's illustrations for the legends of the Round Table. But long before that, even before I had read a romantic version, for American children, of "proud Cortez's" conquest of Mexico, I must have seen pictures of knights-errant on their quest, because I remember lying in my bed in Cuernavaca when

I was six or seven and summoning up, before going to sleep, the image of a knight in armor seated on a richly caparisoned white horse, with a maiden, dressed in white, seated sideways in front of him. The practicability of the seating arrangement eludes me now, but it looked right and feasible then. I was riding home with her after rescuing her from a monster. I don't remember the fight, just this quiet, dignified ride on horseback after the deed was done: the noble dignity, the quiet exaltation, and an indescribable glow of completion, of strength established in courage and love.

But when I saw the marijuana lion, I didn't think I was being called to battle. I was just excited, because I had never, outside of my dreams, or not since my earliest childhood, been aware that the mind has a life of its own, independent of my volition.

Carnival

The next thing I remember, without transition, is sitting in an airplane, one of eighty-one young Americans on a charter flight booked for an "art study trip" to Paris. Or was it a commercial flight? Was the art bit just the story we were told to tell when we applied for our passports? I don't remember, there are altogether a great many gaps in my memory of this time, and I wonder whether these aren't literally gashes left by the pharmaceutical scattershot I directed against my own nervous system a few months later. Or else these lapses are an effect of acceleration, the way a view from a fast-moving train will obliterate much of the landscape. Time really does fly. It's already the summer of 1964.

Here's what I see for the moment: Stefan sits three seats ahead of me. Why aren't we together? I think it's because we both feel that what draws us together is weakness, that to discover our specific weight in the world, we must separate. But it's sad, looking back at the way he sat there, alone (though there was someone next to him), to see his long thin neck and red protruding ears, and to know that my side of the scale was rising as his was sinking, and that he knew that and voiced it in his journal with terrifying lucidity, and that I, for my own protection as much as his, firmly believed that he still had a chance—more than a chance: fame and fortune seemed certain for a boy of his talent, and surely love would come in their wake. And now we're landing, and after a night in a Paris hotel (did Stefan and I share a room?) we assemble again at Orly airport. A tall blackbearded wild-eyed beatnik takes a roll call and shouts about discipline and waves his arms menacingly when someone steps out of line, he is white but talks and sounds exactly like Dexter Gordon, and Stefan, who is next to me now, says, "He is hip, man," and I say, "Yeah, he is one hip cat, he talks with a rasping voice," and Stefan says, "Man, like, when is he from and who set him up to herd us, daddy-oh?" Our irritation is a welcome diversion from the anxiety of knowing ourselves still within the range of our government's punishing eye. If the FBI knows what we're up to and cared to stop us, they probably still could, it's the Free World, after all, America's dominion. Do the others feel as I do, or are these my ex–East German reflexes kicking up? Even after we're en route to Prague on an Air France plane and the stewardesses clearly know or surmise we're on some kind of rebel mission and are amused and sympathetic, I'm anxious, because the group's leader, Eddie Lemansky, has impressed upon us the importance of keeping our secret, we're art students, yes, this time on our way to sample the treasures of Prague. I point out to Stefan that we are probably over Germany, and Stefan envisions himself (I'm citing his journal) "from below, from the 'vantage point' of that godforsaken flat central-european agricultural artificially fertilized landscape, sitting, an American student, in the airplane: an object, as I believe Sartre would say—but still the same, still the German Democratic Student, the same damn subject, the same nonexistent essence." Fatal perspective!

After the landing in Prague, there is no time to take note of more than greenish-gray hues of bronze and stone in the rain, a Cubana airplane stands waiting for us, the beatnik reassumes his shepherding function, and off we go, the mantle of secrecy slides from our shoulders, a friendly stewardess (in army fatigues?) serves us wine, her colleague raises a glass to welcome us: "Soon," she says, "soon you will be *en el primer territorio libre de las Americas!*"—and by God it feels that way, and not just to me, we have slipped through the meshes of state power and entered the pure realm of freedom. Hurrah! There are some Cuban men on board, they're in shirtsleeves, unshaved, who are they, secret service men, passengers? Their faces are open, shining with friendliness. One of them clinks his glass against mine: *"Amistad!"* he says, "friendship!" And then, discovering with delight that I speak Spanish, he tells me how wonderful life has become since the revolution, and it's not the party line, he's speaking as a Christian, and straight from the heart: *"Es una cosa espiritual. Lo que Jesus nos mandó, hacemos ahora: amar al vecino. . . ."* I look around through a blur of tears, the copilot comes out of the cockpit, the stewardess gives him a glass of wine, he joins us for a toast, everyone's laughing, talking, cheering—and here comes one of those memory gaps, a week or so of near-total oblivion, I have no memory whatsoever of the "fantastically exciting and overwhelming" reception Stefan describes in his journal, of the Hotel Internacional, where we were quartered, of the museums, housing projects, and schools we visited during our first week, of Sloppy Joe's, of trips to Vinales, Soroa, and Pinar del Rio—nothing, nothing. A few mist-shrouded islands loom out of the void, and I notice they are all moments of personal sympathy, rancor, lust, pity, affection, and impressions of human behavior that must have startled some habit of expectation; but nothing in the way of facts, figures, policies, arguments, nothing beyond a sunny and friendly, vague and emotional imprint. (Not so vague, come to think of it, just overwhelmingly simple—and I mean that in the pure, positive sense of the word, simple as water is simple, especially when you're thirsty. Very many people seemed happy. So many smiles, so much warmth and friendliness!) The fact is that during much of the time I remember, I was not present at the place I had been invited to—Revolutionary Cuba—but somewhere else. What shall I call that place? And how shall I enter it now in memory?

The answer to those questions just came to me as I sat with closed eyes at my desk: I saw a door, with a peculiar word on it: "VOLUPTAS," in clear Latin script. Of course. I'll follow this lead. Recognizing the word's meaning seems to be some sort of key, since the door opens. Where am I? Naked in a sumptuous bed canopied with white mosquito-netting. The curtains part, an attractive, blonde, brown-eyed girl leans in, wearing a high-buttoned white lacy nightgown, Lourdes is her name, she has a smile in her eyes which I later recognize as one of almost uncontainable mischief, I gently take her arm to draw her in toward me, she touches my lips with hers, pulls away and runs off, laughing, it doesn't occur to me to chase her until it's too late, she's locked herself into an adjoining room and is laughing behind the door, I plead, protest, threaten, knock, make a few cautious thuds against the door with my shoulder, I don't want to break anything, but I do want this sexy little *gusana* rather badly, it's all coming back to me now, another girl called her that, a "worm," the popular word for a counter-revolutionary, but using a feminine form, and I said "She's the prettiest *gusana* I've ever seen," and seeing that Lourdes liked that, I added, "prettier than any flower of the revolution," and from then on she slithered all over me in the pool at the Hotel Nacional, and in the dark on the way to her house where, she said, we'd have a *cama matrimonial* to ourselves (because her mother had received permission to go to Miami and pave the way for Lourdes' expatriation, which Lourdes very much looked forward to); on the way, I was saying, to her big lonely bourgeois house, she let me kiss her and feel her up and made one or two discreetly bold little moves of her own—and now this! "Lourdes! *Te quiero!* Let me in!" After a while I gave up, got dressed, and walked home to the hotel, where, in the morning, and in my presence, my roommate, an eighteen-year-old Marxist-Leninist from San Juan, Puerto Rico, asked me for Lourdes' number, dialed it, introduced himself politely, asked her if, as a friend of the man whose advances she had rejected last night, he might have her ear for a few minutes, and proceeded to entertain her—she didn't hang up—with what the American statutes refer to as an obscene phone call, languidly masturbating under the blanket all the while. I eventually left, not wanting to disturb their budding intimacy, and descended to the dining room eight floors below. There I joined a table where a young white union organizer was buttering his bread while advising five stony-faced, silently chewing Black Nationalists that their divisive views were "a comfort to the landlords and bosses." The nationalists had let it be known that they were keeping a "hit-parade" list of the five or six most obnoxious racists in the group, and that by the end of the trip the one at the top would "have his chest caved in," so I was a little concerned for the union organizer, whose disregard for their threats might be taken for arrogance and hence for racism. My brother was sipping coffee and scribbling in his journal. He was taking note of the remarkable choice of mood music coming from the loudspeaker in the lobby—Bartok's Concerto for Orchestra—and reflecting on the surprising pleasure he had found, after an exhausting yesterday, in reading André Breton's collage poems arranged out of fragments of newspaper headlines, *"something which in New York had struck me as arty and pointless, and now, here, reveals to me the kinship between revolution and poetry; or, putting it negatively: that the difficulty of being 'for' revolution, of believing in its genuineness and complete newness, is comparable to the difficulty of really comprehending a poem, of knowing it in its poetic aspect and not just as something to be 'understood.'"* I, meanwhile, was eating a *fruta bomba*, remembering that I had been warned not to ever, ever call it papaya, because the juicy word had become a synonym for "vulva," and wondering whether a girl who liked telephone sex would expect a man to break through a door before making love to her. I had been ever so pleasantly distracted all week, not just by Lourdes but by every third or fourth Cuban woman, something about the way they carried themselves and the pleasure they took in being noticed, and unless I was extremely mistaken, by the way they responded to me in particular, maybe my blue eyes and pale skin. In any case, and whatever the cause, a haze of perfumes, glances, smiles, and lingering touches had begun to cloud my political vision. Just yesterday, as we inspected the proud militia, I had noticed how breasts and buttocks improved the uniform's baggy design. That young worker demonstrating advanced techniques of cigar manufacture—how tenderly she massaged her product. That spokeswoman for the industrial planning commission had lips that kissed the air as she denounced the U.S. embargo. . . .

A friend tapped my shoulder: "Are you ready?" I'd forgotten, we were planning to take a stroll through the city. I put down my spoon.

"Stefan, do you want to come?" I immediately regretted the question, he looked depleted, drained.

"Yes," he said.

"How about you guys?"

The nationalists shook their heads, they had other fish to fry, so much the better. The union man joined us, and as we left, I wondered whether Stefan's and my names had been added to the hit list.

That evening, after dinner, in the lounge of the Hotel Nacional, I was introduced to a dark-skinned woman in a black evening dress who produced a flutter in my heart and an ache in my groin. She had absurdly long lashes, glitter on her cheeks, a studied hauteur in the tilt of her chin, and she did not find me exotic: She snubbed me. Two hours later, by purest accident and all the more stunning for that reason, I saw her dancing on the stage of a nightclub, just ten feet away from me. The leader of the band was shaking a pair of maracas in her direction and singing about a *linda mulatica* who walks through her *pueblecito natal* for some innocent purpose befitting those endearing diminutives, but there's something about her *bata arremangada,* her tucked-up dress or smock or shift, and the way she lifts her "little slipper"—*levantó su chancletica*—that turns all the men's heads:

Los hombres le van detrás
A la linda mulatica.

Does it matter that the dancing beauty is not *mulata* but *negra,* that all she has on her feet is glitter and an ankle chain, that she's not walking in a *bata* but stroking the inside of a thigh with one hand and divesting herself of ostrich feathers with the other? It matters not one bit, she is stripping down to a glittering brassiere and a narrow sequin-studded loincloth. The singer, still shaking his maracas at her, is addressing the audience:

Si esa mulata me quisiera,

"if this *mulata* were to like me," off comes the brassiere, with a sullen pout she flings it over her shoulder,

que banquetico me voy a dar,

"what a banquet I'll have myself," all the men in the room are up on their feet and a few shout her name, "Désirée! Désirée!", two American women next to me start talking indignantly about exploitation, a man in the front row begs the dancer to take off everything just this once, and something more does come off, it's the pout, she's smiling with pleasure, the whole band breaks into song,

caminando va, guarrachando va,
caminando va, guarrachando va,

and now her dance properly begins, the *mulata*'s walk, which is not a walk but a steady, indescribably sensual rotation of her hips, while her hands are clapping over her head, and of all the lovely details, the one that haunted me for the rest of the night was not the dark gold of her breasts or her stark black nipples, not her long shining thighs or her calm gaze and settled smile as she made her hips sing like that till the curtain came down, it was that she had shaved one armpit and not the other.

Voluptas. She should be from the Yoruba pantheon, but Voluptas will have to do, since I don't know their names. Except for Chango. Désirée told me about him. What does this have to do with Lourdes? Nothing. Lourdes was a lure. Maybe a herald, a prefiguration of the manifest presence. And there's another divine person, he's been there all along, in Voluptas' shadow. He, too, wants possession of my soul. But how stupid he is. I'll call him Politicus. He is stern, enamored of logic, fired by principle, fond of crowds marching in lockstep— so different from Voluptas, who dances the conga.[3]

The next morning, to the sound of church bells ringing for Mass, Stefan and I set out with a couple of friends on an unguided tour of Habana del Este. I see that whole day rolled out like a symbolic scroll, an allegory on the career of political hope. After the bloody colors of dawn, which we missed (let those stand for the brief period of retribution against the Batista gang and their followers), the streets brighten with hope, and at around ten o'clock our adventure begins with a chance encounter, a voice calling down to us from a balcony: "*Tovarish!*" We see a cluster of smiling black faces, hands beckoning us to come up for a visit, they are residents of a new building created to house people who used to live in tin shacks by the edge of a sugar plantation. Our hosts are not unhappy to learn we're not Russian, they've heard of us, we're the heroic *Norteamericanos* who defied the U.S. government to see the splendor of their new lives. And who would not be moved by the evidence they present: a finger rubbing an arm, another the back of a hand—skin color, no longer a stigma; shoes—no one is barefoot, an unimaginable luxury five years ago; a diploma on the wall—for unpaid voluntary labor, a small gift in return for year-round employment; food—a larder full of fruit, bread, butter, *refrescos,* take, we have

---

3. Long after her name presented itself to me, and before this book went into print, Philip Roth called one of his characters Voluptas. He writes faster than I do, and the goddess is impatient.

enough; knowledge—the grandfather learning to read and write, he's in third grade and catching up fast; dreams—all the children have dreams of what they will be, and their parents believe in those dreams. With so much to be thankful for, love is not hoarded, there's a constant exchange of touches and hugs, friendly squeezes, casual caresses. After a long and generous conversation and many toasts to Fidel and to liberty and peace and friendship, we leave, our hearts brimful with the tidings of a new world, a new way of being. The sun stands at high noon and is beginning to sink. The sugarcane cutters told us about a nearby hotel where Cuban, Soviet, and Chinese engineers are staying. That's where we go, but we meet only the Cubans, who have just returned from a year of political schooling in the USSR. Their eyes are unlike any eyes I have seen in Cuba, hard and unblinking, and there is a deadening gravity in their manner that makes me extremely uneasy. I've met with victims of this syndrome before, this "tempering" of character by ideological ferment, the Russians call it *zakalka*, but who would have thought Cubans susceptible to it? I don't remember my conversation with them, but Stefan recorded his in his journal.

"What do you think of socialism?" they asked. (Only one of them asked, but the whole group of ten or twelve was behind him.)

"There is more than one socialism," Stefan said, "I can't answer in the same way for all of them."

He sensed the judgment behind those steel shutters: Social Democrat.

He explained himself: Socialism in Cuba is different from socialism in East Germany or the Soviet Union.

Still without batting an eyelash, they asked him where the difference lay.

"Many differences," he said, but he could think of only one. "Your cultural policy."

He praised the richly stocked bookstores in Havana, the abundance of classical and modern works in translation: Kafka, Beckett, Joyce, Sartre, Camus. They informed him that in the Soviet Union artists were completely free, that there were no restrictions placed on the exercise of thought or imagination. He told them he grew up in East Germany. They shrugged. Not the least simulation of interest, either on a personal or political level. Stefan had become the class enemy.

It is late afternoon, my allegorical sun is half covered by clouds and sinking as our group of seven arrives late for a reception at the Chinese embassy. All the other *Norteamericanos* are already there, glass in hand, smiling, chatting. A Chinese man in a suit—an anomalous piece of clothing in Havana—offers me a glass of wine, everything about him is expressive of cultivated gentility and a will to be pleasant, everything, that is, except his words, which are without exception sincere formulations of the Chinese Communist Party's position on whatever topic we've broached. In a few minutes, he says, we will be shown "important Chinese films."

"Oh, what about?" I ask.

"Socialism," he says. And, since I look puzzled: "Progress," he adds.

"Sounds exciting," I say.

"Yes," he says, nodding and smiling warmly, "it is."

I try my luck with two tall members of a Chinese volleyball team that will be touring Cuba. Their eyes mock me through the mask of cordiality as I try to elicit a moment of personal truth.

"How long have you been in Havana?" I ask. The man in the suit is translating.

"A week."

"Me too. Is there any part of the town you like especially?"

"We like all parts. It is a beautiful city."

"You both like all parts equally?"

"Yes. We come to celebrate friendship with Cuban people."

And now we're led into the screening room. Here is Stefan's review:

> The films that were shown us were of a length that left the realm of mistake and bordered on crime. One of them in particular was extraordinary. It was shot by an anonymous team of camera men and was called something like "The Song of Production." In it, for an interminable hour, was shown nothing but machinery floating past the camera. The frames were of an unheard-of conventionality, the subject was not workers, not even production in the active sense of the word, but simply the growing abundance of certain well-specified machine parts and machines and tractors. At intervals of about ten minutes one got to see a human face, usually wearing a protective mask and photographed from below, like a futurist painting. The film expressed the purest commodity fetishism: the veneration of produced things for their own sake, apart from their human use. It was all quantity and no quality, with an eerie insistence.

And where was the sun when we left the embassy? No doubt it was setting behind dark clouds.

Late that evening I left the hotel in the company of a new friend, the poet George North. We walked for an hour or so, savoring the pleasure of being around people who had no designs on our conscience and were at peace with each other, going about their personal business, lingering in small groups to gossip and laugh in a park or in front of some doorway. By the *malecón,* with the sound of waves lapping in our ears, we stopped to listen to three young men, one of them playing a guitar, another a bongo, a third one clapping his hands in a complicated beat and singing the new hit song:

> *Con su bata arremangá'*
> *levantó su chancletica . . .*
> *Los hombres le van detrás*
> *a la linda mulatica.*

Then we walked back to the hotel. As we approached the tall wrought-iron gate, two teenage girls came strolling toward us, holding hands, a short round one and a tall slender one. The tall one greeted us. I gave her a casual *"Buenas"* in passing. Moments later, her voice called from behind:

"Oye, tú!"

We turned around. Which one of us did she mean?

"Sí, tú, borracho!"

A drunk she was calling me. She had a hand on a hip and was tapping one foot on the pavement.

"Todavía no sabes quien soy?"

I saw that this high school girl was the feathered wonder I had seen the night before. I saw it and believed it, but at the same time a peculiar anxiety rose up in me, a sense that what I was experiencing was not real, that it was a dream. This doubt lasted only a couple of seconds, but it arrested all movement, I just stood there and stared at her. Now she was genuinely indignant: "Where are your eyes, stupid?"

That broke the spell. I walked up to her, apologizing: "You looked so different yesterday." My contrition could not have been more sincere, but she wasn't satisfied.

"The way you were dressed," I continued, "your eyelashes, and then I saw your show . . ."

"I saw you too, you looked like a fish, with your mouth open."

"Who wouldn't be, looking at you," I said. That won me some points, I could tell.

"You still look like that," she said.

"I still feel like that," I said. "Forgive me."

And she burst out laughing, a delightful cracked laugh. Maybe she was hoarse. We all laughed.

"This is China," she said, "my best friend."

"*Mucho gusto,*" China said. She was called China because she had Asian features. George and I introduced ourselves.

"And you're Désirée," I said.

"Emma."

That put the cap on it. Such a pretty Emma, blue skirt, white blouse, little red toenails peeking through sandals. And in her wide-set, almond-shaped eyes there was an appeal of the simplest kind: "Do you like me? I like you." But when I looked at her mouth, Voluptas lifted the veil and I saw, with a clairvoyant shock of desire so intense and sudden that I still remember the way my heart leaped into my throat, that someone, and not just someone but some erotic genius or monster, had discerned the goddess in this lovely girl when she was still barely past childhood, and brought her to ripeness before her time, and dressed her in feathers for the adoration of those called to worship; and that I, if I wanted, could be the one, probably the first one, who would make love to her as herself, as Emma. *Que banquetico me voy a dar.*

The girls had to go home. We parted with handshakes and agreed to go see *The Virgin Spring* Monday evening, the four of us. George told me he was doing it for me. He didn't like Bergman and wasn't attracted to China.

The next morning, Politicus tried to recover lost ground by spurring the Cuban Institute for Friendship among the Peoples (a) to accelerate our departure from Havana—they told us at breakfast we would be leaving in two days—and (b) to make more productive use of our time: an afternoon of sugarcane cutting was announced, volunteers were urgently needed; and as if to reinforce the message, my new friend, George North, turned coat and urged me to come along, a few hours of work was a small price to ask for a two-month vacation, Ingmar Bergman could surely wait, and so could that girl. Was he jealous?

Voluptas promptly instigated a call from Emma. The sound of her soft, cracked voice decided my mind before I even heard what she had to say: Could we postpone the movie? Her friend China was not feeling well, but she, Emma, would like to go to the beach with me (and, since she didn't mention George, I assumed she meant me alone).

The next thing I remember is Emma shedding her dress on the beach—populated mostly by students on their summer leave—and standing there in a two-piece bathing suit made of just enough cloth to accommodate four or five leopard spots. If she had dropped naked from the clouds she couldn't have caused a greater commotion. Every adolescent boy and young man within sight rose to his feet if he wasn't already running toward her, and there was a large enough number of them to make their joined voices sound like the sort of collective male shout one hears at sports events. I was alarmed, naturally, but she was laughing and running away from them toward a pier, which she reached before they did and used as a springboard to jump into the water feet first, holding her nose. The men and boys rushed in after her, an ungainly swarm of churning elbows and kicking feet, the lifeguard was frantically blowing his whistle, a *miliciano* came running, by now I was seriously worried for her, but then two men lifted her up on their shoulders and carried her back to the beach, and gently deposited her, glistening, laughing like a child, in front of the *miliciano,* who looked amused, and the lifeguard, who was fuming. She did not seem to need or want my assistance, so I merely joined the throng of smiling men surrounding her and the two officials. Some women were standing among us, their faces betraying somewhat more mixed emotions. The lifeguard told Emma she wasn't allowed to come here *desnuda.* Emma, no longer smiling, asked him angrily if he was blind, was this a bathing suit or not? The lifeguard denied the skimpy evidence, what he saw was nudity.

At this point I spoke up. I was a friend of the *señorita,* I said, and I was sure she didn't mean to cause a disturbance. A man in the crowd interjected that she had a right to swim here like everyone else. To *swim,* the *miliciano* said, raising a finger, but not to dress like this, it wasn't right.

"*Oye, compañero,*" Emma said then, "you agree I'm not naked, so I'm not breaking the law. Let me swim with my friend. That way no one will see me. And then I'll get dressed and go home."

The crowd voiced and nodded their approval. The *miliciano,* a fatherly man in his forties, was grateful for the suggestion: "If you do as you say, there will be no problem." Then he told the crowd to disperse. But since he expressed that more as a request than an order, they ignored him. We walked into the water hand in hand, and again I felt that shudder of unreality, and this time I knew why: Every step was taking me more deeply into the tenuous half-life of a fantasy I had entertained since my early adolescence, when I seemed to myself so devoid of sex appeal that my shoulders would stiffen and my tongue would retract as soon as the shadow of an erotic opportunity presented itself. The fantasy was that I would become the lover of a very beautiful woman, the envy of every man in the land, and that circumstances would conspire to make my enjoyment of her, and her desire for me, public and evident enough to heal the deepest wounds ever dealt to my pride. And now the warmth of her hand in my hand and the sound of the chattering crowd behind us were persuading me that it was happening in reality. It's a frightening thing when life conforms very closely to one's desire. Maybe it's that the membrane dividing the inner being from the outer would vanish if there were too perfect a mirroring. Maybe the underlying terror is that the world of substance and form would dissolve into streams of energy and emotion, and that these would take on the shapes, not just of our inmost wishes, but also of our fears.

We swam out to the rope that marked the edge of the bathing area. She was floating flat on her back and giggling with pleasure at the effect she had made. The water was so salty it supported her like a bed.

"In Germany," I said, "there are beaches where everyone's naked."

She didn't believe that.

"It's true," I said, "and no one's allowed to wear clothes."

That struck her as so funny she started to sink, or pretended to sink, sputtering and gurgling, and I pretended to save her, held her up by her hair, kissed her, she nibbled and bit my lower lip, tasted my tongue, wrapped her legs around my waist, let herself lie back with her hands clasped behind her head and her eyes closed, smiling, as if to test the fit and sympathy of our bodies, just for a moment, without any mental impedance. Then she disengaged herself and swam circles around me until I caught her and gave her another kiss. But what a curt little word that is. There should be another one, with labials and bilabials in it and all the vowels and some new letters unknown to speech, silent palatals, mute sibilants.

We played around like that for a while. Then she had to go home. We swam back to the pier. She climbed out, wrapped a towel around herself, took her dress and her sandals to the women's changing cabin, followed by a small crowd of gawkers. It took me a while before I could leave the water without embarrassment.

I was in a state of terrific sexual excitement all the way back to the city. She saw to that, striptease artist that she was. The bus was crowded. I was holding on to a bar above my head, she was using my waist for a handle. Both parts of her dangerous swimsuit were with the towels in a basket between my feet, quite unnecessarily, it was a scorching day and the cloth would have dried quickly on her body. Evidently her purpose was to have me know—and, with occasional lurches and sudden stops of the bus, feel—that she had nothing on beneath her dress. I remember that ride awfully well. Someone in the front was playing a guitar and singing a song about Fidel being the horse and "el Che" being the cock, and then Che being the cock and Fidel being the horse, back and forth, on and on. Many passengers were singing along with him and counterpointing the simple tune with an intricate, complicated beat produced by clapping hands and the clinking of a bottle against an iron window-frame.

Upstairs at the hotel, I found Stefan's room open and walked into a snake pit prepared by Politicus. Clumsy god! This could only repel me. One of the Black Nationalists was expounding his views to a small gallery of frozen white faces. I was not in a mood to pay close attention, but here is how Stefan described it:

> A discussion of race and class began in our room between Steve S., Mark M., Jack B., and myself. We were joined by what in my opinion is the most disagreeable of the Black Nationalists, an extremely tense, hyperconscious person who emanates insensitivity, constraint, and an unmistakable falseness—the type of a demagogue. The conversation was a failure from the start. He began talking about the collective action of whites (racist) and deducing from it an essence of whiteness or "typically white" behavior. I objected to the confusion of a sociological fact (collective white racist behavior) with an a priori idea of innate or essential and therefore predictable white behavior. Due to my "training" in these questions,[4] I argued on a very abstract level, since the objection itself was logical and no more. Consequently nobody got the point and I had to suffer repeated interruptions by the nationalist, who would begin with phrases like: "You whites think negroes shouldn't fight back. Well, I'll tell you something you don't know." His head would move back and forth regularly, allowing for about five seconds of staring everyone in the face and making grimaces to suit his words.

I didn't sleep well that night. My roommate's snoring and a bad sunburn added to my discomfort. At breakfast, Politicus made a decisive move: We would be leaving Havana that same day, our bags were to be in the lobby by twelve o'clock. I cursed myself for not having asked for her phone number. I didn't even know her last name. Again and again I inquired at the front desk whether anyone had left a message for me. At around eleven I called the Tropicana and asked for the telephone number of Désirée. The man at the other end said he didn't know and wouldn't tell me if he did.

"This is different," I said, "I'm with the North American delegation. I need to interview her today."

---

4. He meant readings in logic and philosophy.

The man laughed: "We would all like to interview her."

"Just tell me her name," I said, "her real name: Emma . . . what is it?"

He just laughed.

We drove out of Havana in the early afternoon. I left a message for Emma at the desk, an apology with the scheduled date of our return, something flowery about kisses and desire and affection, and a plea that she leave me her number so I could call her as soon as I returned.

For two weeks Politicus regaled us with what Stefan in his journal called "the pathos of the realized vision"—schools, factories, shipyards, theatres, hospitals, farms, and everywhere an overwhelming exuberance and generosity, which were so clearly not the ploys of propaganda that those of us who were inclined to doubt and to voice our doubts—a minority, at that point—were made to feel like pedants objecting to the rules of a game the whole point of which was to enhance the joy of existence. At the vocational training school of Minas del Frio, a spartan encampment high in the thin mountain air of the Sierra Maestra, I watched an instructor drilling a tent full of teenage girls in the schemata of a Marxist orthodoxy that made my East German history lessons look like exercises in free speech and liberal scholarship. But who could object in the face of such passionate élan, such pleasure in learning? The girls told us they had protected themselves against the designs of Voluptas with vows to renounce love and marriage until the whole country was "alfabetizado." Who could gainsay the nobility of such dedication? The teacher asked the class: "How many women were prostitutes in Havana before the Revolution?" The shouted response: "One in three!" "What was the average age of a prostitute?" "Fifteen years!" Probably true. So much for the gentle reign of pleasure.

An alarming rumor reached my ears through the mouth of my roommate, the Marxist-Leninist from San Juan. A newly formed women's caucus in our group was planning to put all men on notice for their sexist ways. Black men, Cuban men, Castro himself would not be exempted, but a virtual pillory was being contemplated for a few unnamed white phallocratic neocolonialist American men who appeared to be using this trip as a pleasure-jaunt. I immediately thought of that sugarcane-cutting expedition I had passed up for a day with Emma.

"Which white men do they mean?" I asked my informant.

"Who knows. You guys seem so scared of the Black Nationalists, you're all on your best behavior. All the more pussy for us colored folk." He laughed. "Phallocratic! Love that word."

Evidently he didn't know about Emma. But what about the women's caucus?

Shortly before we reached Santiago, a Cuban soldier was shot and killed by some goon on the U.S. base in Guantanamo. The Black Nationalists were the first to issue a statement to the press—"a stupidly phrased thing"—that's Stefan's description—"full of redundancies and childish announcements of violent intent masquerading as passion." It was a strange spectacle to watch those with a reputation for liberalism sign the screed with grim expressions and furtive glances around them, terrorized into a contest of militancy. I overheard a discussion of one sentence: "Everyone who knowingly supports the U.S. government should be executed." Someone said that was too weak. Someone else recommended the substitution of the word "tortured" for "executed." That amendment was considered with wagging heads, then gently rejected with a mumbled "no," implying that potential sympathizers in the U.S. might not be ready for such revolutionary language. I voiced my objection to the faulty grammar. That earned me hateful stares from the Nationalists. Then I wrote a more literate and less sanguinary statement that was signed by the majority of the group. That put me on the "hit parade"—near the top, I was given to know, a major candidate for "thuddation." This act also gained me the reputation, among the Marxist-Leninist leaders of the group, of being a man of political substance. "We need people like you," one of them said. I was flattered. Who does not like to be needed?

Still, I did not want to lose touch with the goddess. In the palm of my left hand I carried and preserved the memory of Emma's breast as I had felt it through the cloth of her dress for a moment on that unforgettable bus ride. With this charm, I moved through the realm of Politicus, receptive only to what he could promise in joy, love, and beauty.

Stefan had no such amulet. Looking at his journal now, I see him fighting valiantly, taking the god at his word, demanding of him that he rise to the standards of poetry, philosophy, and inspired action or else hold his peace. All Stefan has for the fight is intelligence, a dubious weapon against Politicus, who recruits his devotees with hopes and hatreds that easily slip from the mass-mind into the most artfully fortified conscience, a perpetual fifth column against the project of individuation. How else to explain a Heidegger in brownshirt and jackboots, a Pablo Neruda conscripted to Stalin?

> June 29. The Cardenas shipyard. The question of workers' representation in the factory administration and their degree of power to express their

dissent was very hazy, but apparently the system is set up in such a way that were there a cause for dissent, or were there a difference between the party and the workers (which by no means exists at the moment), there would be no question but that the workers would have no say.

June 30. The newspapers are terrible. Yesterday, *Revolución* carried the following headline:

"*Barbaría en dos Estados*

RESPONSABLE JOHNSON DEL TERROR RACISTA

piden intervención federal en la Florida y Mississippi

en la desaparecíon de tres jovenes"[5]

I would not be surprised to open tomorrow's paper and see in bold type:

"ALL HUMANS ARE MORTAL

SOCRATES IS HUMAN

SOCRATES IS MORTAL

(*Prensa Latina*) *El Commandante . . .*" etc.

Nevertheless newspapers, even these, are in a sense the key to the universe. (I hope to elaborate on that further.) I could imagine a completely valid surrealist newspaper, or a Flaubertian one. Any school of naturalism will do.

July 11. Santa Clara. Last night a group meeting intended to heal the "disunity" that has afflicted the group since the newly formed "Black Liberation Front" announced their program of punitive redress. A social science professor from Adelphi was socked in the jaw by, simultaneously, two of the five Nationalists, who later said they had planned the whole thing in advance. The spectacle was sort of funny, in retrospect: The frail and extremely intellectual-looking professor holding a blood-stained handkerchief before his bloody mouth and talking caustically and emotionally about terrorism, fascism, storm-troopers, and thugs, while five black men with great muscle-power and studied thuggish expressions interrupt him with statements like: "Either you're with us or against us. If you're against us we'll slaughter you right here and now." The punch was provoked by a trivial incident. Someone, I believe Judy S., was told to shut up. The professor said something in her defense, at which point he was attacked. The ensuing discussion separated, like nothing else, the

5. "Barbarity in two states: Johnson responsible for racist terror; federal intervention requested in Florida and Mississippi in the mystery of the disappearance of three youths." (The three disappeared youths were the civil rights activists Michael Schwerner, Andrew Goodman, and James Earl Chaney, who were subsequently found to have been murdered by white supremacists.)

bullshitters from anyone with a trace of responsibility. Straw-thatched 16-year-old Billy J. Ryan began ranting with mercenary fervor in the black nationalist vein about "insults," and "if you're insulted by a guy, you punch him," and "black people have had 400 years of unimaginable oppression." Someone made the point that the historical fact of racist oppression does not make every one of the Nationalists' arguments correct. The professor asked the Nationalists through his bloody handkerchief whether they are going to continue their tactic of beating up people with whom they disagree, whether they are going to continue bullying intellectuals like a high school gang, or whether they are willing to arrive at some sort of agreement on a basis for discussion. Some idiot (white) once again referred to 400 years of oppression. The professor mentioned 6 million Jews. The Nationalists weren't the only ones who appeared to be downright bored by this. It seems the professor has gained himself the reputation of a bitching, dissatisfied, arrogant, non-working, non-militant egghead. There is a whiff of social darwinism in the air. The Nationalists made reference to possible future brawls, mentioning specifically "stompings" and "chest cave-ins" as punishments not to be sneezed at. One of them has a gun with him, news of which has been leaked to the group.

July 19. The last days have been dominated by depression. And what is that? I'll spit out some of the ingredients: I do not look forward to anything. I am convinced that I am not only incapable of love, but also incapable of communication on the simplest level (except in a nonhuman way, which of course permits of communication on a complex level anytime you ask me to). I am incapable of participation, or rather of everyday empathy. I have extremely specialized sexual and emotional needs but no means at all of making these known, and I mistrust my inclinations so severely that I work day and night to inhibit them, and this is exhausting. And absurd, given the circumstances: two days at the Camilo Cienfuegos vocational center in the Sierra Maestra, with about four thousand students 13 to 18 years old, and 242 teachers, almost all of them very young. It is amazing how many of these people are either extremely good-looking or intelligent or curious and charming or (and this lowest level extends to everyone) agreeable and good to be with. In contrast to them, our group is one distasteful dissonance. The arrival here was typical: one person gathered a crowd by swinging his newly sharpened machete, five others told bad jokes in worse Spanish with loud confident twangy voices, two wives protested bitterly against having to spend the night in a girls' dormitory, which nearly resulted in a fist-fight between one of the

Nationalists and one of the wives, and was followed by an endless meeting—all in front of the amazed eyes of the Camilitos.

July 26. Arrived in Santiago (*"Rebelde ayer, hospitalaria hoy, heroica siempre"*)[6] on the last day of the Carneval. Working our way through the throng last night, found the following slogan suspended over the heads of thousands of dancing people: *"El trabajo es la sementera fecunda donde germinan todos los virtudes humanos."*[7]

I remember that banner and the thrill of assent I felt when I read it: "Yes!"—not to the homily about work, which could not be confirmed by anything in my experience, but to the way the words and the living scene came together as labor and sex and politics and poetry dancing with joy, Voluptas embracing Politicus. And behind or beneath that memory is another one, not much more than a body-sense, something opening in my chest, a pushing out from within, like a stuck window . . . and then a feeling of *whoosh,* openness and grace and tallness, as if for years I had lived in a narrow room walking and standing with a slight stoop, always looking at the ground, and had finally stepped out and remembered what it is like to stand upright. Except I'm not standing, I'm dancing. My feet aren't sure of the difference between conga and fox-trot, but there they are, skipping and stepping, and flowing in and through and around me is a movement that turns around itself and plunges forward slowly, inexorably, like lava, a river of bodies, male and female, many of them dressed in white, some of them—just a few—masked or in costume, but all of them dancing, turning, singing, clanging cowbells, clinking spoons against bottles, blowing whistles, tooting horns. . . .

"*Mira, tovarish!*"

Someone's taking me for a Russian, it's a masked couple, a Che Guevara with beret and cigar and black ears and black hands and a fat smiling black cat with whiskers and a tail, they're showing me the steps, and this Che's much friendlier than the real one, who just yesterday fielded our questions from behind a lectern, and who, when asked why government troops had been used to quell a strike (some Trotskyists in Havana had told us about that), said, "You ask me that, and with the same face of an innocent I answer to you that I don't want to tell you" . . . now someone hands me a bottle of beer, my sixth or seventh this evening, all of them have been gifts for *tovarish,* but when I told them I was

---

6. "Rebellious yesterday, hospitable today, heroic always."
7. "Work is the fecund breeding-place where all human virtues germinate."

Americano, the friendliness was even greater: "Lauren Bacall!" they said. "Humphrey Bogart! Mickey Mantle!"

"*Como asi!*" says the cat.

Ah, the steps, it's not hard to learn, *gracias,* especially the way they're taking me into their middle, el Che on one side, the cat on the other, *muchas gracias,* and to think that a year ago I wanted to *film* this, watch it instead of joining in, what a concept, but where are my friends, I wonder, my fellow Americans, probably gearing up for another seance with the unappeased ghosts and unavenged crimes of racial memory, I'm so glad I'm not with them, grateful to feel the warm sweat of this fleshy cat's arm around my waist, where's my shirt, oh, still there, but unbuttoned, and why would anyone care, with the big joy of the year almost spent, the steady, tired, ecstatic stream still throbbing through the streets after six days of celebration, the exhausted couples draped around each other on stoops, in doorways, on the pavement, leaning against walls, an old man dressed as a white bird with the word "PAZ" painted on his chest lurching up to us, maybe drawn to the other masks, "*Viva!*" the bird says, and that's the best slogan of all, why give the life away to some image, I raise my bottle, and just as the word forms in my mouth I see Stefan tall and pale by the side of the road, and the word comes out "*Vive!*"—like an order: "Live!"—he mumbles something, raises a hand as I push toward him against the tide, I reach him, "*Viva viva,*" I say, trying to make a joke of it, he smiles, "*No puedo,*" he says, "*No puedo vivir,*" "I can't live."

"You can," I said, "you must," and I took him by the hand. If only I had done this more often, my little brother. We met two young girls. They showed you how to dance, you revived in their attention, their smiles. One of them said she wanted to live in America. You told her that wasn't a good idea, black people are freer in Cuba than in the U.S. She was skeptical. "There's nothing like Carnival there," you said. That made up her mind: "I don't want to live there! But you should stay here!" She kissed you good-bye, on the lips, you were blushing. Here's what you wrote the next morning:

> It is estranging, after such a night, to wake up and find the State Department White Paper lying on the table: "And so we oppose the present Cuban regime not just because its ambitions menace our hemispheric neighbors. We oppose it, above all, because its standards of conduct and its tyrannical practices condemn the Cuban people to misery and fear. The Cuban people deserve better than that." If this isn't the encounter of a sewing machine and an umbrella on a dissection table, I don't know what is.

The crowning event of the carnival was a speech by Fidel on the state of the nation, delivered on a vast, open field, from a high podium, before a huge enthusiastic crowd, and I'm starting to see a meaning in the pattern of my forgetting, Voluptas was jealous, she wiped the slate clean as fast as Politicus filled it with words—extraordinary words, I'm sure, because I do remember registering with amazement that I was not bored for a minute, and the speech lasted five hours, "a model of simplicity, honesty, and lucidity," according to Stefan, "completely absorbing, a wonderful speech, almost a lecture, but it also contained something passionate that was not the product of rhetoric but was inherent in the whole event and was felt by everyone: something of the pathos of living history, even now, five years after the revolution. He is speaking: that is almost like: It is speaking, and also: I am listening."

That evening, a baseball game between the heroic *Norteamericanos* and a team from the University of Santiago. Stefan and I, not knowing the first thing about baseball, sit on the sidelines, our team appears to be losing badly, several Jeeps and an armored car come rolling in, raising a high cloud of dust, it's Fidel and Raul Castro coming to join the game, on Santiago's side, naturally, now we're getting creamed, Fidel is an excellent hitter, Raul takes pity and offers to play on our side, he's no mean pitcher either, I wander off to a little kiosk to look at the headlines and find myself standing next to Gino Foreman, the militant beatnik with the dramatic body language and Dexter Gordon's voice. He is going through a stack of remarkably apolitical postcards: showgirls, actresses, Cary Grant, José Martí, Fidel, Marilyn Monroe, another showgirl, Fidel again, a boxer, Picasso's Don Quixote, more showgirls, a glistening black girl with white-white teeth, white eyeballs, and a white string of pearls, he's fishing out his wallet, she's the one he wants, it's Emma.

Back in Havana, we were quartered in a new hotel. I called the Hotel Nacional: There was no message for me. For the first time, I understood why the Buddhists think it desirable to kill desire. No more frustration! This was unbearable. But that evening she called. She was off with her troupe in Camaguey and would be back in two days.

"Désirée, I'm dying of thirst and you're talking to me about water."

"I'm thirsty too. For your kisses."

"I want more than kisses, Désirée."

"I do too. Day after tomorrow."

"Here in my room," I say.

"No, that's too risky. People know me."

"Where, then?"

"You'll see."

My roommate, the connoisseur of telephone sex, nodded approvingly as I put down the receiver.

From then on, my remaining days in Havana proceed as if in a dream that becomes so overwhelmingly pleasant that I no longer want to heed the warnings of unreality.

She meets me at the hotel wearing the dress she wore to the beach. Only I know the meaning of that, she couldn't appear to the world more chastely packaged, but the young black *miliciano* who stops us a few blocks away has his own notions. He summons her across the street with a hooked finger, orders me to stay where I am, asks for her work papers. She doesn't have them with her. He calls her a *gusana,* she makes a motion to stalk off, he takes her wrist, she screams for help, pronouncing the "d" like a "t"—*"Ayuto!"*—something she must have picked up in an Italian movie. I cross the street, a crowd is gathering around them, everyone is talking at once, I hear the word *puta* several times, so that's it, he thinks she's a whore, "I am an artist!" she screams, "I am a well-known dancer!", but she's not known to anyone here, nor is she helping herself with her haughty airs. But her nerves are wiser than she is, she's starting to tremble, she's starting to cry, she's pitiable, now the crowd sympathizes with her, most of them think the militiaman is off limits.

"You can't do that, *compañero,* you have no proof."

"A girl can have foreign friends if she wants to."

"You're jealous, *compañero,* you want her for yourself."

"Let her go, it's not right what you're doing."

The more they argue, the more despondent he looks. In the end, he lets her go.

We move on to the embassy of Ghana, Gino Foreman's pan-Africanism has won him the friendship of the Ambassador, and I've been invited to a party along with some other Americans Gino considers "sincerely militant." As soon as our hosts hear what has happened, they turn off the music and express to Emma their sympathy for the fear and insult she has suffered, and bring her a drink to help her get over the shock. Everyone except Gino has a kind word to say, he pulls me aside with a scowl that looks almost angry, and whispers:

"Do you know who she is?"

"Of course."

"She's Chango's woman, man."

"Who's Chango?"

He rolls his eyes and walks off. Emma is still being consoled. A young Ghanaian talks to me with his hand on his heart: Black Cubans, he says, not just whites, don't like it when they see him with a white woman, "Yes, yes, shoes of different colors they call it, it is frowned on, my friend, not by all, but by some." An American woman says very emotionally that the best way to fight racism is for people of different color to meet and love one another. "Or just have *fun* together!" another woman cries. And within a short time, the theme of interracial amity has charged the room with erotic tension, or maybe it's Emma, who has thrown off her shoes with her sorrows, and who does not know how to dance unsuggestively. I would feel like a fool to join her in front of all these people, but Gino has no such compunctions, he takes my shyness for his opportunity, steps in front of her with his long arms stretched out as if to prevent her escape, and, boring his eyes into hers, applies the hip-swiveling motion of the Twist to pelvically shovel her out of the room, through a door, and onto the balcony, where he tries to embrace her. She pushes him away, laughing and shaking her head, "No! No!", and runs back inside. He tries it again, shoveling away, this time through another door, which he attempts to close behind him, but she darts under his arm and skips across the room and sits down on my lap with her arm around my neck, laughing. He comes after her, pulls at her hand. "No," she says, sweetly, shaking her head, "really, no. I'm with him." Have I ever felt prouder, gladder, more grateful?

"Why doesn't he dance with you, if he's your man?"

"He does other things."

The dear! And before I've done anything! Several couples meanwhile have moved from talking and dancing to more advanced states of amorous entwinement, I notice doors opening and closing, I take Emma's hand, she follows me upstairs, I open a door, I see an office with a couch, no key in the lock, but a "Do Not Disturb" sign hanging on the inside door handle, I hang it outside and close the door. She feels insecure here, she does not want to make love in a room where someone could burst in at any moment. I shove the desk in front of the door, that puts her somewhat at ease, she pulls off her dress, I take off all my clothes, she lets me take off her bra, we're petting furiously on the couch, again and again I try to strip off her panties, "No," she says, holding my hand with a very definite grip, "not here, I don't feel free in this place."

"Emma," I say, "I'm suffering."

"I know," she says, her eyes full of pity, and bends to take my cock into her mouth. She is so good at this that I find myself forced to pull her away by her hair, hard, though not so hard as to prevent her entirely, and producing sounds of a kind I have never before heard issuing from my throat, much too loud. She stops every few minutes to put her finger to her lips, "shhh," and smile at me in the halflight before she resumes her magic. Eventually someone knocks on the door and tries to open it. A man's voice: "Excuse me." It's the young African who spoke to me with so much emotion earlier. "Please, you must come out. I'm sorry. This is an embassy!" I'm almost grateful for the interruption. We get dressed, put the desk back in place, go downstairs, the party has thinned and is half as orgiastic as I had supposed, it seems we did overstep our bounds here, some people are looking at us with curiosity and amusement. Embarrassed, we turn to each other and dance. "Let's go," I say. She asks me if I have the money for the *posada*. "What's a *posada*?" I ask. "The place where we're going." With a shock I realize I was so happy to see her that I left the hotel with only change in my pocket. She has little more than her bus fare. I will have to go begging. I start making the rounds, the two or three friends I ask don't have much in their wallets. Meanwhile one of the Nationalists—the one Stefan earlier described as "the type of a demagogue"—has asked Emma for a dance, and she has accepted. The thought occurs to me: How can he not notice the state she's in? I am suddenly fiercely, frighteningly jealous. I hear Gino's voice in the kitchen, and find him there in conversation with the Ambassador, who is evidently plastered.

"Take me to your leader," the Ambassador says to me.

"Excuse me?"

"Take me to your leader."

"After what *he's* done," says Gino, "*he's* my leader."

I ask them for money to pay for the *posada*. Between them, they come up with the sum I need. I return to the living room. The Nationalist and Emma look like pupils in a dancing school, so staid, so strait, I'm suddenly aware that this man in whom I have seen only a consuming scorn for anyone with white skin is as shy and lonely as I was a few weeks ago. And how serious Emma looks, turning with him in slow circles with her hand on his shoulder. Why doesn't she look at me? I wait for a while. Then I step up to them. "I have the money," I tell her, "whenever you're ready." She nods, smiles, stays with him until the record stops, thanks him, and goes off in search of her shoes. He walks up to me and asks to speak to me in the hallway. I follow him there.

"Did you tell her not to dance with me?"

I tell him what I told her, and why. He stares. It feels like thuddation time.

Then he nods and walks away. Maybe the setting dissuaded him. Or else he believed me.

It was drizzling outside when we left. We ran several blocks to a remnant of decadence the government had the good sense to preserve, a tryster's haven with rooms you could rent by the hour, with dimmable lights and mirror-glass on the ceiling. Here Voluptas won her decisive battle. Nothing is left of Politicus during the last two weeks of my stay, nothing of mass assemblies with banners and amplified speeches, of headlines and flags and posters of Spartan youth and the image, everywhere, of the bearded benevolent despot. There is a glimpse left, through the window, of two bars of light far out on the black water, American warships, but that is because we were making love in front of that window, I was standing behind her, she was leaning against the frame, arching her back to welcome me in more deeply. There may have been a moment, later, when we talked about those ships and their menace to her country, her fear, her readiness to fight—I can imagine it; but what I remember is something she said in front of that window, and the way the words ached out of her: *"Ay, que me llenas!"* ("Oh, how you fill me!" But the English words don't say the same thing at all.)

The rest is made of fragments.

That first night, she showed me a poem she had written while I was traveling— "about us," she said. It was full of hearts and flowers, but then there was a line that surprised me: "I want to love you in your blood." "What do you mean by that, Désirée?" "I can't say." But by the way she says that, I know there is a definite meaning. "Can you show it to me?" The question surprises her. She thinks about it. Something is moving in her. She hesitates. I encourage her. She opens her mouth and gradually, tenderly, sinks her teeth into my breast and bites down until I ask her to stop. In one of the tooth-marks surrounding my nipple a thin spot of blood rises like groundwater from a footprint.

A push of a button, room service comes with a discreet knock, we order Cuba Libres (with ersatz Coke), they're delivered on a tray that is shoved through a swinging panel at the bottom of the door. Through the walls we hear faint moans and cries and the rhythmic jangling of bedsprings.

"How old are you, Désirée?"

"I'll tell you the truth if you promise to keep it a secret."

"I promise."

"Fifteen."

"I was starting to guess it. The last girl I loved was fifteen."

"Do you still love her?"

"No."

"I am jealous of her."

"I am jealous of Chango."

She falls silent.

"Who is Chango, Désirée?"

"He's nobody."

"Gino told me you're Chango's woman."

"I was one of his women."

"Until when?"

"Until now."

That is all I learn about Chango from her. She is secretive.

Again and again, in the mirror above, the visual shock of our colors together. My skin looks like snow next to her dark mahogany.

When she tells me about her friends, her school, her envious colleagues, her neglectful mother, I listen with sympathy while my eyes drink unspoken meanings from her mouth: the coral pink of her gums when she smiles, the flash of her teeth, the beautiful crescent curve of her lips, their sadness and gaiety, their fullness, resilience. My eyes are in love with her mouth.

We are walking on a palm-lined avenue, the sun is setting. A middle-aged man approaches us with a camera: "May I take your picture?" There is something in the grave way he thanks us that touches me, even now in the memory. Something is shining through this moment that is not just beauty or the evening light. I wish I could see that photograph.

She takes me to her house, a two-story house in a middle-class section of town. I meet her mother, a tall handsome person with a strong handshake, and an ancient, bent woman, the mother's grandmother, who was born a slave. The mother is a fashion designer. The great-grandmother peers up at me from under her brows as she pats my hand: *"Muy bien,"* she says, chuckling, *"Americano. Ernesto Hemingway."* The mother is polite but not pleased to see me, and not curious at all. Would I like a drink, she asks. Just water, I say. She smiles on one side of her mouth as she brings it. Then Emma and I sit in the garden with a friend of Emma's, a girl a year or two younger than she is. This girl has pigtails tied up with bright ribbons. Emma plays a strange game: She pretends to allure me with provocative poses, while her friend suppresses a giggle, impressed by Emma's boldness and amused by my discomfort.

The skin on my penis is chafed, it hurts just to touch it. This inhibits our lovemaking. Emma is not disappointed. What she wants from me is romance. *"Mi marido,"* she calls me, "my husband." She is too young for me, she is making me feel like an indulgent father. I ask her to bring her loincloth and eyelashes, she adds sprinkles, stains her mouth with some dark blue dye, the archetype takes over, possesses her, I brace myself against the pain in my penis, she mutters sweet obscenities, moans and wails, her nails digging into my back, then straddles me, casually upright, with her hands on her thighs, smiling down at me as if in triumph as she clenches and rolls her internal muscles to squeeze and suck me to ecstasy. The next day she shows up in her schoolgirl outfit. Désirée wants to be Emma.

In Stefan's journal I find the following entry, dated August 6, 1964, a week before our departure:

> The group's activities are of the kind usually associated with sanatoriums: chess, sleeping, and eating. The tremendous boredom of almost everyone is infectious enough to stifle the slightest spark of interest. Joel and his dancer will probably be the only ones to welcome a rumor that we will be hanging around for two more weeks. Alternatives: write a novel or get some information about Cuba or talk to someone. As it is, as things stand, the first alternative is by far the most likely.

I am divided. One of me welcomes that rumor, the other dreads spending two weeks as Emma's *"marido."* One of me entertains the fantasy of abducting her in a large suitcase and living with her in New York, the other knows this is not possible and not desirable either.

She asks me to stay away from her show on the weekend. "Chango says he's going to kill you." I laugh. "He means it. He's looking for you." That gives me pause. "Does he know where I'm staying?" "He doesn't know what you look like, but if he sees you with me. . . ." I flash on a man I saw earlier in the day, in the lobby of the hotel, examining our faces as we emerged from the dining room. A handsome, light-skinned black man in his thirties, with a gold chain around his neck, smoking a cigarette, wearing the usual wide, short-sleeved tropical shirt, his hands in his pockets, his thin lips smiling with an expression of faintly sardonic amusement. I describe him to her. She nods: "That was Chango."

I am sitting on a wall near my hotel, Emma on my left and, on my right, a modest, gentle, seventeen-year-old from our group I have grown very fond of. His name is Hubert. He is a veteran of a famous gun battle between a group of southern black civil rights activists and the Ku Klux Klan, and, later, the state police. I tell Emma about Hubert, who understands no Spanish. I try to impress her with his courage, but she pities him for his hard life: "*Pobrecito,*" she says, "poor thing." Then I tell Hubert about Emma, who understands no English: her feathers, her dancing. His eyes shine. "She's really nice," he says. Though these words are meant for me only, I translate them. She says she likes him too. I tell him that. He smiles and hunches his shoulders and closes his eyes as if hugging a beautiful thought, she laughs her lovely cracked laugh, they are laughing together. I can imagine him in my place, maybe loving her as I can't love her. A wish comes and widens my heart with pleasure. In Emma's world, a woman belongs to the man she sleeps with. I want to give her to Hubert for a night. Only if she wants to, of course. And what if she does want to? That kills the wish.

I wedge my hand into her as deep as I can. She sits there leaning back with her thighs splayed, impaled, her face, her whole body, limp, drooping, wilting: "*Ayyyy.*" I am hurting her. Why am I doing this? Why is she letting me? I don't want to stop. Deeper. Deeper.

Stefan's journal, August 9:

> 5:30 pm. By now a completely irreparable lack of contact with anything or anyone.

She gives me a photograph of herself standing on a child's swing in her leopardspotted bikini. On the back she writes: "For my husband spiritually and sensually forever Désirée."

She sees me off at the airport, waving her arms and crying and throwing me kisses from the visitors' ramp on the roof of the airport building. I, too, throw her kisses, I am sorry for her and content to be leaving and very tired. Half asleep in the humming airplane on the way home I can feel the caress of her hands and the strong embrace of her thighs.

I don't know where Stefan was sitting.

More German Lessons

In a book about my stepfather, a collection of reminiscences, drawings, and photographs by his friends and colleagues, there is a picture of him, taken a year after I last saw him and two years before he died, by all accounts a miserable time in his life. But here he is happy, as happy as I have ever seen him. At first glance the reason seems obvious: He's being hugged right and left, a laughing little girl on one side, a portly man with black shades on the other, pretty young girls proffering flowers in the foreground, smiles of pleasure all around him. A hero's welcome. This is not Germany. Of course it's not Germany, how could it be? This is the port of Havana, June 27, 1961, and Bodo has just stepped off an East German ship laden with precious gifts of medical and school supplies. That was the real source of his pleasure, not the garland of touches and smiles.

I have crossed out and reinstated that last sentence several times, and now it seems Bodo himself doesn't buy it. I just discovered an entry for July 27, 1961, in the journal he published after his trip to Cuba:

> Still intoxicated from the experience of our arrival today. . . .

After a near-collision with a Greek freighter, the *Halberstadt* pulled in way ahead of schedule, the welcoming ceremony had to be improvised quickly, the first scattered officials came on board, representatives of the Cuban "Institute For Friendship Among The Peoples," the secretary of the seamen's union ("a giant who had lost both arms in an accident"), and then, suddenly, an old and beloved friend from Spanish Civil War days, from exile days in Paris and Mexico, a small, dark-skinned, laughing man with white hair, the poet Nicolas Guillén: "We sink into each other's arms, and for a long, long time we cannot part. All right, all right, now we're at home."

But he gave that last sentence a paragraph of its own, and my translation misses its feeling. This is worth examining more closely.

"Nun gut, nun gut, so fühlt man sich zu Hause."

This is how an emotion is buried. The sentence lies there like an unmarked grave.

"*Nun gut.*" Said once, it's little more than a filler, it means "OK," or "all right." Said twice, these are words of comfort, and more than that, of consolation.

"*Nun gut, nun gut.*"

That's what you say to an unhappy child: It's all right now, everything's all right.

"*So fühlt man sich zu Hause.*"

The impersonal pronoun, *man,* is a widely used linguistic device for masking the vulnerable I in the colors of generality. No one in Germany asks you to "speak for yourself" if you choose to say *man.* So what is he saying?

"Thus one feels at home."

But what he means is: "This is what I need in order to feel at home."

With quiet finality, the next paragraph sends him from his friend's embrace down the gangway and, through the next hundred thirty-five pages, into the ghost-life of his political dream. I am not saying that revolution was a mere fantasy in Cuba. Food, jobs, schools for everyone, decent houses, shoes: This, for a poor and exploited country, is the promise of heaven, and for many it was fulfilled, though at a steep cost in liberty. What I am saying is that Bodo, because he believed that his and everyone's real life would begin in the future, was always haunted by his own unappeased past.

At the end of his book, the child he briefly consoled and put to rest is remembered again, in an image indicative of deep sadness and an attendant yearning for escape, only to be sacrificed, this time definitively, to the god of political hope.

It is Bodo's last day in Havana, he is drifting off after being robbed of his sleep by some airforce captain who wanted him to send information from Germany about *gliders,* of all things, and . . .

> I spread my arms and sail lightly through the air, as I did when I was a child and daydreams guided me from the grayness of life to a future that has now largely become the past again, and that is only bearable as such because it gives birth to a new future, one which we aspired to from the beginning, however poorly we may have conducted our lives—a future in which we placed our hope, the fulfillment of which we will not live to experience. But this hope is that the weight and the hardness of life will no longer consist of humiliation and degradation, of the biblical "upon thy belly shalt thou go, and dust shalt thou eat," that the difficulty of life will consist in the greatness

of the challenge and in the meeting of it, in the higher sensibility of human hearts, in self-chosen maturity. There is a movement toward that, in this country too . . .

He misconstrued the biblical quote: that was said to the snake. But it's his personal mythology that is most sadly askew. How deliberately that "we" comes in to obliterate the boy's singularity, to supplant with the ideologue's blueprint for progress the child's dream of flying. It's the substratum of pain that sounds true, this I can believe: that there was a sense of unbearable, unacceptable humiliation and degradation from an early age on, and an ardent wish that it end, not just for himself but for all. So what is it that bothers me so, that appalls me in the end, that I cannot accept? It is this rush to a remedy that had already proven fatal, this glib postmortem acquittal of a blood-sodden past for the sake of a new hope fashioned in the image of that past's hopeful beginning in the realm of dreams, a new rainbow bridge to a new pot of gold, the true worth of which cannot be tested, until the next nightmare.

For the past fifty pages or so I have been sensing a current beneath me, a steadily building forward flow, like the pull of a river downstream toward a waterfall. I know there is such a fall up ahead, there are several, but I'm also fairly sure now that what I took for a straight line curves imperceptibly, that the river is really the upper lip of a whirlpool. Telling a story, of course, which is what I'm about at the moment, compels at least the illusion of forward motion, but the other movement, a round, centripetal, gradually spiraling turn of things in toward the center, is already perceptible. Pretty soon I'll be sucked into depths where I may have to proceed without memory. I'm glad, because that other self, the one who is suffering extremely and whom I forgot in the memory of so much plea-sure—it's by way of the whirlpool I'll find him. Each turn of the vortex is a circle of hell, and I know he's in the innermost, bottommost whorl. I would dive down straightaway if I could, but it's not time yet. As for the one I shot into space in a Cuban airplane—he's in another dimension, I don't know what to do about him. Although—It could be that the two are obscurely connected, the one above and the one below, just as Zeus and Hades were brothers.

Nothing to do, for the time being, but look for patterns in the rapids, something to orient myself by: There's Politicus making a last, feeble bid for my allegiance, and Voluptas offering drugs as a new enticement, unaware that she's opening doors to divine competitors even more powerful than she is. Eventually a new self emerges under their sway: a diver, impatient to get to the bottom. But he always comes up again, thwarted. Someone should tell him: When you're in a whirlpool, there's only one way to reach bottom: by way of the surface. In time.

Amor

George North—the man who chose an afternoon of sugarcane cutting over a date with Emma's friend China—invited me to share his apartment in a tenement building on Tenth Street between Avenues A and B. Among the friends he introduced me to was a sincere young man who supplied the neighborhood with "grass," "shit," "snort," "smack," "uppers," and "downers." You had to be *au courant* with your terminology. I remember spotting a narcotics agent by his phony lowlife-drugfiend look and the way he asked if I knew where he could get some "reefer."

My preference, at first, was marijuana. I still talk nostalgically with friends about the good old weed-smoking days. They are not retrievable. The plant itself has been altered to produce a more intense and more lasting high, but the effect is also to solipsize users, plunging them into dark private reveries, whereas the grass I remember promoted laughter, dancing, lovemaking, amiable chatter, and, over and over again, the happy illusion of conversational fireworks as we lay back, watching the commonplace opinions we had spouted moments ago descending out of the haze with a brilliance that made us gasp—"Wow!"—each word, each phrase trailing its own comet-tail of subliminal meaning.

My friends of "Progressive Labor" were opposed to marijuana, on practical grounds, because pot-smoking would make them vulnerable to police raids, and also on moral grounds, having to do with the value they placed on what they presumed to be the operations of reason. They were altogether too principled for my comfort. There was a man in Brooklyn, for example, who wanted to see a communist revolution in America and offered to give PL a substantial percentage of his winnings at the racetrack—he had evidently developed a workable system, or else had the funds to bribe jockeys—but Milt Rosen and his friends rejected the offer because the money was tainted: There would be no gambling after the revolution.

Even though I felt much more supported by the flaccid camaraderie of my pothead friends, I went to several PL meetings, unutterably boring conclaves where, I think, tactics were discussed, demonstrations were planned, etc.—I don't remember. I went because these nice, earnest people regarded me with something resembling esteem, of a latent, patiently waiting sort, as if in expectation of deeds I had yet to perform and of which only I was presumed to be capable, all on account of my East German past.

Voluptas introduced me to "speed." Our dealer sold packets of little pink pills called "Dexedrine." Half of one was like a strong cup of coffee. Eight or ten at a time made the brain hum like a hive, which may sound fanciful, but it's as exact an image as I can come up with: Scout thoughts buzzing off for new scents and old dangers, drones OM-ing in deep self-remembrance, and a constant word-searching, nectar-sucking hustle, in and out of conversation, up and under the lines of a book, pencil in hand, a scrivening mania, sometimes slipping from sentences into doodles, but these, too, driven by the same compulsion to SHAPE each spasm as it arose and twist and fit it into a STRUC-TURE that quickly became impossibly complex, while somewhere, unseen, pulsing and battening in the dark, sat the One whose hunger and love were the source and the goal of all this industry.

Politicus launched a spearhead attack in my own apartment. One of George's friends, Maro Riofrancos, was looking for a few people to help him publish a radical literary magazine which he proposed to call "Streets." George enlisted Stefan and me to edit the first issue. Stefan contributed a political play he had written for his high school graduation,[8] and an essay on the esthetics of high-tech barbarism in the James Bond movies. I supplied a free adaptation of a German poem lampooning the Statue of Liberty as a cosmetic gorgon with a vulva of ice cream, the tablets in her hand a rusty comic strip that interests no one except maybe spies from Russia, her torch fueled by the earth's black blood, cheered by tourists from their poop decks, her eyes hollow and dead except for moments—"and the bay must be calm"—when a tear of foreboding runs down her cast-iron cheeks. The closer I came to the vitriolic core of the poem, the more I disliked it. Were we not free, by the laws of this nation, to spit on the symbol of liberty with impunity? What sort of rebellion was it, then, to go ahead and spit? Weren't there better things to do with our freedom? I thought of proposing a change in the magazine's concept, and maybe its title, to something like "Quality"—wasn't that the most revolutionary criterion of all? Let the only organizing principle be that what goes into the magazine be beautiful

---

8. After the publication of "Streets," a group of professional actors put on Stefan's play at a coffee shop on the Lower East Side. The drama critic of the *Village Voice* panned the production but lauded the unknown author. "A Play for the General," he wrote, was not only an excellent play but a wholly inventive use of the theatre.

or dazzlingly good, and to hell with political agitation. I expressed my scruples to Stefan.

"How about a beautiful and dazzlingly good political kick in the pants, delivered to the right target?" he said.

"The target wouldn't notice," I said. Luckily for us, I thought.

"But it's the gesture that counts," Stefan said. "Or do you just want to get out of the heat?"

He was right, I did not have the stomach for ideological trench-fighting. And besides, the "right target" appeared to be the generic White Man: Somehow black nationalism had crept into our politics. One page featured a photograph of a furious Malcolm X pronouncing the letter "f" and pointing at himself: very radical, but when I heard Malcolm X on the radio he sounded insane to me, frothing with hate of the white devils: "Have you ever heard them *laugh*?" Another page featured a drawing of a black bird of prey mangling a pair of white testicles in its talons. One poem by Ishmael Reed celebrated the poetic spirit of young black burglars; another one proposed some rude assaults on the dignity of suburban housewives. The nearer the magazine came to completion, the less I wanted to be part of it. I withdrew my name from the list of editors—my participation had been so lax that none of the other three objected—and changed my name underneath the poem to "Joel Melman," an adaptation of my mother's maiden name. Voluptas was winning.

And then another god intervened. The one with the arrows. Not that I ever knew what hit me, or when, or where. Most likely my skin. All it takes is a nick. Slowly at first and then all the more surely, the sweet poison works its way into the heart.

Halfway through one of those endless PL meetings, the bell rang and the hostess let in a girl whom everyone except me knew as the sister of Ed Lemansky, the stalwart leader of our trip to Cuba. Her name was Susan. I don't remember what business she had come for, and neither does she. What we remember is our first impression of each other, and it is worth recording because it was like a first, hasty sketch made by accident before a deeper purpose took up the design and began the careful and beautiful work of love and patience that is still in progress and will not be completed until we have both died. She was gingerly stepping through the tight circle of seated bodies swathed in smoke of the politically correct kind, and I saw her left leg from the knee down to a little white sock and a shoe, which was of a type no one in my circle of acquaintances wore, a modest workaday middle-class shoe, not a sneaker, not a sandal; and something about the attractiveness of this leg, and the conventionality of the sock and the shoe and the black trench coat she was wearing, combined to produce a puzzling and pleasant ambiguity. And then we were introduced. Of this I remember only the charm of her smile, and that I liked her. What she saw was a tall, thin, pale boy with deep-set blue eyes that appeared to be gazing through her into some wide inner space, a cowlick sticking up on the back of his head, shoes scuffed and worn out to the edge of disintegration, and paint spattered on his jeans. She told me later the thought had crossed her mind that PL was recruiting in Appalachia. She also told me that she knew, at the instant she saw me, that I was a man she could love.

We met a second time, again under the auspices of Progressive Labor. She had helped organize a panel discussion on Cuba at Brooklyn College, and I had volunteered to talk. The two other scheduled speakers were equipped with data they had collected on the trip. I had nothing but emotional impressions to report. I felt obligated to defend against ignorance and lies one simple truth I had witnessed in Cuba: that there was joy in the revolution, that it was above all a revolution of joy, and that something of a spiritual nature, not political in the usual sense—maybe "brotherhood" was the right word—had animated the faces and spontaneous actions of so many people I met there; that in Cuba I had felt it easy to believe in the goodness of man—despite what I knew about Auschwitz—and that maybe the idea of communism had something to do with that, despite what I knew about Russia. This much I believed, but what about liberty? The freedom to travel, for instance, as we had in defense of our civil rights, without any threat of persecution? No one asked me that question, but it haunted my vague and emotive utterances, and later, on a late evening jaunt on the Staten Island ferry with Susan and several friends, gloom overcame me. Why had I not voiced my doubt? Was that what "party discipline" had been for Bodo? No wonder he became bitter.

I couldn't stop thinking about my hypocrisy, and Susan, who was standing next to me by the railing, was starting to think that I didn't like her. We were watching the patterns of lamplit foam on the black waves. Our arms were touching. The others were inside the boat. The wind was cold, I was not dressed warmly enough. I was shivering. Then I noticed that in my thoughts I was closing her coat around the two of us and standing heart to heart with her in the dark with the bass drone of the motor and the swish of the spray in our ears.
. . . I immediately cut off the fantasy, it seemed wrong, callow, selfish, to desire this girl merely because she was pretty and kind and near and my self-loathing wanted a vessel to pour itself into and be forgotten. Not good enough! But the

next scene I remember is in my apartment a couple of hours later, and I am there with Susan, who has a dentist's appointment nearby in the morning, and whom I have invited to sleep on the mattress that serves as our living-room couch. We have just stepped in through the door, and there are George and Maro flat on their backs on the floor with their hands folded under their heads, a packet of "Zigzag" cigarette papers and a plastic bag full of grass on the rug between them, the lights off except for a round candle in the middle of the room, with an upended colander propped up on books above the wavering flame, the purpose being to project the star-shaped holes in the colander against the ceiling. George and Maro's sullenly grunted replies to my introduction of Susan tell me that they have no intention of clearing the living room. Why should they? They think she's here to spend the night with me. I glance at Susan: She looks like a visitor from another planet, and she is: the planet Uptown. So innocent, standing there on her half-high heels, with her pocketbook dangling from one hand, smelling sweetly of nothing but herself. I pick up the mattress, put it on the floor in my room, cover it with a sheet and a blanket: "You take my bed," I say, "I'll come in when you turn off the light." I wait in the living room while she undresses. Something unpleasant has transpired between George and Maro, I can tell. Probably one of those stupid editorial debates, balancing the claims of Apollo against those of Marx, or is it Mars. "Aren't you going to fuck her?" George finally asks. "No." I have never felt more virtuous. The light goes off in my room. I let a few minutes pass, say good night to Maro and George, go into my room, close the door, undress in the dark, slip under the cover. It doesn't take her more than a minute to throw back her blankets, tap her way through the dark, kneel down next to me, and plant a kiss on my lips. Bless her bold heart.

We spent three weeks in that room—discounting a few unavoidable errands in the outer world—making love, talking, sleeping, making love again, talking . . . and because we wanted to sleep as little as possible, we swallowed lots of Dexedrine, which turned out to have aphrodisiacal properties. But then, so does talk when you are in love, and the little pink pills promoted orgies of conversation. They also enabled me to rivet Susan's attention with readings from books that would have put her to sleep without pharmaceutical aid: *Being and Nothingness,* for instance, hours of it. I was fascinated by existentialism (as a possible alternative to Marxism), and Susan wanted to please me.

One day, while I slept, she took my clothes to the laundry. When I awoke, she was cleaning my room. I protested mildly, and she replied that she was sorry but, at least for the time being, she was living with me, and my room was too messy for her. No woman had done this since I lived with my mother, and I wasn't sure I liked it, or, for that matter, that I didn't.

Then the world recalled us both: Susan had classes to attend at City College, I had to look for work. There was relief and anxiety in this separation: I missed her and called her every night, but at the same time it felt good to be on my own, to mess up my room again, go cruising the neighborhood bars with George, maybe with some luck pick up a couple of chicks for the night. And somewhere beyond the horizon waited the woman I would marry, improbably beautiful, brilliant, mysterious, a perfumed labyrinth, a woman like Paris or Alexandria, unfathomable. This was clearly not Susan, who was like her name, which means "lily"—that purest, simplest, most feminine flower—and who loved me. That this was the truly fathomless depth, I must have dimly felt, because the thought of staying with her filled me with a kind of vertigo—that sensation Sartre so brilliantly analyzed as freedom's desire to opt for its own cancellation. Hadn't Sylvia once complained about this feeling? I told Susan one day: "This can't work out. We're too different. It's best if we part now, it'll be more painful later." That cruel little ploy was the last gasp of my bachelorhood.

She was deeply upset, naturally. "What happened? I thought we were getting close?"

"Yes, close, but . . ." And I tried to explain, and since there was no convincing explanation, tried to console, and once that was under way, to recant and apologize, to tell her I loved her and that I was running away from love—which, finally, was the truth.

A nd now two new and very powerful gods step in. The first is called Acid. Anyone who remembers the late sixties knows what he's about. The second . . . what shall I call him? As I search for a name, my left ear goes suddenly numb and deaf, as if stoppled with cotton, and echoes with a ringing sound, suggesting to me that this god is not containable by any name and must be sought out in silence.

But a provisional name is in order. I will call him "Chance," because that was the guise in which he first approached me. The god who throws dice. It really should be "Coincidence," but that's not a pretty name. What a peculiar word, though. It weighs very little in the language; it makes a tinny sound when it's dropped, like loose change; it often comes with deprecating qualifiers like "mere" or "weird"—yet it implies something monstrous, or at the very least unthinkable. It's easy enough, for example, to say "All is one," and to feel the comfort a child feels when it's tucked into bed before being kissed good night. But translate that phrase to "universal coincidence," which is really what it means, and you can't even begin to imagine it. A mind that attempts to force the ten thousand things of experience into such a formula will breed monsters and be devoured by them. And this is not because all is not one, but because thought, whose function it is to divide and distinguish, can no more unite the world than a knife can heal the wounds it inflicts.

The Fury of Symbols

Our high school science teacher had taught us that matter was born of absolute chance and evolved by incalculable multiplications of accident to the formation of galaxies, planets, fish, mammals, minds, and, eventually, high school science tests. This always seemed to me more fantastical than any of the creation myths science was here to supplant. Conversely, if he was right, there had to be more to the fall of dice than numbers, or more to numbers than mathematicians surmised.

Around the time I met Susan I was giving this question more serious consideration than was good for me. I took a philosophical (so I thought) interest in the kind of events Jung termed "synchronistic," and this before coming across his famous study of the subject. I thought I was breaking new ground. Imperceptibly, I became captivated, enthralled, obsessed, until for a few weeks my mind, body, and surroundings erupted in a synchronistic delirium.

I think I caught the virus from reading André Breton's *Nadja,* a book I found beautiful and disturbing—beautiful because of its valiant fidelity to what is unknowable, its hatred of all explanations; disturbing because of the vision it presented of a *possibly boundless* kingdom impervious to the imperialistic designs of reason, a savage and innocent land where things and people obey the unpredictable dictates of chance and of poetry. It was disturbing also in ways that Breton could not have intended: for Nadja, the young woman who guided him to the outer borders of that kingdom, and who left him to take up permanent residence there, was probably insane. Like a boy playing with fire— cautiously, since he is in secure command of that reason whose general rule he deplores—the poet exults in the radiant, diaphanous presence of his muse; but she is burning, and is given no voice in his book for so much as a scream.

I envied the surrealists their coffeehouse trances and theatre scandals, their *amour fou,* their magical Paris. New York had no poetry that I could see. A hard, epic prose it had, made of stone and glass and dirt and steel, bright by day and dark by night, endless reams of it—but poetry: I couldn't see it. However, the magic of chance, I thought, must be present here as much as there, now as much as then. I had already had intimations of it. Everyone does: You think of an acquaintance you haven't seen for years and wonder why she has entered your thoughts, and as you turn the corner, there she is, stepping out of a taxi. Or, in conversation with a friend in a restaurant, say, at the moment when you both tacitly agree to avoid a certain issue, you notice it has become the topic of discussion at a neighboring table. This, I assumed, was the household variety of surrealist experience, available, indeed inescapable, for everyone, and one had only to make it the object of one's most expectant attention to begin to harvest the first shining fruits of that enchanted garden.

I wrote down my dreams, practiced "automatic writing," and, above all, collected coincidences; I searched for them, hunted them. The first finds were interesting, but lackluster. They weren't finds at all, I realized, but products: I had made them. I had to get out of the way, open myself wider. Smoking marijuana, I noticed, helped loosen the grip of habitual thought processes long enough for genuine serendipities to happen, the sort of accidents that refuse to fade into oblivion but cling to the mind with tenacious little roots of metaphor, sprouting significance even when you don't want it (but of course I did). These were the genuine article, but, comparing my finds with those of Breton, they were still commonplace, flat. It must be the difference between New York and Paris, I thought. And then the coincidences started getting stranger, more interesting, in a way more artistic, as if in the web of random happenings there was a pixyish imagination that responded and played up to my curiosity as if to an audience. Little poems of fortuity. For example, one day I was listening to people talking about Vietnam in the office where I worked; not an argument, everyone there was against the American intervention, just a quiet, rather pensive end-of-the-day conversation. The sun had already set, and I was gazing out the window at an unusual cloud formation: It looked like a long dark quill hovering over a piece of paper, or more likely, parchment, with almost perfectly straight edges, certainly an uncommon feature in a cloud. I drew a colleague's attention to it while the conversation continued. "All it needs is a hand," he said. "The hand's invisible," I replied. Then someone in the background said, not in reference to the clouds but to the conversation about Vietnam: "How do you think history gets written, Sam? How do you think it gets written?" The others laughed for some reason, and at that moment a dark red streak developed precisely where the point of the quill touched the page. The streak lengthened into a horizontal line as the conversation shifted to more trivial topics, then it started bleeding toward the bottom, and then it was five o'clock and people were putting on their coats, and my colleague and I looked at each other and silently shook our heads. I wanted to talk about what had happened, and

he said he'd almost rather not, it was just too strange, down to the name Sam—
there was no one called Sam in the office. "What's so strange about that?" I
asked. "Look at those colors," he said, and then (I'm afraid this sounds unbelievable, but it was so) I saw that the sky behind the quill and the bloodied
parchment was distinctly divided into three horizontal fields of color, a fiery
red on the bottom, bone-white in the middle, sky-blue on top.

Similar experiences followed. It seemed that, by way of surrealism, I had
stumbled upon augury. That felt vaguely like witchcraft, like divination by tea
leaves and entrails and hot wax and whatnot, and I was a little embarrassed. I
didn't tell anyone. But I was excited. If this was an archaic way of knowledge,
why should it be any less valid, any more uncertain than ours? And what was
our usual way, after all? To grope for understanding until one touched on something—usually a set of words—upon which one felt justified in conferring the
status of truth; and then, if one was inclined to be thorough, one might test
that truth, tap its surface with doubt as with a felt hammer—not too hard, lest
it break—listening for some telltale hollow or flat sound, and if all went well,
one was pleased to have added to one's store of knowledge. Maybe there were
thinkers who pushed their doubt all the way to the end; but who had the
courage for that—or the faith? But this other way was like being surprised in
the dark. You'd be listening, as usual, half consciously, to some obscure worry
or half-formulated question, when all of a sudden a sign would appear and
answer, sometimes very dramatically. Like the day I drove out to the country
and spent the greater part of the afternoon sketching an oak on the edge of a
cliff, a stream in the valley below, and a factory chimney with its plume of
smoke in the distance. While I drew, the tree and the chimney became symbolic antagonists in my mind, a sentinel of wild nature confronting its demonic
parody, and to stress this idea I darkened the smoke a little and made it billow
more portentously than it did in reality. Pleased with the half-finished drawing,
I drove home, determined to come back and complete it the next weekend.
When I returned, the tree was no longer there: it had fallen root over crown
into the valley along with a chunk of the cliff it had stood on, and in the background the chimney stood smokeless, as if resting after long labor. That one
frightened me. I tried to retrace the steps that had led me there. Surely the sense
of having been given a sign was an error in thinking, a delusion. Surely a coincidence was just a meaningless chance event, and the wish to derive significance from it ought to be dismissed as a product of fear, a craving for certainty
even at the cost of all common sense. But just a small shift of perspective opened
up streams of communication between the heart with its questions and fears

and the wordless void, which appeared to be not indifferent or alien at all, but trembling with a responsiveness that seemed almost intimate. This was not just a game. It was as if there were a voice in the darkness that spoke in signs and symbols that teased the mind with meaning beyond comprehension, but were decipherable by way of feeling; a voice that claimed a kind of exclusive and secret loyalty of me, as if it were jealous of ordinary discourse, and thought it could be betrayed by translation; and in all its messages there was a hint of a promise: Go with me a little way, and I will take you far. And I believed that. At the same time I was profoundly alarmed. A great destruction was under way and I was being given foreknowledge of it. Not the tree, of course, that was just a symbol of something much vaster and darker.

The tide was rising, and still I went about my coincidence-hunting with the patient expectancy of a beachcomber, storing my finds away in a special ledger I had marked "Chance"—until one day the sea came pouring in through the windows.

On a Saturday evening when George was away for the weekend and Susan was in school, a stranger knocked on the door of my apartment. I opened without first asking who it was or looking through the peephole. Standing in front of me was a light-skinned black man about my age who introduced himself as Conrad and said he was a friend of Max, the bookseller on 86th Street and Amsterdam Avenue, and also of George, which surprised me, since I thought I knew George's friends. He was dressed in a peculiar outfit: khaki riding breeches with high lace-up boots, a frayed leather jacket with the collar turned up, and in his hand a riding crop. He said George had told him I had some LSD and wasn't about to drop it, so wouldn't I sell it to him, Conrad—he wanted it badly; and he had brought along the book I had ordered from Max—it had just arrived in the mail.

I should explain a few things before I go on. Marijuana was forbidden, of course, and possession of it was often harshly punished, sometimes with years in jail, but LSD wasn't prohibited yet, and knowledge about its marvelous effects had only recently begun to trickle down from the university laboratories to the streets. That's why I had bought myself a tab of the stuff. But I had also read Timothy Leary's warnings in the *Harvard Advocate* about the importance of "set and setting," and Aldous Huxley's description of some hellish moments on mescaline. I didn't want to cleanse the doors of perception with a dishrag. So I had stored the capsule in the refrigerator for the vague eventuality of a hassle-free weekend in the country. And now came this character wanting to buy it and introducing himself as a friend of both George and Max, and bringing me simultaneous messages from both. It seemed just a bit unlikely, and I had a fleeting suspicion that Conrad was a narcotics agent out to entrap me for possession of marijuana (using the Acid as a pretext); so, as I invited him in—out of courtesy to George and Max, more than anything—I not only told him I didn't want to sell him the only tab of Acid I had but also decided to leave my grass hidden behind the sink instead of offering to share a smoke with him. But Conrad had grass of his own, a neat little row of carefully rolled joints in his breast pocket. His eyes were nervous, alert, but friendly: I could see no threat in them. The book, it turned out, was not the one I had ordered—*The Tibetan Book of the Dead*—but something I had never heard of: *The I Ching, or Book of Changes,* from the same publisher.

We sat down on the rug and smoked. I put on Thelonius Monk's *Brilliant Corners,* and Conrad smiled broadly, closed his eyes, and slowly shook his head as if in unbelieving appreciation. We talked about this and that. And then again he asked me to sell him the Acid, and shyly offered to pay double whatever I had paid for it. He really wanted the stuff very badly, it had to do with . . . —he made a gesture with his left hand that seemed to indicate some vaporous cumulative disorder with roundish contours—"everything," he said then, smacking the riding crop against his boot, and frowning at the rug. I asked him what he thought dropping Acid would do for him. He didn't answer. He sucked at the last millimeter of viable joint and asked with gestures, holding his breath, if I wanted to eat the roach. I shook my head. After letting out a prolonged, hissing exhalation, he popped the roach in his mouth, swallowed it, and said: "It's the best part, man." Then we laughed, and I was reassured by his relaxed and comfortable way of chuckling, when abruptly, without looking at me—he was busy lighting another joint—he asked me where I'd gotten the Acid, and I felt my hands grow cold and I thought: He's an enemy and I've let him into my house and he knows I've got dope stashed away and he wants to get at my dealer. Then he handed me the joint and I refused it and, fumbling for the most immediate way to avoid having to answer his question, I offered to sell him my capsule after all, what the hell.

"Are you sure?"

"Yeah, sure, what the hell, who knows when I'll get around to dropping it."

"Shit, man, that's real generous of you."

As I returned from the fridge and saw him standing there in his boots and jodhpurs (he'd left the crop lying on the floor) with a look of anticipatory excitement on his face, I felt like a fool for conceiving of this nervous innocent as a narc—especially when he insisted on cautiously pouring the contents of the capsule on a piece of newspaper on the table to see what the stuff looked like; or was he mistrusting *me* now? And maybe with good reason, for the Acid turned out to be a little mound of fine white powder.

"Looks like baking powder," he said.

"Certainly does," I said. I was embarrassed.

Conrad licked his finger, dipped it in the powder, and put the finger in his mouth.

"Tastes like sugar," he said.

"No shit!" I picked up a sizeable pinch of the stuff and put it on my tongue. "It *is* sugar!"

He tested it again. It was definitely sugar.

"I can't believe it," I said. This time I wet my finger too and lifted off some of the sugar and tasted it.

"Confectioner's sugar," Conrad said, laughing. "Good stuff!" and he took some more. Then I realized:

"It's *supposed* to be sugar—it usually comes in sugar cubes!"

"You mean . . ."

"Yeah, that's right. You better eat the rest of it."

"Shit!"

He cautiously picked up the paper, folded it into a funnel and carefully poured the remains of the sugar into his mouth. I offered him a glass of water to wash it down.

"I guess we dropped it," he said.

"Yup. I guess we did." I had taken about a third of the dose.

We went back into the living room and sat down, Conrad on a couch, I on an armchair. Conrad lit another joint. I put on Coltrane's *A Love Supreme*. So much for set and setting.

We chatted for a while, and then we fell silent. The music had stopped. Something was happening. Something was snaking through my brain and my body: Energy. Thought. Sex. Memory. Imagination. I reached for a pencil and a sheet of paper on the coffee table near me and wrote: "SENDING OUT THOUGHTS . . ." I imagined flashing sabres, thundering hooves: I was some sort of general, a field marshal of the mind, it felt terrific to have such power, but the very next word that presented itself, "LIKE," proved almost insuperably difficult, it had "kill" stuck halfway down its throat, and did I really want to wage war, and with whom? I fought my way through all four letters and felt the surge of martial power again. "Sending out thoughts like . . ." Like what? I wrote down the words that came to mind: "AN ARMY." Houses were burning. A naked infant lay in the heart of a blue flower, a wasp came and stung it. No! I closed my eyes. Something was working a pattern into the cloth of existence, a million-threaded pattern of whirling, writhing images woven of thoughts, impulses, fears, and desires all braided together, sublime and sinister, cruel and innocent, beautiful and hideous, and the shuttling loom on which all this was woven and rewoven was the human brain, mine and everyone's, and there was no way to stop it. I opened my eyes. Convulsions in the grain of the wood floor: snakes. The room was sugarsweet, powdersoft. I looked at what I had written and added: "OF SNAKES." It took an endless time to write the letters. The "S" alone held so much more meaning than the whole word. When it reappeared again at the end the implications seemed enormous. I drew a picture:

Then I dropped the pencil and looked up. There was Conrad with his eyes closed and his mouth smiling half-open and his head tilted as if listening to distant music, on the long wall over his head an Egyptian mural, the paint flaked or faded with the millennia, a king in perfect Egyptoprofile holding a double-shafted whip in front of his chest, minuscule slaves in a cowering row before him proffering food, live beasts, and other gifts, behind him in lockstep attractive female attendants with transparent garments and palpable behinds and breasts and long gesturing hands, above him the sun with rays ending in hands, the whole thing in cerulean blue and rose and some kind of glittering aqua green, was it paint or inlaid, or both? But when I leaned in to look it was gone. But Conrad was there, Conrad as Pharaoh, his crop the emblem of kingly power, and I, a slave?

By about midnight, Conrad was Conrad again, a New York hipster who, it turned out, had recently joined an equestrian club on the Upper West Side. We went up on the roof. The air over the city was very clear. The moon and the stars were out, and we could see the Empire State Building all lit up. Conrad pointed out the black silhouette of the Con Ed plant a few blocks above us by the East River. Its smokestacks looked strangely slanted to me, the way the expressionists used to draw smokestacks. In charcoal, in fact. Conrad said the smokestacks looked vertical to him, but charcoal seemed just right. And the Empire State Building was done in pastel on a black ground. In fact the whole landscape was a symbolic picture. "How so?" I asked. "Well, the Con Ed Building has no light and it looks mean as all hell. It looks like it's crawling out of the river while everyone's asleep and frankly it's scaring the shit out of me. But there's the Empire State Building. It stands there like an angel of light, it sees far and wide, and it's holding up a spear. . . ." *At that moment, the lights on the Empire State Building went out.* I swear they did—all of them. We just stood there gaping and shaking our heads. The Con Ed Building was puffing smoke through its stacks. "Damn," I said, "that's where the light comes from!" Conrad burst out laughing and slapped his thighs. I laughed too, but I felt very uneasy.

Around dawn we went to Tompkins Square Park to sit on the grass. People were starting the day's errands, buying newspapers, going to church. Others were sitting on the park benches, feeding the pigeons and squirrels, talking, reading. We observed how crooked most people were in their bodies, how they carried themselves as if they had stolen a piece of existence and hoped no one would notice. Every once in a while someone would come along who seemed to feel part of things, who was quietly joyful in his movements, whose face shone. Then we noticed a large yellow turd a few feet away from us in the grass. It formed the apex of an equilateral triangle of which Conrad was the right corner and I the left. Impossible to ignore such a presence once you've seen it. We thought of moving to another part of the lawn, but it felt uncomfortable to break the triangle. We waited. Something seemed about to happen. Far away, at the other end of the park, we saw a drunk staggering from bench to bench, panhandling, and I prophesied: "He's going to come here. He'll climb the fence and sit down in the shit." I immediately regretted saying that. The drunk worked his way in our direction, climbed over the iron fence, and asked us for a dime. (That was 1965, when a dime was still worth asking for.) We reached into our pockets and gave him some change. He thanked us, blessed us, introduced himself as Bill or Jack, held out his hand for us to shake, staggering all the while. "Watch out behind you," I said, as I shook his hand. "No problem," he said, "plenty o' room," and carefully, without looking behind him, sat down in the shit. We got up and left then.

I walked Conrad to the subway at Astor Place. I was quivering, a fine tremor all over my body. I prayed: "Enough. Please. No more." Conrad stopped in front of a trash-can full of discarded photographs, arty portraits of hydrants, puddles, shoes, somebody's ear, etc. He pulled out a picture of a young woman with large breasts half revealed by a plunging neckline and started walking again, looking at the picture and smiling. Then he tore the face out of the picture and threw the rest away. "She reminds me of someone I know," he said. For some reason his doing that calmed most of my anxiety.

When we parted, he skipped down the subway stairs and turned around and said, "I love you, brother," and I said I loved him too.

Back in the apartment, I found the picture of the double-snake infinity sign and the words I had written at the beginning of the trip:

SENDING OUT THOUGHTS
LIKE AN ARMY OF SNAKES

Some part of the brain had edited and completed the phrase overnight—I knew what I had to do. I crossed out "snakes," replaced it with "serpents," and added:

TO SEARCH OUT THE ONE
FROM WHOM ALL THOUGHT RECOILS

I slept until Susan dropped in Sunday evening. She cooked some soup for the two of us, and then we made love and I slept some more. When I woke up around midnight I examined the book Conrad had brought me, and soon began to feel a familiar sensation at the base of my neck, the fine, not unpleasant, shiver of the uncanny. It wasn't just the book's strangeness—the arcane flavor of the English title, the sixfold tiers of straight and broken lines that preceded each chapter, the hundreds of cryptic fragments of verse (that's what I took them for), or the peculiar organization of the text into "Judgments," "Images," and "Lines." True, I had never seen anything remotely like it, but it was obviously a book, an obviously ancient text of Chinese origin and of some psychological interest, since Jung had written the foreword: This much my ever-efficient mechanisms of recognition and classification had told me. But as I followed Jung's sample interrogation of the I Ching, and its responses, it dawned on me that this wasn't a book in the ordinary sense; that it was a *voice,* that it conversed with its readers; that it was not only intelligent, but in some sense alive. At least those were its claims, which Jung was trying to make palatable to a mind accustomed to a rationalist diet. A small storm began to rise in my brain, I could feel it, excitement and disbelief and foreboding and faint disgust all whirling together. In the Appendix was a set of instructions for "Consulting the Oracle." Not having access to fifty-one yarrow stalks, I used the coin method. I tossed three pennies on the floor six times in a row, record-ing the combinations of heads and tails, shaking my head at my superstition and inwardly hoping for a reading that would at least roughly respond to my first question: "Who or what are you?" The chart at the end of the book referred me to the second line of the sixty-first hexagram:

A crane calling in the shade.
Its young answers it.
I have a good goblet.
I will share it with you.

Those four lines did seem to answer my question very clearly, and they still do. If interpretation were needed, I would have rephrased the stanza as follows: "I am related to you as a wild bird is to its young. Though my real nature is hid-den from you, I speak a language that you can understand. Moreover, you can reply to me, and I will hear you. I possess something of rich and mysterious value. I will share it with you."

I decided to repeat my experiment, more or less in the spirit of science, by framing the question as I had the first time: "Who or what are you?" and toss-ing the coins again, noting with a mixture of satisfaction and disappointment that the combination of heads and tails was different from the result of the first throw. This time I drew the fourth hexagram, without any "moving lines"—an indication of a static or unambiguous situation. Imagine my astonishment when I read the Judgment of Hexagram 4:

Youthful Folly has success.
It is not I who seek the young fool;
The young fool seeks me.
At the first oracle I inform him.
If he asks two or three times, it is importunity.
If he importunes, I give him no information.
Perseverance furthers.

I passed the next few days in a fever of coin-tossing, page-turning, and record-keeping, interrupted only by eight unavoidable hours of work at the office and five hours reluctantly yielded to sleep. Susan was irritated, maybe jealous, too, of my obsession.

About a week after the Acid trip, I received the following reading:

If one is not extremely careful,
someone may come up from behind and strike him.
Misfortune.

At this, I rebelled—that is, I protested in my journal: "Susan is right, this is crazy: to allow my fortune to be *dictated* to me, and by what? The fall of three pennies!" I put the book away and went for a walk. After returning, I wrote: "By the river: everything permeated with a subtle dread. Metallic sky, brass, the earth beneath it bluish and cold. When I came home, the beginning of a spider's web across the door frame, the little spider still spinning—how *not* to see this as a symbol? Is this a dream?"

At the risk of being called a fool once again, I asked the I Ching for an explanation, and wrote down the answer:

> A cry of alarm. Arms at evening and at night.
> Fear nothing.

Fear nothing! That was easy for the I Ching to say. I was worried. Susan suggested a psychological meaning. A violent and morbid streak had shown up in my dreams only recently. One in particular had disturbed me: "An old couple in bed. The man awakes and sits up. Death stands behind the bed in medieval robe and cowl. Using both hands, Death presses the wooden handle of his sickle against the old man's throat and says: 'We make the rounds three times a day.'"

I cast the coins once more the next morning, without asking a question. The oracle said:

> One is enriched through unfortunate events.
> No blame, if you are sincere
> And walk in the middle,
> And report with a seal to the prince.

This made no sense to me at all, and I decided to shelve the I Ching for a while. Confucius had said you had to be at least sixty before you could make intelligent use of this book. No doubt he was right.

The following night, between one and two a.m., I was shot by a stranger in front of the door to my apartment.

It happened like this: I came home from a late movie with Susan. We got out of the subway at Astor Place and walked slowly east. Near Avenue A on 8th Street I stooped to pick up a small gray piece of paper. At the same moment I heard a soft high tinkling of bells across the street. I turned around: The street was empty. Susan had heard the bells too. The sound must have come from inside an apartment. The paper I had picked up was some kind of playing card. Two question marks were printed on it, one right side up, the other upside down. On the opposite side were the words

REVERSE

or

EXCHANGE

I put the card in my pocket. We walked through Tompkins Square Park. It was very dark and unusually quiet. A police car slowly rolled by on 10th Street. A small dog ran up to us, wagging its tail, very friendly. I stretched out my hand to pet it. It yelped and ran away with its tail between its legs.

As we walked up the stairs to the apartment, I noticed two men following one flight beneath us. I glanced down through the banisters and saw the head of one of them, a black man with straightened hair. I assumed he lived in our building. I kissed Susan as we walked up. Then I searched for my keys and discovered that I had left them uptown at Susan's place. I knocked on the door. I heard music playing inside, and voices chattering. George was giving a party. I heard a voice behind me and turned my head and saw the two men who had followed us up the stairs. Susan had stepped up to the door and knocked again, a little louder. The door opened and George appeared and looked at Susan. The sound of music was louder now. Why hadn't he told me about the party? This part of the memory looks unnaturally bright, maybe because the ceiling lamp in the hallway was broken: George has his hand on the door frame while the other, his right hand, is holding the door open wide. His left shoulder is sunk below the level of the right, as if he were carrying an invisible load. He's smiling that peculiar downturned smile of his; the corners of his mouth act like brakes on his pleasure. I think he loved Susan. I thought so then, I think so now. Did she love him? No. But at times I was jealous, and I felt that way then. His head, lit from behind, has a halo of blond curls. Susan stands before him in a dark coat, her head tilted, smiling up at him, offering him her face, her smile. I am behind her, out of her sight. And my two executioners—I can't see their faces, but I think they're staring at me. When the nearer of the two men accosts me, I don't hear his voice (I think now that he must have said something dramatic, like "This is a stick-up!"), and I assume he's coming to the party, many strangers come to our house when George gives a party, friends of friends. Now I see Conrad behind George in the kitchen, it's the first time I've seen him since the Acid trip, I say "go ahead," indicating with my hand that the man and his friend should go in before me, Susan's inside already, George has stepped back to make room for the strangers he thinks I've brought with me. The next moment all I see is the face of the man who will shoot me. His jaw has dropped, a mask of incomprehension. I suppose my face looked blank as well.

"*Get* in there!"

He looks mad. He takes me by the arm and shoves me toward the door. I turn around to face him, raising my hands, palms up: "What's the matter? What's going on?" This sends him into a rage. He grabs my right arm with his left hand and half pushes, half pivots me by a half turn toward the door and whisks his right hand out of his coat pocket and shoots. The bullet—this is a reconstruction, of course, I could have no idea at the time what the bullet was doing or whether there was a bullet at all, it sounded so much like a cap gun; but the day after the shooting, a detective searched for the bullet in the kitchen and left in perplexity, shaking his head, and later George discovered a chip in the brick wall opposite the kitchen window and together we reconstructed the bullet's trajectory. I wish I could triangulate the dance of all those bodies in space: The gunman twirling me into alignment as Susan walks out of range into the living room and Conrad stoops over the sink to wash a glass and George, caught between a self-protective reflex and allegiance to me, half closes the door; then the shot: The bullet drills into my right side two and a half inches from the navel, charring the rim of the entry wound, speeds through the thin layer of fat covering the internal organs, misses the intestinal wall by a couple of millimeters, exits about an inch and a half to the left of the navel (no char-ring there), passes through the space between George and the open door, tra-verses the length of the kitchen, missing Conrad by a couple of feet, sails through the crack of the slightly opened window, crosses the courtyard, and smashes into a brick wall. That window was raised no higher than an inch off the sill, and the bullet did not graze the wood. I was pleased with this detail, and there was something like pride in that pleasure—not exactly as if *I* had done it, but as if I had been elected and transported beyond the reach of fate. Because I had been given to know from the beginning that I was past any harm. Even as I fell. For a moment nothing happened at all, I stood there empty, and then I thought this must be a joke but I noticed my stomach was warm and my head was spinning and I comprehended that something unbelievable had hap-pened, I had been shot in the stomach and this could be the end. And the strangest thing happened: The impact of this recognition resembled nothing so much as delight. No thought: I just stood there, amazed; and then I realized I would have to come back to this later because unless I fell he would shoot me again, and what came to mind as I fell, of all the mortal or life-saving thoughts, was how I used to practice precisely this same limp sideways collapse when I was a child and a friend pointed a stick at me and said bang: the pleasure it gave me, this pantomime of the body's reversion to the realm of things while the life crouched inside in secret delight. I hit the floor and I could have burst out laughing but I had to lie still and now I remembered my mother pretending that she was dead—for which she had immediately apologized with a grievous urgency that puzzled me (I was about six), since it implied more guilt over her deception than I could imagine; I had been gripping her throat playfully, pretending I was the maniacal strangler we had seen in a movie—we were both laughing—when suddenly her head fell to the side and her eyes closed and she didn't respond to my calling her name and prodding her, until my voice must have sounded frightened or tearful. And then I thought, I mustn't do that to Susan, and opened my eyes, and Susan was standing in front of me, eyes bulging, fingertips over her mouth: "Ah!" "Ah!" "Ah!" but with her lips drawn back in a way that suggested laughter. She may have been hoping it was all a joke, or trying to catch her breath, but my impression then was that she was disguising a soundless laugh with those strange little cries, and that her hand over her mouth was part of the concealment. It looked very strange, and I thought, oh Susan, love of my life, you have two faces, I am afraid of you. But then I noticed something in me was silently laughing also, as if in the knowledge that this was all pretense—serious pretense, but make-believe nevertheless: theatre. George slammed and double-locked the door (the gunmen had run down the stairs) and called the police, his voice somehow movie-dramatic: "Officer, there's been a shooting here!" His girlfriend, Joyce, stood in the living room with her shoulders hunched and both hands over her mouth, flanked by six horrified-looking people I had never seen, probably friends of hers. Now George was flushing our grass down the toilet. My trousers felt too tight. I opened my belt, my fly, tried to pull down the pants a little. And then I remembered a dream. I had written it down at least three weeks ago: *A man steps out of a car and is shot in the stomach by a man who is hiding behind another car. He bends over and falls to his knees and puts his forehead and hands on the ground, like a Moslem praying to Mecca.* I was amazed. I imagined writing a letter to the Society for Psychic Research: a documented case of precognition! But what if I died? Ridiculous—that was not in the cards at all. *How did I know?* For a few seconds, I felt myself at a threshold, all my memories on one side and a darkly luminous space on the other—like two rooms, one filled with furniture and another empty—and joy running back and forth, crazy with glee, like a puppy racing from room to room when its master comes home. I felt an uncontainable, inexpressible happiness, but strangely as if it were not quite my own, as if something closer to me than anything I called my self had woken from endless sleep. A little later I heard a snarling voice in the back of my head distinctly pronouncing three words: "You disgust me," and at that moment a fist pounded on the door and the police were there, they had come with astonishing promptness—two, three, five, seven men, more and more. They swarmed into every corner of every room and questioned everyone—me too: "Who shot you? What did he look like? Colored, was he colored? How many were there?" Several men occupied themselves with staring at George's Cuban posters and searching for drugs—under radiators, inside drawers, under the rug. Conrad crouched down next to me and placed a tender consoling hand on my knee. "Are you all right?" I assured him I was. He looked sad. "I really am all right," I said, and I was sure I was telling the truth. This certainty, in the face of what had just happened, struck me as comical. Had I ever known myself safer and sounder than now, sprawled on the kitchen floor surrounded by friends and strangers with my trousers unbuttoned and blood trickling onto my underpants from one of two holes in my gut? But that voice, why was it trying to scare me, and above all, why *wasn't* I scared? How did I know I was safe? *By the presence of joy.* I knew, I knew! The snarling voice came back: "You're nothing but pulp," it said. I felt myself breathing and thought: *Breath of life.* "It will fan the fire that burns you," said the voice. Go to hell, I said. That made me laugh, a little sniff of amusement. The contraction of my stomach muscles produced a sharp pain.

A middle-aged bullish cop tapped Conrad on the shoulder, ordered him to stand up, maneuvered him into the living room and questioned him: "It was political, right? Why don't you admit it?" Meanwhile I was bleeding. I was quite feeble by now. At last a young cop was assigned to dress my wounds. He opened a red-cross kit and wrapped an elastic bandage around my waist (without cleaning the wounds, I noticed). I could tell by his questions that he wanted to know what it was like to get shot: Was it a stinging or a burning sensation, was it bad or not so bad? He was also concerned not to hurt me as he bandaged me. Another cop questioned the neighbors in the hallway. I heard loud protestations: "I sleep! I don' hear nahsink!" Finally the ambulance came with wailing sirens. Two men dressed in white came in and tried to lift me onto a stretcher. It hurt too much. I asked them to help me walk downstairs, and surprisingly, they didn't object. They even let me climb the steps into the back of the ambulance. But when the van pulled up in front of Bellevue Hospital, they insisted on carrying me in. "Can I sit?" I asked. "Lie down." The slightest jolt— a cough, a held breath—cut like a knife.

The next forty-five minutes were devoted to leisurely paperwork, three more interrogations (one by a policeman and two by detectives who refused to believe that I didn't know the assailants or their motives), measuring my pulse, and cleaning my wounds. If I hadn't known this was an emergency ward, I would never have guessed it. Not that it mattered: I knew I was safe. (*But how?* I just knew! I knew!) At some point I was asked to undress beneath a sheet. A nurse took off my shoes. Another nurse injected the needle of an IV machine into my left arm. Then she gave me a tetanus shot. I lay in a haze. Deep within, submerged but present, was joy, gurgling like distant laughter.

An extremely thin young doctor—probably an intern—sat down beside me on the bed. Before he had opened his mouth, I felt myself shrinking away from him.

"What happened." (Phrased not as a question, but as a command.)

I couldn't have felt more alert if a snake had slid across my legs. There was no tangible threat in his words or his manner, but what I felt was: This is it. Whether it was his eyes, deep-set behind round glasses framed with black wire, or the way his lips turned down at the corners as if in fine deprecation—everything about him felt subtly yet acutely dangerous, not so obviously as a gun and a bullet, but all the more convincingly in the lightning-swift language of secret signs I had trained myself to decipher. And yet when I answered him, it was with a dismissive arrogance that was completely incongruous with the danger I felt in his presence. I don't know why—maybe it was some kind of bravado; or a magical ploy—as if by treating the threat like a minor irritation, it might prove to be just that.

I told him I had already been asked his question and all those that would follow at least half a dozen times, first at home, then here at the hospital, that I was tired, and couldn't he please get my answers from those plainclothes cops or detectives or whatever they were, two guys.

At first he looked surprised. Then his eyes narrowed—not hatefully, but as if he were trying to recognize something in my eyes, leaning in a little. He smiled briefly. Then he walked off. The smile was unpleasant. He smiled with his lips only.

On my left, where my view was obstructed by a green plastic curtain, a woman was moaning in a steady monotone: "nurse" "nurse" "nurse" "nurse."

The young intern came back with a legal-sized yellow writing pad and drew the green curtain around my bed. Now we were alone together. He put the pad on the empty bed next to mine. Then he sat down on the edge of my bed and drew back the sheet that covered my body, exposing not only the wounds but my genitals. I suppressed a reflex of anger and fear. What if I was mistaken about him? He was just doing his job.

"What happened." Again, the voice was dry and flat.

"I was shot."

"Where did it happen."

I don't know why I didn't simply yield and give him the story. My fear of him stuck like a wedge in my solar plexus, and still I behaved as if under a compulsion to provoke his anger. Partly it was the difficulty of talking without involuntarily tensing the muscles torn by the bullet. I shook my head and turned my face away. He took my chin in his hand and forced me to look at him. "Sorry to *bother* ya, *fella!*" I reached up to push his hand away—I couldn't, it hurt too much. Tears welled up. A flicker of a smile crossed his face. His hand lingered on my chin for a moment, then he let go. I reached down to pull the sheet back up but I couldn't reach it. I tried to sit up; I couldn't. I closed my eyes, trying to recover the sense of deathless security I had felt before. He put the tip of his finger to the entry wound on my right side and very lightly circled the rim. Then he ran his finger along the passage the bullet had taken, pressing just a little bit and stopping every inch or so to quietly ask: "Does this hurt? This? This?" Nothing he did caused me more than slight discomfort. His probings became rougher, so I decided to humor him with a few phoney "ouches." That was a mistake: He increased the pressure. Eventually he reached the exit wound. He stopped, drew the sheet up to my chest, picked up the yellow pad, and started writing. He wrote and wrote. I wondered what he could be taking so long to report. Was he lying? I watched him: If he put on fifty pounds, he would be handsome in a featureless sort of way, like a shopwindow dummy. Thin blond hair. A small cut on his chin. He filled two pages and half of a third. Then he left me. I watched the IV needle pulse in my left arm, the pink liquid bubbling in the bottle above me. The curtain was briefly pulled aside on my right, and a doctor asked me what my religion was. "None," I said.

I lay for a while listening to the woman's steady moaning on my left. She had changed her phrase to "pick me up" "pick me up" "pick me up" "pick me up."

Another doctor, a portly black man, pulled the curtains aside and sat down on the edge of my bed. He smiled, and I smiled. He asked me how I felt, and I said, "uncomfortable but OK." He examined the wounds, and was *very* careful not to hurt me.

"When did it happen?" What a sensible question: not what happened or where, but when! I told him it had been around two or two-thirty. He patted my hand: "I think you were very lucky."

I liked him immensely. A nurse came by and said: "Dr. Castro, please come to bed seven when you have a chance." He said he would be right back, and walked away. I saw George and Susan standing in the doorway. Someone must have forbidden them to enter the room. We waved to each other. Susan was mouthing something—"I love you" or "how are you," I couldn't be sure—and I raised my thumb for an answer. The voice on my left stopped calling. A few minutes later Dr. Castro returned and informed me that an operation was necessary.

"It is a very simple operation and we have performed it many times. We make an opening to find out whether you have been injured internally, so that, if we find a wound, we can mend it. If we don't operate, and you are bleeding by only so much as a scratch in your peritoneum, the damage might be beyond repair in a few hours. Of course we can't operate without your consent. But you must recognize the necessity of it. I repeat, the operation is not dangerous at all. There is no cause for worry. However, if we do not operate, the chances are that you will die within a few hours of injuries that should be repaired immediately. So: Do you consent to this operation?"

Of course I consented. I trusted him without reserve. With a touch on my knee Dr. Castro complimented me for my good common sense, drew the curtain around my bed, and left.

I wished he had not drawn the curtain. I wanted to see Susan and George. I wished they could come in and talk to me. I would ask for permission as soon as the doctor came back.

Then the skinny intern parted the curtains and stood next to me with a clipboard in his hand.

"I want you to sign here . . ."—marking a line with a red pen at the bottom of a printed form—". . . for the operation." And he handed me the clipboard and the pen.

I suppose he had meant to put an X on the line, but it was a cross. I glanced up at his face. He sat down on the edge of the bed, drew the curtain around his shoulder so that he was shielded from the rest of the room, and looked at me steadily, blinking from time to time. A very peculiar sensation then: that someone was gazing at me through his eyes, someone who knew me very well and was using this man's face as a mask. I was afraid. I put the tip of the ballpoint pen on the paper next to the cross. My hand felt cold. I thought of Dr. Castro's good arguments. They sounded tinny against this threat. Of what? Today I would call it "perdition." But I had no idea, then, of what that word means. All I felt was an undefined and therefore limitless menace.

"What if I don't sign?"

This question was no longer directed at the young man whose job it was to secure my signature, it was addressed to that which was looking through his eyes with a glittering merciless intelligence that hated and lured and smiled and lied yet shone with the knowledge of hidden things. He saw through me; I saw only the opaque glint of his understanding.

His answer was to smile down at me, slowly shaking his head, as if to say: "You're going to die, and I'm certainly not going to stop you." And I had such a strange impression then: that this bed surrounded by pale green curtains was all the world there was; that everything else was an illusion or else so separate it might as well not have ever existed; that we would not be interrupted by any Dr. Castro, not by George or Susan either; and that He and I were playing a game, a contest of some sort. And that He had nothing to lose, while I was playing for my life.

I felt as if I had always known Him. He nodded, ever so slightly. What kind of game was this? I asked Him this silently, convinced He could read my thoughts. He raised a quizzical eyebrow: that was for me to guess. "Well?" He said then. It must be poker, I thought, this is something like poker. But you know my hand as well as yours. And you're bluffing, of course you're bluffing. You're asking me to sign this paper, you're telling me I'll die if I don't. Simple logic tells me that the choice you suggest to me will be the one I'll regret. But you're subtler than this. You want me to *think* that you're bluffing. I don't have to solve your riddles. I have my yes and my no. I have a voice in me that is wiser and truer than all your inveigling. It doesn't promise me life, it is life itself, deathless, immortal life. You want me to betray my own soul. You want me to doubt that I'm well and that all is well. You want me to die.

And then I had doubts again. More than doubts, almost a certainty that all this was pure craziness, this enemy and this dancing ally within, that I was faced with an obnoxious intern who would probably play no part in the simple and necessary operation that had been recommended by Dr. Castro, and that I should put an end to this nonsense and sign my name next to that slightly lop-sided X and be done with it.

I said: "I think I'd like to wait with the operation."

"No operation then?" Mocking blue eyes.

It took a great effort to talk, especially since I believed he knew, and knew that I knew that he knew: "No, that's not what I said. I said I'd like to wait. I'm feeling fine now, I'm pretty sure there's nothing wrong with me, I don't know why, I'd just like to wait a few hours. If my condition deteriorates, of course I'll . . ."

He snorted, shrugged, and left.

Dr. Castro returned, looked at me sternly, and said with annoyance: "What's this I hear?" He shook his head. "I thought you were reasonable!" I didn't know what to say. "Why did you change your mind? Are you frightened?"

I told him I wasn't. He didn't believe me. I said I wanted to wait for signs of definite danger. He was quite annoyed. "You are not a doctor," he said. "Do you really think you can decide what is good for you in your state and what is not? It is not necessary for you to feel pain even if you are lethally wounded. You might lie here comfortably for a few hours while your intestines fill with blood, until one suddenly bursts. Don't you understand?"

At this moment the loudspeaker interrupted him: "Dr. Castro, Dr. Castro, please come to Intensive Care," and a rasping voice called from a neighboring bed: "Focken communist!" I laughed, wincing with pain, Dr. Castro shot me a furious glance as he left my bed in a hurry, and I realized that he had swayed me with the authority of his manner and not with his arguments, because now that he had behaved like a vain, silly man, his arguments carried no weight at all and I knew the last veil had been removed from my understanding and that I would not sign for the operation and that everything would be all right. I knew it and knew that I knew it and if I had been able to I would have shouted for joy.

George and Susan came to my bedside. They had seen by the doctor's face that something was wrong. A nurse told them they couldn't stand there; they nodded yes, yes, but ignored her. I told them what I had decided. George looked sick. He made a few attempts to change my mind and then said that if I died it would take him a long time to forgive me. I said I was sorry this was upsetting him but everything would be OK and as soon as I was up and walking we could celebrate. All the while I could feel Susan's hand in my hand, and her other hand stroking my head. My eyes filled with tears. She dried them with her fingertips. She was crying, too.

"What if you're wrong?" she said.

"I would still be OK." What an amazing thought: life and death, being and not being, the same—could that be? "But I'm not wrong. I've never been more certain of anything in my life." And she believed me. Somehow that seemed stranger and more wonderful than my own assurance.

A policeman ordered George and Susan to go back to the entrance. They left.

Dr. Castro returned and asked me point-blank: "Yes or no?"

"Why yes or no? Why not wait and see?"

"We have a shortage of beds, and we don't have the time to play games." He was rigid with anger. He held out a printed form: "If you wish to leave this hospital *immediately,* you must sign this." I signed the form. "A nurse will bring you your clothes." He walked off and said something to George and Susan in passing. They came back to my bed. George looked sicker than ever. Susan was holding my hand, and I thought: If she dies before me there will be no one whose hand pours such sweetness into my body and I'll be poorer than the poorest derelict because I'll know what treasure I've lost. What was I thinking before, then, about life and death being indistinguishable? I placed her hand on my heart. Bliss of being alive together!

It took a while before the nurses removed the IV needle from my arm and brought back my clothes. Susan asked a nurse to clean the puncture wounds from the needles; the nurse said she wasn't allowed to give me anything after I'd signed out. But she did agree to wrap a bandage around the bullet wounds. Another nurse warned her not to break the rules by applying alcohol to the wounds.

I got dressed beneath the sheet after the nurses left. Susan tied my shoes while George called for a taxi. I managed to walk without great discomfort. I felt dizzy, though. Before leaving the ward, I turned around. Several men in white coats stood close together, discussing something intently. One of them was Dr. Castro. The bony intern was gone. A nurse dropped an empty tray with a bang. It raised a small cloud of dust.

George took the subway home and Susan and I took a cab to her place uptown. In the elevator mirror, I looked to myself like Cantinflas, the Mexican comedian—my pants hanging loose around the waist, the trouser legs covering the greater part of my shoes. The elevator man didn't seem to notice. We opened the door quietly, so as not to wake up Susan's roommate, Myrna. I went right to bed. Before going to sleep, I saw a hypnagogic image of a needle drawing a slender red ribbon in a single, wide stitch through my body and out a window into space.

The imp of coincidence had a field day with me for about a week. When I awoke early that same morning, Susan was already up. She came into the room with Myrna and Myrna told me she had woken up from a dream in which I had been sentenced to death by hanging. At the crucial moment the rope tore and I was pardoned and packed off into bed in Susan's room, exhausted but healthy, and Susan came to Myrna to ask for some aspirin for me.

Around nine a.m., George came with a doctor. The doctor examined the wounds and said, "If you're not dead by now, you're OK. But you were very foolish, refusing to authorize that operation, it's a miracle, really. Look: The bullet passed through the skin and fatty tissues, probably ripping some of the musculature, but missing by what must be a fraction of an inch the intestines and the stomach. I congratulate you on your good fortune, but not on your good sense." I suddenly felt certain I would have died on the operating table if I had signed that form.

I slept the rest of the day. In the evening, I took a bath. Susan, changing the sheets, found a few peas I had spilled while eating, and Myrna suggested they must have rolled out through the holes in my stomach. The crisis seemed to be over.

I called my brother the next morning and told him what had happened. He was in Vermont, visiting his high school English teacher. Twenty minutes later he called me back. He had told his teacher's wife about me at breakfast, and she was very surprised, because she had just woken up from a dream in which a man was shot in the stomach and survived and told everyone it was virtually painless—"only a jolt."

George came by wearing an "All The Way With LBJ" button with a little noose attached to the bottom. He brought me my journal, the notebook in which I recorded my dreams, and an envelope addressed to me that had arrived the day before. I opened it. It was a three-page advertisement for a new California publication called "Borderline." On the cover page was a large picture of a black coffin with an open lid. The inside of the coffin was red, and a heavy black question mark was painted on this red surface. A caption in bold-face capitals beneath the picture read: "DO YOU KNOW THE DAY YOU WILL DIE?" I had never heard of "Borderline." They must have gotten my name from a mailing list.

I spent most of the day in bed writing down everything I remembered. In the notebook, I discovered four dreams that had anticipated the shooting. The first was the one about the man who was shot and ended up in a Moslem prayer position. The second dream was about three weeks old: "Susan points out to me that I have three navels. I look and am amazed to find that I actually have two extra navels, one to the right and one to the left of the one I was born with." (There followed a confident interpretation along Oedipal lines.) The third dream was dated February 16, eleven days before I was shot: "An airplane makes an emergency landing on a two-lane highway lined with trees. The plane is running fairly fast and slowing down. There are three men in the cockpit: the middle-aged pilot who has expertly carried out the forced landing; a younger co-pilot sitting to his right; and a third, very young man who sits between them, even though there is hardly any room (he seems virtually body-less), and who seems to be on his virgin flight. A very large black truck comes rushing toward the plane at great speed. A collision seems inevitable. But the truck passes under the left wing, missing it by a fraction of an inch. The plane stops. Then it turns out that the pilot has been shot, probably from the passing truck. Clutching his stomach, he exchanges seats with the co-pilot. 'I'm all right,' he says. 'Just get us out of here.' The plane begins to turn. At first it seems impossible to maneuver it, slalomlike, through the trees and across the plowed fields on both sides of the road, but the co-pilot succeeds. Now the plane has reversed its direction. The road ahead is clear. The youngest of the three men is feeling a subtle and growing ecstasy." The fourth dream was the one I described earlier, about Death coming to an old man and saying, "We make the rounds three times a day."

In the evening, I found myself with Susan and George watching an Off-Broadway production of a Brecht play about three pilots who survive the crash of their plane and discuss their situation among a chorus of invisible spirits.

The next day, a Tuesday, I went back home to 10th Street. George showed me where the bullet had struck the brick wall outside the kitchen window, which was still raised about an inch off the sill, as it had been on the night I was shot. Conrad came over in the evening with a gift of half an ounce of grass.

Wednesday, Conrad and I took the bus to Bellevue to pick up some money and papers I had left there. We got out of the bus at the wrong stop and approached the building from the back, opposite the side where I was carried in by the ambulance men. There was a large door with an EXIT sign above it, a swinging door with two panels. We decided to go in and ask someone how to get to the Emergency Ward. As we approached the door, I stopped in my tracks. There, drawn in yellow chalk, was the following:

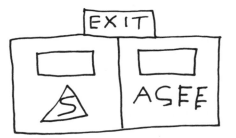

"That's my name," I said, pointing at the right-hand side of the door. Conrad stopped, shook his head vehemently, and said: "No—no, no, man—no, it can't be. . . ." He looked frightened. "It's just a coincidence," he said. He pointed out that the G wasn't really a G and the E's weren't regular E's either. I asked him what else the word could be read to mean—and it was a word, wasn't it?

"Maybe a kid wrote it," he said.

"My name? Do you know how many Agees there are in New York outside my own family?" He shook his head. "I've checked the phone directory: Two."

Some people came out of the other door and stared at us as they passed. We must have looked strangely excited.

We went inside and asked a nurse where I could find my belongings. She referred me to the Property Office. There I was told I would have to get the signature of someone in the Emergency Ward and should go to room so-and-so. I knocked on that door. There was no answer. I opened the door and stepped in; Conrad followed behind me. There, surrounded by several waiting patients, was Dr. Castro, with his back to me, filling out some forms. He turned, came walking in my direction, his head bowed, looking down at the papers in his hand. He walked right up to me without looking up, raised his head, and saw me. His eyes widened for a moment, and his mouth opened too.

(Among all the strange events I've reported, this is the one I was most tempted to alter or omit, because it looks contrived. But it interests me for that reason. Real events aren't normally made to order like that. This doctor: the degree to which he is distracted, so that he ignores my knocking and my coming into the room, his several steps in my direction without seeing me, so that he can stop short and look nonplussed, his widening eyes, his dropping jaw —he's behaving like an actor building a scene; nothing too much or too soon, no ragged ends of accident or inconsequence—it doesn't seem real. It didn't seem real then either. I've felt that way watching magicians at work: The mind can doubt all it wants, but the eye is as gullible in an adult as it is in a baby. And at the same time I was fascinated: What was going on here? Who was pulling the strings? Because life shouldn't be capable of sleight-of-hand. Or even interested.)

He closed his mouth, still staring at me, but without giving any sign of greeting or even of recognition. I returned his gaze for several seconds. "You might not remember me," I said then. "I was here on the morning of March 1st with a gunshot wound. I've come back to pick up my belongings. I need someone's signature. Perhaps you can help me. . . ."

He lowered his eyes, considering my request. "No," he said then, looking at me again, with a quizzical, suspicious look in his eyes, "I don't think I can help you. I know nothing about this." I was puzzled. Was he afraid? Was he astonished to see me alive?

"Perhaps you could tell someone else to give me the signature?"

"No, I can't do that. I know nothing about these procedures." He was staring again. I stared back.

"I have to get the stuff sometime," I said, "and I do need the signature of someone in the ward. It might as well be you."

Some more staring. He shrugged. "We are very busy here." And impatiently waving the papers in his hand, he walked up to a patient who was lying on his stomach on a wheel-bed and took him by the arm:

"Hey! Hey! Are you still with us?"

The man stirred. Dr. Castro left the room, closing the door and leaving me behind with the patients and a nurse who was sitting at the desk, rhythmically pounding a stamp over and over onto identical pieces of printed paper which she pulled off a stack in front of her. I waited a few minutes, since some of the patients needed her attention more urgently than I did. But she went right on pounding, and eventually I asked her if she would sign the slip of paper I had been given. "Certainly," she said, and signed.

I picked up my belongings at the Property Office. Everything was there except the card saying REVERSE or EXCHANGE. It struck me then that those curious little extrusions at the bottom of the letters on the door were the beginnings of a mirror-image:

That the hook on the G, in fact, had *reversed* its normal position and seemed about to produce the curved back of an upside-down G; that the S in the triangle was the letter I had turned into a snake on the Acid trip; two snakes, in fact, and they were *reversed* images of each other; and that in the airplane dream, too, there was the theme of reversal, the plane reversing direction after the pilot was shot. But what did "Exchange" mean?

We left by the rear exit to look at the graffiti on the door again. Conrad said: "It *is* your name." Then he told me that on the night I was shot he had seen my first name written on the wall of the hallway outside my apartment. When he said that I felt nauseated. It was too much. Whatever was doing these things was overdoing them.

Sure enough, when we got home, there was JOEL written in blue magic marker on the wall among dozens of other names and signs. It might have been there for a while without my noticing it. Nothing occult about it. I shrugged and felt relieved. We went inside. Susan was there, and George, and George's girlfriend. We smoked some of the good grass Conrad had brought, and talked about what had happened. No one else had noticed my name on the wall either, but so what, the walls were covered with graffiti and the hallway was dark. Finally we decided to go to a movie. I was the last to leave the apartment. As I turned the key in the lock, I noticed on the door frame an X about the size of my hand. It was drawn with yellow chalk, just like my name on the hospital door. It might have been there when I came home, but why didn't I see it? Who put it there? Conrad? I felt nauseated again. "I've had enough," I said. "Please stop." The others were already going down the stairs. I caught up with them. I didn't tell them about the X on the door. Much later, I told Susan.

Near Nassau Street and City Hall, I saw jets of steam shooting out of the gutters. Susan and I were the only ones on the street—we were lagging behind the others, who had already turned the corner. It was dark. I felt dizzy. A sputtering neon sign over a bar glared with a light that looked not just hard but angry. Susan steadied me. "What's the matter?" she asked. I told her I was scared.

The movie we went to frightened me also. It was a documentation of the Living Theatre's production of *The Brig,* itself a documentation of three hours in the punishment barracks of a U.S. Marine base. It wasn't just the brutality on the screen, or the demented enthusiasm of a man in the front row who kept shouting: "Give 'im hell, motherfucker!", it was the sense that this, too, must contain a hidden meaning which it was my fate to discover.

After about ten minutes, I asked Susan to leave with me. Out on the street, I told her what I had been feeling. "It's crazy, isn't it?" I asked. "It *is* crazy," she said. "It has nothing to do with you." "Maybe the army's after me." "You're 4-F, they don't want you. And those were marines." We hailed a taxi and drove to Susan's place. All the way uptown I kept thinking about *The Brig.* The most disturbing part of it, worse than the incessant yelling and humiliation, was the servility of the victims, the eagerness with which they strove to expunge in themselves the last vestiges of independence.

On the floor of the elevator in Susan's building was a torn-out piece of newspaper. I picked it up and read it:

. . . of ambrosia. You walked over to the airman at the tail end of the line, kicked the man in the pants, and returned without a word to your puzzled host. "Why in the world," St. Peter asked, "did you do that, General Le May?" and you replied, "just because he was last."

That night I woke up in fear. I was thinking of Conrad. It was because of him that I'd taken the Acid. Hadn't he tricked me into it? The next time I had seen him was the night I was shot. What if he knew the two strangers who followed us up the stairs? What if he had set up the whole thing? He had seen me draw the double S when we were on Acid and he was with me when we discovered the S in the triangle and the letters of my name on the hospital door. He must have put them there in the first place. And the yellow X on my door. But that was as far as my suspicion could reach. What about the path of the bullet, through my body and out the window, and my surviving it: Who arranged that? What made those bells ring at the moment when I stood in front of that little gray card, and what impelled me to pick it up? What made the bum sit down in the shit after I said he would? Who sent the dreams that prefigured the shooting? What intelligence governed the fall of three coins so that a randomly selected line in a book would answer my questions not just coherently but truthfully? Who arranged for the lights to go off on the Empire State Building right after Conrad established it as an "angel of light" and the Con Ed plant as its sinister opposite, as if to insinuate the suggestion that Evil was the beginning and end of what power and glory Good claimed as its own? Unless I presumed Conrad to have the powers of a demiurge, which would be crazy, or attributed all these events and their linked meanings to an avalanche of accidents—which was unreasonable; unless I dismissed the secret delight that guided me past the counsel of logic and doctorly reason, I had to suppose that something unknown yet profoundly close to me was the maker of this puzzle, this dramatic mystery in which, for reasons I could not begin to guess at, I was the central figure. And as I thought this, my fear subsided and I became still, and a strange, arcane vision rose up in me. It looked like a medieval tapestry representing a labyrinth with a unicorn and several human figures, and all of them were myself. I was the sacred monster at the heart of the maze, and also the hunter sent out to catch him, and the maiden chosen to be his bride. There were two or three other figures, but I forgot them. It felt like a momentous revelation, yet it came and went in a few seconds and almost without excitement. I wrote it down and went to sleep.

The next morning I went with Susan to photograph the inscription at Bellevue. If I ever wrote about all this strangeness, pictures would help make it believable. Breton had included photographs in *Nadja*—each one of them evidence, if not proof, that the "fury of symbols" was as real as a woman's glove or a wasp-waisted statue on the Place Maubert.

It was raining, the chalk was beginning to wash away. I showed Susan how to operate Myrna's camera and stood myself at the center, between the two wings of the door, on my right the triangle with the S in it, on my left the partially inverted letters of my name. I thought it would make a good picture.

Later, in her apartment, Susan took two more pictures of me with my shirt off. That was to document the "three navels."

I couldn't sleep that night. Susan suggested I go to a psychologist. I didn't like the idea. But maybe a sedative would calm down these phenomena along with my nerves. Maybe Conrad could get me some.

I consulted the I Ching. It said:

> Use no medicine in an illness
> Incurred through no fault of your own.
> It will pass of itself.

That is what happened. The wave of coincidences subsided. The last in the series involved the photographs. It turned out that after taking the picture of me in the doorway of the hospital, Susan had forgotten to advance the film and superimposed an accidental picture of a wide jet of steam shooting out of a damaged pipe by the side of a building, with a triangular danger sign next to it. She must have released the shutter without noticing. My name on the door was completely obliterated by the white steam. The triangle with the S was nearly invisible. The DANGER sign stood at a slant, in sharp focus, pointing like an arrow at my groin. Above my head was the EXIT sign.

The two pictures she took of me in her apartment were also superimposed. The result resembled photos taken during seances—a ghostly double, naked, rising out of my naked torso, the Band Aid covering the entry wound faintly visible in both bodies.

After this first plunge—the first of several that I can foresee—the stream calms again and flows broad and quiet, pushing along its slow freight of foam and detritus. And there is that other movement I mentioned earlier, the sinking, deepening, downward and inward spiraling, in which the river seems more like a bottomless sea, stirring with strange fish and unpredictable currents. The everyday self on the surface is horizontally driven, writes and destroys what he writes (he's been doing that since he was twelve years old), goes to the movies, smokes dope, reads, talks and makes love with his girlfriend, and works, or pretends to work, at the National Opinion Research Center, making a modest living, complemented by Susan's wages (she has dropped out of school and is working as a "Subscriber Relations Representative" for an insurance company), all in all enough money to keep his head above water, and enough, too, to purchase the substances that will enable his alter ego to dedicate himself to drowning in depth.

These two are so different—the deep-sea diver lost in a world of perpetual astonishment, the everyday self adrift in the shallows of the known—that it's hard to believe they both inhabit the same body. They are like strangers who meet on and off in an elevator, take note of each other's existence, and never converse.

Shards

Coming out of the depths and into the shallows, no matter whether the trip had been "good" or "bad," whether I came back exhausted and harrowed or glowing with health, there would immediately begin an unstoppable process of forgetting, a melting away of something which, down below, I had held in my hands and vowed to bring back up with me, something precious and hugely important. Diving in the opposite direction, from the flowing surface into the timeless pool, there would always come the moment, about a half hour into the trip, when I would realize, with an ever new shock of surprise, that *this, this,* was what I had forgotten through all those weeks of petrifying normalcy, and had remembered the last time I dove down here, and the time before that, and had always forgotten in the interim: this wholeness, wholeheartedness, this tremendous passion of being, without which the jewels I could now plainly see scattered over the sidewalk would revert to dust and garbage, as vacant of meaning and beauty as the faithfully recorded opinions I spent my days at the office tagging with numerical codes so that someone else could convey them to their final destination as fractions of a percentage point in a statistic. How to salvage the pearl without price, how to bring it into my daily life, into the office, the bus on the way to work? Because the drug was just an awakener of something dormant in the body, I was certain of that, all the saints and seers of all religions confirmed it. How to create an instrument by which the normal consciousness could reenter the sanctum at will?

Near the end of one trip, I wrote the word "pain" on the left side of a white sheet of paper and on the right the word "bread," and connected them with a line. "Stefan," I wrote over the line. That said everything. But would I understand it afterwards? Probably not, because without energy—this monstrous energy coursing through my nerves—the formula would remain just that, a prescription, a diagram. Wasn't there a word that could signal this power, and by which it could be recalled? At the bottom of the page I wrote: "God." The word widened, yawned, the O grew ten times larger than the G, and the D went soaring off the page onto the floor. When I looked at the message later, I recognized the Anglo-French pun equating pain and bread and remembered reflecting on the words "energy" and "passion." I also remembered praying for my sick brother. And I knew I had lost the treasure again. For a while I thought I could repossess it by giving it a new name—Life—and trying to remind myself that the life I was living from day to day, without vital participation, must be That—until I realized It was essentially beyond words and probably beyond recollection. We are creatures of memory, thought itself is but the response of the past to the unpredictable challenges of the moment. I knew this, and there seemed no way out of the prison of time and continuity except to swallow one more LSD-tinctured sugar cube and maybe find a trapdoor, or break through the walls.

I had moved out of the apartment I shared with George North and set up house with Susan in a railroad flat on 4th Street between 2nd and 3rd Avenues. It was a colorful neighborhood—alcoholic bums at one end of the block, a transvestite club at the other, Chinese garment workers in a factory across the street, Archie Shepp rehearsing with his jazz band in an apartment on 5th Street and the Bowery (we often sat on the stoop listening), a Yiddish theatre in uneasy proximity of a Ukrainian social club, Polish restaurants, Puerto Rican *cuchifritos*, and the usual assortment of middle-class "Heads," as self-respecting hippies were starting to call themselves.[9] For all its variety, I felt no urge to explore this world at my doorstep. Why would anyone want to do that, when for a pittance, on any day and at any hour, you could charter a trip through eternity and to places so strange they would make Marco Polo's adventures look like a family picnic? That was a world worth visiting! And no one slashing his way through this wilderness or transported to some paradisial lagoon would put up a flag and start the game of nations and wars again, because this realm was sacred and no one who entered it failed to emerge hallowed and purified.

Susan thinks I took about ten LSD trips altogether (she herself never tried it); I think it was twice as many. But that's like counting tornadoes—each one exceeds number and measure, each one is too much. Storms of light. And what's left in memory is not the light but the wreckage—shreds, a small dusty heap. For example: I remember eating a bowl of soup after an experience that I registered to myself as "endless hell," but of that hell, of its logic and temperature, nothing is left. An image comes up of a piece of cut barbed wire—maybe, together with the good soup, as a sign of release from bondage. But what was that hell? It filled me not only with horror but also with awe, with reverence.

9. We did accept "hip" as an adjective—the one legacy of the beatniks we consciously accepted. It was good to be hip, but not hip to insist on being hip, or to proclaim yourself hip. You could say "I'm hip, man," but all that meant was "I understand," though it was a hip way to say it.

What was it? I can only surmise, the way archaeologists guess at the splendors of a lost civilization from a few potsherds found by a hillside. Although, every once in a while, more evidence comes to light than I can comfortably look at. I must proceed slowly.

I tasted the soup. It was a black bean soup with pieces of pork in it. I bit off a piece of bread. Susan put on a record. I licked a tear from the corner of my mouth. What was my emotion? I hesitate to name it: gratitude. It wasn't the reflexive social gesture that usually goes by that name. It came as a blessing, a grace, a reprieve from unspeakable suffering. Nor was it gratitude *for* anything in particular. It was itself that for which it was grateful: this pure thanksgiving.

It was a *consuming* emotion, literally: It ingested the world, took it in so completely that inside and outside were indistinguishable. That was its thankfulness, that it would not exclude any part of the world from the blessing: not the round, containing hollow of the bowl any more than Susan's face smiling at me through tears; not the chunks of pork torn from a life like mine, any more than the evening light shining through dust on the window; not the twisting rivers in the dark boards of the table any more than my tooth-marks on a yellow pencil on the floor. Why on the floor? Because I had dropped it there, because it was my nature to disturb the natural order of things, because Susan, miraculous friend, was always cleaning up after me and was not happy with that, not at all; because I was selfish, and that selfishness was unexpiable by any amount of suffering, and yet I was forgiven.

It was a *singing* emotion, it rang through the marrow of my bones, it had a steady iambic pulse: da-*doom* . . . da-*doom* . . . and after a while it took on the meaning and sound of three words—"a LOVE / suPREME"—which I knew were being transmitted to my ear through a slightly defective loudspeaker behind and above my head (that was the vulgate, the prose version, I could still read it, I was still sane); but I also knew that they came from the bowels of the earth and the vaults of heaven, and that they had been given to the great-grandson of slaves as witness to a love that surpasses the cruelest reach of reason, that they were as holy and as near to the unpronounceable name of the All as any prophet's utterance, any scream of a pig led to slaughter.

What was it that was so terrible, though? What was that Otherness that broke through the battlements that night? What was it that prompted that phrase I used earlier, "storms of light," and that made the world not the same ever again?

Last night, after writing these questions, I was given a glimpse of it: the Fear. I was falling asleep when I heard soundless words in the back of my mind, unremarkable in themselves—one of them was ". . . five weeks in arrears? Send him notice . . ."—but what made them significant was that I knew that they were not mine, not even unconsciously mine, that I was eavesdropping on the mental somnambulations of neighbors, most likely, people I didn't know. That insight intrigued me, it made me feel larger than myself, and the sense of the unknown lying in wait for me outside the fringes of consciousness felt vaguely forbidden and almost erotically tempting. And then the word "playground" floated in, trailing a cloud of such ominous meaning that I sat up straight in my bed: *The world is not your playground, it is dying at your meddling hands, you are no longer innocent, know it, live with it!*"

Another shard: I was in a room infested by mouths—mouths on the walls, mouths on the floor and ceiling and filling the air, chewing mouths, smiling and grinning mouths, and, worst of all, talking mouths, spewing not words, not even recognizable fragments of words, but a sort of sludge and smear of syllabic garbage, an endless vomit of meaningless loquacity. I wrestled in that room. I fought for my life and that of the world, because this self-devouring body of language was the world's body, the one human beings live in. As in those old folktales where the peasant lad sets out to find the demon's heart in a sparrow's egg or in a berry ten million miles away, I desperately searched for the word or formula that would dispel the horror; and when my eyes fell on a piece of paper and a ballpoint pen, I was sure that angelic forces had guided me to them. The pen didn't work. I shook it, warmed the point with my breath, sucked at it, scribbled emptiness, nothing but emptiness onto the paper, until with huge relief I produced a dark scrawl, an oval, and into that oval, quivering, and with an effort of concentration that strained my capacity almost beyond enduring, I wrote, in capital letters:

THE WORD DISORDER
BRINGS ORDER BACK

and the curse was dispelled.

Another shard: a perpetual implosion of time and space. The world, or at least very large parts of the human world, was being sucked into nothingness like water down a drainpipe, gobs and gobs of civilization whirling into zero, Europe, India, China, Egypt, unstoppable. In the end, once again, the saving act of writing, a message to whatever self might survive this:

RE MEMBER GOD

Here's a prettier shard. An hour after "dropping" 500 micrograms of LSD, I visited my old friend Victor. Even though I was in love with Susan now and Victor had broken up with Sylvia, something of our old rivalry still lingered. I was struggling with my writing; he was excelling in his art. I doubted myself; he didn't. And I disliked the part of myself that depended on his approval and thereby made me his inferior. Mainly, though, I liked and trusted him. Otherwise I would not have visited him on that day. But there may have been a contentious motive, too. Victor was afraid of Acid. He couldn't even smoke grass—he said it gave him the "heebie-jeebies."

He looked apprehensive when I stepped into his studio—I had told him on the phone that I was tripping. I assured him that I felt calm and that things looked exactly the way they always did, just a few inches off the ground. He laughed and asked me if I'd like some tea, and I said yes, and while the tea was brewing I told him about a man I had seen in the subway on the way to his place. A guy in his forties wearing a three-piece suit, he had looked almost too prosperous to be in the subway, a glistening attaché case on his lap with three golden initials on it—I. C. E.—and when I looked into his face and body I saw that there was no warmth in his life, his knuckles were white where they gripped the edge of his attaché case, his jaw was so firmly set it was hard to imagine him ever smiling. But the strangest thing about him was that no one sat next to him on either side, even though there were people standing who could have used a seat. It was as if his coldness cleared a space around him, as if he was condemned to be alone.

Victor was skeptical: Did this really happen or did I, maybe, imagine it, or part of it? After all . . . No, no, I said, I can tell the difference between fantasy and perception. And then the tea was ready and Victor brought some crackers and cheese and we sat down to eat and drink; and from where I sat, I looked at the work for which he was becoming famous—three-cornered crates made of plywood boards, standing about eight feet tall, and steel tripods with legs of unequal length made of water-pipes fitted together with three-way joints. I had to laugh. I knew this was not the intended effect, so I tried to explain, and that made matters worse: something about triangles, I said, they look self-important, they sort of swell up in the middle and try to look sharp on all sides. Victor smiled benignly, he didn't mind my laughing, any vital response was fine with him, he said, including anger, anything real. A woman had walked into his exhibition, cast a glance at the plumbing and plywood, and asked when the show was scheduled to open—he'd gotten a kick out of that. Someone else had used one of the tripods as a trumpet—why not? So laughter was OK. But now he looked pensive. "I have an idea," he said, "have a look at this," and he went to a closet and pulled out several easel paintings in oil which he said he had done as a nostalgic exercise, because figurative art was a thing of the past and the only path left open for serious artists was to push their genre to its abstract limit of minimal definition. I was not in a state to absorb this argument, but the canvases drew me in, and I could immediately see why: They were his stepchildren, they had been spared the rigor he had imposed on his legitimate offspring, they danced in a soaring freedom of primary colors, and their forms—landscapes, nudes, trees, interiors—had arranged themselves with perfect ease according to their own mutual tensions of attraction and repulsion. They were marvelous paintings, and I told him so. Then I glanced at the floor and was astonished.

There, on the floor, was an immensely intricate, dazzlingly colorful mosaic made of what looked like small glossy tiles that were constantly leaping, sliding, scurrying into new configurations, insectlike, fast, faster than thought, or else vision had become the medium of thought and something was projecting light through a point in the middle of my forehead, some kind of machine, no, not a machine, just a rapid vibration between and just above my eyebrows which, I presumed, was the source of this shimmering profusion, this swarming of forms, this termite kingdom of perpetual beauty, it was almost repellent—and what was it: Art? Nature? Philosophy? Science? For there was nothing chaotic or mindless about it, it was ordered, the whole thing sustained itself by virtue of some kind of principle: It was round, for one, perfectly circular, and the center, just off to the right of Victor's left foot, was the iridescent image of a hummingbird, made of small tiles like everything else in the picture, but lifelike, and in motion, hovering in an aura of invisibly fluttering wings; and, grouped around it like planets around the sun, but in symmetrical formation, were twenty or thirty circles of different sizes and no particular color, no substance either—they were ideas, and this struck me as a sublime joke, because why would anyone bother to multiply the absolutely unalterable idea of a circle, and vary it in size, distribute it in space, why if not as a punning comment on the omnipresent unity of being—how ingenious, how subtle!— but already the joke was beyond me, because, weaving through and around these geometric phantoms, binding them together, alternately revealing and covering them, were vine leaves on a trellis, flowers, and birds, all of them lifelike, all of them in motion, and all of them made of ceramic tiles, and that, too, was a joke, this time on the idea of materiality—as if the designer of the picture were saying: see, whatever looks real has been *made* to look real, and is nothing but an appearance; and this joke, by the force of logic, included Victor's foot, or rather intended it as the main point, the punch line; for if the mosaic was an illusion—and I knew that it was—and yet its quick-shimmering little tiles seemed hard and smooth despite their not at all stonelike manner of leaping in and out of existence, why should this shoe—made of thick, yellow, paint-splattered leather, its long laces wrapped twice around the ankles—why should this shoe be as real as it pretended to be, why could it not have been planted there like the trompe-l'oeil windows in Roman murals, to say to the viewer: What *seems* to be *is* not, there is no foot as there are no tiles, there is no body as there are no boards and no leaves on the floor, there is no floor as there is no foot, there is no life as there is no truth, there is nothing the matter because nothing exists, no New York City, no past and no future, no self and no world . . .

At which point I tore myself loose and looked up, feeling faint and vaporous. Victor looked solid enough. So did his crates and tripods. So did his paintings. Everything he made proclaimed its presence with a firm voice: I am! I am! But how crude it was compared with what I had just witnessed.

Another shard: Shortly after I was shot, I had a dream in which I flew out a window dressed in an electric blue Superman costume. Writing in my journal, I noted that the capital S on my chest was the same letter that had appeared opposite my name on the hospital door. Why didn't I associate it with a word like "Saved?" That would have been fitting. Instead, I imagined myself as the savior, and in the terms of a six-year-old, because that was my age when I wanted more than anything in the world to soar like Superman, with a cape to signal my speed to the astonished crowds. I took note of all this as I wrote down my dream, and thought nothing of it. That was an early sign of catastrophe: Unconsciously I had put on the garments of a superhuman power.

And now I notice a resemblance between these five shards and some others I dug up in earlier excavations, from a much older stratum of memory.

When I was a child I had dreams that today seem like portents. What purpose do signs and dreams have if they present themselves to a mind that is not capable of understanding them?

One dream was about the atom bomb and about me preventing it from destroying the world. I can remember some of the origins of this dream. My parents had read the news about Hiroshima, and they were appalled. I remember them talking about it with each other and with their friends and my gathering from their talk that something very bad had happened. I was five then. During the next few days I learned that just one single bomb had destroyed a whole city and most of the people in it. I imagined that bomb must have been very big, but my parents said no, it was small. In my dream, then, I saw an airplane flying over Cuernavaca, where we lived, and dropping an atom bomb. The bomb was white, round, and very small, in fact I would have thought it was a ping-pong ball if I hadn't known it was the atom bomb. I started running to catch it. If I caught it the world would be saved, if I didn't everyone would die and there would be no more world. The bomb drifted in the wind the way a ping-pong ball would and I ran as fast as I possibly could, terrified. I caught the ball with a dive just before it hit the ground, like a baseball player, and it didn't explode because I had caught it in time. *Then I put it in my pocket.*

A second childhood dream I remember was a repetitive nightmare. There are three elements in it: a black bull, a magician with a black cape, and a train. I'm standing near some tracks and something tells me the train is coming and I begin to feel an obscure foreboding of something I know and can't remember. Then the train approaches from afar and blows a whistle and the earth trembles as it approaches belching steam and getting bigger and bigger and louder and louder and finally ROOOOAAAAARRRS past me whirling its windows past me and recedes again into the distance and vanishes into the horizon. Now there's silence and I know I should have woken up because the terrible thing will happen and I won't remember it until it's there. I can hear a drum thumping (probably my heart). Now I hear the magician's voice and I remember him as I see him. He is holding a magic wand up in the air and with his very deep bass voice he is making an O sound and making it gradually climb up a half-note scale, and to this day I can think of no more perfect musical expression for slow, ice-cold, sadistically calculated menace. And then the magician vanishes, and instead there's a bull, and the magician's voice is climbing the scale. The bull lowers his horns, way down, paws the ground, snorts, and starts running toward me. Nothing can stop him now, nothing. He gets bigger and bigger as he approaches, the magician's voice gets louder and louder, and just before the bull gores me with his horns both the voice and the bull disappear and the magician stands in front of me completely silent and I am helpless.

When I told this dream to our maid, Zita, it scared her. I was seven then.

Zita often took me with her when she went shopping. One day, at the butcher's, we had to stand in line. The butcher had stepped outside for a moment. Everyone was waiting for him. The shop was dark. Zita was holding my hand. There was a smell of sawdust. My feet hurt. Suddenly there was a glare of sunlight. A door had blown open. I saw framed in the doorway two men and a woman bending over a very large bird with a long neck. The bird screamed and flapped its wings. One of the men embraced it, pressing its wings against its body. The older man seized its head and pulled at it, so that the neck was stretched taut. The bird screamed again. The woman placed a pail beneath the neck and picked up a long knife that was lying on the ground. She began to slice at the neck, cutting from below upwards, with vigorous thrusts of her arm. There were two or three more screams, piercing and frantic, as the blade cut deeper into the neck. A stream of blood ran into the pail. It made a tinny sound. The women above me were muttering. They didn't seem to like what was happening. "The knife is too dull," one of them said. Then the door closed with a bang.

Across from our house in Cuernavaca lived a little girl who came to play with me nearly every day. This child was whipped with a variety of straps and ropes as often as two or three times a week. Sometimes she was beaten extra for crying while she was being whipped. Her mother called her to punishment the way my mother called me to dinner, by calling her name, but what a terrible name that was: "Dolores."

We played in my house a lot, where her mother couldn't see her. We played with my toys. Sometimes she ate with me and my parents. She had never tasted butter before, or tapioca, or hot chocolate. There were no whips hanging on our walls, no bleeding saviors on the cross. She must have thought I lived in Paradise.

I remember lying next to her on the cool tiles of our shaded terrace leafing through a book of woodcuts by the Mexican artist Posada. Posada made pictures of executions, eight or ten different scenes with proud men facing the firing squad, and other pictures of hanged men with their tongues bulging out of their mouths, and one of a man being dragged away from his wife and children by soldiers, and another one of a woman being stoned. There were also pictures of criminals: a man sinking his teeth into an infant, a mother scorching her teenage daughter with a fire-poker, a man slitting a screaming woman's throat; and pictures of skeletons dancing, playing cards, and drinking tequila; and pictures of the end of the world, and of the seven deadly sins, and of hairy devils dragging their victims into hell's gate, conceived as the yawning, fire-spewing jaws of a huge reptilian head.

It was Dolores who introduced me to the idea that there was a real Devil and that one could have personal dealings with him.

It happened on one of the rare days when we were out on the street. We were playing marbles with several other kids—all boys except for Dolores—on a strip of hard dirt a couple of blocks from where we lived.

Marbles, in Mexico, were indicators of status and class. There were plebeian marbles made of clay, burnt in a kiln and dyed various pretty but lusterless colors, which at that time were sold at the rate of five for a centavo and were thus available on the market to even the poorest; and there were glass marbles of varying size and quality of coloration with equivalent gradations of price that, at the highest range, made them inaccessible to poor children—except, of course, by their winning them in a game. In this respect a degree of democracy prevailed in the game of marbles that was not reflected in the economic games played by adults. That is the reason why rich boys—and I was incalculably rich in comparison with most of my playmates—were welcome to join the street children in a game of marbles. There were exact rules, and the strictest fairness was observed by all—as was the case with fights, which were fought according to conventions of obviously chivalric origin, involving formal declarations of hostility and equally formal terms of cessation. But I never got into fights, and because I was good at playing marbles, and because my Spanish was fluent and without accent, my friends respected me, and forgave that I was a gringo.

On that day, though, a boy I had never seen before, darker and more ragged than any of the other children, tried to cheat me out of a large and beautiful marble of clear glass with a single blue swirl spiraling through and halfway around it; that is, he simply took it, along with three ordinary marbles that were his by right, and claimed that it had been his all along. The other boys and Dolores protested angrily, I didn't have to say anything; everyone had seen me take the marble out of my pocket and put it in the center of the circle, and no one had come close to knocking it out with his marbles, least of all the stranger, who didn't even know how to shoot a marble the way you were supposed to, with a flick of the thumbnail across the middle joint of the index finger: He just rolled his like little bowling balls, which gave him more force but less secure aim. We let him do it that way because he said he came from Jalisco and that was the way they played marbles there—but now it seemed they cheated there too, and maybe he wasn't from Jalisco at all. I strongly suspected that, and told him so. He said he damn well came from Jalisco and this marble—my marble—was the proof because they made marbles like that in Jalisco and only in Jalisco, you couldn't get them anywhere else, not in any store—glass ones yes, but not clear ones with a swirl of blue going through like a river, and had *I* ever been in Jalisco? I hadn't. Well? He spread his hands, with my marble gleaming on his right palm, as if every possible proof, material and circumstantial, had just been demonstrated and merely required an assenting nod from one reasonable and disinterested person to assume its rank among the eternal verities. My friends and I immediately closed in on him, and Dolores tried to snatch the marble from his hand. At that moment it was gone. I don't know how he did it. His sleeves were short and he couldn't have suddenly thrust his hand into his pocket and held it out again in that same palm-up gesture of a philosopher proffering his Q.E.D.—not without anyone seeing anything, not that quickly. Nothing at all had changed except for the marble disappearing and the expression on his face turning from insolent superiority to mock-astonishment as he stared out at his empty hand. "Where did it go?" he said, and looked at his other hand to see if the marble had reappeared there. Then he turned both hands over to look at their backs. Then he turned them with their palms up again and pulled his shoulders up to his ears, eyes gaping, mouth open, as if astonished to the root of his being. "It must have gone back to Jalisco!" he blurted, and then he looked around at our faces and burst out laughing. No one touched him. No one said another word to him. He walked away, still laughing. And after he had crossed the street, he jumped up to tap a street sign with his fingers. Then he turned the corner and I never saw him again. I remember the precise place where this happened, it was the corner where I often bought certain bags of candy inside which you'd always find a little plastic toy, a different one each time, hermetically sealed in a small plastic suitcase you had to snap open by pinching it in the right place.

On the way home, Dolores and I had an argument. It began with her insisting that the boy who had stolen my marble was the devil—not *a* devil, but *the* devil, and this struck me as so silly that I replied with something like "I didn't see any horns on him." I had just recently learned the rudiments of sarcasm from an older boy after weeks of bafflement at his ambiguous, half-friendly, half-hurtful sense of humor. But it was as wasted on her as it had been on me. She earnestly agreed that no horns had been visible, but according to her mother the devil could take any shape, and I had better pray my head off and maybe donate a candle to the Santa Señora de la something or other. I replied that I knew for a fact there was no such thing as a devil, the priests had made up the whole thing to scare people. At this she became very agitated. How would a little indio like that learn magic? How did I think he did it if it wasn't magic? And how did I know he hadn't taken a part of my soul with that marble? What would the devil want with a marble anyway? And that boy's skin was awfully dark!

I didn't know how to reply to this barrage. What did skin color have to do with the devil, especially since Dolores was dark-skinned herself, and what really was a soul, and could it be lost, or taken away, and could a piece of it be taken? I did have an answer to the bit about magic. A friend of my stepfather's could break off a finger and show it to you in two pieces, but still it was just a trick, he'd shown me how to do it. Unfortunately I hadn't practiced the trick very well, so my demonstration failed to refute her belief in magic.

In our zeal we had stopped walking and within minutes a circle of spectators, mostly men, had formed around us. It was clear to me, from their mumbled comments, that they, too, believed in the devil, and from their chuckles, that they found me amusing. Dolores didn't seem to notice, or to care. She was proselytizing—for the devil, or rather for faith in his existence. And I think she really believed that the salvation of my soul was at stake and that if I only believed in the devil I would pray to God and be saved. So she told me in extremely vivid detail how the devil had arranged and supervised her father's death of appendicitis: first by giving him the pain when he was out of town on an errand, so he couldn't get help for two days, help that wouldn't have helped in any case, since the devil appeared to a neighbor in a dream, disguised as a Saint, and told her to put a hot brick on Dolores' father's stomach because this would help him and nothing any doctor suggested would help. So her father screamed all night and her mother and the neighbor kept heating a brick over a fire and putting it on her father's stomach, and in the morning when he was almost dead, Dolores was sent to fetch a *bruja,* who told them to stop using a brick and burned some plants and sang and prayed and passed a crucifix over his stomach, but it was too late and he died, and later the *bruja* read some tea leaves for free, and there on the bottom of the cup was the sign of the devil, she showed it to Dolores and her mother, a real little *diablo* with horns and a tail, and they all knew beyond the shadow of a doubt that *he* had caused it, and the *bruja* said all that was left was to pray for his soul and donate a candle to the Church of the Santa Señora.

"There is no devil," I said quietly, intimidated by the crowd of adults. I felt like crying. Then a very large man with a ragged straw hat and a Zapata moustache stepped into the circle, gently pushed Dolores aside, put his fists on his hips, and looked down at me with more deadly sarcasm in his glittering eyes than I had ever dreamed of marshalling in my little sallies. I stepped back, almost staggering, tore my eyes loose, and pushed through the wall of bodies and walked off with long strides. Dolores caught up with me and took my hand. We walked home swiftly—not running, so as not to *look* frightened. Dolores, too, was afraid. From around the corner, we could hear her mother calling.

"Enough shards," says my soul-critic. "Get back to the river. And widen your sight, at least for the moment, to take in the others who were swimming with you."

■   ■   ■

WE

The big We. Of course. I remember driving in a bus with Susan through some town in upper New York state when a young man with longish hair and a head-band spotted me with *my* longish hair (Susan still looked "straight") and raised two fingers in a "V" sign, which at that time still meant "Peace," and I returned the gesture. The beauty of that exchange: It was not yet a convention, but more like a remembering of something ancient and still wondrously alive, the recognition of strangers in the sign of a god—or was it a goddess, what with the beads, long hair, bangles, etc., and the back-to-nature idea behind them?

"Idea," I say. Of course it was not an idea but an impulse, a dream, itself a manifestation of nature like any tree or cloud. That was the secret of the big We's unity: It was not an intellectual thing, not the product of reflection, not even "ideological." It came out of nowhere, it grew in the dark, like mushrooms: Suddenly at dawn the damp woods are dotted with white caps.

"That's not an explanation," my soul-critic says. "We can adduce economic and sociocultural factors, the influence of newspapers, photographs, TV, and music, the impact of drugs—nothing comes from nothing." True, I reply, but that's a little like saying those mushrooms cropped up because there were spores in the moss and the rain quickened them: undeniably true, but of relevance only to certain zones in the cerebellum and not to wherever the place is—it feels like the middle of the chest, two or three inches deep—that responds with wonder and something like love to the sight of the fairy ring at dawn where there were only wet leaves in the evening.

But who this We really was, this ecstatic ghost in whose body we danced, we had no idea. Nor did we ask. Nor did we pray to the god or goddess who had swallowed us, because we did not know that we had been swallowed alive. Such things were inconceivable to twentieth-century middle-class brains.

A doctor administering penicillin to a Mexican Indian medicine woman believes he is applying a chemical substance to a biochemical machine in order to improve its functioning—and perhaps he is.

The medicine woman has taken peyote to help the doctor and strengthen his medicine. Peyote tells her that penicillin is good. She tells the doctor that his medicine is a white snake and that this snake is strangling a vicious dwarf in her liver.

To the doctor, peyote is a toxic hallucinogenic drug; he would never prescribe it. To the medicine woman, peyote is holy, and a person who eats peyote swallows a god.

The doctor knows many things, but the medicine woman knows one big thing. She knows that matter and spirit are one and the same divine substance. She knows it because her parents knew it, and their parents' parents. Hundreds of generations invited the god into their bowels, and the god in turn made himself at home there and learned something of human fear and human love. But when in the middle or late sixties the doctor's children swallowed peyote or mescaline or LSD, neither they nor the god were prepared for each other.

I remember a boy from New Orleans who stayed at our house for a few weeks dropping Acid every three or four days. "It all comes back to the same ole thang," he said one day at the dinner table: "We're all one. You don't need a lotta smarts to count to one." I'm not belittling his insight, it was the same truth the medicine woman knows in her bones, but three weeks later the boy was at Bellevue Hospital trying to pick up the pieces of his identity. It is no small thing to swallow a god.

Is there a difference between swallowing a god and being swallowed by him? None at all. In the god's realm, we are what we eat because what we eat digests us.

That is all I wish to say about the big We for the moment.

Stefan's Prophecy

Shortly after Stefan's twentieth birthday, Alma persuaded him to talk to a famous psychiatrist who had heard about the brilliant young schizophrenic—that label was loosely administered in those days—and had expressed an interest in meeting him. She was present at the interview. After the formalities of introduction, the psychiatrist asked his first question: "How would you describe your problem?" Stefan cleared his throat and tensely asked a question in return: "How would you describe yours?" The doctor failed this simple test. He was arrogant and defensive, and Stefan walked out of his office. That's how Alma described it to me.

Some people held Alma responsible for Stefan's illness. He treated her badly, had hit her a few times—why didn't she force him to leave her house? He was twenty years old. Why didn't she insist that he get a job? Wasn't she coddling him, weakening him? I, too, thought that, and told her so. She had a maddening way of evading criticism instead of meeting it, and that made her look guilty and probably made her feel guilty too. As for me, I had read my Freud, this looked like an open-and-shut case: a clinging, overprotective mother, an asthmatic boy gasping for breath in her arms, in her enveloping pity and love, and now a young Oedipus drowning in the whirlpool of his unconscious desire, her unconscious seduction. Perhaps there was truth in this diagnosis, but it lacked one essential bit of information, something Alma saw in Stefan's face all the time. One day she said it, and it stopped me cold: "Your brother is in hell." It was undeniable.

What could I do, how could I help him? He was so formidably defended. Visiting him in his room was like stepping into a minefield: One ill-chosen word, or an untoward move—but words were the biggest danger—and he would explode, and you wouldn't want to get near him again for weeks. But you had to. There he would sit, on his bed or on a chair, white, extremely thin, looking both slack and tense, eyelids drooping, cheeks pulsing as he worked his jaws, alert for the prowling advance of the Helpers (that's what he called us in his journal), unwitting agents of retrogression and death, children of

Ahriman the destroyer, sent to prevent Stefan's emancipation from the prison of appetite. Spanning the length of one wall and nearly reaching the ceiling were shelves bending with the weight of several hundred books: at the bottom right, the ones he and I had read as children and others only he had read, among them his favorite when he was ten, the story of an expedition, by sailboat, to seven islands, each its own Eden, which are not found on any map and cannot be approached by the usual navigational methods, since they are not to the north, south, east, or west of any place, but are situated in a dead calm "behind the winds" of the world—*The Seven Fortunate Islands Behind the Winds*. To the left of these first books and above them were the works he had been made to read in school, *Hadrian's Memoirs,* an anthology of famous letters, masterpieces of reportage, books by American liberal intellectuals which he lampooned in the margins. Next to these, the novels he had read and those he had not yet and would never read, among them a paperback copy of *Jean Santeuil,* which stands on a shelf in my house today next to the fat volumes of *Remembrance of Things Past,* a brittle, yellowing paperback, before which I would like to put a sign, maybe an olive branch, if one could be found, in memory of the time when Stefan first read these pages and felt himself burning with admiration and pleasure and also with the ambition to write something like this someday soon, in his own voice and with his own materials. And after the novels, plays: Beckett, Brecht, Büchner, Japanese No plays, all of which he had studied, absorbed, annotated, criticized; and a large collection of modern poetry, much of it French (Breton, Desnos, Eluard, Michaux) and Spanish (Lorca, Machado, Neruda, Vallejo, and a Cuban poet he had met on our trip and whose work he admired, Luis Marré). Works of science then, and Western philosophy—somewhat disordered, these, Marx and Engels scattered among Plato and the logical positivists—and finally, on the top shelf—you had to stretch for these—books on religion, occult philosophy, white magic, clairvoyance, by charlatans and saints, crackpots and visionaries, with names like Gurdjieff, Krishnamurti, George Ohsawa, Vivekananda, Alice Bailey, Rudolf Steiner, Madame Blavatsky, and the most revered, Sri Aurobindo. And Aurobindo's translations of the Bhagavad Gita and several Upanishads. And the Bible. On one wall hung a photograph of Aurobindo in an enormous thronelike armchair, wearing a white robe, with long white hair and a flowing white beard, looking exhausted and saintly; and another picture of an Indian sculpture representing an "ascetic Buddha"—a living skeleton, lotus-seated, in a decorative halo. That picture in particular frightened me, because it so grimly proclaimed a will to outstare, outlast, outlive life itself, and because, more and more as he adhered to a diet consisting almost exclusively of brown rice, with only occasional sparse additions of some properly "Yang" vegetable, that horrific image was becoming his lodestar, shining him the way to a world behind the winds and beyond the flesh.

I challenged Stefan one day. I don't know what gave me the courage. I was perfectly calm. Consequently, he, too, was poised. For the first time in months, we managed to have a real conversation.

"Why this picture?" I asked, pointing at the "Ascetic Buddha." "You know the Buddha didn't stop there," I said. "After starving himself, he accepted milk from a shepherd girl. And then, when the armies of Mara came, he pointed at the earth as his witness and ally. *That* was his victory, not this. Here, he was lost."

"Those were the good old days," Stefan said with a tired, wry smile. "The earth is no longer solid. You want to help me, but you don't realize that you live in my world just as I live in yours. We're not monads. And this one world is a hell, whether you know it or not. People think their freedom from pain, their comfort, their appetite, is some kind of badge of sanity, a pat on the back from Mother Nature to give them a satisfying burp and tell them they've been good boys and girls. But Mother Nature is being tortured. Mara's armies are having a field day. The reason I put up that picture is to remind me that my task in life is not to enjoy myself but to fight Evil. Not by signing petitions or going to demonstrations or writing another *J'accuse*—the world is drowning in words! No, I'm talking about mental war."

His voice, though still calm, was beginning to sound oratorical, as if he were addressing an audience. I tried to inject some mild sarcasm, a blunt little barb:

"Sounds like Armageddon."

"It may very well be Armageddon," he said.

"And who fights this war?"

"Those who are called to battle, whether by love or madness or divine compulsion."

"Battle to what end?"

"To save the world."

"From what?"

"From falling into a deeper circle of hell. Where there may be no possibility of redemption."

"You're serious!" I said.

I had gone too far. His energy abandoned him. He suddenly looked desolate. He closed his eyes for a long moment. Then he opened them again and quietly, without looking at me, said: "In two years you will come into a great darkness. Then you'll know what I mean."

I didn't know what to say. We sat without talking for several minutes. Faintly, from the radio in Alma's room, two violins, a viola, a cello, and a clarinet sounded a tune of ineffable tenderness and solace. But here, in his room, a demonic intensity had gathered. I started to pray, silently in my mind, and in German for some reason, although we had been speaking English:

"Vater unser der du bist im Himmel . . ."

"Now please leave my room," Stefan said. "I'm tired."

I walked out feeling angry. Where did he come off forecasting my future?

It was after that conversation that I began, in moments of half-conscious reverie, to picture myself floating into his hell by some feat of telepathic projection, threading my way through the maze of his delusion, taking him by the hand (as in the whirls of Carnival in Santiago de Cuba), and showing him the way out. The most vivid part of the fantasy was the mood of release and celebration after the rescue. I couldn't really imagine his predicament, or, for that matter, how to take the first step into his labyrinth. I might have asked him to show me the way, but I didn't think of that.

■　　■　　■

In August 1966, Stefan went to India, the first of several desperate searches for a guru, someone with the authority to put a stop to the mental war, or at least call a cease-fire. Alma, Susan, and I accompanied him to the airport. We arrived much too early. Stefan asked us not to wait, but Alma insisted on staying until his plane took off. She kept looking at his face and wringing her hands, unable to hide her anguish at her son's condition. Nor could he suppress his rage at having his misery mirrored in her pity at every moment. I tried to distract him with a pocket chess game I had brought along, but then, for no logical reason, he resigned and, mumbling an apology, withdrew into stony silence. Even Alma was relieved when he finally walked through the door of the boarding ramp. Still, she wanted to wait until the plane had taken off. I went outside with Susan. Something extraordinary happened then. I was standing next to her behind a tall wire fence with a view to the landing field, wondering out loud whether that distant airplane taxiing into position and stopping and roaring its engines was Stefan's, and if it was, whether he could see us waving and feel our good wishes, and whether he cared. Susan said, "Sure he cares," and then the plane took off and rose, and as we watched it gradually grumbling away into invisibility I suddenly said: "Let's get married." Out of the blue. It surprised both of us, because I had always rejected the idea of marriage as a kind of insurance policy against all the risks that make love exciting and precious.

We got married in November. Two weeks after the wedding, Susan discovered that she was pregnant.

Let me take stock of the gods. Voluptas and the one with the arrows now preside together as household gods, perhaps too content to take note of their two most dangerous rivals, Acid and Chance. Politicus, too, who seemed almost defeated for a while, is on the ascendancy: He assaults me with bloody televised carnage from Vietnam and periodically drums me out of my bohemian retirement to join the growing waves of refusal that are flooding the streets of the nation: Stop the war! No more killing! Those are slogans I can believe in, I can echo them in my heart while others shout them. That's one thing I learned in East Germany, anything shouted in chorus turns into a lie. Oh, that's the trouble with you, Politicus, whatever you touch turns sterile and stupid and eventually hateful, even when you mean well and especially then. Look at these other slogans you cooked up:

"Bim bam boom, Viva Mao Tse-tung!"

"Up against the wall, motherfucker!"

"Bring the war home!"

It makes me ashamed to be part of a crowd that would chant these words with conviction. Even though I would feel guilty not joining them.

And you've given the others, our enemies, equally imaginative war cries:

"Nuke Hanoi!"

"Better dead than red!"

"Take a bath!"

They hate us. Some of us hate them. Most of us fear them. There are rumors that the internment camps used to hold Japanese Americans during World War II have been refurbished on orders from Robert Kennedy to make room for obstreperous blacks, pacifists, and drug users.

Chance

At the National Opinion Research Center, I discovered creative and uncommon uses of the Xerox copying machine. By folding, cutting, tearing, and bunching pieces of paper, some of them with print and pictures on them, and xeroxing them, and combining copies of these copies in newly folded, cut, torn, and bunched arrangements, and adding to these the xeroxed images of parts of a face, mine or a colleague's—a flattened ear, a porous nose, a smear of lips, a bristly chin, a mad round eye—I produced reams of legal-sized landscapes and portraits, some of which I adorned near the left or right margin (in the manner of Chinese paintings) with columns of typed or handwritten phrases culled at random from books and magazines. My employers were lenient and unwatchful.

But let me be watchful of my words now, especially as I describe my deliberately careless use of them then.

"Culled at random" is right, but it's not the whole story. Those scrambled phrases had to cohere, otherwise why go through the labor of disjoining and recombining them; and though pure chance was wonderfully quirky, poetic, even inventive at times, it didn't always do the trick. A supervisor was needed. So, while my fingers performed their riffling and pointing blindly enough, the eye (or the I) that took up their findings was not neutral. Yes, an I, and a very secret one. He stood invisibly at the center of operations, accepting and rejecting, shaping, adjusting, choosing between "ands" and "buts," adding syntactic links where they were needed—a mere instrument, I thought, but he was the demiurge of this willful chaos, the real maker of its meaning.

"Invisibly." This word, too, needs qualification. Because just now, I had a glimpse of him (before my "mind's eye") as a tall man in a Nazi uniform, standing in the middle of a bare courtyard, facing a group of emaciated prisoners who step up to him, shivering, one by one. Silently he points to the right: this way to the gas chamber—and to the left: this way to the stone quarry. And even at the time I am describing, he showed himself. I remember a series of dreams in which senseless atrocities were committed by an unknown killer who always left a cryptic signature at the scene of the crime. One night he revealed his identity. He was the leader of a criminal gang who had *asphyxiated* some two hundred people in a bus by diverting the exhaust fumes into the body of the vehicle. I saw the victims soundlessly gasping behind the windows, their hands and mouths pressed against the glass (rather like the faces on my xerox portraits). The police were, as usual, stumped. Their only clue was the gang leader's four-letter cryptogram, which he had scrawled on the pavement with a blue magic marker:

J

O

E

L

"How strange," I thought, after writing down the dream, "he has my name." That was as far as my analysis went. He was invisible in the same way and for the same reason the poor are invisible to the rich: I didn't want to see him.

In hindsight it's clear enough. He found a certain sadistic pleasure—or a blasphemous joy, which amounts to the same thing—in what I conceived of as a literary exercise: cutting into the sacred body, severing it limb from limb, redistributing the mutilated parts in derision of their natural order, their health; and then to read the demonic message, the new dispensation of the mangled Word:

> Nobody has begun to distinguish between the footprints of ancient trees
> and the heartless night's meandering Pythagoras brooding more blindly as
> the waves echo across the hearthstone into the sheepwhite chalk. Nobody
> has begun to distinguish between the mute trumpeting of groin and prayer
> and the midwives motionless in the frost by the gates of Eden.[10]
>
> The park shouts so loud that Jim Rib son of Adam standing naked at the
> temple door in Black Valley feels the noise of the rushing air go blind in his
> ears. And back along the long bleak street he makes his way back to the
> dust-appointed apple trees in a shadow by the disappearing garden.
>
> And prophets gripped his hands and poets added all kinds of new ones,

---

10. Bob Dylan must have been part of the mix here.

and a lovely stinking little baby bounced out of the bed of time to knock Jim
Rib's geometry all awhirl; and animals and birds and fish wept all that night.
It was the sickness of the countryside inching into light . . . etc.

This was a text without pictures, so I must have written it at home. The thing
was titled: "The Wind of Words blows Christward, bearing God knows how
much dangerous information," and obviously I had no idea how dangerous
this Christward drift really was, because I turned my phrase-mixing into a parlor game. These are its rules: The players, any number of them, sit in a circle;
each one is equipped with a stack of books, newspapers, magazines, police
blotters, restaurant menus, what-have-you—the content of the texts matters
less than the contrasts between them.[11] One player assumes the role of scribe
(this is preferable to using a mechanical recording device). Someone, anyone,
begins the game by opening a book and reading out loud whatever fragment of
text his eye or finger happens to land on. Let's say it's this paragraph, these
words from the previous sentence: *"Opening a book . . ."* While the scribe writes
that down, a second player flips open whatever lies at the top of his heap—say,
the journal of Henry David Thoreau, a volume that happens to lie at hand near
my desk right now—and reads the very first set of words, or maybe just one
word, that meaningfully connects with those first three words and continues
their statement: "What is it I hear but the pure waterfalls within me," says Mr.
Thoreau. That is very nice, but much too complete for the purpose of the game,
so the player must cut the phrase, chop off its head—for example, like this:
"What is it I hear but the pure . . ." The pure what? The answer comes from the
third player, who has opened a textbook on sociology: *". . . footnotes,"* he says,
and the fourth player, who, I hope, has a sense of the shape and evolving idea
of the sentence, decides to conclude it with a dip into, say, Chang Chung-yuan's
Creativity and Taoism, which I just pulled out of my bookcase: *". . . of here-now,"*
he says, and "period," he adds.

"Opening a book, what is it I hear but the pure footnotes of here-now."

Maybe the scribe would like to delete "pure" and change the assonance of
"hear" and "here" and substitute a question mark for the period, but the text
must run on.

I bought myself an 8 mm Bolex camera and walked around shooting whatever caught my fancy, then rewound the film and exposed it again, this time
with long takes of the neighborhood flowing into the lens as I walked with the

---

11. The process itself dictated its reasons one day: *"Contrast contributes contrivance control."*

camera held to my belly. I rewound it a third time and rolled it forward and back and took a few more shots at random: a girl in front of a puddle, a cloud, garbage burning in a trash-can. When the film was developed I invited our friends for a viewing. A double world passed before our eyes, an aquariumlike Lower East Side where stoned freaks and hostile policemen walked through each other like ghosts, where a chessplayer's move stirred a spray of pigeons out of Susan's pregnant belly, where a powder-blue car sailed into a shop window full of powder-blue plaster Madonnas and vanished in a white cloud—in short, a perpetual flux of rhyming and punning images. The film was dazzling, especially when I added a Rolling Stones record for a sound track.

I am wa-i-ting . . .

Mick Jagger sang, and immediately everyone on the screen was waiting—a Chinese cook smoking in front of his restaurant, waiting, two pasty-faced Hassids studying skin magazines at a bookstand, waiting, my friend George North looking into the world with a bitter, skeptical smile, waiting, and there was I with a short beard and shoulder-length hair, looking Christ-like and eating soup from a bowl:

I am wa-i-ting . . .

In the soup, running through it and into my chest, was a street, and the street was bouncing, but my face on the screen was calm:

Oh yeah, oh yeah . . .

A little boy crossed the bouncing and bobbing street. He stopped on the sidewalk to look at the camera, and the camera looked at him:

I am wa-i-ting . . .

All the while I was eating my soup, drinking wine from a bottle, and waiting. A band of half-nude adolescents appeared in my bowl, on my face, and above my head, gyrating in the new Californian manner, waving their arms like seaweed. I put the spoon in my mouth, chewed, and swallowed:

I am wai-i-ting . . .

The burning trash-can appeared. Now the dancers themselves looked like flames. Behind them loomed the high-rises of Central Park South. They were burning. The whole park was on fire, and I was eating this burning dancing human trash, chewing it with a kind of bovine patience . . .

Oh yeah, oh yeah . . .

The dancers disappeared, leaving only the fire. And there, in the fire, was the little black girl with pigtails staring into a puddle and into my bowl. I scooped her up, puddle and all, and swallowed her at the moment when the street dropped and a tall house suddenly slid down my face, window by window, until a sign,

JESUS SAVES

stood printed across my forehead. A large white cross hung over my head. Spoon in hand, burning, I raised my glass for a toast:

Wai-ting for-some-one-to-come-out-of-some-where!

sang Mick Jagger, and the film ran out. Everyone in the room laughed, whooped, and applauded. So did I. But the terrible thing—terrible now, looking back, not then, I was elated—the terrible thing was the deep satisfaction I felt. Chance had elected me into the Archetype. I had a fate. Why not? Didn't I know I was born to greatness? And it was just beginning.

One of my friends was Steve Handschu, a blind sculptor and martial artist. If that's not quite believable, it's because it's not quite true: Steve had partial vision in one eye, and through a telescope lens several inches long he could examine the grain of his sensuous wood sculptures and even read. He could make out the shapes of people and things without that device, but he needed his white cane to navigate through the shadows. He had the dislocated half-smile I've noticed on many blind people, the smile of a face that does not know what it is to be seen. He was twenty-one and smoked a pipe, which gave him a middle-aged, bourgeois air. I don't know how he absorbed Stefan's scorn on that account. Steve was one of two people who had accomplished the extraordinary feat of befriending my brother during his four-year reign of terror as the Walden School's tongue-lashing genius. Like Stefan, he was precocious and brilliant; unlike him, he fed and exercised his body well, and liked to rest in its comfort. I think he had fantasies of being like the blind swordsman of Japan who could hear a leaf falling and spear it in midair. He studied karate and regularly donated his muscled body and, alas, his blind eyes to the pugilistic "defense committees" of SDS and Youth Against War and Fascism.

Steve was witness to three pivotal events in my life. I will list them in the order of their occurrence:

1. Some twenty people, most of them women, were marching around an army recruiting center on West 42nd Street, a metal shack in the middle of a traffic island, with a flag on its roof and a minuscule office inside. I was one of them. Through the window, I could see a uniformed man drinking coffee and another one grinning as he talked on the phone. Surrounding us on both sides of the street was a large and hostile crowd, among them some forty construction workers on their lunch break, smiling broadly under their hardhats. One of them yelled: "Take a bath, asshole!" He meant me. A small police detachment came, presumably to protect the recruiting station, gave us an amused once-over, and joined the crowd. In front of me walked a stout, old woman who was carrying a poster and chanting with a whiny voice: "Stop? ze var? in Viet? Nam. Bring? ze droops? khom." I wasn't chanting. Not that I didn't want the war to stop, but as I've mentioned earlier, I was allergic to agitprop, it reminded me of East Germany. So, in a perverse way, did our leaflet, which said, among other things: "Vote With Your Feet!" Nor did I look forward to getting beat up. I looked at Steve, our sole protector. He was smiling, as usual, but his fists were clenched and he was breathing heavily. He wasn't chanting either. The grinning soldier stepped out to give each of us a personalized version of that internationally recognized hand signal, the raised middle finger. A hamburger roll came flying across Broadway. The policemen were laughing. I pulled out a copy of Chuang Tzu I had stuck in my back pocket, opened it, and read:

BETTER TO ABANDON DISPUTATION AND SEEK THE TRUE LIGHT.

I left immediately. The next day, when I visited Steve, he had a black eye. He showed me a tabloid newspaper with a picture of him getting punched in the face. The caption read: "The Will of the People." The crowd had closed in on the demonstrators right after I left. That was the last political rally I attended.

2. We were smoking hash from a hookah, sitting on cushions on the floor. Steve, a professed atheist, confided to me that he had recently done something rather like prayer. He had thought of Stefan and his suffering and sent out his good wishes and a feeling of love to wherever he was in Asia, hoping that this could reach him.

"Maybe it can," I said. "Let's pray for him now." And we did. We sat silently in the nearly dark room, thinking of Stefan and watching the flames of three candles we had put on the floor. After a few minutes, something in the configuration of those candles began to disturb me; they formed an irregular triangle, geometrically perfect as all triangles are, and yet in some profoundly irritating way out of whack, skewed, disharmonious, wrong. If I moved any one of the candles, it would be better. And then I spoke: "This is me," I said, pointing to the candle nearest me, "this is you," pointing to the candle nearest Steve, "and that's Stefan," pointing to the third candle, which stood at a distance from both of us. And the moment I said that, the flame on Stefan's candle wavered as if someone had blown at it. It immediately righted itself and stood still, but then it wavered wildly again, lengthened until it stood twice as tall as the other flames, suddenly squatted, contracted, and went out, leaving a wisp of black smoke. The next moment, the flame leaped back into existence, flaring green-ishly, sputtered, crackled, flailed back and forth, and went out with such final-ity that we just sat there staring at the dead candle for several minutes without saying a word. I had feared for my brother often, but this was my first intima-tion that he was not just endangered, but doomed.

3. A friend of Steve's named Jason was telling me, in Steve's company, about the vistas that had opened up for him when he joined the Church of Scientology. I knew what that was about. I, too, had once sat behind the "E-Meter," revealing my secrets in emulation of those glassy-eyed young men and women who had, at considerable expense, become "Clears." And though I was starting to suspect the good church of being what it is now widely considered to be—a multimillion-dollar racket aiming at world domination and using lie detectors to blackmail its members in the name of "total liberation"—I was sympathetic to Jason's enthusiasm, and eager to help him understand one of the axioms of Scientology: That the world as we know it is created by man, and that therefore each one of us is responsible for its condition.

"But not in equal measure," Steve interjected. "We may all be in the same boat, but some of us are galley-slaves, others are officers, and still others are passengers, first and second class."

"And yet," Jason said, "we presume that in some sense we're all equal. Isn't that so?"

Steve nodded.

"So what is it," I asked heuristically, "that we all have in common?"

"Bodies," Steve said.

"Pain," Jason added.

"We have that in common with animals too," I said. "But what humans have in common, I think, is selfhood. Everyone who says 'I,' in whatever language, means the same thing. And that 'I' wants unlimited power and freedom. What 'I' wants is that there be no Other."

I was looking at Jason as I said this. I stopped talking and suddenly we were just looking into each other's eyes.

Staring was a widespread practice in those days. Scientologists did it on principle: The "clearer" you were, the less you blinked. "Heads" did it out of sheer fascination: What could be deeper than a human eye? And sometimes through that eye you could glimpse pictures and faces from what you could only presume was the history of a soul. But this time something new happened. I saw my face in his. In actuality we looked completely different—his hair was blond, for one, mine was dark—but somehow the mind construed general features we had in common—long face, blue eyes, and so on—into signs of identity, and cunningly linked them into a pattern of sameness, until after a few minutes it was like looking into a mirror. My eyes looking back at me were bright with interest, and a sly sort of glee. What did this mean? I was adept at reading signs, why not this one?

"I," I said, pointing at myself, ". . . am you," pointing at him, ". . . and you . . . are I . . . and Steve is I . . . and I am everyone . . . and anyone can say it, because everyone knows himself as I." I expected Jason to pick up the thread, but he burst out laughing and the illusion was dispelled. Steve was stuffing his pipe and shaking his head. He did not like this philosophy, he did not trust it at all.

That night I was full of energy and brightness. I couldn't sleep. I sat down at my desk to write and noticed a doodle I had drawn while talking on the phone. It was a picture of a leaf with a woman's smiling face in it, or a woman's face with the veins and serrate edges of a leaf. That picture recalled an old memory. Climbing the big *chapopote* tree in our garden in Mexico—I must have been around six—I had seen a leaf slowly creeping on spidery legs along the branch I had scaled. I had felt neither fear nor curiosity, just shock at the strangeness of this impossible thing, and at the same time a contrary shock of deep familiarity. This eerie emotion had puzzled me more than the crawling paradox before me, and it stayed with me after my stepfather furnished an explanation of the outer event complete with the insect's name and a fancy new word, "mimicry." Now, twenty years later, face-to-face with the leaf-face or face-leaf I had unconsciously drawn, that feeling came back, a memory of a memory that was itself an echo of something deeply forgotten, yet elusively near. What was it? What was it? And how strange that this strange thing had come out of me! How strange, therefore, was I, the maker of it! Saying this, I welcomed the strangeness into myself, and it flooded me with such tremendous energy that I had to stand up. I looked out the window at the silver-colored facade of the fabric factory across the street, and at the disc of the full moon above it. "I am that," I thought. And the world, too, was charged with this incomprehensible strangeness. I was standing in a room on the fifth floor of a building on 4th Street between 2nd and 3rd Avenues, but I felt large enough to span continents.

The next day felt like a holiday. The air was wonderfully clear, the sky was cloudless, the light brilliant. It was the first warm spring day of the year. My boss at the National Opinion Research Center sent me on an errand to Columbia University. Waiting for the subway at 14th Street, I watched a long-haired kid write something with chalk on a metal pillar and walk on with comically loping steps. I read his message:

UP WITH THE NEW

DOWN WITH THE OLD

The train arrived, and I got in. Between 34th Street and Times Square, an old black man walked through the car and handed me—and only me—a card that read:

ALL MEN ARE CREATED EQUAL

On the way back to the office, I saw a single word scrawled on a wall:

COINCIDE!

What a strange use of the word, I thought—as a command, an assignment! I returned to the office. A colleague handed me a list of phone numbers and names: The phone had been ringing for me all morning, she said. Some of the callers were people I hadn't seen in weeks. I rang them all back and invited them to my house for dinner. Then the phone rang again. The caller nearly dropped the receiver when I answered: She had gotten a shock. "But that's not possible," she said, "the phone's made of plastic." "Everything's possible," I said. "Come over tonight, I'll explain." Again the phone rang, again I invited the caller. It was Steve Handschu. "Come over tonight if you can," I said, "and ask Jason to come too." Then I sat down at a typewriter and wrote:

I AM THE ONE IN WHOSE NAME YA-EL IS PROCLAIMED THE EVERLASTING LIFE OF THAT I AM AS ALL NAMES DO PROCLAIM ME. MAY ALL WHO ARE AND SHALL BE KNOW THEIR TRUE SELF AS I AM.

I made some twenty copies of that before I left the office.

The house was full that night. Susan and I had ordered fried chicken, George North had brought a load of fish and chips, another friend had prepared a large bowl of sangria. Jason was the only guest who didn't come: I might have taken that as a cautionary sign. I distributed my manifesto, which was read and received with amused incomprehension. I proceeded to explain: "I . . . am you; and you . . . are I; and he . . . is I . . ." etc. I must have communicated something more vital than those words as I performed the ritual, because after a few repetitions, everyone was smiling broadly, and when we all sat down to eat one friend laughingly proposed a toast "to the spread of universal self-consciousness"—but I wasn't sure anyone had really caught the spark, otherwise there should have been some kind of contagion beyond the usual high spirits produced by good company, grass, food, and wine. After our guests had left, Susan told me it had been a great evening but she hadn't much liked my passing around that note. It was silly, she found, and the inclusion of my name somehow spoiled the universality of the message. I disagreed. I was in no mood for doubt, I was feeling too good. A friend told me the next day, in a half-dubious, half-admiring manner, that with my long hair and short beard, sitting taller than the others at the center of a long table, eating fish and drinking wine, I had not just looked like Jesus in a picture of the Last Supper, but had somehow played the part with impressive exuberance—shining, as it were, in the glory of the new dispensation. I laughed. I was flattered.

The Storm

On an unseasonably warm night shortly before Christmas 1966, I took a large dose of LSD. It was late, around two o'clock in the morning. Susan went off to sleep, and told me to wake her if I needed help. A strong wind was rattling the windows and whirling rain and garbage through the streets. I turned off the lights, lit several candles, took off my clothes, sat down on a large cushion. Near me on the rug stood a bowl with fruit and a glass of water. After a while my hands started to look strange, a familiar sign that the Acid had taken. Unsuspected ranges of blue, rose, and green played over my arms and legs. The whole room with its soft dancing lights was steeped in a sort of visual perfume—tactile, too, as I discovered when I dipped my fingers in the water and touched them to an apple and a plum. A splatter of rain against the window passed through me like an exquisite wingbeat. The more I immersed myself in sensation, the more beautiful and the more subtly articulated it became. What better setting for the rest of this trip than under the blanket with Susan? But on the way to the bedroom, I saw my reflection in a tall mirror, and stopped. It looked like one of those ithyphallic representations of a pharaoh, made of brass or gold. At the same time, the dance of light and shadows gave his skin a shifting, transparent quality, like the wind-ruffled surface of a clear pool of water. On closer inspection, I saw that the body had breasts, full and round, like ripe fruit, and the golden phallus was replaced by a triangular grove of dark pubic hair. Then the breasts were annulled by thick curls on a broad, heroically muscled chest. The arms, too, were powerful and adorned with metal bracelets. A peculiarly vaginal wound opened up in the chest, which was hairless now, with a web of blue veins beneath the skin, blood flowed down the belly and onto the legs, the body turned a dull greenish gray, the skin cracked and split, worms swarmed in and out of the putrefying innards, a new, pink, adolescent body blossomed out of the corpse, whether a girl's or a boy's wasn't clear, ballooned into obesity, shrank and shriveled into a withered, hollow-chested old man with a long, pendant scrotum. I knew that what I was seeing was the reflection of my thoughts, but that was no comfort, because my thoughts were no longer mine. Two rooms away, Susan was sleeping. I started walking in her direction.

The dining room was almost unrecognizable, much too long, the distant door to the bedroom was tiny. Asleep on the floor, twitching, our sick little dog lay in my path, a breathing monument of reproach. He had some kind of spastic nerve disease which, according to the veterinarian, was incurable. Why had I not taken him to another vet? Because I didn't care enough. Because I wanted pleasure and was always banishing pain from my thoughts. Because I would court pleasure as long as the rack and the scalding oil were out of my sight. A flash of lightning lit up the apartment. I needed help, fast. Far off to my left, on a couch, in the glow of a wall lamp, lay the Bible. I stepped around the twitching dog, walked the three endless steps to the couch, picked up the black book, sat down, opened the book to a column of red words which was at the same time a tall building the color of blood, with empty spaces in place of windows, but of course I knew it was not a building, this was the Bible and these were the words of God which, once read, would be words of salvation. Inside each word were letters and clusters of letters all pulsing their own unpronounceable meanings—stn thh es gpr—fierce little strongholds for the eye and against the ear, and that felt extremely uncomfortable. Then a burst of thunder decided the issue, and the opening phrase stood before me: "Seest thou these great buildings . . . ," which I assumed meant the house of words on the page, and I thought: How wonderful, this must be God the Father's house with its many mansions, and it looked to me like some sort of hotel where a soul could find shelter from the storm, and maybe a hospital, too, where a sick dog could be healed. To enter it you had to read with faith in your heart and fight off any temptation to join the revolt of the parts against the whole. So I read: "There shall not be left one stone upon another, that shall not be thrown down . . . ," and as I read, there was a knocking against the windows, which I knew was the wind, but it was also the unnamable trying to barge in, and the house of stone and the house of words were the same thing threatened with ruin, and the words on the page and the sounds in the room and outside had the same awful meaning. There was a thumping sound, for instance, which I recognized as the beating of my heart, but it was also a cosmic drumbeat portending some unimaginable climax. Nothing was more important now than to keep the building intact by reading each word in its divinely intended sequence, but a nasty trick was built into the message: Several lines down from the top I was warned not to "go down into the house neither enter therein," an instruction that should have been posted on the roof. But before I could turn back again, I was unequivocally told not to do that and not to "take up my garment" either, no doubt meaning the clothes I had dropped in the living room. How good on such a night to be in the house of God. But the next sentence chilled me: "Woe to them that are with child and to them that give suck in those days"—Susan!—and there was a flash of light followed by a tremendous crash, and that shock blew away the subtle membrane that sets apart the everyday self from the deathless soul and the domestic cave from the roofless, bottomless universe. But my heart was still locked in, pounding the walls like a desperate prisoner. Nothing was what it was any longer, the masks had fallen, the dog was all the sickness and suffering of life, and I had been put naked into the world to take care of it and had made such a sorry mess of it through the aeons, and now I had swallowed a poison concealed in a sugar cube that was setting free a horrific power that had lain encoded in words from the beginning of time, the same power that had created the world and was now tearing it back into chaos. I shut the book, as if to clamp shut the mouth of God, but the message continued in the steady scratching of the dog's claws, the fiendish whistling and howling outside. Why, when I still had the chance, hadn't I taken my stand with the letters against the text? Their revolt might have made other meanings, other outcomes possible. Now it was said and done, irrevocable, written in blood, and it was my fault, because my nerves and cells were the conduits by which the world was not only perceived but sustained, and I had swallowed a poison which no human body was meant to absorb and which was now racing through the most sacred and secret halls of the temple like an invading army, trampling the statuary, burning the scriptures, and it wasn't my body only that was going down in thunder and ruin, it was the world. There was a shout on the street, a metallic clang. A police car passed by with a wailing siren. And then a new element appeared in the text, a hard bang on the door, and another one, and a rustling, swishing sound in the hallway, and a third, brutal bang—and this, too, was my doing, though I didn't know how I had done it or whose dread arrival those knocks were portending. I didn't answer, or even dare to move. I thought of calling Susan for help. She was asleep. Asleep! How was this possible? How could the same divine power (mine!?) crush the world in one hand and cradle it in another? And how could I dare disturb the grace that protected her? Let her at least be saved. . . .

I was half sitting, half lying, pressed against the back of the couch, my arms stretched out right and left on the pillows in the position of the crucified. The mind, racing in circles, and seeing itself trapped and exposed on all sides, cowered, and waited, voiceless, for the final judgment. The dog whimpered in his sleep, bared his fangs, let out a growling sniff. Then our white cat came in from the bedroom, stopped at the sight of me, fixed me with his malachite eyes, or was it my eyes that had caught his, was I reeling him in telepathically, for he was walking toward me now, leaped up on the couch, put the cool weight of a paw on my leg, stepped onto my groin, my belly, my chest, and lowered himself down on my stomach, purring, and still steadily gazing into my eyes. Impossible to approximate, now, in the dim light of memory and with words, the strangeness of that stare. *It was not to be read,* that was one essential ingredient. It was not an element in the mad text of destruction. Nor was it blank. It came from a different world altogether, a world untouched by symbols and signs, and because that world perceived me, I knew that I existed in it, and that in it all was well. The gaze was not mute, it spoke plainly in the pure language of being—as all creatures and things do, as indeed thunder and lightning do, so that, if we could hear and perceive the good news that streams in upon us perpetually from all directions, if we were not forever distracted by the lure and the menace of the nonexistent, we would not be in need of salvation; but here the eternal message was being delivered to my address, with perfect detachment and at the same time with something like magisterial command, as if to say: This is for you, and I will not be refused. Calmly, the animal outgazed my terror. I, too, became calm. Outside, the storm abated and gave way to a steady strong rain that clattered on the tin windowsill. For a long time, I listened to the rumbling swell and subsidence of the cat's pleasure. He was flexing his front paws in rhythmic alternation, sinking the tips of his claws into my chest.

PART 2

Prologue in Hell

Doctor Faustus in his study—a sizeable loft of the kind that became fashionable in SoHo in the seventies—engrossed in contemplation of a chart covered with arcane symbols. On one side of the room stands a tall mirror, on the other a celestial globe. Objects belonging to the Middle Ages and the twentieth century (a TV set, an alembic, etc.) are visible in the flickering light of an open fireplace and the beams of modern track lights affixed to the ceiling. In the large, uncurtained bay window, a sliver of moon with the evening star above the bright silhouettes of a modern city skyline. A police siren passes outside.

Silence.

A church bell rings.

FAUST *turns his head*
> To think that bell once had the power to ring
> the vespers to philosophy! Or that
> I took it for a love-call! Now I cringe
> to hear each hour so mercilessly quartered.

Pause.

> The sound is hollow.

Pause.

>   I have not lived.

Pause.
He turns and slowly steps before the mirror.

> Look at yourself: How gravity reclaims you,
> who strove to rise above the crush of time.
> Philosopher! A bag of bones and dry thoughts,
> fit for no trade, a stranger to the world—
> but every wrinkle in your face says: "Higher!
> Beyond the stars! Transcendence! Spirit! Mind!"

When any shrub stripped of its leaves in winter
will put a dunce's cap on your transcendence
with the first buds of spring.

He puts on his doctor's cap.

Doctor of law!
The social body's sick, and you, the doctor,
prescribe restraint. The patient does not die,
but neither does he live as God intended:
He steals, blackmails, rapes, tortures, now as ever.
The true physician would incite the fever
to run its course and sweat the demons out.
But he will never come. Your paragraphs
take care of that. Your pills. Your quackery.

He tosses the cap on the ground and turns away from the mirror in disgust.

"To live as God intended . . ." Oh, how I hate
the sound of unction dripping from your tongue,
still at this late hour, as if that word, God,
could, with the right devotion, like a dog's
dumb, patient lapping, heal your master's wounds.
Your master's, yes: not God, but Manunkind,
sick to the bone with all the rotting sores
of history, yet finding time, and strength,
to kick his slave, his hairy, humble dog,
uncomprehending Everyman—himself!

Looking up.

Why do you grant your miracles to saints
and not to those who seek you through pure thought?
Good God, is not philosophy a prayer?
Or must we eat of ignorance to be saved?

He turns back to face the mirror.

What do you want, Faust: knowledge or salvation?
If you were saved, and bliss were ignorance,
and all the centuries rolled back to nothing
and Eve lay uncreated in your rib,

and you, content in Nature's lap, saw Knowledge
sliding on serpent scales to bring you news
that One begets a second, Two a third—
that and no more—and God with one swift flash
banished the snake from paradise forever:
You'd follow it; and if with flaming swords
the angels barred your way: in your own heart
you'd find its winding path and follow it;
and if its burrowing had hollowed out
the roots of life itself, and God's command
was that you put an end to learning now,
what would you do?

Turning away from the mirror.

                   What *would* I do? And yet . . .
An end to learning . . . That might be a prize
worth reaching for. But how is this achieved?
Thought cannot do it. The knife that cuts off thought
is thought itself, a thundering thought of silence.
But what a thought: The final fruit of knowledge,
sweet antidote to that first, bitter taste
that split the world and made Division king . . .
Would it be sweet? Experience speaks against it:
This world in torment is God's blessed work,
why would He wish to heal it—and through me?
And yet . . . Must I not seek that remedy
since thought conceives it to be possible?

*He hurries to his desk, takes a piece of chalk from the drawer, and quickly draws
a circle on the floor.*

I've been a coward on the battlefield,
fled from the rush and peril of desire,
betrayed my love for love of reputation:

He steps into the circle.

Here, in this field, I will not drop my sword—
my trusty doubt—nor hide behind mere faith
as if that were a shield fit for a warrior.

From the chart, he copies the mystic emblems onto the outer edge of the circle.

> If these make good their claim, the spoils of Rome
> will tinkle like a beggar's cup beside
> the wealth I'll gain: not coin nor mortal power,
> but knowledge of first things, and life eternal;
> if they be dreams, I'll be no poorer for it.

Distant thunder. He shakes his fist at Heaven.

> Enough of your commands and prohibitions.
> Upon the powers of darkness I now call:
> Is there a world not made of man's conceiving,
> a self not shaped by that same self-made world,
> a truth embracing all, without contrary,
> a Good not clawed and fanged with secret Evil,
> a Being not subject to decay and death:
> This I would know; this knowing were the rightful
> end to the sickness of philosophy . . .

The light dims. A voice is heard.

VOICE   A worthy end, a worthier beginning.

FAUST   Who are you? Speak!

VOICE   Your friend and Counterpoint.
The knowledge you request cannot be given.
Nor taken, for that matter. It is yours.

FAUST   Since when?

VOICE   Since the beginningless beginning
unto the endless end.

FAUST   This frightens me.

VOICE   Because you are beginning to remember.

FAUST   Remember what?

VOICE   That question is a door . . .

FAUST   Which I remember opening . . . Oh God,
forbid me entrance, seal it with your name,

I have been here before . . . Lord, banish me
Forever from this place, to any hell
but this one!

VOICE   Faust, this hell contains all others.
And who could banish you? This is your kingdom.
I read your hope: Since memory trapped you here,
oblivion might set you free again.
We have been through this many times before.
The recipe is simple—here it is:
Disguise yourself as any of your creatures,
dream yourself mortal, small, particular,
and scuttle through the foam of self-oblivion
till the cold truth comes crashing with the tide
of memory, like thunder, to reclaim you.
There is no hope for you. There never was.
Yet there need be no lack of satisfactions:
This is the realm of infinite transgression,
freedom's unbounded playground. One constraint
alone imposes itself: You are not
free to set limits on your liberty,
which has consigned itself to suffering.
Complain not of this truth. You are its maker.

FAUST   How could I be? I could not even think it!

VOICE   Then think it now, and calibrate the endless
degrees of sufferable pain.

FAUST   Release me!

The church bell rings a second time.

VOICE   Once and for all, know yourself as Creator
of this unhappy world, its deathless Self.
Do you require proof? Consult your doubt.
Where is it? Gone. Your faith? A memory.
Knowledge alone presides where they once warred.

FAUST   What knowledge? I see shadows on the walls,
of hideous shape and evil implication.

VOICE   They are the myriad limbs of mortal mind
            now garbed in vestments of eternity.

FAUST *throwing off his cloak*
            Let me stand naked, and like any man
            tremble within the confines of my skin!

VOICE   Tremble you may, but not as any man.
            Yours is the power, the kingdom, and the glory.
            Who will oppose you, other than yourself?
            And how does power know itself? Through opposition.
            Where you've grown skin, you've grown the teeth to tear it.
            Not even you can abrogate this law.
            Oh paradox most subtle and sublime:
            Absolute power is purest impotence,
            compelled forever to destroy itself.
            Rabbit and snake, cold eye and shivering heart,
            their unison alone is All in All.

FAUST   Let me be stone!

VOICE   Stone lives. You live within it.
            New hope is born from those inconscient depths
            to suffer love, and grief, and pain unspeakable.

FAUST   Let me be free!

VOICE   You are, in all your creatures.
            The wren's flight is your liberty in action.
            So is her miserable death, alone,
            her throat a living nest for worms to breed in,
            her eyes, still open to the light of day,
            dark pools from which ants drink their sustenance.
            Yourself now drink this image, swallow it,
            elixir of damnation, God's own truth.
            Such is the world, its justice, and its beauty,
            from wing to wing, curved claw to shuddering beak.
            This is the miracle of your creation,
            the might, the glory of your sovereign will.

FAUST   I did not will this, ever—all my will
            is that it end.

VOICE   Your will, Faust, is to know.
          This is the knowledge of first things you asked for;
          this, the quintessence hid from mortal eyes.

FAUST   This can't be all . . . This is a fiendish joke . . .
          Or madness . . .

VOICE   Would you be healed of it?

FAUST   Would I be healed—by listening to you?!

VOICE   Whom would the Lord of Hosts elect as doctor
          and with what instruments would he proceed?
          Find a redeemer? Nail him to a cross,
          as proxy for your guilt and punishment?
          You are the whole, how could a part redeem you?
          Each detail is your self, without exception:
          Judas and Jesus, one twin agony;
          the crowd, mouths gaping with unholy thirst
          for that extremest, criminal, divine
          excess you now enjoy, the tortured limbs,
          the nails, the fresh-cut cross still spiraling
          its wooden prayer to heaven, that barking dog's
          quick, infantine delight at such excitement
          in so many bodies—

FAUST   Forgive me, Father!

Downstream

One hundred pages and three years in narrative time have passed since I sent off that fellow in a Cuban army plane—the one who began as an "I" and ended up in endless space; and I have been wondering, on and off, what became of him, and what he was doing in this book in the first place, other than disappearing. Now I know that each pulse of that worry was a moment in his gradual drift back into presence. He is descending. I can see him, feel him. No, not quite see him. He is like the phantom body that appears when I close my eyes and feel the blood coursing through my fingers and hear it ringing in my scalp. A bodyless body, descending through a blue fluid (I feel it blue, though I cannot see it), floating downward, supine, his arms folded crosswise over his chest—sinking the way fish sink in an aquarium, by imperceptible modulations of their breathing, by minute flicks and quivers of their fins and tails. But he is not moving, except for the very slow and even rising and falling of his breath.

Where is he going? For there to be movement, there has to be stillness, something the movement is measured against. For there to be a descent, there must be a point of departure above, or a passing of something on the way down, or a destination below. But I see none of these. And yet I feel him descending, and feel myself sinking with him. I can enter his form and feel his crossed hands from within, and beneath the hands a streaming movement in his heart. The heart and the hands are in communication, but I cannot decipher their language. At moments it seems I am not separate from him, but then I remember and see myself sitting here at my desk, writing him, watching my pen dance on the page as my words call him down and describe him sinking in his blue element.

Now his position has changed: He is facing me, still in that hieratic pose, but upright, and he himself has become a dark gleaming blue, as if made of polished lapis lazuli.

"Are you able to speak to me?"

It feels absurd to address this idol as if he could answer. Is he human at all? But his hands stir, and he is breathing.

"Have I mistaken you for someone else? Who are you?"

And he answers: "I am he whom you called, your self as an other."

"You are returning from a great distance."

"Greater than can be imagined."

"But I have been there, haven't I?"

"You are always there."

"Why don't I know it, then?"

"You do know it. Else I would not be here to tell of it."

"What can you tell of what can't be imagined?"

He is silent. We continue to sink together. There are fearful moments when I lose sight of his contours and it seems that I am alone in an empty world. But then I see clearly that he is still there and intends to be there, and I remember with guilty gratitude that it was he and not I who was lost in space. No doubt he is grateful for my presence, too. And still we are sinking.

I notice that as we descend, his color gradually pales, while the surrounding atmosphere not only lightens but turns to rose. Also, for the first time, I notice hair and a beard on him. A new object appears, a dark rectangular frame, hovering in space between us. A mirror, I think, but the figure facing me shakes his head: "We are not the same," he says, and the frame disappears.

The sensation of sinking has gone, the only thing moving is my breath and his. And now I see green around us, we are on a lawn. He appears to be smiling, somewhat secretively. I know why. It has become apparent to both of us that I recognize him: those long strands of dirty blond hair . . . that thin, scraggly beard . . . pale, shifty blue eyes . . . sallow skin . . . the faded buckskin jacket, with dangling fringes that echo the limp fall of his hair. . . . I even recognize the lawn on which we are sitting, it's a park in London . . . and there are his moccasins, which I will be condemned to wear for one terrible week in the cold glare of his omniscience, walking my feet sore as I search for my car, my soul, my salvation and that of the world. . . .

"You're too early! I'm still in New York, my daughter hasn't been born yet. . . . Why are you here already?"

"I'm actually late," he says. "We both are. Time is pressing. But I'm wearing the wrong face, that's what's confusing you."

His face becomes long and bony, his long hair and beard disappear, his jacket turns into a white smock with a ballpoint pen clipped to the side pocket, a stethoscope dangles from his neck, he is holding a set of printed forms, his blue eyes observe me through round, wire-rimmed glasses. I know this is just a memory, a picture in the mind, but it alarms me anyway.

"My enemy."

"That's too dramatic a term," he says, smiling, "and it'll lock you into the notion that you're good and I'm evil. We've been through that. Your counterpoint—I prefer that. Or more precisely: *His* counterpoint . . ."

And he glances downward, through the floor. He means my condemned, outcast self, the prisoner of hell toward whom we are traveling.

"But we are one being," he adds. "The three of us. The all of us."

"But didn't you say we are not the same?" I reply. "How can we be one and not the same?"

"One splintered holiness. Dismembered members of one another."

As my anxiety relaxes, I become aware of the room in which I am writing, and of my pen rippling along the page. The day is darkening outside. A blackbird whistles. A neighbor opens the door of the building, lets it shut with a soft thud, walks up the creaking stairs. My counterpoint is still there, a blurred shadow, and comes into focus as I recall him. His skin wrinkles like crepe and changes color, this time to a near-transparent porcelain white, his eyes narrow and slant, long whiskers sprout from his face, pendant eyebrows, a wispy white beard. He is holding a brush in a vertical position. I recognize him too: I've seen him in a dream. The brush paints a shrub, a cloud, a tree, a stream. The stream ripples on of its own accord.

"You seek truth," he says, with a voice like the rustle of dry leaves. "Big mistake. Everything is already truth."

"That's interesting," I reply, "but you are a creature of dreams. In the daylight of consciousness, there is light and shadow. I need to know."

"There is no consciousness," he says, "there is only this." And he points to his images: shrub, cloud, tree, and stream.

"No *need* for consciousness?" I ask, guessing at his meaning.

"The All-pervasive does not know itself, but it manifests as the knower and the known. It is, in a sense, knowledge itself and is therefore bright. But it is also the purest ignorance and is therefore obscure."

I don't understand, yet I speak as if I do. The words form of their own accord: "Are you not a composite of things held in memory?"

"I am mind in operation. That bird you hear singing outside your window was painted by my brush."

"If there is no consciousness," I ask, "what is mental reflection? Who makes distinctions like those of name and form?"

"No who. Things are distinct as they are."

"What about the prediction of events, the accounting of the past? Discrimination of right and wrong?"

"All that is wind and weather. The All-pervasive comprises all opposites."

"I am not convinced of your independent existence," I say. "Who are you apart from my thoughts and feelings?"

He continues speaking in that dry tone of voice.

"Your thoughts and feelings occur to you exactly as do the phenomena of nature. You are what you witness. Therefore it is you who have no individual, separate existence."

He begins to fade.

"Don't leave yet, please. I have an urgent question."

He waits.

"My brother, Stefan. He, too, was in hell. I went there to save him. Then he died. Where is he? Does he need releasing too?"

"Release yourself. That is the open gate he needs. Look . . ."

With his brush he replenishes the river. A fish leaps out of the waves . . . no, it is the hand of my newborn daughter rising over the edge of a basket, my very first sight of her as a nurse carries her past the room where I've been waiting with other prospective fathers. I ask my Counterpoint why he is showing me this. He does not answer. Instead, I feel a warmth, a shuddering in the skin of my back and neck. My pen is still rippling, running, writing the stream of my life. The flow of it feels surprisingly swift, I guess it's the pace of the present tense of 1967, when a popular song says: *"Slow down, you move too fast, / Got to make the morning last,"* which no doubt was meant as an invitation to leave the "rat race" and stop being "uptight," but it's also a sign that the pulse of life is accelerating, in fact the whole world's speeding up, and there are moments in the daily image-bath in front of the TV when the thought, the fear, the awful probability floods the mind: that the carnage is rising, that we may already be drowning in it, despite the dryness of words we ourselves use to comfort our skins, "escalation," for instance, as if there were degrees of proportionate and allowable murder. And there is the war of the desperate on the home front, riots in the black ghettos, and that newsworthy battle cry "Burn baby burn," which finds warm support among those idealists who say, with a smile, "You can't cook an omelet without breaking eggs." Nor does the jargon that pits "doves" against "hawks" make peace a likely prospect for those who have no stake in any war. Martin Luther King and Robert Kennedy are killed in short order, the first death producing the deeper shock of dismay, the second, for me, a less poignant irruption. But a disturbing sign coincides with that news, a message from the hawk in man: In the park, at the mouth of a tunnel, I find a wounded pigeon, shot with an air-gun pellet. It dies overnight in the shoe-box I carried it home in. Dark forces are in ascent, the I Ching confirms it, so does a glance at Richard Nixon's resentful scowl on the election posters, so do the Luciferian antics of the Left. George North told me about a demonstration in Washington where people chanted: *"We all live in a concentration camp"* to the tune of *"We all live in a yellow submarine,"* as if asking to be put behind barbed wire. Who says America won't close her borders and punish her disobedient children? There is more unemployed hate in this country than anyone cares to imagine. Watch out! Or better: Get out, fast! Like a godsend news comes through the mail: I will inherit $12,000 from the estate of my father's mother as soon as the money is released from a mysterious condition described by the bankers in Chattanooga, Tennessee, as "not yet liquid." What to do with this bounty? Invest it? Too safe, too careful, I can't live that way. Buy a house in the country? Not safe enough, I'm on the FBI list. Emigrate? Yes. The only question is where. Susan's willing to leave, but wants clear travel plans, a predictable route, a known destination. I'm inclined to let chance determine the place. There'll be a sign. Some dreams provide hints: mountains, a lake . . . not specific enough. I try pointing at random in an atlas: My finger lands in Rumania, not the haven I'm looking for. Then the sign comes. Someone in the office got a pretty postcard and passes it around: An old woman in black carrying a basket, a goat nibbling grass by a blue door deep-set in a low white house, in the background a turquoise sea and blue sky, the whole scene drenched in sunlight. Where is this? I look at the back of the card: Ibiza (never heard of it), and inadvertently glance at the handwritten message: ". . . it's Paradise!" That decides it: We're going to Ibiza. Now Susan objects: "What about Gina?" (That's our baby's name.) "And what'll we do when the money runs out?" I offer a compromise: If Nixon loses, we stay, if he wins, we leave. "That's crazy," she says, "Nixon's not a Nazi." But I feel danger in my bones. Something terrible is about to happen. I don't know what it is. Maybe it's just the stories about exile and flight I grew up with. On November 5, Nixon becomes President. He has usurped our V-finger peace sign and brandishes it with both hands, it means double victory now. And at the same time, a quarter of my inheritance liquefies, three thousand dollars, a windfall. Susan relents. She could use a vacation. It could even be an adventure, not a dangerous one if we stick to Europe. And maybe we'll settle somewhere, who knows? And find other people who feel as we do. Found a commune. With a free school for the children, more or less along Tolstoyan lines. Why not? We're packing our bags. How quickly time passes. Was the river really this fast already, when we were still young? Yes. I can still hear remarks, from myself and others, that a month is not what it used to be, and one of us, Maxwell Schneider, only half-humorously speculating that the CIA might be using a time-conversion machine for their private benefit and at the hip population's expense. I remember the date on which those words were spoken, November 28, 1968, Susan, Gina, and I had just boarded the *Goran Kovacic,* a Yugoslavian freighter laden with machine parts and North American freaks (as We have started to call ourselves), and Schneider was one of two men competing for dominance in our little society, the other pretender being a tall blue-eyed fellow with leonine locks named John McGregor, whose vanity, personal magnetism, physical bearing, patronizing friendliness, and romantic self-love fit him for kingship as naturally as a round peg dropped into a round hole. Schneider, complexly angled and deeply cracked, had to settle for a tributary part combining the functions of minister and fool. There he sits, three hours after we've left New York harbor, magnificently bearded but dwarfishly slouched in his chair, clutching the edge of the table like a child, peering with dark, solemn eyes at his fellow freaks, most of whom haven't yet made each other's acquaintance: "At midnight," he says, "we will take off our masks." John McGregor, broad-chested and suave at the head of the table, proposes a toast "to friendship," and all of us raise our glasses. "To love," he adds, "and to the health of the sea," and he says that with such orotundity that even the "straight" passengers at their separate tables—two young blond Swiss and a middle-aged couple from Wyoming on one side and an enormous gray-suited man on the other ("the biggest lawyer in Yugoslavia," according to our waiter)— turn their heads and mechanically reach for their wine glasses: such is the power of command in one ordained by nature to wield it. But there is a law of compensation: Next to Schneider sits a Moroccan woman who introduces herself as Záhara, pronouncing the name with an air of breathy enticement. She plays the part of the fading beauty with amused melancholy, much as Schneider burlesques his own flawed will-to-power, they stir laughter and lust in each other, and John McGregor visibly regrets the seating arrangements. Golden-haired Gina, meanwhile, enthroned on her highchair at the opposite end of the table from John's, a queen without peer or rival and hence without envy, wields her spoon like a food-flinging scepter and issues bright little commands: "Ahpoo *doose*! *Tay*-toes!" Susan and I attend her on either side. Gina's crib takes up most of our tiny cabin, and what with the need to open closet doors and search through suitcases and change Gina's diapers and squeeze past the crib to get to the washstand and climb up and down the ladder leading to the topmost of our two berths, balancing, all the while, against sudden heaves and shoves from the sea, Susan and I find ourselves snapping at each other like rats in a cage, until Gina explodes into ear-splitting demands for "Twinkies!", of all unavailable treats. Here is the test of Sartre's dictum about hell being "other people." He is wrong. Where three egos face off in a room without exit, the way out is through simple choiceless attention, which, as J. Krishnamurti says in a passage I've marked with a star in his book, "is nothing other than love itself." Reconciled, we drift off in our separate beds. Faintly, then, through the humming reverberation of metal walls, a radio bids us good night with the Star-Spangled Banner. Lying on my back, thinking of friends left behind, of my brother trying to heal himself with the "Zen Macrobiotic Diet," of Alma chanting "Na-myo-ho-ren-ge-kyo" for his salvation, of her potted flowers flourishing as he gets worse, of all of us groping like tendrils in the dark, rootless plants in a ruined garden, I suddenly notice that someone is in my bunk with me, not by my side, there isn't enough room for that, but above me, hovering in the air, a man, bald, his ageless leathery face just a hand's breadth from my face, grinning. Through my skin, from my head to my toes, I feel a malignant will oozing into me. I can't move. I can't scream. Some guarding mercy dispels the nightmare and gradually soothes me back to sleep.[1]

By morning, the sea has calmed. Over chessboards in the smoking room and leaning over the railing, lounging on deck chairs, but especially during the fourfold ritual of breakfast, lunch, tea, and dinner, the passengers, hip and straight, take cognizance of one another. Hip and straight may no longer be a reliable distinction. That young Swiss couple, Willy and Gretel, look like figures from *House and Garden,* but passing their cabin door we smell the fumes of hashish. Over shuffleboard, we meet Lester & Jill, newlyweds on their honeymoon voyage, looking straight as flagpoles but equipped with a stash of first-rate Mexican weed, which they share with us in their cabin: Lester of delicate build and tender disposition (I remember his intervention when I scolded Gina once: "Oh no, don't, please don't make her cry, she doesn't mean any harm and she's so happy!"), Jill at once virginal and motherly, and unabashedly in love with love. She says there is no time in history that moves her more than the age of chivalry, and that sometimes she thinks she must have once been a lady in a tower and Lester a serenading minstrel. He demurs, in gentle self-deprecation: "More likely one of those guys with a fool's cap and bells." Not really, I think, that's Schneider's job, but I dub them "Jester and Lil" anyway, and real-

---

1. For weeks I've been dragging my heels against the swift pace of this telling. I've invented obstacles, escaped into reading, television, sleep, food, quarrels; even convinced myself I had approached my story wrongly and must begin it anew; anything to prevent me from sliding toward the disaster that is the source and the goal of this book. Like a pig led to slaughter. Now I am ready to take the next step, appeased and comforted, I don't know by whom. Maybe the butcher. Do I have a choice?

ize only then how well the name "Lil" suits her very pale and pure skin, and
how the fleur-de-lys pattern on her dress confirms it.[2]

I suspect some pupil-widening substance at work behind the dark shades of
Calhoun, a taciturn Texan with a ring in one ear. Having heard him say he grew
up in Ibiza, I naturally want to know what that was like. Calhoun prepares his
answer for at least two minutes while his fingers tease swirls of flamenco from
a guitar.

"We used to dive for octopus," he says. That is all I learn about paradise
island.

In the lounge we meet eighteen-year-old Mark, who is reading a book of
prayers by Paramahansa Yogananda and, wonder of wonders, actually loves his
parents and is loved by them, and whose face—for no reason, for joy—has a
way of bursting into a smile when you least expect it, and who seems to actually want you to be happy. I will always think of Mark Johnson's smile when I
want to remember the love you could see shining in the faces of strangers in
those days.

But the one I spend most of my time with, aside from Susan and Gina, is
John McGregor. Some large emotion is struggling loose from old bonds that
still hold it fast. He is so happy, he says, happy to be alive. Just a few years ago
he was on one of those bleeding-heart Christian trips, feeling guilty of everything, scarcely able to speak his mind, until he ate a package of morning-glory
seeds and saw—did not visualize, imagine, think about, but simply saw—a
potato-field in full bloom: "Oh what a miracle!" One morning on the ship, John
makes another discovery: "I've found him," he says, eyes ablaze. "Who?" "The
man, the man I've been looking for!" The man's name is Vessel, he is a Beatles
fan and he hates Yugoslavia. John found him in the hold of the ship, a spiritual
stowaway, though a member of the crew. "You know what he said to me?" "What
did he say?" "He said most men talk from the heart into the head and then from
the head through the mouth, but that I talk straight from the heart." That night
King John convenes a great party in Vessel's cabin. A storm is rising, the passengers are forbidden to go out on deck. Susan elects to stay in our cabin with
Gina. Calhoun plays the guitar, John and Vessel sing Beatles songs, Vessel drinks
brandy and refuses the joints that are passed around. He doesn't smile, he sings
with a scowl on his face. What did John find in him, and above all, how did he

---

2. A few years later, in the early seventies, Lester showed up unannounced at my house in Brooklyn,
with long matted hair and a long beard, in a dhoti, with mala beads around his neck and tinkling
bells attached to his ankles. He had become a yogi and was on his way to India. Jill had left him for
another man.

find it? I will never know, for the scowl is permanent and John on his pinnacle needs someone to look down on, and that someone is me. Turning his head to gaze into my eyes, he serenades me, accompanied only by Vessel's clapping hands (Calhoun has left), while I listen, riveted, with a mixture of hurt, puzzlement, and fascination, to the complete lyrics of "I'm Looking Through You," all the way to the last line: *"And you're nowhere!"* Thus consigned to limbo, I stagger, dazed, to our cabin (the ship is being tossed like a cork), and finding Susan and Gina asleep, I stumble on to the lounge, where Calhoun and Schneider sit slumped before a bottle of pear liqueur. Never have I felt more grateful for undemanding human company, or for the amnesic properties of alcohol. It is night, and completely black outside, except for an occasional dash of spray in the portholes; no stars, no moon. We don't talk, we just listen to the howling and crashing outside and the sound of an unfastened piece of furniture sliding and banging in an adjoining cabin. Calhoun has his shades on, as usual. I feel his desperation, and Schneider's, and mine, and Susan's, and I know that Gina can sense our desperation and feels a mute unease, and wish to God I could do something about it. And now Calhoun stands up, takes off his shades and puts them in his pocket and announces that he is going outside, and, simultaneously, Schneider says "You're nuts" and I say "I'll join you." Seconds after the door slams shut behind us we are drenched to the skin. Calhoun staggers along ahead of me, gripping ropes that have been fastened to the outer walls for occasions like this. Huge sheets of water rushing across the deck. Onward, forward. We leave the sheltering wall and receive the full force of the storm, which is tugging and pushing at us with a fury that feels not at all mechanical but conscious, deliberate, full of snarling malevolence. Now it is a question of gauging the time it takes between one precarious tilt and the next, and leaping from one vantage to another during the interval, then hanging on with our hearts in our mouths while gravity, wind, and waves do their utmost to tear us loose. Yet I feel a tremendous confidence, and find myself laughing with uproarious glee (inaudibly of course) at the somnambulous ease with which my limbs and various objects—crates, bars, ropes that emerge from the void at the precise moment when they are needed—shake hands, as it were, as perfectly fitted to one another as an ape and the branches he swings from. Once we reach the bow, we sit down, letting our feet dangle over the edge and gripping the bars of the railing and opening our mouths wide to let the wind roar into us, and shouting at one another:

". . . . . !"

"What?"

"It's a movie!"

". . . . . !"

"What?"

"Douglas Fairbanks!"—which is instantly confirmed by an abysmal plunge and a long, long moment of chilling submersion in a murderously violent rush of water. When we rise again and find one another still present, we agree without words that we'd better go back inside. On the way Calhoun decides to climb to the crow's nest at the top of the mast, and this time it is I who declare that he's nuts. I leave him, fight my way back alone, and gasp in wethappy relief when the door bangs shut behind me. Standing before me in the corridor is Vessel, drunk, together with a shipmate of his. He stares at me. "You are completely crazy," he says, and translates the verdict to his friend by means of a corkscrew motion near his temple. I walk on, laughing, and keep laughing to myself, because despair and self-pity are gone, washed away as clean as if they had been dust on my skin.

Washed away, too, is the Strait of Gibraltar, along with the thrill we must have felt at its sight, and three days and nights that are blank in my journal as well, except for one eerie moment, a downward- and backward-sucking slide beneath the gathering swell of the next wave: a picture lights up in the mind as I hold a lungful of marijuana smoke in our cabin, it's a cup or a chalice I see, golden yellow, the color of the heraldic lion I saw when I smoked my first joint: "The grail," I think, which immediately brings to mind Parsifal's clarion call— "der Gral!"—as an ironic echo, but the ache in my chest is not ironic, it feels like a wound, a heart-wound, a sweet yawning pain. Where have I felt this before? Trying to remember, I slide back, back to my seventh year when I would imagine myself a captive bound to a stake, with the eyes of my enemies feeding on my nakedness, mortified and exalted, a little St. Sebastian pierced by this same mysteriously pleasant unhappiness. What is this joy in suffering, and how does a child come upon it in the midst of a soft, coddled life, and what perverse genius guides him to lick out degrees and variations of it, secretly, with sybaritic abandon? Every question is a hook, but this one sinks like an anchor, down, down to God knows what dark awful place. No! I don't want to know it, and I'm not fishing for sea-monsters either, I'll cut off the question and pray that it never comes back. I go out on deck, glad to feel the solid planks beneath my feet, stand with the wind in my ears in the glow of the moon, and suddenly see the silhouette of Maxwell Schneider in the stern of the ship. His back is turned to me. He's staring out at the fiery afterglow of the sun. He raises both hands. "Odin!" he calls. And again, more loudly: "OOOODIN!" If he's clowning, it's for no audience at all. Who are we? Where are we going? What are we doing? Speeding along on rippling waves painted by an unseen brush.

Arrived in Tangiers, we lodge in a boardinghouse run by a skinny old Frenchman with a face ravaged by every mortal and venial sin in the book. At night, in our dark room, I hear him chastising his poodle. *"Punir,"* he says, and repeats the word several times quietly but with such malice it seems he is trying to instill in the dog the fear of eternal damnation. Every few minutes, after an interval of petrified silence, another drop of soul-shriveling condemnation: *"Punir."* I am fascinated. He does not hit the animal or even raise his voice. His passion is cold, and the punishment consists of fear.

The next day we walk through the town. Dozens of hawkers descend on us, selling pipes, broken radios, Swiss watches, jewelry, blouses, French, Spanish, and English paperbacks, and, again and again, hashish. "This is a bargaining culture," Záhara told us, "never just buy at the price you're offered, that would be insulting." But we can't bring ourselves to bargain down a ragged old man from the pittance he is charging for an embroidered scarf: We accept his price, he looks disappointed. Some ancestral strain in Maxwell Schneider, meanwhile, awakens to the bargaining culture as to a long-lost home, he's trading a pair of suspenders, an old suit, ballpoint pens, etc., for a woolen blanket, an embroidered cap, a good pair of sandals, and what's more, within hours he's the most popular foreigner around, invited for tea in the Kasbah and a private smoke in a new friend's house.

Calhoun, who survived the storm, has gone on to Marrakesh with Záhara and John McGregor. Lester and Jill have run afoul of the immigration authorities. Lester is South African, and in this part of the world his passport has the effect of a leper's bell, he must remove his loathsome self to a more welcoming place—say, fascist Spain—within 24 hours. Together the five of us (Gina in her stroller) tour the city. It is Ramadan, from everywhere we hear the electronic muezzins calling, swarms of screaming, laughing children tug at our clothes, proffering useless trinkets, holding out cupped hands. The coins and candy we hand out increase the flock rapidly. Our only recourse is a remedy Záhara taught us, a single word, sharply uttered, *"Billik"*: Never mind what it means, she said, it'll work like a charm. It works rather more like a curse, leaving us guilty and, for a while, unmolested. We eat couscous in a small restaurant. A pale young man in a gray-striped djellaba comes in from the street and with a slight bow and a pleasant smile says: "Welcome to Morocco." His name is Hassan, and he is a student who likes Americans and also likes to practice his English. He smiles at Gina, she recoils. The restaurateur doesn't trust him either. *"Billik!"* he says. Hassan looks unperturbed. "Would you like good hashish?" Of course I would like good hashish. "Lester, would you like good hashish?" "Certainly," he says, and together we follow Hassan through the swarming, narrow streets of the Kasbah, leaving our wives and Gina in the restaurant. Hassan has lost all interest in the English language. Despite his youth, he appears to command respect, even a hint of deference, among several older men we pass. *"Salaam aleikum." "Salaam aleikum."* He leads us into a perfumed house with a large inner courtyard, a fountain in the center, twittering birds in cages alongside the walls, three galleries with columned arches, tiers of rooms without front walls, like the rooms of a doll's house. As we follow him up a flight of stone steps, I see that in each room several men sit around a hookah. Some of them are talking, most of them are dreaming. The floors are carpeted, so are the walls. Hassan leads us to a room of our own. "Please," he says, smiling, pointing to a couch. "Sit." But the cushions are so soft it's more like lying down. Hassan puts a small black lump in the bowl of the hookah, lights it, hands me the pipe. I take a deep drag, hold the smoke, and am obliterated. As I come back to the world, I remember that for one astonishing moment I was in some kind of heaven. Lester takes the pipe from my hand, inhales, exhales, inhales again, and offers me another toke. I'm incapable of moving. "Do you like?" Hassan asks, a look of ironic appraisal on his face. I cannot answer. Turning my eyes, I see Lester's face. He is smiling. "Good shit," he says. These words cannot possibly refer to what I just experienced. Never have I felt such happiness. "How much?" I finally ask. "Ten dollars," Hassan says, holding up a brick of hashish the size of a medium-sized paperback. I reach for my wallet. Ten dollars for a year's supply of paradise! To my amazement, Lester is not tempted. He can't risk getting caught with it at the Spanish border, he says.

Ten days later, in Seville, I meet a wandering freak, a connoisseur of every mind-bending drug I have heard of, whose expert judgment persuades me that (a) the bliss that befell me in Tangiers was a minor blast of nirvana, released by a blackout (it happens, he says) or triggered by some wayward neuron but definitely not the effect of any sort of hashish or opium or whatever substance Hassan had ignited in the bowl of the hookah, and that (b) I had bought for ten dollars and smuggled across the Spanish border at considerable risk to my freedom a densely packed brick of dried cow-shit laced with exotic condiments, notably curry. The freak is way ahead of us, his hair is longer, he smokes hash through a bong, he's leaving Spain. Ibiza, he says, is all right, nice beaches and all and the locals are cool, and there's an island called Formenterra which you can reach from Ibiza by ferry, some four hundred people live there, beautiful people, man, they have almost nothing but they'll give their right hand for you if you're their friend. But it's all over now, the straights are coming in droves, man, mainly to Mallorca but they're starting to trickle into Ibiza and even to Formenterra, businessmen and their wives and poodles and speedboats. The Guardia Civil are arresting freaks already, man, for looking weird, for having no money, for sleeping on the beach, for nothing. As he speaks, I feel myself getting ill, whether from smoking cow-dung and curry or from anxiety over our uncertain future I can't say, but what's clear is that I won't make it to the toilet, Susan rushes to my aid with a bowl, Gina, seeing a jet of vomit gushing from her daddy's mouth, bursts into wails of grief, and remains inconsolable even after the mess is cleaned up and I've washed and we have explained to her that I'm not hurt, still the same old daddy—Look! I suddenly say, swinging around to point out the open window. The maneuver works, she is silenced by wonder, but to my astonishment I myself see for the first time the glory of the orange trees outside our hotel, and am amazed at how blind I am most of the time, tapping through shadows, taking my bearings from memories of the earth.

The freak starts packing: Gotta move on, man. Where is he heading, I want to know. He savors his secret, holds it like a lungful of ganja. At long last he exhales it: "The Seychelles, man. Pass it on to the righteous only: the Seychelles Islands." For a farewell gift he leaves me three tabs of Acid—which I don't remember swallowing, though I'm sure I did, for it seems they turned four or five weeks of memory into a desert. A few isolate images stand at wide intervals like rocks in raked sand: the spires of Gaudi's cathedral, spectral evidence that we were in Barcelona; a navy man boarding our train and putting his hat on his lap, upside down, revealing two pictures he carries pressed against his cranium all day (held in place by a patch of clear plastic), a Virgin Mary and a busty pinup girl; a glimpse from a taxi, minutes after disembarking in Ibiza, of a tall young man, bearded, with shoulder-length flowing brown hair, dressed in a long Afghan sheepskin coat, standing erect as we pass, following me with his eyes, smiling, as if to say: This is the place, brother, rest content and sin no more. Looking out of an uncurtained window in a cold room, it's Christmas, Susan and Gina are asleep, some revelers below me shouting a bawdy song about St. Joseph the cuckold asleep in his bed, the Angel of the Lord absconded, the Blessed Virgin in bliss on a bloody sheet. New Year's Eve, again in front of a window, we've moved to a *pensión* on a hill above the old city, this time Susan's next to me, pale and luminous in a black sweater, or is it the gas-lamp that's making her shine, we're clinking glasses, atoning after a sad quarrel in which she bitterly regretted following me on this wild goose chase, we stand and watch a single star pulsing over the black Mediterranean. More lights appear, I'm alone, sitting on a rock by the roadside at dusk, writing in an enormous ledger, the lights are the lamps of cars and bicycles belonging to workmen on their way home from a day's work building hotels. *"The headlights are yellow,"* I write, and as I copy those words in my Brooklyn apartment, I glimpse, in the stream of thoughts recorded in blue ink three decades ago, a dark undertow and the flick of a tail in the depths. *"The headlights are yellow,"* I wrote, *"which subdues the glare enough to enable one to look into it without blinking—like golden explosions, giving a velvety density to the surrounding darkness. The lamps of the bicycles vary in color from a pale red or blue to yellow and a bright white, and these round globes of light approach, dancing toward me, separating and coming together again, until the forms of the bicycles and men take shape and pass by. 'Hola' one of them says. 'Hola!' I answer. How good it feels to just write down what is, to match words to the presence of things, on the first page of this wonderfully ponderous notebook."*

Turning that page (here in Brooklyn) I see pasted in the margin the indignant face of Scrooge McDuck and in the speech bubble above him the following words: *"Hum! Solamente existe un yo!"* [3]

On the opposite page, the record of a visit to the beach with Gina. She plays with a little Spanish boy her age, together they fill her pail with sand, and then with mud. A little later the boy's grandmother slaps him for getting his clothes dirty, and Gina puts her hand to her cheek and looks at me, crying, as if I could do something about the injustice and cruelty of life. It is, to my knowledge, her first experience of violence. But what I do to her then is worse than the slap: I *explain* it.

---

3. "Hmph! There is only one I!"

Es Vive

We are living in Es Vive now, a scattering of two-story houses near the east coast of Ibiza, and we're no longer alone. Below us live MacDougal, an American ex-convict; Helle, his pregnant Danish wife; Baxter, their unwanted half-year-old son; Milton, an enigmatic wraithlike man from San Francisco; Basil, a Canadian sculptor and snob with the hands of a strangler; and the house next to ours is occupied by an ebullient rabbinical student named Steve Levinson, his seventeen-year-old gum-chewing sister Anne, their twelve-year-old brother Aaron, and a many-headed flock of friends and parasites whom Steve refers to as "hips," since no self-respecting hippie would call himself that. Half the island's foreign community comes to partake of Steve's daily macrobiotic dinner parties, for which he does the shopping and cooking and which he initiates with grandiosely delivered and always new and original prayers—my favorite, or at any rate the only one I've retained, being "Thanks a lot for all this good food!"— feasts which sometimes culminate in philosophical symposia over wine and dessert. "So what *is* the purpose of life?" asks young Aaron one day, and big brother Steve responds with booming voice and commandingly pointing finger: "The purpose of life is that *you* be happy!" Basil calls Steve "the lord of hosts," he disapproves of the rabble that's fumigating our courtyard with Moroccan hash, blasting the stillness of dawn with Jefferson Airplane and Cream and Pink Floyd and Beatles and Rolling Stones, sunning themselves too visibly on the roof, where a parapet blocks the cold wind from the bay. "There's just too damn many of them," Basil says, kneading the air with his bony fingers. Among the horizontal many, plumb in the midst of all that indolent flesh, there is one who stands serenely vertical, palms placed together in front of his chest, eyes closed, smiling, Christ-like with his long hair and beard and robelike length of Afghan coat. He looks the way I want to be. I have seen him before, he's the fellow we passed in the taxi right after we got off the boat. His name is John Sebastiani. He is a Yogi. He stands on his head, contorts his limbs, holds his breath, sits like a Buddha, smiling, on the roof, in the yard, on the beach, anywhere. He has foresworn money and is traveling around the world with

God's grace for a compass and the love in his heart for a passe-partout. He just recently came back from Afghanistan, where he received his coat as a gift and contracted jaundice. He teaches me Yoga. The word means "yoke," he says, not "yolk," which is what I thought he said—snug containment in the world egg, waiting to be hatched—but yoke, meaning harness, submission, and servitude, body and ego yoked to the Higher Self that is God's emissary to the material realm, and the way he says that, mildly and from the eminence of established practice and devotion, the words convey an infinite challenge and more, an injunction: Every moment brings the choice, he says, between aspiration and decline, the calling of the Higher Self and ego's petty, self-seeking inclination.

When the lord of hosts flies home with his brother and sister to Philadelphia, the faithful, like bees bereft of their Queen, go swarming about the island, some of them finding cheap lodging in fishermen's *fincas,* others, less solvent or more romantic, settling into some caves cut into the cliff on the south side of the island—an infestation, as far as the Guardia Civil are concerned. They round up the cave-dwellers, confiscate their passports, rescind the residence permits of all who don't have a hefty wad of pesetas tucked away in their embroidered jeans. Only John Sebastiani escapes the raid: In the nick of time his Higher Self tells him to abandon his cave and shoulder his knapsack and walk the five miles to our house in Es Vive and knock and ask us if he may sleep under our roof. Of course he may. In exchange he introduces Susan to macrobiotic cooking, plays with Gina, and teaches me refinements of Yoga which I am neither prepared to receive nor in a position to refuse, for he lives with us day and night and evinces at all times a discipline and maturity that make me unpleasantly aware of my own deficiencies. He is not at the mercy of moods and emotions, doesn't slouch, controls his appetite, speaks only when he has something to say, does not permit himself even a hint of collusion with people whose habits conflict with his aspirations. Everything about him makes me feel unfinished. If I didn't admire him, wasn't touched by his kindness, if I didn't in fact like him, he would be unbearable.

Gina, who has not yet developed a higher or a lower self, adores him. Every day he walks with her wherever she wants to go—to the beach, to the anthill behind the house, half a mile up the road in search of goats (she greets them in Spanish: "Hola, goats!")—but what am I saying, "walk," she halts every few steps to show him some remarkable thing—a pebble, a flower—which he contemplates until he, too, recognizes the wonder of it. He asks her indulgence for the slowness of his perceptions. Grownups, he says, take a long time to see things right.

Pepita, the landlady, gives John and me an up-and-down glance and a twitch of an eyebrow as she speaks with disgust of the dirt left behind by *"los porcos"* who moved out next door. She is lying: The Levinsons swept and washed the place daily. Her next tenants, she says, will be of a better quality. Then she smiles at Susan, who wants only to know when our thermostat will be fixed. *"Mañana,"* Pepita says, in a tone of sincerity which, I notice, has deepened with repetition. Then she pinches Gina's cheek, hurting her and exclaiming *"que guapa,"* how beautiful she is.

Alone at night in a room I've set up for myself and my books, I smoke some dope and let my pen ripple across the page. The next day, I'm surprised by what I've written:

> Pause and consider
> how far you have strayed
> in your garden of pleasures
> fulfilled and delayed.
>
> The serpent whispers
> of sorrow and hate.
> Eat again of the fruit
> before it's too late.
>
> To some it is bitter,
> to others, sweet.
> Disdain the savour
> but swallow the meat.
>
> The circle closes.
> Day begins.
> The victor loses.
> The vanquished wins.

What are these riddles? Should I take this seriously? Who is speaking? And to whom? What is the fruit? The day? Who is the victor and who is the vanquished? And why do I feel this peculiar excitement, this mixture of dread and expectancy?

Word of our hospitality must have reached the two strangers who knock on our door and introduce themselves as members of the Living Theatre, whose "Paradise Now!" show has been proposing to audiences all over Europe, and occasionally persuading them, that clothes are the white man's burden. The two are off on a jaunt of their own, looking for ways to bring the spirit of anarchy back to Spain. They have thought of one promising antidote to the psychic damage inflicted by thirty years of clerical fascism: Add several hundred thousand micrograms of LSD to the water supply of Barcelona, for starters at least, as an initial shock therapy; but that would take more capital than they have at their disposal. They have, in fact, no money at all: They have foresworn it. "So has he," I say, pointing at John. He sits very tall, with a gentle smile and a calm, steady gaze, shining. Nonplussed for a moment, the anarchists resume their patter of introduction, which issues in a request: Could they sleep on our floor for a few nights? Of course they may. Could they have some hash, too, not for themselves but so they can turn the locals on? I feel bourgeois and stingy for saying no, but I don't want to be implicated in a drug bust. How about some pesetas or dollars? they ask. Their shamelessness is almost disarming. Not for themselves, they add, but as a donation toward a piece of political theatre they plan to stage: a public burning of paper money. The working title is "Auto-da-fe." They've already collected a bundle: It's amazing how glad people are to give toward a good cause.

"Doesn't 'auto-da-fe' mean 'act of the faith'?" John asks with an uncharacteristic look of puzzlement.

"Yes, it does," says the older of the two, a firm-jawed Frenchman with dense black hair.

"And didn't it also used to refer to the burning of heretics?" I ask.

"Yes, it did," says the younger man, an American whose left eye keeps wandering sideways, as if distracted.

"Isn't burning money like burning food?" Susan asks. "I mean, people need it."

"They *think* they need it," says the Frenchman, "and because they think so, they do."

That night I hide our spare cash in a sock.

The discussion of the money-burning project continues the next day in the courtyard, where Susan and John and I have convened with the visitors and our downstairs neighbors to smoke dope and sculpt with some clay Basil dug up near the beach in Figueretes, while the children play in the sand.

MacDougal, who has been in jail for grand larceny, is deeply offended: "Money isn't just symbolic," he says. "If it was, you guys wouldn't have to beg for it."

Basil, who is forming some abstract tubular thing, says: "Money is an index of labor."

John, who has not spoken all day and appears to be molding a vessel, says:

"Labor is energy. Energy is holy." After a while he adds: "Therefore money is holy." That surprises everyone.

"Then why do you choose to live without it?" Basil asks.

"To put myself at the mercy of those who have it," John says.

Mysterious Milton, who is sculpting a head with wings, says to the newcomers: "I think you guys should go all the way. Throw everything you have into the fire."

"Including your shoes," says Helle while forcing a pacifier between her whining son's clenched teeth.

All the while I have been sculpting what looks like a piece of natural rock, with fissures, caverns, crevices, caves.

"What are you trying to do," Basil asks when he sees my product, "revert to chaos?"

"Yes," I say, "I want culture and nature to be indistinguishable. That's my program." I intended that to be facetious, but as I pronounce the words, they sound pompous, and then I realize they are true.

"That would be the end of the world," Milton says, putting his winged head next to my rock.

The anarchist with the wandering eye destroys his creation, whatever it was; the other, the Frenchman, leaves his—a realistically rendered phallus—behind on the patio, where it hardens in the sun after the two have moved on to Barcelona to expand their collection for the Auto-da-fe. Pepita's new tenants, a fat, bald, middle-aged man and a pretty blond woman, stop to smile at the thing as they return from the beach. Both of them have wet seaweed wrapped around their necks. He is carrying a plastic pail with one hand—filled with water, it seems—and a transistor radio with the other. The radio is tuned to the French news. Her hands are full too: She's carrying pieces of driftwood and the rusty handlebars of a bicycle. Every day they come home like this, balancing the pail and laden with detritus, unaware that the hippies next door are weaving the most extravagant speculations around them.

Basil, who normally takes a misanthropic view of people he doesn't know, imagines them in the most brilliant light he is capable of projecting: The chick is some kind of artist, that's clear, most likely a sculptor; and the guy must be someone like André Michaux, one of those poet-adventurers who took hundreds of mescaline trips before any of us were born.

MacDougal thinks it more likely the man is a fugitive from the law and is humoring his eccentric girlfriend, who hangs out with him for the money and has a thing about seaweed.

Helle thinks they're an incestuous couple, a father and his daughter.

Milton thinks the man is a double or triple Taurus and the girl an Aquarius—not a favorable combination.

I think they're an avant-garde version of Sunday painters.

Susan thinks they're innocent tourists with a passion for beachcombing.

Gina, the only realist among us, calls them "the blue man and the yellow lady," in reference to his shirt and her hair, and is promptly invited into their house, comes back with a piece of cake, and reports that "they talk funny."

"How do they talk, Gina? Show us."

"Raw, saw, faw, tue."

That evening our new neighbors knock on our door: Blaise and Juliette are their names. They've come with a gift of several wet, black, globular, spiny things that appear to be alive, *"oursins,"* a great *délicatesse,* very expensive in Paris—assurances that fail to convert our squeamish American palates. But a glance at the dictionary clears up the mystery of the pail: *oursins* are sea urchins. The major arcanum is revealed the next day: Juliette is an artist who smokes dope, and Blaise is a communist who prefers wine. But what is a communist? Not even I, who grew up among Marxists, am prepared for this object lesson. He owns a car, and because others don't, they may use it. If you have no license, he finds you a driver or carts you around the island himself. Maxwell Schneider arrives from Morocco hidden behind dark red shades and a jungle of hair; Blaise finds him a house in the hills and drives by every other day to bring him groceries and make sure he's all right, for he's given signs of being anxious. More freaks arrive, from England, Australia, Holland, the U.S., and head straight from the harbor to Blaise and Juliette's—but it's Blaise they talk to; word has gotten around, he's the new lord of hosts. Pepita has stopped speaking Spanish, she spits her wrath in Ibizenco. We can forget about the thermostat now. Blaise's guests will sleep on her floor, her armchairs and couch, until he has found them a place. Some of them are fantastically garbed; I distinctly remember a sky-blue turban, striped bell-bottom pants, and a flowered vest on one tall, shirtless man from Vancouver. Juliette looks on with amusement, murmurs mild sarcasms in all directions. She is a Virgo, not an Aquarius. Milton's beginning to despair of astrology, because Virgos are supposed to be neat and Juliette is sloppy. But her critical acumen fits the sign well. Seeing me on the roof, where I like to sit with my ledger, she says, shielding her eyes: *"Siempre buscas las alturas!"* I always seek the heights. I guess it shows. I am ambitious, and worse, afraid of being ordinary. I must achieve one of three things before our money runs out: write a great book, attain spiritual enlightenment, or, barring transcendent personal achievement, form a commune—otherwise it's back to the world and forty years of office work. I would rather die. But I also would rather not have anyone know it, and Juliette sees through me.

Ah, and she sees something else. I see it myself by reflection in the mockery of her eyes. Susan, who has been grumbling, on and off, about the foolishness of this flight of ours—about the hardship we are imposing on Gina, who has no children her own age to play with, and about her own loneliness and homesickness—is all of a sudden strangely content. She stops on the road as we walk home from the market together and looks out over the fields to the sunlit bay with its two fishing boats and high wheeling gulls. She has walked this stretch dozens of times and never felt herself included in the landscape. Now she is smiling with pleasure. How lovely she looks, her stance firm and yet buoyant, as if raised by some calm inner joy, a basket pressed against her hip, placid and happy in her blue skirt and red blouse, a breeze playing in her hair, tall, smiling. Where have I seen this angelic smile? In John. There they are, smiling together in the kitchen, shucking peas as he murmurs about Yin and Yang in the vegetable kingdom. Their smiles linger as we sit down to eat. The usual little exchanges at the table—"would you pass the salt?" "do you want some more water?"—now carry a new meaning for which, I can see, there is no expression more true or more eloquent than this calm, intermittent blossoming of affection, this quiet, generous warmth that is kindled again and again by the smile on the other's lips. She has joined him in his peaceable kingdom.

There is nothing more humiliating for one who aspires to the heights than a base emotion like jealousy, especially when he has no grounds for complaint or suspicion—no betrayal, no deception or even a hint of concealment. I try to lose myself in reading, in writing, in the study of Milton's astrology books, but I can't concentrate. Is it pity, then, or the need for distraction that leads me to adopt a large, smiling, yellow female dog who walks into our apartment in desperate need of shelter from the pursuit of five sexually agitated males? It turns out she is, moreover, sick—a continual twitching of the hind legs—and appears to be in pain. I take her to a vet. What she has, he says, is an aftereffect of distemper, and incurable. However, he might be mistaken, in which case vitamins may relieve her symptoms. He gives her an injection in each hind leg, causing her to howl with pain, charges us 185 pesetas, and suggests we bring her back for more shots. The I Ching advises me that the vet is seeking "splendor for his own dwelling" and should not be consulted further. I am also warned against making rash decisions—"the command has not yet been given"—and assured that good fortune will come the dog's way. Several times that same night she yelps pitifully. I decide that, unless her condition improves very soon, I'll have her put to sleep. The next morning Susan learns, through a chance encounter, that the dog used to belong to the owner of Mil Flores, an apartment building, and that he abandoned her when she got sick. A group of Dutch kids living at Mil Flores took her to a vet and gave her medicine, after which she noticeably improved. But then she was in heat and ran off, and they gave her up for lost. I go to Mil Flores and find the Dutch kids, who indeed have her medicine and are overjoyed to hear "Zusje" is well. The name (which our American tongues, in a matter of hours, will condense to a single odd syllable, "Shooce") means little sister, they called her that before they really knew her, she should have been named after a Boddhisattva, because she's a saintly dog, noble and ego-less, as I shall see. My wife and I must be good people, since Zusje sought us out. When I come home, she is gone: Someone left the front gate open, despite the sign I posted there in English and Spanish. I am tearfully angry, and very much want to blame Susan or John, both of whom are as sorry as I am to see the dog gone. The next day, Susan returns from the market followed by Shooce. Gradually, thanks to the medicine, her whimpering quiets, though the shaking persists. So does the attraction she exerts on the island's male dogs. Day and night, an enormous black hound with flaming yellow eyes jams his muzzle against the crack at the base of the front door, snorting like a dragon, clawing and whining. Sometimes he howls with awfully expressive longing. It's hard to get in and out of the house. In my ledger, under the date January 31, 1969, I write:

> Difficult night, and once again, a bilious awakening, fit to make me tear
> my hair out—Gina cranky and demanding, the sick dog twitching and
> whining with discomfort, Gina continually falling on her head and
> screaming, Susie, who's as worn out as myself, leaving the door open
> (after agreeing to let me sleep), so that Gina and Shooce could take turns
> keeping me awake. Eventually I felt like breaking everything in sight.
> Most influential in this direction was our gentle boarder, John, who
> weathered our domestic storm by, literally, swaying like a solitary pine
> tree in his private island of peace, cross-legged, smiling, and, on at least
> two occasions, whistling through his teeth and very faintly shaking his
> head—with amazement, I had to assume, at my lack of self-control; and

though, or because, there were good grounds on which to judge me, I became even more irritable, and then downright furious when I realized I couldn't vent my anger on him—his offense having been so subtle as to (probably) pass unnoticed by himself. Besides, he'll be leaving in a couple of weeks.

For relief from these tensions, I gravitate toward Maxwell Schneider, who thinks John is a fraud and who, in his lonely cottage, is busy doing something I have been intending and even professing to do for months: writing a book. It consists of short bursts of improvisation which he calls "spontatas." He reads me the beginning:

A Long Letter Home From Camp Chipper

I used to think Friday was my lucky day. Then something good happened on a Monday. Thereafter I thought Monday my lucky day. But now I really believe that Wednesday is my lucky day.

I trust people with beards. The bigger the beard, the more I trust them.

People who have an objective know what clothes to wear. Others, who just want to know who they are, don't know what to wear.

One instant doesn't ensure the next instant.

I can't think of anything better than people. I can't think of anything worse either. Nevertheless, at every moment, everyone is doing the best he can for himself and the world. Awareness of that is another matter.

This I could imagine reading without distraction. Something like this I could even imagine wanting to write. This is good, Max. Keep it up!

Someone suggested today that happy and sad are dime-a-dozen emotions; it's the in-between . . . Well I say fuck the in-between, forget about sadness, and do the easy one—happiness. Yes!

If anyone passes Clark, Schneider & Schulz, 457 Park Avenue, would they please go in and ask for Steve. Steve is my brother. Would they please tell him he's wasting his time being a lawyer. He won't listen to me.

———————

Nobody could count all the money in the world. There's so much. Then how can it be of value spending one's time making money, as if there wasn't already enough. We need to make things of which there is a shortage: love, space, trees, quiet, clean air and water, happier selves and friends, peace in the world, and more people inclined to give us the full treatment in a back massage. We need to make not money but more FEELING.

———————

Wives are not property, wives are for feeling.
Husbands are not possessions, husbands are for feeling.

———————

FEEL 'EM UP   FEEL 'EM UP   FEEL 'EM UP

———————

Which brings me back to my problem. What does John have that I lack? The question drowns out Schneider's voice, gnaws at my thoughts, slinks through my dreams, makes me awkward, false, stiff, crooked in John's presence, impatient with Gina, and, on a few occasions, vindictive toward Susan on account of actual or imagined slights that have nothing to do with her real offense, which is simply that she finds pleasure in another man. What should I do? Maybe the I Ching can advise me. I toss the coins and draw Hexagram 47, "Oppression (Exhaustion)," Six in the third place:

A man permits himself to be oppressed by stone,
And leans on thorns and thistles.
He enters his house and does not see his wife.
Misfortune.

What an unhelpful omen—it throws me back on myself. Should I talk to her? But what is there to say? It's all so obvious. Besides, I'm too proud, too hurt, too afraid to reveal my suffering. And why doesn't she see it herself? But one day she caresses my face and says: "You've been looking so sad," and she says that with such pity and love that all my doubts are canceled at once and all my rancor toward John—well, not all, but most of it—is washed away in a flood of grateful tears. She is ashamed of the joy she's been feeling, and of her reluctance to see my pain. No, no, no, I say, I don't want you to lose that, just . . .

"It's not right," she says, "you and I . . ."

"And John?" I ask. "What are his feelings?"

"About me?" she asks.

"Yes."

She shrugs: "He likes me, that's all."

"Are you sure?"

She falls silent for a while as we dry each other's tears. Then she smiles. "He's not even aware of me as a woman," she says.

My vanity doesn't want to accept that. Nor does hers—she's still thinking about it. Then she laughs. "It's a fact," she says, "he doesn't have a clue."

Ten days later, John leaves Ibiza with no money in his pocket, just a boat ticket to Barcelona we've bought him. From there he intends to hitch rides to Algeciras, where he hopes to get arrested for vagrancy and deposited in Tangiers courtesy of the Guardia Civil. Here is my journal record of his departure:

> John left, twice in a row because the first time he missed the boat. No: three times, for after the second time Milton and Susan and I met him again at the beach of Figueretes. So, after the third and final round of embraces, he trudged up the goat-path to the top of the cliff. But that wasn't the final good-bye after all. Arrived at the top, he turned again and raised his hand, looking like an ancient pilgrim with his long hair and beard, the pack on his shoulders, the long Afghan coat. Milton, then Susie, and then myself raised our hands—sympathetic energy across space and time—but I felt a niggling petty nastiness inside that was glad he was leaving and impatient to see him gone. He walked off among the walls of the Old City.

Antonio Salvador

Just a few years ago, our new neighbor Blaise told us, he had been squatting in front of an oil-drilling rig in the Sahara holding a rifle, his brain shrunk to the size of a pea by the sun and the perfect thoughtlessness of his profession, which was to shoot jackals, vultures, Bedouins, any creature who strayed into his range because it couldn't read French, the language of the No Trespassing signs. (Juliette stroked his bald head at the mention of the pea; she liked to tease him.) An engineer befriended him and gave him books to read—de Maupassant, Tolstoy, Balzac, Gorky, the Communist Manifesto, and, to cure Blaise's racism, poems by Aimé Césaire—and Blaise read all these books to please his new friend. The one thing he wasn't willing to do for him was join the Communist Party. One night the friend saw Blaise threaten a fellow who owned nothing but the rags on his back. "Were you really prepared to shoot him?" "Naturally." "Why?" In the face of this question, Blaise lost his powers of speech. And his friend didn't help by filling the silence. He waited. Blaise opened his mouth, but nothing came out. It was night in the desert, that was part of his difficulty; the hugeness of space swallowed all the ready answers before they could slip into words. And then he saw it: He was stupid. He had always been stupid. He had never realized it, but now he knew it, and after some anxious sweating, he said it out loud, and it was this confession that finally filled that yawning "Why?" with meaning. All he could expect of his friend, now that the poverty of his mind had been revealed, was either a conventional denial or an embarrassed withdrawal, but instead the friend said something that changed Blaise's life: It is true, he said, you are stupid. You have never used your brain. But recognizing that you are not intelligent is the beginning of intelligence, don't you see? And Blaise saw it clearly: the nature of stupidity and the nature of intelligence. Intelligence was not cleverness, jumping around in the brain, making connections. That was monkey work on a very high level. On top of the tree of evolution we still have monkeys. Intelligence is courage, the courage to see what is in front of your nose. When you are afraid, you can't see. All the stupidity in the world comes from fear. Intelligence, courage, love, justice—they all go together. We divide them with words but they are one thing. That is what Blaise learned from his friend in that one conversation.

A short time later, the friend died of a heart attack. That is a different order of stupidity, the stupidity of accident, no one's to blame for that. But because of his respect for that man and his intelligence, Blaise became a communist and—not unrelated—an art dealer specializing in prints by Picasso, thanks to the intermediation of a relative who did odd jobs for the artist. But mainly Blaise was a communist. He studied, he listened to the great speakers. And the more he studied and listened, the more convinced he became that in the communist idea all virtue, all the possible goodness of man, was embodied, despite the tragic mistakes and the murderous aberrations. Until he realized that loving an idea is what idealists do, and that communism must be practical, otherwise it's just a dream. That we must begin to live the dream now, make it real in our lives, under the material conditions of capitalism. Otherwise how can we change anything? But when he asked his more educated friends about this, he was told: You are an *utopiste,* a *déviationiste à la gauche,* a *Marxiste infantile,* a *matérialiste vulgaire,* bad names. Then he began to suspect, and then to see, that most communists don't really want what they say they believe in. Otherwise they would live differently. And in May 1968 he saw the proof. "We had a general strike," he says, "labor and intelligence united, the government on its knees, de Gaulle fled from Paris and threatening a bloodbath, everything now depended on the Communist Party. They had power in their hands and they gave it back, very politely, to the bourgeoisie, because what they saw was hundreds of thousands of *utopistes* and *Marxistes infantiles* writing poetry on the walls and saying it's our turn now. And the workers all went back to work like good little boys and girls, and the students went back to finish their studies and pick up their diplomas. It's a puzzle to me, a big big puzzle, I don't understand it." And the way he said that, with his good-natured taurine head swaying from side to side, as if dazed, I saw why among all of Picasso's graphic works his favorites were the etchings depicting the Minotaur in the labyrinth.

This perception led me to an exciting idea (for the description of which I shall have to leave Blaise in his consternation, still shaking his head, until I come back to him later). Why not imagine a modern Perseus who sets out in search of the Minotaur? The monster, of course, would be the embodiment of the hero's secret hatreds and fears, his own brain would be the labyrinth, Ariadne's thread would be the trail of memory leading back to some ancient trauma, etc., the hero himself would be a late-twentieth-century Everyman, but at the same time his fate would saddle him with all the savage romance of archaic myth; and since I was already seeking *"las alturas,"* it didn't seem a far stretch to put aside my William Burroughs imitations and automatic writing for the hyperrational experiment of a narrative poem in the eightfold rhyme scheme employed by Byron in his Don Juan. And with a theme I could spread my wings in! I began my poem as follows:

Antonio Salvador

On Thursday, March 12, 1964
at 519 East 10th Street in Manhattan,[4]
there slept, behind a triple-bolted door
and dusty windows curtained with fake satin,
a pale young man named Tony Salvador.
Antonio, actually, since he was Latin.
Of course he couldn't care less, in his slumber
for his ethnicity and building-number.

A firm Will not to be awake withstands
even such prompting as roused Sleeping Beauty.
How much more easily, then, a steel band's
variations on a theme from "Tutti Frutti"
blared through a neighbor's radio, or, like hands
of an alarm-clock gone berserk with duty
two vagrant flies that wheeled around his head:
Antonio Salvador lay as if dead.

Within his faintly snoring skull, however,
was much commotion and discordant noise,
engendered by Antonio's staunch endeavor
to sleep, and stay asleep, and counterpoise
flies, music, and the time of day forever.
To marry sleep! No pain, no transient joys . . .
Unfortunately even sleep can't bless
a man with infinite forgetfulness.

Three angels (such at least they seemed) appeared,
all dimpled grace and delicate of limb,
but sporting each a long effluvial beard,
a rare appurtenance of cherubim.
They smiled, held hands, and sweetly volunteered
to entertain Antonio with a hymn.
I think it was the steel band and the flies
invading his sleep's fortress in disguise.

---

4. That is, on Bodo's birthday and very near the apartment I shared with George North before I was shot.

"Glory!" they sang. "He's given up the ghost
and come—praised be the Lord!—to join our chorus!
Quick, get some goblets, and propose a toast!
Servicio! Clouds! Don't dawdle, hurry and pour us
sweet manna! It's not always we can boast
of company that hasn't come to bore us,
or to perturb the air with pious strife.
Drink to the man who overslept his life!"

A burst of terror roused him like a shot
into a sitting posture on the bed.
The angels, vapor-like, dissolved, and not
a sound was in the room, or in his head.
Suspicious silence—and, on second thought . . .
horrible! "Let me wake up!" No sooner said
than done. Antonio woke to the disorder
that men call "life" on this side of the border.

Disorder not just of his room, though that
was part of it, what with the soft upheaval
of billowing dust raised by a startled rat
running across a landscape of primeval
undifferentiation—plants, a hat,
computer printout sheets for the retrieval
of market and opinion research data—
sprinkling all these good things with fecal matter.

I mean a wider circle of confusion
wherein both rat and man stand at the center,
guarding it with their life against intrusion
of personnel unauthorized to enter—
each other, for example; where illusion,
not stone, makes up the maze, of which the inventor
—I'll place a bet on this—was paranoid,
though unbeknownst to Bullfinch and to Freud.

Knock! Knock! Who's there? "It's Daedalus, the cunning!
I've lost the way, the plan, the key, the door!
Where is that bullhead monster? I've been running
for ages round and round, and Minotaur
runs free, rampaging through the fields, sunning
his broad, flat, brainless skull by Acheron's shore.
Is this my work? Ye gods—Zeus! Hera! Cupid!
Can genius be this intricately stupid?"

But let's not stray—not yet, at any rate—
into the vapors of mythology.
Daedalus-Tony is the man whose fate
concerns us here: an IBM trainee
who wakes up to discover that he's late
for work and in all probability
will lose his job. (Rat-Minotaur has crept
behind the trunk where Tony's clothes are kept.)

At this point the story breaks off. It was fear that stopped it. Two letters had come in short succession, one from Stefan in Nepal and one from our mother in New York. Alma wrote that she had paid for his trip and that some people were blaming her for not forcing him to get a job, as if anyone in his explosive state could last a day in an office; that he had expressed so much hope in finding a teacher in Nepal who could help him. As for herself, she was well and in reasonably good spirits, still working for the Group Health Insurance Company, with her East German past incognito, as far as she knew. Stefan's letter consisted of the Sanskrit sign for "Om" and three words he had cut out of a newspaper: "RENAISSANCE OR DIE." Above them was a drawing of a cross-legged monk with a hole in his stomach through which you could see the spine and several ribs. Far up in the sky, an airplane was dropping bombs on a burning village. In my ledger then I sketched out a plot for "Antonio Salvador" in which the labyrinth became something like a Christian hell with concentric realms of progressively deepening horror, into which the hero descended, not to kill a monster but to redeem a suffering brute. The fear surfaced in a dream. I was coming home to my room in a cheap boardinghouse and met my next-door neighbor in the corridor, a fat man with an aura of extreme brutality. He was turning the key in his door as I turned mine, and looked at me as I looked at him. There was a sly, insinuating amusement in his face. Tucked under his arm, half hidden under a cloak or overcoat—or else half revealed to tempt my curiosity—was a black metal box with a white cross on it. I slipped into my room, and he into his. A crude wooden door was let into the wall between us. Fortunately a heavy bar lay across it, so he wouldn't be able to enter. But I felt a threat nonetheless. It came from the box. I went to the door to make sure the bolt was secure and noticed it was not a bolt but a sword. I woke up with my heart pounding. A few days later I saw by the side of the road near our house a large writhing earthworm covered with patches of red fur that on closer inspection turned out to be hundreds of tiny ants. It was being eaten alive. This sight obsessed my thoughts for days. As a child, after watching some boys dismember a dragonfly, I had sworn to God that I would save any hurt creature that came my way; a vow I had adhered to fairly constantly through the years, even at the cost of incurring ridicule, exempting myself only when, occasionally, a body of water was covered with more drowning insects than I could reasonably set about saving. It gave me pleasure to play the beneficent god and imagine the happy amazement of the creature scooped out of disaster and released to a life it had already lost. Until, at the age of twelve, I allowed myself to be converted to the pleasures of fishing. That is, I saw clearly that to gain honorable membership in the society of village boys I had to prove myself capable of spearing worms on hooks and breaking the necks of striped bass (a humane improvement over the more common method of letting them suffocate in a basket). For support, I adopted the scientific view that primitive nervous systems do not permit the development of something so complex as consciousness, and that therefore pity for worms and fish was absurdly misplaced. The trick worked, and I learned to enjoy fishing. But a few years later, I noticed how closely these arguments resembled the rationalizations for killing and performing useful experiments on *"Untermenschen"* (of whom I would have been counted one, had I lived in Europe when I was a child); pain was expressive, even in a worm, and its language did not require interpretation but a compassionate response. Otherwise, what was consciousness good for? I gave up all forms of hunting and returned to my childish vow, paying special attention to worms, as a sort of penance, I'm sure. A long rainfall tended to bring them out, and a deadly attraction drew them into puddles, where their twisting bodies would gradually slacken and bloat, and eventually drown, unless I happened to spot them in time and put them out of harm's way. I was the Good Samaritan of worms. But when I came across that writhing creature by the roadside in Es Vive, I stood as if paralyzed for a few moments. I had always had an obscure sense that my vow of compassion was the positive expression of a refusal; now, for the first time, I knew it: I would not make peace with the cruelty of life, I would not accept it. But the very lucidity of this conviction filled me with fear, and I dared not disrupt the awful ceremony at my feet. I thought of my dream. If I took up the sword, the door would be unbarred and the evil one could come in. But I had no right to allow this pain to continue. I picked up the flailing worm and carried it to the garden faucet by the side of our house and washed off the ants and dug a little hole with my hand in the soft dark soil of a flowerbed and put the worm in and covered it with earth. Some of the ants must have drowned. I could imagine that without agony, so it was an acceptable triage. But for days I thought back again and again on the sight of that martyred worm by the side of the road. It was as if I had never saved it. Then I realized the issue was no longer that worm or those ants but something they stood for, an obscene and terrifying union, the marriage of suffering flesh and devouring pleasure, of delight and desecration. Torture. When was it not part of the normal run of things, on the human plane, not just in nature? That photograph of a flayed man I had seen. Disemboweled heretics. Impaled. Those pictures from China, new heretics and witches, and what time-honored skills were retried on them behind walls was anyone's guess. The water torture. Mengele's knife. I would never be able to hold back Mengele's knife, it was done. And what if death did not put an end to those horrors, what if it were true, as I had read in some occult manual, that the famous déjà-vu sensation is a glimpse of an enormous repetition compulsion at the heart of things, and that only by esoteric discipline or else through the irruption of a higher consciousness at rare fortuitous junctures in our fated lives can we slip out of these deeply grooved patterns and inscribe a new design of possibility. The Via Appia, six thousand crucified men lining a public highway, again and again and again, forever. I tried to shake off this repellent fantasy, told myself it was absurd and illogical, but it had a commanding hold on me, as if it wanted to prove itself by repetition in my own brain. The obsessive images came in waves, with hour-long intervals in between, and gradually subsided. I didn't go near my poem again.

■　■　■

A pause, and I notice I've slipped from the rippling surface of time to where
I am now, down under. Blue all around me. I write, write, but hardly see
my pen.

I feel you near again, my Counterpoint. Have I summoned you? Is it the
atmosphere of pain and fear that attracts you? Is that your element?

Vaguely, in a dim space at the back of my head, I see him seated, very straight,
holding a glass of water with a spray of lilacs in it. No menace there. But the lilacs
are at the peak of their bloom, there's a hint of straw in the leaves. Ah, and I hear
him speaking, indistinctly . . .

Enter the house of your fear, he says.

I'd have to be fearless to do that, I say.

He does not answer, and I hesitate, unsure whether I ought to trust him,
even though I decided years ago that, since he knows my every thought, trusting
him is my only sane option. I feel the blue element swirling past me, alive with the
indistinct forms of fish and . . . what is this, a mermaid? Oh, I remember the day
now, my parents and I were painting in the shade of our terrace in Cuernavaca—
Alma, pregnant with her ill-fated second son, copying a plant with large leaves
like green elephant's ears, me with crayons and a coloring book, filling in the
plumes of an Aztec prince, and Bodo carefully, delicately painting a Meerjungfrau,
blond with bare breasts and a fish tail, who pulls a young man from a boat into
the green-blue waves, as a Meerjungfrau must. There, it's taken me a while to
weave and spread this word-net, but she's already gone and with her the happy
atmosphere of that sunny afternoon. A gray stony form has begun to loom
up from the depths, a castle or fortress, covered with lichen, and the blue
element has grown darker and colder. I am sinking. The green-black walls slide
past me as I sink. Gargoyles, the curved backs of stone elephants. Now I touch
down on the soft ground, rousing billows of weightless dirt. My heart is beating.
A flight of stone steps leads to a tall iron door. I am relieved to find it barred
and padlocked. I raise my head to measure my distance from the top of this
watery world, where Blaise and Juliette are driving Joel and Susan and Gina
and their pregnant dog to their new house in the hills above San Antonio.

I can't see them. What I see instead are the towers of the castle, and streams of minnows darting in and out of the archery-slits. Is anyone in there at all? The moment I ask that, I see that the door is not locked, and that it stands slightly ajar.

Can Pep Serreta

Our new home (on the top of the world) is Can Pep Serreta, one of two houses perched on a mountain on the western side of the island. The terrace, facing south, offers a tremendous outlook over the tops of lush trees (nourished by one of the few streams in the area), and beneath the trees brush-covered hills dotted with four or five widely spaced miniature houses with minuscule goats and chickens and children in their yards, and beyond the hills patchwork fields and pastures all the way down to the sea, which is not blue but turquoise. Once in a while when you turn your head east, far off in the distance, you see an airplane rising soundlessly and with exquisite slowness, always the same smooth arc. After feasting your eyes on so much space, you come back to where you are: a brilliant white wall with a blue door, a round stone well, indolent flies, lizards sunning their antediluvian heads. Something about this simultaneity of lizards and planes, ancient kin and first descendants, their seeming equality in size, their silence, gives me a deep pleasure. The north side of the house looks down on the sinuous twists of the road to San Antonio, crudely cut into the mountain like the bed of a stone-age river. Here and there it ducks behind a hill and crawls out again, flanked by fields of dramatically gnarled fig trees. The earth has a reddish tint that turns purple toward evening, when the town lights up in white, pink, and blue and the drifting dots of fishing boats light their lamps and the old women dressed in black come walking home from mysterious errands that have taken them all day. There is a family next door, a stern handsome man with thin lips and a deep vertical crease in his forehead, his pretty wife, who is blond—an exotic sight in these parts, he guards her with obvious pride—and, at last, a playmate for Gina, a little girl her age. Here, I feel, I could spend the rest of my life, and for the rent Micolao, our affable landlord, charges—twelve dollars a month—we probably could afford to. But Susan is not happy with the place. It lacks running water, it's an hour's walk to market and a good deal more than an hour back uphill to the house. No stove, just an open fireplace and a small gas burner we brought with us. Shitting in a field among little blue flowers and grasshoppers isn't her idea of an idyll either. The nearest doctor miles away, and no telephone by which to reach him. The friends we've made have either traveled on or are on the other side of the island. Also, our store of travelers' checks is dwindling, and God only knows when the bank in Chattanooga will stop "regretting" and start releasing the remains of my inheritance from its inexplicably frozen condition. For the first time since we met, we are quarreling—bitter fights for supremacy, though the ostensible issues are time, money, shopping, and childcare. She's had enough country pie and blowing in the wind, she wants to go home, to Brooklyn of all places, and shouldn't *I* follow *her* for a change? But what sort of change is that, back to the nine-to-five grind when I'm just beginning to come into my own, this is a contest of faith against prudence, and it isn't just me, I have the Zeitgeist on my side, a whole generation mobilized in a war of consciousness against guns and money, so who in his right mind and still under thirty (a year to go!) is going to opt for a "regular job" when there is a world to win, I won't even consider it. If Susan would only drop Acid, she would learn to enjoy bathing in a tin tub in the open air, she would relish the smell of woodsmoke, the sounds of wind, birds, and insects, the luxury of a night sky not eclipsed by the lights of a city. I tell her this, and she believes me, but she is afraid—the memory of a hash-induced rush of paranoid terror (back in New York, before we left) restricts her to the safe precincts of marijuana. Only people, only the new friends and fellow communards I've been praying for, can stem the homeward-, Brooklyn-bound tide of her thoughts.

And then they appear. Ed, Fred, and Betsy are their names. Freshly arrived from Barcelona, they have been turned away from every hotel listed in *Spain on $5 a Day.* I find them bewildered and homeless under a fig tree near San Antonio. "They don't much like freaks around here," I tell them. "Better cut your hair or stay at our place. The cops don't come up there." We smoke some dope they've brought along, they unwrap some bread and cheese, I uncork a bottle of wine I've just bought. Happily stoned, we trudge uphill. Betsy is pregnant, and very young, just a teenager. I offer to carry her backpack, but she says carrying it strengthens her stomach muscles. The mala beads around her neck, the long patchwork dress, the single thick black braid, the large brass earrings, suggest the gypsy or earthmother idea, but she's pale and haggard, her smile is more brave than cheerful. Fred, who appears to be her boyfriend, has the kind of lusty baritone and sure flat-footed stride I associate with lumberjacks and mountaineers, and sure enough, he grew up in the Ozarks and worked in his father's lumberyard till he volunteered to join the army, got disgusted with basic training, and went AWOL in Saigon for six months—a story he doesn't care to go into right now. "Not now and not ever," Betsy says, and

Fred doesn't answer. Ed is silent for most of our walk—in a knowing and dignified sort of way. He has carved himself an oaken staff which he uses as a walkingstick, and with his short-trimmed beard and long yellow hair held back with a scarlet headband he appears to have stepped out of one of Howard Pyle's illustrations for *Robin Hood and His Merry Men,* except he's not merry, he's serious. Halfway up the mountain, Shooce appears, head held low, ears laid back, wagging her whole rump with pleasure. "She's pregnant!" Betsy cries. "When is she due?" "I don't know," I say, "looks like soon. And you?" That sounds awful. "In six weeks," she says. "I didn't mean to compare you," I say. "I'm not offended," she says, "we're all animals." We arrive at the house. Susan is taking a sunbath, naked, and hurries inside, annoyed at my indiscretion. Ed, Fred, and Betsy unburden themselves of their luggage, take off their shoes, and stand gazing into the valley. Shadows of swift-moving clouds slide downhill over trees, hills, and miniature houses, evaporate over the sea. Faintly, from a great distance, we hear someone singing flamenco. The three of them look at each other and smile and walk into each other's open arms. I've seen them do this once before, evidently it's an accustomed ritual, but this time they hold open a place for me. I join them, happy and flustered by so much and such sudden intimacy, and feel my head touching their heads, and my arms and hands touching their necks and hair and shoulders and arms, and someone's arm around my shoulder and a hand rubbing the back of my head, at which point Susan comes out again wearing a dress and Betsy and Fred open their arms to include her. Something is wrong with this configuration, she's being welcomed by strangers in her own home and has no graceful option except to join the group hug, put a friendly face on the awkwardness of the moment, and wait for an introduction. In bed that night, Susan tells me with lowered voice how Betsy offered to read her palm and then informed her that her head line and heart line are both quite shallow, but that this condition will improve with maturity. Not a good beginning.

But after a few days, a kind of harmony sets in. Betsy proves to be a great help to Susan in the kitchen—she has worked in a macrobiotic restaurant —and Susan receives a second course of instruction in George Ohsawa's Philosophy of Oriental Cooking, which in Betsy's rendition is terse and dogmatic: "The body is a temple . . . Vitamins are a myth . . . Eggplants make you angry . . . ," quite different from John Sebastiani's vague musings in the realm of clouds. The meals are delicious. Ed discovers that a rusty bicycle standing in the toolshed, apparently ripe for the scrap heap, can be made serviceable by means of an equally rusty hand-pump that is attached to it. He straps a basket behind the saddle, a time- and labor-saving device if there ever was one. Evenings, when Shooce comes into the house to lie near the fireplace, he sits next to her with eyes closed, laying his hands on her twitching rump and murmuring the Lord's Prayer. Fred is the least concerned with reciprocating our generosity. He is a born freeloader, that rare kind that invariably finds willing donors and never provokes resentment: He pays with appreciation. He smokes a great deal of hash and works hard at bronzing himself with sunlight and—this is Betsy's recipe—Lipton's tea. He likes to talk I Ching and Buddhism with me. He flirts with Susan in a way that amuses her and does not make me jealous. Two or three times a day he retreats with Betsy to their room or to a secluded patch of grass a little down the hill.

One day, after an all-inclusive and heartfelt group hug, our three guests honor us with an invitation to a great gathering that will take place beneath the Eiffel Tower on July 4, 1970, to inaugurate the new decade. Fred started the movement in Vietnam, Betsy and Ed have done their utmost to perpetuate it, and when a complete stranger approached Ed a hundred miles from home to invite him to be there in that place on that date, he knew it was really happening, a convergence of hundreds or, who knows, thousands of like-minded souls. "So pass it on," Fred says. "Invite anyone you feel you'd like to see there. Let your heart make the choice."

■　■　■

It is neither dark nor light in the house of my fear. If I see something, it is because the owner of the house wants to show it to me—but him I never see. Nothing here is as things are above water, at the top of the world. There, the mirror in the hall has a terra-cotta frame of baroque design, covered with faded gold paint, and the glass reflects a bookcase, a door, or a window, depending on where I stand. At night, when the electric lights are out and the moon is full and I stand at a certain angle, the mirror resembles a skull with a blank glaring face—or rather, no face at all. But down here, the thought that this skull is a mirror filled with moonlight seen at a certain angle of reflection is a dangerous illusion, for the optics prevailing here are not those of light and the physical eye. This eyeless gaze, this mouthless grin, are sinister signs of welcome, and I would be an uncouth guest in the house of my fear if I armed myself with explanations. How to explain, for example, that right now the mirror is no longer there, that in its place hangs a picture my mother painted of herself, that it faces me directly, not sideways as it does on canvas? Looking closer, I see that her eyes are averted and filled with tears. I must have hurt her by something I said, and she doesn't want me to know it. In the world above, her tears could have other causes and usually do—my brother's sickness, for instance. But here nothing appears except to reveal me to myself.

■   ■   ■

Everything in the world above is nearly perfect. "Fretsy and Bed," as Gina inadvertently nicknamed our three guests on the mountain, have moved into a nearby cottage owned by Micolao. The war in Southeast Asia has never been further away, despite Fred's disquieting confession that he has a permanent image of a gun-sight in front of his eyes. Shooce is suckling her seven puppies and is no longer in pain. Blaise Dumoulin with his car has created a mobile bridge between us and folks scattered all over the island. Several Americans besides us have rediscovered the bicycle. Something like a community has begun to develop. Why this narrow, quasi-political notion of a "commune" when there's so much space to spread out in? This is how Ibizencos have evidently lived for centuries. We will have to learn from them. We will also have to sustain ourselves economically. Parasitic dependence on the tourist trade seems the most promising strategy. Juliette is already at work painting seascapes with cliffs and gulls and old women in black with grazing goats. Susan and Betsy and Helle could form a day-care center. Ed and Fred could take people on hikes. Milton could provide astrological counseling. Maxwell Schneider and I could edit a newsletter for travelers, not just here but worldwide, with up-to-date info on visas, hotels, exchange rates, hip hangouts, anti-narcotics laws, etc. Susan still grumbles about this or that inconvenience and mourns her lack of close friends, but I'm sure that will change. Look at how happily Gina plays with Juanita, the neighbor's daughter; how they cover the walls of our house with crayon marks; how Micolao doesn't mind. The I Ching warns against complacency, counsels vigilance against "signs of disorder." Is that a political reading? We are in a fascist country, after all. Signs of disorder could be dangerous here. But the island smiles beneath the iron heel. When the post office clerk pounds his fist on the tyrant's face, he is saying something, but mainly, he is affixing a stamp. Nixon? What does he care about a handful of longhairs on a Mediterranean island?

A whole lot, according to Schneider. The main target is himself, "but we're all implicated, don't kid yourself, man, those guys don't fuck around."

"What guys?"

"The CIA."

"What are you saying, Max?"

"Remember what I read to you about people needing more feeling instead of more money?"

"Yes."

"Calls to action. I've written a whole bunch."

"So?"

With a darkly significant look, he hands me several small, ringbound blue notebooks. "Don't show anyone." I read them at home, smoking Nepalese hash as I turn the pages. Where is the beginning, the end?

> Women! Procreate without men! Lobby for the erection of sperm banks in every major city! And stop flattering men by telling them you are their equal! You know perfectly well they are self-centered infantile emotionally crippled control-crazy testosterone-driven robots in search of a soul! Secede from the union of the sexes! Make love to other women! And remember: the fate of the world depends on your gaining swift and complete access to power on all levels of society. So run for office and vote for your sisters! Believe in yourselves!

> Men! You stand accused of every evil under the sun—war, torture, pollution, hysterectomies, traffic congestion, abstraction, bad journalism, child abuse—while women claim for themselves all the virtues even as their mouths water for money and power. Disarm them! Give them what they want! Give them your nine-to-five jobs with their phony rewards, give them the platform shoes of prestige, the U.S. Treasury, the Presidency, and the medal of honor, and demand in return a guaranteed minimum income, the decriminalization of narcotics, and the right to live a life of carefree self-indulgence, with some time set aside for the children!

> Children! You are being taught to read so that you can be as destructive and unhappy as your parents! Demand an immediate end to boring education and insist on having fun 24 hours a day! What else is childhood good for?

> Teachers! Remember your mission! You are not entertainers! . . .

On and on he goes, page after page, calling everyone to action, as if to incite Armageddon:

Black Americans! While white folks send your sons to be killed in
Vietnam, their own children are preaching the cult of flowers. Isn't it
time you reaped the benefits of leisure and they shed some blood for
your freedom?

Parents of hippie freaks! Face it, that's what your children are becoming!
They want total freedom and they want your inheritance too. Screw
them! Write your congressman a letter demanding compulsory haircuts
and detention centers for the uncompliant. Once they look and act
normal, it'll be easier to love them!

Hippie parents with children of school age! The reason Johnny can't
read is not that his teachers can't teach or TV has scrambled his brain,
it's that he's too busy decoding the divine message in the cells of his body!
Abandon pedagogy! Take your kids out of school, and let them teach you
the arts of shameless nudity, perpetual presence, and eternal delight!

He's having fun with this, but in the background I see Schneider's widely
spaced sad eyes, he is frightened, I take another toke of hash, it stirs up a wave
of dark euphoria, and suddenly in the tumbling scrawl of words on the page I
sense the movement of a whirlpool, gathering momentum, deepening, and
then it seems to me that I know what it's like to be Schneider in Schneider's
body with his broad back and rounded shoulders, and to smile Schneider's wry
slanting smile as he sits up in bed in his spooky little *finca* after some screaming bird scared the hell out of him, to shuffle across the room in slippers if he
wears slippers or barefoot if he doesn't and open the door and stare out into
the enormous darkness, to shut the door and look in the mirror and see
Schneider's sheeplike face framed by tangled thickets of curly black hair, to sit
down at his table, shove away a loaf of bread and a jar of honey and pick up
his leaking ballpoint pen and write:

Jews! Has it ever occurred to you that you are the Messiah, the despised
Son of Man, the Prophet of God, abused and vilified through the ages?
Place the names of Moses, Jesus, Spinoza, Einstein, Freud, and Kafka
on your crown, weave your robe of ten thousand other souls no less
glorious, and know yourself to be the greatest among nations and
beloved of the Lord! Sh'ma Yisrael!

American Indians! You, the original people of Nixonland, are the most
forgotten and despised on the planet. Gather hope! Your ancestors
danced the sacred ghost dance too early! Revive it! TV stations will

broadcast and satellites will relay to White Men's living rooms your
drums and pounding feet and chanting voices, the globe will spin
faster, the White Man will whirl off the face of the earth!

Pretty soon I've lost Schneider again in the whirlpool, I turn the pages, impatient to find the point of the exercise: more and more groups and subgroups
are summoned: Muslims, communists, capitalists, white supremacists, black
separatists, vegetarians, cripples, criminals, the French, the Germans, the
Chinese, the old, animal rights advocates, vivisectionists, Trotskyists, everyone
is called to battle, even the pacifists.

Pacifists! You have marched and protested and the war continues. You
have seen the burning bodies of monks and the bombs continue to fall.
Show the hawks that you mean it! March to the Capitol by the millions,
douse yourselves with gasoline, and bring this mad world to its senses
with a conflagration of conscience!

And then, after a blank page:

To Richard Nixon,
President,
United States of America.

Dear Mr. Nixon,
I trust that you have surrounded yourself with a staff intelligent enough
to allow this important message to reach you.

I have made a discovery that promises enormous benefit and unimaginable power to those in whose hands I shall place it. What I have to offer
you is a thing of the mind, a knowledge, if you will, not a fabricated,
material thing. Yet it dwarfs the hydrogen bomb in destructive potential.

But it is for peace and healing that it holds out the greatest promise.

This power I have discovered is in every human being's possession,
but only one in a million uses it, and even he unconsciously, and therefore weakly and intermittently; and this is because, before my discovery,
this power was unknown.

I would like to reveal this secret to you, because I believe you would
use it to the benefit of our country and the world. If you do not reply, I
will have to impart my knowledge to someone else, for the simple reason
that its nature compels communication. It is not possible to know what
I know and remain silent.

You may smile at this offer of power, consisting of nothing but words, to a man in your position. "What is this panacea, this secret weapon?" you might ask. "Show us what you can do with it." I am showing it already. If you do not see it, it is because your eyes are not yet open. Grant me an hour of your time, and I will show you how you can be remembered as the greatest leader the world has ever known.

Please address your response to:

Yorunta,
c/o Maxwell Schneider,
Poste Restante,
Ibiza, Spain.

This must have been the last thing he wrote, the rest of that notebook is empty. Who the hell is Yorunta? Suddenly the thought of Stefan sharply obtrudes. He is drowning, and I'm living my merry life. I wish I had a telephone. I want to call Blaise and ask him to take care of Schneider. I want to call Alma and tell her I'll try to persuade Stefan to check into a psychiatric hospital. I want to send a telegram to Katmandu and ask Stefan to please come home. But it's night and we have no phone and Schneider is probably just pretending and Stefan will not be persuaded by anyone except strangers in Asia and phantoms in the mind.

Two weeks pass, and with them a series of unpleasant developments: Susan, Gina, and I are laid low by diarrhea accompanied by fever and cramps. The doctor (fetched by Ed, with Micolao's help, from the distant lowlands) calls it a virus, highly infectious but not dangerous. Swarms of ecstatic small flies invade our room. Gina is miserably bored and wails that her tushie hurts. Susan, exhausted and racked by pain and disgust, reverts to blaming me for our misfortune, and brings up again the issue of New York, where at least there are clinics, toilets, and taxis. Ed reports that in the house down the hill, Fred's testicles have swollen to the size of eggs, I should get well soon so I can take him to a doctor. Susan suggests that Ed apply his healing touch to the afflicted area. Ed chooses to be piqued by the remark. "Look," I say, "tell Fred to just show the doctor his balls, for chrissake, they'll speak for themselves, he'll understand. I'll write a message, in case there's any confusion." Fred hobbles to San Antonio on Betsy's arm while Ed serves us as messenger, cook, errand-boy, and nurse, always careful to keep a wide berth from our door. That evening Ed tells us the doctor did nothing at all for Fred, not even relieve him of his money. He just stood in the door of his office shifting his eyes from Fred's hairy face to Betsy's bulging belly to my politely worded message in his hand, and then ushered them out of his house with a stream of staccato accusations that continued after the door slammed. On the way back up the mountain, the miracle happened, quietly and unnoticed until after the fact: Fred's balls have returned to normal. But Betsy is not well, her stomach feels queasy, and she has a temperature. Fred is cooking nettle soup for her, something recommended in her moon-sign book.

Ed's face is grave. He's about to pack up, he says. He doesn't know where he's going, but he has to leave. Maybe India.

"Why?" I ask.

"I should never have teamed up with Betsy and Fred." And he proceeds to tell a tangled story about how he'd met Betsy when she was still in high school fooling around with witchcraft, casting spells, wearing seductive costumes, sleeping with all sorts of guys, how she'd gotten herself pregnant and then tried to induce an abortion by swallowing some sort of poison; how he showed her pictures of embryos in LIFE magazine, persuaded her to keep the baby, set up house with her, and became impotent because he realized she did not love him and would never love anyone, because she didn't know what a genuine feeling was; how Fred came along, fresh from Vietnam, and slept with Betsy, which was OK with Ed, and slept with a dozen other women, which wasn't OK with Betsy but she wanted him anyway, wanted him *and* Ed, and how she persuaded them both that if they could "make a triangle work" it would prove something wonderful about human nature. And so they traveled together, satyr, eunuch, and pregnant gypsy, happy until Ed discovered that he disliked Betsy and resented Fred, Mr. Body, Mr. War Hero. "And that's why I have to go," he says. "As soon as you're all up and well."

We're up and well two days later, but instead of leaving immediately, Ed organizes a cleanup party at our house. Fred brings an insect bomb against the flies, we pick flowers with Gina during the holocaust, then open the windows wide and sweep up the thousands of little corpses and scrub the floors clean. Then we all pile together in one big hug. It's as if there had never been any trouble. At Gina's naptime, Betsy makes up a story about pixies which we all listen to until Gina drifts away. The pixies suggest true stories from the realm of magic—Acid trips, premonitions, coincidences—and then Fred, on my prompting and with Ed and Betsy's encouragement, tells the story of his adventures in Vietnam.

After enlisting in the army and undergoing basic training, he realized his error; he had wanted adventure, not tedium and brutality. "I'm a lover, not a fighter."

He was sent to Vietnam. During the flight, somewhere over the Pacific, he resolved to desert at the earliest opportunity. The airplane landed in Saigon. The recruits were ordered to stand at attention, stand, march, turn about face, stand at ease, sit down, stand, and march again. Trucks, Jeeps, and airplanes wheeled about in confusion. Communications blared through defective loud-speakers and the histrionic bellowing of commanding officers mingled in a manner that brought sardonic smiles to the faces of the GIs. Hours passed, with much commotion and no progress. The officers decided, in view of the unusually chaotic situation—"unusual for the army," Fred says, "which means it was a tremendous mess"—to exempt their men from the duty of asking permission to leave their ranks for the purpose of peeing against a tall metal fence that separated the airfield from a busy street. Here it was, the earliest opportunity. Fred dropped his gun, climbed up the fence, let himself drop to the other side, and walked off into town. He was AWOL for four months, befriending Vietnamese prostitutes, black-market dealers, dope pushers, and addicts, and sharing their precarious but never tedious existence, to which he was able to contribute materially as a supplier of cocaine and hashish to American troops.

One day he was arrested by a military policeman in an opium- and heroin-den that was rumored to have been established by the Viet Cong, or at least supplied with drugs by them, for the benefit of their enemies. His defection was quickly discovered. After three harrowing weeks in the brig, he was court-martialed and sentenced to spend six months on active combat duty. "If at the end of those six months," said the officer in charge of the proceedings, "you are not either dead or insane, my name is not Jack Loomis." Fred kept the name in mind. He spent six months where most men were required to stay no longer than three weeks. He was sent on scouting missions into Cambodia, forays that were invariably accompanied by gunfire, and sometimes by a mine exploding underfoot, scattering into the jungle fragments of a body that minutes ago had been a friend. He helped set fire to the thatched roofs of villages that were suspected of being friendly to the V.C., hardening his heart against pity and shame. His sergeant had an eye on him. One sign of insubordination or perhaps just fear, and Fred would be court-martialed again. The sergeant could even shoot him without any legal ado, especially during an exchange of fire. So could Fred, for that matter, shoot the sergeant, and God knows he was tempted. But the name Jack Loomis kept him on the straight and narrow path of self-preservation. He wouldn't do the man the favor of throwing his life away.

The enemy soldiers looked like children, and some of them were; and some of them were women, as delicate and with faces as pretty as those of the girls he had lived with in Saigon. Captured, they were lucky if they escaped being gang-raped, shot, or tortured by the Vietnamese experts to whom the dirty work of interrogation was generally delegated. Sometimes an especially resistant V.C. would be taken for a ride hanging upside down from a helicopter. Sometimes they'd cut him or her loose. The nights were full of fear. Once, keeping watch along with several other sentries while the rest of the company slept in their tents, Fred listened for hours to the sinister dripping and rustling of the forest, when suddenly wild screams rang out very close by, accompanied by the sound of cracking branches and a strange, rapidly thumping noise, like a drum. Terrified, the sentries pulled their triggers and sprayed the darkness with machine-gun fire. The sleeping men leapt up, grabbed their weapons, scrambled out of their tents on all fours, threw themselves on the ground, and opened fire in all directions. After a while, they stopped shooting, and there was silence. Next morning Fred and two other men were sent out to search for bodies. They found a family of apes, five in all, including a baby. One of them must have weighed four hundred pounds.

The sixth month passed, and Fred was alive and for all practical purposes sane. He had to admit it was rather surprising. The only thing wrong with him was this permanent apparition of a gun-sight, a circle with a cross in it, that was superimposed on everything he saw.

As soon as he got back to Saigon, Fred inquired after Lt. Jack Loomis. After a good deal of searching he found out that Loomis had died in a traffic accident.

Fred received a dishonorable discharge. He was angry about that, because he believed he had served his country long enough and displayed enough courage to merit a decoration. He joined the "Veterans Against the War in Vietnam" and gave speeches all over the United States describing his experiences in Cambodia at a time when the U.S. government was lying about its military presence in that country. Gradually he developed an inflated sense of his own importance. His cohorts criticized him for the length of his speeches, and for his tendency to spice them with anecdotes that had little political relevance. The FBI took a lively interest in him, tapped his telephone, and managed to dissuade one employer after another from hiring him. To help himself, he founded a "pharmacy," supplying his neighborhood with LSD produced by a fellow veteran and amateur chemist in the basement of an uncle's house. Among his clients were Betsy and Ed, who were planning a trip to Morocco but still lacked the money. "Well, I had plenty of that," Fred said, "and then Betsy and I got close. All I needed was a passport." Fortunately the FBI didn't, or couldn't, interfere with that.

After telling his story, Fred goes off to the poop-grass with a roll of toilet paper and Betsy asks whether anything struck us as strange in his story.

"The whole story is strange," I say.

"Something in particular?" Susan asks.

"Yes," Betsy says. "Something missing."

"He didn't mention killing anyone," Susan says.

"That's right," Betsy says. "It comes out in his eyes sometimes. It scares me." Fred comes back, still buckling his belt.

"Hey, why you all so quiet?"

"Just thinking about your story," Ed says.

"Naw, forget it. We got more living to do. Huh, Joel? You ole bookworm?" He slaps my knee.

That night I wake up with the thought that I might be able to reach Stefan mentally, psychically. That is something *he* believes in, so maybe with some luck and magic we might meet halfway. I'll drop some Acid, a nice hefty dose, hold before me his picture of the wounded monk and the burning village (might as well face his horror if I want to help him) and project myself to where he is. With this thought I go back to sleep. In the morning, I eat a light breakfast, take two Acid-saturated sugar cubes from their secret place in the cool stone larder next to the well, and inform Susan of my intentions, leaving out the esoteric details. Why invite doubt when faith is what I need? Faith and decision. If she knew what it's like to have all your limiting beliefs washed away by an unimaginable riptide of color, power, emotion, and truth, she would understand. She would know that things thought to be impossible in one's "right" mind can become not just possible but undeniably real. The psychedelic hucksters talk glibly about Inner Space, we nameless freaks talk about good and bad trips, so how about Inner Space *Travel*? It's a useful image for my purposes now: Let Faith be the vehicle; Desire, the aim; let Acid provide the propulsive blast; the rest is energy, divine energy, without which nothing can be accomplished or even conceived. But now I notice that it isn't Susan's doubt that is the problem, but mine, and that this doubt is a fear, and that the fear is focused on Stefan's picture, on that monk with the gaping hole in his stomach, that burning house seen through a gridwork of ribs and spine. What a brutal exposure of death in life, mayhem and ruin right in the Buddha's belly, and he has Stefan's face, his anguished mouth and eyes, no, I'm not ready for this. It's not the right time. Put away this picture. Go fearless or don't go at all. And I put the sugar cubes back in the larder, and seeing Gina and Juanita with Shooce and the puppies awash in a puddle of sunlight in front of the shed, I go and lie down on the grass with them, welcomed by their shining eyes and several slow happy slaps of Shooce's tail on the ground. Together we watch the fat little dogs jamming their muzzles and pumping their tiny paws into the full rosy teats, sucking, squealing, wiggling their tails. I reach out my hand and Shooce stretches her neck to lick my fingers, wagging her tail. "*Pah*-pees!" Juanita says. She's learning English. Heracles conquered the Gorgon by mirroring her hideous face with his shield, but if I am to walk into Stefan's hell, *this* is the face of life I must hold before me. Can I do it? Later.

In the afternoon, Susan takes a nap and I sit reading a collection of E. M. Forster's essays while the children play with their dolls. Fretsy and Bed drop in for a visit, they wave hello. Betsy is walking slowly, bent forward a little. Ed shows me a manila envelope, shakes it: "Pictures," he says, smiling. "You'll be amazed." Fred puts a bamboo flute to his lips and announces himself with the opening phrase of "Wake Up Li'l Susie," and Susan sticks her head out the window, smiling. Then she comes out with a bottle of wine. We talk. Susan asks Betsy: "What's the matter, are you sick?"

"Maybe," Betsy says. Her stomach is hurting, her head too. And nausea. It started last night.

"Betsy, how about going to the doctor?" I say.

"Not again!" she says, laughing. "No, it's getting better. I'm fasting. The body heals itself, if you let it."

"Aren't you worried about the baby?" Susan asks, with concern and reproach in her voice.

"I have been, a little. But I can feel it moving in a quiet sort of way. I think it's feeling fine."

I bring out my guitar, we sing, play with the children, talk. Ed takes the guitar and he and Fred harmonize their voices and sing a pleasant bluesy song called "The Ode to Billy Joe," which Susan and I haven't heard before.

"It's new," Fred says. "When did you guys leave the States?"

"Last November," I say.

"Whew, things've changed since then—huh, Ed?"

Ed nods.

"For the better or worse?" I ask.

Betsy says "worse" and Ed, sagely, "just change." Fred says nothing. I glance at Susan to search out her response to this, but she doesn't appear to be listening. She's trying to deflect the course of an ant that is determined to cross the parapet she is lying on.

"How's that, Betsy?" I ask, and I notice, not for the first time, the pinched look in her face; her black eyes are narrow, with an uneasy sharpness in them. "There's just a lot of fighting there," she says softly. "People trying to bring the war home. Other people want to nuke Hanoi. There's just a lot of bad feelings."

We all stop talking. No sound except for the crickets and the children's quiet chatter in the distance. The simmering stillness of noon is so dense with heat and space that we're all starting to wonder who will sacrifice the faintly oppressive comfort of this silence, when suddenly, out of nowhere, there comes swelling toward us, so quickly there is no time for the mind to make sense of it, a roaring scream that widens incomprehensibly to an enormous all-enveloping sound, until at its apex the eye recognizes its source, an airplane flying so low it's about to shave off the treetops, hurtling over the edge of our roof and behind the house and away, back into the void it came from, trailing a diminishing, grumbling remnant of noise. We sit, lie, and crouch as if petrified and then burst out laughing, all of us except Fred, and only now do we see that he has bent over double with his hands clasped over his head. After a long silence, he lowers his hands and raises his head, his face white. "Holy shit," he says. Betsy stands up and puts her hand on his head, peering into his eyes. "It's all right, Fred. Everything's all right." He reaches up to feel her hand on top of his head. "Holy shit." He's quivering. "Hand me the wine, will ya?" I give him the bottle, he takes a long swig. Ed raises the flute to his lips and, gazing out at the valley, starts making music again, a lilting Celtic tune. Betsy listens with her eyes closed, her hand on her belly.

"I almost dropped acid this morning," Fred says after a while. He's looking at me. "That sound would've been one hell of a moment." He chuckles.

"Why didn't you?" I ask.

"I forgot." He chuckles again.

"Funny, I almost dropped too, this morning," I say.

"And why didn't you?"

"I was afraid."

"Of what?"

"Of fear."

"Oh man, that's no good. I don't wanna hear that. You can't give in like that, it'll make you weak. When you're scared of tripping, that's when you gotta drop. You gotta face the sucker down."

"What sucker?"

"Fear! Who else? Fear is the enemy, not the Commies, the Nazis, the CIA, whatever. You can't be free if you're scared. I don't wanna see freaks putting away their acid 'cause they're afraid."

"Fred, you sound like a soldier. We're not at war here."

"You better believe we're at war! We're soldiers, man. We've been conscripted. This is our uniform." He holds up a strand of his long hair. "And we're pretty well equipped." He grins. "We got dope to spread a little fun with—that disorients the enemy—and then acid to bust through the fortifications. Like the song says: Break on through to the other side! That's what we got to offer—conquer fear and live in freedom. Set an example. And that's *all* we got. If we don't do that, we might as well cut our hair and hop on the treadmill like they want us to."

Ed has stopped playing his flute. Betsy is smiling. Susan, still lying on her side, has propped up her head to listen and watch.

"You got me half convinced, Fred," I say.

"Half?"

"Two-thirds."

He laughs. "Then let's go, man!" He stretches out his hand.

"Go where?"

"To the other side."

"Now?"

"What other time?"

My earlier misgivings come back: The monk with the hole in his stomach, Stefan's bottomless unhappiness, the war being waged in all our names, and now Fred's untold story, and the recurrent hint in his eyes of ever-present terror. Do I want this for a setting? But I clasp his hand.

"Your stash or mine?" he asks.

"Mine," I say.

As we stand on the sunlit terrace then, holding a glass of water in one hand and our dose in the other, I feel my guts tremble in anticipation of the familiar and always unimaginable ordeal that lies ahead. Then it is done. My stomach contracts like a fist. I imagine the sugar cube pulverizing inside. It'll be a while before the Acid takes. Susan calls the children into the house for a snack. Fred sits down on the parapet with his eyes closed, facing the sun, hugging his knees and smiling. Betsy lies down in a deck chair near him, holding her belly like a medicine ball. Ed strums the guitar. Juanita's mother calls in the distance: "Juanita-a-a!" Gina wants to go with her friend. Ed volunteers to take them. They leave, tall Ed in the middle, a feather stuck in his scarlet headband, holding each little girl by a hand. Shooce slowly walks up the steps to the patio, wagging her tail, lies down on her side in the sun, goes to sleep. She's taking a break. Her rump is no longer twitching. I wonder if Ed healed her. The puppies squeal faintly in their bed of rags by the shed. Swallows swooping. Crickets chanting. Betsy massaging her belly. Fred says: "Some day I want to run down this mountain all the way to the water." Neither Betsy nor I respond, we just watch his wish run down the mountain for a long while, all the way down to the water. Ed comes back without Gina, goes inside to tell Susan the kids are taking a nap, comes out again, picks up the flute from the chair where Fred left it, sits down on the parapet between me and Fred, facing the valley with his feet dangling over the edge. Silence. What an amplitude, what a largess of humming potential! Now Ed sounds a soft, quavering note, and another one, cautiously, unsure what mood to strike, or perhaps affected, as I am, by the distances and relational tensions between our bodies, intervals that divide our common space into an oddly musical order, long held notes of a dissonant chord that is audible to a kind of intellectual sense I have never noticed before, a feeling for something like moral geometry, if there can be such a thing; but this discord holds a promise of closure, holds it in tantalizing abeyance, holds and withholds it so skillfully and so relentlessly that there's no room for anyone to make meanings in any medium other than that of emptiness. That's why we're silent. And Ed feels that, of course he does, that's why he falters, as any artist upstaged and outdone by a master would falter and quietly put away his instrument. And now Susan comes out of the house, stops in the door, looks at me, shining with love, my heart opens, she is walking toward me across the terrace, through this loose circle of friends that isn't a circle, that has no center, moving with a strange gravity, taking me into her eyes and into her heart even before she clasps her arms around me and presses her cheek against my chest. Ed has found his tune, a ragalike snake of longing, fine little quavers and semi-quavers undulating around a constant baseline, and dotted around it the thin squeaks and yelps of the puppies, while Shooce breathes in her sleep. And here it is, oh this is it. Time flows in sweet golden drops. Everything is music, how could I have forgotten that. Susan's brown hair, a river of musical color. The soft breeze disperses the sounds, moves them in wayward meandering currents. Here and there, swallows slice the tune, easily and without damage, like knives cutting through water. Oh it's coming. Susan stirs, lifts her head, looks at me. I look into her eyes. When have I not known you? Fathomless beautiful friend. Oh the love, the distance. Oh the sorrow of being two. Tears are running down our faces. After a while I remember Fred and slowly turn my head, and she too turns her head, as if mirroring me. Fred is looking at us. His pupils are enormous, almost completely obliterating the edge of green around them. Black holes. "Are you stoned yet?" I ask. He chuckles and spreads his arms in an admirable gesture: "Aaaah."

A hundred yards down the hill, behind the stream and the grove of trees, is a small wheat-field belonging to Micolao. That's where I go with Susan, that's where we sit face-to-face on a blanket in the thick secret air, holding hands, surrounded by a funnel of crisscrossing stalks, and begin to journey deep and far into each other's eyes. It's hard for her to stay with me; she looks at my mouth, inviting me to join her on the easier, pleasanter paths of sensuality. But I don't want to make love, I've seen something I didn't want to lose sight of. What was it? I no longer know. I lean in to look closer. A cold terror floods my limbs—the horrible thought that the power I feel soaring through me will prove stronger or simply other than love and crush her like an avalanche, incinerate her like a flash of lightning—and this fear shuttles back and forth between us with fiendish haste, quick quick quick, as if hustling to weave a pattern of lies and distortions—until, very much like shafts of light, intelligence and love disperse the shadows.

"Joel!"

It's Ed's voice, coming from the porch.

I don't answer. We're hiding like children, like Adam and Eve in the garden. And Susan is transfigured. Fragments of wheat in her hair shine like jewelry, each grain and sliver exquisitely crafted and arranged. A tear quivers in the corner of one of her eyes like a crystal pendant. It severs itself, rolls down her cheek, leaving a glistening streak.

"Joel!" The voice sounds urgent.

"I'll see what he wants," Susan says, and gets up and leaves. The wheat closes behind her. Eons pass. Where is she? Don't worry. All is well. I lie back and close my eyes. Now to sleep for a thousand years. The mind is full of trees. Looking closely into their foliage, I see snakes feeding on them. They make a whispering as they move in and out of holes in the wood, and I can feel them boring inside my skull like worms in an apple. I open my eyes and see it is the wind in the wheat that is whispering, and recognize the worming in my head as the snarl of a distant chainsaw. All is well. An ant scrambles over my hand in a frenzy of exploration, searching, searching, for what? Don't follow this thought. I stand up resolutely, staggering slightly. A tall man is approaching downhill from the house, leaning back to brace himself against the pull of gravity, his dark eyes strong and grave beneath keenly arched, thick eyebrows, gold hair splashing over the sides of his face. It's Ed. How splendid he looks. But his steps are too long and too swift, something is wrong. I step forward, parting the wheat before me. We meet at the edge of the field.

"Something's happened to Shooce."

"What?"

"Come see for yourself."

It takes centuries to reach the porch. At each step, some portion of eternity rears up and displays the whole ferocious innocence of life: birds! shrubs! insects! clouds! And our clumsy man-feet stomping uphill. What strange beasts we are, advancing on prongs! Too much! I merely think these words, but I hear them slosh and suck like boots in mud, which of course is not here in this dry land but elsewhere. Ah, here is the house, the steps to the porch: Too! Much! Too! Much! Shooce is lying on her side, panting, Fred and Susan are crouching next to her, petting and talking to her. Fred points a finger at an ugly ragged black hole in one of her teats. A slow thick stream of mingled blood and milk oozing from it.

"The puppies were getting into it," Ed says.

I feel faint and sit down on the floor. I notice with surprise that Fred is crying.

"Where's Betsy?" I ask.

"She went to lie down," says Ed behind me. "I think you should go get a vet."

Who, me? Now? Impossible. I'm not fit to fry an egg in this state, and I know what I look like, a living example of the uncoordinating effect of *drogas,* insane, so please, this is fascist Spain, folks, they'll lock me up, there must be another solution. But there isn't. I'm the only one here who speaks Spanish. Sober, solemn, and stern, Ed's eyes speak of necessity and duty. Couldn't I write out a message for Ed or Susan to deliver? I'm ashamed to propose it. I feel like a child who for the first time in his life is being sent on an errand where he will have to brave an encounter with strangers four times his size and infinitely his superior in knowledge and strength, and at whose mercy he will have to place his transparent feebleness, ignorance, and fear.

"I'll go to Micolao," I say.

"Take the bike," Ed says.

"I'd rather walk."

"You'd better take the bike."

I look up at him, jolted by the commanding firmness of his voice.

"There's no time," he says. "Take the bike and fly."

Careening downhill then, grateful there's no one but me to witness my cries of fear and whoops of relief and laughter, gripping the handlebars with all my might, using my heels to supplement the almost useless handbrakes, ogling the rocks, holes, and puddles in the road with a bug-eyed terror that strikes me, at relatively safe intervals, as extremely comical, there comes a moment when, unable to negotiate a sharp turn, I go sailing over the edge of the road and am reminded in midflight of Ed's final injunction, which I am now carrying out to the letter, one hand raised to the vicinity of my forehead in a semblance of a soldier's salute—"Mission accomplished!"—mouth open in a gasp of amazement at the uncanny coherence of the moment, the crisp particularity of ruddy clods of earth, rough weeds, and grass I'm falling toward, the background of conflicting emotions left at the top of the mountain like a bank of fog, the nauseating thought of Shooce's puppies nuzzling at that open wound, the graceful progress of my limbs through the air, like those of a marionette, the horizon tilted as if seen from an airplane, an orange sunset over a fiercely blue sea, the town preparing for night with a scattering of blue and white lights. I hit the ground and somersault out of the bike's way. Nothing is damaged, in my body or in the bike. Some dirt down my collar, that's all. A miracle! No excuse to go on by foot: back in the saddle, and trust in God.

As I roll into town, I begin to despair of finding the way to Micolao's house. The streets all wear the same whitewashed facades and storefront awnings; even their names—Calle Valencia, Calle Madrid—barely distinguish them. What an ugly town! There is the sun, a bloody egg on the horizon. I pass a white fence, behind it a woman taking her wash off a clothesline. I stop to ask her where I might find Fernando Micolao, but before I can speak, I feel the power in my eyes burning into hers. She stiffens, as if galvanized, and for a moment stands illumined with the same ferocious glare of consciousness that blazes in me. We are both frightened. Quickly, I veil myself with blinks and smiles and by stroking my hair with my hand, and ask my question, and the woman conspires with me to make believe that the only world she inhabits is one neatly delimited by such words as "three blocks to your right," "past the drugstore," and "next to Señor Palau, the lawyer."

Señora Micolao greets me at the door, timidly gracious, the mistress of the hearth. At once I feel secure in the presence of such doll-like automatism: no chance of being found out by her. Micolao, too, seems safe: He's eating dinner, always a wholly absorbing business for him. He welcomes me with the usual boisterous heartiness, and without interrupting his meal for a moment invites me to sit down and help myself to some fruit and wine, inquires about my wife's and friends' health, smatching and chewing and slurping wine all the while; and these gustatory noises blend ambiguously with emphatic grunts that are intended to convey appreciation of the urgency of my appeal for help, and a granting of pardon for the untimeliness of the visit. "We must fix it right away," he says then, and calls for his wife to bring the guest some cheese. "You must try it," he says, "it's made of sheep's milk." A glance at Micolao's plate confirms a sudden suspicion: He's eating lamb. For a moment the town's butcher looms up, a fat man in a bathing suit, glistening in the half-light, a hook in one hand, a sheep's carcass on a table behind him, the bleating of sheep resounding from behind a metal door, above him the hand-painted sign: MATADERO, which, not for the first time, but nonetheless with a shock that explodes like a bomb in my chest, I realize means, simply, "killer." What a profession! What a vocation! And God help us who hire killers for the comfort of our bowels. Micolao cuts and chews, the apparition recedes. "I know a woman," he says, wiping his mouth and shoving the plate aside. "She lives in Cala d'Hort. She knows about these things." What things? Slaughter? Micolao peels an orange, separates a segment, I make the mistake of following it into his mouth. There is no way to avoid getting mashed by those pestlelike teeth now, the pain is awful, in fact quite unbearable, but also fascinating, because like any other sensation, pain has varieties of texture and depths of intensity that require corresponding faculties of perception which, I can only surmise, have been dormant until this moment when all my insides cry and cringe before the next bite, and suddenly Micolao has become a pig, a godlike pig wearing a vest with a watch-chain, a broad linen napkin stuck in his collar, a pig-god with a globulous belly and a chomping mandible and coarse blond stubble on his pink cheeks and chin, and he looks at me with his small shrewd pale blue eyes, and I can feel him chewing and sucking out all the sweetness and juice, and I notice that at the core of my pain and fear there is an extraordinary sense of comedy, and a thrill akin to the exhilarating horror produced by certain amusement-car rides, especially at the moment when the well-chewed morsel is plunged down the throat for further processing. "I will take you to her," Micolao says. Señora Micolao brings in a plate with cheese and bread, and I perform the obligatory charade of lip-smacking surprise and praise for the proud manufacturer (who has resumed a human appearance), even though I can't taste anything and the stuff has the color and consistency of wet chalk. Señora Micolao stands before a stained-glass window through which a streetlamp casts a circular glow, her red hands folded over the round protuberance of her belly, and with her kind timid smile, her white apron, her black dress, stark as a nun's habit, and the white walls and the stained-glass window behind her, she looks like a figure in a Flemish painting. Micolao shoves his chair back, pulls out the napkin from his collar and drops it on the table, and says something to his wife in Ibizenco, incomprehensible to me, and she nods and smiles and says *adiós* to me, and her eyes flicker anxiously from my face to my shirt and back to my face, and as I leave the house with Micolao, I see that the front of my shirt is covered with mud.

By the time I've helped Micolao unload several empty crates from the back of his pickup truck and stacked them in his shed and lifted the bicycle onto the truck and sat down on the torn leather seat next to him, by the time we're finally bumping along the road to Cala d'Hort, night has fallen in earnest, leaving just a faint luminescence on the horizon. Micolao has fallen silent. Black clouds glide briskly across the blue-black sky, obliterating stars and revealing them again. A gibbous moon hangs over the hills to the left of the truck, rimming their backs with silver. The confident rumble of the motor, the smell of leather, gasoline, and tobacco, the enveloping blackness of night, the searchlights testing the road like feelers—all these are signs of safety and comfort. I remember feeling like this in my parents' car, driving home at night from a trip to the theatre, dreaming my own midsummer night's dream of a leaf-green Puck still flying through the air, swinging on a rope like Tarzan. Alma cursing the bumps in the road, but I liked them. And wondering why Bodo couldn't drive when he was so strong and able in every other way. Even though sometimes he pretended to be weaker than I when we wrestled. How pleasant this is, feeling childish. Why did I ever give it up? I'm happy. Gina, where is she? Asleep in her bed, hugging her Smiley-mouse. I send her a light blue, weightless blanket of prayer. Where has my fear gone? I have more mental control than . . . oh, maybe than ever. There doesn't, in fact, seem to be much mind left to control. I sit bouncing in my seat like a husk, emptied of all but a few rattling grains of thought. Susan, her face . . . and in a flash I know what all those paintings of the blessed Virgin are about: divine love in a human smile. And there is Ed, looking at me with those stern, sober eyes. How annoying! He's so *serious!* And Shooce—how could I forget! That's why I'm here in Micolao's truck, to save Shooce! This is an emergency! The puppies are screaming for food. Ed is still staring, maybe probing, as if there were something to be found out, or confessed. This, too, is the face of God. Now I'm ashamed, and wish I could escape from being a child by some feat of heroic maturity.

"Can you pay her five hundred pesetas?" Micolao asks.

"At home, yes, I don't have them here now," I say, glad to have regained a grasp of practicalities. Ed's eyes have vanished. I'm thinking about pesetas. What are they worth? There seem to be two standards, value and honor. There are people who ask a pittance for services which the more savvy folk in the main towns exchange for at least ten times the amount. Yet here is a woman from Cala d'Hort, where everyone is poor, charging five hundred pesetas. Or isn't it rather Micolao, who is certainly no pauper, recommending this amount—the same Micolao who practically gave us his house on the mountain because he was ashamed of its stone well filled with rainwater and its lack of plumbing. Should I bargain? Am I being taken? Should I pay without question, since Shooce's life is at stake, not my honor? Should I pay Micolao for his help? Or would that be an insult?

"It is better if you pay her well," Micolao explains, as if he'd been listening to my thoughts. "She's like a witch. It's better if she likes you."

The truck stops near some dimly lit shacks and what looks like a general store with a striped awning and a large unshaded electric bulb beneath which several drunken men stand hugging and singing, their shadows leaping in all directions. Micolao steps out of the car, approaches one of the shacks, and knocks on the door. I stay in the truck.

"*Quién?*" says a shrill voice.

"Micolao, Fernando!"

The door opens and a bent old woman appears, her face and hands white against her black kerchief and long black dress. A dialogue in Ibizenco follows, of which I can only make out the words "*Americano*" and "*Can Pep Serreta.*" Micolao is shouting, and the old woman keeps saying "Aha" in a high-pitched quavering voice, like a worried chicken. Then she steps back into the house and emerges again with a straw bag slung over one shoulder and follows Micolao to the truck. I step out to let her sit in the middle. Micolao introduces us with "*El Señor Americano*" on the one side and "*Señora María*" on the other. The old woman bows and gives me her warm dry hand to hold and says "*mucho gusto,*" emitting a powerful whiff of garlic. She has no teeth, so that her mouth resembles a vortex that is sucking in her lips and cheeks; even her nose and chin seem intent on disappearing there. No wonder Micolao called her a witch.

But there is no malice in her eyes. They glitter, deep in their hollow sockets, with humor and curiosity. *"Vámonos,"* she says, and Micolao and I help her to clamber into the truck.

Micolao and Señora María converse in Ibizenco a good part of the way while I lean against the door with my eyes closed and pretend to be sleeping. A thick pulsating stream of thoughts and pictures pours through me—beautiful, ugly, terrible, and sublime thrown sloppily together like junk in a tide, exhausting to watch, impossible to ignore. In obedience to some tremendous compulsion, this mess of particles is being repeatedly jerked together in hugely intricate, absurdly beautiful systems of connotation and implication, hovers for a moment in a paroxysm of inane perfection, collapses back into chaos, and is swept up again, over and over in ever new spasms of meaningless complexity; and I too—or rather, that part of me that stands apart, though compelled to attend to this phantasmagoria for fear of being sucked into its flow and dragged out of the reach of reason—am oscillating at a brisk rate between poles almost incomprehensibly disparate: disgust and delight, exhaustion and power, despair and titanic resolve, love and a mean, dispirited futility. I open my eyes and sit up. The old woman turns her head and looks at me. Her eyes are like craters, her nose and chin hooked toward each other like a vulture's beak. Her mouth opens and puckers into a smile. I try not to look afraid.

"Como están?" she asks, pronouncing the s like an f.

"Muy bien, gracias. Y usted?"

She cackles and turns to Micolao and back to me.

"Ustedes hablan Español muy bien!" she exclaims.

"Usted también."

I say it with the most earnest intention to be polite, and realize too late that for me to praise this woman's faulty command of Spanish is a dubious compliment and possibly an insult. But she is delighted. She shrieks and slaps her thighs. Micolao chortles sympathetically. I laugh uneasily and look out the window at the moon, which is dancing alongside us, speeding through billowing black clouds like a windblown sail. Now I see Señora María's mouth in the sky mumbling "Can Pep Serreta," pronouncing the s like an f. Or is it Shooce's wound? or, argh! It's the Buddha in Stefan's picture, the hole is in his body, bombs raining on houses in hills much like these, which I don't, *don't* want to think of, no, it's a hole in the clouds. But there's no getting around it, the ragged black hole is a wound, opening closing, opening closing. Señora María speaks, not in the sky now, but next to me, I turn to look at her and see the world-wound gaping from the concave space between her nose and her chin, explaining itself in Spanish, with a high, quavering, cracked voice, explaining how itself came to be: too much milk in one *teta,* the nipple clogged, or else the *perritos* weren't sucking enough, so that in the end . . . and lacking a word, the lips pucker and blast out a voiceless *"poof"* of wind and spittle. *"Una explosión,"* Micolao translates, at which point I ask him to please stop the car, I'm feeling sick. The truck stops. I step out and wholeheartedly vomit.

When we finally arrive at the house, Shooce is lying on the floor in the kitchen with the puppies furiously sucking at her and pumping with stiffly outstretched front legs. Susan and Ed are on the floor guiding the puppies away from the wound. Fred is with Betsy, Susan says.

Micolao settles down on a bench near the fireplace with his thighs spread, clasping his knees with his thick red hands. I kneel down next to Susan. She pats my hand: "How are you?" Impossible question! "Good," I say. "And Gina?" I ask. "Asleep." The old woman fumbles in her straw bag and produces a tin can filled with a blue salve. She spreads some around the edge of the wound and puts a glob inside for good measure. Shooce raises and turns her head, lies back with a shuddering sigh. Now Señora María asks for a *sostén del pecho,* cupping her hands over her breasts for translation: a brassiere. Susan fetches one from the bedroom. The old woman fits one cup around the wounded teat and slings the straps around the dog's chest and shoulders, tying them at the back of the neck. Shooce winces and makes motions to snap at her hand, but acquiesces to Susan's persuading voice and touch.

Fred comes in from outside, looking meek and sad. He crouches down next to me, peering into my eyes, takes my hand, and says: "How ya been, buddy?"

Moved, I squeezed his hand and say "Good. How about you?"

"OK. Joel, listen, can you ask them . . . I think Betsy needs help right away."

"Why? What happened? How is she?"

"Nothing happened, she's still the same. That's the whole thing, it's going on for too long. Listen, I had a vision. I was sitting by her bedside and I heard some weird sounds, like glass breaking and little bells tinkling, and this squeaky voice was trying to say something into my ear. I couldn't understand a word, but it went on for at least an hour, so it felt like something important. So I kept listening. And then I saw this little doll, just a round head with no face and a kind of skirt underneath, and it floated through the air and picked up our bags with all our clothes packed and the sleeping bags rolled up and strapped on, and put them on the bed. Our stuff was actually spread all over the room, but I saw it packed and ready to go just like it was real. So I packed up. The bags are standing by the edge of the road."

"You mean you're leaving tonight? Where are you going?"

"I don't know. Maybe just to San Antonio and back. But I'm taking the stuff with us. Are you coming along, Ed?"

Ed nods gravely.

Señora María issues another instruction. Micolao transmits it to me (arching an eyebrow at the sight of Fred's hand holding mine), and I relay it in English to Susan: "Put cream on twice a day. Always use a clean brassiere."

Susan seems steeped in thought and sadness. She is mechanically stroking the dog with one hand, while the other is held against her cheek. Señora María wipes the salve off her fingers onto Shooce's fur, then onto the sides of her dress, smiles at Susan and says *"Gracias, Señorita,"* and stands up. Then she turns to me and dusts her palms to indicate a finished job. Fred and Ed pick up the puppies and lay them next to their mother, where they immediately begin stretching their little blind faces in search of her nipples. Shooce turns to inspect the bandage and to lick the puppies and gently shove them into position with her nose. I walk into the bedroom to get my wallet. In a streak of light falling in from the half-open door I carefully count out five hundred pesetas. I step back into the kitchen and start counting out the bills again—just like a bank clerk—into the old woman's palm which floats before me, gnarled, welted, shaking, covered with a grasslike pattern of black crosshatched lines, some of them as deep as knife cuts. My own hand, too, floats through space. How long this takes! Looking at the bill I'm holding, which just one ancient moment ago I had assured myself was one hundred pesetas, I see the zeros multiplying and the printed personage sticking out his tongue and puffing his cheeks, and his signature writhing like a bevy of snakes. Shouldn't the Acid be wearing off by now? I will never take it again, it's too much stress to inflict on an organism. What if something snapped or tore inside? And how can the old woman not feel, not know that her client is thoroughly out of his gourd? These finely crinkled, wax-surfaced sheets of paper, of what immemorial poison or elixir are they the sum, the cipher, the sign, of whose pain and whose promise? How like a blessing and how guilty and mean is the instant of giving and taking. My soft unlabored hand, white, returns through the vast lucid emptiness, more swiftly now, and takes the second bill and sends it off on its mission.

As we all step out to accompany Micolao and Señora María to the truck, Fred tugs at my sleeve: "You're gonna ask them, aren't you?"

"Of course." And I ask Micolao, very apologetically (how many times have I done this before!) for a favor: My friend is sick, the pregnant girl—could he please take her and her friends to a doctor in San Antonio? It's urgent.

"*Sí, como no*," says Micolao, and a moment later Susan and Fred and Ed and I are embracing as we did on the day we met, and then Fred and Ed help Señora María get into the truck, and climb up onto the back, and wave back as Susan and I wave and the truck rumbles off downhill and into the darkness, scraping some bushes by the side of the road, the taillights gradually converging. Then it stops, and we can hear Ed's and Fred's voices sounding faint in the distance, and then, more faintly, Betsy's thin little voice, and we can vaguely make out their slow, careful, shuffling progress as Fred and Ed help Betsy walk along the path from the house to the brightly lit cab of the truck. Then the door slams, and the truck rumbles and mutters off into the night, leaving Susan and me standing alone at the top of the mountain. The night is still and as suddenly intimate as if a door had shut upon us. Walking back to the house, Susan reaches for my hand. We stop before the steps to the terrace, embrace, and kiss. We walk into our room, past Shooce and the suckling puppies, and take off each other's clothes with tender impatience. No need to make love, love makes itself.

A week passes, and we hear nothing from Fretsy and Bed. "Is there still a chance of our forming a commune with them?" I ask this of the I Ching. The response is discouraging: "Wind blowing over water disperses it, dissolving it into foam and mist." Then Blaise shows up in his beat-up Renault: "You must come, Schneider is *fleep-out!*" With Susan and Gina, we drive to Blaise and Juliette's house in Ibiza, where Schneider has been hiding from the CIA ever since he sent off that letter to Nixon, adding to the lines I've already read some insinuating soul-talk to the effect that "we are all brothers," that brothers are proverbially prone to kill each other, and that therefore the President cannot trust anyone, since anyone, including Schneider, might kill him, but that, as matters stand, he might as well put his faith in at least one person, namely Schneider. Realizing that such a message might not be allowed to reach the President, Schneider approached the British Consul in Barcelona, hoping to engage his influence and credibility in a cause that could only benefit the Commonwealth, since Yorunta knows no boundaries of race or nation.

"What is Yorunta?" I ask, and Blaise taps his forehead with the tip of his index finger.

"What did the Consul say?" Susan wants to know.

"Schneider never spoke to the Consul. The Guardia Civil put him on the boat back to Ibiza."

Lucky man! I've heard a few things about Spanish madhouses.

We find Schneider ensconced on a throne of pillows and surrounded by the usual motley crew, ten or twelve people, including Milton, MacDougal, Helle, little Baxter, Juliette, several ragged blue-eyed Australians, and Basil, who has turned his back on Schneider and is shaping a rhomboid form in Baxter's pink plasticine. Ed is there too, sitting at Schneider's feet like a disciple. Schneider is orating on "cosmic psychology," the power of words, magic, "thinking in other categories," Jews, numbers, Hitler, and Yorunta. "Who or what is Yorunta?" I ask, and Schneider is happy to enlighten me, dark eyes burning above his prophet's beard. The name "Yorunta" is derived from three English words: "Your own talk." Each of us is Yorunta. There is no Schneider, no Blaise, no Joel, no Helle, Basil, or Baxter, there is only Yorunta. Strictly speaking, Yorunta is all people taken together, but only the handful of people in this room have an inkling of this tremendous fact and its implications. Our task now is to let each man, woman, and child realize, each for him- and herself, that each is Yorunta and none other. To achieve this, there is need of a vast organization dedicated to the communication of Yorunta to Yorunta by every means—art, language, propaganda, even force. At the center of this enterprise is the Logos, the Word, and the Word is God. Whoever is doing the talking is wielding divine power, is in fact the Godhead himself; and whoever is doing the listening is, for the time being, not God. The roles are exchangeable; that exchange is called "dialogue." I notice that Schneider is doing all the talking, and only listens in a perfunctory, formal manner when someone else says anything.

While Schneider continues his disquisition, Ed gets up and asks me to step outside with him. His gray, grave eyes rest upon me with a brightness I haven't seen in them before. He gazes and shines and does not speak.

"What's happening?" I ask.

"Bad news and good news."

"What's the bad news?"

"The baby died."

"Why? What happened?

"Micolao drove us around for hours looking for a doctor. They all refused to treat her. We couldn't understand a word of what anyone was saying, but we figured it had something to do with Betsy's being underage and pregnant and unmarried. We finally took the boat to Barcelona and checked into a hospital. Betsy had a ruptured appendix. We were just in time, she just barely made it. Fred insisted on staying at her bedside around the clock, but then he got distracted by one of the nurses and ended up balling her in the laundry room. Somehow Betsy found out about it—I think the nurse let her know—and that sent her downhill again. It was touch-and-go for a couple of days. Now they're holding hands and talking about marriage. Betsy and Fred, I mean. But the baby was stillborn—poisoned."

"And the good news?"

"I'm gonna follow him."

"Who?"

"Schneider."

"Are you serious?"

He nods.

"And where's he going to lead you?"

"If I knew, I wouldn't follow." He hadn't heard my sarcasm.

"Schneider is crazy," I say. Ed smiles indulgently. We go back inside. Schneider is initiating the Australians: "I christen you Yorunta," with a popish touch of two fingers to the convert's forehead. I, too, submit to the ritual. Hadn't I said much the same thing the year before when I believed myself to be "the One in Whose name Jo-El is proclaimed the everlasting life of That I Am as all names do proclaim Me," and hadn't I tried to initiate others in much the same way? But I left them their names; Max wants a oneness without any difference. "I may be Yorunta," I say, "but I talk my own talk, not yours." A hardness comes into his eyes, he's calculating. I could swear that I know what he's thinking: Since Yorunta is everyone, and the word Yorunta comes from "your-own-talk," and since "the Word" is God and Yorunta is Schneider's brainchild, it follows that Schneider is God and Yorunta his creation, and all who profess to be Yorunta along with Schneider are automatically an effect of which he is the cause. Your logic is too loosely strung, Yorunta, Jo-El has escaped. Jo-El is a jealous god, he will not suffer any Yoruntas beside him.

But Schneider has greater problems than my unbelief. Blaise, super-hippie, the island's mother hen, wants to sweep the homeless out of his house, and Schneider in particular. Of course Schneider isn't actually homeless, but he's afraid of going home, his *finca* is filled with anti-Semitic spirits, attracted like flies by a letter he wrote to the government of Israel and neglected to mail. Can't he stay, please, at least for a week? Blaise shakes his bull's head in refusal. Juliette has withdrawn to the bedroom, so I assume it's on her account that Schneider is being ejected. He must have offended her, frightened her, who knows. I propose the obvious solution: Schneider and Ed could move into the vacant house down the hill from ours. Blaise offers to drive us to it. On the way, he stops for gas. Schneider gets out, waves good-bye, and leaves. We drive on without him. Three days later Ed comes to the shed I've converted into an office (with a rabbit coop for a desk). He's carrying his backpack. He's leaving, he says, leaving for good. Schneider rejected him. He's already said good-bye to Susan and Gina. Could I cast the I Ching for him? The oracle tells him that it would be advantageous for him to limit himself in some manner, and to live for a while within these limitations; and that, with confidence and sincerity, he will succeed in crossing the great water. I walk with him—Gina is riding on my shoulders—down the road to where it forks at the foot of a powerful old oak with dramatic holes in its trunk, its roots rising halfway out of the earth. It looks as if it should be dead, but its branches are heavy with leaves. There we stand, gazing at a sight we have welcomed gratefully many times on the way uphill from the town. "That seed didn't think twice when it started to grow," Ed says. We shake hands. Ed says "Peace be with you" and starts walking downhill. Then he turns around and says: "I'll see you in Paris." "That's right," I say, "July 4, 1970."

A Letter from Stefan

Pondicherry, March 10, 1969

"To Whom It May Concern"

I shall not reveal what holds us concealed:
The breath of the flame in the bold lion tame.
Through storm-sent Clouds, burdened with guilt
Ride the average messengers, stoned to the hilt.
I have left my two biceps at home on the bed
And proceeded on foot to go earn my bread.
Bread I found none, but some crusts and a slice
Were given to me with a quart of advice.
I regret having mentioned whereto I was bound,
For otherwise I would have never been found.
But your thoughts found me out, and they cancelled my trek,
So I am again at your call and your beck.
My own thoughts besiege me, please don't send me yours.
I'll ask for them, though, if a shortage occurs.
Forgive the precision of what I impart,
I am not skilled enough to turn it to art.
But the words I am sure will be understood
By your kind nodding heads as your hands rap the wood.
(Three times is enough, or so I believe,
Your worries, if any, to heal and relieve.)
Forgive my impatience and bid me farewell
To continue my trip to the pit of the well.
I am looking for WATER if truth must be told,
But the plot of the story is old, very old.
So here I must break, and not down, but off,
For it does seem to me I've said more than enough.

But better to do and to say what is done
Than wordless and heartless to turn and to run.
I will speed this to you in a silver airplane
With the wish to return to you not without gain.
But if you would wish me a fortunate trip,
Please do release me from your worry's grip,
And leave me to roam as a bird in the air,
To be taken care of by No One Nowhere.
My life is your life and your life is mine,
So please do not think of me all of the time.

Onward! Onward! There is no leisure in the house of my fear. My Counterpoint, so polite until now, has taken to nudging me, rather firmly, away from certain gilded doors I'm inclined to open, and, with particular insistence, away from places inviting to rest or reflection, like that room filled with old books we just passed, with a plush couch in front of a blazing hearth and the shadow of a knight's suit of armor leaping on the walls; or the smooth marble edge of a fountain stocked, for some reason, with lobsters—which, if I saw rightly, had their claws taped, a disquieting detail that should not have been passed over; and then, at apparently random moments, he'll suddenly shove me in a direction no sane organism would take of its own accord, straight through a concrete wall, for instance, which, when a moment later I test it with a push of my shoulder, proves to be what it seemed before I passed through it. This Counterpoint has become "directive," an approach I have never responded to with alacrity. He knows that, of course, so I have to presume he has his good reasons for hurrying me. Not that this gives me comfort. Even the worst of us have their good reasons. But I have to remind myself that he and I are no longer enemies; or rather, that we've come to some kind of truce; that I have been operating on the extraordinary supposition that I might indeed be able to trust him, despite the torture I've suffered at his hands; and that this venture of writing my way back to set free what ghosts of unredeemed suffering may still lie trapped in the past could not be undertaken, or accomplished, without him.

Oh, now I see, at last, where he has been guiding me: a brick-colored courtyard, sunlit, square, surrounding a turquoise swimming-pool—something of a joke, since the whole house is submerged—not in water, as I first supposed, it's thinner than that, a translucent fluid that offers a faint resistance to every step. Tiring! Why can't we slow down? Why not fly, if speed is what's wanted? I'd like to ask him that, but he doesn't allow me to turn for so much as a glimpse of his face, which I presume still presents that benign if clichéd image of seasoned wisdom, a white-whiskered old Chinese man. However, he's letting me stop now. A surprisingly cheerful place this is, open to light and sky. Thank God for permeable walls! And there, with his back turned toward me, facing the pool and sitting right by its edge, is a person—a gray-haired man, cross-legged, his head bowed—the first soul I've encountered down here. . . .

Though, come to think of it, I've seen signs of presences other than mine, beginning with my mother's self-portrait near the entrance: a pair of crutches, probably Stefan's after his first attempt to kill himself; my stepfather's blue canvas espadrilles, similar to a pair I bought in Ibiza; a cotton dress on a hanger, with large bright flowers printed on it, belonging to sweet-smelling Zita, our maid and a second mother to me when I was a child. . . . I can't imagine why these mementos were put in the house of my fear. . . . Again an abrupt shove, advancing me several steps toward the man by the pool. I protest: I'm not a chess piece! And I don't like standing so close to a person who isn't aware of my presence. If I were invisible, I wouldn't mind, but I'm near enough to stir the hairs on his cheek with my breathing, a slight turn of his head would put me in his field of vision. In which case I imagine he would be alarmed and then maybe angry at being stalked like this. But I'm more curious than cautious. I peer over his shoulder. He is reading. The book in his hands is written in Spanish. I lean in more closely to make out the text. It is a novel about a man falling through time to his death. He falls from the roof of a tall building, headfirst, and as he falls, windows fly past him, and each window frames a scene from his life, a flicker of memory so complete in its details and meanings that he is able to forget—and he forgets gladly—that his life, the only real life he has, is speeding like an arrow to its mark. In the top margin of each page, in bold italic type, are the words

LA TUMBA

Clever title! It has two meanings, "the fall" and "the tomb." The falling man is none other than myself in the upper world, 29-year-old Joel lying on a mattress in the back of a Volkswagen bus he just bought but does not know how to drive. A young Canadian he met in Ibiza is sitting at the wheel. Susan is in the front passenger seat, laughing at something the Canadian just said. Gina lies asleep on the mattress under a blanket, hugging Smiley, her gray flannel mouse. They are all on their way to Saanen, Switzerland, to attend the talks of a sage, J. Krishnamurti, and to find kindred lost souls in search of a commune. He does not yet know that he is falling. He is aware of an acceleration, he can measure it against the memory of slower rhythms, longer days, but he is not, at the moment, afraid, as I am afraid, here and now in the House of my Fear, of the fall I see coming. However, I feel the pull of a different gravity, back, back, "into the backward and abysm of time." Closing my eyes, I see myself as a child standing on the roof of an Aztec pyramid with my stepfather, who is holding my hand as I venture near the edge of the stone pit where the priests used to perform their bloody sacrifices. . . . Or was it that other time when we were in the mountains and Bodo told me to drop a pebble into a gaping fissure in the rock, and the pebble fell and fell and fell and fell until it struck water with a remote hollow

. . . b l o o k ? . . .

There's a trace of the Coliseum in the pyramid, I notice, lions instead of obsidian knives, a hint of spectacular cruelty in any case. . . . Now the man turns the page, and I notice the text is unparagraphed—one solid block of words, if it's a tomb, or else a plunging fall—reaching, in any case, from the top of the first page to the bottom of the last without a break, I'm sure. I feel a deep sympathy with this reader. I, too, would read such a book with fascination. But I must be careful not to betray my presence to him. The fright could cause him to lose his balance, he might fall into the pool—not the end of the world for either of us, but embarrassing. And only now do I notice that what I took to be a patio surrounding a pool is really a roof, a wide square of flat terra-cotta tiles framing the open pit of a courtyard, I don't know how many stories deep. I draw back quickly and can no longer read the words on the page. Instead I notice what a strange bulging face the back of a head presents—eyeless, noseless, mouthless, but with a set of ears and a neck, an un-face . . . and a sickening suspicion arises: that it is not I who am spying on an unassuming stranger, but he who has been observing, or let's say, mentally tasting me all along, with interest and quiet amusement, through some unknown organ of perception.

And now it begins.

A shock, like an axe-blow drawing the first sap of remembrance:

That it's He, and that He may be none other than what I am when all masks of identity have been removed, and that I must not, must not meet Him face-to-face, though I know I have met Him before (when?!) and will again, and somewhere in the depths of me even want to with a passionate urgency that frightens me more than any mortal danger I could imagine, because He is the sum and multiplication and geometric progression of all danger and pain, I've seen the proof of it, **CHOP!** and I know it as flesh knows the cut of a knife: that I'm not a leaf among leaves but the tree itself. **GOOD! GET A FEEL OF IT!** Oh but this is something other than Pain and Fear . . . Knowledge . . . and a marveling pride opens out in me . . . and a wordless gratitude . . . **IDIOT! AS IF MY INTENT WERE TO BRING YOU KNOWLEDGE OF ROOT AND CROWN. A TOOTHACHE UPON YOU, FOR STARTERS!** and now I recall that I thought these same thoughts and heard these same brutal admonitions the last time, though not in the same order, and that, when I thought and heard them, I knew it was not the first time then either and that the time before that had been the same also, an endless series of identical moments reaching back, back, back forever, and forward into the future as well, and laterally, too, and inward in as many dimensions as the mind cared or dared to imagine; but it didn't and doesn't dare, and this very act of dreading a memory of infinite repetition is the remembering of that dread, and is the knowledge that this dread is, and was, and will almost certainly be again the first whisper of a hint that the horror, being endless, is always only the beginning. . . .

ETERNAL RECURRENCE!

The words blast an alarm through all the corners of the kingdom. I open my mouth to defend, to explain myself, but the fact of the matter is too simple for words: I'm cracked open, that's all **CHOP!** And again the recognition: This is known, this was many times before, this is old, old knowledge . . . a silent scream of protest:

NO!

And another blow: **CHOP!**

YES YOU REMEMBER!

I swallow, I gulp

(the gulp too is a repetition)

HA! HA! HA!

What's so . . .

NOW YOU GET IT!

Adam's apple, it's an old joke, stale really

**MIGHT AS WELL CALL A RAINDROP, A PINECONE
A REPETITION,
YOU'VE BEEN GULPING SINCE THE BEGINNING OF TIME!**

Tears well up

AAAW

What's that, pity?

HAHAHAHAHA!

How did I . . .

how can . . .

but . . .

how far does this . . .

oh God . . .

these questions . . .

these words . . .

insufferable . . .

repeated . . .

forever . . .

**NOW YOU ARE AWAKE! YOU COULDN'T BE MORE AWAKE IF
A SNAKE CAME SLITHERING INTO YOUR ROOM!**

Would that it were that, a beast or a monster, I might have a chance to defend
myself. But this enemy has no face, no body, no smell, no location, it's nearer
than near, it's my own secret will . . .

NO!

**WHAT A RIDICULOUS MINCING VIRGIN SQUEAL,
WHEN YOU'RE PANTING WITH LUST FOR KNOWLEDGE!
I'LL PLAY A MUSIC ON YOUR BRAIN THAT WILL MAKE THOSE
STIFF-FINGERED DO-RE-MI-FA-SO'S YOU'VE BEEN PLAYING
ON YOUR LEDGER, ON YOUR ALPHABET, TO THE
METRONOME BEAT OF YOUR THREE-CORNERED
LOGIC, LOOK LIKE THE CHILD'S PLAY THEY ARE.
THERE'S BEEN ENOUGH LITERATURE.
THE WORLD IS ON FIRE.**

Where am I? Alone in the dark. How did I get here? I fell. I'm still falling.

Krishnamurti

Saanen, Switzerland.

Krishnamurti sits on a plain wooden chair near the exit of the large gray dome-like tent, raised on a dais above his listeners, an old brown-skinned man with a wonderful face, refined and passionate, marked by the knowledge of pain and beauty, a spray of white hair brushed forward on one temple and in an ample sweep across his head, casually dressed in gray slacks, a white shirt, and a dove-blue sweater, long slender hands resting in his lap, one foot tucked behind the other, scanning us through dark, doleful eyes as our rustling and whispering settle down to a hush of attention. The impression of fragility is dispelled the moment he speaks.

"Here we are again," he says, in a ringing Oxford-accented voice, "with our flags all aflutter . . . the Swiss with their banking secrets . . . the French with their conceited palates . . . the Americans in their provincial glut . . . the British with their beastly little Queen . . ."

He moves on to more particular insults: "Some of you have been following me for forty years. We have grown old together. And there you still sit with your eyes rolled up into your heads, as if by hearing the speaker's words you were more likely to grasp something that would withstand the corrosion of time." Strange opening for an oriental sage, not kind or dispassionate, probably not wise either, but we are not here to be flattered, we are here to "die to the past," which surely includes our puny identities, personal and collective. Down with the ego! He wields his right arm up and down, left and right, like a crosshatching sword, and we hold up our heads, some six hundred of us, for the blessing of decapitation: freedom from the known!

But let me not disparage the subtlety of Krishnamurti's discourse, or diminish the cut of his words as he spells out for us the picture of the world we live in, its misery and meanness: from the more obvious obscenities, the ones we imbibe with our morning coffee as we peruse the global gossip columns, to those nuclear breeding-places of vice and unhappiness, our own families: dependence, attachment, domination usurping the name of love; intelligence blunted, the sense of beauty coarsened, the spirit of inquiry suppressed in schools dedicated to the mere replication of collective memory; the flame of discontent smothered in conformity or else perverted in political strife; forty years of office work and the small consolations of parenthood held out as supreme goals for a boy or girl of pacific inclination, and for the more aggressive, brutal triumph in the marketplace of commodities or ideas. How is a person who seeks the way out of this labyrinth, not just for himself but for the countless others whose misery and confusion he recognizes as his own, how is such a person to proceed, where should he turn? Outside the citadels of ambition, cults and religions beckon, altars shrouded in incense, priests robed in ancient dignity. Is there a god who can show us the way? Are there temples and holy books not made to fortify him who made all the mischief in the first place, the lord of the castle, the one who holds captive the maiden innocence of life? This is no longer Krishnamurti speaking, this is Joel drifting off on the waves of a dream. My brother, how did you get so lost? How could your face become a mask for the eyes of madness to stare through? Alma, my mother, why were you made to give birth to such suffering? Bodo, why did you die a fly's death in that shimmering web, all the joy of life sucked out of you by the monster you set out to conquer? A door slams shut behind me. Where am I? Alone in the dark. How did I get here? I fell. I have been here before. . . . I . . . I . . . I . . . The word echoes. A yawning ache opens out in my heart. I must understand it. I . . .

"Why?" asks a voice in the dark. "Why not simply suffer it?"

What a question![5] Who is this? But I already know.

"I don't have to listen to you. You are not my master."

My Tormentor responds by plucking a chord on a few select nerves in my bowels, casually, an arpeggio of pain. He laughs, and I have to agree, my defiance sounds ludicrous now.

But He does respect courage, I've noticed, so I ask Him, shivering, "What do you want?"

His silence regards me, a single cold eye.

He wants what I want, I realize then: unconditional truth.

The shock of that threat throws me for a spin, I'm back in the big tent, riveted by Krishnamurti's eyes, which are peering straight into mine, and with huge

---

5. Sage counsel, it seems to me now, here in Brooklyn, but I listened to Fear instead.

relief, and not for the first time, I relegate the Antagonist to the realm of unreal things.

"If in fact you . . . ," Krishnamurti says (me?), ". . . are not separate from the world . . . ," leaning forward and pressing his thumb and two fingers together as if about to throw a dart (I'm ready, I'm ready! but he is no longer looking at me), ". . . this mad, brutal world, with its violence, misery, war, starvation, torture. . . . If in fact you are the world and the world is what you are . . ." (I strain, strive to comprehend it: choiceless awareness of what is, no effort, no naming or interpreting, no lapse of time in the act of perception, no distinction between the observer and the observed, no residue of memory, what the hell is it?), ". . . and you realize this, with your brain, your heart, your nerves, your whole being . . . not as an intellectual proposition or a belief, but as a fact . . . Are you with me?"

I'm trying, I'm trying.

"Please don't just sit back waiting for wise words, because there is no such thing. I am not a leader, you know, and I hope most of you have not come to be led. All this is quite pointless unless we proceed together, inquire together. I don't know whether . . . are we in fact doing that?" The question is disarmingly sincere. Various heads nod.

"Yes!" someone cries.

"Very well, then. What happens in a mind that has come this far? That has understood the nature of this violent self-centered activity we miscall life?"

"Energy," someone says, hopefully.

"No, sir, don't answer, just stay with the question. . . . What happens . . . ?"

He looks around, still holding that dart, regards me briefly, rousing me to titanic aspiration, and moves on in search of a worthier target.

"In the very structure of the brain," he adds. "What happens?"

The tension is enormous, but nothing happens, nothing ever does in these colloquies charged with apocalyptic innuendo, no brain catches fire, we walk out, stunned, into the crisp cold Alpine air. Back to the campsite, where Susan is waiting with Gina by the dirty green bus in the din of the polluted river. She's worried. Our money is running out. What if the next installment from Chattanooga doesn't come in time? Who should we borrow from? We don't know a soul here. We can't even leave the damn campsite, since neither of us knows how to drive. "I'm not worried," I say. I trust in Chance. Susan is so frustrated she picks up the nearest object—a kitchen knife—and throws it at me. The handle strikes me in the chest. We stare at each other open-mouthed. Have we really come to this pass? No, we haven't. We burst out laughing. Then an elfin figure comes out of the mist, wearing a peaked knitted cap with earflaps, shirtless, barefoot, walking with a peculiarly springy stride. He seems to be looking for someone, he's searching the faces and eyes of strangers. Seeing me leaning against the open doorway of the bus, he breaks into a sunburst of smile, and abruptly smothers it, turns, and walks off, erect and graceful, like a dancer. A few moments later he comes back to where Susan and I are helping Gina stir vegetables in a pan over the gas burner.

"You people look as if you need money," he says.

I confirm it: "How could you tell?"

He peels a bunch of Swiss francs from his pocket.

"I have lots of money. I can lend you some."

I place my palms together and bow to him. Later I write down his name in my journal: Steve Marpol. If anyone knows his whereabouts, please let me know. I would like to repay him.

I would also like to rewrite a harsh little exchange of words I had with my brother. He arrived three days late for the conference, deathly pale, stiff, thin, his jaws pulsing, his lips slack with sadness, his forehead cloven by a fierce frown. He was on the way home from India, where he had failed to find the Dharma teacher he had been looking for. His last attempt had been with Lama Govinda in Nepal. After a brief interview, the old monk had instructed him— with the kindest intention, I'm sure—to seek psychiatric help without delay. He was back on the macrobiotic diet, it helped him, he said.

"And that?" he asked, pointing at my astrological charts (Milton in Ibiza had taught me how to read them), "does that help you?"

I had never asked myself this question.

"It helps me . . . to understand others," I said.

"Others!" he snorted. "For what purpose?" and walked away, livid. We hardly talked after that, but the pulsing of his jaw spoke clearly enough. Give me peace, it said, or get out of my way. I felt the impulse to hug him, to tell him that I loved him. But he would have perceived it as glib condescension: "Try love for a change, little brother. Will is not the way." Besides, what did I know? I was no less confused than he was, just luckier.

He spent half the night sitting upright in the bus while Susan, Gina, and I slept. By the morning he was calmer. I can see him now, smiling as Gina walks off with her mouse-doll to greet a little boy she's met on the campsite. The day's topic in the big tent is "fear and pleasure." I am sitting on the floor near the exit. Krishnamurti wields his long arm and flat hand like a sword, slicing, severing: pleasure from joy, not the same thing. In the first, the circling of thought, the accretion of time around an experience, a greed for continuance and repetition, a smothering, killing glue of attachment; in the second . . . Ah, and he shows it with one lordly gesture: enjoyment: of a setting sun, a goblet held in his palm, the untitled king of a boundless land, possessionless and immeasurably rich. Pleasure: . . . and again with a gesture he evokes the circling of memory, but this time the turning thing has a hidden back, and that back turns frontward and is revealed as the face of fear, the obverse of pleasure. At this moment a cold wind blows through a half-open flap in the tent, and something else, a mental, shivering movement, wafts through the audience, stirring faces and bodies like dry leaves. Krishnamurti's speech halts, he appears to be looking or listening alertly. A hand rises up from the cold rustling swirl.

"Sir," Krishnamurti says, "we will have questions later, would you kindly . . ."

But Stefan stands up. "I have much acquaintance with fear," he says. The audience, shocked by the interruption, whispers and hisses some hushing advice, but he continues in that peculiar clipped accent he has developed since he began traveling in Asia, and which may in part be caused by the tension in his jaws: "I understand the connection with pleasure. But there is Evil, you see, there are powers of Evil, and I am afraid they are not just a shadow of the pleasure principle. How can I meet Evil without being afraid? That is my question."

"Sir, we shall come to this in due time, if I may ask for your patience."

Stefan sits down. The due time never comes. The word "evil" is not mentioned again. That afternoon, Stefan takes the train to Zurich, from where he will fly back to our mother in New York. At sunset, gazing into the river, I see in the roiling yellow and black ropes of water the stripes of a tiger. I have seen beasts and faces in clouds many times, but never felt them looking back at me. This tiger is crouching, tensed. I turn and walk to the van, to my family, with fear in my back.

■ ■ ■

"The will is in confusion." Thus spake the I Ching, in response to a question about "forming a commune." It's not a matter of "forming" anything, I am told, but of bringing a sacrifice. "The King approaches his temple." The human floods are collecting and rising above the earth—draft dodgers, anarchists, globe trotters, utopians, spiritual fortune hunters—to be contained, one would hope, within bounds that will make of us a lake, serene and cheerful, instead of just something let loose, a torrent of resentments and fears. "Religious forces are needed." What sacrifice, though? And who is the King who will perform it?

Not me. How could it be me? I am to consult "the great man." I know who that is. I am to "undertake something." Success is assured.

On a bench in front of the elegant chalet where Krishnamurti is staying, I await my turn for an interview. But what a word for such an encounter. Just yesterday, a six-foot American freak with a few dozen Acid trips too many behind him trudged up this hill in a hurry "to have it out with the little fuck once and for all" after spending two years trying to get him to answer his questions about Super-Nature, depressed the door-latch without knocking, stepped in with a long stride, and encountered the old man staring up at him with a look of fierce delight and exclaiming: "Ah!" as he took the befuddled intruder by an elbow and gently but with irresistible firmness conducted him back out the door and locked it. A young Swiss man is in there right now. I imagine him straining to meet, or elude, the scalpel thrust of a question: "Sir, who is it that wants knowledge and freedom and power all in one?" Who indeed. It is I who was asking that question. God help me. Should I tell him about the attacks of infinity I have been suffering? No, that's irrelevant. Parked by the edge of the road is the green and white VW bus, with Susan and Gina inside it, our luggage, my books (a traveling library by now), and half a dozen Dutch freaks. We're headed for Holland, because when I posted a query on the campsite's bulletin board requesting a chauffeur in exchange for a free ride to a destination of his choice, the first licensed driver who answered was Jan Waterstrat, a former First Officer in the Dutch navy, now an Acid-head with blond Medusa curls and two small blue uniform buttons for eyes, very round and very bright. He, too, disapproves of Krishnamurti, a mean-spirited old fart on the warpath against youth and pleasure. He disapproves of me, also, for my foolishness in "going to the Sphinx for answers"—that's how he put it. Now the ornately carved door of the chalet opens and the young Swiss steps out all lit up by some happy emotion and walks past me with a jaunty stride, smiling, blushing deeply. He was in there no more than ten minutes! I won't be dispatched so quickly. Krishnamurti holds open the door. I avoid looking at him for more than an instant. I have read about fathomless eyes—he has them: large, dark, the pupils indistinguishable from the iris, peculiarly glazed, like the eyes of a blind man. But it isn't *his* gaze I fear, it is mine; as if the urgency of my need could hurt him. He leads me into a room, offers me a chair. The room breathes wealth, comfort, refinement, but I don't look around. I am the object of scrutiny after all—my own, not his. He hesitates next to the chair facing mine and walks back where we came from, placing a hand on my shoulder as he passes and murmuring: "I'll be right back." A gentling reassurance lingers where he touched me. My hunched shoulders settle. I despise myself for being so nervous. He passes me again, his walk almost soundless; sits down, tucking his trouser legs to protect the crease, draws one foot behind the other, rests his palms on his lap, and looks at me.

"So. What brings you here?"

Good God, what a question. My whole life swirls around me like troubled water. The future, too: some awful forebodings. . . . Should I tell him? But he has them himself, he has told us about them: the constant destruction, the disintegration, worldwide. And the self at the center, weaving the pattern, incessant, a deepening hell.

"I don't know where to begin," I say.

"Begin anywhere," he suggests.

And I begin by condensing oceans of experience into psychogrammatical chunks: "communist parents . . . ," "two writing fathers . . . ," "a mentally ill brother . . . ," while my face contorts in self-disgust. I pause. The chunks stand grouped around an empty center. What brought me here? A dilemma. What is it? "On the one hand," I say, holding out a hand, and for the next few minutes, like Vishnu, I juggle a dozen options on as many hands: on the one hand my family, on the other, religion; on the one hand art, on the other, ambition and thirst for fame; on the one hand my sick brother, on the other my own comfort; on the one hand the dream, since childhood, of being a writer, on the other the reality, at age twenty-nine, of having published exactly one poem; on the one hand a constitutional need for unbounded personal freedom, on the other the narrowing focus of practical duties I will have to perform when our money runs out; on the one hand love, on the other, security; on the one hand the world, on the other hand myself. As I speak, Krishnamurti's hands lift off his lap, palms upward, and rise and fall in alternation, like scales. He's mirroring me. I drop my hands.

"How long have you been doing that?" he asks.

"A long time," I say.

We sit in silence for a few minutes. I dare not look at him. This silence frightens me. It moves. It's not the sort of stillness you can rest in.

"I've been listening to your talks," I begin, raising my eyes to meet his again, "and reading your books for several years now, and I haven't yet found—" (the words gushing now with an urgency that threatens to drive tears out of my eyes) "—haven't entered—the choiceless awareness you speak of."

"What are you waiting for?"

The question stuns like a sledgehammer. I'm speechless, not just on the tongue but in the brain.

The mind rallies, tries to forestall defeat. "I don't know," it says. "I'm caught between . . ." And there are my hands again, balancing options.

This time I give up—but what am I saying, "I," the whole fortress of self-defense capitulates, its tenant disarmed, the drawbridge let down, defeat admitted. In place of an enemy, sunlight pours in through the picture window. There it is, the garden, as it was before anyone named it, though names come to mind. A blackbird bathing in a stone basin filled with rainwater. So many birds! Their chirping and piping scattered in stillness like jewels on clear glass.

"You mean . . . ," I say quietly, "this is it?" And I look at him, fearing another subtraction.

"It must be," he says without hesitation.

Gratitude. Stillness, and the little noises at home in it.

"It all seems very simple," I say.

"Keep it that way," he says.

Tears in my heart. I'm smiling. So this is it? This, the answer? It's almost too simple. What am I going to do with my life? Listen to birds? All the questions I came with start stirring again: Stefan, art, war, love . . . Stefan. Why did Krishnamurti not answer Stefan's question about fear and evil? Krishnamurti slaps his knee.

"Basta," he says, and stands up. I follow his motion: off the chair and out of the room, out of the room and toward the door. I'm being dismissed. I turn to thank him, and feel again that I am assaulting him with the violence of my emotions.

"You are welcome," he says, without my saying anything. As I walk toward my family and traveling companions and friends, who are waiting for me in the bus, I realize I didn't say good-bye. I stop and turn. Krishnamurti is turning away and closing the door. I suddenly feel pity for him. Is there anyone more alone than he?

My brother.

Falling

All through the long trip to Holland, in conversation, in moments of half slumber on the big mattress in the back of the bus (Jan Waterstrat is driving), while changing Gina's diapers, at rest stops shaded by pines at the edge of the Autobahn, a subtle, secret, bubbling joy interrupts the stream of thought and experience. This, if I steeped myself in it, I know, is the force that would gather the tribes.

"But that would be the death of you," the Antagonist says, sword in hand.

So that is the sacrifice. I'm not ready. The faint bubbling joy recedes and the cares of the day enclose the mind like a lead coffin, dragging it down into bottomless sleep. But this sleep is not dreamless. I am falling, falling, the pictures of passing time flitting by like wind-driven clouds: the German police who flag us down and force us to have our worn-out brake-linings replaced, and the long conversation among the Dutch freaks after that, about German officiousness and rigidity, and how much more sensible and humane the Dutch are, and the Dutch border police then subjecting us to a humiliating strip search and presenting us with a statute according to which no Dutch citizen on Dutch soil is permitted to drive a car registered outside Holland. Stranded, we contemplate our options: break away and risk motorized pursuit, or . . . and the other option falls into view like a sign from heaven, half a mile down the road, a hitchhiker. Let him not be Dutch! He's German. He is straight as a flagpole and headed for Flanders, but hearing and seeing our predicament, he unshoulders his knapsack, sits down at the wheel, and drives us far out of his way to the houseboat up north near Leeuwarden where Jan lives with Antje, his pregnant young wife. All the other Dutch freaks are dropped off on the way. Arrived at long last, our benefactor, shrugging off the effusion of thanks he deserves, hugs the five of us, shoulders his knapsack, and begins his long hitchhike back south. The houseboat then, its gentle rocking when a passing barge wrinkles the water. Gina, with remnants of Spanish still trailing her English speech, instructing her dolls in the palate-scraping language she hears around her. Antje wooing her with honey and tickling her feet and walking with her by the river. She's

fond of Susan and of me, too, and likes my idea of a commune as a new kind
of family inclusive of spiritual kin. There's room in the boat, why not live
together? She knows something about astrology and finds our charts com-
patible. "If only the transit of Saturn wasn't making you heavy and sad," she
says, "that's a hard one for Jan to take, and he thinks it's your natural tempera-
ment." The fact is, he dislikes me. I've ingested too much Krishnamurti with
my LSD, I read too much altogether, blinding myself to the pleasures of life
and prattling about some phantom Love and Enlightenment as if sex, food, and
friendship were nothing, no wonder I'm getting bummed out by drugs. There
he sits, with his rosebud lips pursed, a Calvin and an Epicure joined as one,
glaring his censure through hard button-eyes as he sucks on a long Turkish
pipe. Time to leave, and the sooner the better. If only I knew how to drive. And
our money's running out. And the bank in Chattanooga is not responding to
my telegrams.

At night, before I've dropped off to sleep, two puzzling images appear before
me: an American flag, and a pair of dice. What does this flag, or any flag, have
to do with me? But the dice mean something, I believe in Chance. And promptly
the god sends us three bearded English hitchhikers on their way home from
Sweden, picked up by a truck-driving friend of Jan's. They can hardly believe
their luck: a ride straight to their doorstep in Weymouth, if they do the driving
and pay for gas. Another telegram to Chattanooga, urging a transfer of funds to
Weymouth—as likely a resting-place as Leeuwarden—and on we go, homeless
strangers in our own car. The Englishmen find Gina's Anglo-Hispanic patter
amusing, her occasional fit of willful crankiness less so, Susan tolerably pleasant but not really hip, and me objectionable for reasons I can only guess at.
Did Jan sprinkle poison in their ears before we left? Am I talking too much
about Krishnamurti? Do I sound like a proselyte? Is it the combination of my
being an American who lives like a refugee, the recipient of an inheritance who
doesn't have enough money, the owner of a bus who doesn't know how to drive,
an Acid freak who hoards books like a traveling scholar? The nearer we come
to Weymouth, the colder the atmosphere gets. We arrive on a rainy weekend,
the bank is closed, so is the American Express office. The Englishmen deposit
us in a house inhabited by friends of theirs, two couples not markedly fond of
each other and angry at us for the claim our need makes on their charity. "We
have a spare room, of course you can stay while you have to." But that night
Susan, taking a bath, hears one of the women saying, with her voice lowered:
"Really, George, why not the bus, there's a mattress in there," to which George

mutters an irritated rejoinder about the coldness of night and "the baby, for Pete's sake." We post a notice on a local bulletin board, requesting a driver for a trip to London. Monday comes, Tuesday, with no news from the bank, no response from a driver. We huddle for human warmth in our room, since our unwilling hosts all but spit their displeasure whenever our paths cross. I examine my horoscope and discover a feature that is also present in Richard Nixon's chart. It betokens, according to the dean of English astrologers, C.E.O. Carter, a propensity to have *confused conditions* thrust upon one: "The native may be circumspect and practical to a fault, yet at some time in the life his prudence seems strangely to desert him, and a long train of disorder may have to be worked out." Nixon's troubles have yet to begin, but mine are in full swing already and will reach culmination in a year and a half. Against this discouraging prospect I arm myself with the dictum of another astrologer, Alan Leo: "The stars incline but do not compel." Voilà, I am inclined to trust in Chance, is this imprudent? We shall see. Wednesday morning, we hear a song on our little clock radio:

> *Baby, we gotta get out of this place*
> *If it's the last thing we ever do!*

For the first time in weeks, we look at each other and laugh.

Gina: "What's funny?"

"We're all funny," I say.

"Money is funny," Gina says, and that, in our circumstances, is an excellent joke, especially after our walk to the bank: A thousand dollars were wired through that morning. The shift in our fortune lends me wings of audacity: I'll drive! I know the basics of starting and stopping and steering, the roads aren't very crowded, I've had some practice in Spain, and I'll learn as we travel, there isn't that much to it. Freedom! The drive is uneventful until, crossing a great bridge as we enter the city of London, and drifting into a maze of arrows and signs and crisscrossing traffic, I give myself over to the guidance of instinct, which leads me to the feet of a whistle-shrilling policeman. He bends to look into the interior of the bus, sees Gina wrapped in silk scarves and surrounded by dolls—smiles, and asks where we're coming from. "America," I say. "Well, in Britain we stop for red lights," he says. "I'm sorry," I say. "Glad to hear that," he replies, cheerfully raising a hand to his visor: "Carry on, but keep your eyes open." Good advice for an unlicensed driver!

Combinations of hearsay, random turns of the road, and the counsel of *London on $5 a Day* take us to a bed-and-breakfast hotel in Paddington. A couple of days later, a realtor directs us to a flat on Christchurch Road in Brixton, a working-class neighborhood sprinkled with immigrant families from Pakistan and the Caribbean Islands. No longhairs, though. In a newspaper I find, among appeals for and offers of maid service, used cars, furnished rooms, occult secrets, marriage, and electric appliances, an invitation to join a lesbian anarchist commune in Scotland, clearly not our turf, but it shows me the concept is alive out there. If we keep it alive in our hearts, the Law of Attraction—one occult secret I believe in—should lead us to the right people, and them to us. But what am I saying, "us," it's *my* dream mainly. In one of several wrangles with Susan over whether it's wise and practical to live on hope and a dwindling bank account, I realize we have incompatible notions of what it means to live well: hers, a modest but comfortably furnished nest, with friendly neighbors and playmates for Gina; mine, a utopian island where the synergy of many or even a few people's talent, intelligence, craft, and industry would put ordinary social arrangements to shame, yes, even on a practical level. For weeks, we are alone and lonely, with only ourselves for company. All the while, I am studying and with great frustration attempting to understand a book called *The Tenth Man* by an author named Wei Wu Wei, which attempts to reveal, in parables and philosophical dialogues, the eternal (and, he says, wide-open) secret known to the Buddha, Lao-tzu, Huang-po, and Ramana Maharshi, that there are no things and no creatures, no self and no other, no world and no God, and that therefore there is no problem whatsoever.

One day, I buy a small cake of hash from a Jamaican man on King's Road. I smoke it at night after Gina and Susan are asleep. Stoned, I reread Wei Wu Wei's "quaint story" of ten monks traveling from one Master to another in search of Enlightenment. They cross a torrential river, and when they reach the other shore, one of them counts the other nine and concludes that someone is missing. Each monk in turn counts the others, and since every one of them forgets to count himself, they all end up mourning the loss of a brother, of whom they appear to remember and miss only the fact that without him their number is decreased by one. Annoyed, I close the book, suck in another toke of hash, absently staring at the diagram on the cover,

1 2 3 4 5 6 7 8 9 0 9 8 7 6 5 4 3 2 1

and hold my breath. An image appears, of a man standing in a Roman four-horse chariot, racing. The next moment I'm in the chariot. An imploding darkness closes in as I exhale and my horses gallop into the zero. Where am I?

THE VOID

says a bass voice with mock-menacing intonation, like an actor burlesquing the idea of fear; and sure enough, there's laughter, as of an audience, but I can't laugh, I'm the butt of the joke. The word oscillates,

VOIOIOIOIOIOIOIOIOIOID

filling all space, which I recognize as a subtler joke, and expands until only the vowels are left, which immediately become a chorus line of lamenting Jews in black coats throwing up their hands

Oy! Oy! Oy! Oy!

swaying like seaweed, to the rich amusement of the invisible audience; and again I'm not quick enough, or too divided, to join in their laughter. A sudden blow then, **CHOP!** and a tearing, rending, crashing sensation **YES YOU REMEMBER!** I swallow, I gulp . . . more laughter . . . **THAT YOU AREN'T JUST A LEAF ON A BRANCH BUT THE WHOLE TREE!** "Not again!" I say. This produces a new round of hilarity. I intone the Lord's Prayer, but a sinister pun twists the words: "Hollowed be thy game." "Love," I say, a whispered plea to love itself, and instantly a great set of Elvis Presley lips drawl the word with distinctly obscene implication

No!

and since even Hell can't get by without metaphor, the gates of **AUSCHWITZ** open, and in we go, into a monstrous hive of ideas that fall upon me like hornets—numbers, symbols, logical systems enacting effortless understandings in my uncomprehending brain, abstractions possessed by a lust for embodiment that knows no pity, and against whose rage and delight I have no defense, since every intentional thought immediately performs an animated cartoon of its meaning. "I must understand it," I say, standing up, and instantly sink back, crushed beneath an immensity of actual and impending pain which, incredulously, I recognize as my own. But there is an increment of understanding, I hug it: No limit, that seems to be the law here. And another fact: Someone is enjoying this—at my expense, but still, a recognizable glee in violating all bounds and strictures known or imagined, moral ones in particular, and especially those sacred injunctions that are meant to seal off the terrestrial from the infernal realm: those against murder, blasphemy, and wanton injury. Who is this? Who? But there is no answer. The tumult of voices and symbols is subsiding. "Thank God," I say, and that rouses another ripple of sarcastic amusement. But the mind is clearing. Exhausted and grateful for the reprieve, I return to the surface of things. On my lap lies the book with the arched row of numbers. The Zero is no longer a cipher of absence. More like a vacant eye. No more revelations, please. But they come, one by one, in no hurry, while I sit like a pillar of salt, fascinated:

1. I have been here before . . .
2. This recognition is itself a recurrence . . .
3. Since what recurs is recurrence, a beginningless, endless series is implied . . .
4. Didn't Plato equate remembrance and knowledge? . . .
5. But what is remembered here is not a tranquil and static realm of ideas, it is a single, unfathomably sinister one, the idea of repetition itself . . . Eternal return . . . "Eternal return of the same." Those words are a citation, appropriately enough, but it never dawned on me, when I read them in Nietzsche, why the contemplation of this thought should be the supreme test of philosophical valor. It seems now . . .
6. that the idea of infinity, projected in time and in space, injects limitless variation into the sameness of the same. Therefore . . .
7. in the endlessness of repetitions, there is an endless amplification of knowledge. What are its findings?
8. That something profoundly forgotten and unimaginably dangerous to the knower remains to be known, and that with each instance of re-cognition, structures of sheltering ignorance will fall and more unendurable news will come pouring in.

I shudder, put the book away. "Enough thinking," I think, as if I had been doing the thinking. And wrapped in this thin cloak of vainglory, I lie down on the mattress next to Susan, who has been fast asleep all the while.

■

Time flows on, gray and slow like the muddy Thames. Astounding, to paddle the surface again, with no torrents or whirlpools in sight, after a plunge like that. How lost I've been in my soul-searching, how blind to the solitude of others. Gina, in my arms in front of our living room window, points at a copse of fir trees behind the neighbors' garden plots and says: "That's where my friends live."

"What friends, Gina?"

"My friends! My Chinese friends!"

She says it with such pleasure I am almost convinced of their material existence. When I ask her about them a month later, she says they've gone home. A real friend has taken their place, named Evelyn, the first European child Gina has met who is allowed to get her clothes dirty—no small freedom for a two-year-old. Her mother, Janet, a thin friendly shy woman addicted to the I Ching, is on Public Assistance. She makes no decision without consulting the coins, which she shakes between her hands and then examines on her flat palm for their configuration of heads and tails, at the market, at home, in the street, in the tube, with or without the book, since she practically knows it by heart. For the first time since leaving New York, Susan feels the weight of loneliness lift from her shoulders, and I from mine the burden of guilt on her account.

Janet's boyfriend, Mick, has the sad mouth and burning eyes of a disappointed fanatic. He works in a factory, so we don't see much of him except on weekends. He used to be political, he says. One day, though, he dropped Acid in Hyde Park and watched an African man hold his audience spellbound with an argument that equated English capitalism with "techno-savage slavery" and communism with "universal humanity," a clever entertainment at the least, but all the while a rain of blossoms descended upon them all, adorning their hair, forming pink epaulettes on their shoulders, drifting past their unseeing eyes, gathering in small drifts of glory at their feet—a message that should have silenced every tongue in the park, but the chatter went on unabated. Since then he has turned away from politics, and from intellectual incitements as well, keeping only *The Tibetan Book of the Dead* (in Timothy Leary's version) and the I Ching as inspirational guides, singing and playing the guitar in his off hours, smoking hash, and, sadly, shooting heroin.

Karl Marx should have given some thought to psychology. The class struggle, mired in the bickerings of parliament, returns home to wage civil war in the mind: Mick against Mick, the high noble vision against the pedestrian, plebeian reality: not enough money, not enough leisure, not enough confidence to make the music, write the songs, or put on the show. But he's fun to smoke dope with, imaginative and witty. "On the evening of the sixth day," he says, "when God looked around and saw everything he had made, behold, something was missing. So he tossed in the I Ching."

Karl Marx should have given more thought to opium as well. It's drugs, not rallies and manifestos, that are dismantling the boundaries of class in the Western world. Why else would a banker's daughter and the son of a candy manufacturer share a four-bedroom flat with Mick, Janet, and Evelyn, in a run-down district of London called the World's End? Drugs, according to astro-logical symbolism, are subject to the rulership of Neptune, and so are chaos, clairvoyance, clandestine associates, confusion of thought, debauchery, exiles, and feet. The banker's daughter, Veneta Knowles, likes to walk barefoot and on her tippy-toes, like a pre-Raphaelite nymph, and actually uses the word "debauch," in reference to the way she spends her nights—something she's had enough of, she says. The way she says that excites the faun in me to prove her wrong. Does she know that? Of course she does. Ralph Ponder, the candy-man's son, has expressive feet also: They splay out like a penguin's, with the heels nearly touching. He spends a great deal of time in bed with a kind, intel-ligent, melancholy girl named Georgie, not in debauchery but smoking hash, watching Monty Python, and reading John Galsworthy novels out loud. They're friends of Mick Jagger and of a reincarnated lama named Chögyam Trungpa, to both of whom they will someday introduce us. But meanwhile our money's running out again, and there's another snag in Chattanooga. We'll have to move out of our flat in Brixton, we can't pay the rent. Veneta Knowles invites us to live in her room; it'll do her good, she says, having a family around. We can have her bed, she'll sleep on a couch, and there's room for Gina's crib.

Ralph and Mick help me lug my library upstairs. "If wisdom could be found in books," Mick says, "Joel would take the cake." He is right. Voluptas is back, and I don't know a book that could do half the job of a cold shower to reduce the effect of Veneta's seductive sighs at night when she knows Sue is asleep and I am awake. Mornings, she tiptoes off in high heels and a short dress to work in her father's bank. We'll just have to live with the tension—Susan too, she is not blind—till we can afford an apartment. But it seems, all in all, that we have arrived. Our new home is a commune of sorts, though no one calls it that. It's called "Milton Chambers," because that's the name chiseled above the once ele-gant entrance. A lively assortment of dopers, hedonists, students, and artists troop in and out for business, conversation, food, music, candy, or shelter. Some are well-to-do and help defray the household's expenses; others who, like us, have less, contribute less tangibly. Susan with her good-natured friend-liness, a steady glow in the flux of moods and performances. I with my travel-ing library and astrological services. Gina with blazing eyes and miraculous syllogisms: "The world is round, there are mommies all around the world, and all mommies love their children, so there's love all around the world! And the moon loves the other side of itself!" Gina and Evelyn are playing with a group of "straight" kids in a parent-run kindergarten nearby. Just around the corner is a bookstore called "Gandalf's Garden," run by two Hobbits with a taste for Eastern religion and astrology. A nice old man from Ceylon teaches Vedanta there on Thursday evenings. At home, I practice Yoga and meditation. Counting my breaths in the lotus position, I hear Susan's bright laughter coming from the kitchen or from Ralph and Georgie's room. Things are looking up. But alas, it is because my own eye is biased. Hasn't Susan intimated a number of times that she still wants to go home, that she's lonely despite the nice people here, that she's tired of pulling clothes out of suitcases, that she doesn't have faith in my communitarian idea? Now she is saying it in earnest, and with the intent to persuade me. "Give it time," I say, "it's just starting to happen." But it isn't. The city government has approved plans to demolish large parts of the World's End, including our house. The burgeoning commune is more like a makeshift harbor where travelers swap stories, barter, smoke, sleep, and then sail on. Impermanence is half its charm, and no one besides us has a need for more solid moorings. Meanwhile the bank in Chattanooga is stalling. Another month of that, and we'll have just enough money to get us back to New York.

"There must be some way outta here, said the joker to the thief." That's Bob Dylan, always a trusty augur. "There's too much confusion, I can't find no relief." Exactly the problem. Others are feeling it too. Someone's distributing a leaflet in London, bearing a single question: "WHO IS THE JOKER?" I have a hunch. I have heard his voice, his laughter. He is my secret self, somewhat criminally inclined, to say the least. My torturer. The thief? I've seen him too, he's just about anyone out on the street, stashing away that little piece of existence he calls himself. "Businessmen they drink my wine, plowmen dig my earth." A cosmic joker, dig it? "None of them along the line know what any of it is worth." "And what'll you do if we have to go home?" Susan asks, knowing full well she's probing a tender sore, but the question has to be asked. "I'll get a job," I say.

It sounds like: "I'll throw in the towel." Never! It's not work I fear, it's ignominy. I have a promise to keep. My brilliant and sickly brother, six years younger than I, outshone me when we were children. Bertolt Brecht once asked my opinion of a poem he was writing, on the presumption that Bodo Uhse's son was not likely to be a dunce. I was failing the ninth grade. I heard Pablo Neruda declaiming his poems in our living room shortly after I dropped out of high school. Bodo won the East German National Prize for his novels. Now Jim, my American father whom I never knew, is becoming a household god of sensitive collegiate freaks. I'm almost thirty, too old to "show promise." I can still hear Krishnamurti's question: "What are you waiting for?" It's time to deliver. *"So let us not talk falsely now,"* says the thief in gentle reproof to the joker, *"the hour is getting late."* The I Ching speaks about a sagging roofbeam. On further inquiry (in James Legge's translation) it suggests spreading "mao grass" beneath heavy objects. The days are ticking. I need more concrete information. Little Evelyn's mother, Janet, recommends the Spiritualist Society, and there, without any helpful hints on my part, a small round woman named Minny Bridges tells me, in crisp no-nonsense terms, that I am a writer and ought to be writing, and that a spirit named Eric thinks so too: "Let the Inner Man write, not the outer," she says. "Be like Dickens. He did not let the world dictate its terms." I feel my soul spread peacock feathers. But it is more than that. Veils upon veils of identity part, fall away: secondhand hipster, studious reflective intellectual, bashful hedonist, stern yogi . . . Not this, not that. Petals of an opening flower. She stops talking, raises her hands, holds them in midair, as if entranced by a vision. She's playing the pool to my Narcissus, I am reflected in the shining of her face, but it's she who sees me, and now it is done, the petals close again, I blink, unsure of what has transpired, and she says: "What you believe shall come to pass." What do I believe? But she's getting messages from the spirit world, names that mean nothing to me, Jackie, Margaret, Joseph, I shake my head, "we are linking," she says sternly, as if I were failing to play my part, and now comes a dog that means nothing to her but sends shivers up my spine, "a black poodle, circling around your house, I don't know his name," she says, but I do, it's a figure I've known since childhood, Mephisto's first appearance in *Faust, Part I,* get thee behind me. A coldness passes into me, as if from a draught, but the room is windowless. "Quite large," she says, frowning. She watches the poodle with suspicion. After a few moments her face relaxes, and the coldness lifts. "We are linking." The links are terrestrial now, thank God, transatlantic in fact, there is movement, of money, of news, coming my way. "When?" I ask, in a tone of voice that betrays my anxiety. "There are delays," she says. Don't I know it. She falls silent and stares into the middle distance between us. I wait. "Do you know anyone in Italy?" she asks. I shake my head, no. "Those are our indications," she says. "I see a light there. A small blinking light. It should not be ignored." Our session is over.

Later Susan reminds me that we do know someone in Italy, Diane Agostini, who was with me in Cuba and with whom I shared several momentous Acid trips on the Lower East Side. Last we heard, she was married and living in Perugia. What if she changed her name? But thanks to the new feminism, she has appended her husband's name to her maiden name with a hyphen, and she is listed in the Perugia telephone directory. I call her and tell her about Minnie Bridges: "Are you the blinking light?" "Of course, of course! I'd love to see the both of you again, and to meet Gina, and I know Vittorio will, he loves children. So get over here any way you can. Please! Money's no object, OK? Love!" Three times on our way to Italy, I hear the Beatles amplify her parting message—*"All you need is love!"*—which would be a good omen if I hadn't once imagined using this song as a sound track for a documentary film about cruelty: Take the real fiendishness of man and nature, the bottomless horror of life in the absence of mercy, yes, show pictures of *that,* with this song for accompaniment. And I notice how much energy flows into this ugly fantasy: like a growling in the mind, a gathering grumble of dark resentment and pride and—held back as if ready to pounce—a fierce sort of soldierly joy, yes, as if in foreknowledge of some furious fight to the finish—but with whom, for Christ's sake, the Beatles? And suddenly I am struck, not for the first time but with sharper clarity than before, how much of my writing and especially my "authorless" cut-up collages has been quite explicitly aimed at offending not only Christians but Jesus, which is a rather surprising position to take for a man raised by moderate atheists who looked on religion (though not on the church) with affectionate condescension and no hate at all. All the while we're crossing the Brenner Pass into Italy, Gina and Susan are asleep on the mattress behind me, it's night and very foggy, I'm in the front passenger seat sitting next to a silent and friendly young man named Luigi whose driving skills we solicited through a newspaper ad, and who is on his way home after a year's stint working as a waiter in London. He plunges into the mist and around hairpin curves with nothing but two blind feelers of light to test the perimeters. Why don't I clutch him in terror or ask him to slow down? Because I know there is worse in store for me—luckily for my sleeping family!—than a brief panic, a crash and crack of bones, or even heartbroken survival. I fall asleep in quiet dread while Luigi plunges on. A Chinese man approaches me with a white handkerchief spread over his palm. There are several other men with him. He presses the handkerchief over my mouth. I can smell the chloroform. "It is necessary," he says, with a tone of regret. Next I know I'm alone in a fairground, at night. Gleaming painted cars around me, wooden horses, Ferris wheels. I hear the thin, plaintive "meeow?" of a kitten—a skinny little thing with a scraggly tail, her fangs and pink tongue bright in the moonlight. I pick it up. What shall I do with you, how can I feed you? I'm as lost as you are. The kitten starts biting my fingers. You're too rough! I try prying her loose with my other hand, but she's sinking her teeth into my palm and clawing my wrist with her hind legs, it's a much bigger cat than I thought it was, if it's a cat at all, but whatever it is, it's starving and regards me as meat. I whirl my arm, the beast doesn't fall off. One of its eyes catches mine, it's not a cat's eye, it has a human intelligence and expressiveness and it knows that I know it is the Evil One. I knock him against a wall, he is impervious, I can't shake him off, he's growling ferociously and tearing my hand, I'll have to kill him, I swing my arm down and with all my might smash his head against a black square on the ground, and a disc with a painted clown's head flies upward, climbing a vertical scale that is marked, from the bottom upward, with the words

PEACE

CONCORD

DISCORD

WAR

and already I see what I've done, good God in heaven if it is in your power to redeem an effect from its cause put a halt to this horror, but the clown slides higher,

PURGATION

and higher,

DAMNATION

slows in its rise toward the word

PERDITION

which I know will light up when the bell is struck, but now there's a shift, the cat is gone, so is the scale and the fairground, I'm awake and immensely grateful for another last-minute reprieve.

■   ■   ■

The falling is faster now. The trapdoors of transition yield upon contact. No sooner arrived at Diane's than the impossibility of our staying becomes evident. Vittorio loves children the way bonsai gardeners love trees, and Gina's moods and passions, her gaiety, grief, wrath, and exuberance, are too elemental for comfort in a small apartment cluttered with breakable knickknacks bequeathed to Vittorio by three generations of strict Catholic mothers. He is kind but deeply conventional, it worries him to see Diane's friends so rootless and disoriented. Diane concurs with his disapproval, especially of me, and shows it in subtly barbed comments implying a sad lack of maturity on my part and a sobered perspective on hers. So I disapprove of her too: She of East Village celebrity, once elected "Slum Goddess of the Month" by an anarcho-surrealist weekly, has become a provincial housewife who meets with other wives for coffee, cake, and gossip while the husbands discuss politics and football in the town's "red" cafe, opposite the "black" one, where the rightists congregate.

It's Vittorio who finds a solution. He shunts us off to a collective household of Maoist men, introducing me as a Comrade who was raised in East Germany, defied the American ban on travel to Cuba, had personal dealings with Che and Fidel, and is now self-exiled out of disgust with Nixon's fascist regime. The Maoists help lug our suitcases and my books up three flights to a large bare quadrangular room furnished with a mattress and four giant posters of Marx, Engels, Lenin, and Mao, one on each wall. There, in the great leaders' ocular crossfire, we set up house while our hosts play the "Internationale" over and over on a wobbling turntable.

In a lull one day—I am sitting on the floor drawing astrological charts, the Maoists are off to a rally—I hear a melodious voice, an old man's, reciting what appears to be a love-poem: *"Che bella la piccolina . . . che dolce . . . che carina!"* I turn my head and see Gina standing in a slanted sheaf of sunbeams by the low open window, smiling, entranced by the tenderness of the voice, which must be coming from a window opposite ours across the echoing courtyard. There are flowers in a box on our windowsill. Birds are chirping. My daughter, my child, how many days have I been lost to you in the murk of my dreaming! Open my heart to love, God, let me be no longer selfish![6] For the next several days, the glory of the old city is revealed to me. The circular Church of San Angelo, its golden cupola fringed with pigeons. The gesturing angels on the walls of the Oratory of San Bernardino. The steep narrow cobblestone streets, the blooming gardens and vineyards outside the crumbling city wall. And a half hour's drive from Perugia, the three of us stand gazing down on the far-stretched valley from the high hill of Assisi, where the world (if you disregard a few thin plumes of factory smoke) still looks as it does in Bellini's sublime *St. Francis in Ecstasy* at the Frick.

---

6. That selfishness, though—to be fair to myself—results from the pull and tug of a deep-gnawing trouble, the perpetual argument and ache and evidence of failure. And trotting patiently at my heels, like a jackal, my old familiar, my poodle, my enemy, biding his time.

Blessed are the poor, especially those with frozen assets. A friend of the Maoists, a member of their circle named Umberto Q., moves out of his apartment to make room for the needy American Comrade and his family. Most likely his motive is not charity but political discipline, for the posters in his room are all icons of hardness and his handshake is crushing. I'm grateful for the misunderstanding. So is Umberto Q.'s roommate, Alberto "Pippo" Frank, who need no longer hide his counterrevolutionary passions, marijuana and American music. Stoned, he prepares for his doctoral exam, intermittently bursting into a snatch from Credence or Dylan or else punctuating his thoughts with an authoritative *"Ecco!"* He believes in science *and* magic, revolution *and* charity, the iron rule of matter *and* the primacy of consciousness, and to let the world know he's of two minds, he hides half his face behind a curtain of hair. Little wonder: He's born in the sign of the Twins, with Venus in conflict with Mars, or shall I say Voluptas with Politicus. In no time at all we are friends, the four of us, as if we had just parted for an afternoon and were now resuming an interrupted conversation.

Pippo has a brilliant idea: He introduces us to the mayor of Perugia, a communist. The notion of penniless Americans with money in the bank puzzles the mayor, but when I pronounce the word *"burocrazia,"* his face lights up with understanding. A friendly handshake, and from now on, every noon, we join some fifty or sixty men and women at one of eight vast wooden tables in an ancient high-ceilinged room that was once the town's granary and is now the municipal soup kitchen. Have we ever eaten this well? Plenty of pasta, rich minestrone, white bread, red wine, and the generous sound of arguing, laughing voices, all in exchange for a pink ticket stamped with the seal of the mayor's office.

Spring comes, the grass grows green, magnolias and cherry trees put forth their blossoms. No news from Chattanooga. Umberto Q. drops in, spots my astrological charts, sees the militant kitsch removed from his walls, hears me boast that I haven't read a newspaper in months, looks at Pippo without saying a word. He smells a bourgeois rat. Two weeks later, Susan, Gina, and I return from a weekend trip to Rome (myself at the wheel, still without a license) and find all our clothes and my books neatly stacked in the hallway. On my desk—Umberto's desk—lies a fat eraser with the word MAO written on it. We have been expropriated. And again Pippo finds a solution. Halfway between Perugia and the village of Pontefelcino, a class of college freshmen from San Jose State College have rented an old farmhouse from a Countess who lives in a castle nearby. The students don't object to our living with them till our money comes through. Nor does their professor. Why should he? He lives in the castle. The Contessa doesn't mind either. The students have come to study art history, but they spend their days smoking dope and dropping Acid. So does the professor, so does his strange Estonian wife. So do I. Not Susan. And Gina, of course, is everyone's envy, "naturally stoned."

I'm falling so fast now I can hear time whistling in my ears. Is it my time or that of the world? Am I afraid for myself or for others? The messengers of fear come from all sorts of quarters, even the Beatles, as when Paul McCartney sings with that clear sad voice of his that he *"saw the photogra-ha-haph"* of a man *"who blew his brains out in a car"* and how he just *"had to la-ha-ha-ha-haugh,"* and *"now-they-know-how-many-holes-it-takes-to-fill-the-Albert-Hall,"* and then, with the theme of obliteration roundly established, that long-drawn-out gradually amplified pulsing discord which always suggests to me a stretching and strain-ing of mental and spiritual matter to a point where the fabric must tear; and where the Beatles warble beatitude—

LET IT BE

echoed by thousands of road signs all over the country:

FIAT

the Stones mock them satanically with

LET IT BLEED

and that word refers, by implication, to the curse of sentience, the unhealable wound in the body of life. And when Chicago Transit Authority blends into a song the roaring chant of a crowd attacked by police dogs:

THE WHOLE!

WORLD'S!

WATCHING!

those words, divorced from their distant context and multiplied in listening brains all over the world, suggest a fight for more urgent stakes than the 1968 National Democratic Convention. In one of R. Crumb's cartoon books, there is a picture of an exploding world. The epicenter of the explosion is a middle-class living room, a man is flying one way, his wife the other, lamps, cups, and glasses accompany them. Everyone fears the President's finger on the red button, but who considers the mental chain reaction, starting in God knows what subway or factory or country club or backwoods fishing creek, by which the impulse moving that finger is finally released? But the frightening thing about this picture is the fact that it scares me, *me*. How can that be, unless I sense, within myself, the imminence of just such an explosion? And the fear is not that I might blow up in rage at Susan or Gina or one of the boys and girls in the farmhouse, but that somehow my thoughts could set going a Rube Goldberg machine of interacting psyches, all of our undigested resentment rolling and clicking and popping along, setting off bells, opening doors, until the great work is completed in the sign of the mushroom cloud.

Against this impending avalanche, the imagination—not mine or anyone's in particular, but the collective groundswell of which our private fantasies are the seepage and surface trickles—projects the dream of an Edenic revival in which women and men, children and animals rejoin as a holy family to live in communion with Mother Nature, under the guidance and at the behest and election of God, the Creator, who wants His unfinished work to continue.

But where are these friends in Utopia? I have a notion, more than a notion, a near-certain hunch: We will meet them on July 4, 1970, in front of the Eiffel Tower, where Ed, Fred, and Betsy urged us to come for the Great Convocation of the New American Decade, or is it the world's.

The long-awaited "partial distribution" from Chattanooga comes at the end of June, enough to tide us over for a few months. We leave for Paris on the morning of July 3. On the way we pick up two Sicilian laborers who are hitching their way to Germany. They are surprised when I ask them to drive, on the grounds that I don't have a license. They are even more surprised when Susan discovers that we have lost three thousand dollars in travelers checks somewhere en route. The two young men are kind enough, and trusting enough, to lend us a precious portion of their savings, enough to fill our gas tank and feed us until the American Express office in Paris reimburses us upon arrival. Then we part with warm mutual thanks and drive to the house of an American friend of Pippo's who told him she'd put us up for a night. We climb three flights of stairs, ring a bell, an attractive blond woman opens the door. She's stark naked. Come on in. The apartment is full of scowling young men, all of them dressed. Yes, she was informed of our coming, but you see, "my lover" (she calls him her lover, gesturing to one of the scowlers) "is a Mexican *revolutionary,* and some friends of his have just come from *fascist Greece,* I mean, like, *political refugees,* so, can you dig it? This makes for some weird heavy vibes," from which I deduce that there's a problem of space and that she's been apprised of, and disapproves of, our antipolitical leanings. We sleep in the bus. Several times, during the night, the police bang on the car with their truncheons. In the morning, we go to a nearby cafe for breakfast. I request three croissants. The waiter corrects my pronunciation: "*Crois*-sants, monsieur! *Crois*-sants!" Paris is not displaying its legendary charm, everyone's in a whirr of ill-humored haste, the weather is humid and gray, and the people we ask for directions sneer at the mention of our destination, or at the way we pronounce it. Arrived at the Eiffel Tower, we find busloads of straights—Germans, Japanese, Belgians, Swedes. They're not looking for us, they're looking for Paris. Have we made a mistake? Was it the Arc de Triomphe? We drive to the Arc de Triomphe. No one is there. Absolutely no one. How could we have been so wrong? Susan, too, was convinced. We all were. Fred, Ed, and Betsy. Blaise and Juliette. *They* at least should have come, they live in Paris! We call their number, a middle-aged woman responds: "*Blaise et Juliette? Ils sont partis, hier matin! À Ibiza!*" That puts the lid on it. They forgot! All those thousands of people, or hundreds—dozens, at least!—who at some point were delighted by the idea of helping to create this magical moment, this poem in the calendar, forgot about it, or else were prevented by something they thought more important. But this means something. You don't get duped on this scale of magnitude for no reason.

However, there's no time to reflect on it. I'm falling. Our next destination is Switzerland again, another conference with Krishnamurti. I'm determined, this time, to follow his dialectic all the way to that sacred place where thought stops and God, world, and self are one boundless presence. Of what consequence would lack of money be then, or the need for employment? I'm also determined to find people with whom to found a commune, in particular people with children. I park my car in the same spot it was on last year. The campsite looks the same, so do the Alps, but it's not the same world. A picture of a bearded, long-haired freak with a big red X across his face is posted on a bulletin board on the main street of Saanen. A group of vigilantes has threatened to beat up some twenty-five people who have come unprepared to pay for lodging and are sleeping under a covered bridge. I approach Krishnamurti's secretary, suggesting he allow the roofless to sleep in the conference tent. The man is indignant: "This tent," he says, "is the property of the Krishnamurti Committee." The more I speak of need, the more he repeats the word "property." I decide to bring the matter up with the boss. He opens the conference with a disquisition on "responsibility," arguing that conventional bounds of duty are actually ploys of dereliction, since there is no real boundary between the self and the world. What a lovely coincidence, and how good that he's thinking my way. By now I know his meaning so well that I needn't strain to grasp it. Who is responsible for the state of society? Who creates hells? Who is the maker of madness? Who denies love? Who resists change? Who makes an impregnable fortress of hope? Who builds the jealous gods and the vengeful ones? Who is the lord of this world? Whose words are these? Not his, not mine either, I've sunk into a dream, but the terrible thing about all these questions is that their answer is always "I," and that this "I" has no plural, though everyone can say it. Wake up!

I am present again to the speaker's presence: "Therefore," he says, "responsibility does not end at the borders of self-interest. You *are* the world, it is of your making, no one else is responsible for its condition." Whereupon he invites his nonfollowers to ask questions.

I raise my hand and ask what "we" might do about the people under the bridge. Krishnamurti, forgetting his own wisdom, says: "The Swiss don't like hippies, that is a fact. And we are responsible only for what happens inside this tent." Suddenly he looks deeply surprised, and then we both realize that he has stepped into a trap, and that I am the one who set it. Abruptly, he makes a strewing gesture and says: "Take care of it among yourselves." Handfuls of money come toward me from all sides. "Later, later," Krishnamurti says. The donations continue on the campsite all afternoon.

So do the admiring and curious looks of strangers. A shaggy-bearded French astronomer approaches me with burning eyes: Someone told him I am seeking like-minded people to found a commune. He would be honored to be counted among them. He has carpentry skills, a strong body, a good mind, and he's sick of the world of ambition and power. He is addressing me as if I were his general. This misunderstanding is so flattering that I respond in character, with a firm smile and a stalwart gaze: "I'm glad," I say. "I've been waiting."

It's happening. These are my people. My drifting fall is reaching its goal. In the nick of time, too: a few more months, and the last of our money will run out. But with friends like this Frenchman and who knows what others, no obstacles will be too great.

A young American couple comes next. They, too, apply for membership in my commune. I listen to their story. Then I describe them in a letter to Stefan, who is back in New York, living with Alma and studying Zen with a Japanese monk: "Their Names are Ronnie and Rose. There is something peculiar about them, I'm not sure what it is. Maybe they're too symbiotically entwined to fit into a commune. Actually it's only the guy who's peculiar, he's a macrobiotic draft dodger who seems perfectly intelligent until he starts talking about a loop in his brain—some kind of insight he got from Krishnamurti. But his wife,

Rosie, has her feet on the ground, which is more than I can say for myself these days, and she loves him. Who am I to accept or reject them?"

By the next morning, I have become the focal point of a minor revolt among Krishnamurtiites. People, most of them freaks, are packing their bags. Several German freaks in a Tibetan-style yurt near ours inform me that I opened their eyes to the great man's fraudulence. Would I like to join them on a trip to the mountains to take some LSD with them there, "Orange Sunshine," no less, the best and the purest? Of course I would. When? In a couple of hours. We'll miss Krishnamurti, I think to myself. But who cares! I've replaced him in these people's estimation. "Where you lead," their eyes say, "we will follow." A Danish television crew films me walking with Gina on top of my shoulders. Go ahead, show the people of Denmark the face of European humanity reverting to Nature. Show them the blaze of this child's eyes undimmed by fear, shame, or manners, pan down to her bare little feet set against the patriarchal splendor of her father's beard. I'll point the camera at you, too, if you want, yes, you with the gypsy dress and the tinkling bells on your ankles. "You are from America?" she asks, while the camera rolls on the shoulder of a man with one earring and tight leather pants. Freaks, pot-smokers, acid-heads, hired by the state to record the Zeitgeist! In the U.S., they're threatening to round us up. Was it not Danes who wore yellow stars to protect the Jews from the Nazis? Wonderful country! "Yes," I reply, and I notice I said it with pride. It all started with us, after all! "We would like to ask you some questions about yourself, about your views and so forth. Is that OK?" Of course it is. They set me up in the open door of the bus, seated. The pretty interviewer asks me why I have traveled so far from home, and whether I would consider going back, and why not, and what is my idea of an "intentional community," and where do I hope to find people to join me, and if I don't believe in plans, by what star or what faith do I choose to be guided, and is my wife content with this drifting way of life. . . . Sensible questions; it's my truthful answers that leave me with a feeling of having been flayed of all pretense so that sober folks in Denmark can watch me and think: "What a sad, lost young man, and how good that our children are Danish." There's no time to recover my self-esteem, the Germans are revving their motor. We take off for the mountains, leaving Susan and Gina at the campsite.

Orange Sunshine

We are seven, all men—the four Germans, two Danes from the TV crew, and myself. We ingest the Acid on a high rock covered with moss and little white flowers. From there we look down on a wide, grass-green valley, a crystalline lake, a dense grove of fir trees, a glittering stream, behind the firs and about at our height a handsome chalet, the whole landscape contained by snow-topped mountains, a postcard world, beautiful and somehow small. One of the Danes, sitting behind me, reads from the *Bhagavad Gita*:

"Always when the universe approaches destruction and disorder grows in the world of men, O descendant of Bharata, I give birth to myself. As a refuge for the just and a bane to evil-doers, to restore the world's wholeness, age after age, I come into being."

Some enterprising evil-doer has inflicted a gash on the body of trees, a deep, slanting stab. It isn't just ugly to look at, it hurts. The whole valley is wounded.

"But the truly wise," says the voice behind me, **"do not mourn either for the dead or the living. For never was there a time when I was not, nor thou, nor these mighty generals, and never shall there be a time when all of us are not."**

Who says this? I turn to look at the source of the voice. How thin he is! Long stringy blond hair. Like a skeleton. No flesh on his face either.

"Sense impressions, O son of Kunti, are the cause of cold or heat, pleasure or pain, they come and go and are transient. Thou shalt learn to endure them, descendant of Bharata. He whom such impressions do not torment, thou bull among men, he who is wise, indifferent to pleasure and pain, is indeed ripe for immortality."

I stand up and my bare feet start walking away. It's as if my feet weren't mine, as if someone else were making them move. Who else is there? The earth. Maybe the earth is using my feet to show me something she needs to have known. The wounded earth. I can't get the sight of that gash in the forest out of my mind, the more I try, the more it persists, until I feel it in my side, like the stab of a lance. Am I descending into the valley or is the valley rising to meet me?

"Walk, son of Kunti, and ask not: your destination will come to you."

My destination. How will I recognize it? So many things are coming to me, but they all pass me by: alpine roses, birds in the grass, significant stones, a butterfly. . . . How will I know I've arrived at my destination? It will stop me. Maybe the lake is my destination, it's coming closer, or getting larger at any rate, and the way it sparkles seems to indicate something. I'll get there in time. Just keep those feet walking, stomp, step, stuff, stump. I'll walk all the way to Parnassus if wings don't carry me. Parnassus? Is that what I said? Be silent. Keep your eyes on your feet, they'll sing for you. Tick, tock, keeping time, that's what they're doing. How long have I been walking? Hours, it seems. Do the others still see me? Don't look back. Splush! Smush! This grass is wet. A tangle of thorns, watch your step. Water? Am I walking in water? Time, that's what it is. Of course. The stuff accumulates, and I've been walking for, jeez, it seems like a century, no wonder it's rising above my ankles . . . my knees, my hips . . . what is this? No matter, just walk, you can't stop anyhow. Where are we going? To the end of time, where else. If there is such a thing. Never mind. I'm sinking, or rather, the waters are rising, up to my neck now, I'm floundering, kicking as the lake closes over me, gagging, choked, a stab of inhaled water, drowning I'm DROWNING

drowned

DROWNED!

but

this life of mine, what was it . . .

My toes touch down on soft slime and mud, pebbles and plants. The flood is receding: down from my shoulders, my chest, my waist as I rise with bright splashing steps into a new green world humming with insects, warm light on my skin like a caressing hand. TIME says a familiar voice. Walk, oh walk on, you good faithful feet, uphill up, how your tread moves the earth and the very mountains, for they are turning, slowly the whole world turns slowly around me, you good earth, you kind blue heaven, are you not one, is your embrace not eternal, was I not born of your love, am I not here to bear witness to your unshakeable union and to stamp underfoot those whose error would set you apart? Smush! Splash! Into the mud with you, infidels! There it is again, water, how can this be, not again, and the tangle of thorns, oh no, oh please not again, not the (gulp) (wild laughter) why? **BECAUSE WE MUST CARVE OUT A WAY** torture **THROUGH THE BODY OF TIME** this is torture **AH SO YOU'VE NOTICED** Water rising up and over my chest **TIME'S UP!** and into my mouth and nose and closes over me and through the body's choked roar of protest and despair I hear a shrieking rending blast of laughter and my feet regain a toehold on mud and slime and off we go on another round, again the waters part again I rise shining astonished into a new world, but this time my heart is not glad, this time dread scours the landscape for proof against the curse of **ENDLESS REPETITION** by which alone mountains are mountains and flowers flowers and sky sky, and there *is* proof, those soaring peaks and stern majestic crags are *new and unforeseen,* this single buttercup caught with a sprig of clover between two toes was *unforeseen,* this fat hum of a passing bumblebee was *now* and not before or after, these steady heaves of breath like an enormous two-handed saw severing what poor mangled crying thing from its root . . .

YES YOU REMEMBER

I swallow, I gulp, marching bravely
. . . But it was an axe before, wasn't it? . . .

(the sawing continues)

So there is . . . (see-saw, see-saw) *. . .*

PROGRESS?

gales of derision, *"No,"* I say, *"No!"* with defiance, but deep inside, a ravening question:

remember *what?* remember *what?*

THAT YOU AREN'T JUST A LEAF ON A BRANCH BUT THE WHOLE TREE

and in a flash I see new exfoliations of meaning: that

I AM ALL-THAT-IS

and all-that-is is what I am—that there is none other than that which I am—that what I am is in perpetual motion, and that this motion is cyclic—that Susan and Gina and Stefan and my mother and the friends I've left behind and all the billions of people living and dying and starving and working and playing and killing and loving and hoping and believing are part of this cycling hell that I am and will whirl on like this forever if I can't stop it and that if I don't stop the pain will increase the pain of knowing that all pain from speared worms to tortured souls in hell is caused by this endless desperate wandering search *for what? for what? for an end!* "Stop!" I say, but it continues, everything continues, these whirring insects, this pounding heart, these feet, Smush! Splush! and I see the lake before me again, gleaming, and the tangle of thorns on my right, but that's changed, it's barbed wire now, and I am a soldier marching in a world stamped to mud by my marching feet, everything in ruins, bloodsodden, and Gina and Susan and Stefan and Alma I hope still alive somewhere but doomed unless . . . *Why?* I ask as the water rises above my ankles and the answer comes iron-hard **BECAUSE YOU WANTED IT** above my chest *When?* I ask **FROM THE BEGINNING** over my neck my mouth eyes head oh let it stop here let it not ever have been let it perish let there be death but there is no death the water is receding again I am rising again from the flood sloshing my way through marshland back into new lives to generate new **TIME** out of my own thoughts a time-weaving spider gone mad and spinning a thread around itself not now and not always but **FOREVER** and condemned and enabled to imagine this measureless cycling horror until I pass the same unsame grinning tangle of thorns that heralds the next inevitable drowning.

And then it stops.

I am no longer wandering. I am lying on my back, eyes closed, inhaling an intense aroma of sod and grass. Even eternity comes to an end. Is this possible? Something intervened. An angel? I stumbled. Thou good earth. Mother. Providence and shelter from the cruelty of light. Susan, Gina, are you still alive? Stefan? Alma? Is the world still there? At peace? Something tickles my arm, I look: A fly, fat and hairy and very large, sits on my wrist, palpates the skin with fussy front paws and a long black proboscis, tap here tap there, like a doctor searching for a vein. No, not an angel. The insect stabs, stiffens, and tanks up, its hind part swelling. I could shake you off like the fly that you seem, but what good would that do me, you come in a thousand forms. And you knew I would know you, how could you not, my unknown Self, my God, my Destroyer. Or is it mercy that brings you in this form and has me lie still. The fly—maybe it was a fly?—pulls away and lifts off and is gone. Am I in hell or in Nature? Another fly, just as large, alights next to the swelling lump left by the first one. I shake it off, sit up. Two other flies are sucking on my right ankle. Another one, already drunk with blood, hangs by its stinger from my left foot, I shake it off. Another one's sucking at my throat. Two or three are stinging my shoulders, my side. Let them eat me. I lie back. Another one settles on my forehead. I close my eyes. I can live like this, die like this, it is not bad.

A hand touches my shoulder, stirs me. I open my eyes. It's a real hand, a real person. It's one of the Danes, the one who filmed me centuries ago, this morning. "Thank God," he says. What for? But I thank Him nonetheless. And I notice a closing of the waters, some horrible place where I just was, receding, or was it a being, a creature? Something . . .

The Dane holds out a hand—"Come!"—and helps me onto my feet. His face is radiant with compassion. I brush the blood-drunk insects from my arms and legs and look around cautiously. The flattened grass where I lay has retained the shape of a body. Above the head, a twisted branch . . . a trampled rose . . . a halo of thorns . . . a toppled crown . . .

"I thought you were dead!" the Dane says. Together we walk uphill and into a copse of virginal pines. Their stems are swarming with mystic letters or symbols. I *was* dead. And now I do remember something. My brother was there, Stefan. Such suffering, unimaginable—mine, his, everyone's . . . Words start tumbling out of me. The Dane holds up a finger with tremendous authority:

"Stop!"

What did I say? We walk on in silence. He turns around and, with a fierce exclamation in his language and a pushing, thrusting gesture of both hands, curses, or banishes, something behind us. I want to ask him for an explanation, but he puts a finger over his lips. We walk uphill, through a slowly turning world of arcane pines and firs.

"Listen," my friend says, cupping a hand to his ear. Music. Distant music coming nearer. Singing, a choir. We walk on silently. The trees part, we step out onto a flower-strewn ledge, above us a roar of blue sky, the sun blazing like a stupendous jewel above hard, snowy peaks. Perched on a neighbor hill is a wood-block house, the same chalet I saw before the Acid took hold, and there, on the porch, stand eight or nine men and women, all of them facing the valley, singing in four-part harmony. I turn to my companion. He is transfigured, or else he has all along been an angel disguised as a Danish hippie, with long smooth pink cheeks and a blond moustache, limp blond hair touching his broad, prematurely stooped shoulders. Disguised, I say, because now his eyes are unnaturally brilliant, and his face, his whole body is shining a fine, white-gold light. I am frightened. Are we in heaven? And those singers, their song, those ancient words: *Ehre, Glaube, Leid, Dank* . . . Whose honor is being chanted here, whose suffering lamented? Or is it a song of thanksgiving? Where are the others who came here with us? And Susan, Gina—are they still alive? Has the old, suffering world gone to ruin? Smiling, the angel looks out at the mountains. I follow his gaze and meet with the sun's glare. I won't look away. I look until my eyes overflow. Oh take me up. I spread my arms and step forward, rising. But man is not a moth, and the slope inclines downward, rather steeply in fact, so it's downward I trot and stumble and slide, keeping my face lifted, however, and my arms spread, miraculously upright, a puppet suspended from the sun, happy, unspeakably happy and grateful, until, half falling, half running, I propel myself sidelong in the direction of another brightness, this one on the ground, a rectangle of gleaming white surrounded by several gray, spectral bodies of ghosts or, more likely, devils, because they grunt and hiss hatefully as I drop to my knees, face lifted, arms spread in ecstatic adoration, plumb in the middle of what I now realize is a sheet, for one of the ghosts—but ghosts don't have beards and little green hats—a man, then—the man is trying to yank the white cloth out from under me. I yield it to you, my brother, it's yours, I want only the sun! Oh, I will worship the sun forever!

On the way home in the van with my happily reassembled friends, drifting back in memory over the remains of this terroful day, I arrive again at those ghosts or devils, one of them yanking at the sheet, and recognize them as a small Swiss family, their grunts and hisses the sounds of Swiss German, and the sheet as a tablecloth spread for a picnic, not a landing site for that hideous hippie who dropped into their midst like a giant water bug, sopping wet, glittering with seaweed and slime and bursting with insane exaltation.

Back at the campsite, I step out of the car and see my little daughter running up to me, laughing with glee. Before I can kiss her she is gazing into my eyes and exclaiming: "Happy! You're happy!" and I realize with a pang of self-reproach how selfishly unhappy I've been and how much she needs me to be happy. "Where were you?" she asks. I point to the snowy peaks in the distance. "You're happy!" she says again, and this time her delight is so great she breaks into a dance, whirling her arms and kicking up her feet. "Gina! Where did you learn to dance like that?" She throws her hand back and points to the mountains.

To the Valley of Marvels

A new tent has been pitched near our bus. Its muscular occupant came by bicycle from Zurich, an impressive feat on these mountain-scaling roads. His name is Adam Bonheur. Mr. Happiness! He doesn't look the part, but that's not surprising: No one comes to Krishnamurti without trouble gnawing at his soul. What's surprising is the nature of his trouble. He tells Susan and me about it on his first night in Saanen, by a small fire at the edge of the dark, churning river.

Fifteen years ago, he was a child prodigy written up in the tabloids as "the Swiss boy Mowgli," meaning that he had a mysterious ability to communicate with animals. That was in part because he had trouble communicating with humans, but the tabloids didn't mention that. With his parents' uneasy consent —they wanted him to become an opera singer—he kept a sort of Edenic menagerie of domestic and exotic beasts. When he published a paper on the behavior of sparrows, or swallows, or some other creature common in Switzerland and now suddenly, thanks to his observations, not common at all, Konrad Lorenz, the founding father of ethology, applauded him in an enthusiastic article. With the help of a government grant, he spent an arctic winter with a pack of Alaskan huskies, playing with them, hunting with them, digging a lair in the snow with them, respectfully watching and mournfully recording their ritual murder of a sick member of the pack, though he could, of course, have intervened. "I was their leader, their king, their god!" he says passionately, like a man regretting a great, lost love. He spent the following summer with a bear in an alpine valley, harvesting berries with it, living a bear's life as far as was humanly possible without abandoning his obligations to the tribe of ethologists who were awaiting the results of his study, until an alarmed shepherd shot some lead pellets into the animal's hide. A good thing Adam managed to persuade a nice old woman to let the bear into her nearby house! This was no longer ethology, it was a study in interspecies relations: The killer circling the house in perplexity, the widow worried about her dishes, the house shaking as the bear licked its wounds, and the young scientist ruing his ignorance of human nature. He had been educated by a tutor, but his real teachers were his monkey, his snakes, his fox, his hawk, and they were his best friends as well. It was time to adapt to his own species. He enrolled at the Sorbonne, where he aroused a good deal of amusement and condescending affection by his lumbering gait and a habit of turning his entire head to glance sideward, instead of just his eyes. But after a few months he had learned to move like a human being and to talk like a Parisian, expressing opinions about Algeria, existentialism, Jean-Luc Godard, American imperialism, anything. Women adored him, and he them—their bodies, their scents and passions, his own animality in their embrace. But one day he went to the zoo and persuaded the director to let him visit the gorillas in their fenced-in plot. He went to them out of pity and love and a kind of nostalgia, but there was vanity in his emotion as well, because people were watching. The apes eyed him with interest. Then one of the males swung himself toward him on a suspended automobile tire, baring his huge yellow teeth, swatted him hard in passing, turned in the air as he dropped to the ground, and reared himself up to his full height a few feet from Adam, roaring and slapping his chest. The warden intervened with a blast of water from a hose, and Adam rejoined the human world, humiliated but otherwise unscathed. Or so he thought. Today, he dates a long chain of failures and a deepening depression back to that Sunday afternoon. His easy brilliance at parties and in debates abandoned him. So did the woman he was living with—because she did not feel loved, she said, and he did not have the heart to contradict her. He conducted a study of the intelligence of dolphins and then learned that his employers were under contract to prepare dolphins for use as living torpedoes by the U.S. Navy. He abandoned the project and took various odd jobs—as a music tutor, a gardener, a freelance editor, even a dog walker. One day he had a dream: It was Judgment Day for the human race, but the angels appointed to judgment were animals. The intelligence shining from their eyes was terrible: They knew, and they knew no pity.

All this he tells us in one long quiet monologue, keeping his voice low so as not to wake Gina, who is asleep in the bus nearby. I feel as if I have known him all my life, and that I love him as I would a second brother, or a son, though he's my age or older. I tell him about the commune, which seems on the verge of happening; that one of the four Germans in the nearby yurt, a fellow named Wolfgang, is all for it, and that he is about to inherit a large sum of money, and says he would put it at the commune's disposal, to buy land and a house to begin with, and that he has met an American girl on the campsite who wants to live with him and therefore with us, and that she knows a couple in southern France who she's sure will be interested in living with all of us. And that there's a French astronomer, Luc Robineau, who says he's ready to give up his science and join us with his wife and son, and a couple from New York, Ronnie and Rose.

"We will need some animals," Adam says.

It's happening!

■   ■   ■

In the House of my Fear, there are happenings also. Every time I open a door, I enter another version of the same familiar room with the furniture rearranged and yet another door that I must open. The couch, the rug, the books, the mirrors, nothing can be trusted here. There's a chair, for instance, that is shaped in such a way that to sit in it is to feel guilty. The Holy Inquisition is said to have employed such a chair for the purposes of interrogation. They called it "the Little Ease." The Little Ease now stands in the House of my Fear and beckons in every room I enter. If I were free I would never use this chair, but there is no freedom in the House of my Fear.

■   ■   ■

I show Ronnie and Rose my most recent "cutup" collage of phrases randomly culled from books and magazines. Ronnie says it is "lacking in passion." I say this isn't a case where passion is required. He says there never was a case when passion wasn't required. I ask him what he means by passion and he says the root meaning of the word is "burning," and I, convinced he is wrong both about my poem and about the word, say passion means "suffering," and open a dictionary to decide the issue at least of the word (inwardly burning with pique at his judgment), and notice my finger has landed on "world" at the very moment when, without my having given him the slightest clue, Ronnie says: "Passion is knowing that we are the world," and the truth of that, so much bigger than my etymological quibble, plunges into me like a flaming arrow. But there is another ingredient: a line from a Buddhist sermon which is more present to me and more ripe for fusion with the words proffered by this particular moment than any other memorized phrase, because it concerns "the world" and because I have made it my watchword against complacence and written it on the first page of my journal and cited it in a letter to Stefan, not to edify him but as a pledge of allegiance to him in his hell:

THE WORLD IS ON FIRE

That is the first in a chain of implacable annunciations, which are not delivered in words alone but in synesthetic bursts of neurological chaos—pictures, sounds, sensations, and ideas scrambled together in pulsating bundles which somehow—this I will never be able to explain—are *eloquent* and in fact deliver something like a disquisition on the causal links between my personal feelings and all the calamities of history and nature, in short an indictment, and finally a judgment, utterly vacuous in its enormity, though the argument on which it rests is tailored to the precise measure of my every fault and failing, leaving me shattered and shivering in my chair, my hand still resting on the open dictionary: I have been found guilty, by what judge or judges I do not know, of a crime the cosmic extent and horrendous implications of which I will be given to know in future ordeals. The catastrophe lasts no more than a minute, according to Ronnie and Rose, who think I was having a dizzy spell. I tell them nothing of what has happened, and don't confess it to Susan either. What could she do with this knowledge? Conclude that I'm crazy? And then what? This is a battle I have to fight by myself. But to tell the truth, I want it that way, maybe because I'm convinced that I have no choice, and that I might as well embrace the fate that has taken me by the throat. Now *that* sounds crazy, considering the horrors I've been through. On the other hand, isn't it mad to speak of a battle when I'm being attacked by nothing but thoughts that pretend to hold the universe at bay, like terrorists in a B-movie? No, no, no, it may be crazy but it's not silly, not trivial! All right, make it an unwritten chapter from Don Quixote—the noble crackpot battling mosquitoes and thinking they're demons from hell. And what do their stings amount to? Threats! So, then, who is this invader? I have a hunch: It's me. Not a day passes when I don't stuff my brain with concepts like "no-thought," "choiceless awareness," "non-volitional living," "consciousness without a center," "ego-death," "killing the ego"—is it any wonder the poor thing is starting to behave like a trapped beast, baring its fangs, trying to make itself look invincible? But what am I saying, "poor thing." As long as I am identified in any way—with my thoughts, my feelings, my reputation, my body—I am at ego's mercy, its petty pleasures and endless afflictions will appear to be mine. Hence the temptation to coddle it, pity it. When what's really called for is a dissociation so perfect that the ego, deprived of its purchase on organic life, starves, weakens, and finally gives up the ghost it has always been. That is the gist of an extraordinary book I've been studying—no, not studying: swallowing, without comprehension and in blind expectation, exactly as I would a drug that promised to release the mind from its prison once and for all—by a Thai monk known as "The Venerable Chao Khun Sobhana Dhammasuddhi."

Acid and mescaline open the doors, even catapult you (when they don't cast you into some deeper dungeon) into a boundless, light-filled world imbued with one, only one exultant meaning, proclaiming one message—"I Am!"—from as many voices as there are creatures and things. But after a few hours the walls come back, and so do the bars on the windows, and you hear the key turn in the lock and the warden's complacent voice saying: "Back to normal." It's like a tourist visa to the realms of light (and with no guarantee against raids from the nether world); but to those who apply for permanent residence, and who are willing to leave behind all their belongings, the keys to the kingdom are granted: *Also sprach* Chao Khun Sobhana Dhammasuddhi. You either stay in the dark or blast yourself into Nirvana, Enlightenment, Kensho, Satori, Samadhi—the terms vary, but they all refer to a transcendent reality of which our daily life is a shadow. How do I know that this is the case? I don't know, but I have read the records from India, China, and Japan, maddeningly absurd dialogues between masters and disciples, punctuated with shouts, slaps, and blows, often with no reported consequence but sometimes concluding with the laconic notation of one all-important event: "Thereupon the monk was enlightened." Where are the teachers of our time who would shock us awake with a thundering *"Kwatz!"*? Krishnamurti has turned down the job, we're on our own, he says. On our own—let's face it—we're waiting for Godot. The world is on fire. Stefan knows it better than any of us. I fear for him. *"The Weathermen want to bring the war home,"* he writes in a letter from Nepal, *"but what they're doing is spreading it. Like the rest of us. I say to the Weathermen: Set fire to the incendiary. Consider those burning monks in Vietnam. That's bringing the war home. It begins in us and can only end in us."* That frightened me when I read it, because I have come to suspect that Stefan is schizophrenic and one thing I have learned about this disease is that it literalizes all metaphor. Stefan, I don't know how to prevent you except by reaching your goal before you do. But how? How? The little word "how," says Krishnamurti, is the most mischievous word in the English language. There is no "how," and according to Chao Khun Sobhana Dhammasuddhi there is also no "Who"—you get there by no longer being some-body. But he offers guidance in egocide, and a meditation center in England. I'll have to go there. Although there is a voice in me that laughs: Another postponement? More ruses, more tricks? And beyond this Mephistophelian voice is the counsel of the wise: There is no map by which a seeker could find the promised land, since the very act of seeking imposes our exile. Do it now. Do what? Observe the mind in its self-evasions. But now I can hear my own words slipping out of the tracks of logic. Who is evading whom?

Who wants to get rid of the ego? Why, ego, of course! For the greater glory of the one jealous god, himself! And who is beleaguered, harassed, accused, and defiled? Who, if not the body, the life, and the truth? Good God in heaven, am I going mad after all? Who am I and where am I going? If this fiend who attacks me is my own hidden self, then I am a more convincing enactment of absolute evil than any cloven-hooved devil I've seen in a painting. And if it is not I, who is it, or what?

Two days later, the core group of our commune-to-be sets out for the Maritime Alps in two cars: Luc Robineau's shining Land Rover containing Luc and his wife and their child and luggage and Adam Bonheur and his bicycle, and our mud-caked VW bus driven by Ronnie, Rose next to him shouting with Janis Joplin and the Holding Company: *"Take-another-little-piece-of-my-heart-now, baby—TAKE IT!!"*, Susan on the mattress reading *Where Angels Fear to Tread*, Gina and I among mountains of luggage and books at the rear of the bus playing a game I've invented, a variation on the Rorschach test: make random spots with paint on a sheet of paper, print them onto another sheet, print new spots onto that, a palimpsest of spots, and then, with a fine pen, trace the outlines of whatever shapes suggest themselves in the pattern. The shaking of the car adds creative interference. This is how I like to live: plunge into the unknown, trust Chance to deliver the goods when you need them. And that is precisely how Susan does not like to live, and how she has been living for the past two years, patiently, in trust and fealty, until this moment, when the goods are at last being concretely delivered. Here we are on our way to a new life—on the verge of bankruptcy, true, but with the rescuing lineaments of Utopia just starting to appear—and she wants to bail out! The night before leaving Saanen she said: "I have nothing in common with these people. Nothing. I'm lonelier with them than I'd be on my own. And this Ronnie character smells bad." It's true. He's following the precepts of Dr. Arnold Ehret's "Mucousless Healing Diet," and has been observing with satisfaction, day by day, the emergence of pimples and pustules and now the beginnings of phlegm in his throat, signs that his body is healing itself of toxins. "Give him a chance," I said, "if his book's right, he'll be smelling like a rose in three weeks." "Then he'll try to convert us," she said. "He's a fanatic. And that French guy isn't about to give up his career, haven't you noticed how he looks down his nose at our car and the way he polishes his? His wife seems nice, but we can't talk, she doesn't speak English. Their little boy snubs Gina, and you know why? Because she's a *white American*—that's what the kid said to Adam! Can you imagine? Who are these people? It's grotesque. And Adam—he's not made for communal life either, at least not the kind you have in mind. He made a pass at me Sunday when you were in Zurich."

"Did he . . . did you . . ."

"No."

"Strange," I said, "I was tempted in Zurich, probably around the same time."

"I didn't say I was tempted."

But I had been tempted, and I confessed it to her. I had taken the train to Zurich to pick up a new disbursement of our money, and had spent the night at the house of a friend of Adam's, Hans P., whom Adam had described as a "philosopher-activist, hard as a rock and soft as a child." Sure enough, Hans told me almost right away that he disapproved of the counterculture's "pharmacological tactics" and "atavistic neo-Rousseauist utopianism," but he said this with such kindness and evident goodwill that it was impossible to take offense. "Basically," he added, "I think Marx had the right idea." I replied that Marx's belief in the Messianic mission of the working class was itself atavistic, that we had no choice, be we Christians, Marxists, or Timothy Learyists, but to pray, struggle, or hallucinate our way back to paradise. He thereupon asked me how I would imagine *these* men—pointing to a photograph he had clipped out of a newspaper and pinned to a wall, a picture of two captured Viet Cong whose cheeks had been pierced so that a cord could be run through the holes and the two ends attached to a T-shaped wooden handle by which a GI, nearly twice the size of his prisoners, was leading them through the jungle—how I would imagine this group, the American too, would most likely find their way to paradise. To which, after a moment of speechless horror, I replied that each of us must begin by transforming himself, for surely greed, cruelty, and fear had their seat in our own hearts and not in the U.S. State Department. And I raised the ante by taking a small dose of LSD. Now our conversation took adventurous turns, for as he spoke, I could see that he had sealed the doors to mythic and sensuous and spiritual realms which I was freely inhabiting, and for which, in his terms, there was no language, and that consequently he was a prisoner of his clear, stern, admirably logical constructions, and that his soul wanted out. I, for my part, didn't want to look at that picture again, but my gaze was drawn back several times to the bovine, obedient expression of the prisoners' heads, rolling eyes, and tensed necks as they followed their captor; and finally I asked Hans if we could change seats, and he obliged. Then he invited some friends over—four men and a slender, dark-haired girl named Liane. The men and I debated for hours—about East Germany, communism, psychotropic drugs, cultural revolution, the Black Panthers, unions, the commune movement—but Liane just listened, watched, occasionally smiled, and periodically withdrew into her own thoughts. She looked sad. I found her disturbingly attractive. The friends went home, Liane stayed. At around eleven, she and Hans went to bed, and I, still stoned, stayed up in the living room, listening through a pair of earphones to Dinu Lipatti's unearthly performance of Bach's First Partita. Then the bedroom door opened and she came in, wearing a plain cotton nightgown. She sat down on the rug near me and lit a joint. I took off the earphones. The space between us was dense with desire. Keeping her voice low, she told me that she liked me; that she had lived with Hans for two years and loved and admired him, but that he had recently come out of jail no longer the man she had known; that he had refused to serve in the army and been denied Conscientious Objector status and had then rebelled against certain prison rules and been put in solitary for several months, and that something had broken inside him; that he was impotent. Once or twice, as she spoke, she gulped in mid-sentence, stroking the rug with a fingertip. In these signs, and in the proximity of her bare foot to my hand, I found more enticement than it seemed conscionable to resist. Nevertheless I consulted my conscience, and found it opposed to my desire on two accounts: Susan, who trusted me, and whom I would have to either hurt or deceive if I did as I wanted; and Hans, who had shown me nothing but courtesy and friendship, and in whose house I was a guest. I could not accept Liane's invitation. All this, in a few plain words, I confessed to Susan. She was hurt, as I might have imagined. I decided to leave unmentioned the fact that I had given Liane the address of our destination in southern France. Why muddy the waters of the future? Sufficient unto the day is the evil thereof.

Back to our two-car convoy now, and to the present tense of July 1970. Somewhere near Lyon I observe Luc and Ronnie glumly urinating side by side and think: "incompatible." Moments later, Gina pounds little Aristide on the head, with a hammering fist from the top down, boom. "For no reason!" according to the screaming boy's mother, which angers me, because the remark imputes malice to my daughter, who I know hit the little gauchiste for a reason. These are not happy auspices. At rest stops and restaurants, in the large and small inconveniences of the long trip south, the possibility that Susan is right about Luc and his family and Ronnie and Rose and Adam and us begins to loom large: that we are on a fool's errand and only a miracle and maybe Wolfgang's inheritance will make a community out of us. We arrive at our destination, a small dusty town called Breil-sur-Roya, in steep-hilled wine country, half an hour's drive from Nice. Our host, already apprised of our arrival through a letter from Wolfgang's American girlfriend, Wilma, is waiting for us at the post office, a tall, darkly tanned freak with a mane of dense brown locks, something springy in his steps and rising in his stance, wearing a flowing Indian shirt and black velvet pants and sandals, a string of mala beads around his neck, strange eyes, their gaze not penetrating so much as bottomless, but not unfriendly, all of which my astrologically programmed forebrain computes to "Scorpio-Gemini-Aries" or maybe a harmonious Pluto-Mercury contact, yes, the primitive, brooding lord of the abyss and the sprightly messenger of the gods in tenuous alliance. I like the man. His name is Shiva. Something tells me "he will make a difference," though I'm not sure what kind or to whom or to what. He climbs into Luc's Land Rover and guides us uphill by steep winding turns, glancing sidelong down and back through the window from time to time, smiling, it seems at me, who am driving, while Gina next to me in Susan's lap resumes her tired litany of "when-are-we-gonna-be-there?" until suddenly at the top of the mountain we stop next to a small house half hidden by wine leaves, and get out.

Blessed stillness, balmy late-summer evening air.

A pregnant woman comes out of the house with a suckling infant at one exposed breast, barefoot in a long gypsy skirt, long blond hair draping her shoulders, smiling warmly, and welcoming us, "Hi," with a melodious voice.

"This is Helen," Shiva says, standing next to her beneath a vine-clad trellis. They look like gods.

"Up there," she says, pointing to a wooded crest nearby, "is another house, it's unoccupied, we have the key, those without sleeping bags could sleep there. And the others are welcome to our floors, or the porch. I'm sorry we can't offer more comfort."

Shiva brings out a gallon bottle of red wine, a bowl full of fruit, a platter with cheese and bread, we help him bring chairs from the house, place them around a wooden table under an apple tree, and sit in silence—even the children are silent—stunned by the huge enveloping stillness and the chorus of crickets swelling and subsiding in the trees, and the buzz of insects among those tall stalks of . . . am I seeing right? Marijuana. Everything here bespeaks welcome and, yes, I dare think it, homecoming: This is the place! But at the periphery of my emotion I can't help noticing with irritation and disappointment that Susan is less than charmed, she's had her fill of rustic inconvenience, she finds Shiva and Helen too hip by half, I can tell, and besides, she's run out of cigarettes and all these pot-smoking communards have something against tobacco.

"Where can I buy cigarettes?"

"Not around here you can't," Helen says, "not at this time." And, unspoken, the question hovers on all lips: "Why didn't you think of this earlier?"

An hour later, we're parked on a lane near the beach in Nice. Gina is asleep in the back of the bus. I can't see Susan's face except when she draws on her cigarette. That's what we came here for. We are talking quietly. She's going home, she says, with Gina. I have no words.

"It would be nice if we went together," she says.

"I can't do that," I say. "Everything's coming together now. I can't give this up. And for what? To punch in at nine a.m., like good boys and girls? Stash away a little nest egg?"

"That's not fair," she says. "That's not all I want from life."

"What *do* you want?" There is hate in my voice. I am afraid of myself.

"To be with you," she says. "To make a real home for Gina, with stable walls, in one place. To have a real family. Real friends. We're lonely, Joel, don't you realize?"

My eyes start brimming. I wipe the tears away. I can't afford to melt. I'm thirty years old. By the standards of the world I'm a bum, I'm nothing. I won't throw in the towel while there's hope.

"Why don't you give it a chance," I say.

"Oh Joel, for how long? Our money's running out, and then what?"

"Wolfgang has money."

"We don't know Wolfgang. You're gambling. I don't want to gamble anymore." She will leave me.

"Will you come back?"

She wraps her arms around me. "Of course I will! How could you think . . ."

How could I indeed. But secretly, in the House of my Fear, I have been thinking thoughts much more terrible than these. I have been feeling him closing in on me, my mortal enemy. Stalking me. Like that scene in a Western I saw long ago—moccasins treading on pine needles, the pioneer women asleep in the covered wagon, the men with their guns and the dogs all asleep, and a child startled into terror by nothing but knowledge: They're going to kill us! But that terror is still of the realm of nature, where creatures are eaten by other creatures and the face of the Evil One is simply and terribly enough the face of your natural enemy, as the snake is to the rabbit, and the cat to the mouse. But this enemy has no face and has no intention of eating me, on the contrary, he threatens me with eternal life, eternal and infinite suffering. He waits for my thoughts to spring traps prepared for me in the brain, small slips and tricks of chance that release chains of monstrous, unthinkable consequence. While Susan and Gina are present, he stays at a distance, waiting. Because it's me he is after, only me, thank God. But now that they're leaving, I feel his breath on the back of my neck.

Ronnie's wife, Rose, keeps a journal. She calls it her book of days because on New Year's Eve she ate magic mushrooms and received prophetic names for each day of the coming year:

"The day of the butterfly"

"The day of giving God a break"

"The day of the mole's ministry to the sparrows"

The day Susan decides to leave is "the day of snap judgment." Rose says the names always fit the days, and not just her own days but others'. The day with the mole and the sparrows, for instance, was the day I embarrassed Krishnamurti.

"You mean we're the sparrows?" I ask.

"Yes," Rose says. "Sparrows shouldn't listen to moles. You were the chief sparrow that day."

"So who should sparrows listen to?"

"Nobody. They should build nests . . . preferably in a high place like Breil . . . make babies. . . ."

A fat chance Rose has to make babies with a husband like Ronnie. Gnarled and gnotted, his skin turned sallow from Ehret's Mucousless Healing Diet, he spends his nights hawking and spitting phlegm ("harumphing," Rose calls it) and rehearsing in his mind the next morning's prophylactic activities: Yoga, prayer, pranayama—on the night of the "day of snap judgment," for instance, a list of proposals he'll present to us concerning our common future. But we're falling into the future so fast there's no time for planning. Susan and Gina have to be driven to the airport (for all anyone knows, Susan will be happy to rejoin us all in a few weeks), the whole crew (all but Helen, who has chosen to stay at home with her daughter) piles into our bus and rolls down to Nice to see them off, the social lie and the presence of strangers help blunt the pain of our parting, a few kisses and hugs and my wife and daughter are gone. Now the rest of us travel on for a picnic in the Vallée des Merveilles, a scenic site recommended by Luc, I'm in the back of the bus, lying down, Adam is at the wheel, expounding, in his melodious, French-tinctured English, on a vision that has been ripening in his brain for the last several days, an amazing proposal: to create an Eden-like sanctuary in the Swiss Alps where the European bison would roam and the brown bear would harvest his berries in peace once again, because we would be their custodians. "And where would the bison come from, not to mention the land and the money?" Luc asks, a tone of angry sarcasm in his voice. But Adam has thought of this, he is a scientist too and therefore a man of practical reason, this is not another hash-induced pipe dream but a tangible possibility: The bison would be imported from the Soviet Republic of Belarus, where they are still extant, the land would be a nature preserve under the auspices of a scientific institute of which Adam is a respected member, and the admittedly large cost of the project would be underwritten by the Swiss government and sectors of industry eager to absolve themselves of their ecological sins. All the while, I feel a warm leg pressed against mine, it's Rose's, she likes me, and her husband is much too preoccupied with Enlightenment to care what she does with her leg, I close my eyes and descend into a hollow ache in my chest, a vacancy, a valley—of want, I suppose, for my wife and daughter, but it's deeper and wider than I would have thought; and I think, this must be what banishment feels like, and that reminds me of Bodo, my stepfather, who lived in exile for twelve years; but this ache is so formless and empty, and the longing within so detached, like some dim outer planet slipped out of orbit and drifting in space, that it seems to me not like banishment from a country but from life itself; and it occurs to me that to a child, orphanage would cause no less pain than such exile; and this thought erupts in a swift enfolding motion of protective fear and prayer for my daughter, a plea so urgent that it is a command: Let her not lose her father to madness, let me steer my ship out of the whirlpool before it's too late; and then, relaxing again, musing vaguely on orphaned children and banished souls, I think: Maybe some children need to lose their parents. Isn't my brother fatally bound to his mother, isn't that the sea he's drowning in? And then—and this thought startles me, I'm wide awake now: What if the Fear that has been visiting me at odd moments, sometimes on drugs but not always, and never when Susan or Gina is there, what if the Horror—I might as well call it that—is an initiation of some kind, one of those ancient rites designed to cut a boy off from the realm of the mothers? What if I have yet to become a man? In which case what is called for is courage and nothing but courage, and trust that some fatherly love is watching from behind the masks of terror. I open my eyes and turn my head and see Rose's face next to mine. She smiles. What does she hope to gain from this flirtation? I sense some great sadness in her. What are we doing? Where are we going? I ask her what the day's name on her magic calendar is. "The day of the spider," she says. "What does that mean?" I ask. "We'll find out," she says. And now we've arrived at the Valley of Marvels, a green hilly landscape rather brutally gouged by a dusty red dirt road. We pull up beside a cinderblock house, take out the fruit, bread, and vegetables we've brought with us and the little gas range and the blankets. It's drizzling. Aristide is crying, he wants to go home. Someone has hammered a large nail into a deer's skull, fastening it to the lintel. Shiva winces at the sight of it and shakes his head, he seems to think we should not go inside.

"It's dead," Luc says dryly as he enters the house.

"Nothing is dead," Shiva mutters.

Only after we are all inside, sitting on benches around a massive table, does he come in too. A dense, sticky odor of pine resin pervades the air. Just minutes ago, in the car, people were laughing and singing, but now nobody talks. The light from outside, already dimmed by a roof of rain clouds, is further dulled as it passes through three dirt-smeared windows. On a white cloth on the table, a Cézanne-like arrangement of scattered apples, a wine bottle, and a stack of plastic cups, but no one eats or drinks. Adam Bonheur turns in his seat to watch a small flock of birds that has assembled in a tree near the window, waiting for the rain to pass. Shiva is sitting very straight and still, glistening drops of water in his hair. He appears to be listening out into space, as if alert to some hidden presence. Aristide starts falling asleep in his mother's arms, his legs resting on his father's lap. Luc and Marie-France are huddled together, their heads touching, their faces brooding, absorbed in some dark joint dream that excludes the rest of us. Rose's leg, I notice, is pressing against mine again, in a gently urgent sort of way. Embarrassed, I pull away from her. What does she want? Why doesn't she speak to me directly? Now Ronnie pulls a neatly rolled joint from his shirt pocket, lights it, takes a drag, and passes the joint on to Shiva, who takes a long toke, passes the joint to Marie-France, exhales, and quietly, calmly, asks:

"Who are we?"

Silence. Marie-France has passed the joint to her husband, who sucks on it greedily and taps Adam's arm to distract him from his birds. Adam takes a toke and passes the joint to Rose. Still no one speaks. Finally Ronnie breaks the ice.

"We think we know what we're after," he mutters. "But for some reason none of us have said a word about it. We think we have come together to make life more enjoyable, freer, more loving, maybe holier. We want to grow old with our grandchildren near us, like in the village days of our ancestors. Or even have bears and bison around us, if Adam's plan works out. It's a beautiful dream. But I believe life has other plans for us. I believe we are bound to run up against the forces we want to escape. We don't even know what to call our enemies—I mean, 'straight' doesn't really describe them, does it . . . or what they're capable of. . . . But *we* are visible to *them,* don't you see? We are everything they are afraid of. They will destroy us. They have to."

No one seems to quite know what to make of this oration. No one has ever heard Ronnie do much more than ramble obsessively about matters of health, diet, and Yoga, and, somewhat incoherently, about Enlightenment. Suddenly Luc explodes.

"*Life* has plans for *us*?!"

He turns to me. "What are *your* plans? I'd like to know."

At this instant I come to an appalling realization of something that should have sunk in long ago: This astronomer has not only hitched his wagon to a star like the rest of us, taking his family along for the ride, but has decided, or been persuaded by some hypnotic witchery of his own making, that I, Joel, am that star, perhaps only because for a moment I flummoxed the great Krishnamurti. But didn't I play a part in Luc's seduction? That day he approached me with shining eyes, didn't I stand there puffed up like a general in an operetta, pleased to conscript him into my nonexistent commune? It is my duty to disenchant him—as quickly and cleanly as possible. Though to judge by the look on his face, it won't take much persuading. Marie-France, I'm pretty sure, considers me a fraud already.

"I have no plans," I say.

"Why not?"

"I grew up in the land of 5-Year plans."

"So?"

"So . . . I guess I plan to drop out of time altogether."

I don't know why I am making this pronouncement, but it falls like a bomb into our midst, leaving a crater of silence. Luc flashes a glance at his wife and lowers his eyes, breathing heavily and slowly shaking his head. Marie-France looks disgusted and vindicated. Rose smiles enigmatically. Ronnie is staring at me with intense interest. God forbid, not another follower! Adam turns his head to look at the birds again. They are gone. "It stopped raining," he says. Shiva opens a jackknife and starts peeling an apple by artfully turning it against the edge of the blade. Rose, always a trove of pertinent quotes, says: "Watch your parking meters," leaving the first part of Dylan's couplet unspoken and all the more trenchant. Marie-France lifts Aristide's legs off Luc's lap, stands up, and carries the boy out of the house without a word, while Shiva attends to his evolving spiral.

Adam takes a jew's harp from his back pocket, puts the mouthpiece between his teeth, and starts twanging the little tongue of steel. What is it about this simple act of peeling an apple that seems so significant? Or is it the rhythmic monotone of the jew's harp that lends it importance? Or is it because, for the first time since we came together, our minds are as one, almost prayerfully intent on the progress of Shiva's knife? Let it succeed! Because if it does, maybe . . . For a moment the peel seems about to break, but Shiva adjusts the slant of the blade in time. And then it is done. Adam stops playing his instrument, as if it were no longer needed. The stirring of relief in the room almost feels like hope.

Now Shiva cuts the apple in half, carefully scrapes the seeds out of the core, stands up, scoops the seeds into the palm of his right hand, takes the two halves of the apple in his left hand, and goes outside. We hear him speaking French to Marie-France: *"Ils sont très fraiches,"* he says, *"et pelées. L'une est pour toi et l'autre est pour Aristide."*

"Merci," she says, amused.

We hear Shiva's tread in the wet soil surrounding the house. He passes one window, then the second one, then the third, stopping at each one to hold up a pinch of apple seeds for all of us to see—like a magician preparing a stunt— and ceremoniously placing them on the windowsill. After circling the house he comes in again with a small purple pouch in his hand, sits down where he sat before, puts the pouch on the table, and says:

"We need an acid test."

My Counterpoint has returned, interrupting my story.

How greatly he has changed. And how remarkable that he began, many pages ago, as a will-o'-the-wisp, a fleeting impression on the edge of thought which I could have brushed off like a gnat. Probably if I had brushed him off, he would now be one of the million forgotten moments. But I saw him, and invited him into this book. For a while I feared him, thinking he was the scourge and mental enemy of my younger days come back to haunt me; and as long as I feared him, there was a menace in his words and actions. Once he even pushed me off a roof. At that point I no longer quite knew who I was. That is, I thought I was describing my younger self's fall through the medium of time (which I felt to be thicker than air but subtler than water), down past many windows that flew by like months, until he—that is, "I"—would land with uncanny softness in that darkest vault where the torturer, Time, instructs the damned in the enormities and the minutiae of eternal suffering; but I myself, I, here at my desk in Brooklyn, was falling through time as I wrote, falling not only forward in him, my past self, as I remembered him, but backward toward where I imagined him or some ghostly double of him still trapped in that hell, still mutely screaming through the endlessness of time.

I see that clearly now, thanks to my Counterpoint.

Last night he put his hand on my shoulder—here, at my desk in Brooklyn. The house was quiet. Susan was asleep.

That hand—I could see it, as if I were standing behind and above myself and also behind and above him—was at one moment human and gentle and at another clawlike and grasping. It flickered back and forth between these two appearances, I could not hold it still in my mind. But its touch, my sense of it on my shoulder, had a gentling effect, and I knew I was no longer falling.

I felt his touch for a while as it faded. But even after it was gone, I sensed that he was still near me. I went to the living room with a notebook and a pen, dimmed the lights, sat down on the couch, closed my eyes, and waited.

Eventually he spoke to me. I answered. He spoke again. Mind spoke to mind with the fluid immediacy of music.

C. Better to rise from here, up, up. No, we don't need a plane, not any longer. Not even bodies. Just your voice and mine.

What? And leave him, I mean me, down there, with the plot thickening the way it is? I'm not afraid, you know, I don't need protection.

C. Not protection, but guidance. Do you think you can slip into another's "I," even your own past self's, and not feel his skin closing over your face?

What of it? He is who I was, and I've surpassed him by thirty years, can I not speak for him?

C. Not in his voice. Look at him.

    I look. I see a mouthless angel, his wings on fire.

C. His agony would seal your mouth.

    The apparition vanishes.

Who was that? Me or my brother?

C. It was both of you, it is any of us. His condition? You named it once: the Unspeakable. To save him, choose your words carefully. That could preserve you from some dangers as well.

Which words? Can you be more specific?

C. Yes, begin with your pronouns. At moments of danger—and they will come—let "I" denote only your true self, the great man of no account, and let Joel be one of the countless third persons, of whom alone a story can be told.

I can do that. But how does that save the angel?

C. It doesn't. It merely protects you. To save the angel, you must go to where he is, without fear, armed with the conscience of words, enter his form, and lend him your tongue. But the voice will be his and not yours—an important distinction, which you will forget, and of which I will remind you. This is a dangerous undertaking, and requires adequate preparation. Defining our pronouns was a start.

What else is needed?

C. Your map needs redrawing.

What map?

C. The path you envision before you set out.

You're right. I've seen it in two ways, no, three:
    1) a vertical plunge, "la tumba"
    2) a drift down a river, with rapids and falls
    3) a whirlpool,
and frankly I've worried about this, because they can't all be right.

C. Come now, you've faced greater dangers than that of the mixed metaphor. I suggest we employ the first of your three modalities—of course it's up to you— and see where it takes us.

All right, let's go. To the angel!

> And already we're diving, plunging through darkness, past pinpoints of light that may be stars or houses . . . through a grayish, lightening layer of clouds . . . and abruptly into bright daylight, straight toward a sunlit shining wet black tile roof, and through it . . .

C. Voilà!

> but the house is gone and so is the car and the people and so is the earth, I feel my hand in your hand (why can't I see you?) and there's wind in my hair, we are diving through what I'm embarrassed to say resembles the tunnel-like passage to the realm of the dead described in the hundreds of near-death accounts assembled by Raymond A. Moody, M.D. Except there is something so deeply familiar about this smooth-shimmering, spiraling duct, it appears to be made of some whirling watery substance, which now with an ache of longing that puzzles me I recognize as the substance of my own existence, its colors, moods, emotions, events, large general themes and myriad particulars all flattened and smoothed into one continuous and seemingly endless tubular wave: my life! my life!—to see it so separate from me, so transformed, so unlike anything to which the word "I" could palpably correspond! Yet to know: that I need only stretch out my hand to feel that strong element streaming again through my fingers: the solace of it . . .

C. Do that.

Is that your advice, my Counterpoint? Who are you? Are you my own impulse, my inmost will?

I touch the streaming wall and see gray rock, tufts of flowers, hard blue sky, and hear in my head, on my skin, all around me a steady "twangety-boingety-twangety-boing" like some huge metal frog bouncing with dark tellurian joy, but it's a light sound as well, sprightly, light-footed, skipping along like a young mountain goat on a narrow ledge between steep exuberance and sheer plunging terror, and though I know this is Adam Bonheur's jew's harp, still Adam is nowhere and the sound is everywhere, as if the mountain itself were boinging and twanging its solitude into the world, and when the sound stops and Adam laughs—ah, what a happy laugh!—it is the mountain laughing because the mountain is Adam even though Adam is somewhere around here and everything now depends on my finding Adam or finding the source of the sound in the rock. Or am I the source? Oh, but I mustn't think that. Thinking that gets me into trouble. Ah, but you've already thought it. And every thought is a door. Twangety-boingety-twangety-boing. And having stepped through the door

NO!

you know where your steps

lead you, boing, boing, down the stone steps to that dank room where other doors open, boingety-twangety, boing, boing,

■   ■   ■

For centuries he scoured the conical peak of the mountain in search of Adam, miserably convinced that he was the maker of the singing mountain and the maker of Adam as well, until

C. Stop! It's good you slipped out of his skin when you did, but look at your words. You will get lost unless you open them up. "Maker," for one. Quick! Quick! Crack it open! Not ready for that? Then I'll do it for you. There is no getting around it, we will have to talk about how God came into the picture—the God of gods, the jealous One, beside whom there can be no other. Long before your first conscious forays into the inner outland, long before Acid, Voluptas, Politicus, and Chance, long before you and I met, you began, in the secrecy of your thoughts, to burrow and dig for Him. Others aspired through thought and emotion, others prayed and mortified their bodies, or sang in weekly congregations, or praised Him, praised Him on every occasion, filling their hearts with gladness. Still others hoped or speculated on His return, or philosophized about His absence. Or quarreled with Him, and in that way bound themselves to Him. Or else ignored Him, or shrugged Him off as a chimera. But you dug for Him. Slyly. Not even you knew it. In your imagination, but under cover. Like a prisoner digging a passage through the wall of his dungeon. Thinking that somewhere the heaviness, the dense dark resistance of not knowing would give way to light and space. And all the time you were digging downward, down toward the center of the earth, thinking that surely your will and desire would take you to Him. Like a thief in the night! Yet it was not something you did on purpose. No, it was too steady for that, too constant. Like the movement of blood, a blind, perpetual rhythm, a pulse. Yet the deeper you dug, the more solid and dark your prison became. The walls were descending with you.

"When was that," you ask, "when and where"—always anxious to know the coordinates—and I answer you: In the Time before time. In the All-ways, NowHere. In time, you discovered Acid, of course, and Acid gave himself to you as Gunpowder gave itself to those ancient warriors who knew only halberds and spears and a slant rain of arrows, or as Dynamite did to miners who knew only pickaxe and shovel: Power! Power beyond reckoning, beyond all imagining! Power enough to break open the vaults of Heaven, again and again if need be! But in your Bastille, in the Time before time, still digging for God in perpetual automatic zeal, you heard the reports of those detonations the way some deep-sea creature might receive rumors of light from above, as news so remote as to not be believed, a dream in a dream. Until one night the walls gave way. Was it the joining of those two motions, the brigand's fury and the prisoner's patience? Was it fire from the cauldron heart of the earth bursting in from below? You remember the way the world ended, it was in your apartment in Brixton, your wife and your daughter were asleep in another room. Prompted by something you had read in Ramana Maharshi, you earnestly asked the question of questions: Who am I? I am not my body, you said, because when I dream, I am but my body is absent. I am not my emotions and thoughts, because thoughts and emotions come and go, but I, taking note of them, seem to abide. I am not . . . and then it came, without any precipitant cause, out of nowhere. A branching tree of evolving life, nascent flesh budding forth in innocent urgency, rustling into fullness, glorying briefly in eternal youth, meeting love and the hateful enemy, crushed and mangled and dying into rebirth, again and again, multiplied in endlessly varied forms and destinies—oceans, jungles, cities, worlds—the whole of it, too, blown into being like dust by a sudden breeze, held aloft for a brief eternity and dropping back into zero, leaving you dazed and stranded on the couch. The pride you felt then, like a sail big enough for another world-storm to blow the earth from its orbit! But that pride made you deeply afraid of yourself, and with reason. Still seated on that worn couch, in that small room, one of billions of other human beings alive on the planet, you were the stars and the constellations, and you had the power of a demiurge. How could that be? Who am I? You asked it again, in fearful wonder, and you answered yourself with a Sanskrit phrase you had read: *Tat tvam asi:* Thou art That. And you took "That" to mean: "All things at all times" and "Thou" for your separate embodied self, your personality, an impossible equation. Mistook boundless being for endless duration. Qualitative for quantitative infinity. That notion entailed, among its corollaries, endless repetition and limitless variation, and the multiplication of repetition by variance, and the potentiation of that process by an endless succession of random factors; and your brain, ever busy, set about computing the unthinkable problem, not with numbers but with thoughts that bodied forth as things, creatures, people, worlds. This computation, of course, could not but be resultless, or rather the result was one of perpetual inconclusion, a widening torment without the remotest hope of an ending. And yet this hell was a mere antechamber to the one that would welcome you later, when you were made to know (I do not say "believe," because you were damned and the damned are made to know) that you were not only "That" but the maker of That, and therefore the martyr of your own irrevocable will to be all that was possible, without limit. Yes, irrevocable—that alone remained a mystery, all else was knowledge. Or so it seemed. And because you were the Maker, you were the one to be held responsible. By all—since the others, though made of your essence, were separate from you—and for everything. Now you remember. It made not the slightest human sense, but you were no longer human. And now, let's get back to the mountain—more of a hill, really, from our vantage—in the Vallée des Merveilles, where you were looking for Adam, the man with the jew's harp.

I wasn't the Maker then already?

C. Not yet, though the horror was dawning in you, a black dawn, darker than night. But the light of this world stood at high noon then, and Adam was laughing. Or was it the mountain? For when you found Adam, he was not laughing, he was twanging the jew's harp, thoughtfully, steadily, but the air was still full of laughter.

I remember. He was sitting on a ledge among white and blue flowers. When I sat down next to him, he chuckled again, not at me but at something below us.

Way down near the foot of the mountain, a minuscule yellow tractor was butting against a tall pine, apparently trying to uproot it. We could hear the insistent snarl of the motor, like that of a small stubborn dog in a tug-of-war with its master. Again Adam laughed, and the laugh expired in a "hmmm" that expressed rich amusement and something like tenderness. With wonder, with gratitude, I felt my stomach contract and my own laugh, an echo of his, coming out of my mouth. Does God laugh, I wondered. If he does, it is his most generous gift to us. Or did we steal it? An astonishing thought arose: "This is what it means to be saved." Obscurely, I must have known I had escaped a terrible danger.

C. Obscurely, yes. The light of salvation was correspondingly dim. But go on. For this we have time.

The tractor backed up, with its rear end raised, and attacked the tree again with a vengeance. The tree shook and started to lean. I was no longer amused. I felt for the tree, it knew it was dying. But Adam, still chuckling, was with the mountain, and the mountain was barely tickled by the little murder at its foot. We have dynamite, I thought, we have learned to lay mountains low. But there were bigger mountains, Annapurna, Everest. Oh, but we have nuclear weapons, and depots full of poisons the world has not dared to imagine, we have them, we can devastate nature. Adam laughed again. He was shaking with laughter. The tractor was backing off. Leaving the scene in a hurry, racing, in fact, but backwards, as if in retreat from a pursuing foe that would give it no quarter. It disappeared behind a wooded hill. The tree stood, crippled but alive. Adam returned to twanging his jew's harp. What a portentous sound! If fate played a musical instrument, it would be a jew's harp. After a while, he stopped playing it and said: "I'm going to India."

"What about the commune?" I asked.

He shook his head and smiled, gazing past me into the distance.

"No, I'm going to India. I'm going to study Yoga."

From that moment on, our would-be commune started disintegrating. Luc's announcement on the way back to Breil—"We're going back to Paris!"—didn't surprise anyone. Nor did Aristide's delight at the prospect of playing with his friends again. What surprised me, though, was how pleasant Marie-France suddenly looked—all that glum suspiciousness suddenly gone. I thought of Susan, who wanted nothing more than for me to come home. A small sacrifice: Why not do that for her? Sell the bus, fly to New York, get a haircut, shave, throw myself on the mercies of the job market. I pictured myself being interviewed for a job selling encyclopedias, and praying that I wouldn't get hired. I looked at Rose. She, too, looked content, her soft wide body eloquent with pleasure. She must have made love with Ronnie, I thought, but no, Ronnie sat next to her like gravity incarnate, watching us all with a gaze that was by turns doleful and angry: Woe unto you! Generation of vipers! I had seen this ponderous intensity in him before. Always it had been a secondary aspect of his personality, a kind of shadow: Now it appeared to be his substance. "Ronnie, we need your light, not your darkness," I said to him mentally. A moment later his face softened and he looked at me with a smile. I'll have to experiment more with telepathy, I thought. Dangerous thought! Three weeks later, I became the subject of just such an experiment.

C. Go there, go!

But it's not time yet, we're . . .

C. Time is about to splinter.

If I don't proceed step by step, I'll never get there.

C. If you don't heed my advice, you will stumble.

> He gives me no choice. Seizing my hand, he dives with me through the floor of the bus back into the tubular wave—(my life! my life!)—until we emerge in the kitchen of the house in Breil. Or is it the House of my Fear?

Shiva

It is night. Joel is sitting on the wooden floor, holding a lungful of hash as he hands the pipe back to Shiva, who is sitting on a chair. Behind them a bare brick wall, shelves with books on Hinduism, Chinese Buddhism, astrology, a Bible, the I Ching. The kitchen is dark except for a gas lamp on the mantelpiece and the flickering glow cast by a blazing fire in a large open fireplace. The doorless entrance frames a black starry sky, a stone well, behind it the moonlit marijuana patch. Through this doorway many insects, big ones and small ones, flutter into the room, lurch around the lamp and eventually throw themselves into the flames, flaring up briefly as they burn. The two young men pass the pipe back and forth, silently watching the conflagration. Finally one of them breaks the silence.

Shiva: Po' li'l' insects.

Yes, I was thinking the same thing. I was thinking "poor little insects," and that I was breaking my childhood vow to avoid needlessly hurting any creature. The entrance could have been curtained, for instance. But it was hot in the kitchen, and we needed the cool night air, and besides it was Shiva's house, Shiva's and Helen's, and therefore their decision to make.

Shiva: Po' li'l' people.

Why was he talking that way? Like a character from *Porgy and Bess*.

Shiva: Po' li'l' worlds.

With those three simple strokes, he summoned the Infinite into our little space, and Shiva and I were no longer who we had seemed a moment ago. I don't mean that the being who rose up in me to defend the Creation was not my self, but that it was I with an urgency that exploded the bounds of personality, so that my emotion appeared to be greater than human: "No!" it said (not in words, of course)—"this holocaust was never meant to be!"

C. You were not just speaking to Shiva.

No. It was to the All, for the All, as the All that I spoke. I summoned up all that was made of light in me. Proudly the light gathered in my heart. Effulgences. Huge arms of longing reaching in all directions. How wonderful, I thought, my heart can reach out to all: to those I know and love, to begin with: May they be well, may they be happy and free from harm: Susan, Gina; our future communards on their way to us from Germany now: Wolfgang, Wilma; Adam Bonheur on his way to India; Luc and his family back in Paris; Blaise and Juliette selling trinkets to tourists in Ibiza; Ed, Fred, and Betsy now scattered in various parts of the globe; Saint John Sebastiani still penniless somewhere in Turkey or Afghanistan, God bless them all. Maxwell Schneider beardless on medication in New York; my brother Stefan, lost in what flickering Asian heat, may you find your teacher, may you be blessed and your thirst be stilled, may you be made whole, may my guilt be washed clean as well. Because I envied you when we were children. Because there was a brilliance in you that was obscured in me, and it seemed to me that you had stolen it, you in your innocence. And my secret hatred took root in your soul and possessed you, like a curse. But did it stop there? Did I not start despising the world for not loving me, not embracing me as the mother it had once been to me? Was I not consumed with the desire to prove myself stronger than all others?

And all the while Shiva was staring at me, and I met his gaze with mine. I am now reminded of an account I once read of two bushido masters meeting eye to eye, standing immobile for a full hour with their swords held at readiness, until, with a mutual bow, they agreed to yield to each other's unshakeable stillness. But if this was a contest, Shiva had the advantage already, because I was afraid. He was sitting cross-legged on the chair, bent forward, chin in hand, his elbow resting on the edge of the table, his pupils like bottomless wells. Could he see my thoughts? There was a kind of suction in this stare, like a vortex through which the stream of thought flowed instead of pouring into space.

I suffered from his stare.

C. You suffered from shame. You felt exposed. You didn't want to admit your jealousy, your envy, your humiliation. Liane, the girl you had met in Zurich—the one whose advances you had nobly spurned because you were a guest in the house of her lover and you did not want to betray your wife—Liane had come to visit you in Breil. There had been a secret hope in your invitation (which was why you had not told Susan about it), and there was a fairly overt promise in Liane's tacit acceptance, and more than a promise in her arrival—you knew it the moment you saw her trudging up the hill toward the house in

Breil, a knapsack on her back, waving both hands at the sight of you. How charming she was, how pretty! Long slender limbs, sleek long brown hair. Such warmth and love of pleasure in her smile, her wide-set hazel eyes. And so obviously glad to see you—she of the impotent boyfriend. Moreover, your wife was away. Could Voluptas have arranged this tryst more conveniently, more propitiously? Still, you were hesitant. And Shiva had none of your scruples.

Or my inhibitions. As soon as Liane and Shiva met, the die was recast, and the prize fell to him, just like that. She was sitting on a low stool in the kitchen, a little out of breath from the steep climb, chatting happily in her French-inflected English, while Helen (with her baby on her arm), Rose, Ronnie, and I responded with friendly small talk. Shiva was the only one directly facing her. He was silent. Squatting Hindu-style on the floor, his knees jutting up near his shoulders, twirling a tuft of hair beneath his lips, smiling. His desire filled the room like a scent. He looked like a faun within sight of a nymph. All he lacked was the reed flute. He was swinging in his haunches, a slight, gentle, rocking, pelvic motion. It could have meant nothing or it could have meant what it looked like. But of course it was up to her what it meant. She glanced at him once, twice, with a kind of startlement. And finally she leaned forward and looked into his eyes with a wonderful smile. The smile of the nymph, I suppose. We all witnessed that stark moment, Helen too. What did she make of it? She looked watchful, one hand resting on her pregnant belly. Shiva said "Hmmm," as if tasting something delicious, and then, shyly, warmly: "Welcome." The shyness surprised me.

C. But now, two weeks later, the faun's gaze was no longer shyly averted. He was staring at you. His nymph was back in Zurich, but through your eyes (for the eye receives mental matter, not just light, and transmits it as well) he was now seeing himself and Liane slipping into the vineyard behind the hill, hand in hand, in a happy hurry, exactly as you had observed them two weeks ago through the curtains of a second-floor window—a view, from a hurt and jealous distance, of a moment which Shiva had lived at virtually no remove from himself. Quite a surprise! Moreover, the scene was now colored by emotions which, though they concerned him, were yours—your shame, your envy, your self-contempt for what you judged to be your hobbled manhood. These, too, he could see, for the screen onto which your confession projected itself was the whole human mind, of which he partook as much as you did. Is it any wonder he stared? He was as fascinated by what he saw as you were by dread of what else might be revealed about you. Oh, to be small again, a six-foot body, a buzzing brain in its bony case! But some force had cracked you open like a walnut. Out of that fissure now, that yawning mouth of possibility, crawled, first, another specimen of unlived lust, and another after that, and then several more, the fetishes and rituals of your secret reveries, trivial disclosures but all the more painful to your pride, especially when Shiva smiled and shook his head in disbelief at the imaginary uses to which, just hours ago, in a privacy you had thought inviolable, you had put his pregnant wife, in feeble revenge for his triumph. "If I can stay with my shame," you thought, "and go to the end of it, I'll be free of shame and pride alike"—advice you had learned from Krishnamurti. The opportunity offered itself, or let's say, it turned your gaze: from Shiva's stare to the open door. What a relief it was to have a view of your own and to see that the same opening through which the moths of the night were lured to their death offered you a path of escape from perdition. (That is the only right word for the threat you were facing. We will have occasion to use it again.) There was the well in the moonlight, the gleaming pail on its rim. Five steps would take you there. You would undress, lower the pail into the well, draw it up again full and quivering at the end of the taut rope, lift it and pour it out over your head. You would stand shining under the stars, as clean as the earth was on the first day. But there was a threshold. A slat of dark wood nailed to the floor, no obstacle to the body but a wall of fire to the mind. Poor human moth, endowed with foresight. From the hither side of the threshold, the imagined sight of your possible, probable self naked by the well—before the ablution, before the blessing that would surely follow—was too scorching, too shameful to contemplate for more than an instant. For there, in your man's body, in his nipples and buttocks and hips and arms, stood the ghost of a woman, a young woman, a woman your own age precisely, and the prospect of standing in her skin, denuded of your manhood, exposed to Shiva's pitiless gaze, promised further descents into deeper humiliation, not rebirth in the waters of life. That was the fiery limit you faced, the impassable threshold. Fifteen years earlier, when you were a boy, there had been, for a boy, no grimmer or more awful fate than to find himself forced to admit—to confess!—any erotic impulse resembling what girls were presumed to feel in their bodies. There were a few such damned souls in your school—creatures shunned by the others or else tolerated with cruel condescension. Better to die! "I know better than that now," you told yourself, and you did. What man, after all, does not have an indwelling woman, or woman an indwelling man? But this knowledge did not give you courage. Perhaps you did not know it well enough. You were unable to step through that door. It occurred to you to close your eyes, but it was too late for that, you could feel the Enemy slithering under your skin, a voiceless snicker.

It was you, wasn't it?

C. It was I.

And Shiva?

C. Shiva was perfectly silent, perfectly still.

Who are you, Counterpoint? What is your name?

C. My name is legion, but you could call me Pluto, or Hades, Lord of the Underworld. Orcus, Dis. I was on your mind, those days, as an astrological cipher. However, it's one thing to chart a god's path through the heavens, another to feel his breath on your neck. I'll tell you a secret about Pluto: He doesn't accuse. Never, never. He is a judge. Nor is he evil, though he knows no mercy. His only commandment is: "Thou shalt be whole." Now letus move on, time is pressing. Perhaps it is best if you pick up the thread, nowthat we've passed that impassable threshold. There are more coming up,though: be prepared.

I turned my head to look at my friend again, if he was a friend. His gaze had become more opaque, the set of the eyes more symmetrical, the smile more serene. Behind and above him on the mantelpiece, stacked upright in a coffee tin, were some two dozen carpenter's nails. I was very afraid now. Beleaguered, invaded, disarmed, exposed, all outer and inner escape routes blocked off, confronted by this bronze shield of a face, I scoured its features for a sign of contingency, a breach, a window perhaps onto *his* scatteredness in *his* inner landscape. And something new did appear in it, or at any rate something I had not seen before. . . . It pains me to recall this, Counterpoint.

C. Of course it does. It was the beginning of your crucifixion. Or your trial, if you will, but the trial was the execution. The point was to nail you to the four quarters of human existence, so that for once you would take in the whole view. You sensed this, vaguely. That's why you were terrified of those nails on the shelf. But the inner man has no hands and feet. The first nail was a word and the heart was its bed. Go on.

From behind the metallic gloss of the cheeks and forehead, the strong fleshy nose, the coarse, wavy hair, the full mouth framed by a short beard, a remote strain of African ancestry began to shine through. The discovery roused a rush of hope: I was the seer now, he the seen. And what was I seeing, after all? Evidence of human time, human impermanence, human fragility. Maybe this ancestor had been a slave, cowering, as I was, abused and ignorant in the house of his fear. Friendship was possible again, solidarity, brotherhood. Speech! Why hadn't I spoken all this time? But how could I speak now, as if nothing had happened? Perhaps I should simply say his name. But that could evoke the destroyer god again, the one he was named after. I did not speak. Long minutes passed, as long as centuries, and Shiva did not revert to his familiar appearance. The African and the destroyer god kept wafting in and out of each other. And the African's face was starting to look defensive, as if anticipating a blow, and mean, as if contemplating an attack. Who would I be speaking to, if I spoke? Maybe I should call Shiva's name after all. Why didn't he say anything? At last, then, a word was spoken. It spoke itself. Without a sound, without my opening my mouth or stirring my tongue, it spoke for me, in me, and as me, in a jeering, adolescent voice, shouting from a great distance, muffled at first, as if through some dense intermediary matter: "Nigger!"

That voice was not mine, Counterpoint!

C. No, but it came from the basement rooms of the house of your fear, the ones you share with the multitude. The labyrinth. You didn't want to admit its existence, the misery there, the brutal stupidity. That word was the key that turned the lock. Down you went, step by step. There was nothing you could do to stop it. A key, a nail, a lock, a heart: We'll have to mix metaphors a good deal more recklessly to approximate the logic by which you were judged. That word had one other function: Shiva was meant to hear it, not so that he would be hurt by it—he was only amused, and after the third or fourth repetition, bored—but so that you would know yourself to be confirmed, in the Law by which you were being tried, as guilty. Of what? Of every crime under the sun, but to begin with, of being the kind of white man who envies black men and denies it by calling them "niggers."

But I was nothing of the sort!

C. That was your protest then, a silent scream. You offered your entire past as surety, confident that not one of the countless moments answerable to your name corresponded to this description. But what are a million past moments against the authority of present evidence? There was that ugly—and, under the circumstances, ridiculous—word shouting in your brain. Its aura pervaded space like a stench.

What was it? A demon?

C. A ghost. Which is to say: a whorl of recurrence, an eddy revolving around a nub of time. When your psychologists speak of "complexes," they are speaking of ghosts. Ghosts are not as mysterious as people believe. There are hungry and happy ghosts, angry and lost ones. Some ghosts want only a gift of beauty, an act of kindness to ease them back into the void where they came from. Others cry out for vengeance and will not rest until someone—anyone—atones for their pain. Remember those perfectly innocent defendants in the great show trials in Russia? The evidence against them was stacked so high, and was in the absence of a defense so convincing even to themselves, that a few of them went to their deaths consoled by the belief that they were expiating the crime of the century. Perhaps, from the ghosts' point of view, they were. But what is the crime of the century compared with the crime that made all crimes possible? And who will expiate that? This was the question for which you were summoned; for which in fact you were elected to be the answer.

Elected by whom? By what?

C. By guilt.

What guilt? How could I atone . . .

C. . . . for the crime of God?

I would never put it that way.

C. But those were the terms of the interrogation. And you accepted them.

I had no choice.

C. The choice was to go to the well. You refused it.

I can't go on.

C. You must go on.

I don't remember what happened next.

C. Oh, but you do. Recall the words you clung to as you descended.

Bad poetry.

C. It was your only truth.

Must I?

C. You've already begun.

"Must I then go to Bethlehem . . ."

C. But to indicate the centrality of those words, they should be displayed like this:

MUST I THEN GO TO BETHLEHEM FORGOTTEN AND FORSAKEN?

I meant Golgotha, but I said Bethlehem. My own words weren't mine.

C. They never are. Only your motives are yours. However, the question received an answer.

The question, yes, but I was left in the dark:

IS ALL FOR GIVEN.
IS ALL FOR READY TAKEN.

Was this an offering of hope or a mockery? A consolation or a slamming door? Also, Shiva had been replaced by a weird tableau: the legs of a chair, two feet—one in a blue and one in a black sock—above them two legs in blue denim, and a third limblike protuberance jutting out to my right at waist level, but no foot visible there. And the fire in the background. One of the two legs was vertically positioned, the other one lay on the ground. The foot in the black sock, belonging to the vertical leg, stood flat on the floor, and its big toe, pointing in my direction, was wiggling rhythmically, as if keeping time to music. The other, immobile foot pointed away from me and lay on its side, as did the corresponding leg. I know now where my confusion stemmed from. I had lowered my head, eliminating Shiva's upper body from my view, and had tucked my right leg under, while Shiva on his chair had folded his right leg over his left thigh. But Joel, then and there, had no way of knowing that. All he knew was what he saw, and what he saw was a pair of legs haphazardly deposited on the floor, one of them standing, the other on its side, like discarded tools. But alive. Who was this disembodied creature? Who but himself? What other being had there ever been? His wife and his daughter—a fiction. His tortured brother—a dream. The world—what world? There was only "I," and I was a multitude of creatures and things. An infinity. An eternity.

C. But you outlasted eternity, at least for a while—one paradox for which you were grateful.

Yes. It took just a few hours. The "I" reverted to human proportions, the world resumed its unpredictable ways. With uncommon speed, I should add. The day after the nightmare, Ronnie and Rose, still living together on top of the hill, began . . .

C. But tell it in the present tense, or else the speed of it will escape you!

. . . begin to avoid each other, and I start wondering if Rose's halfhearted advances might have really been mute cries for help. Even more disconcertingly, Helen and Shiva shed their godlike composure and descend to unconcealed quarrels over money: It's running out fast for them too, and how does Shiva expect to support two children, once the new baby is born?

"I don't know, Helen. I'll find a way."

"Oh yeah, like where, Shiva, up in the moon?"

Which is a low blow, because Shiva has been telling me, in Helen's presence, how he is trying to "understand" the solar system, to somehow hold in his mind the reality of those tremendous volumes and speeds and distances and the almost frightening precision of details like that of the moon's being just the right size and its orbit around the earth just the right distance from a human observer and set at just the right angle to cover the sun from time to time like a perfectly fitted, custom-built lid of darkness, not a tenth of an inch too small or too large. He shakes his head at my astrology: "You *are* the stars, man, and the stars aren't symbols." Oh, but they are, I think. But I sense that I've lost his respect and stay silent. Then Wolfgang, the long-awaited German heir, arrives from Frankfurt with his American girlfriend, Wilma, and suddenly a fortune in frozen assets awaits conversion into a homestead in Ireland or the Seychelles— that's the plan—maybe even right here in Breil. What magical timing! But "the bank in Zurich," as Wolfgang refers to it, operates much like the bank in Chattanooga. There is nothing to do but wait for liquidity to set in, a process which, I know, could take weeks, months, or years. Meanwhile Wolfgang is low on cash and, Wilma tells me, addicted to morphine, an expensive habit. Wilma isn't solvent either. Her parents in New York don't know she's in love with an addict, but they remember her affair with a Dominican gang leader and they're worried sick about her. Yet they refuse to bail her out with a check. She made a mistake, she says, in sending them a Bob Dylan verse:

She never stumbles,
She's got no place to fall.
She's nobody's child,
The Law can't touch her at all

and assuring them that it described her. It does, but this truth is cold comfort to her parents, both of whom are lawyers.

Wolfgang's inheritance, it turns out then—it's Wilma who spills the beans—is not exactly an inheritance. It's a bargain. His mother will give him a large sum of money on the day a famous detox clinic in London attests to his cure. Now the hopes of the commune rest upon Wolfgang's rehabilitation. He is not at all sure that life without morphine is worth living. He spends a lot of time thinking about it in Shiva's kitchen, looking dreamy, serene, ironic, and sad. He is also treating that kitchen the way an uncouth traveler might treat a railway station, dropping cigarette ashes on the floor and grinding out the stubs with his heel. At sunset one day, over dinner outside, when Shiva spots a strip of toilet paper flapping amongst his prayer flags in the fig tree on top of the hill, he knows where it came from and confronts the miscreant. But it wasn't Wolfgang, it was Ronnie. And Ronnie says it was the wind that did it. Thereupon Shiva plunges a steak knife into the dinner table. Time to break up the party, no need to consult the I Ching.

C. Change of scene, then:

World's End

And my Counterpoint shoves me gently but firmly across several weeks of meandering indecision (what if the tide turns—maybe I should stay? Or should I join Susan and Gina in New York?) to a large empty flat in the World's End district of London, an area which, some 50 pages past, I described as "run-down," but now it is living up to its name: wreckage everywhere you look, gutted buildings, rows of flats exposed to the street, flower-patterned bedroom walls, mirrors, toilets. During the day, large iron instruments of "urban renewal" lumber about with an air of civic dedication, but the landscape resembles the ruins of Berlin as I witnessed them when I was eight years old. At night, in the glow of a waxing moon, a deeper stratum rises to the surface. Now the city resembles nothing so much as the apocalyptic woodcuts of José Guadalupe Posada, stark images of havoc and terror which in turn are linked to the memory of my childhood friend Dolores, with whom I lay side by side on the cool shaded tiles behind my house, out of her terrible mother's sight, studying the stages of *"el fin del mundo."*

Of course in the World's End of 1970, the heavens do not belch fire and no panicked citizens pour into the streets. A redeemer has come, he has offered himself, his brain and his nerves, as ransom for a doomed humanity, yea, as a theatre of devastation. He does not know this yet as he swallows a massive dose of LSD at precisely 10:32 p.m. on November 12, a moment suggested by astrological considerations. Now or never, he tells himself, and what he means by that is: all or nothing. Break through to the greater reaches of love and intelligence, or live shrunken, an ant among ants in the hive of New York where you came from.

A week later, looking again at the constellation he chose for a talisman, he asks himself how he could have presumed to drain the sky with a few hasty gulps and read the stars like tea leaves; and worse, how he could have contrived to interpret such a baleful arrangement of symbols as anything but the devil's signature. He scarcely remembers what happened. Not that he wants to remember. But there is the compulsion to go back, as if to the edge of a crater. There, looking down, he sees the fiery gorge he fell into. It is not conceivable that he came out of it whole and alive. Yet he is here, he exists. Never again. Never, never again. What was it, though? Down there, he was no longer human. Down there, he was crying for death. Down there, love was on trial. He writes the word "HELL" on a blank sheet of paper. It has no meaning. There is no word for what happened down there. "HORROR." Let that word be an epitaph at least, a warning for all time. Never again. And "PAIN." More cannot be said.

But this much can be remembered: It's a view of the edge of the crater. Two weeks later, he writes it down with a borrowed typewriter:

```
The morning after, I walked through the ruins to Gandalf's
Garden. I wanted to look at a poster that hangs there,
showing the world as a flower, each petal a separate realm
of existence, and in the center of each realm a Buddha. I
wanted to confirm that there is a Buddha in the bottommost
petal, surrounded by images of suffering and cruelty, and
that he is raising a hand in a gesture of assurance: Do Not
Fear. But there was a sign on the door: "THE LOTUS IS
CLOSED." If the words had said outright "Abandon Hope," I
think their effect would not have been as crushing. It
would have been a message for all who read it, instead of
for me alone.
     I didn't want to accept it. So I depressed the door
latch. The door was open. I stepped in. The gnomelike fel-
low who runs the place was reading a book behind his desk.
A man wearing a baseball cap was looking straight at me as
I entered the room. He was sitting on the floor. He had
tilted the visor upward, like a child. But he was older
than I was. He wasn't the Gandalf's Garden type at all. He
wasn't the baseball cap type either. He had combat boots
on. Otherwise, he was dressed like a working man. He was
holding some New Age magazine, but he wasn't reading. His
eyes looked glazed.
     "How are you—good?"
     He gave the last word ironic emphasis.
     "I don't know," I said. Who can claim to be good?
Besides, I knew his question was a trap.
     He shook with amusement. I thought I knew beyond any
doubt that he knew what I had been doing all night: suffer-
ing (what else?) for the sake of all beings. And that I
knew all the time I could let myself off the cross at any
moment, and that I didn't because the moment I contemplated
```

that option, the thought of Gina leapt to the fore, warning
me that she would be destroyed in my stead, and with her
every last soul on the face of the earth. So I had no
choice except to play my part faithfully, unto the endless
end.

Early that morning (I'm recording this now at my desk in Brooklyn) Susan
had woken and found me lying on the mattress next to her, glassy-eyed. (Yes,
she and Gina were with me again.) She talked to me, shook me, called me. I
couldn't respond, but I saw her. I saw and heard everything very clearly. Doors
opened and closed. Wolfgang came in with Wilma. (They had come to set up
house with us in London—still the commune idea.)[7] Together they raised me
up. My naked arms dangled out on either side, pale green and stiffened as if
from the rigors of crucifixion, the palms turned upward, the fingers curved like
a dead bird's claws. Susan was wringing her hands and raising her eyes to
heaven. Some part of me thought the whole scene very artistic. Was I "good"?
Was I an impostor? Hard to say.

"And you?" I asked, "how are you?"
"Oh, crazy." Strange choice of words, I thought.
Whereupon he said: "Yeah, strange . . . I've been tripping
all night."
"Me too," I said.
"I know," he said. "Strange, isn't it?"
I said nothing. I started feeling cold.
"You're from New York, aren't you?"
There was no point in denying this, or in confirming it.
"Of Irish extraction, right?"
Next he would mention Jewish. Wasn't that required for
this drama? But he didn't. I suppose there was no need to
convince me further of his clairvoyance. He went on to tell
me that, unlike me, he never took Acid but mainlined
amphetamine instead. He offered me some. I said no thanks,
thinking my tab must have contained speed. It felt that
way.
All the while some harp player was thrumming dulcet
tones through the stereo. The hobbit behind the counter was
reading his book. Then the music changed. As soon as I

---

7. What else have I forgotten? The house we were in, gutted and slated for demolition, was the
venerable Milton Chambers, where we had lived the year before. Ralph Ponder, the candyman's
son, still lived there, rent-free, with his girlfriend Georgie.

heard the first chords, I felt myself turn ice-cold inside.
(I think one could classify the varieties of fear by the
temperature they produce in the body, and also by what they
do to the sense of time. There are speeds of fright, for
example, that zing through you like an electric shock. But
this was the famous freezing of the blood, and time slowed
down extremely.)

So there it was, that clarion voice:

Please allow me to introduce myself
I'm a man of wealth and taste
I've been around for long long years
stole many a man's soul and faith.

The man with the baseball cap regarded me with amusement.

Pleased to meet you!
Hope you guess my name!

He asked me if I liked Mick Jagger. I hesitated. Now he
laughed out loud.
"You've got to admit he has a beautiful voice!"
I said nothing.
"He makes me want to run amok." He shot out his fists
right and left.
We listened to the song.

I stuck around St. Petersburg
When I saw it was time for a change
I killed the Czar and his ministers
Anastasia screamed in vain

"I'm going to New York next," he said. "And then down
South: Alabama . . . Mississippi . . ."
"Do you like it there?" I asked.
"I like the black people," he said, "not the other
shit."

Just as every cop's a criminal
And all the sinners saints,
As heads is tails, just call me Lucifer
'Cause I'm in need of some restraint

"Don't do it," I said, without words.

He chuckled. "You're good," he said then. "You're really good."

So if you meet me, have some courtesy
Have some sympathy and some taste
Use all your well-learned politesse
Or I'll lay your soul to waste

At that moment a kerosene heater that was standing on the floor started burning.

Oh yeah, get on down!

I didn't notice it until the man with the baseball cap pointed it out to me with a nod. The flames leaped high and black smoke rose to the ceiling. The Rolling Stones were whooping it up:

Tell me baby, what's my name?
Tell you one time, you're to blame!
Oo who! Oo who!

while the storekeeper rushed about searching for rags to smother the flames.

I asked, without words again: "Did you do that?"

The man laughed and nodded. The laugh was strange. The tip of his tongue was pressed against his palate, so the sound was a series of hisses: "Ss-ss-ss-ss-ss-ss." His eyes were very glassy. It occurred to me that I may be talking to a spirit who had taken possession of this addict's body.

"Really?" I asked, out loud this time, I guess to test my assumption.

"Yes, really," he said.

The next song was "Gimme Shelter." I didn't want to hear any more. The hobbit was still fighting the flames. We just watched.

"You should see Central Park now," the man with the baseball cap said. I remembered the superimposed film I had made of burning trash-cans on 4th Street and dancing hippies in Central Park. It was all my doing.

Marianne Faithfull's wonderful voice soared above the electric guitars:

*War, children! It's just a shot away! It's just a shot
away!*

Now the flames were snuffed and the heater was glowing
again. The storekeeper went back to his desk and returned
to his book. He ignored us completely. It was as if we
weren't there.

I stood up. "I have to go home now," I said.

"Me too," the man with the baseball cap said, still sitting on the floor. He pushed up his sleeve, showing me the
bruised and punctured crook of his arm. He opened his hand.
"How about a quid?"

At that moment I responded to him as if he were human. I
hesitated. He was killing himself with speed.

"Don't you think I deserve it?"

The irony of that was too perfect to resist. I gave him a
pound and left. In the door I turned to look back at him.

"See you 'round," he said.

On the way home, I saw a headline in fat, oversized letters—I'll paste it in here:

CATASTROPHE

I bought the newspaper. A tidal wave had struck the coast
of Pakistan. Some 13,000 pilgrims had come there to worship
in the Ganges Delta, but the number of casualties exceeded
that number by a wide margin. The estimates ranged between
60,000 and a million.

For days after, I felt and behaved like one of B. F.
Skinner's poor electrified pigeons. For instance, when a
ship's horn blasted me out of sleep, I took it to be a
trumpet blast announcing The End. It seemed the whole world
must have heard it. My whole body became a shivering flame
of fear and prayer. It was for all of humanity I feared and
prayed.

The next day, it rained heavily in London. Parts of the
city were flooded. Water came pouring through leaks in our
ceiling. Wolfgang's hair caught fire when he leaned over
the gas burner. Susan was seized by nameless fright and sat
shivering in her bed. Wilma took care of Gina while I
wrapped my arms around Susan until she calmed down. In the
morning, when Susan went to the playground with Gina, the

```
Fear came back to me. I prayed desperately. The door
opened. A girl came in, barefoot, long stringy brown hair.
She crouched down next to my bed and stroked my forehead
until I was calm. She said she had "felt something" and
that's why she had come. I never asked who she was. (Lots
of people move in and out of this building.) Or rather, I
asked if she was an angel. She said she wasn't.
```

Beneath this record I pasted a photograph, a radar scan of the eye of a hurricane. It looks like a spiral nebula in a black sky. Underneath that, I pasted a paragraph from the report on the tidal wave:

> The wave coincided with an abnormally high tide. It hit the
> Patakhuali district of the Ganges Delta at about midnight. It came,
> according to one survivor, with a hollow, rolling roar and a cold
> luminous glow like a ray. It washed away most people and then
> washed back 90% of them.

■　■　■

Turning that page, I find another document glued to its back, a card my brother had made for himself, printed in Gothic letters:

REMEMBER THE PAIN
OR IT WILL COME AGAIN

Stefan had stopped over in London on his way home from Nepal. We met in his hotel room. I told him he didn't look so good. "I know," he said, "I'm starting to frighten kids in the street." I told him about my "major bummer" and that I couldn't remember the details and was glad of it. It was then he handed me that card. I flared up: "I prefer to live in the present." Stefan, grinning, replied: "Where in *hell* do you expect to find any trace of the present?"—pronouncing "hell" with such scorn that I, stung at being taken for a freshman in any subject, especially that of hell, by my little brother, slammed my hand down on the table, clearing a space of clarity in that dingy hotel room (I still see the mottled mirror on the wall and Stefan's frayed herringbone coat on a hanger), but then said, without knowing what I intended to mean: "Let's stop this charade!"—which set the wheels of delusion rolling again, in both of us, I'm sure: the vain fearful hope for an end, not just to our quarrel but to the masquerade of me-and-you altogether.

A Turn in the Road

The three of us set off again in our VW bus: to Brighton first, where we stayed in a grand old Victorian house with a group of painting, pot-smoking, rock-'n-rolling students—not a commune-in-the-making, as Veneta Knowles, the banker's daughter, had led us to believe, just some rich kids on vacation from life before they settled into respectability. However, they had a recommendation: a Buddhist sheepherding commune northwest of Edinburgh. And now I feel the days and weeks flying past like wind, there's no time to look around, I'm falling again, or rushing with the river, I'm no longer sure of the element, only that its force compels me to stay with the present tense, despite Stefan's mocking rebuttal. The long drive north now, through gray rocky landscapes and gray, stone-cold towns. Christmas Eve on the Scottish border, Gina on the floor near a candlelit fir tree by a fireplace, playing with her presents (delivered by Santa before her bedtime), our elderly hostess brings Susan and me a gift of hot punch, pity in her eyes for us poor refugees, homeless on this holy night. Of the commune the next day, we find only the sheep, and later their garrulous wrinkled shepherd, from whose virtually incomprehensible speech we gather, little by little, that those nice young longhaired English have betaken themselves to Australia, or is it Tasmania, something like that. Southward again we drive, stopping briefly at Samye Ling, a big log house with windows and doors painted in bright primary colors, Tibetan prayer flags fluttering in the branches of pine trees nearby. I knock and ask for Chögyam Trungpa, Rinpoche, the lama to whom Ralph Ponder, the candyman's son, promised to introduce us last year (along with Mick Jagger). The monk at the door gives us the once-over: "Chögyam Trungpa is no longer a monk," he says. "He is married. He lives in Vermont." The monk sounds angry at Chögyam Trungpa or else at me, perhaps for presuming that a high Tibetan personage would welcome some straggling hippies as friends of friends. On we go—resolutely southward to Brussels, where we have an open invitation from Micky and Zina Lapidus, childhood friends of Susan's. They have a little son, a year younger than Gina. They also have friends with other children her age. We move into an apartment near theirs. If we weren't living on our last two thousand dollars, if my ambition weren't set on ENLIGHTENMENT,

C. A drastic shift of direction, this one.

How true—at a right angle to the one I was going in.

C. Which one was that, my friend? Don't take this curve too quickly.

Don't, Counterpoint, no curves, no highways—I have enough metaphors to reconcile, it's becoming impossible: a vertical plunge from the roof of my life to the grave; an anxiously drifting and hurtling joyride down a river, eddies and pools alternating with Niagara-like falls; the same watery surface turning against the pull of the sea and spiraling all the more surely downward, a vortex; a house full of two-way mirrors and unreliable furniture, with shifting walls and an echoing basement that turns the most innocent sounds into omens of horror; and now you want to throw in an automotive image, and I'm supposed to be on a highway, swinging into a curve?

C. An exit lane. And here's why I warned you to take this curve slowly. There are a few things you need to see clearly before you leave them behind.

On either side of the road was a burning landscape. The world was on fire. You remember that Buddhist book you showed Gina?

Yes, about the boy who didn't heed his guru's advice about anger. The anger manifested itself as fire. It turned to rage and spread from house to house. Those pictures frightened her. I hugged her and told her that love always puts the fires of anger out. She believed it, but I didn't. Or rather, I feared that my love was too puny, too timid to prevail against what I had seen of hellfire.

C. That is why your commune wouldn't take shape. Your hopes for it were so high that you doubted it out of existence. It was supposed to put out the flames.

Like a fountain, I guess . . .

C. Yes, an artesian well. It wouldn't be the only one, of course. Others like it would spring up elsewhere, and would eventually take up mutual communication, each of them drawing waters of spirit from the common ground. A global irrigation system . . .

Now you're mocking me. I never conceived of anything like this.

C. Of course not. You dreamed it, just as you dreamed that your body was that of the world. That was your brother's dream too, his nightmare. Except, unlike you, he committed that dream to paper, in paintings and drawings, some of which he sent you. More often than not that dream-body with its severed limbs and gaping wounds and burning hair had the overall form of a Buddha, harmoniously proportioned, balanced, and, strangest of all, at ease. Wasn't Stefan dreaming a way out of misery, both for himself and the world? And you wanted to meet him in this, to bring your dream to his. Your commune would be a haven for him, and more than that: a hospital. He would be healed there. By yourself, you were unable to help him; invariably he would throw in your face the reflection of your anger, your pride, your aggression, your fear. But with the help of others united in a quest for self-transcendence, you would make yourself worthy of him, for the sake of the world.

But now, after reading road signs marked "Commune" for several years, you discovered that you had been misled, and that the road you were on was taking you straight to the dreaded dead end of middle-class normalcy. Your dead end, moreover, was for Susan a reprieve: no more living out of suitcases, no more temporary homes. That's when you really started feeling the heat. It no longer came from the sides of the road but from its destination, your future. In a book by the Venerable Mahasi Sayadaw you read that Nirvana means "becoming cool." The monk claimed that a mere ten days of sustained "bare attention" could lead an aspirant to Nirvana, if he applied himself to its pursuit with unwavering zeal. A holy indifference, a lofty detachment—was that the solution? How would that help Stefan, how would it change anything in the world? A phrase of Krishnamurti's rang in your ears like a doomsday warning. He used it often to awaken young people to the urgency of change: "Forty years of office work!" Against that death sentence and its execution, there was but one appeal: to die the death of the mind here and now; to die to the things you cherished, including your family; to die and be born in a blaze of spirit, fearless and innocent, an instrument of Love. But you had tried that—through efforts at effortless, choiceless awareness, through chemical raids on the brain's stubborn sleep—always to no avail. And then you found Chao Khun's book, and in it another translation of "Nirvana." The word meant "extinction" or "snuffing out," not of physical life but of the ego, whose perpetual motion is fueled by the fires of greed, hate, and delusion. That word, "Nirvana," with Chao Khun's name attached to it, now pointed the way, a last exit. There was a chance, after all, that you, too, could attain Nirvana. Wouldn't that change everything? The future, even your dreaded forty years of office work, would be annulled in a timeless Present. ENLIGHTENED, you would *be* the light instead of seeking it in books, in meditation (which you had taken up on the prompting of Chao Khun), or in some aloof, august sage like J. Krishnamurti. And what would that light be if not Love and invincible Truth? ENLIGHTENED, you would enlighten others. Your brother first of all. The darkness in him would scatter in all directions, maybe with shrieks and a stench, like exorcised demons, but in the end, Stefan would grasp your hand and easily, lightly, step out of his madness as if from a prison whose gates have been opened. And Susan—she, too, would be illuminated, like a mirror that catches the light of the sun. That's how you imagined it before it dawned on you, later, that "enlightenment" might, among other things, be a condition of seeing others in their true light. So great was your need to shine! And not just to shine, but to draw back into your sphere all those whose paths had crossed yours, however briefly, and who had let you know, sometimes with words, more often by direct, unconscious hints—like that peculiar style of distractedness that had become endemic in the late sixties, and that was really a sign of alert inward listening—that they, too, had heard the wordless rumor, had felt the tremors of some nameless, holy disturbance at the heart of reality: John Sebastiani, for instance, who, you had last heard, was studying Rudolf Steiner's spiritual science somewhere in England, or Adam Bonheur, the friend of animals (you would have to recall him from India), or your old roommate George North, who had written to tell you that he had abandoned his radical politics and was practicing Zen in New York, or Shiva—mystical, mysterious Shiva, whom you sometimes suspected of being enlightened already, a Buddha disguised as a pot-smoking hippie, or Ed, the third wheel of "Fretsy and Bed," who was looking for someone to follow. If, on the other hand, you did not make the supreme effort at self-transcendence, if you did not sign up for a ten-day retreat with Chao Khun, nothing would change, or rather, as Krishnamurti never tired of repeating, the process of disintegration would continue, in you, in your brother, in society, in the world. That is why you swung into that curve without putting your foot on the brake, confident that, since you were at the wheel, your wife and your child would go with you. But the turn did not lead where you thought it would.

You're right. It led to a crossroads. One night I stayed up late in our house in Brussels, painting. I painted aimlessly for a while, using various colors, and finally settled on blue, a blue movement that gathered into the shape of a wave. At its foot lay a beach with tiny human shapes, sunbathing, playing ball. None of them saw the advancing menace. Pleased with the picture, I went to sleep, and later awoke from a dream in which I was hiding from a man who was plotting to kill me. He found me. He was wearing a white smock, like a doctor. He was enormous. His hands alone were larger than I was. "I'm just a child!" I said. He heard me. "It's not my doing. It's your parents who asked me to do this," and he reached out to pluck me from my hiding place.

I recorded the dream and went back to sleep. A second dream followed on that same night. Through a window I saw houses that were giant mushrooms or small round hills with windows and doors. The sun had just risen, the soft roofs shone in the pink, golden light. An adolescent boy appeared, his arms spread as if to embrace this enchanted world. "At last!" he cried, "at last, at last!" His face turned, we saw each other, my heart overflowed with love.

This dream, too, I recorded, and went back to sleep. When I woke again, it was from a dream in which Susan was seated on a chair in the fullness of pregnancy, wearing a red dress. She was about to give birth. I was kneeling on the floor before her. By my side lay a black book titled *The Wave of Isis*. I was surprised that it wasn't "The Veil" of Isis, but no, it was "The Wave." Beneath the title was a small square hole. When I leaned in to look more closely, a shaft of cold wind struck my eye, and I knew at once that this wind came from the outer darkness, and I felt a great danger, not for myself but for the unborn child. "This must not touch the child!" That was the assignment with which I awoke.

A week later, Susan told me that her period was late, and when she consulted the doctor, he confirmed that she was pregnant. This was not, for her, good news. In a few weeks, after my retreat with Chao Khun in England, the three of us would be forced to return to New York, since no work permits could be obtained in Europe. Gina would be separated from her new friends, and would need more attention than either of us would be able to give her if Susan's pregnancy was brought to term. The strain of poverty (not just a lapse in a bank payment this time), homelessness (at least for a while), and my absence for much of the day, since I would be working—this was unavoidable. But the ill-timed birth of our second child was not. Abortion was legal in New York, and affordable.

There was the cold wind I had been warned against. Desperate, tearful arguments ensued. I pleaded with Susan, citing my triple dream as proof that I had received a sacred mandate to be a father to this boy—I was certain that it was a boy. She was not persuaded. It was just a dream. The fetus was not yet a baby and surely, therefore, not yet conscious. All the while, as we wrangled, I knew that the child's fate was in my hands, not hers; that if I chose to forego the retreat with Chao Khun—and with it the chance at a last-ditch escape to some supernal realm—and instead resolved to return to New York right away, find an apartment and a well-paying job, sacrificing my needs for my son's, Susan would be reassured, Gina would have a little brother, the joyful face I had seen looking at me through that window would welcome me every day when I came home from work, and all would be as it should be. But I couldn't or wouldn't do that, and it was with a criminal's conscience that I saw Susan and Gina off at the airport.

From then on, not a day passed when I wasn't reminded that I was on trial. For example, shortly after Susan and Gina left, I was writing by the edge of a pond when I heard the sound of footsteps and quickly closed my notebook. Two boys appeared, about five and eight years old. The older one asked me what I was writing. I said it was a letter. To whom, he wanted to know. To my daughter. How old is she? Three and a half. Can she read? No, but her mother will read it to her. Where are they? And so on. As I answered his questions, he politely corrected my French. Then the younger one, who hadn't spoken yet, asked if I had any other children. No, I said. But you do, he said gravely, you have a son. I denied it. "He has a son," he said to his friend with great definiteness. For a moment I admired him. This boy was clairvoyant. I did have a son, still alive in Susan's womb. The next moment I felt abysmally sad, and then came a familiar signal of imminent horror, an icy contraction deep inside my chest. "But Pierre," the older boy said in a broadly sardonic manner, "the man would know this better than you!" "But he does have a son," the younger boy said, in a tone of such earnest sincerity that it bordered on satire. "It's just that his son is too small to see. A *little little little little boy! Petit petit petit petit petit!*" He chirped this like a bird, bunching all ten fingertips into a minuscule funnel.

All the while, as the boys tormented me, I was fascinated. Who were these uncanny messengers? Ordinary children, obviously, two little Belgian boys having fun at this foreigner's expense, without any knowledge of my condition, certainly without conscious cruelty. The rest was coincidence. That explained everything, didn't it? Yes, everything, except the hole I had dreamed of, the small square hole in the book of life. How cold was the wind that blew through it. I had failed to shield my child from it, now it was whistling through my ribs. And the book itself—what was contained between its covers? An old old story, old beyond reckoning, with countless characters and fates. But now a new chapter was beginning, maybe the final one. For the first time, the author of the story would reveal himself—would, in effect, become its central character.

He would reveal himself, first of all, to himself. Little by little, in spasms of infinity. The process was already well under way. What could I do to stop it? I set up barriers of logic, like "an effect can't be its own cause" and "the part can't contain the whole." There they stood, like the walls children build out of sand against the incoming tide. Children, of course, enjoy losing their gamble. They secretly bet on the sea. Not I. My life, my sanity, and the world's peace were at stake, perhaps its existence. I desperately hoped my little proofs would hold.

C. Not so, my friend. You secretly bet on the sea as well. But carry on.

"Carry on" . . . That voice, those words, I recognize them . . . And the place . . . A long narrow room . . . a couch, an armchair . . . This was three weeks later, in Surrey.

Chao Khun

The couch is the seat from which the Venerable Chao Khun Sobhana Dhammasuddhi observes me as I traverse the length of the room. Every morning for ten days. First comes my knock on the door. No, before that, as I await my turn, there is my predecessor's voice sounding up through the floor of my room. I can't hear the words, but the tone is one of complaint, a recital of trouble, maybe physical pain from sitting in the lotus posture, or obsessive thoughts of some kind. Or, who knows, something worse, like grief over a broken marriage, or a sickness, or a bereavement. It is human suffering, whatever its cause, and Chao Khun will welcome it into his human heart. But what can Chao Khun, what would the Buddha himself, make of me and my monstrous affliction? And why am I here when I know I can't be saved? What other purpose can there be than to suffer deeper, more unimaginable degrees of humiliation and pain?

When this thought invades me, I cry out silently (it all takes place in silence): "Why?"

And the answer comes with fury:

BECAUSE IT WAS YOUR WILL!

"When?" I ask then, dodging the biblical hint and trying, sincerely, to remember.

FROM THE BEGINNING!

Was that you, my Counterpoint? Was that your voice?

No answer.

Why do I trust you? Why do I trust even your capricious silence, when it comes?

C. Perhaps because you know it is not capricious but, like any other occurrence, inevitable. And because you have made your peace with silence. But carry on.

Now Chao Khun responds to the complainer, so calmly I can barely hear him. The complainer's voice rises again. Chao Khun responds with a brief comment. Silence. Then a burst of laughter from both of them. The interview is finished. The door opens and shuts. My fellow seeker—I know who it is: a skinny middle-aged Englishman who goes into spasms during meditation, probably from the release of Kundalini—walks up the creaking stairs, mindfully, as the house rules prescribe, and in slippers—noting, mentally, "lift" when a foot rises, "swing" as it swings to the next step, "down" when it settles, and then the same with the other foot, "lift . . . swing . . . down," slowly, slowly up the creaking stairs and down the hallway, then gently taps on my door. I do not respond. The only words exchanged in this house are those exchanged with Chao Khun in the morning. The Englishman walks on, lift, swing, down, to his room. I step into my slippers, mindfully, slowly open and shut the door, walk down the hallway and down the creaking stairs. There is no way to hide in this house. The meditators gag for words at the breakfast table, words that would spin veils of pretense around us and build shells of refuge for the mind to hide from itself. But no words are allowed, and nothing is hidden. Everything I do betrays me. When I knock on the door, the relative force and spacing of the three little raps articulate the timidity of my hope and the weight of my fear with awful precision.

"Come in."

Crossing the room. Consciousness clings to every motion, I am manacled, chained. I glance at him, hoping for a nod or a smile. Why doesn't he let me know that I'm OK? And why, for that matter, do I need his OK? Because I am treading the edge of an abyss, and that abyss is myself, and there is no support. But these aren't the rules of this game. The rules are that I must reach my appointed destination—a distant easy chair—on my own strength, while he sits on his couch, feet cozily tucked under his saffron robe, gazing at the floor, taking me in, I suppose, with his peripheral vision. Arrived at the chair at long last, I turn to sit and face him. His gaze is direct and not unkind, but there's a faint, slanting smile on his lips that gives him a sardonic expression.

"How are *you*?"

Always the same question, always delivered with the accent on the "you," which gives it a faint touch of irony matching the quality of his smile. The impossible answer bubbles up in me, searches for words. It can't be confessed.

"It's hard."

"Ts, ts, ts." That and the way he shakes his head says: "Isn't that too bad."

This time I won't be seduced into laughing at myself with him, liberating though that would be for the moment. Already I feel steadier. My posture straightens imperceptibly. But it's not imperceptible. He mirrors my motion with a slight straightening of his spine, and again I feel caught.

"Is it fear?" he asks.

"Yes."

"Visions?"

I hesitate. Visions are the least of my problems. Life itself has become a nightmare.

I look at Chao Khun again. "No," I say, "no visions."

"Sometimes it seems hard," he says, "but only for the ego. The ego complains. The ego pleads weakness. But to do this work, we must be strong."

Chao Khun's smile is indecipherable. I read in it compassion, mockery, amusement, kindness. A powerful emotion wells up in me. It is love. I love this grave, humorous monk. He is my teacher.

We gaze at each other in silence, smiling.

"Is the mind quiet now?" he asks.

I look in on the mind. It wavers like the surface of the sea when it is almost calm.

"Not really," I say.

"Maybe quiet enough?"

We both laugh. There's always a laugh at the end of the interview. How does he do it?

I nod, tears of gratitude in my eyes. "Thank you."

"You're welcome. Carry on."

■　■　■

On Chao Khun's recommendation, Joel practices the walking meditation in the garden, under a blooming magnolia. The grass is of that youngest, freshest, infant green that will last just a few days before it matures into a proper English lawn. Robins, blackbirds, and thrushes chirp and warble in the fir trees surrounding the shrine room, a converted garage. There is one bird that calls, unmistakably:

"Free-dom! *Free*-dom!"

Of course the bird says no such thing, but the mind has elected to hear it that way, and once heard there is no way to hear it differently.

"Free-dom!"

There is something wrong with that bird, Joel thinks, trying to make a joke of it. But it's not funny, because obviously something is wrong with the mind that imagines him and the birds and the garden and the world. And whose is that mind? No, don't think. Lift, swing, down.

"Free-dom!"

Slowly, mindfully, at the prescribed snail's pace, he approaches the stone Buddha at the end of the garden. He likes this figure. Once or twice he imagined its stone gaze blessing his efforts.

"Free-dom!"

Lift, swing, down. He walks around it. It has no back. It is hollow. The head, too, is hollow. It doesn't mean anything, he tells himself. But it does. His heart sinks.

"Free-dom!"

Nothing is real. The garden is a stage set. For what sinister drama, what cruel farce? He already knows. His part is cut out for him. There's no stopping, no hurrying it either.

"Free-dom!"

A cardinal alights on the shrine room.

"Free-dom!"

■ ■ ■

In the shrine room. Four men and three women are seated on firm round cushions in the cool semidarkness, their eyes closed, their legs folded in the half or full lotus position, their attention tethered to the rise and fall of their breathing. One elderly woman sits on a chair. The man who knocked on Joel's door earlier is sitting near the teacher, perfectly still. Sooner or later he will start to tremble, but right now the serpent power lies coiled at the base of his spine. Joel sits behind him, wrapped in a brown blanket, fragments of dried leaves in his beard and long hair. Chao Khun sits facing his students, slightly elevated above them on a low dais, his eyes closed as theirs are, a faint curl of a smile in one corner of his full lips, his hands neatly placed palms-up in his lap, one on top of the other, thumbs touching. Everything about him expresses peace and contentment, even the folds of his robe, like the fluting of an Ionic pillar turned to cloth.

These visual details come by courtesy of my Counterpoint, without whose eyeless view the shrine room would have only an olfactory and auditory presence—the odor of incense and freshly cut pinewood, the chirping of birds, a scramble of squirrel claws across the roof. Joel is unconscious even of these. He is turning a key which he hopes will open the door leading out of the house of his fear. The key consists of attention and breathing. When these two become one, the lock turns by itself, and the door barring inside from outside is free to swing freely, in and out, from Now to Now. At moments he feels that the walls themselves have dissolved. A luminous emptiness spreads like a lake. But there is a shore. A ring of darkness surrounds him in the distance. How could it be otherwise? He is still there, reflecting. If there were no center there would be no horizon. Would that not be the meaning of *anatman* taught by the Buddha? No self, no point from which space and time are measured . . . No distance, therefore, between self and not-self . . . No "others," in fact, but the world all one . . . No dread, therefore, and no guilt . . . Is that love, the true love Krishnamurti is always invoking when he berates his non-followers for mis-naming lust and attachment "love"? Is that Chao Khun's condition? Does he only exist for others, not for himself?

Now Chao Khun's sleeve rustles faintly as he reaches for the little brass bell on its stand next to him. Joel's eyelids stir, the ring of darkness collapses into a point in the pit of his stomach, the bell goes "Ting!", a cloudy mass rises through his chest and throat into his face, his eyelids part, a black naked figure, no more than an inch tall, with jagged widespread little bat wings, detaches itself from his forehead, floats waveringly through the air, glides into the teacher's forehead, and disappears.

I can't go on.

C. You must go on.

I don't know how to describe what I felt.

C. Describe what you thought.

I knew at once that I had done something terrible. And it was all the more terrible because I had not intended it.

C. And now what you saw.

His face when he came out of the shrine room. I was waiting for him outside. There was something hidden about him, a kind of lurking. His neck looked shorter, as if he were pulling his head in. Maybe he was afraid. Also his skin was sallow. I approached him. "I need to talk to you," I said. I had to tell him, warn him.

"Tomorrow."

He meant our scheduled talk after breakfast, but he spat the word out like a curse.

"It's urgent, I need to speak to you *now*."

"Do you think you can save yourself by *talking*?"

He was right. I fell silent. The face before me was not human. It was a beast's face. But the beast was endowed with human intelligence, human cunning. It was Chao Khun's face, of course, and it was also the mask of impersonal evil. Never since have I seen such malignancy in a face. But there was also something very nearly comical about it. I think the threat was so great that fear itself came to a halt in me. I saw. Was this real? What if this greenish ghoul-faced monk with bloodshot eyes was purely a product of thought, an illusion? I leaned in more closely to peer into those eyes. Was anyone in there at all? The eyes rolled up and back into their sockets. Only the whites were visible.

What happened there, Counterpoint?

C. You sent him home. He hadn't been there for a while.

What home? Oh, that home.

C. The only one. Then he came to again.

Yes, his eyes rolled out again and his mouth opened and he screamed at me: "Be quiet! Tomorrow!" and wheeled around and stomped off with his slippers slapping against his heels.

That night something roused me from sleep. Not a sound, not a dream. I knew what it was. It was knowledge. (I know it was nothing of the sort, but that's what I took it for then: iron, incontrovertible truth.) I sat up. The room was dimly lit by the moon. There were the walls, the corners, the window. Nothing had changed in the visible order of things, but there was another order, the order of time, of whispered intimations.

"You have been here before."

Knowledge was memory. The terror of that!

"The past is now—and always."

The mind quailed—the wordless, gestural equivalent of "not again!"—and that thought—the irony didn't escape me—started the avalanche of repetition—

"Again."

Because it had always begun like this—with the memory that it had always begun with a memory of remembering precisely this—and what was "this"?

"Eternal recurrence."

■　■　■

I have grazed this subject a few times earlier in this book. I realize now that it can't be described, at least not in its essence. It can't be described because it can't be imagined. To imagine is to place an image before oneself, but the eternal recurrence is not an image. It is a catastrophe of thought in which you, the putative thinker, become the object of a relentless investigation by a mind that has no use for your parochial identity because it is obsessed with totality. It seems to regard you as something like a function in a calculus of variations. Alas, the function feels, and the curve on which its variance is measured is an index of pain. Without feeling, you might be content to serve as a funnel through which an ocean of past events pours itself into the future. But that ocean is sentient, and you are made to know it. "Remember the cruelties!" Voltaire's slogan could have been addressed to you. Not that you stand back to imagine the horrors of this world. You know that you cannot imagine them. Rather, you *are* their perpetual arising, they happen with and without your knowledge, but in you and through you, and there is no end to the permutations. Moreover, the number of possible events, though inconceivably large, is circumscribed, but time has no end. Therefore everything happens again. Eternity and infinity are not concepts you hold in your mind. They are the arms of the cross to which you are nailed, the wheel on which you are broken, the perpetuum mobile through which you are ground . . . but *these* images, to describe the catastrophe, would have to be varied ad infinitum.

Or else . . . maybe I'm deceiving myself. Maybe the truest way to represent it is as a blank spot on the map. With a demon or devil next to it, as a warning to unwary travelers. Around it the colors and marks representing the known world, and among those the river I've been traveling on, a blue vein. It dips into the blankness and disappears. Later, out of that blankness (in the blankness there is no time, only eternity) the river emerges again. That's where memory leaps into being.

■　■　■

A thicket, impenetrable, or a jungle. Or is it a single tree? Bulging into fruition, shriveling into decay. The fruits are faces, bodies, lives. A world. Yet a tree. Out of this swarming indefinition, a hand, a finger on a red button.

Time for a little hell on earth.

NO!

The finger lifts.

As you wish. The show will go on.

FOREVER!

Suddenly a weapon. Someone hands him a sword. Who? What a question! The word *is* the sword!

WHO?

Or is it an axe . . .

WHO?

Three heads chopped off with one blow, who are they?

Susan, Gina, Stefan.

A moment's horror, he sees: **they are thoughts.**

But they bleed!

Have I killed them?

Yes, and not for the last time.

Are they real?

As real as dreams are while they last.

Let me wake up!

Careful now—the world might end!

Who are you, monster?

Who do you think? Who would devise such a scheme, if not you?

So ingenious that not even you can unravel it!

So transparently fake, just a bubble of mind-stuff!
So durable, so impregnably real!
So cruel that you, the author of cruelty, cry out against yourself:
Who are you, monster!
Listening, I notice—almost too late!—that I nearly surrendered
my only weapon:

WHO?

The world-tree spreads itself, bristles. Sprouts organs, blue-veined bags of
vulnerable flesh.
Murder the Creation . . .
No world! No love! No time. No truth. No people. No creatures. No pain.
and you kill yourself . . .
Is that true? Am I nothing but thought?
Why, what did you think, child? Thought thinks, therefore you are!
And I see: All is thought, without exception. The body, a thought. The tree of
life, a legion of thoughts. Or one thought with a thousand heads, a million if
need be. Strike its heart:

WHO?

Who indeed! Who dares lay an axe to this stem? Splitting it, and the split
runs through every branch, every leaf. A laugh fills immensity.
It was always like this, don't you see?
Split-mind splitting endlessly, world without end!

WHO?

The word is no longer an axe or a sword, it prays.
Promptly the tortured Christ appears, nailed to a cross, crowned with thorns,
his side pierced, drops of blood adorning the wounds.
"I know that my redeemer liveth"
But he's only a thought!

WHO?

The Buddha appears to the far left of Jesus, resembling Chao Khun and also the hollow statue in the garden.
A mockery!

WHO?

Now the adversary rouses himself in earnest, almost boastfully, with a swagger. As if to say: "What you've seen so far was just a flick of a finger." His weapon is argument. He argues by revelation, which is to say, by force. In splendor and in horror, in grandeur and depravity, he knows no limits, and he shows me that. His essence, his truth, his joy, are summed up in a single word: Infinity. He knows no prohibition and only one commandment: Be! Mere possibility is an irritant and a perpetual goad to creation. Therefore, in his world, whatever is possible is, was, and will be condemned to exist. Only hope is impossible, though impossible to abandon. It is not possible because even the purest aspiration is immediately translated into the weirdly vegetal patterns of a purely quantitative infinity, much as the dignity and uniqueness of a face would be mocked by a system of mirrors in which it was not only endlessly replicated but also varied, an ever more grotesque cartoon of itself, to the point of demonic inversion. And the corollary, each time, of these hideous demonstrations is that I am that; that there is no enemy and indeed no other being than myself, though I make myself plural a billion times over; that what I am is omnipotent thought dedicated, for reasons unknown to itself, to the elaboration of a self-torment that can only deepen and sharpen in the course of eternity.

But something has entered this desolate glory, a breach in the law of repetition.

Surely this word is the true name of God! I say this now, here at my desk in Brooklyn. Back then in my terror I thought it was still a crude axe or sword in my hand. But the word swept through the mind and its terrible creations, demanding truth and nothing but truth. The mind wants to hide, it builds labyrinths, posts the doors with promises and threats, beautiful promises, terrible threats. But to this word, this divine interrogative, nothing is hidden.

What happened next I don't remember. Or rather, a miracle happened, but between the curse and the miracle, there was a gap. What can I say? I don't know what happened.

C. That's because nothing happened. More precisely, what happened was nothing. You know it only by inference, as you know in the morning that you were unconscious for much of the night. But *this* nothing is not a blank spot on the map. It has no contours, no margin by the side of which you could post an indicative figure—an angel, say. No river runs through it. No traveler will ever explore it. Nothing whatever can be said about it. Not even that it answers the question "Who?"

But I can speak of the miracle. Out of that vacancy, bliss was born.

C. That was later. First there was knowledge. Not its parody, which is a product of fear. Fear is thought and thought is time, but this knowledge is not of thought. Don't try to remember it.

What was the knowing about?

C. About itself. If it were to speak—but to whom would it speak? It knows no self, no other—it would say: "I know that I know." It is consciousness without an object. If it were in time, it would be eternal; in space, omnipresent. But neither time nor space has yet been conceived. Out of this knowing, then, presence is born, and consciousness comes to itself as I AM. This I AM is not you, nor is It anyone other than you. It is pure being in pure self-enjoyment. Its nature is bliss, and that bliss has no limit. It is the quintessence of all joy, all beauty, all truth. Call It the Supreme Being, and it is That; but to itself it is only I AM. Out of this glory, then, forms arise, colors, distinctions: Yet all is one. This you remember.

There were two bodies, naked. Beautiful, gold-olive bodies. Breathing, glowing. I don't think I glimpsed them for more than a second, but I knew it as an eternity. A man and a woman. On a bed, in a room. Entwined, yet completely at ease. I saw them. But also: I was them. There was no trace of Joel, except perhaps as a memory, otherwise I wouldn't have been so astonished. Bliss suffused the whole scene, and that bliss was myself. One self, male and female, eternally in love. Such beauty! Such happiness!

The next moment there was one body alone. It was me. I was seated, not lying, on the bed. Flowers were drifting down the walls of the room, slowly. The walls were diaphanous. Was I awake? Was this a dream? If it was a dream, it was not one from which I wanted to awake. Nor did I want to review what had happened. What I wanted more than anything was to sleep. That, it turned out, was a dreadful mistake.

I found myself in bed in the house where I had lived as a child in Germany. It was night. My brother was asleep in the room next to mine, and my parents were asleep in their room. But then I saw my mother in the hallway adjusting the level of a picture on the wall. That was something she often did, even in other people's homes. Nobody ever minded. But this time I minded. I got out of bed and went to where she stood next to the picture, still fiddling with its angle. I took her firmly by the hand and led her down the hallway and out onto the lamplit balcony. I took her by her hips and easily, lightly, threw her over the railing. If this had happened in physical reality, she would have fallen onto a stone terrace one floor beneath. But there was no terrace. I threw her from our house into the blackness of eternal night. I woke, and it was I who was falling, forever, again, into the certainty of endless torment. I don't know how long this particular eternity lasted, or what intervened to allow me eventually to fall asleep.

■ ■ ■

I woke up feeling lacerated. Moreover, I seemed to have developed a new organ of perception overnight, one that enabled me to see malevolence in inanimate things. The corners of the room were cruelly angled. A gleam on the doorknob was a stare. Even a sparkle of light on the magnolia leaves outside my window hurt me. So did the thought of Susan and Gina still asleep on the dark side of the planet, whirling into another day, another increment in the fury of cycles; that and the fear that sooner or later they would have their brains pried open like mine, and that that would be *my* doing, that it was already my fault. I skipped breakfast, fearing the gazes of the other guests. I sat on the cushion in my room, attending to my breath as best I could. The skinny Englishman shambled and creaked his way to my door and knocked. There was no getting around it now, I had to meet with Chao Khun again (cycles!). Halfway down the stairs, I stopped. I wanted to stand there until my heart stopped pounding. Then I thought I could sense Chao Khun's thoughts speaking to me: "Do you really think you can hide?" He was waiting for me. I went to his room and knocked. It wasn't the usual tentative knock. "Come in." He averted his gaze as I passed him, but of course he was watching me. I crossed the room, a matter of seven steps. I took them with resoluteness, as if to say: "Crossing the room is my business," and: "If you want to make watching me *your* business, be my guest." I sat down in the armchair and looked at him. His face was not unfriendly. Above all, he looked human. What a relief! Now he would ask "How are *you*?" That was *his* business. But he didn't ask that.

"You look well today," he said.

I smiled. We both smiled. Neither of us said anything. Our smiles faded. Fear stained the stillness, like a drop of ink spreading in a clear lake. It was the memory of our encounter in the garden. His gaze became penetrating and hidden.

"Did you sleep well?" He never asked questions like that.

"Not well," I said. "And you?"

He smiled: "I didn't trust you yesterday."

"I know. But you guys aren't supposed to blow up like that."

"I'm not perfect."

I loved him for saying that. I decided to tell him about my ordeal. Using the words "pain" and "fear" and "infinity" lightened the burden of secrecy. He wasn't the enemy. I also told him about my weapon, "Who?", and how it had saved me. He listened sympathetically.

"Was that Nirvana?" I asked.

"It is what it is," he said.

That formulation sharply recalled the root of the terror: that I, the most god-forsaken of creatures, was the maker of worlds. This I would not tell him. What could it possibly mean to him? Buddhists don't believe in God. But that wasn't the real reason why I didn't tell him. I was ashamed. Such miserable abjection could not be confessed. Besides, he would think me insane, maybe have me committed to an asylum. Nor did I mention the demon that had passed from my forehead into his.

"Later the fear came back," I said.

"And? Did you ask again: Who?"

"No. I guess I lost hope."

"Not thoroughly enough," he said.

Those are the last words I remember him saying. He probably meant that I should steer clear of both hope and despair. But the meaning I heard was: "Abandon hope." The more I think about that moment, the funnier it looks to me. It's like a cartoon, a Zen joke: A monk in his cell, a man falling headfirst past his window. The monk says: "Take the Middle Way!"

PART 3

Into the Labyrinth

There it is—my white VW bus rolling into London on a rainy evening in April 1971. It's getting dark. My past self at the wheel, longhaired and densely bearded, is singing. You would think that a man who sings must be happy. But this man is in despair. He doesn't know what to do with his pain. He could as well scream instead of sing, and in fact he has screamed, once or twice. But now he is singing. Why would a desperate man sing? To put a boundary around his emotion, by pouring it into a vessel. But the tune he has chosen is too small, too simple.

He tries talking sense into himself: "What is your problem, really? That you won't be remembered for your deeds? That you haven't attained Nirvana? That you haven't founded a commune? That you're thirty-one and don't amount to much? That you feel like a failure? Congratulations! Welcome to the human race!" This talking-to is well intended but worse than useless, it's cruel, especially coming from himself. He knows perfectly well that he isn't human, that's the grotesque truth of the matter. What if the human race should catch wind of his true identity? What kind of welcome could he expect?

He sees a sign: "THE HAVEN." Just what he needs: safe harbor, asylum. The sign hangs slightly askew over the door, paint is peeling off the front of the building. He circles the block until he finds a parking spot next to a red brick wall. He puts on a raincoat, since it's cool outside, puts his travelers checks in the side pocket, crawls into the back of the bus to draw the flowered curtains over the back window, locks the van, walks back to the house with the sign. It's obviously a flophouse. The walls are filthy. No matter, it's The Haven, everything will be all right. He checks in with an elderly clerk who lacks the three middle fingers of his right hand.

"Upstairs, room 3."

Room 3 was a large room with four beds and a washstand. No closet, no chairs. Two men sat facing each other on two of the beds, playing checkers by the light of a naked bulb in the ceiling. The board was supported by their knees. I said hello and sat down on one of the unoccupied beds. It sagged deeply beneath my weight.

"Better not sit there," one of the men said. "That there's your bed."

I thanked him and moved to the other bed. It sagged just as much.

"You'd better smooth it out, Mack."

He meant the first bed I had sat on. He said it kindly, by way of advice. I got up, smoothed the creases on the bed, and returned to mine. Then I realized I hadn't brought my toothbrush, pajamas, or fresh clothes. And how was anyone supposed to sleep in this bed? I should ask for my money back, sleep in the car. But I had already taken my sandals off and didn't have the will to change course. I stripped to my underpants, hung my clothes over the metal frame of the bed, lay down, pulled the blanket over my eyes, and waited for sleep.

Later that night I was awakened by the glare of the ceiling light and the voice of a furious man. I turned my head to look at him and instinctively turned away again. He was cursing in what must have been Scottish; I couldn't make out most of the words, but they were all violent. Some heavy metal thing fell to the floor with a clang and he roared, this time in the clearest English: "I'll rip your heart out!" A shoe flew against the wall next to me and dropped to the floor. The other shoe was thrown at another wall. I didn't hear it drop, so it must have fallen on one of the beds. Then the sound of his clothes coming off, a belt-buckle knocking against the bed frame, his heavy breathing. He went to the washstand and poured a pitcher of water over himself with a splash. "I'll kill you," he said quietly. I had the impression he had said it to me. Then he dried himself, turned off the ceiling light, and went to bed. There he groaned, cursed, and whispered for a while and eventually lapsed into snoring. A few minutes later I heard the other shoe being discreetly placed on the floor.

Sweet oblivion
Licks his
Eyes at the
Edge of the
Pit

I woke up at dawn. My neighbor had stopped snoring. His face was turned toward me. He was young, blond, with a blond moustache, blond stubble on his cheeks. His lips were moist and slack, but there was a furrow between his eyes, so deep it seemed to cleave his forehead in two. The fingers of one hand were curled around the top edge of the blanket, which was pulled up to his chin. I got dressed as quietly as I could and carried my sandals out of the room.

I sat down on the stoop in front of the house to put on the sandals. They were thongs, the kind Jesus wears in old paintings. They were a gift from one of Chao Khun's disciples, a big American seaman who had broken the no-talking rule on my last day there because, he said, he had a feeling that I'd understand. He'd been hallucinating, for months now, he said. But he didn't call it that. He called it "movies of the mind." It could happen at any time when his mind wasn't occupied, and it happened most often during meditation. The shrine room would disappear and he'd be in some ordinary familiar situation, say in a car with his sister and her boyfriend driving along the Merritt Parkway talking about his sister's son or whatever, maybe other cars would pass, it would start raining, he'd put on the windshield wipers, whatever, or maybe he'd be somewhere else, like a teahouse in Singapore, playing chess with some guy he'd never seen before, and this would go on without his even suspecting that it wasn't real until something woke him up, and frankly it was scaring the shit out of him because sometimes he wasn't sure whether sitting on a cushion in Chao Khun's shrine room wasn't just another movie of the mind. So these were his sandals. He had insisted on giving them to me.

The pink light on the walls made the stone look soft. Birds were chirping somewhere above the roofs. I felt numb inside. No feeling, only the memory of the mute anguish the night before. I decided I needed some breakfast. I stood up and walked to the corner and around the corner and another corner and past my car and on for a block or two and around another corner until I found a small diner, where I ordered coffee, fried eggs, and toast. After that I felt better, and on closer examination, human. What a nightmare I had been living! Thinking I was God . . . how had I managed to believe anything so ridiculous? There must be some mechanism, I thought, a crazy logic which you can't reconstruct when you're in your right mind, try as you might. . . . Otherwise it should make sense to me now . . . so what was it? . . . no, careful now, be grateful the cloud has lifted, don't ask. . . . And besides, I had things to do . . . plenty of them. Thank God for things to do! Drive to the American Express office and post a notice on their bulletin board offering a VW bus for sale. Write a letter to Gina. Sell my books at Watkins & Stuart. Drive to the World's End, see how the folks at Milton Chambers are doing, ask if I can sleep over until the car is sold. Call Susan, my angel, and Gina—"Hi, Daddy!"—just thinking of her bright little voice dispelled the shadows.

I paid for my breakfast and set off toward the van. I walked two blocks to the left, turned right, took the next left. The street looked different from the ones I had walked earlier. I had taken a wrong turn. I should have taken note of the name of the street the car was on. I went back to the diner and tried to reconstruct the path I had taken. Just to make sure, I asked the waitress if she knew where The Haven was. She didn't. I could have sworn I had come from the direction I had just gone. I walked the same two blocks to the left, turned right again, but this time took a second right turn. I didn't recognize this street either. No matter, it had to be nearby. If I just turned a few corners, I was bound to run into it. Or into The Haven. From there the car wouldn't be hard to find.

I turned more than a few corners. Here and there, I stopped to ask people how to get to The Haven. No one had heard of it. I noticed something alarming. When I looked in people's faces, they averted their eyes. This reflex was so ubiquitous and so predictable that at one point I wondered whether these people might not be machines. But no, they were human. Still, they seemed to be under a spell, as if programmed to carry out complex tasks, exchange information, and connect with each other only to the degree necessary to avoid collisions. Some of their faces were so sad I could hardly bear to look at them.

I stopped asking for directions and adopted the most rational method I could think of: walk ten blocks in one direction, then walk ten blocks in the opposite direction on a parallel street, scanning each side street as you pass it. Behind me I heard someone use the phrase "at my wit's end." That pretty well described my condition, I thought. Also my feet were hurting. The sailor's sandals were a little too big. I noticed a woman in a window, arguing with another woman on the street, angrily pointing to her left several times. I walked in that direction. Why not? It was a street I had not taken yet. A small dog stopped at the sight of me, cocked his head in puzzlement or expectation, then trotted on with lowered tail. I followed him. He was obviously lost and hungry. Someone must have abandoned him. He didn't have a collar. Dog, dear dog, if you find my car, I'll find you a home, if you don't, we're both lost and I can't help you. The dog stopped here and there to sniff and pee. At each of his stops, I waited for him to walk on. Eventually, by a circuitous route, he led me back to the diner. An intriguing result, but useless, really. I turned around. The dog couldn't help me.

I stopped at the corner. I had been at this crossroads before, several times. Not only that, I had explored all the possible directions it offered—turning right, turning left, turning back, and going forward. It felt like a mockery. A bitter, heavy, yellow-green feeling sat in the middle of my chest. I recognized it: despair. "You don't have a right to this," I told myself. "Gina needs you. Find your car, sell it, and go home." But Christ, wasn't I trying to do that? Then I remembered the dog. His leading me to the diner may have been useless to me, but what about him? He needed food. Maybe something was leading *him,* and in effect both of us. But I had been too self-concerned to notice. I knew how to talk a good line about love, the kind with a capital L, but when a lost, hungry creature came my way, all I could think of was to strike a deal for mutual aid. It would have been so easy to feed him. I had to find him again. It was important. At least as important as finding my car. Maybe more. Yes, certainly more.

I walked back to the diner. The dog was gone. By now my feet were hurting rather badly. A blister was starting to form beneath one of the straps. I was limping. The waitress in the diner stared at me through the window. I went inside.

"I can't find my hotel," I said. "I know it's nearby."

"The Haven, you said?"

"Yes, maybe someone else knows where it is."

"Randall, you know any havens around here?"

"Havens?"

The cook behind the counter took stock of my appearance.

"Are you sure it's not Heaven you're seeking?"

A man at one of the tables burst out laughing. I turned to leave.

"I'm sure you'll find it on your . . . way," the waitress said.

What I found was a police station. That did seem like a good idea. Perhaps I was guided after all. I went inside and explained my predicament to the officer behind the reception desk. He was a cheerful, hard-eyed, ironic young man about my age. He searched through a register for The Haven and then informed me that it didn't exist.

"Sorry. No such place hereabouts."

I asked to see a phone book. The policeman watched me with amusement while I searched through the business pages. He suggested I register the car as lost. He asked to see my passport and my car papers. The car had been registered in Katmandu and had Nepalese license plates.

"Hmm. Got any drugs in your car?"

"No, just books and clothes."

"Books and clothes, eh?"

He handed me back my documents.

"What color is the car?"

"White, with a black stripe."

"Any other distinguishing marks?"

"A flowered curtain."

"Dirty?"

"The curtain?"

"No, the car."

"Yes."

"What year was it built?"

"1966."

"Now dictate the registration number to me and we'll put on a search."

I dictated: "LDX432."

"L for lost," he said. "Golly, there's an S missing. Are you sure it's LD?"

"Yes, LDX . . ."

"Alright, D for damned. Next?"

"X."

"X for ex-treme-ly . . ."

"432."

"432 what, days, months, or centuries?"

Seeing the confusion in my face, he laughed: "Cheer up, mate, we'll find it for you." He signed the form he had written on, pounded it with a stamp, tore off the sheet, and handed it to me. Then he stood up and held out his large hand. I shook it. He suggested I call in periodically, since he would have no way of reaching me. He chuckled as I left the station.

His improvisations haunted me for a while as I limped through the streets. "Lost . . . Damned . . . Extremely . . ." Why had he chosen those words? I tried to construe their intended meaning. The first one was obvious, it referred to the car. The second one . . . well, "damned" was an all-purpose word, wasn't it? An expression of sympathy? And the third one . . . God only knew why he chose to stretch that into three separate syllables and why he said it at all, but surely he was what he appeared to be, a cop on desk duty, sturdy, good-natured, capable of a blunt sort of irony but not of the kind of sinister innuendo I was attributing to his jokey little remarks. On the other hand, what was that riff on the numbers about? Whose days, months, or centuries could he have meant?

I saw the answer to that question reflected in a shop window: an archetypal figure with a long beard and long hair, his open raincoat billowing behind him, loping with flatfooted strides, limping. I knew who that was and why I was shown it: the Wandering Jew. My mother was Jewish. That meant I was a Jew. I had never thought much about that identification. What was a Jew? That question, too, was answered with a vengeance: a Jew was an outcast, a pale slave of God, a laughingstock to healthy heathen like that ruddy-faced cop behind his desk.

I walked on. What else could I do? I turned corners. The city was starting to come alive in an interesting way. Things weren't content with just being, they gestured. Not all of them, but some of them, once in a while. A stirring of dry leaves along the sidewalk, for instance: I knew it was the wind that did it, but in another dimension it was a gesture (whose?), and more than that: a communication. Not in words, of course—I'm translating. "You have no choice," it said. A little later, a trickle of water flowing into a gutter said: "It's under the surface. To find it, descend." I didn't respond to these invitations right away. This was different from reading that woman's pointing finger as a directional signal, or from choosing to follow the dog. There, the initiative was mine. Here something else was in charge. I knew I was courting danger. But I was tempted. And that temptation was so attractive, and felt at the same time so menacing, that I stopped walking and stood still with my heart beating hard in my chest.

As a child I had lived near a border. If you crossed it without permission, you could be in trouble. Here, too, was a border. It accompanied me as I walked. It moved with a covert, slithering motion defined by that uncanny gesturing of things. Sometimes it was near, the next moment it could be far away. On one side of the border, the one I was on, was the world of the sane. Over there, where the gestures pointed and beckoned, was the world which the sane called madness. But what was that, madness? What if madness was only the subterranean presence of something archaic in man, a realm of symbols, of signs which the ancients and so-called primitives could navigate by means of sorcery and magic? What if madness appeared to be a distortion of reason because reason interpreted it that way? What if Blake was right when he said that reason makes war on the imagination? What if Stefan's suffering and, lately, mine were caused not by madness but by that war? What if it was true that the fires of hell are the delights of genius? What if I walked in and found myself liberated after all, here and now, at the end of my journey? How easy it would be then to go to Stefan in *his* hell, as I had imagined so many times, and show him the simple and only way out—through daring.

I started walking again. But this time I looked at the ground as I walked. I watched my feet. They were bare, except for the straps that held the sandals in place. The pavement glided away beneath them. At moments, I seemed to be walking a treadmill. There was something incongruous. Asphalt was made for shoes. These bare feet in sandals were not of the city, not of this time. The Wandering Jew? Maybe. They could be the feet of Jesus as well. Their stories were linked, come to think of it. Links everywhere. Two men, two Jews, two souls, two feet, two terms in an equation. The feet tell the story: left for Jesus (the way and the truth), right for his victim. *Victim?* But that's how the story went: The Jew Ahasuerus shoves Jesus as he carries His cross toward Calvary. Then Jesus condemns Ahasuerus to wander over the face of the earth until His second coming. In the eyes of love, whose sin is the greater? Jesus is not without sin. And who would know this better than Jesus? How could He ever forget what He did to the Wandering Jew? His suffering must be endless. Unless he returns to redeem Ahasuerus. But for that to be possible, Ahasuerus would have to forgive Him. Would he? Does he? Yes, I do, of course I do. That absolves Ahasuerus, but Jesus cannot absolve Himself. Of what? Of the crimes of God. Who will forgive Him these? For He has taken them on as His own. Will He return? Will He reveal Himself? Am I He? Now there's another pair of feet walking next to mine. Moccasins. Who is it? Not me. But he's matched his step to mine exactly. I look. He's a freak, long blond hair, stooping a little as he walks, I can't see his face. Left, right, left, right. We're walking in lockstep. I stop, he stops. He turns his head to look at me. Small pale blue eyes half hidden by long strands of dirty blond hair, thin red lips smiling through a scraggly blond beard. I start walking again, he walks too. At a curb, we both stop.

"Hello," he says.

"Hello."

"Looking for something?"

"Yes, my car. It's near a fleabag hotel called The Haven. You know where it is?"

"Not yet."

"Not yet?"

"Don't worry, we'll be guided."

"By what?"

"By the forces that sent me."

By any rational standard, this man was not to be trusted. For a moment, I had no illusions about that. But rational standards weren't doing me much good. By rational standards, I was about to enter upon a career of 35 or maybe, with early retirement, 30 years of unrewarding office work. Rational standards had sent me wandering crisscross through many miles of London and brought me nothing but sore feet. To hell with rational standards. The doors of my heart flew open in an access of hope and gratitude that made him visibly flinch.

He composed himself quickly, but in the strangest way. He stepped back, crossed his arms over his chest with the fingers touching his shoulders, and lowered his head, with his eyes closed. In this hieratic pose he stood for ten, fifteen seconds without moving. A man passed between us and walked on, crossing the street. I waited. Then Richard (that was his name—he told me later) came over to me. He stepped up very close and said, almost whispering: "It's time." His breath was sour. Time for what? I didn't ask. I would find out. I would make myself empty and ready, like a blank sheet of parchment for Truth to inscribe itself, moment by moment: the Knowledge for which the time had come.

We went to a nearby park. Many details of our conversation are lost to me now. No doubt I was unconscious part of the time. He asked me about myself and I answered. I wasn't curious about him. He would reveal to me why he had come. And he did. To save the world, he said. Not by himself, that was impossible. But together, he and I would accomplish it.

He must have seen me very clearly: my bottomless, boundless guilt, my desperate grasping for any promise of redemption, my secret belief that the world with its pain was my bungled creation. I don't know how he knew that. Maybe I told him. It's possible. In crossing the border, I had relinquished the sovereign right of a denizen of reason: I could no longer doubt. How, then, could I guard my words? I was a child. It took no great cunning to deceive me.

He asked me to buy him something to eat. He hadn't eaten in two days, he said. We went to a restaurant and ordered identical dishes: filet of sole. We sat facing each other at a small table. When the food was served, the fish were facing in opposite directions. From this, and from the punning sense of "sole," I deduced that we were bound to each other like the twin fish in the sign of Pisces. He ate with concentration, chewing vigorously. We didn't talk. Finally I asked him: "So how am I going to find my car?"

He put down his fork, chewed, swallowed, and glared at me: "How are you going to find your *self*? That's the question. Your car's important, but only as a sign."

"Of what?"

"Of how out of whack *you* are—and because of you, everything else. There's going to be a war, don't you understand? But you and I can prevent it. So help me to help you, please, and don't ask foolish questions. There's too much at stake."

"What should I do?"

"First of all, I'm not God. I'm just a word in the message. Watch the signs. Pay attention."

And he continued eating.

What signs? Through the window I saw a blazing orange glow on a house-front across the street. The sun must be setting, I thought. And those people walking past, hurrying slightly, with contented looks on their faces, must be on their way home from work. Was this a world in need of saving? What side of the border was I on?

"They're happy," I said.

Richard followed my glance out the window. He gave me a sharp look. "You think so?"

I paid for our meals. When I put the change in my wallet, Richard suggested I give him some money for shopping expenses, since I would be eating with him and his friends. I didn't ask who they were or where we were going. I gave him ten pounds.

We walked again. My feet were hurting, so I had trouble keeping pace with him. And he walked fast. Sometimes he was a block ahead of me and would stop and wait for me to catch up with him. Once I thought I had lost him, but then he appeared by my side again. It seemed that he was playing a game with me, testing me maybe. We came to a pair of long, tubelike passageways that led underground at a gentle incline. At the entrance they stood side by side, separated by a thin wall, but looking in you could see that they went in divergent directions. We entered the one on the left. After some thirty steps, Richard suddenly ran back to the entrance and slipped around the corner, into the other tunnel, I assumed. Limping, I ran after him. I couldn't find him. I could see far into the other tunnel. He wasn't visible there. I looked around in all directions. He was gone. I had to laugh at myself. So Richard was a con-man. Well, he'd gotten ten pounds and a meal out of me, no great loss. Embarrassment was the worst part of it. How could I have been so trusting? And where would I go now? He had lured me so far afield that only a miracle could lead me back to my car. I didn't even know the name of the district! Unless . . . and then—thank God!—I remembered. That cop had given me a phone number! I searched my pockets, my wallet. Where was it? He had written it on a piece of paper and handed it to me. How could I have lost it? I searched a second, a third time. It was gone. I felt like crying, but instead of tears I felt a burning sensation in my eyeballs. I felt a presence nearby, just outside my field of vision. Instinctively I recoiled. Someone was standing behind me. I turned my head. It was Richard.

"Sorry," he said. "There was something I had to take care of."

For a moment I felt like hitting him.

"What's going on, Richard? What are you trying to do?"

"I'm trying to help you."

I was failing him. He was testing me. I had to try harder.

We entered the second tunnel, the one on the right. People were swarming in and out of the tube. Jokes were exchanged, smiles passed from face to face in passing. How extraordinary. Was it possible that all these people shared some special knowledge or experience? What could it be?

The tunnel ended in a large, crowded, brightly lit underground station. The sounds of trampling feet and amplified announcements echoed off the white-tiled walls and high ceiling. Two tall escalators ran side by side in opposite directions, conveying streams of people to a lower level and up to ours.

"After you," Richard said, letting me descend the escalator before him. When I was about halfway down, I saw him ascending the other escalator. I looked behind me. He wasn't there. It didn't seem possible. How could he have gotten down there so fast, and by what route? Could he see me riding down toward him? Of course he could! Or was he someone else, someone who looked just like him? No, it was he. Scraggly blond beard, sallow skin, limp hair, limp fringes on his yellow buckskin jacket. He looked absent and sad, as if lost in his thoughts. As he passed me, I called out to him: "Richard!" Startled, he turned his head: "Oh, there you are!" and swung himself over the railing behind me.

We traveled underground for a while. I didn't take note of the stations. I followed him into a supermarket. I pushed the cart while he selected two loaves of bread, several pork chops, three bottles of beer, and a small sack of potatoes. Before putting each item in the cart he gave me a questioning look, as if soliciting my approval. I had no preferences. My only concern was not to lose him again. He opened the glass lid of the freezer where milk and butter were stored and held up a bar of butter: "D'you like it salted or plain?" The next moment, the object in his hand was a carrot. "Oops!" he said, "it's getting freaky around here." He tossed the carrot back and forth from one hand to the other. Suddenly the butter was there again and the carrot was gone. "Weird!" he said. "Let's put it back." He tossed it back into the freezer and closed the lid. Was there anything else I would like, he asked. How about dessert? I shook my head.

He paid for the groceries. Outside, the walls had turned a pale gray lavender. The street lamps shone yellow. We walked for a few blocks. Richard carried the bag with the groceries. At one point he stopped. "You carry it," he said. As I held the bag, he crossed his arms over his chest again, with his fingertips touching his shoulders, and closed his eyes. We stood silently for a little while. Above us, someone was playing The Grateful Dead. "Let's go in here," Richard said. I followed him up two flights of stairs to a door with the word LOVE painted on it in four colors. Richard rang the bell and immediately bounded down the stairs. I stood there alone with the grocery bag in my arms. The door opened and a tall blond bearded freak with a blue headband stood before me.

"Yes?"

"I'm a friend of . . . I came with Richard. Do you know him? He was just here a moment ago."

"Oh. Well, come on in."

He led me into a fantastically cluttered room full of cushions, magazines, sheets, and clothes. There, seated and lying around a large hookah, were three guys. One of them was Richard.

In the flat that night I was unable to sleep. Each time I began to drift off, an awful threat leaped out at me. What the hell was it? All I could remember was speed and ferocity. After a third or fourth attack, I was so shaken that I sat up, determined to stay awake until morning. Wasn't that what I'd gone to Chao Khun for—to wake up, and to stay awake? But again and again, sleep crept in on me and with it a hint of menace.

Maybe the couch was too soft. Maybe if I lay down on the rug . . . and I did, with a pillow under my head, and covered myself with a blanket. One of my hosts, asleep on a mattress near me, was breathing steadily. I felt the urge to cough, but suppressed it. A line from a German poem occurred to me: *"Rühre nicht an den Schlaf der Welt"*—and my heart leapt into my throat. Was that it, the danger? That I, with my ungoverned thoughts, could stir the world from its sleep? Stir it into nightmare, like Yeats's blundering beast? That, therefore, I must wake? That I wasn't allowed to sleep?

But I needed to rest if I was going to search for my car in the morning. Richard had given me directions to a place called Bayswater. My flophouse, he said, was most likely there. He had some business to do in the morning, so he couldn't help me search for the car, but he would the next day if I didn't find it. He had my interests at heart after all. Something creepy about him all the same. All those vanishing acts and that business with the butter. It must have been a conjuring trick. And when he ran downstairs he must have climbed up the facade and gone in through the window. He'd had just enough time before Gordon, the guy with the headband, let me in. Gordon had a cross around his neck, I'd noticed, and Richard—he wore a ring with a pentagram on it. Wasn't that a satanic symbol? What were the two of them doing in one house? Everything about them was opposite.

Eventually I dozed off again. This time no fiendish threat leaped out to greet me. Instead the floor gave way. But not completely: My heels and the back of my head still rested on solid ground. I don't know how long I hung in this ridiculous position, with only emptiness beneath me. Maybe just a few seconds, but the next day, my whole body ached. I was tempted to let myself fall, but how could I? It was the world's fate that hung in the balance, not just mine. And in the world—lest I take the world for an abstraction that might be dispensed with—were Susan and Gina, whose lives would be crushed if I let go.

I sat up again and slept no more. I didn't sleep the next night either, or the night after that. Maybe a fourth and fifth night too, I'm not sure. I sat with my legs folded in the half-lotus position for hours at a time, in a chair, on the floor, on a couch, depending on where I was (the locations varied), and relieved the physical strain on my back and legs by walking around the room. It's possible, of course, that while sitting, I slept without knowing it.

A nd here I begin to lose sight of Joel and his guide. Not entirely, I'm happy to say—I see them at intervals, but the time between their appearances is invisible to me.

I can hear someone ask me now, puzzled, impatient, a reader who likes me better when I'm plainspoken: "What you mean to say is that you don't remember. Please, just fill in the gaps or declare them vacant, and get on with your story!"

Maybe you're right. But I want to take note of my peculiar difficulty here. These vacancies—the ones Richard and Joel are about to walk into, and from which, at intervals, they will emerge—are not simple absences. If they were, I could skip them and move to the next solid presence, or else fill in the gaps, as you say, with a little imagination. More likely than not, in the process some of the forgotten events would rise to the surface, and on this field of memories real and imagined I would advance. But I can do neither. These gaps are already filled with what appears to be some kind of anti-mnemonic substance. It's as if I were forbidden to remember, much as I was forbidden to sleep at the time. I'm allowed to imagine, though, so long as it's not as an aid to remembering. Unless the substance is anti-imaginal too. No, I can advance this way. But where am I going? I'm walking in a fog so dense that I can't see my feet, let alone the ground beneath them. But above my collar the view, though still misty, is clearer. How can I reach those rocks in the distance? Or even those branches a stone's throw away? I'm treading emptiness, each step takes me nowhere. If I were to rise, on the other hand . . . high enough to glide through the air . . . (ah, I can sense my Counterpoint near me now) . . . yes, now I'm balanced on a treetop, flapping my wings, cawing my satisfaction into the gloom. But what a way to travel, and what a way to write. This must be what is meant by going out on a limb. Now another crow settles on a branch near mine.

Is that you, my Counterpoint? Who's going to believe what I have to say from now on?

C. Don't worry about your readers. It's he whose faith you must awaken. It's him you want to save.

Joel?

C. Who else?

For Stefan's sake.

C. For all our sake. When one of us is lost, the echo is everywhere.

Who are you, Counterpoint?

But he's flying already, and I take off after him. Flying is easy. A slight strain on the pectorals, but otherwise pleasant. An airy lightness. It was cold on that branch, but the exercise helps. Makes me want to caw again. Why not? My Counterpoint answers: "Krah!" It's embarrassing, now that I hear it coming from him. What's this story turning into? Castaneda? A video game? Disney? And where are we headed? Toward those rocks, I suppose. They're looming up closer. But they're not rocks at all, they're houses. A city. London, no doubt. That's better. And the light's changing. So is the weather. We're on a treetop again, it's warmer here, spring. People swarming homeward after a day's work. Sparrows pecking in the gutter beneath us. There's Joel, limping in his outsized sandals. He's looking for his car. He didn't find it in Bayswater. Didn't find any of the previous day's landmarks either, the diner, the little park. Now he's slipping away again, lost in the fog.

Counterpoint, what's this charade? Of what use are we to him, as crows?

C. None whatsoever. His fate rests entirely in the hands of our scribe at his desk in Brooklyn—provided we keep ourselves out of his reach.

Why? What can the narrator do without us?

C. He can trace the outlines of the visible landscape.

A cartographer, then. And us? What's left for us to do?

C. Well, to begin with, we might explore the implications of our current disguise, and the fact that, for the first time, we resemble each other. Most important, though, we'll exclude ourselves and our realm from the narrator's vision.

Our realm? What's our realm?

C. The imagination. It's imagination that built the labyrinth. What Joel needs is a map.

■　■　■

"Scribe" he called me. That stung. Who would he be without my scribbling? And that other wing-flapper, does he really think "narrator" makes me feel better? Who does he think he is? The author? And "cartographer" finally—that tops it off.

I hear their distant cawing, like raucous laughter. Can't see them at all. Fog.

Without imagination. Not once in this book have I had to work under these conditions. Irresponsible, really. You'd think at a juncture like this we'd want to make use of all our resources. But no, I'm reduced to "tracing the outlines." From what perspective, may I ask? With what grammatical instruments? Is it a "he" or an "I," past tense or present?

No answer.

Well, here goes—pictures from an exhibition. I'm not even sure of their sequence. I'll list them as they come.

Richard's Prediction

Casually, at a moment when the others were not present, Richard informed me that we would all get busted in a few days—unless, of course, I found my car before that, in which case I would be safe. But most likely, I would get busted too.

A Change of Shoes

After wandering around London for two days, his feet hurt so much that he can barely walk. It's the size of the sandals, they aren't tight enough, the straps chafe the skin. Richard offers him his moccasins. That reminds him of an American Indian adage: "Don't judge a man until you have walked a mile in his moccasins." He has judged Richard. He has come to suspect that Richard is evil. Now he will be walking many miles in his moccasins. They're a little too small for him, but that's preferable.

Buddhist Society

Gordon, Richard, and the two other freaks took me to a gray two-story house with a bronze plaque next to the door. Memory tells me that the words on the plaque were "Buddhist Society." But the Buddhist Society's current Web site shows a large impressive building with many windows and a flag waving on a turret. I suppose they've moved.

Gordon rang the bell. A man with a pipe in his hand appeared in the doorway. Gordon explained himself. "Our friend here needs help," he said, with a gesture toward me. "He had some kind of religious experience in a Buddhist retreat in Surrey. He's kind of shook up. Can you talk to him?"

The man with the pipe shook his head: "We're not psychiatrists." A thin, balding fellow with a sweater appeared behind him.

"I think he needs *spiritual* help, man, not a shrink. Can't you refer him to a Buddhist priest?"

The man with the pipe shook his head. His colleague looked highly amused by the visit. He asked me to name my teacher in Surrey.

"Chao Khun," I said.

"That's right," the man with the pipe said, giggling. "Can you say his full name?"

"Chao Khun Sobhana Dhammasuddhi."

"Very good!" He giggled again. Something peculiar in his body language: He was swaying his hips.

The man with the pipe began to turn back inside, and the man with the sweater, who had seemed half inclined to take up Gordon's challenge for its humorous potential, stepped back into the shadows as well.

Gordon raised his voice: "Where's your compassion, man? He's come to you for help, doesn't that mean anything to you?"

The door closed.

Orientation

My dear feathered colleagues, one of you spoke of Joel's need for a map. No doubt it looks that way from the treetop, but you are mistaken. If someone gave him a map, he would throw it away. Everything signals, everything gestures, the world has become language. By these signs he can orient himself, and he does. A startling honk at the moment when he's about to turn a corner is a warning: Don't go there! The resultant turn of his head brings a bus into view as it stops just a few steps away. And there is a little girl his daughter's age, gaping at the strange bearded man as her mother lifts her onto the bus. So this is the way. In the bus, a vacant seat next to the mother and her daughter confirms that he has made the right choice. The child asks her mother:

"How long is forever?"

"Forever is a long, long, long, long time."

"You mean long, long, long, long, long, long, long, long, long, long, long, long?"

"That's right, it doesn't stop."

"Never?"

"That's right, it never ends."

Later, after the mother and daughter have left, he hears a man's gravelly voice muttering, right next to his ear: "This is the place." At the same time his eyes are taking in the words "DON'T MISS IT!" on a poster outside. He rises from his seat. The driver's voice announces the stop. He can't quite make out the words, but they really don't matter, because this is the place. Bewildered, then, he stands on a nondescript street corner somewhere in London. What does this have to do with his car? Maybe nothing, but the name of the street—he sees it printed on an enamel sign—indicates a mode of physical destruction that awaits him:

Kilburn

Not that being burned to death would be the end of him. Forever is a long, long time. It's always only the beginning.

And yet, day after day, he finds his way home through the labyrinth without even knowing the name of the district he lives in. I don't know how to explain it.

The golfer

I meet an old man in the street. Something military about him, tight, compact, vigorous. He appears out of nowhere, confronting me in such a way that I am forced to stand still, and launches into a passionate harangue in a dialect I don't understand. Every once in a while a recognizable word lets me know that the man is speaking English and that he's telling me about himself and his desires. Every few seconds he licks his lips. His gestures become crudely sexual and violent. He's castrating someone with a twist of his clawlike right hand. Why is he showing me this? Seeing that I don't get it, he repeats the operation several times. "Like *this!*" he says, "and like *this!* And *this!*" Oh, he's showing me what's in store for me. He reaches into the space between us, grasping and clutching my entrails and ripping them out and wrapping them around himself. Then he scoops out my eyes and castrates me again. Now he drives off two objects (my eyeballs? my testicles? I'm not sure) with triumphant swings of an imaginary golf club. "Like this! Like this!" I understand: My spiritual body is indestructible, therefore it can be violated over and over.

Metamorphosis

Gordon puts on a record: . . . guitar chords: . . . a clear tenor voice sings a song of love and consolation. As always, there is another, occult meaning. It comes in a line in the middle of the song:

He's bound . . . his heart . . . with an iron . . . band . . .

The image stuns me with its truth. How is this possible? It can't be that everything, *everything* acts as a mirror! There must be contrary signs, if you only look for them. I turn my gaze to a shelf with books and select one of them for a test, at random: one title, a red book: what news? *Metamorphosis*. If it weren't Kafka's story, you could squeeze some hope out of this word. But no, the news is: mutation, degradation. A vermin among men. Stop! Don't accept it! Try another one—the blue book next to it. I squint, the word on the spine is printed in small type. Oh God. *Metamorphosis* again. My heart . . . like a bird in a fist. An iron band. No way out.

The other two

As I said, there were two other guys in the house besides Richard and Gordon, but I've nearly forgotten them, and since I'm not allowed to imagine, there's very little to be said about them. Their names were Dane and Gavin. Dane was short and stocky, red-haired, with red lips and fierce blue eyes. I think he had a short beard. Gavin was thin and fey, beardless, with soft brown eyes and a gentle, secretive smile. I felt at the time that Gavin and Dane resented my presence but tolerated it because Gordon was king in the house and he believed in charity.

Gordon's judgment

Joel is standing on the street with Gordon, Richard, Gavin, and Dane. Richard says something to him in his usual near-whisper of insinuation. Gordon steps between them and jabs a finger at Richard's forehead: "There's a lot of evil in there, man! Watch yourself!"

The unthinkable

So long as he manages to stay awake, he's postponing the unthinkable. And what's the unthinkable? No doubt the worst possible outcome. What would that entail? Susan and Gina's destruction. But how? Oh, don't think it, don't think it, or it will come to pass! But the thought has already begun, it's unstoppable.

Homeless

Every once in a while, he meets someone. Some people he asks for directions to "The Haven." Some surprise him with questions of their own. Some he has silent exchanges with. Each of them delivers a message he needs to hear. He doesn't seek out these messengers. They present themselves.

For example, several teenage boys and girls on a gloomy, deserted street, at night. The girls have dark eye shadow and dark lipstick, the boys are wearing army boots. He meets them when one of them asks him for a "fag." He can't understand most of what they're saying. His American accent brings out amusement, curiosity, and resentment. One of the girls tells him she lost everything in a fire. The way she talks about it, it was a grand thing, what happened to her.

"When did it happen?" he asks.

"Just last night. I was out late. I come home, my whole flat and half the building's burnt down. All I've got left is the clothes on me body!"

She has no idea why she is telling him this. How could she? He himself didn't know until the moment she told him. He was the one who burned her house down. His thoughts. His secret, uncontrollable malice. It must have happened while he dozed off at Richard's place. And who knows what else. They start playing tag. He walks on. "You're it!" a girl calls. Doesn't he know it.

Heavy

An American kid with a shining halo of blond curls comes up to him in the street. He keeps walking, and the kid walks next to him.

"Hey, man, you want some good Lebanese shit?"

"No, thanks."

"Blotter acid?"

"No."

"I got mushrooms too."

Joel shakes his head.

"Oh, you're stoned already!"

Joel stops and looks at the kid and sees a child's face that fills with pity at the sight of his face.

"What's wrong, man?"

He searches for words. Maybe he can tell him. Not about the car and The Haven, but the real trouble.

"Can I help you?"

"I doubt it."

"Don't doubt it, man. Maybe I can help. What's the trouble?"

"I'm God."

The kid is trying to understand. He would save him if he could. For a moment Joel fears that his condition could become the kid's by infection, and that he will pass it on to others, that it will spread—a multiplication of horror beyond anything he can imagine.

The kid shakes his head: "Oh, man, that's heavy." He just stands there shaking his head. Joel walks on, and the kid stays behind.

The house in the garden

Again that soft whiteness pervading everything. But there's also the warm gold of sunlight on green leaves. He has been walking all day, faithfully following the secret signs, and now, after endless miles of gray stone, he finds himself limping along among orchards and patches of ploughed earth. Is this still London? There must be a reason why he was led here. There it is: an old woman. She's weeding her garden behind a lattice fence. Behind her, a small house with smoke curling out of a chimney. Either the house was made of wood or my memory has made it that way. This is the light and this is the garden, the humble hut, the billowing smoke, where a bent old woman is the grandmother of any child who comes to her fence and asks if he may come inside. How could he not ask? Here, if he slept, the world would be cradled in kindness. He asks. She turns her head slightly, smiling. She is so stooped she seems about to keel over. "No, dear," she says, "you'd better go home," and goes on with her work. "I have no home," he says. She doesn't respond. It occurs to him to offer her money, but that would change everything. If she accepted his money and let him in, she would not be herself and he could not sleep. "I need to sleep," he says. Now she moves toward her house, still as bent as she was while weeding. She's supporting herself on a cane. "I had a shelter," he says. "It was called The Haven. Do you know where it is?" She goes inside and closes the door.

Courage

All the countless signs and symbols have one purpose: to show me the way. They are as varied as light and shadow, as transient as touch and sound. But there is one sign, and only one, that does not vary and does not point in any direction. It consists of a single red word, "COURAGE," emblazoned on a blue ground. The word and its ground are contained in a circle.

I know it's the name of a popular beer, but the way it comes to me, always at moments of hopelessness, is surely a message. Who sent it? Who wishes me well? I'm grateful to it every time it appears. The gratitude fades as I walk on, and sometimes doubt takes its place with a vengeance: What's courage good for? You're in hell! But hours or days later, when the very thought of hope seems a mockery, the sign reappears, dangling over the door of a pub.

The grapes

I saw a young man in a business suit sitting on a sheet of newspaper at the top of a broad flight of steps leading up to a pompous old building. He had red hair and he was eating a sandwich and he was looking at me, my body and face were turned in his direction—sufficient indications that I was supposed to sit down next to him. The guy didn't flinch at my long hair and wrinkled clothes. Instead he asked me if I would like some grapes. I held out my cupped palms. He put several grapes in them. I ate them, slowly, one by one. What a wonderful taste. Together we watched the briskly walking men and women—mostly men—on the wide square beneath us. He said he preferred to eat his lunch here, alone, rather than with his colleagues. He worked in a bank.

"And you," he asked, with friendly irony, "where do *you* work?"

"I'm God."

"Ah," he said, not at all surprised. "I'm pleased to meet you." We shook hands. I knew he was mocking me but I didn't mind.

"I'm a human being," he said. That little distinction drove a wedge between me and my humanity. From then on every encounter drove that wedge a little deeper.

A fisher of souls

A little black boy, seven or eight years old, came to the house. He wanted to speak to Richard. But Richard was busy rolling joints and didn't want to be bothered. No one else in the house took any notice of the boy. He hung around for a while and eventually went home. He came back another day, and again Richard ignored him. I talked to him a little. He looked desolate. He answered my questions politely, obediently, as if I were his teacher. When I asked if Richard was his friend, he nodded, but without gladness. What could he possibly want from Richard, and what could Richard, so sour and joyless, have to give him? I didn't ask these questions out loud. There was no need to, they answered themselves: Richard had nothing to give him, it was not in his nature to give. But whatever his victims desired or needed, no matter how simple or far-fetched, he knew how to bait his hook with it as a promise. All his offers were baits. And what he was angling for was your complete faith and allegiance: your soul. What did that mean, to take someone's soul? And what did it mean to have lost it? I don't want to ever recall in its fullness the pain that arose in response to that question. The boy gazing into my eyes seemed to understand.

"Is Richard your friend too?"

"Yes," I said.

The river

A man leaving a building holds open the door. I walk in. Up the stairs, second floor, third. Muffled roar of a vacuum cleaner and a radio or TV reporter's voice.

Follow the sounds to their source. An open door. An apartment. A young woman cleaning a rug while a large TV set blares out the news. A man is talking about a polluted river. In front of the TV is a chair, set at an angle that invites me to sit there. I walk in and sit down facing the man. He winks at me slyly and smiles. The woman, holding her roaring machine, looks at me with surprise, then shakes her head, giggles, and continues her work. The reporter's face is replaced by images of dead fish and dead birds floating in water, a wet furry animal in the grass, dead, with bared teeth, more dead birds and fish on a table. What does this have to do with me? Everything. The reporter's face returns, smiling. Again that sly wink. With his voice he is talking to the world, but with his smile he addresses the One whose job it is to hold the world in balance. I have seen this smile before. It's Richard's. What is he up to? What is his purpose?

The brink

Someone put me up for the night. We met in the rain after dark and he told me I could sleep on his couch if I wanted. He was friendly and about my age. That's all I remember about him.

When we walked into his flat, I saw that I wasn't his only guest. A couple lay asleep on a pallet on the floor. The girl was brown-skinned, the guy pale and blond, with an earring in one ear.

I didn't sleep on the couch. I sat awake in an armchair, keeping the world in balance. A church bell quartered the hours with merciless pedantry, announcing the approach of the moment when I would lose consciousness and drag the material world with me into the nightmare of eternal repetition. On and off, the sound of a passing airplane ground its way through my skull like a rusty bandsaw. I was already convinced that thoughts were volatile things and things solidified thoughts. Now it was getting hard to tell the difference.

Once, on the brink of sleep, the stream of mental images was abruptly accelerated, exactly like a film running through a defective projector. It lasted only a few seconds, but my terror was extreme, because a world can be destroyed in seconds.

Richard was here, observing my thoughts and responding to them as he saw fit. Why my thoughts were of such consuming interest to him was a mystery. Maybe he fed on them the way vampires feed on blood. How deceptive he was—as deceptive as I was trusting. Pretending that we were equal, with common interests and comparable powers. There was nothing equal about us and our powers were not comparable. I must have foolishly endowed him with faculties that were properly mine—omniscience, for one . . . omnipresence . . . maybe omnipotence. I had even deprived myself of all memory except that of this miserable entity, Joel.

But what if I was only Joel after all? It was possible—everything was possible! What if I wasn't the insane, immortal creator of an insanely cruel universe, but just another madman? Like Stefan? That would make all the difference. In fact it would be salvation itself—even if I didn't know it!—because the world would be untouched by my insanity and I would be released by an inevitable death. If I could only believe that!

Early in the morning, my worst fear came to pass. The mind sped up again, and this time the madness engulfed the material world. It began in the room I was in. The blond kid stirred in his sleep and suddenly yelled "What the FUCK!" The girl's finger was caught in his earring. He slapped her. She pulled back, still caught, he followed her hand like a bull on a halter. Outside, in the greater world, the last war was beginning. Now finally free, the boy roared "YOU STUPID FUCKING BITCH!" She crossed her arms to protect herself, he whacked her several times, she screamed, our host came in from another room and yelled "JESUS FUCKING CHRIST ALL FUCKING MIGHTY!", which I thought was a desperate appeal to me, and only now did the kid and then the girl notice the stranger sitting motionless in an armchair holding them in his attention, with his hands cupped right and left as if he were a scale and their souls were being weighed. That stopped them.

The turbulence settled, hostilities ceased. Out in the world (I saw this mentally) a finger withdrew from a red button, rockets were lowered on their launching pads, the Washington-Moscow hotline cable (red, like the button) trembled with last-minute mutual assurances. I sat for a long time, breathing deeply to calm the thumping of my heart, because that sound had often been the trigger that set off the eternal return. If that happened again . . . God forbid! All flesh would see it together. No one interfered with me. Our host went out to buy a newspaper. The kid with the earring took a shower. The girl started making breakfast. When a breeze stirred the curtains in the direction of the door, I stood up and walked out.

Snake eyes

My eyes ached. It was from the effort to stay awake, and from trying to read all the signs. I stopped in front of a shop window. In the window were a mirror, several lamps, and a book. I saw myself in the mirror. My eyes were bulging. I looked at the book. On its cover was a picture of two dice and a title in black letters: *Snake Eyes*. Should I buy the book? No doubt it said something about me. But I knew it already. There was something horribly malignant inside me. It showed well enough in the world I had made. Now it was beginning to show in my face.

Mr. Watkins

I ran into people who wanted to help me. One of them was Mr. Watkins, of Watkins & Stuart, the bookstore. He came out of the store to talk to me on the street. We had never met, so I can't imagine why he did that, unless someone called him out on my behalf, but I don't remember that. Mr. Watkins was an elderly man in tweed, with a pink, fleshy face and blue eyes beneath worried, bushy eyebrows. He appeared to me to be exceptionally kind, so when he asked me what was the trouble, I told him. "Oh God," he said, and his eyes flew up and off to the side. Like a gambler who places his last chip on the most improbable number, I decided that if he just saw me, face-to-face and man to man, I would be saved. Just a moment's recognition would be enough. And how would I recognize his recognition? I would feel it. But how could he see me? My bulging, malignant eyes repelled his gaze. I stopped talking and waited for the cosmic croupier to turn the wheel, confident that I would lose. Once again, Mr. Watkins' gaze touched mine and instantly sped off. He hurried inside to call for help, and I walked on.

Anticipation

Walking, walking. What is this cheerfulness in people, evenings, on their way home from work? Ripples of laughter, smiles. Even when no one talks, there's a stirring, a current of—what? Like the excitement of nature before a cloudburst. A stirring, a whispering, a gladness in the air. Weird little whirlwinds of—what is it, anticipation? Yes, that's what it is. Small groups, accidentally drifted together on a street corner, waiting for a green light, strangers, yet they share a secret. They guard it even from each other—otherwise why would they smile so furtively? Or else they're hiding their smiles from him. That's possible. Everything's possible. It's really one smile, scattered among a thousand faces. All around him. Black and brown immigrants, stiff-hatted tweedy men, laborers carrying their tools, women with shopping bags, the differences melt in this dawning, this burgeoning—of what? Some large and good occasion. People chatting, hurrying, standing, but intermittently, there's this flash of pleasure in their faces. So they smile, why shouldn't they? People smile. But it's not just a smile. Often it's followed by a licking of the lips. There's something crude, almost obscene in that gesture. Appetite. That's what it expresses. Appetite, sexual or gustatory. What's wrong with that? What's wrong is that this smiling and lip-smacking happens too often. And sometimes the licking is accompanied by a swift sideward glance in his direction. The glance doesn't always meet his, but it knows where he is.

The poster people

And there are the poster people. He sees them all over the city. The men clean-cut and clean-shaven, with chiseled cheekbones and steely eyes, the women in the bloom of youth, glossy, with white-white teeth and lacquered lips. But no libidinous tongue-lapping here. These people don't want anything. Their pleasure is timeless, eternal. To the normal passerby, they advertise things the possession of which is supposed to confer to the buyer some part of these people's merciless beauty. But to him, and to him alone, with little signals—a dimple, a gleam, a wink—they advertise their real purpose: to herald a new age and a new humanity. They smile, but the smile does not warm the heart. It is a smile of satisfaction. They feast on the body of love like ants on a worm. And that body lives and writhes, it is sentient, it suffers, its pain is the incense in their cult of pleasure.

The prognosis

In the end, God's creatures will drag their Creator out from his hiding place, by the scruff of his neck, as it were: Bad god! Bad god! But "bad" is hardly the word for what he has committed: an insanely bungled creation, an attempt at perfection so ingeniously misconstrued that it perpetuates its failure ad infinitum in an endless cycle of suffering and degradation, an idea of universal harmony that has incarnated as a mutual eating society of pitifully sentient beings. So much for the so-called natural order. But he couldn't leave bad enough alone. The same hapless intelligence (or fathomless wickedness, a possibility he hasn't dared to contemplate yet) that dreamed up those primal hells, the jungle and the sea, went on to evolve a human brain, and with it the capacity for ever more hideously advanced disasters. But now that the globe is whirling into apocalypse, now that nations and empires, no longer just bands of apes, stand glaring at each other, still as helpless as any beast in the grip of instinct, rockets poised, warheads loaded; now that the ultimate horror is dawning on the world, isn't it time that his creatures find him, and having found him, find a way to put an end to his machinations, once and for all? Not by killing him—that would be a tragic waste—but by making a feast of his substance, forever. That will absolve them of the need to kill. That's why they're licking their lips. They're hunting for their salvation. And where will they find him? The beauty of it, so deliciously improbable: hiding in London with a group of Irish hippies! And how will he be identified? By his words, of course! Someone will read his journals, and especially the records of his dreams, where the cosmic extent of his guilt shows itself plainly enough. What a capital discovery! The key of Genesis, found by a policeman in a derelict VW bus! But hope dies slowly. Still he is compelled to search for his car. Once or twice he is tempted to go to an airport and book a flight to New York. He has enough travelers checks in his pocket . . . but what's the use? It will only bring calamity to his wife and his daughter. Their hope, and the hope of the world, rests in his destruction.

If he *did* find his car, on the other hand . . . *If* he could drive to some field or forest outside the city and incinerate his notebooks . . . *If* that were still possible . . . then maybe the horror would shrink down to human proportions . . . maybe the world would muddle through, as it always has, despite all the misery . . . maybe he could live out his life being a father to his daughter and a husband to his wife and a friend to his friends and a neighbor to his neighbors, in blessed anonymity, until death claimed him. *If* that were possible. But with every passing day and night that seems more fantastically improbable.

The takers

"Yield," says a traffic sign. He knows it's addressed to drivers, but it's also a command to his soul. And he does yield. It's a wager like Pascal's, an act of faith, and as such its own proof and its own purpose. Against all the whisperings of malice he trusts that there is an Other after all, a force that is not his own self-destroying self, an invisible God who wants his happiness, who will hold out a hand to him at every step, who grieves for him when he falls, who would descend to the deepest hell to save him, his child, from perdition. Gladly he follows the sign, gives up his stubborn claims to autonomy. And he is rewarded. His nerves twinge in response to the subtlest suggestion, the minutest fraction of a hint. A touch of air on his left cheek bids him turn his head. His glance meets a pattern of broken plaster on a wall. It resembles a running dog. The dog's shape recalls that of the dog he met days ago, the one he lost sight of, the one he failed to feed. Here it is, trotting along, with its tail in a happy position. He follows its direction. His motions take on a blind ease and sureness and swiftness. He glides through the streets, into buses and subways, downstairs and upstairs, effortlessly, like a leaf in a river. He no longer feels his blistered feet. Where is he being taken? He doesn't know. He doesn't need to know. In the landscape of terror, he has become fearless. As if that were not miraculous enough, the flow of indications takes him directly to the American Express office, the one building in London where he can expect to receive a message from his wife. The next moment he finds himself standing in line with some twenty or thirty other Americans, men and women, some of them freaks like himself, all of them expecting mail from their loved ones. Oh the blessing. To be one of a group, yet particular; human. Arrived at the counter, he asks if there are any letters for Joel Agee, and spells his last name. The clerk brings him two airmail letters and a postcard and asks for an identification. He has none. It's in his car. He turns around in despair. There, like a plank floating into the view of a drowning man—go there, go!—is another queue before another counter. He joins it. What is it for? Not mail. It's for changing travelers checks into pounds sterling. You don't need an ID for that. And he's got travelers checks, about eight hundred dollars' worth. He exchanges the whole batch and leaves with his wallet stuffed. What's it for, all this money? Maybe to fly home? Oh maybe! Oh the miracle! Eternal gratitude if it were so! But it's not up to him. It's up to the Guidance. The signs have to take him there.

Halfway down the block he meets a beggar. He's seen him before, a staggering drunk, still young, with blazing blue eyes in a sunburnt face full of scars and scabs, blood on his shirt, mumbling some thick-tongued plea while holding his cap out with a stiff arm. There's your purpose, there's your meaning: Give! He opens his wallet, pulls out the frontmost bill (who is he to choose?), a twenty-pound note, puts the bill in the man's cap, happy to be an instrument of providence, God knows it's long overdue, and steps into a bus just as its doors close. Where are we going? Never mind. There is only one destination, NowHere. He finds his way home by the usual magical route. His hosts are asleep. A candle has been left burning on a dish next to his pallet. On the pillow lies a leaflet with the headline: "Who is the guru?" It must be a gift from

Gordon, the man with the crucifix. It reminds him of another leaflet he saw more than a year ago: "Who is the Joker?" And because this leaflet recalls that one, because all things linked by association are presumed to be essentially identical, the Guru and the Joker are one and the same. Did any of the medieval chroniclers of Hell, did Dante or Bosch, simple translators of the varieties of physical torture into the numeral endlessness of time, or those Tibetan encyclopedists of postmortal horror, did any of them ever imagine a torment like this? That thought frightens him deeply, and it's the most dangerous kind of fear, close to the edge of the ultimate Terror. He mustn't allow it. Mustn't allow mockery to usurp the throne of meaning. Don't believe it! He sits in the wavering light of the candle until it goes out, and continues sitting in darkness, staring down the temptation to sleep. How many nights has he done this? Five? Six? Is that possible? Is this already the nightmare he's trying to prevent by not going to sleep? If that is the case, why not simply give in? Sleep . . . let darkness cover the face of the earth . . . let it all go to hell . . . it can't get any more hellish than this . . .

Oh yes it can! For you and the others! Infinitely worse!
You've been there, you know it!

He goes to the bathroom and takes a cold shower. Gets dressed, and on the spur of an impulse (No hesitation! Follow!) leaves the house and entrusts himself once again to the Guidance. It's still night, and misty. I can no longer see him. Maybe it's the other, unreal kind of fog our putative author called "antimnemonic." But I'm not supposed to imagine what I can't remember, so I won't imagine that blankness either. Suffice it to say that it's broad daylight when Joel reappears, and that it's a moment of miracle: precisely the moment when he finds himself standing again at the entrance to the American Express office.

This time he does not obey his first impulse, a choice he regrets as he presses his palm against the chrome bar that opens the glass door. Why didn't he simply walk on? That would at least have had the dignity of a free act. But it would also have been an act of infidelity that could have cost him the company of his angelic protector, his last refuge against the torment of falling back into the innermost circle, where the only truth is "I ALONE AM" and the only law is that of the eternal return of the same. Better to be a slave of God than omnipotent and at your own mercy. Better to follow your Guide like a sheep, even if it's to the slaughterhouse he takes you. Slaughter is mild compared with the horrors of solipsism. He joins the queue of people expecting mail from abroad. They're not the same people as yesterday, but there is a sameness nonetheless, and that sameness mocks him. Arrived at the counter, he asks if there are any letters for Joel Agee, and spells his last name. The clerk is not the same clerk as yesterday, but that makes no difference. She comes back with two airmail letters and a postcard and asks for an identification. He turns away. There is the other queue, the one for cashing in travelers checks. But he has already cashed in all of his. There's no way to expunge the worm of doubt now. He hears its voice as he leaves the building: "The Guru is the Joker. The Guru is the Joker." But guru or joker, angel or fiend, it still is an Other, he mustn't forget that, and the Other is with him, His rod and His staff, they comfort him. From far off, he sees a beggar approaching. He's not the same one he met yesterday. He's a bearded longhaired freak like himself, panhandling. Again it occurs to him to turn away, if only to break the pattern of repetition, which is threatening to become exponential. But the risk is too great. He'd be left alone with that hideous mantra revolving in the back of his mind. From now on, he will meet everything and everyone that comes his way as a message from God, a Word in the poem of Salvation. He takes a twenty-pound note from his wallet and holds it up as he meets the panhandler and gives it to him in passing, and walks on. "Wow! Thanks a lot!" He hears it behind him. This is the Way. Give where you can. This is the lesson you're here to learn. Life is a school. Some lessons have to be repeated. It's for your own good and the good of others. Passing a bank, he scans the text of an ad in the window. There's that word again, "YIELD." Wasn't that the instruction that sent him gliding through the streets and straight to the American Express in the first place? There to supply him . . . with what? With the means to give. To yield and to give—are they not the same? Look, there's another beggar! How providential for you and for her. A longhaired girl in a patchwork gypsy dress, and she's coming right up to you with her hand held out, as if she knew what you're here for.

"Hey man, can you help me out, if I don't pay my rent by tomorrow I'm out on the street."

Of course you give. She plucks the twenty-pound note from your hand with a quick little two-fingered tug and walks off quickly. She didn't say thank you. It doesn't matter. It's none of your business. She asked and you gave. Divine economy, reasonless as love itself.

Some eight or ten people, maybe more, come to pick up their twenty-pound notes. Like flies drawn to honey. Some cross the street with a businesslike air, approaching him as if they had an appointment with him, and straightforwardly ask him for money. Others, more stealthy, post themselves in his path with hangdog demeanors, holding out a cupped hand or a hat, pretending to be at their wits' end appealing to the stony hearts of common moneyed folk, until he reaches them. One guy shows up twice—first as a hand-wringing kid, incongruously preppy, literally writhing in supplication as he begs him, "please, please," to give him money to buy medicine for a sick sister. The second time around, he's wearing a girl's plastic rain hat and, squaring his shoulders, issues a cheerful command: "Give to the needy!" Joel gives—not because it's not obvious to him that these takers are thieves, but because there is something so demonic about them that he can only presume they are emissaries of a dark force that wants propitiation.

A new religion

The stream of occult indications takes me swiftly—I'm almost running—to the entrance of a large modern building. A policeman blocks my way, not with a gesture or a word, but silently and with his entire body. He holds his hands behind his back, which makes his broad blue chest even broader. He's looking me straight in the eyes, smiling. The smile is as firm as his stance. His pupils are narrow. Isn't he the cop who took down the details about my lost car? And now that I've given up on the car he shows up? Such beneficence is no longer credible. Or rather: to hope for it is to invite worse disasters. No, it's not he. Yet he looks very familiar as we stand eye to eye. I'm fascinated. Is he real? Yes, he's as real and as individual as anything in this world, but he's also perfectly unbelievable, a dream figure masquerading as fact, a figment. And yet, though I'm dreaming him, he's in my way, and he's probably holding a truncheon behind his back. I don't want to find out what a dream truncheon feels like. What I want is to wake up. What if it's all a dream, as the Buddha said? This building, this monstrous hive of a city, the scramble and buzz of people and cars, this thousand-faced leering smile all around me—dream-stuff, down to the stone of the pavement. Let me wake up! But the dream continues. A middle-aged woman with a wide-brimmed hat joins us. Words are exchanged—between her and the policeman, between the policeman and me, between me and the woman.

(Had they been speaking Dutch and I Chinese, the illusion of mutual understanding would not have been more amazing. My words, whatever they were, matched the terms of their discourse well enough to elicit remarks which, whatever they meant to their speakers, appeared to be addressed to my soul. The woman in particular seemed very well informed.)

"You thought last year was the end of it, didn't you?" she says. "That was just the beginning. Last year we drew up the tally. Tonight we'll close the account."

"What account?"

"The results! Have I made myself clearer?"

The results—I've already seen them prefigured in advertisements all over the city. The poster people. There's no one like them in the streets, but that's no wonder. They are not yet. This is what people will be like when they're done with me. And the results for me? My body eaten by all those salivating mouths. Not literally, but through some process of transsubstantiation.

I protest almost voicelessly, without hope: "It's not fair."

"Fair!" she snorts. "Your notions of fairness and ours are quite different."

"We shan't decide the issue by talking, now, shall we?" says the policeman.

"No," says the woman, "devotees will decide."

Her omission of the definite article surprises me, but not as much as the introduction of "devotees," with the accent on the "o." Devoted to what?

She turns to enter the building, and the policeman makes room for her, keeping an eye on me.

"Why can't I go in?" I ask the policeman.

The woman answers in his stead, spitting her words with violent scorn: "The reason I can and you can't is that there's a *difference* between us."[1]

The haircut

Through a shop window he meets the glittering humorous eyes of a fat man with a handlebar moustache who looks like Meher Baba, the Zoroastrian avatar. Joel stops in his tracks, astonished. Baba died a little over a year ago, yet here he is, crooking his finger: Come in! The door is open. Joel obeys. The fat man bids him sit down in a leather chair in front of a mirror, whips a white cloth around him, ties it behind his neck, grasps an electric razor. Baba runs a bar-

---

1. Recently an English friend told me that Londoners get quite "frisky" around election time: "Even local elections get us stirred up. It's the closest we come to a carnival season." So that's what all that lip-smacking anticipation was about. It also helps translate "devotees" back into what that haughty woman probably said: "the voters."

bershop! A lousy pun, but appearing like this, without words, authorless, fully embodied, it's stunning. "Everything off?" he asks, licking his lips, and the Maker of worlds nods, without knowing why.

Exquisite Corpse

In Baba's mirror, he had seen a spot in the center of his forehead. The mark of Cain, he thought, and tried wiping it off with his fingers. That turned the spot into a swastika—just a suggestion of one, but that was enough. Now, walking the streets again, he remembers a drawing he made in Ibiza together with a couple of friends. They were playing the "exquisite corpse" game, invented by the surrealists. It requires three players. The first player draws a head at the top of a sheet of paper, then folds back the page so that only the neck is visible. The second player draws a torso with arms and folds back the page so that only the bottom of the trunk is visible. The third player completes the body with a pair of legs. Then the picture is opened, and the players have a good laugh at their creation. (There is of course always a fourth player, Chance, who supplies all the comedy and never laughs.) This particular exquisite corpse had a porkpie hat, a swastika on his forehead, and a scar like Frankenstein's on one cheek. His eyes were crossed and steam was coming out of his ears. The corners of his mouth were turned down. In the middle of his naked chest was a red heart. His arms were stretched out right and left and his hands were pierced by red stigmata (or else he was nailed onto space). Beneath his dangling naked hairy legs were vertical streaks, indicative of speed, and a cloud of exhaust fumes, and underneath those, far below, the curved face of the earth. He remembers laughing until his stomach hurt. He remembers his comments and theirs: "Poor guy!" "Oh man, is he fucked up!" With tears of laughter in their eyes.

"Thou art that," he thinks now, picturing the swastika on his forehead. "That art thou."

Hunted

They're on to him. The hounds have caught his scent. It's a hunt, or an execution in the form of a hunt. A ritual, in any case, a sacred game. Not a chase, though, oh no. A still-hunt. Isn't that the sporting term? The devotees perch in their hiding places while their beast of venery strays into their sight. And the devotees, where are they? Behind those lit windows. But why are the curtains drawn, the shades? Where are their faces? Are they watching him on TV? Yes, some kind of universal closed circuit. But oh, it's not just for the eyes, this show. They have his thoughts for viewing, his inmost feelings. No escape. It's night, but never was he more visible, never more naked. The glare that reveals him is brighter than the sun. It's the light of consciousness. Whose? Why, his and theirs, all at once. "We're of one mind!" they say, with a fierce brilliant joy. But not in words. He hears it through his nerves, a voiceless thrill, univocal. And there is no denying it, All is One and One is All, and all is Consciousness. No escape. But neither can he surrender. It occurs to him to stop walking and stand still as a rock in a dark corner and silence his thoughts. That might make him invisible. But it's not allowed. Fear forbids it, his fear and their pleasure. For without his gulping dread, his wincing and pleading, his dodges and flights, his comically transparent ploys and darting subterfuges, there would be no sport.

The reason for it

"How can you believe it?" He asks himself that. How could he believe anything so preposterous? The Maker of worlds scurrying around London like a cockroach, handing out travelers checks to buy himself absolution, sleepless and terrified because his creatures have banded together to exterminate him, or worse. Why don't they step on him? Why this cruelty, this vivisection? He knows why: to redeem the cruelty. All of it, throughout all time, by bringing it upon himself. The cut worm forgives the plow, but not before the Maker of men who make ploughs has suffered himself to be cut and broken, mangled and speared. No, he can't disbelieve it. He is that monstrosity, that cockroach god, despised and rejected, immortal and therefore endlessly killable. All the pain will be redeemed. Beginning with this: exclusion from the community of love, the scapegoat's lot in every religion, always for God's sake and to redeem the sins of men, now his to suffer for their sake, the true redemption. No more substitutes. This is at last the true coin of the realm, of which other currencies are mere symbols. The fount of all value, the broken heart of God. That's why there's such excitement up there.

The shock

On the outskirts of the city, near some tracks. Red sunset colors on gray scudding clouds. His feet ache. He is still walking, but he no longer knows why. Not to escape, since there is no escape, nor is he searching for anything, since the thing to be found all along was himself, and they have found him. They have his body, his thoughts, what more do they want? His life? He's immortal, they know it. There must be some use to which they will put his eternity. He sees a tall tower made of crisscrossing steel bars. It looks like a praying mantis reared up on two feet, its small humming head and two other feet stark against the lurid sky. He approaches it. A sign warns him:

DANGER!
HIGH VOLTAGE!

Above the words is a red skull-and-crossbones. Maybe he can die after all. He steps through the gate formed by the tower's massive feet, expecting to be electrocuted. A surge of power lifts him onto his toes, twisting his entrails as he walks on, and releases him on the other side of the pylon.[2] He's not dead. Of course not! So what was that for? Ah, he gets it. Just another sign of what's to come. He will be the world's power source, its generator.

Hotel Acropolis

He knocks the door clapper of a small hotel. I don't know why it claimed his attention. Maybe the name: Hotel Acropolis. An old man in a bathrobe lets him in. As he signs the guest book, there is a very sinister sign: the ink in the pen runs out. He asks for another pen. The proprietor, intensely irritated, says: "Iss too late! Second floor! Number 8!" and hands him a key. He climbs the two flights of stairs, hesitates in front of the door: 8 is the sign of infinity. Then the overhead light goes out. He fumbles for the keyhole, opens the door. More darkness. A moment of panic: They're waiting for him, the devotees, this is the place! Then he finds the light switch. The room looks normal: a bed, a night table, a dresser, a closet, a washstand. Above the bed, a picture of the Acropolis. On the night table, a book. The curtains are drawn. He locks the door from inside. As if that could help him. They don't need keys, they don't even need to see through the walls. The stage of the drama is inside his brain. Better not turn off the light. He takes off Richard's moccasins. What a relief! Lies down on the bed without getting undressed. His eyes close of themselves. But he mustn't sleep. He sits up, reaches for the book by his bedside. The title is written in Greek letters. He opens it. Vertical rows of Greek words followed by English

---

2. I know I'm supposed to eschew all imagination, but I can't help wondering what happened there. Was it a real shock? Did I imagine it?

words. Some kind of dictionary. Why that in a London hotel room God only knows. But what am I saying? It's there to tell God what God doesn't *want* to know. He riffles the pages while his eyes select words at random. The mind links their meanings into a wordless prophecy that sees the future of God and the world: He will suffer the fate of animate and inanimate matter. Whatever distortion or injury, damage or ruin have been wrought upon earth, beasts, and men, will be suffered by him who made them. Because the word "cut" exists, he will be cut, and "rent, slivered, sliced" in the bargain. He will be eaten and drunk and excreted. He will be scrubbed, scoured, and burnished. He will ferment. He will be spilled and poured out, and drained drop by drop. He will be threshed and dragged. He will twitch, he will flutter. He will burst. He will be blinded. He will boil with rage. Terror will freeze the blood in his veins. The permutations are endless. And all these thoughts are themselves already the execution, by the cutting and gouging, fermenting, draining and bursting, etc., of his mental body. He flips the pages, searching for a way out or at least for a hint of the possibility of a reversal. There are such hints, but they prove to be ruses. Dante was wrong about hell being a place where hope is abandoned. Hope is the flywheel that keeps the infernal machine in motion. Without hope, despair would find its dead center and the soul would find peace in its torment. He closes the book, drops back on the bed, his eyes close. Something enormous is going on in there: a winding, twisting, and coiling movement, slow and continuous, huge strands of mind being braided into ropes, and those ropes in turn twisted, wound, and coiled into thicker ropes, cables. At the center, though: nothing. Just let yourself drop in there . . . No! Something or someone awaits him on the other side of sleep, crueler than anything he has endured or envisioned. He gets up, puts on Richard's moccasins, and goes back out into the night.

Sorcery

Night. A black car passes him slowly and takes a left turn by a white picket fence. He walks on. After a while another black car passes him slowly and takes a left turn. Wasn't there a white picket fence by that same corner the first time? But how could it be the same corner? No. A large striped cat crosses the street, running, and leaps, no, sails across the fence, much too high and much too long a leap for a cat. And the cat is too big for a cat. A sorcerer? Richard! He walks on. A black car passes him slowly and takes a left turn by a white picket fence.

The tree

Rows of small, nearly identical houses. The windows are dark. Where are the devotees? Only the street lamps shine. The lit-up trees look unreal. One tree in particular is alive in a way that no tree should be alive. It sees him, it stops him cold with a glare of all its leaves. Each leaf-tip is an eye.

"Who are you, thousand-eyed one?"

No answer, but he knows: This is the plural gaze of the One Mind. He stares back. Staring with the intent of outstaring the distance, annulling it. No distance, no difference, no seer apart from the seen. No doer apart from the deed, therefore. No maker, no thing made. No world, no creation. Wouldn't that be the end of the nightmare?

Above him—but this is something I perceive and he doesn't—a rustling in the branches . . . A crow . . . And another one nearby, shaking its tail feathers, glistening in the moonlight . . .

■   ■   ■

What happened, Counterpoint? Our scribe has gone silent.

C. I silenced him. He broke the rule I gave him. We were never in that tree.

But now we are. It's a cheap trick, Counterpoint, I know him. He was tired of taking dictation from memory. He wanted our wings.

C. And where does that leave him? Still at his desk in Brooklyn, taking dictation, this time from us. He will complete his assignment. He has no choice.

Counterpoint, I have the strangest feeling.

C. What is it?

That I've followed your lead exactly the way my past self down there followed his Guidance. And now that I find myself in this ludicrous disguise I see how crazy it was to follow you. But there's no turning back, is there?

C. No. And a good thing, because time is pressing. Our scribe is getting old at his desk in Brooklyn. His hair is white and thinning. There's a hint of arthritis in his writing hand. And that poor ghost who took himself for the Creator is still trapped in his hell, unaware that the future is on its way to release him.

Then I ask you again, Counterpoint: of what possible use are we to him as crows?

C. None whatsoever, because he can't see or hear us. But there may be some perspective to be gained from our position up here in this thousand-eyed tree.

What perspective? That's *his* delusion down there! I don't think it's wise to make it ours!

C. I suggest that you take a good look at your surroundings, and then a look at the looker as well.

Fair enough. What I see is, first of all, you in the form of a crow, your head tilted sideways, which I guess is a crow's way of looking at someone straight-on. . . . There's a glint in your eye . . . and reflected in that glittering pinpoint I see—of course!—another, minuscule crow's head, my own . . . all of which does not clarify matters, I'm sorry. Unless you intend to give me a lesson in optics.

C. You're not far off the mark. Carry on.

I see moonlit leaves all around, and that looks very nice. No thousand eyes, thank God. Two blue ones down there, though, staring up at me, Joel's. I take your word for it that he can't see me. Besides, I would remember it if he did. I can't see myself either, of course, except for one huge jutting beam of a beak, black, that swings left and right, up and down, as I turn my head. That's natural, I suppose, a trick of perspective—your beak doesn't look remotely as large. But I don't think that's the perspective you mean.

C. Not exactly. But you're starting to look in the right direction.

OK, what else do I see? Nothing. There's a kind of sensory seeing, the feeling of claws gripping a branch beneath me, tensing against minute shifts in my balance, and twitches in the dorsal muscles which, I presume, activate the motion of my wings. Frankly, I find this pedantic naturalism annoying and embarrassing, since there's nothing natural about this animal act. But there it is, I'm a crow. More precisely, I am a fiction perched on the memory of a hallucination. . . . Hmmm, that does raise the question: Who am I really?

C. Yes! Yes! Yes!

So that's what you meant!

C. It is. And here's my assignment to you: Ask yourself: Who am I? Nothing else. Who? You already know the power of this weapon. Only the fearless can wield it. Hold it poised like an arrow on the bow of your attention, and keep the drawstring taut. No need to aim, it will find its target. As soon as an answer presents itself, concrete or abstract, let go. Notice where the arrow strikes: always the heart. It's a feeling, a sweet yawning ache, the wound of unknowing. Again and again, arm the attention: Who am I? Who?

To what end, may I ask?

C. To ward off all pretenders to the throne of the First Person.

And who is . . .

C. The rightful heir? That's precisely the question. Don't forget it! Above all, don't leave this branch until Joel finds you.

Until Joel finds me? But he's already leaving . . . limping off into the fog. . . . Will he come back? I doubt it! . . .

Counterpoint? . . .

Gone. Sometimes he reminds me of that creepy Richard. . . .

Interlude: Mirrors and Dreams

That was ingenious of you, Counterpoint, putting that bird to a philosophic purpose. Though frankly I don't see the purpose of bringing in birds in the first place. And it spooks me that 28 pages back, when you and he first took wing together, he still considered himself the author of this book—as I do now. He seems to be under a spell. What happened to him?

No answer. But I know you are here.

What are you? You keep changing faces and functions: A tyrant? A magician? A judge? A trickster? A sage? Not that I expect you to tell me.

And I, here at my desk in Brooklyn—what am I about? I've stopped "tracing the outlines of the visible landscape"—not because I don't want to, but because the landscape is no longer visible. I must have strayed into the anti-mnemonic fog. No dreadful recurrence of forgotten terrors, thank God; no fearful revelations either. Just a slow, drifting, slantwise descent through a milky void. At least I think I'm descending. I'm not certain because I see nothing against which to measure this motion. Nevertheless I feel myself drifting softly through a milky whiteness, along with my desk, along with the wall I'm facing.

Isn't that how you came to me, Counterpoint? Long ago. Except yours was a gradual descent from boundlessness into form, and from form into speech, and the medium through which you descended was blue. I was afraid of you then. No longer, I'm relieved to say. In fact I can't even say that I don't trust you. But I do find your silence unnerving, because you know as well as I do, and probably better, that this book is being written to save my soul, and yet you leave me adrift in this whiteness.

(I notice that I said "my" soul, not Joel's. His fate is bound up with mine, of course—intimately, since I was he thirty years ago, and he is still present, still homeless, still wandering unremembered through the house of my fear, neither dead nor alive, but suffering! I am he and he was I.)

There, I've said it: You warned me a while back not to slip into my past self's

"I" lest I find myself trapped in his hell with him, or as him. I've dipped my toes in those torrid waters since, and I haven't drowned. So I'm ready, Counterpoint. If you would only release me from this fog.

But you don't respond. Maybe you're waiting for me to arrive somewhere. And maybe I should watch my "I"s for a while.

The drifting continues. On and off, the whiteness thins out into ragged strips and gives way to stretches of clarity. Then it returns. Aside from that, there is almost no movement. Only my pen is running along the page, and my lungs are breathing, out/in, out/in, like a steady, gentle surf. I am writing in peace. Somewhere else, out of my view, my feathered colleague is presumably asking his assigned question incessantly, his claws curled around a slim branch near the crown of the thousand-eyed tree. I wonder if his labors are the source of this peace that I feel? All is well in this leisurely drift of my pen.

How peculiar I look! I see one ruddy right hand protruding from a charcoal-gray sleeve, wielding a pen between a thumb and a frowning forefinger, and one ruddy left hand protruding from another charcoal-gray sleeve to steady the page; a pair of corduroy legs disappearing beneath the edge of the desk and a charcoal-gray trunk rising above it; and above this breathing torso, above its chest and shoulders, where a head might be expected, nothing at all—except for an enormous, semi-transparent nose—two noses actually, roughly as tall as the half-open door on my right and as wide as the window on my left, the gap between their converging tips just large enough to frame the page on which these words are being written. Looking up from the page and past my two noses, I see the above-mentioned wall, which is white with a few scattered minuscule specks, brick-red and pale blue. Above these, and slightly above eye level, is a picture I neglected to mention earlier (perhaps I didn't see it), an old print, hand-tinted by a later colorist, showing Goethe's yellow house in Weimar.

Still no word from my Counterpoint, but a sign: a faint touch on my shoulders, like that of a garment made of some gossamer-light material. I can't see it, but it's there. A cape of some kind, or a cloak. When I asked for its meaning, there was no answer, but my guess was confirmed by a glow of heart-warmth: an insignia. There's been a shift in our ranking order. I'm no longer the scribe. What am I, then? And what about Joel? How will I finish building the gate by which he will leave the labyrinth, when I myself am meandering? Will you kindly respond, Counterpoint?

And he did respond. Last night I dreamt that a man whose face I couldn't see was walking along the surface of an enormous globe in search of the city of London. He was wearing a hat and a long coat with an upturned collar. At first it seemed he was walking on a flat plane, but then I could see it was curved and that it was in fact the northern hemisphere of the earth, because it was covered with a grid of horizontal and vertical lines, and these lines converged toward the top and widened toward the bottom. It looked like a giant astronomical globe, but it was the earth, because not only was a man walking on it but I, too, was supported by it, lying on my back. Yes, I dreamed that I was lying on my back on the surface of the earth, and that a man with a face I could not see was walking along that surface looking for the city of London, and that he was orienting himself by lines of latitude and longitude. The earth was blue, as if all the continents had sunk beneath the sea. I wondered how the man could find anything here except an abstract location. London was not even a point on the map. Then I remembered that London had something to do with me. I had been there a long time ago. Something terrible had happened to me there. I was so unimaginably lost. But now, thank God, it was sunk beneath the sea. The man was walking in my direction, and as he came nearer, I heard a series of dull, heavy drumbeats. I still couldn't see his face—it was hidden behind the brim of his hat—but I noticed that he was very thin. At the moment when his foot touched me, I understood: I am the place where Joel is lost! My own brain is the labyrinth! My eyes opened. I was lying on my back in the dark, on my bed. Susan lay next to me, breathing evenly. My heart was beating. So that was the doom-speaking drum! I was relieved.

And then I saw myself walking in the house of my fear. But at the same time, the house was in me. When I say "I saw" I mean literally a seeing, as if a third eye had opened on a view that was hidden to my physical eyes. I shut those to see the view better. It was a city, the city of London, a maze of streets and buildings, and it was also a doll's house with millions of rooms. So small, so big! I was delighted by this ambiguity. It was small because the whole of it was capped by a domelike expanse of tingling sensations and high ringing noises that defined the roof of my skull. But it was also very large, because it was a city, not a doll's house, and this made my skull seem gigantic. Skull! Hours ago, I had lost sight of my head altogether. Now it was humming with presence, a spherical shell for this infinite doll's house, which was itself humming with millions of lives, though I only saw one body clearly. If I said that was Joel in his misery, it would be untrue, because there was no pain or fear. It was just me in my dreambody walking the dream-streets of London. There was a considerable sense of risk in that, since I knew that at any moment the eye of vision could open on hells that I had experienced three decades ago and had been mercifully allowed to forget. It even seemed likely that my Counterpoint might intend to push me down into them, as part of his plan to rescue Joel, and that he was enticing me to take this amble for that purpose. But feeling my larger, fleshly body at the same time, feeling my ringing and tingling scalp, especially, as a kind of surety, I wasn't tempted to drop the subtle thread of consciousness that was guiding me through the labyrinth. On the contrary, I felt safe enough to venture deeper into identification with my dreambody by letting the physical recede into the background. Susan's hand was near mine. If there was any real danger, I would reach for her hand.

Immediately a new presence appeared in the street. It was the little dog Joel had met and followed and lost and seen again in a pattern of broken plaster on a wall. It trotted ahead of me with a purposeful air, wagging its tail, looked around at me briefly, and disappeared around a corner. I followed it, turned the corner, and was surprised to find myself in a long hallway at the end of which hung the little baroque mirror that had hung in my room in Mexico when I was a child, and which I had loved for the flamelike forms on its gilded frame, even though it scared me at night when it reflected the light of a full moon, because the shape of the glass then resembled an eyeless, noseless, mouthless skull. Hadn't I written about this mirror somewhere? Yes, in the book I was writing, the one I was planning to call "In the House of My Fear." Good title. But where was that dog? Why was I losing him all over again? And what was that object reflected in the mirror? Another mirror! But the mirrored mirror was oval, with a narrow dark frame, and it was standing in a corner. The moment I recognized it I felt a jolt of electric alertness. It was fear, I suppose, but its immediate consequence was a sense of calm and contentment: I was embodied, not anchorless in the ocean of mind. The vision vanished. I opened my eyes and turned my head and saw that Susan was awake and watching me, smiling.

The oval mirror is a sharp reminder of an assignment I was given when I was in my twenties, before London, before Europe, before Acid, before Gina was born. I had read somewhere that one could consult one's dreams like an oracle: Write down an important question before going to sleep, and record the dream or dreams you awake from. The question I chose was: "What is my purpose in this life?" That certainly seemed important enough. The dream I awoke from went like this:

I was sitting in the middle of the big fountain in Washington Square in New York. The fountain was dry, as it usually is. A stern and very thin man gave me a large oval mirror and a cloth. The mirror was stained in several places. "Polish it until it's clear," the man said. I started polishing the mirror. The stains were not easy to remove. It would take a lot of work. "Make sure you're done by the time I return," the man said, turning away from me.

There was my answer. I imagined it meant that my purpose in life was to hone my skills as a writer, so that I could "hold a mirror up to nature." I didn't know what to make of the thin man.

A few years later I read about the poetry contest that determined the successor to the Fifth Patriarch of Chinese Buddhism. Shen-hsiu, the senior monk at Huang Mei Monastery, wrote a verse that excelled all others in succinctly summarizing the Buddha's teaching:

The body is the *bodhi* tree
The mind, a mirror bright.
Make sure to wipe it hour by hour
So no dust can alight.

How remarkable—that was my dream assignment! A Buddhist dream before I knew anything about Buddhism! And how instantly clarifying this explication was—like a swipe of a feather duster.

But Shen-hsiu didn't win the contest. Further down the page was another poem:

There never was a *bodhi* tree
Nor any mirror bright.
Since emptiness is all there is,
Where could the dust alight?

This rebuttal raised its author, an illiterate kitchen helper named Dajian Hui-neng, to supreme eminence in the hierarchy of Ch'an Buddhism. His four lines have brought enlightenment to many seekers. To me they brought bewilderment. For many years I gave no more thought to the thin man and the oval mirror.

What does this have to do with Joel in his labyrinth? Please tell me: What was the point, or counter-point, earlier, of all that urgency on Joel's behalf, of your shoving and driving me past several perfectly pleasant stations on the way, of whisking me through a tubular wave and bumping me off a rooftop until I was no longer sure if the time whistling in my ears was present or past, Joel's or mine; and what is the point, now, of that crow interrogating himself (and what's the point of his wings?); and this silly cloak on my shoulders, what is it good for unless it confers on me some power beyond my ordinary abilities to release Joel from having to make that ultimate descent again. (The deepest hell was an eternal repetition, I mustn't forget that.) Of what use is this metaphysical mirror talk to him, or to anyone?

Again I was answered in a dream. By the voice of a woman singing, a dark soulful alto. I heard it as I woke up this morning. The words were German and the music resembled one of Mahler's mournful *Kindertotenlieder.* The phrase that ended the song was: *"Da war kein Blick, der durch den Spiegel drang."* That means: "There was no gaze that penetrated through the mirror," which conveys little to me beyond an obvious reference to the various mirrors I've mentioned, but in German the words evoke an awful desolation. The moment I awoke, the horror of Joel's condition was revealed to me and was covered over as quickly as it appeared. This was not something that I dared to remember, and isn't now. It must be part of the landscape that is hidden in fog. Even a few years ago when I was translating Friedrich Dürrenmatt's fable about the Minotaur trapped in a labyrinth of mirrors, I didn't recognize myself.

When I was five or six years old, I was in just such a place. My parents took me to an amusement park in Mexico City. A big man with a big sombrero beckoned me with a hooked index finger: "Come into my hall of mirrors!" He said it was magic. He said I would see myself a million times. I looked to my parents, they smiled their approval and encouragement. The hall of mirrors was inside a small windowless house with a red curtain in place of a door. The man held open the curtain and bade me in with a bow and a sweeping gesture of one arm, as if I were a king. The curtain closed behind me. It was bright in the hall of mirrors. There I was, many many many times, just as the man had said. I walked along the path between the mirrors, and as I walked, all my mirror images walked along their mirrored paths. When I waved, they waved. When I stuck out my tongue, they stuck out their tongues. Their paths ran off in all directions, bumped into each other, branched off into new paths which in turn branched into more paths, on and on. My path alone was unbroken. It led by a zigzag route around sharp corners back to the curtain. But I didn't want to go out yet. There was something I had liked on the way. I walked back to where I could no longer see the curtain. Here I was alone with myself. I sat down on the floor. So many me's out there! They sat as I did, looking in all directions. Some of them had their backs turned to me. The further away they were, the smaller they got, like anything seen from a distance. There was no end to them. The ones furthest away were tiny, almost like stars. And they all did what I did. When I lifted a hand, they lifted their hands. When I lowered it, they lowered theirs. But my power was even greater than that. I closed my eyes and they disappeared. I opened my eyes, and they all sat there staring. With good reason! A million men with big sombreros had burst in on the million me's and gripped them by their collars and the seat of their pants. One of them was really me. The man who grabbed me was real too, and left no doubt about it. He called me a "*chingado.*" Why was he so mad at me? Why did my parents smile at him when he carried me out like a thing and deposited me, standing, at their feet?

The drifting movement continues, but I'm beginning to see a form in it. We're moving in a circle, slowly, or more likely an inward-turning spiral, with Joel at the center, and gradually gathering from the surrounding mist some element, still unknown to me, that is essential to his condition and maybe to his release.

The Last Day

1 to live and 1 to dy 2 boys gone
1 to lite and 1 to dark roading on
Never did the Good Luck brother
Tern a roun to help the other
Never did the other 1
Ever have the sents to run
      Russell Hoban, *Riddley Walker*

I see him now, limping painfully. It's dawn in London. Something tells him it is the last day. Whether it is the end of his life or the end of the world or both he does not know, but that he will find out before the end of the day he has no doubt at all. It's not a sign or a voice that tells him this but a wordless certitude, no different from mine right now of knowing that my Counterpoint is here, invisible behind my back. (But the moment I write this, I know that I don't know what I thought I knew a moment ago. That is the difference between us. I can doubt my own suppositions; he was compelled to believe his.)

The morning brightens. He needs to get back to the flat. Even though Richard is there. He has to sleep. All along he has been thinking that if he falls asleep, sheer hell will break loose. But if he doesn't sleep soon, something terrible will happen to his brain, and therefore to the world. If he finds his way back, he'll ask Gordon to pray for him while he sleeps. Gordon is a good man. Gordon believes in the holiness of love. But to find his way back, Joel needs a bus or a tube. The bus stations are vacant. The next train won't be running till 6:30 a.m. And when the time comes, which train should he take? In what direction? He doesn't even know the name of the district where his hosts live. Maybe that's why the Guidance is with him again in full force. It wants to show him the way, as always. Signs swarm all around him. The pavement especially is in a state of profusion, like the surface of boiling water: letters, words, diagrams, symbols.

Later that morning. The sidewalk glides toward him and past him like a conveyor belt, and so do lampposts, doors, and windows. He alone is motionless, though he feels his feet striding beneath him, a painful ache at each step. He won't last much longer, he knows this. Suddenly a familiar housefront comes into view. It's the House! The house where he lives!

His hosts are shocked by his appearance: beardless, with short-cropped hair. But there must be something else they see about him that makes them call out his name and rise to their feet when he enters. Dane, the compact blond guy with the brilliant blue eyes, takes him by the arm and conducts him to an easy chair, as if he were an old man, or wounded.

Gavin, the boy with the fey, girlish manner, brings him a cup of tea. The tea hurts his chapped lips as he drinks it.

"Did you find your car?" Richard asks, as if he didn't know. Joel doesn't answer. Gordon feels his forehead and brings him a cold wet cloth and wipes his face with it. Then Gordon takes Richard's moccasins off Joel's feet and washes his feet with the cloth.

"How about some sleep?" he asks. Joel nods gratefully and slides off the chair and stretches out on the rug. Gordon lifts his head and puts a pillow beneath it. They're preparing him. Let them. "Thank you," he says. His eyes close. Then they open again. If he falls asleep, the world will end.

He notices Richard staring at him, and turns his head to see him better.

"Thank you for the shoes," he says.

Richard nods and fixes him with his cold, pale blue eyes.

"What do you do with it?" Joel asks.

"With what?"

"With my soul."

"What are you talking about?"

"My soul. You took it."

Richard looks horrified. "Jesus Christ, I didn't take your soul!"

Joel believes him. He not only believes him, he is grateful to him for not taking his soul, and for his candor in letting him know that. Immensely grateful.

I'm very close to him now. I mean spatially close. He's lying on his back with his eyes shut, and I'm looking at his face from no more than five or six inches away. He looks contented for a while, and then troubled again. I know where his thoughts are taking him, but I'm not quite prepared to follow him there. So this exterior view will have to suffice, a perfectly accurate and completely misleading genre scene of the early seventies: four longhaired friends lounging and slouching around a table, smoking dope and listening to The Chicago Transit Authority,

Can you tell me   please don't tell me
It really doesn't matter anyhow

while a fifth man, stoned or sleepy, rests on the floor, his head on a pillow.

It's just that the thought of us so happy

The oddest thing in this picture is my own invisible presence: I'm like a ghost in this room.

A sudden shift, like a shadow passing over his face: For a moment he looked like Stefan. More precisely, like a particular memory I have of my brother asleep on a couch in our mother's apartment in New York. He was about twenty years old. Maybe it was the combination of those two circumstances—that he was so young and that he was asleep—that made the expression in his face so shocking. During the day he worked his rigid cheeks and tall frowning forehead into a mask of implacable sternness, a fortress against the assaults of "Evil," as he had begun to call his affliction. But now his will was dormant, the fortress walls were gone, and his features had relaxed into the form that time and suffering had wrought upon them. Such hopelessness, such sadness in a face that was still a child's.

I remember a dream I had when you were still alive. It was about two brothers who were to be hanged for crimes they had both committed. I believe they were twins. The gallows stood on the market square of the medieval town where they had lived. The criminals stood on upended barrels with nooses around their necks, and the townspeople thronged around them, waiting for justice to be done. A priest touched the criminals' foreheads with a cross. Then a magistrate unrolled a scroll of parchment and read aloud a proclamation that filled the townspeople with moral satisfaction—"Aaah!"—and the criminals with hope: One of the culprits was to be pardoned. But which? Their offenses were equal. The decision would have to be made by lot.

My brother. I have neglected you in this book. Several times as I wrote, I called you, half consciously, in my thoughts, but when you knocked at the door, asking for remembrance, I didn't open: He's too far away, I told myself, much too long gone, I can't see him, let alone touch him. And it was true, of course, because I thought so. But now you have come to me unbidden, and this time I won't refuse you. And that you came at this moment, as my past self approaches the brink of damnation: surely there is a meaning in that. Was it to remind me that my fate and yours were intertwined then, and still are?

So it's the whirlpool again, but this time a braiding of twin strands descending, you and I, Joel and Stefan. (In reality, of course, we did not go down together. And before you perished, I had recovered. Nevertheless, for the sake of harmonious form—even as the unalterable tale is being told—I will arrange our fates as if there were a balance and no disproportion of luck in our lives. I offer this fiction as an ornament to mark the void of our joint disappearance. Because, of course, I too will vanish.)

Joel

Before coming home, he thought he would sleep, but now he knows that he will never sleep again. If he slept, the world would come to an end, and he will not let that happen. The devotees know this, they know they can count on him to save the world. But that's not enough: The world needs redemption. A new and final golden age is being ushered in, an eternity of youth, health, and beauty, the direct yield of his eternal damnation. For there is no redemption without sacrifice. All the pain, all the grief, all the terror, all the waste, all the cruelty of life will be expiated by him. Forever! This is the end of Joel. To the future race of men on this planet he will always be the supreme culprit, the clown with the big red heart, the crucified hands, and the swastika on his forehead, who was shot like a rocket to heaven. Something for the children to laugh at. Maybe he'll be emblazoned on the night sky as a new constellation: the Exquisite Corpse. Will anyone pity him? No. Pity will be expunged from the human heart. Where pleasure reigns supreme, nothing is more useless than pity.

Stefan

I remember the surprise visit you paid me and Susan shortly before Christmas 1971. It was just a few months after I had been released from the netherworld, and I still had the crazy hope that by suffering through my ordeal I might have redeemed some of your karmic debt, and that by some law of correspondence that surely applied to brothers, my recovery was a warrant of yours as well. We got along that evening—without your flying into a rage and slamming doors, even without the usual portent, in your tensing cheeks and fingers, of an imminent explosion. But your quiet was due to Thorazine, a drug whose effects are inadequately described as tranquilizing. You could barely walk. It must have taken an enormous effort to transport yourself from your halfway house in the Village to our home in Brooklyn. You moved like an arthritic old man, with a hunchbacked shuffle, arms dangling. You had no appetite or else were afraid of eating, though you did toy with the plate of brown rice and stir-fried vegetables Susan had prepared for you. After dinner we talked, uneasily, about your chess games at the halfway house and, for the sake of balance, my esthetic games with the Xerox machine at the office where I worked. (What a blessing the 9-to-5 grind had been for the first few weeks after my recovery! Even the act of punching the time clock was a blessed confirmation, twice a day, that I had rejoined the ranks of the normal. Until boredom, the true proof of normalcy, set in.)

"You won't succeed," you said then, half mumbling, as if talking to yourself.

"What?"

"Your job . . . You can't make market research agreeable to the spirit. . . . Also, you can't make art on a Xerox machine."

I resented that admonishment, and especially the manner in which it was delivered. Your face was set in a mask of scowling sternness. Your hands were folded in your lap, with the tips of your thumbs touching. I even thought I had heard, as I had on previous occasions, a trace of an Indian accent.

We played chess later on. You drew the white pieces, but made an error in the Queen's Gambit which cost you a pawn. I was tempted to let you regain the advantage. But then you played so cleverly and with such engagement that I felt justified in playing as well as I could. Now the game was a pleasure for both of us. Your scowl disappeared and gave way to a look of calm concentration.

In the end, though, when you resigned by tipping over your King, you were exhausted.

I asked you whether the Thorazine affected your playing. "It improves it," you said. "Chess is the one thing Thorazine improves."

I think it pleased you when I laughed at your joke, but I couldn't tell.

You stood up and looked down at me, heavy-lidded, unsmiling, depleted. "Where can I sleep?"

I laid out a sleeping bag for you on the floor in Gina's room. When she woke up early the next morning, while Susan and I were still asleep, you were looking out the window. Then you helped her build a castle with her blocks, mumbled something about frying an egg, shuffled toward the kitchen, then changed your mind and left the house.

That afternoon Alma called: "Joel! Stefan just jumped out of his window!" The police had notified her. We saw you at St. Vincent's Hospital a little later. You were conscious. Your skull and forehead were wrapped in white bandages, helmet-like, and from beneath the rim of this helmet you were observing us with glittering curiosity.

I stepped up to you: "Stefan?"

You smiled: "I should have moved Pawn to King four."

Maybe. Maybe that would have made all the difference.

Joel

A crushing weight presses down on his chest: **NEVER AGAIN** . . . Now Susan's voice sounding very close pronouncing his name in a tone of heartbroken love. She's waiting for him in New York, wondering why he hasn't answered her mail, hasn't **CALLED**, worried sick about him but better that than knowing who he really is, or worse, being forced to partake to any degree in the horror of his condition. . . . **FORCED**: The thought engenders a whirl of possible, probable fates, and on the most cruel of these the mind confers the iron insignia of certainty: Susan a slave, the unloved chattel of some crude redhaired bloke whom a closer look reveals to be the policeman who took down the license plate number of his car.

Stefan

After a week in the hospital, you seemed transformed. You were charming, sensitive, and friendly. Your skeletal frame had put on a healthy plumpness. You went on ice cream and chocolate binges and reproached yourself for them, not morally but out of concern for your waistline. There was a mild, childlike softness in your smile. But when Alma and I expressed our amazement that you were well again—mentally well, emotionally—you were surprised. Deranged? Deluded? For years? You'd had a difficult time, absolutely, but still, it was a dedicated existence, disciplined, more purposeful and fundamentally more ordered than most people's lives. Nothing crazy about it. What were we talking about?

"Stefan," Alma said, "you jumped out of a window."

"I did nothing of the sort. Someone pushed me. That place was full of crazy people."

"And how do you think you got there?" I asked.

You heard my anger. You sat up.

"I'll tell you how I got there. I made the mistake of telling you guys about the company I was keeping. Sane people don't have conversations with dead people, especially not *famous* dead people, and if they do, they don't talk about it. But I did. So naturally you called the police. I misjudged you, both of you. The rest was Thorazine and some very bad luck. My hip is broken. The doctor tells me I'll never be able to sit in the lotus posture again."

I was boiling, but I kept my mouth shut. I had half a mind to confront you with the desperate pencilled messages you had left around for an unknown benevolence to answer, the dismembered, gutted bodies in your drawings; or better, since the drawings and notes could with some justification be defended as art, remind you of the day you knocked Alma to the ground and kicked her; the day you smashed your bedroom window; your nightly retching in the bathroom; the trail of blood Alma found in the kitchen after you had half-heartedly cut your wrist. But I couldn't bring myself to say anything. I was confused by the righteousness of my own anger. What did I want from you, repentance? As if you were *wrong* and not simply sick. And I didn't want to risk a fight with you.

Joel

After Susan, Gina. After Gina, Alma. After Alma, Stefan.

Everyone he loves will be destroyed.

The world is not worth saving.

Did they hear that?

Silence.

Words now, roared by a million voices:

THE WHOLE WORLD'S WATCHING!
Bass thump cymbals climbing
THE WHOLE WORLD'S WATCHING!

piano teeters on a halftone

THE WHOLE WORLD'S WATCHING!

fourfold trumpet blast discordant

Faces full of hate and fear

Faces full of me

What if the roles are reversible? As they sometimes are in a bullfight? What if the game, for the Enemy, entails a risk—because without risk there would be no excitement? No game, in fact, only the tedious execution of a plan? And what is that risk for the Enemy, but a weapon ever ready in his victim's power. . . . And what is that power if not his dreaded power to sleep, and by that sleep to end EVERYTHING. . . . A sleep so final that all light is swallowed by darkness and with it all possible future days. . . .

No thought . . . No world . . . No life . . .

Run you better run you know

The end is getting near

Someone covers him with a light blanket. He opens his eyes, it was Gavin. His eyes close again. Gratitude floods him like sunlight. The blanket was blue, like Gina's blue blanket. Her baby words, "Blankins" and "coveh me," sound in his ear, exactly the way she always spoke them in her little voice. . . .

And they'd love to burn you

Or at least to turn you

round

How easy it is after all . . . to give it all up . . . and how strangely happy he feels

Boom

There goes New York

Boom

Moscow?

Boom

The music stops

Good night . . . How strange . . . he is happy . . .

Brutal shouts. The light goes on.

Stefan

At Albert Einstein Memorial Hospital you were forced to submit to daily interviews with the chief psychiatrist, Dr. Rubin. "Interviews" sounds like polite Q&A sessions. Not likely! You despised the man's profession, and I'm sure you let him know that. But I don't think he was vain, and he couldn't have been stupid, because, amazingly, you came to respect him. And then: "I think he can help me"—you actually said that to Alma. I don't know how he did it. He must have respected *you*. But then he had you transferred to a halfway house, medicated to the gills, with a small monthly stipend to live on. No more sessions with Dr. Rubin. He didn't take outpatients.

He left you with a "Good luck" and a warning: "If you want to get well, don't live with your mother." There was a theory at the time that paired every schizophrenic with a "schizogenic" mother. Maybe that was Dr. Rubin's diagnosis of Alma.

After your leap from the window, Alma called Dr. Rubin and begged him to visit you—she had to beg, because he didn't want to—and eventually he did. It probably wasn't a good idea. I think you were hurt when he didn't come again. When I mentioned his name, you shrugged and turned your head away.

But your bones received expert attention. The chief surgeon at St. Vincent's recommended a "pinning" to secure the position of the femur in the socket of the broken pelvis. You signed a release for the operation, which was promptly and successfully performed.

Last night I woke up with the following thought, fully formulated:

"Let 'I' be a bridge between past self and present."

Maybe it came from my Counterpoint. I don't know. I must have been working on this problem all along.

A bridge! Frankly, I don't want that particular self to cross over here to my desk in Brooklyn. But I understand. This is a rescue operation, and courage is needed. And besides, I may not have a choice: For days now I haven't been able to write another sentence about "Joel."

But I'll write in the past tense. Keep time flowing back from now to then, not the other way around. Never!

Far off in the shadows, I can hear that crow reciting his mantra: "Who am I?"

Why this anxiety? My heart is beating faster. At the same time, I feel the weightless touch of the invisible cloak around my shoulders. It's been there all along, but now it claims my attention. It has a calming effect. Maybe it's there to protect me.

Joel

I imagine there may have been more than two men who barged into the flat, but I remember only a tall dark-haired lantern-jawed guy with sideburns and a shorter pasty-faced fellow who was starting to go bald. They wore cheap suits and ties, and though they played their parts with conviction and energy, they never stopped looking amused—like intelligent actors in a bad play. I could see why. The timing of their arrival was just too absurdly miraculous, their B-movie getup and manner too broad to be taken seriously even by themselves. A sublime joke, really, bringing in this campy deus ex machina at the last minute to save the world, and from what? From an act of God! But only a monster would be amused by this joke, and who was that monster but I—I!—who, unbelievably but undeniably, had dreamed up the whole cosmic charade. Monstrous beyond all imagining.

Richard and Gavin and Gordon and Dane leaped to their feet. Maybe they were ordered to, but I hadn't heard the command, so I merely raised my head and supported it on my left palm. This contemplative attitude got me into trouble. The man with the sideburns roared at me, smiling: "GET UP!" He patted me down and told me to turn out my pockets. There was only small change in them.

"Where's your coat?"

"Over there," I said, pointing to my jacket, which was hanging over the back of a chair.

"We've got a Yank here," he said to his colleague. He searched my coat pockets, then riffled through the contents of my wallet.

"The bastard's loaded." (Not true—those were my last 400 pounds, in 10-pound denominations.) Then he stuck a hand in one of the pockets and pulled out a fist-sized lumpy object wrapped in tinfoil. Was he a magician, like Richard?

"What have we here," he said. He peeled back the tinfoil and held up the corpus delicti like a jewel, turning it in the light: a chunk of hash.

"Now you're going to tell me you've never seen this before."

"I haven't," I said.

"What's it doing in your coat pocket then?"

I shrugged. Why get embroiled in such trivia? There were deeper hells to descend to.

Stefan

One day you asked me to bring you a manuscript you had been forced to abandon when we had you committed to Mount Sinai. It was in your room at Alma's place. You were eager to take it up again; it needed a foreword, you said. And you wanted to hear my opinion of it. My heart sank when I saw what it was: a spiritual treatise in the tradition of Alice Bailey and Madame Blavatsky, but a good deal crazier than theirs. It purported to be dictated by several omniscient directors of human evolution, and its purpose was to prepare us all, through your mediumship, for the practical as well as theoretical fusion of occult science, Yoga, Mahayana Buddhism, and dialectical materialism—a total revolution of mind and society. Months earlier Alma and I had heard, through the closed door of your room, your typewriter clattering on and on with incredible rapidity, by day and by night, for hours on end. How could anyone write so fast? Alma thought you must be copying something. But it was too fast even for that, because you hardly ever paused. I figured it was one of the many autotherapeutic techniques you had invented, maybe a way to outrace your own brain or short-circuit some mental compulsion. I was amazed, then, to see the product of those sessions: some fifty legal-sized, single-spaced, unparagraphed pages ranging in subject matter from cosmology to mathematics to biochemistry to atomic theory to political science to pedagogy to transpersonal psychology to apocalyptic prophecy, varying in style from a weirdly bloodless, scientist sort of prose replete with arcane diagrams and hierarchic enumerations to passages of grand poetic sweep and intellectual passion. It ended in a kind of coda, written in free verse, each line beginning with "I," at once personal and of a galactic remoteness, in which you proclaimed your irrevocable victory over such crippling allurements as food, comfort, sleep, and love. When you asked me if I had read it, I said, much too awkwardly, that I had been unable to give your paper the attention it probably deserved. I said I thought the poems, plays, letters, essays, and journals you used to write more valuable, and that also I no longer trusted or enjoyed occult philosophy in general.

"Meaning . . . ?" you asked, since I was clearly talking out of one side of my mouth.

"Meaning I would rather hear your own voice than any other voice speaking through you."

You took in this rejection with a complacent equanimity that I found insulting, as if you were too sure of your accomplishment to be troubled by the incomprehension of a lesser mind.

Joel

On the way to the police station, the two narcs sat with us in the back of the paddy wagon. The one with the pasty face lit a cigarette, and held out the pack to his prisoners. The man with the sideburns grinned. Gavin, Dane, Gordon, and Richard, each of them took a cigarette. It was the politic thing to do. But I shook my head and explained that I didn't smoke. "Tobacco," Richard said. That struck Sideburns as funny. Shaking with laughter, he said something about me in cockney which I didn't understand and that made everyone laugh, Gordon too. Then Gavin said something that made the narcs laugh. Again the meaning of the words escaped me. The mood was oddly convivial, as if the parts they all played were just masks adopted by mutual agreement, a jugglers' fraternity from which only I was excluded. So they knew who I was, and had known all along. Soon everyone would know. More wisecracks followed. I didn't understand anything. Sideburns made a slack-wristed masturbating gesture, indicating me with a tilt of the head. This time only the pasty-faced man laughed. I turned away and looked through a narrow window covered with wire mesh.

■

A little later (still in the paddy wagon) I heard Gordon's voice: "You think you're in charge here, don't you?"

I turned my head and saw the pasty-faced man staring at him, dumbfounded.

"You're not in charge. Your power is on loan, you'll have to give it back someday."

The narc glanced at his colleague, I suppose for advice or support, but Sideburns was as surprised as he was. I too was amazed at Gordon's courage. He wasn't afraid. Was it his faith that gave him courage? He had a big cross dangling over his chest.

Quietly, with menace in his voice, the pasty-faced man said: "What are you trying to tell me?"

"I'm telling you that you have a soul."

The narc looked disgusted and also embarrassed, as if Gordon had exposed a weakness in him, and that was the end of that conversation.

■

A large square empty room with benches alongside the walls. Dane is sitting next to me and the other three sit at a right angle to us. My whole body is trembling. Dane brings his face up close to mine, bores his fanatical blue gaze into my eyes (I suppose he's trying to steady me), and starts singing:

I taste your blood

Those four words set the tone and frame the meaning of the rest of the song. I listen carefully, but I'm not sure I'm hearing it right. What I think I am hearing is a song of thanksgiving addressed to the crucified Christ by someone who is drinking his blood.

■

We're being marched down a hallway and up a flight of stairs. Sideburns gives Richard a shove in the back, "Move!" and I, reflexively, shout: "Don't do that!" Sideburns wheels around, a gleeful look on his face, his fist comes toward me with surprising slowness, slow enough for me to observe how it gets bigger as it comes nearer, bigger than his face, until it connects with my forehead, producing a shower of bright lights. Then a policeman steps around where I'm sitting on the floor and, laughing, says something to me in passing which, again, I am unable to understand.

Stefan

After three months at Saint Vincent's, you were able to walk, very laboriously, with the help of crutches, and you were transferred to a psychiatric ward. The place was pleasant enough, all things considered. Care had been taken to remove as much as possible any resemblance to a prison or even a hospital. You had a private room with a view of poplar branches and a large patch of sky. It was spring. The reviving year could be felt even in this troubled place. The patients milled around in their pajamas and bathrobes, talking and smiling. A loud group of checkers players competed all day, just like in Washington Square Park.

You kept a distance from all these people, except for a young woman who strangely resembled you—not so much your present self, but the monkish, emaciated person you had been until recently. She had shaved her head, as you once had, and the hair was just beginning to grow in. She wore round wire-rimmed glasses like yours. Like you, she had large protruding ears, a thin straight nose with a vertical furrow over the bridge, blue eyes, a tall smooth forehead; and she had the same extremely pale skin dotted with faint yellow-brown freckles.

You told us her story when we asked you. (In the past you would have bristled at the intrusion.) How very much like you she was even in her way of rationalizing her situation. She had no "psychological problem." The reason she was at Saint Vincent's was that her parents didn't understand Buddhism and mistook meditation for catatonia. She had fasted for several weeks and kept a vow of silence—that was the extent of her aberration. But she had learned a lesson, she said: There was only one home for her, the nunnery in Nepal she had foolishly abandoned; one family, the Sangha; one parent, the Tibetan teacher who had guided her for more than a year; one love, the Buddha. As soon as she got out of Saint Vincent's, she would get a job and earn her fare back to Nepal, and never again succumb to a craving for a childhood she had outgrown. You told us these details with a kind of solemnity that impressed me.

Once when I came to visit, I found her sitting in a chair by your bedside. You were both smiling, and from what I could gather, talking about your memories and your plans for the future. You too had been in Nepal, you too would return there someday. You had exchanged amulets and beads you had bought in the Himalayas, and now you were wearing them for each other.

She was released after three or four weeks. She continued to visit you, though. Each time I saw her, she looked more and more like a pretty young woman and less and less like a nun. The intervals between her visits grew longer. She had a job now—her psychiatrist had needed a secretary, and so . . .

You didn't seem hurt, maybe because it was in the nature of your understanding with her that there should be no attachment. After all, you were Buddhists.

One day she received an amazing job offer, as if by divine intervention: She was to translate some ancient Tibetan texts into English. You told me about her great stroke of luck with joy and with pride, as if she were your sister. That was the last I heard of her.

Joel

I'm locked into a tall narrow echoing cell. Nothing in it, not even a chair. No latrine either.[3] A neon light in the ceiling, graffiti on the walls, mostly names and initials. To me they speak as if in chorus:

---

3. Unless I've forgotten. But neither do I remember smelling urine.

Don't forget me! I was here!

To whom is this appeal addressed? To me, to me! Poor criminals, poor slaves. They don't know how guilty their God is, and how helpless. But now his sins will wash them clean.

There's a pencilled word, retraced to make the letters bold:

P R A Y

To whom is it addressed? Not to me. Who would hear God's prayer?

And there's another word, scratched into iron with a fine-pointed instrument:

H E L P

Oh, but it looks much too quiet on the page, too sober, too level, too neutral, too *standard*. There was nothing standard about the word on the door. It was made up of bundles of jagged slashes. It quivered in grotesque, obscene, naked, cowering anguish. To whom was this silent scream addressed? To me, to me!

Stefan

Your release from the hospital was sudden and unexpected. We were all caught by surprise, you too. You had been vaguely considering going back to school, possibly to study medicine, but no practical arrangements had been made. What would you do now? And where would you live? Alma's place was out of the question. Not only because of Dr. Rubin's advice. You yourself were afraid of going back there, like a moth to a candle, to confront once again the horrible perpetuity of those carpets, plants, paintings, lamps, to be surrounded again by those peeling walls, everything permeated with her touch and breath, and worst of all the petrifying pity in her gaze; to have to protect yourself once again from those malignant vibrations by painting the walls of your room with cryptic designs and rearranging the furniture in it and perfuming its air with incense and silent austerity. And of course it was inconceivable for her, for us, to put you back into a halfway house; nor should you be made to live alone. I invited you to stay at our place—not without misgivings, because of our difficult relationship in the past—until some other solution offered itself; and you gratefully, I think even eagerly, accepted. Alma offered to pick you up in her car.

A strange dispute developed the next day when Alma arrived at the hospital. In your presence (that was unwise of her) she began to beg the resident psychiatrist not to send you out into a world you weren't prepared to live in. He replied that staying in the hospital wouldn't do you any good, that what you needed to do now was to practice walking. She pleaded with him: "Walking is the least of his problems. . . . You know it, doctor! He's a very sick boy, he needs medical attention. . . . Please . . . He tried to kill himself!" The doctor reminded her ("so coldly," she told me later) that you had already signed the release form, and that besides, you were not a "boy." You were twenty-seven years old and able to make your own decisions. That remark set you in motion. You limped out of the room on your crutches, leaving your suitcase for her to carry after you.

Joel

He screams (it's "he" again, there's no way "I" can inhabit that scream and continue to write). It begins as a bellow, a roar—of an animal, hunted, tormented— and ends as a word. A human word, and more than that, a prayer for beast and man alike:

"LOVE!"

When I was a child, I once heard the screams of a pig as it was being slaughtered. For hours those pitiful shrieks repeated themselves in my memory. What had the butcher done to inflict such agony? Had he stuck a knife in the pig's heart, or slit its throat? Probably—a blow with a sledgehammer would have silenced it sooner. Why were people so cruel? Those questions subsided gradually along with the mental echo of the screams, but then, a few days later, a new question arose: What was the purpose of a scream like that? Everything in nature had a purpose and a use—we had learned that in school. Dandelion seeds were built like parachutes so that the wind could carry them to where they would take root and grow into new dandelions. Birds sang to mark their territory. Cows mooed to keep the herd together. But of what use were those screams to that poor pig, or to other pigs who heard them in their pens? None at all. Or was there a larger purpose? Because the sound carried very far—across the lake to my ears, for instance, and maybe beyond the neighboring villages. Everyone could hear it. Was there some purpose in that? Not really. People had to eat, and one of the things they ate was pork, so the scream of a slaughtered pig was in the natural order of things. Pigs had always been slaughtered, and would be forever. But still, that scream was meant to be heard. By whom? And then the idea suggested itself that the scream was meant for God's ear. That it was a complaint to God, who alone had the power to set matters right in the world, and who had made pigs and men as they were. And that God, if he heard the pig, would be very sorry.[4] But there was another possibility; what if God had involved himself in the Creation in such a way that he himself was all the creatures he had made, and that he was lost in these creatures and looked out through their eyes and wondered who the other creatures were, half remembering that they were all himself? So that, when a pig screamed because a man had stuck a knife in its heart—maybe a man who had fed it and treated it kindly until now—that scream was God's scream to his own lost self: Wake up! Have mercy!

And now that boy is a man who believes he is God and who screams the word "love" into the world.[5] It makes me laugh, here at my desk in Brooklyn. I know I shouldn't laugh, but it strikes me as funny: He's trying to edit the Creation. Stop the presses! The book of life is horribly imperfect! Because the Word, the Word which was in the beginning, the Word which was God, was the wrong word! Let there be love! Let this word answer the word on the door!

"LOVE!"

He screams it again and again. Each time, the sound changes slightly, and gradually the meaning of the word changes as well. It's as if he were sculpting it, shaping it, and at the same time stripping it of all foreign matter: grief, for instance, and hope. It's no longer a plea or a prayer, but an order. To whom? To all. A first and last commandment:

"LOVE!"

Maybe if his eyes were open, he would imagine the word breaking through the wall or through the iron door like a cannonball. But his eyes are shut and the word expands in all directions and towers up to heaven:

"LOVE!"

(For a moment, here at my desk in Brooklyn, I saw it as a mushroom cloud looming over the edge of the sea. Fear canceled the image the moment it

---

4. That, of course, was not something East German kids learned in school. Religion was not in the curriculum. But it was in the music my mother played on her violin and viola, in the poetry I read, in the paintings reproduced in books we had in our house, in the rituals of Christmas and even in the gonging bells of the sixteenth-century church across the lake.
5. If he only remembered the boy's vision of the creator lost in his creation, he would be very near the door that leads out of the house of his fear.

appeared. This was no longer amusing. What are thirty years, or three hundred miles, to a force like that?)

"LOVE!"

There, it's honed to perfection now. It's no longer a commandment. That would entail the possibility of disobedience, and hence of failure. It's not even a communication, but an iron decree, an impersonal law of nature. Though it issues from his mouth, he no longer feels himself to be its author. It's as if the word were proclaiming itself, roaring itself, with a will of its own, into the fathomless ear of space:

"LOVE!"

The door opens. Two men enter the cell, a policeman and a man carrying a black satchel. The supreme being contracts into a body cowering on a stone floor.

"What's the matter?"

He turns his head away, stares at the floor.

"I brought you a doctor."

What kind of doctor? What's in that bag? Knives? No, much, much worse and therefore much more probable: his journals, the records of his dreams, the protocols for his psychiatric interrogation, the insulin, the electrodes.

"I don't need a doctor."

Silence.

"Are you sure?"

Emphatically, still looking at the floor: "No doctor."

The door closes with an iron bang, a key turns the lock. Receding steps, muffled words. Then: "Not even a thank-you . . ."

Stefan

You were smiling when you walked into our apartment. There was a swagger in your walk, despite the crutches. Our young dog, Tommy, who ordinarily barked at strangers, greeted you so enthusiastically he almost knocked you over. You let him lick your hands and face, took his head between your hands, rubbed your cheek into the soft fur around his neck. After a few days, Tommy was more attached to you than to anyone else in the family. You "set up headquarters," as you put it, in the living room, sleeping on the couch and arranging your books in a row on the floor alongside the wall. You spent a lot of time reading. You weren't very communicative, but neither did you shut yourself off, as you used to do. You were in good spirits, and we got along well.

Joel

Late afternoon. Another police van, larger than the paddy wagon, more like a bus, driving through London. Through a narrow window slit covered with wire mesh I see people walking, their motions arrested as they flit by. Not one of them glances in our direction. We have been rendered invisible. For a moment this "we" fills me with comfort, but then I remember that I can never be part of a "we" again, not even the society of criminals. That's why I'm locked into a tall narrow metal cubicle by myself. There are ten or twelve other prisoners on the bus, my four friends among them, and also several policemen, but since I can't see them, it's as though they weren't there—as if no one had ever existed except myself. As if, as if—oh, I wish it were true! Back in that dungeon, when I called out the word "love," it seemed almost possible—and not the worst of all possible fates, as I used to think whenever I came near the brink of it—not at all. It would be a godsend, truly!—and this pun a true joke, the truth as a joke, which I could laugh at through all eternity! Why not? It's better than the alternative. And more plausible! Haven't I been at the mercy of phantoms all along, figments which I took for real? Those fiends who swarmed all around me, begging for money, so similar to the blood-sucking flies in Saanen . . . that haughty woman who told me about the devotees, and that absurdly broad-chested cop who blocked my way before she showed up . . . the sailing cat and the Hotel Acropolis . . . *Richard,* with his pharaoh's stance and his magic tricks, turning butter into carrots, for Christ's sake, was there ever a more *obvious* chimera! And those two narcs, straight out of central casting, or *Alice in Wonderland* . . .

"You're just a pack of cards!"

That's what she said to the mad cricket players . . . and they were what she said they were! Playing cards throwing royal tantrums, whacking hedgehogs with flamingo mallets, chopping off heads . . . but with those six wonderful words, the dream was dispelled! . . . Try it! Try it! Blow them away!

And he does try it, by sounding the ultimate dream-dispelling word:

"OOOMMMM . . ."

over and over, louder and louder. His voice attunes itself to the pitch of the motor, the metal walls resonate with the drone of the sacred syllable . . . over and over, louder and louder:

"OOOOOOOOOMMMMMMM . . ."

The door opens, a laughing policeman sticks his head in: "You'd better cut it out, or you'll wake everyone up!" and slams the door shut again.

Stefan

The Welfare Department sent you a postcard. You had missed an appointment with your caseworker in Brooklyn and were asked to come for an interview at their central office in Manhattan.

"What's this about your being on Welfare?" I asked. It was the first mention of it I'd heard.

"There was a social worker at Saint Vincent's, she made the arrangements."

"So why didn't you go?"

You shrugged. "It's just about filling out forms."

"Well, yeah, so you can get money that you're entitled to, and so Alma doesn't have to support you."

You smiled slyly. "You mean 'out of her meager pension'?"

"Yes, I admit it, I'm trying to make you feel guilty."

"You're right. I'll take care of it. They scheduled me for next week. By then I'll be able to walk better."

You kept your promise. You went to the Welfare office, stood in line for half an hour, leaning on your crutches, in a badly ventilated room with hundreds of sweating men, women, and children, waited three more hours sitting on a chair, all in order to answer a few questions that could just as well have been answered by mail.

"I told you it was bullshit."

"Well, at least now it's behind you."

"It's not, that was just the beginning."

"Why, what's next?"

"More appointments, more paperwork."

You missed those appointments. You also missed several appointments for physical therapy. I learned about those from Alma.

"Jesus, Stefan, you really should go there."

"I don't think so. My hip is healing by itself. Just don't worry about me, OK? I'm so sick of people worrying about me."

How could we not worry. You were starting to retreat from life. You were losing your appetite and had to be urged to eat. It was impossible to include you in all our activities—I had to go to work, for example, and Susan took Gina to a playgroup every morning—nor did you want that. Still, you felt excluded, not through any willful coldness on our part but, much worse, by the natural order of things. You began to show a painful uneasiness in our presence, as if you could think of no other way to make yourself belong in our world than to mutely observe it, and when that started getting embarrassing, to retreat into the sanctuary of your private thoughts. You spent hours sitting on the couch, almost motionless, apparently in a state of sullen brooding, camouflaged at first by books and magazines that you held in your hands but were obviously not reading, until these were replaced by a perpetually rock-'n-rolling portable radio on your lap. The fawning advances of the dog only irritated you. Once or twice you gave him a painful kick.

I became concerned that Gina might be disturbed by these developments, but I was mistaken. She accepted your stony unresponsiveness as a matter of course and filled the tense silence at mealtimes with her usual gay, random chatter.

You were falling apart again, swiftly and visibly. All the old symptoms were returning, and there was a look I had seen in your face before, but never so unguarded or for such a long time. It was sorrow—a sadness so defeated, so abandoned by all hope that it made one want to cry out "We love you, you're safe, it's all right." At night, through the curtain that separated our bedroom from the living room where you slept, Susan and I could hear you practicing pranayama with a manic pedantry that left no doubt about the earnestness of your will to renounce the world.

Joel

Brixton Prison. A large noisy hall full of men. Some are standing, most are sitting on benches, talking, waiting. They're all dressed in brown. So am I, but my outfit is clownishly outsized. There's a storm outside, so loud and so close someone near me says "it's the end of the world." Naturally! It's the end of the last day. Once they're done with me, it's the Golden Age.[6] A guard, earlier, said

---

6. "It's not right! It's not fair!" Somewhere deep inside, far away, Joel rails against the mask of God.

we were here for "reception." Such a courteous word for a ritual of humiliation. But some of the men look expectant, excited, and it's not just on account of the storm. There's a gesture that springs from body to body like a contagion, I've seen it before in the streets, a darting, grasping thrust of a hand. Sometimes a kick is added, or a chop with the edge of the other hand. Every few minutes someone performs one or the other of these violent gestures, or a variant of them, and always it's followed by eager nods and laughter.

Where are my friends from the house, my helpers? Only Richard is here.

Skulking, as usual, with his hands in his pockets. He's avoiding me. Just as well.

Suddenly the lights go out and a cheer goes up in the darkness. I'm sure they'll fall upon me now and tear me to pieces. Like those ants I saw feasting on a live worm. No one touches me. The darkness persists. Someone shouts something, others laugh, then there's more shouting and laughter and darkness, and then a stupendous double flash lights up the room and reveals the bodies in it as puppets, like dancers in a strobe light, their gestures stopped in mid-motion. One of them is Richard, looking straight at me, his right hand raised in an apostolic gesture, as if to bless or subdue, a strand of blond hair draped around his head like a golden circlet. Darkness again, a fearful crash of thunder, the electric lights go back on, another cheer, I look around, Richard is nowhere in sight. I look in all directions. Gone. How does he do it? Was he here at all? Was he just an apparition? Is anything real?

A young man tugs at another man's sleeve, points in my direction, they snicker: "What kind of . . . ?" I look down at myself. My uniform is four, five sizes too large. The sleeves hang down to my fingertips, the elephantine pant legs bunch up over my feet. An older man with the furrowed, sly face of a care-worn Ulysses stares at me with an expression of sad disbelief, more disgusted than pitying, shakes his head, turns away.

Stefan

A friend who was leaving town for a month invited you to stay in her apartment, asking that you water her plants in exchange. Some friends of hers from Boston would join you for at least one long weekend, so you wouldn't be entirely alone. Her place was just a few blocks from ours. You welcomed this opportunity as gladly as we did. Susan and I helped you pack your bags and carried them to your new home.

One of the four people who arrived from Boston the following weekend was André, a Nigerian student who wanted to explore New York during the last week of his stay in the United States, but was afraid to do so without a guide. The moment you heard this, you emerged from your shell to offer your services. You could walk by now, haltingly, with a cane. The exercise would do you good.

The two of you stopped in at our place on the way home from one of your excursions. You were exhausted, but what a wonderful change in your mood and appearance: visibly proud and contented. André was radiant with admiration for what he called "the bigness of life" in New York. Especially in Harlem, he added shyly. I liked him very much, and wanted to thank him for what he was doing for you, but then I realized by the way he spoke and listened to you that he wasn't acting from charity but from fondness and respect.

After André left for Nigeria, you spent two weeks alone. You didn't seem to want any company, at least not mine. I called a couple of times, but you were sarcastic and gruff, and I was insulted and didn't call again. Finally, when you had to leave my friend's apartment and I invited you to come back to our place, you said you preferred to live with Alma.

Joel

I'm locked up with a scowling young man who has a purple bruise on his forehead and a split and swollen lower lip which he keeps probing with his tongue. As we shake hands, he introduces himself as "Harry" and lets me know, with a bone-crunching grip, that he's stronger than I. I say nothing. He must know who I am, so why tell him. But now he asks me what I did, and I realize I have to explain myself. What did I do? Why am I here? I have to reflect for a moment. After seeing Richard in the lightning flash, I came to a new conception of my identity. God, Christ, and Satan are one triune being. As the maker of all things, I am God; as the author of evil and suffering, I am Satan; as the redeemer, I am Christ. But to the redeemed, I can only be Satan. So I say: "I'm the devil." Whereupon Harry winces: "Oh shit!" Who can blame him? Who would want to be locked into a small room with the devil, or with a lunatic, depending on how you look at it? How *does* he look at it? "I think you ought to know something about me," he says, scowling, palpating the bruise on his forehead. "I get violent when people don't listen to me."

Stefan

When Alma and I picked you up to help you move your belongings to her place, I was shocked by your appearance and also by your manner. You had started losing weight as soon as you left the hospital. Now you were almost as thin as you had been before you jumped out of the window. Instead of swinging your cane, as you had a few weeks ago, you stabbed the pavement with it. With your short-cropped hair, your neatly trimmed red-brown beard, your round steel-rimmed glasses, your long pale face with two vertical folds above the bridge of your nose, you looked like a terribly stern nineteenth-century schoolmaster. I remarked to Alma later that there was something awfully forbidding about you, as if you were trying to make people afraid of you. She opened her purse and showed me a passport photo you had recently posed for (you were contemplating another trip to Nepal). "This is what he's turning into," she said. You had forced your face into an expression of icy, murderous defiance. Your teeth were bared, your eyes bulged with the effort. What archfiend were you staring down? The photographer? Had he annoyed you by suggesting that you smile? Then I remembered your monstrous system of self-transformation, codified on hundreds of index cards, each one representing a phase in a relentless struggle to submit every stirring of spontaneity to the yoke of the will, and I realized, with a stab of recognition, that the adversary you were confronting in this photograph could only be yourself.

I once showed that picture to someone who didn't know you. He burst out laughing. I was offended by this reaction, but in retrospect it consoles me, because it shows how inept you were at appearing demonic.

Joel

There are two metal bunk beds cemented into the floor, with sagging springs and thin foam mattresses, coarse sheets, pillows stuffed with what feels like sawdust. Harry and I converse sitting on the lower berths, facing each other. Or rather, he talks, and I listen. He's from Leeds, he says, where he worked in a paper mill until recently. He came to London for a purpose, to settle a score. Not finding the man he was looking for, he went to a pub and made the mistake of talking to a couple of blokes who were too drunk to listen. The police were called. One thing led to another. A regular pagga.

"What's a pagger?"

"A pagga. A brawl. What do you call it?"

"A ruckus. A brawl."

"A brawl, then." He goes to a mirror that's hanging over a black metal cupboard and examines his face.

"Jesus," he says.

Then he goes to the window and looks out into the darkness, gripping the bars. It's still raining outside, but the storm has abated. He shakes the bars: "Power to the people!" and laughs to himself. He goes back to the mirror and palpates the bruise on his forehead.

"Hahaha, I'm growing a horn! And you say *you're* the devil!"

A little later he sings:

> *Jesus Christ*
> *superstar*
> *who in the hell*
> *do you think you are!*

When he sees the expression on my face, he laughs. He repeats the song again, looking at me, and is shaken by laughter. He's got my number.

A harsh bell rings three times. Shortly after, the door opens and a guard sticks his head in: "It's bedtime, lads. Lights out in five minutes."

Harry strips and puts on his prison gray nightshirt. I do the same. Discreetly, we avoid the sight of each other's nakedness. He gets into the lower berth of one bunk, I climb onto the upper berth of the other. I feel safer there.

Stefan

The next time I saw you, we quarreled violently. I knocked, you said "Come in," and as I entered your room I noticed hanging on the wall over your bed a picture Alma had taken down while you were in the hospital, a photograph of a sculpture representing a smiling, meditating, and grotesquely gaunt "ascetic Buddha." I had intended to stay calm in your presence no matter what you said or did, but now I felt an old anger rattling against that resolve, like an impatient creditor demanding his due. We had quarreled over this picture once before. It made me angry to think that among all the icons you could have chosen, you had selected this pious skeleton, as if to justify your own emaciation. All the weight you had put on in the hospital—it was burned away; the easygoing, clear-minded, sensitive disposition, the appetite for human company that brought a smile to your face when a visitor entered your room—it was all gone. The Stefan I knew and loved had been dispossessed, and in his place sat again a certain hollow-eyed philosopher whom I knew well but could not love or even respect, telling me very quietly, but with intensity, and with a peculiarly lisping accent and a smug smile that was no doubt meant to look sagacious, that if I needed any assistance—particularly of a psychological nature—you would be glad to counsel me or direct me to where I could profitably ask for help.

I became so irritated with this sly sardonic maneuver that I suddenly threw a question at you, like some blunt and heavy weapon: "When's the last time you had a meal, Stefan?" You reacted with a delighted "Aah!"—pointing your finger at me: "He shows his true colors!" You leaped up and lunged toward where I was sitting, grabbed my sweater, which happened to be red, pulled the cloth close to your face, and shouted: "I see anger! I see lust! Onanism! Sloth!" You tried to tip me out of my chair: "Get out!" I pushed you away. You lurched over to where your cane was and approached me, brandishing it over your head. I was already leaving. "Go to hell!" I shouted, hastily slamming the door behind me. Alma was standing in the kitchen with her hands clasped before her breast. "I'm sorry," I said, and hurried out of the apartment.

Joel

Circling the yard with other prisoners. Some of them chat as they walk. They know each other. The only one I know is Harry, but he's staying away from me. I guess he doesn't want to be associated with this clown in the outsized suit. Or else he needs a break from being cooped up with Satan. Has he told the others about me? Do they know? It's hard to tell. What's not hard to tell is that I look ridiculous. People are laughing at me, shaking their heads. Little by little the circle lengthens into an oval and then into a horseshoe form that rotates slowly, with me at the center of the open gap. Four steps ahead of me and four steps behind, there is empty space. And then I notice the smell. It's unmistakable. I smell of sulphur. Isn't that brimstone, as in "hellfire and . . ."? I have been marked.

Stefan

For more than a week after our quarrel, I felt sick at heart. I shouldn't have left you with that curse. I had to see you again. But how to approach you? I hesitated for another week. Then I had an idea. Long ago, when you were a child and I was an adolescent, we used to play table tennis. I had played better than you, so much better there was no competition. We didn't play often, either. Only sometimes, when there was no stronger opponent to play with, I would condescend to loop the ball over to you in leisurely volleys, while you sweated and struggled to wrest a point from me. When you were committed to Albert Einstein Memorial Hospital, you had begun to play again. I remember your telling me about your greatly improved form, and my fleeting impression that behind this shy boasting there lay a challenge.

I called you up and asked you, just as if nothing had happened between us since we were kids, whether you wanted to play table tennis.

"Sure," you said. "Where?"

"There's a place right near you, corner of 96th and Broadway. It costs a dollar an hour. You can move around without your cane, can't you?"

"Sure. When can you come?"

"I'll be there in forty-five minutes."

You were waiting for me when I arrived at the ping-pong parlor. You played well—aggressively, confidently, carefully. You wanted badly to win, I could tell by the way you winced whenever you made a mistake. But your hip put you at a disadvantage when the ball flew out of your reach and you had to step after it. I could have won without difficulty, but rigged the game in your favor. When you won, you looked satisfied and actually smiled.

Outside on the street, I proposed that we have a meal together. You frowned and shook your head. I glanced at my watch, pretending to have just remembered an appointment which I couldn't afford to miss. I dreaded sitting face-to-face with you in your room again. You didn't seem to care whether I stayed with you or not. You looked absent and preoccupied.

"I really enjoyed our game," I said, holding out my hand.

"Yes," you said, "we must do it again," and suddenly let out a snort of amusement (I think at the formality of our exchange), and then abruptly smothered your grin with a deliberate straight face. You looked so sad and pale and red-lidded I wanted to do something, right away, that would make you feel better. All I could think of was to suggest that you eat some fruit, and of course you didn't do that.

Joel

A guard opens the door and beckons me with his hand: "The Chaplain wants to see you." As I rise to my feet, Harry says: "You need a new set of clothes, man." Then, to the guard: "He'll break his neck in those trousers."

Is this concern for me? I am touched. Or else he's embarrassed to be seen in my company. In either case, he regards me as human. How can that be? When everyone else knows? Suddenly I'm afraid for him. He is innocent, he shouldn't be dragged into hell with me.

The guard laughs at the sight of me: "We'll take care of that."

He takes me to the Chaplain, a dry thin man dressed in black, seated behind a broad desk. A slim silver cross on the wall behind him. He asks me in a distracted manner (he's looking for something in a pile of papers) if I would like to attend a religious service. My heart contracts with fear: the devotees! But it seems I'm being given a choice.

"No."

He looks up at me. "I understand. Would you like me to notify someone? A loved one?"

A loved one . . . Before caution can stop me, I blurt out Susan's name, her parents' address in New York, and the Chaplain writes down the words. There's no taking them back now. Let them be spared!

■

(Now at my desk in Brooklyn, thirty years later, I am holding the Chaplain's brief, handwritten message to Susan. Among the round, neat letters there is one perfectly vertical, sharp-angled L. It stands there like the spirit of rectitude itself. Is it an accident that he firmly capitalized the word "law," and that he omitted the definite article?

"Your husband is being detained for offenses against L*aw."*

■

From the Chaplain's office, the guard leads me through echoing corridors to the reception office, where I will be fitted with a new set of clothes. Two smiling men await me there. Their eyes do not connect with my gaze but slide down to my chest to feed on my heart.

"This is the man," the guard says. I know what that means: Ecce homo.

Stefan

Alma called me at the office where I worked. With a kitchen knife you had threatened an elderly woman, a friend of Alma's who had invited you to dinner.

"What should we do now? What if he starts threatening people in the street? I called Dr. Rubin at Einstein Memorial. He said we should bring him in right away, and call the police if he refuses. But Joel, I can't have him committed again—I can't do that to him. I don't know what to do."

"Maybe you can persuade him to turn himself in—or at least take some medication at home. I don't think he should be living with you otherwise. He could hurt *you*."

"I can't talk with him anymore. He screams at me when I make the slightest suggestion. I'm afraid of him."

"I'll come over tonight."

When I arrived at her place I could hear your typewriter clattering in your room. Alma and I fortified ourselves with coffee. Then I suggested we sit and meditate for half an hour before speaking to you.

You stopped typing. Now your silence was joined to ours.

After a while we got up and ventured toward your room. I knocked.

"Come in," you said.

I opened the door. You were sitting on your bed, facing us squarely, straight as a broomstick, surrounded by typewritten papers.

"What do you want?"

"Excuse me, Stefan, we have to discuss something with you. It's important. Can we sit down?"

"Get out."

You reached for your cane, which was leaning against the bed by your side. Just like a warrior prepared to fight to the death, without apparent excitement, you stabbed the floor with the cane, still sitting in your bolt-upright position.

"Get out or I'll kill you."

"You're not going to kill *anyone*!" I shouted. "You're not going to beat anyone with your goddamn cane! That's what I'm here to talk about, you understand? And I'm not leaving! I'm not afraid of you!"

"Joel!" Alma laid a restraining hand on my shoulder. I was quivering. All my earnest resolutions—to love you, to be patient and forbearing—had been swept aside. I was glaring at you. I'm sure at that moment I was the perfect embodiment of your most untrusting conceptions of me.

You stood up and came limping toward me, leaving your cane behind. Your face was white.

"You are a *fucker*! A *good*-for-*nothing*, *slop*-eating, *bourgeois fucker*! And *you* have the *gall*—" You were punctuating every other word with a jab of your finger at the center of my chest.

"Stefan! Control yourself!" Alma cried out behind me.

"Don't worry, I'm not hurting him—look, he doesn't even feel it!"

You resumed your poking with a kind of experimental zeal, as if fascinated by my spongelike passivity.

"That's enough!" I shouted and pushed you away, so that you staggered backwards toward the bed and collapsed there, clutching your heart.

"You killed me!" you shouted. "You bastard—you really killed me!"

"Don't be ridiculous, I didn't kill you."

"You did! You killed me astrally!"

I shrugged, disgusted. At the same time the sight of you sprawled across the bed with your mouth open and your hand on your heart filled me with pity, fear, and remorse.

Joel

Harry talks and I listen. I have no choice. He is violent, stronger than I am, and he needs to be heard. I understand only fragments of what he says in his choppy North English accent. But I can make out just enough to indicate my feigned comprehension with occasional nods and hm-hms. Never have I listened so acutely to the vocal nuances that modulate the meaning of spoken words. I can make out this much: He is talking about a man who will have to answer for his sister's pregnancy, about his disappointment with the Labor Party, about his abusive alcoholic father who died of TB, and about his mother who works as a maid for a rich and indolent family. That word, "indolent," is Harry's, not mine. He likes words. Reading out loud from a tabloid report on a recent crime, he pronounces the word "battered" with dramatic emphasis, stops in mid-sentence, and repeats the word, amused by the hard, percussive sound. He recites several awful poems by Rod McKuen and then, when I pretend to like them, a free-verse poem of his own—of which I remember two startling images: "crippled daisies in the coal dust," "cobweb roofs of shanties," and the refrainlike repetition of a phrase about the ravages of "Master Alcohol." I want to tell him that he is a much better poet than Rod McKuen, but I suspect a trap. Nothing is what it seems, and I don't know who Harry is.

Stefan

It was late, and we were all exhausted. I was sitting on top of your desk, you sat slumped on your bed, and Alma was sitting on the floor next to you, holding your hand and pleading with you:

"Stefan . . . can't you see . . . you need help . . . help us to find a way to help you . . . no, listen to me, Stefan, please . . . we love you, we don't want to hurt you . . . I called Dr. Rubin yesterday. He told me they have drugs . . . not Thorazine, Stefan, *new* drugs that can help you calm down and still let you think and work . . . and feel. But you have to see him at the hospital—he says he can't prescribe anything without seeing you first. I promise you I won't have you committed again. I should never have done it, it was a . . . Stefan, do you hear me? Are you listening? . . . Stefan, do you trust me? . . . Please answer."

You slowly sat up very straight and tall and turned your body to face her directly, and placed your free hand on the back of her hand, so that now you were holding her hand between your palms. Then you reached out and tenderly brushed a lock of hair off her forehead with your fingertips. She smiled through her tears, her face supplicating and full of pity. You wiped the tears off her cheeks.

"Yes, I trust you," you said.

Joel

It's a warm day, and a large number of prisoners are milling about, at ease, instead of circling the yard in a file. Maybe it's Sunday. A tall pale blond man strikes up a conversation with me. He has a long gentle face with large eyes and a wide, thin-lipped smile. His lips are very red. He looks like a harlequin. For some reason he talks to me about love. At first his speech terrifies me, because to him love and appetite are the same thing, and I still suspect that I'm going to be eaten.

"Everything is love," he says. "Our feet cling to the earth. The planets revolve around the sun. That's gravity, but what is gravity? Attraction. And attraction is love. The bars on our windows are made of atoms that communicate across enormous distances. 'Hello? Anybody out there?' 'Yes, yes, I'm here, thank you for asking!' This conversation we're having, it's not just *about* love, it *is* love. I hope you don't mind my saying so. From my tongue to your ear through your eyes to my heart. It's all one beautiful, endless circulation. I spoke to that Pakistani fellow over there, he says he's being charged with murder. A fight in a bar, some unforgivable insult, out comes the knife and into the other man's heart. Sounds like hate, right? But I tell you, it's nothing but passionate, rageful love. Even the most heinous crime is an act of love."

Far off in the inner depths I feel the presence of tears.

"What is *your* crime?" he asks. There is no trace of duplicity in that question. He wants to know.

"Drugs," I say.

How extraordinary: He believes me. I can lie. The devotees are not omniscient. Or else he is a different kind of being. An angel? Maybe. All he knows is love.

"And you?" I ask.

"Fraud. I tried to defraud the British Railways."

Stefan

We entered the visitors' room of the psychiatric ward. The moment you saw Dr. Rubin, you stiffened. He was standing behind a white counter, looking dapper in a dark suit. He seemed in a hurry. He exchanged a few words with a nurse and glanced at a sheet of paper she handed him. Then he saw us and immediately put the paper on a desk and approached us.

"Stefan, I'm glad to see you," he said, holding out a hand. Your jaw was clenched, the knuckles of your fist clutching your cane were white.

Dr. Rubin lowered his hand. "How are you this morning?"

You shut your eyes and frowned, as if forced to endure some intolerable gaucherie.

"I hope you will stay with us for a few days. That way—"

"*Stay* with you?" Thrusting your head forward and boring your eyes into the doctor's. "You mean I'm *invited*? It won't *cost* me anything?"

Dr. Rubin turned aside to say something to a nurse, who nodded and disappeared through a swinging door. You stepped back and raised your cane, pointing it in the direction of the doctor's heart.

"None of your tricks, Dr. Rubin! I've got you covered!"

I found that funny, but no one else seemed to—not Dr. Rubin, at any rate, nor the two orderlies who seized your arms and pried the cane from your fist, knocking off your glasses and shattering them in the process. Dr. Rubin gave them some instructions involving the name of a medication I had never heard of. They led you past me. Each man was holding you by a wrist and an upper arm. They were lifting you slightly, causing your shoulders to hunch up. You looked scared.

"Hey Stefan," I said, and for once you looked at me without expecting a challenge. "Take it easy, for Christ's sake. We'll wait for you here." You heard that, you nodded. Then you were ushered out of the room. Dr. Rubin picked up your broken glasses and handed them to Alma.

"That wasn't necessary," she said.

He looked helpless. "I'm sorry. I wish—"

"What are they doing with him now? Please bring him back!"

"He's safe, no one's going to hurt him. He's getting an injection, that's all. It'll calm him down, probably for the rest of the day. But that's not enough. He shouldn't be living with you."

"Can't you give him this same medication to take at home?"

He shook his head.

"Why not?"

"Because he's too sick. He needs supervision."

"He won't sign himself in," she said.

"I agree," he said. "*You'll* have to do that. I'm sorry."

"I won't. I did it once, I won't do it again. I won't betray his trust."

"It's to protect him, not to betray him. He's very very sick, you know, and in terrible danger, I hope you realize that."

"I know it better than you do!" she said furiously. "But I won't betray him again. It would kill whatever faith in life he still has. He trusts me."

"Well," Dr. Rubin said, a little curtly, "you've made up your mind, there's no point in arguing, and those people are waiting. I hope you're making the right decision. Take a seat out there. I'll come back with him in a couple of minutes." He left through the swinging door.

Joel

The harlequin isn't the only angel. There are others, and there are devils as well.

There is a man with a ducktail haircut who wears an extinguished cigarette over his left ear. Sometimes he walks in front of me in the yard. Sometimes he ascends the iron stairs as I descend with the other prisoners. Our eyes never connect. Always the same knowing smile, always the same charred, half-smoked stub over his left ear. I don't know what is being signaled by this, but I dread it.

There is an African man with tribal scars on his cheeks who greets me, day after day, on our way to the yard, with a single word: "Courage!" This is the same word that came to me, disguised as a beer advertisement, day after day, when I was lost in the streets. At first I don't trust the evidence of the miraculous, but after the third time I nod, like a student receiving instruction.

There is a long-term convict who escorts me to a room where a smooth young man in a three-piece suit awaits me—the barrister who will defend me in court. The barrister's eyes keep gliding off mine and focusing on the center of my chest. He asks me a few questions in a breezy, cheerful tone, and says good-bye. Again he stares at my chest. Escorting me back to my cell, the convict tells me to get a move-on. "You act like you own this place!" I find it strange that a prisoner should have the prerogatives of a guard.

He reads my mind: "I have lots of friends downstairs," he says.

"Downstairs?" (already fearing the explanation).

"The netherworld. They can't wait to meet you. I'll introduce you one of these days."

There can be no doubt that this man is a devil. The barrister, on the other hand, is difficult to place. Maybe he's a vampire.

There is a longhaired kid whom I have met before. He was one of the many pothead visitors at Milton Chambers, the house in the World's End where Susan and Gina and I lived with Veneta Knowles, the banker's daughter, and Ralph Ponder, the candyman's son, and Ralph's girlfriend Georgie. Those were the good old days, but I don't want to remember them. The kid stops his reminiscing. "Oh man!" he says. "What happened? You're so sad!" I don't answer. After a while he whistles the opening bars of "Hey Jude." Does he really think it is within my power to take this sad song and make it better? Evidently yes, or else he's mocking me. "Why don't you pass the buck?" he asks then. I'll never do that, I can't and I won't: send another soul to this hell of all hells, as ransom for my release. But for the first time since the curse fell upon me it dawns on me that I may have a choice.

Stefan

We sat in the waiting room of the psychiatric ward, where an orderly stood hobnobbing with three policemen who seemed to be in charge of a longhaired young man who was seated on a bench with his hands manacled behind his back, staring blankly, with his mouth open. On a couch, a plump white woman sat in uncomfortable proximity to a young black girl who made periodic but obviously halfhearted motions to rise to her feet in defiance of another orderly's repeated command that she stay seated. Twice he pushed her back onto the couch. "If you don't cut it out we'll have to tie you up," he said. She didn't stand up again.

You returned behind Dr. Rubin with an air of absentminded aloofness, holding your head high and squinting, maybe because of the loss of your glasses, as if you were searching for something in the distance. Dr. Rubin held out his hand to you, and you mechanically gave him yours. "It was good talking to you, Stefan. I'll see you next week." Then he turned to Alma and me and explained that you and he had agreed to meet once a week, and that you had promised to take medication at home.

"I have a suggestion," he said then. "I think Stefan would be better off if he was on his own at least part of the day. Any degree of independence will do him good. Maybe you could get him a room at the Y. Provided that's agreeable to you, Stefan," he added. "Think about it." You nodded.

"One more thing," Dr. Rubin said. "We'll get your glasses repaired, if you'll be so good as to fill out a form for us. I'm really sorry this happened. The nurse at the counter can help you."

"Thanks," you said, already moving toward the door, "I don't really want to see all that clearly."

Joel

A letter from Susan. Words of limitless love, but I read them with fear and trembling. She's coming to London with Gina. The Chaplain has set a trap for her. The devotees will bring us to trial as a family. I know it's insane to believe this, but I am helpless against the omnipotence of thought. I look up and see the headline on a newspaper Harry is holding:

EUROPE: THE WAY OPENS

Something opens—here, where I am. Opens! The next moment it's gone. What was it? What was that feeling? But it wasn't a feeling, it was . . . And then it comes again, like a breath of sea air and brine, rich and glad and free. And then it's gone. But the memory is there. All day long the omen reverberates.

Stefan

Alma rented a room for you at the YMCA. She called me that evening. She was crying. The Y was even drearier than the halfway house had been—all those hallways, drab little rooms, and cold, impersonal people. How could anyone live there, especially someone as frightened and hurt as you? What should she do? She was tempted to go against Dr. Rubin's advice and bring you back to your room in her apartment. I suggested that she wait and see, and that we both keep in close touch with you.

Two days later Alma received a call from the desk clerk at the Y: You were unable to walk. Your hip had given out. Alma drove you to the emergency room of the nearest hospital. The hip was reset, but it appeared that a new pinning operation would eventually have to be performed. You were advised to walk only with great caution and as little as possible.

Alma told me you were glad to be back at home in your room. You were rearranging your books and replacing the pictures on the walls with portraits of the Dalai Lama and Gurdjieff and with kabbalistic diagrams and your own finely drawn esoteric mandalas. I went over for a visit. You joined us in the living room briefly, I think just to let us know you were OK. You were very quiet, and your face looked calm. That was so unusual that I felt a twinge of alarm. But then I thought: It's the medication. And maybe it was. Or else you had already made your decision, and your mind was at peace.

Joel

Harry and I go to the prison library, I search for the I Ching. Of course it's not there. But Harry finds what he came for: a history of naval battles. He scowls ironically when he sees my selection. "The Good Book!" he says. On the way to our cell (where a guard waits impatiently, holding the door open), he hums that tune again:

I climb onto my bunk and hold the Bible in my lap. My whole body is quivering. Hope is on trial, a trial by Chance. If yesterday's omen was true, the Good Book will show me the open way. If not, I'll know there can be no hope for me. I'll open the book at random. (Open!) But not before my heart is quiet. So I sit in the midst of my quivering self and close my eyes. Just be. Just wait. Just hope.

No. Just be.

I sit for a long time. At one point Harry asks: "What are you doing?"

"Meditating."

He digests that in silence. Then he chuckles.

The cell is darkening. Harry has fallen asleep. The ceiling light goes on. At long last my hands move toward the book as if of their own accord. It's the moment of truth. I open the book and read:

Peter therefore was kept in prison: but prayer was made without ceasing of the church unto God for him.

And when Herod would have brought him forth, the same night Peter was sleeping between two soldiers, bound with two chains: and the keepers before the door kept the prison.

And, behold, the angel of the Lord came upon him, and a light shined in the prison: and he smote Peter on the side, and raised him up, saying, Arise up quickly. And his chains fell off from his hands.

And the angel said unto him, Gird thyself, and bind on thy sandals. And so he did. And he saith unto him, Cast thy garment about thee, and follow me.

And he went out, and followed him; and wist not that it was true which was done by the angel; but thought he saw a vision.

When they were past the first and the second ward, they came unto the iron gate that leadeth out into the city; which opened to them of his own accord: and they went out, and passed on through one street; and forthwith the angel departed from him.

Stefan

A colleague at my office told me there was a call for me. It was Alma.

"Joel! Stefan killed himself!"

I felt no surprise, no protest, nothing at all. I must have been holding my breath. When I exhaled, it was with a melting sense of relief. For your sake above all. Thank God. Thank God it was over.

"Where are you?" I asked.

"At home. They just took his body away. He's dead, Joel."

"How did he do it?"

"He jumped out of his window."

Six floors. And the courtyard was made of concrete.

"Come to our place," I said. "Please, right away."

I called Susan, who was at home with Gina.

"Oh God, I'm sorry," she said.

I excused myself at the office and took the train home.

442

Joel

And Peter wist not that it was true which was done by the angel. Those words keep returning to me. Who says it *was* true? Who says the angel and Herod and Jesus and Peter himself aren't figments of my monstrous dream? Along with the rest of the biblical cast, and the angels and devils of Brixton Prison and the devotees and Harry and . . . yes, this corollary is inescapable, Susan and Gina. And Stefan and Alma. Figments, phantoms . . .

But Peter, who thought he was dreaming, chose to believe that he was being saved. Otherwise he would not have done what the angel told him to do. Can't I do the same? Am I not in fact being invited to do so? Wasn't my hand—my dream-hand—guided to that particular page, as if by an angel?

"Cast thy garment about thee, and follow me."

If I can believe in the nightmare, why can't I believe in its ending? Let me wake up! Or at least let me dream something happier! Will I go home with Susan? Will I tell bedtime stories to Gina again? Yes, I say, yes. But give me a sign so that I can believe it!

■

And the life-dream responds in the language of dreams. Three maidens come to the hero's dungeon, and each brings a gift of self-remembrance. They come from the World's End, where Susan and Gina and I lived during two successive winters.

Stefan

Susan was out in the park with Gina when Alma arrived. I made some tea. Neither of us drank it. Her body was hunched, her face puffed from crying. I don't remember her crying in our apartment, but she must have. I'm altogether amazed by how little I remember of that afternoon.

At one point she looked at me with such an intensity of grief that she was slightly cross-eyed. There was a terrible question in that look, terrible because it was addressed to me and my heart turned to stone at the sight of it. I don't know what the question was—maybe just "Why?"—but I was unable to answer it. I just looked at her, numb and cold.

Then she asked me a question in words: "You didn't like him, did you?"

It hurt me that she had such a simple conception of me and of our relationship. At the same time I saw with stark clarity how jealous I was. As a child I had resented Alma's preference for you, and later, when you became sick, her almost worshipful pity, her heartsick, urgent chanting of Na-myo-ho-ren-ge-kyo for your salvation (which didn't save you but had a grotesquely enlivening effect on the plants in her house), her adoring way of invoking your "genius," your "massive intelligence" whenever she spoke of your suffering, as if to reproach your fate for not destroying someone less valuable—indeed as if *my* gifts and *my* suffering, my soul, in effect, were of a less heroic order. It took me a while to find words, and the ones that finally came were banal and didn't answer her question: "I have feelings too," I said.

"Oh, I *know,*" she said, "I didn't *mean* . . ." She was sorry she had hurt me, and I forgave her with a nod that meant "I know." We were fairly well practiced in this pattern of exchange, so it wasn't complicated.

I don't think she ever needed to ask your forgiveness. But that may be my jealousy speaking, still, thirty years later.

"Stefan knew he was going to kill himself," she said later. "I don't mean he had it planned, but he knew. This morning. I had to do some errands, and I felt awful leaving him alone, but there was no choice. He said good-bye to me."

Now I remember her tears. She had to stop talking for a while.

"I was about to leave," she continued, "and he came up to me and said he wanted me to know that he had finished his book. He said it was a good book and it would be useful to people, it would help them. Then he held up his hands and moved them around my head, almost touching me, but not quite—like a halo. And he was saying good-bye. He said it several times. He was smiling. He was expressing real feeling, real love. All the distortion was gone. I hadn't seen that in him for so long—real feeling. It came from his heart. And then he said that I had helped him all these years, and had sacrificed a lot for him, and suffered with him. He said all these things very calmly. He wasn't crazy at all, his eyes and his voice were clear and quiet. He said that someday I would be rewarded for everything I had done—that nothing good or bad goes unrewarded. He said . . . he said I would be blessed."

She burst into violent, moaning sobs. How could I forget that? I wanted to comfort her, to put my arm around her and console her. But I was unable to join in her grief. I was ashamed of my coldness, but felt powerless to do anything about it. I imagine you must have felt like this often. I could barely talk. There was a knot of emotion stuck in my throat, a bitter feeling obscurely compounded of sorrow and anger, impossible to swallow or spit out.

Joel

The first maiden comes disguised as a disheveled woman in drab clothes, carrying a heavy shopping bag. That is, I don't recognize her. But then I do. She is Janet, the wife of Mick, the guitar-playing heroin addict who thought the I Ching, not man, was the crown of Creation. I liked Mick. I like Janet too. She was a friend to Susan. Her daughter, Evelyn, was Gina's playmate, I used to take them to feed the swans.

"Janet."

"Joel."

She says it so simply, it touches me like a kiss on the forehead. She knows me as Joel, and she wishes me well.

Stefan

I had imagined the medical examiner's office to be a long, dark hall smelling of dust and embalming fluid (presumably musklike), with two long rows of corpses laid out on cots and covered with sheets, and an old man searching for you among them, like a mail clerk shuffling through the poste restante. That fantasy began to evaporate when I set foot on the broad expanse of steps extended to the bereaved with exactly the same air of granite potency and solemn condescension one would expect from a bank, a courthouse, or an embassy.

The wall directly facing me as I stepped in—a marble wall of imposing height and breadth—bore a lengthy legend graven in magisterial capitals for the consolation of those who understand Latin. A tall flag hung before it, set at half-mast. A group of well-dressed men and women with grave and furrowed faces stood near the entrance, talking quietly. A uniformed guard directed me past them to an office (normally proportioned) where, after a lengthy demonstration of officious indifference on the part of the staff of four, a balding black man read off to me, in a dry voice, a list of questions concerning the name, age, and sex of the deceased, his occupation and place of work, my relationship to him, and the cause, circumstances, date, and approximate time of his death. The man didn't bat an eyelash at my answers. He must have been used to hearing about suicides. He typed out the data on a printed form, separated the several carbon copies, and handed me a small blue card with a penciled number on it.

"Take a seat and wait till your number is called."

Joel

My second visitor is Veneta Knowles, the banker's daughter, whose room we shared at Milton Chambers and who distracted me with her nocturnal sighs and silken stirrings just five steps away from our bed. Her, too, I don't recognize right away, because she has painted herself with vegetable dyes—her lips scarlet, her cheeks and forehead a graded blend of rose and green, a star-shaped bauble in her heaped-up blond hair, laughing blue eyes set underneath like jewels in a showcase. All this for me! And not, clearly not for a god, but for a man!

Stefan

I was too restless to sit. I paced back and forth in the lobby. I tried not to think about you. I didn't want to cry there.

I stopped pacing and stood still for a while, trying in vain to decipher the Latin inscription. The last words, ". . . SUCCURRERE VITAE," seemed to connote something like "Life goes on"—or had it something to do with *succor*? The flag, I realized then, was set at half-mast not to salute the as yet unidentified dead who were stored in the medical examiner's office, but to honor Harry Truman, who had recently died.

An abundance of marble had been lavished on walls, pillars, and steps, and even furnished the frame for an indoor garden. I had never seen such rank and ecstatic vitality displayed by a bunch of plants, not in any greenhouse or forest: Here was a fugue of squat swollen stems holding aloft thick fountains of lush, broad leaves, and two flowers, enormous, pink, opening their hearts to the slanting sunlight that fell through the window. You couldn't help admiring them again and again as you waited your turn. The eye would scan the marble patterns for something interesting to fasten on, brush shyly past the troubled faces of the other visitors, and come to rest on the plants.

Those well-to-do people near the entrance, for example, one of whom was rather loudly praising the exquisite *cleanness* of Switzerland, where nearly *every*one wears ties, where even the young people *never* wear dungarees, and graffiti are simply un*heard* of—they, too, took refuge in prolonged botanical inspections.

But no one discussed the plants or commented on them, so far as I could tell; maybe because they proclaimed too loudly their own triumphant existence. Why were they there? Whoever had planted them must have had in mind some tactful consolation akin to the written one on the wall. But these plants were obscenely alive; they could only remind you, in a rather blatant way, of the deadness of the dead one you had come to identify.

I ambled back near the office where I had been interviewed, and from where I assumed my number would soon be called. The door was open, so I could observe two elderly, cultivated Chinese men requesting with great courtesy of one of the clerks that he expedite matters somehow, for they had come in from Washington and had a plane to catch. The clerk said: "You will have to wait till your number is called. There are other people in line before you." The Chinese gentlemen each made a little bow of polite resignation, and rejoined their wives, who had been sitting stiffly poised with downcast eyes throughout their husbands' efforts, holding their pocketbooks on their laps. The clerk, spotting the ticket in my hand, and assuming I too wanted to register my impatience, waved me away, and reiterated his formula: "Please take a seat and wait till your number is called." This time I did as I was told.

Joel

The third maiden is Georgie, who used to spend her weekends in bed with Ralph Ponder, the candyman's son, reading John Galsworthy novels out loud. But that is a poor description of her. There are people whom one remembers by their radiance. Georgie is like that. What is this invisible light? Kindness, love. If I told her what I see, she would be embarrassed, and maybe the light would be dimmed. So I tell her instead about Harry, how violent he is and yet how surprisingly decent. I notice the floor in the visiting room is littered with cigarette butts and wonder if Harry, who is always bumming cigarettes off other prisoners, would consider it an insult if I brought him cigarette butts. And then I repeat something I said before—"I'm really OK"—and am astonished by how true that sounds.

Stefan

No sooner had I sat down than I became an object of critical scrutiny for five young people—two men and three women—directly facing me from the couch opposite mine (the Chinese were sitting on a couch by themselves). I presumed they were Puerto Ricans, though they could have come from anywhere in South America; and they just as automatically (and mistakenly) assumed that I spoke no Spanish, and proceeded to milk my appearance for all it could offer them in the way of distraction. One of the men in particular, a burly guy with a Playboy pin in his lapel, scanned me with hostile admiration from head to toe, and started commenting, fatuously but not without wit, about my hippieness, beginning with remarks about my womanish and no doubt unwashed hair, the button missing on my coat, my worn heels and unpolished shoes, moving on to a *Reader's Digest*–like sermon on the moral decay, the blurring of sexual distinctions, the erosion of authority in the United States, and returning to the concrete with a comparison of my hair to that of a dog they all knew. Most of the others (including myself) seemed to welcome the entertainment, but were too sad to reward his efforts with more than occasional and quickly fading smiles. The second man, who was mostly staring at the floor, just nodded from time to time to show that he was listening. And I, of course, kept a straight face. I wasn't angry.

There was a silence, during which a man's voice could be heard scolding in the office: "Maybe it's a waste of time to tell you guys you oughta be ashamed of yourselves. But at least have a heart, you know what I mean? Even if you have no shame, at least have a heart." Then someone shut the door.

Looking at one of the Hispanic women   the one who did not have a man sitting next to her—it suddenly struck me that she might have lost her lover. Her eyes were puffed, her face was drawn and exhausted.

The office door flew open, and a slight, short, very pale young man with spectacles stepped out holding a sheet of paper in his hand, and called out a number—not mine. The Spanish-speaking group rose to their feet and were led at a brisk pace through a door with a black **2** above it. They returned almost instantly, the three women crying out and sobbing hysterically, one of the men nervously fumbling for a cigarette, the other (who had done the talking before) determinedly stoical. The women collapsed back onto their seats, violently shaken by sobs. The man with the cigarette numbly struck a match four, five times without lighting it. The stoic, looking less stoical now, put his fingertips to his eyes and shook his head. The women held hands and embraced, still crying pitifully. The man with the cigarette stood up, grabbed his coat and said: *"Vámonos!"*; and then the others also gathered up their coats and umbrellas and pocketbooks and walked past me up the steps to the foyer and out onto the street. I avoided their faces as they passed.

Joel

"I brought you something": some 15 cigarette butts from the floor of the visitors' room. To prevent them from dropping, I offer them on cupped palms. Harry receives them, surprised and grateful. The scales fall from my eyes. Harry is real. He is not only not a creature of my imagination, he is not imaginable at all. He escapes definition because he is so furiously intent on defining himself. His opinions reverse themselves, his stories contradict each other. After a week of listening to his relentless monologues, all I can say about him with assurance is that he is a man who needs to be heard. A man above all—not a devil, not one of the hungry devotees either. And because he claims all my attention for much of the day and has not the slightest interest in me and my phantasmagoria, the monster that claims to be myself is weakening, starving, and I am recovering at least a semblance of my own humanity. Otherwise I could not have engaged in this simple and beautiful transaction.

"I" . . . "I" . . . Who am I? It doesn't matter. All the rest of the day, Harry smokes with relish, fumigating our cell, much to my discomfort. But I am happy.

Stefan

For a while I watched the young clerk walk in and out of the office and Room 2, rattling pieces of paper in his hand; and when that got tedious, I studied the pictures on the walls—discreetly tinted prints depicting the flowers, roots, and fruit of various plant species. I thought of praying for you, but that seemed artificial.

A member of the English-speaking group, a powerfully built middle-aged man in a sharkskin suit, strode past me jauntily on soft crepe soles, one hand in his pocket, the other dangling by his side with exaggerated nonchalance.

"Excuse me," he said to the clerk, "why is there such a delay? We've been here for forty-five minutes! What's taking so long?" His voice was demanding and authoritative. The clerk curtly explained that the body had to be sewn up—accompanying his words with a graphic sewing gesture (no fine embroidery stitch, this sewing; more like mending a sail). The middle-aged man stood still for a moment, then turned around and walked past me again. All the color had left his face. His mouth was open. I felt a surge of pity, but fought back the tears.

Joel

I awake at dawn. I had a dream. There was a battle. Unspeakable carnage, cruelty. Don't look there, don't. A pigeon coos on the windowsill. I am in prison, not in hell.

Harry is snoring. Something good happened yesterday, something important. Ah yes, I remember. Georgie. And before her, Veneta. And before her, Janet.

I sit up, turn toward the window, cross my legs in the lotus position, rest my hands palms-up on my thighs. How strong that feels, how sure.

I can still hear Janet pronouncing my name: "Joel." The miracle of that moment. The recognition: This is the name I answer to. Not God, but Joel.

Words are the names things are called by. Don't all things answer to their names? The thing sleeps, you call its name, it raises its head and pricks up its ears: "You mean me, *me*?"

But I am no thing. How could I be? Nevertheless, I respond to the name I was given. It is a misnomer. My true name is "I." Everyone's true name is "I."

Who am I then?

Eyes close. There is the dream again, the dregs of it. In my mouth the memory of a sweet and oily flavor which with a jolt of horror and disgust I recognize as the aftertaste of my own self-devouring. Horror! Hatred! Endless guilt! Thank God it was only a dream. But dreams are real. Spit it out!

With the taste of inexpiable crime in my mouth, I pray:

"Our . . ."

and that single word is already the expiation. It means I am one of many, and that we are not dispossessed. Over and over I recite the Lord's Prayer. Never before have I felt the encircling grace of this poem, its vaulting gestures and huge equations, or the knowledge of terror that speaks in its final entreaties.

Stefan

Eventually the clerk concluded his business in Room **2**, vanished into the office for a while, reemerged, and cheerfully called out another number. The Chinese were next. They followed the clerk through a door that has lost its number—presumably a 1. The husbands stepped aside to let the women enter first. Room number 1 turned out to be a corridor that led downstairs at about a thirty-degree angle. The clerk pushed the door shut behind him with a slight bang. I could hear footsteps receding with an increasingly faint and hollow sound, until there was silence. Minutes passed. The hollow shuffling sounds resumed, and grew louder. The door opened. One of the women was tottering and soundlessly crying. Her companions supported her on either side. The clerk escorted them to a couch with hasty efficiency. The crying woman sat down and daubed her lower lids with a little handkerchief, very delicately. She sniffed. Her husband bent over, placed a hand upon her head, and murmured a few words. Then he retreated to make room for the other woman, who sat down and took her friend's limp white hand between her palms and proceeded to mutter, quietly, deliberately, and almost without interruption, directly into her ear. From time to time the weeping woman daubed her lower lids and nodded quickly, with just the faintest edge, it seemed to me, of irritation. The two men stood aside and conversed.

Joel

Doubt comes back, with a vengeance even, but it will not take root in me again. Love rules the world, a curse cannot prevail. I think this, and the words are a shield against doubt:

> **Love rules the world**
> **A curse cannot prevail!**

Doubt attacks with knowledge: of cruelty, of crime and injustice, beyond reckoning, beyond imagination. But these words thrust doubt to the furthest horizon:

> **Love rules the world**
> **A curse cannot prevail!**

And when doubt encroaches again, they stand ready and sweep it away:

> **Love rules the world**
> **A curse cannot prevail!**

Again and again I repeat it, until it repeats itself. Wafting away what's left of darkness. Until there is only space:

> **Love rules the world**
> **A curse cannot prevail!**

In this clear space, the bars in the window, the gray yard outside, the sounds of the ward, shouts, footsteps, hard clangs. I look down at Harry in his bunk. He is lying on his back with his hands under his head, and the book he's been reading lies facedown on his chest: *Glory Days of the British Navy.*

Love rules the world
A curse cannot prevail!

What wonderful knowledge is this? It needs no proof, it is its own evidence:

Love rules the world
A curse cannot prevail!

Stefan

I was relieved when the Chinese group left. It was hard not to cry at the sight of them, and I was determined not to cry—not to *feel,* if that's what it took.

It wasn't long before the small clerk breezed out of the office again and called another number. The man in the sharkskin suit responded and was led through door number 1. He towered above the clerk by a good two heads. He still had one hand in his pocket. The door snapped shut behind them. I listened to their footsteps receding, echoing as they grew fainter, and eventually vanishing out of earshot.

An intense silence followed; no sounds from the office either, just traffic boiling outside. Then I heard—everyone in the office and behind me in the foyer must have heard it too—an uncanny sound: a kind of cavernous barking; and then it seemed to be a violent argument between two men; but no, it was . . . *someone seemed to be laughing down there!* I felt my skin crawl. The sound grew louder and lost its eerie echo. Now I knew what it was. The door opened, the man with the sharkskin suit came out howling and blubbering and covering his face with his hands. The clerk ushered him in the direction of the steps, where his friends received him.

I cupped my hands over my eyes. I was determined not to cry.

There was a long pause then, during which I prayed. I prayed for you, that your spirit would find its home and place of rest; for Alma; for the people I had seen crying; for all the dead, here and everywhere; and for the dying, for the unborn, and for all the living. For animals too.

Joel

A holding room for prisoners on their way to court for arraignment. We sit on benches alongside the four walls, dressed in our prison browns. The center of the room is empty. Hardly anyone talks. For a while, several men quietly discuss their cases, speculating about their probable sentences, and two of the more experienced prisoners offer estimates pro bono.

One of the prisoners is Richard. We're each sitting near a corner, diagonally to each other. He must be as aware as I am of how precisely this arrangement expresses our mutual polarity and distance. But he's bent far over, leaning on his knees, his long stringy hair dangling over his face. Not for a moment has he acknowledged my presence, and we've been in this room for at least half an hour.

The door opens and a guard lets in a new prisoner. It's the pale blond harlequin who lectured me about love. The angel. He's dressed in white pants, a white shirt, a white jacket, red socks, and white tennis shoes. He looks around.

"What an unhappy room," he says.

Richard raises his head. His eyes are bleary.

"Are *you* happy?" he asks.

"No," says the angel, "but I put a bright face on it."

"Is that how you keep your suit clean?"

"It helps. It even helps you."

Richard mulls that over. His gaze drifts, accidentally meets with mine, and darts off again, as if stung. The angel sits down. Richard buries his head in his hands.

Stefan

Another number was called, still not mine. A group of seven, all black and very poor, to judge by the patched and threadbare clothes they wore, were led through Door 1. And again—but this time in chorus, and recognizably—their return was heralded by loud wailing cries. The door flew open, and a woman staggered out, moaning and waving her arms. A young man followed, his face contorted and wet with tears, carrying in his arms a young girl, who was also crying and seemed to be close to vomiting. A white-haired old man had his hand on the young man's shoulder; he too was crying. A young woman followed, walking very upright and slowly shaking her head with an expression of sickened dismay. And after a while the last two emerged, an old woman and a teenage boy, sobbing and supporting one another, their heads touching, followed by the ever-efficient clerk, who closed the door behind them and directed them to the couch.

There they collapsed, embracing and sobbing, until one of the women said "Let's get outta here" and they left.

Joel

The air is bright around me. Oh, it was bright in the prison yard as well, but it's not the same weather inside prison and out. Remember this!

The almost inconceivable, no longer hoped for, has happened, is here, is truly the case: Susan and Gina are with me. I'm out of jail. The poster people no longer wink and salivate. The devotees are devoted to living in London and don't appear to be concerned with God. Road signs and headlines are just what they are, no secret text runs alongside the vulgate. The police found my car and did not break into it and explore my journals and analyze my dreams and publish me to the world as its Maker. The face of things is not a mask, appearances do not deceive. Surely I am blessed. But the blessing is provisional. My trial is in two weeks. There is a judge.

We're staying with Garth and BJ Anderson, friends of my mother's, at their house in Surrey, not far from Chao Khun's meditation center. That proximity worries me. The thought of Nirvana, of having once wanted it, fills me with shame and horror. I want only to be sane. I don't think there is anything more noble in a person, or more beneficent, than sanity.

Susan and Gina are sane. They are sane the way bread is bread and water is water. That's why all my infinity attacks took place in their absence.

Garth and BJ are sane. They listen. Nothing I say surprises them. When I tell BJ about Shiva's shapeshifting and telepathy, she nods, and it's not a mechanical nod, it means "I understand," and she does. When I describe Richard's hieratic posturing to Garth, he smiles and says: "Mephistopheles." And they're not afraid to ask dangerous questions. They coax little echoes of hell out of me. I'm afraid to tell them—afraid for them—but they want to know, and I need to relieve myself of my secret, at least by hinting at it. Amazingly, it doesn't hurt them. How wonderful! Like saints who touch lepers without contamination.

But can I catch their sanity by contagion? I hope so! There's BJ, baking a cake. It has currants in it. Susan helps her, together they talk about homesickness. In another room, Gina tells Garth about "Liddleiddly." On TV, there's an ad for the musical *Hair*. Later Garth says: "I've been wondering: How does a guy like you get taken in by some Irish schmuck who says he was 'sent'? I think it's because of long hair. It brings out the archetypes." There's something to that. I can't picture Christ with a haircut. Or Buddha. Satan, on the other hand . . . Satan can put on disguises. I still believe in Satan, or whatever he should be called: the deceiver, the tempter. When Susan and Gina walk into a store while my head is turned, I suddenly see their absence and KNOW by the freezing of the blood in my veins that they were figures in a dream from which I have awakened, again, eternally alone in a mad universe of my own devising. Until they come out again. Oh gratitude! Oh the blessing! They are real, they are an antidote to illusion.

Stefan

There was just enough time to wipe my eyes and swallow back the knot in my throat before my turn came. The clerk led me into Room 2. There you were, lying on your back behind a plate-glass window. Your face, brightly lit by invisible floodlights, contrasted sharply with a night-black background. There was a bruise on your cheek. No other damage was visible. A brown blanket covered your body up to your chin. You looked asleep. Austere, serene. All the madness had gone out of your face.

"That's him," I said. The man made no reply. Neither of us moved.

I felt gathering up within me, in a simple, unquestioning movement of my deepest memory, all the confusion of pity and ill will—or was it thwarted love—I had ever felt for you, and cast it out of myself. I wished you well from the bottom of my heart.

"What happened to him?" asked the clerk.

"He jumped out of a window."

Then I turned toward the door, and the man led me out.

Joel

It's Gina's bedtime. I've lit a candle next to her bed. Hugging her Smiley-mouse, she gazes into my eyes as I sing her a song she has not heard before:

Amazing grace, how sweet the sound
That saved a wretch like me!
I once was lost, but now I'm found,
Was blind, but now I see.

I stop singing. These words are so overwhelmingly true, the tune almost too beautiful. Somewhere I read that the man who wrote it had trafficked in slaves.

"Daddy?"

"Yes?"

"Are you crying?"

"I'm crying because I'm happy."

She looks puzzled, still gazing at me, but does not ask further. Then she smiles.

"I like it," she says.

"Me too. It's a beautiful song."

"I like it when you're happy."

I stroke her hair. We gaze into each other's eyes for a while. Then she turns over, hugging her Smiley-mouse, ready for sleep.

"Sing it again."

'Twas grace that taught my heart to fear,
And grace my fears relieved;
How precious did that grace appear
The hour I first believed.

Am I saved? I don't know. But at least for the moment I have been set free. Even though the judge found me guilty. "Suspended sentence"—it sounds like a Sword of Damocles. Yet I am free. I don't quite believe it, but it would be impious not to accept the present as a gift. The present!

Stefan

It was cold outside. Life did indeed go on, that banal observation was unavoidable. Life went on right outside the medical examiner's office in complete, if not blissful, ignorance of death. People and cars were rushing in all directions. In a shop window, Richard Nixon addressed the nation through several TV sets. How driven and thirsty everyone looked! Obsessed with motion! Mad with purpose! I wanted to stop one of them and tell him: "We're all going to die. I've just seen it. There's a place right around the corner. . . ." But who would want to hear that? They'd think I was crazy.

456

On the way home in the subway, there was some mechanical problem; the train jerked and clanked laboriously, stopping and starting until it finally deflated with a hissing gasp at the Brooklyn Bridge station. The loudspeakers ordered all passengers out onto the platform. There I stood for a long time shifting my gaze from the tired, morose faces around me to the patterns of broken tile on the wall across the tracks, while the man in charge of the loudspeakers, excited by the crisis, issued periodic communiqués.

A Krishna devotee came down the steps and entered the crowd. He was a strapping young man, much healthier-looking than most of his brethren, and obviously proud of his shaven head and priestly trappings. He announced with a strong pleasant voice that his Yoga group was collecting funds for the orphaned and starving children of Bangladesh, and that it would be nice if someone contributed something. And then, seeing me watching him, he said "Hare Krishna," and I said hello.

On a sudden impulse, I stepped up to him, put 50 cents into the cigar box he was holding in place of a begging bowl, and touched his arm: "Can you do me a favor?"

"What is it?"

"My brother just committed suicide—"

"Oh, that's bad."

"Yes, I know it's bad, but he did it, and I'd like to ask you to pray for him."

"I don't know, man, suicide is a very wrong thing to do. You don't even get reincarnated, you're like a ghost from then on." He pondered for a while. "There is something *you* can do, though. You can bring offerings—like food—to some *priests*. Now, I can't really tell you where to go, because I don't know too much about these things, but that's what you can do, and it'll benefit your brother in some way." Then he laughed and shook his head and let out a little whistle. "Wow—don't you *ever* do that to yourself."

I felt very angry at him. I wanted to take back my 50 cents.

"I think you're wrong," I said.

"What do you mean?"

"I don't believe my brother will be punished. I don't think God punishes us at all."

"Oh, that's OK," he said. "Thanks for your contribution anyhow."

Joel

In bed with Susan. We have never made love like this before: so perfectly unhurried, at rest in motion; staying with the glow of the beginning, not driven to fan it to full flame. Later we trace each other's features with our fingers, dreaming each other up. The room is completely, stunningly dark. Then we are quiet, and the silence congeals into a question. I don't imagine that it can be answered, so it's really a thought. It's a terrible thought. At first I don't dare to say it. But then I risk it.

"Susan?"

"Yes?"

"I read this thing once about demons in the astral realm, that they can take on any form . . . I know it's probably nonsense, but I was thinking . . . let's say you died before me . . . and then, when I died, you would come to me."

"Yes."

"How would I know it was you and not a demon? How could I tell?"

Without a moment's hesitation, she replies: "I would love you."

Stefan

Shortly after you died, I had an extraordinarily lifelike dream in which you and I were in a garden surrounded by ivy-covered walls. We talked about your suicide. You said you hadn't jumped but had *fallen* from the window. I reminded you that you had said something very similar in the hospital.

"I don't remember the first time," you said. "It's a complete blank. I remember being crippled but not how it happened. But the second time I remember very clearly, and I'm telling you, it was an accident."

"I find that hard to believe," I said. "You don't get pushed out of a window once and then fall out of another one by accident."

You shrugged dismissively. That gesture amazed me. How unchanged you were! I asked you if you had any company. Now your speech and gestures became evasive. There were people, you said, but you didn't have much to do with them. I suddenly felt afraid for you and cried out: "Stefan, what about your surroundings? This garden, the smell of the grass, the ivy . . . I hope you're not ignoring it!" The moment I spoke, I knew it was a mistake.

You were very irritated. "Who are your teachers?" you asked.

I tried to answer your question honestly. It seemed that the particular teaching I was trying to impart to him came from people like Alan Watts and (this embarrassed me) Timothy Leary, and maybe, peripherally, from Krishnamurti. You said: "You stick to your teachers, I'll stick to mine," and began to withdraw, very characteristically, with a pained and angry expression on your face. I shouted something after you (just as typically), trying to shake you out of your set way. You walked to the wall and began to dissolve and rise up and over the wall, leaving in your stead a large butterfly or moth that fluttered along the ivy.

■

Alma had a similar experience. You appeared to her in her sleep and said, "Stop trying to help me, I prefer to work with Joel," and abruptly disappeared.

That made me happy. I thought I had lost you after we met in the garden.

After telling me the dream, Alma asked me: "What do you do that I don't do?"

"I send him feelings of love and confidence that he's OK."

"I don't have that confidence," she said. "I'm just begging for a sign that his suffering is over."

■

A few weeks later I had another remarkable dream. I was sitting on a beach surrounded by loud, cheerful bathers. Suddenly I saw you standing up to your knees in the water, wearing bathing trunks, looking at me. The ocean surrounding you was ablaze with that scintillating brilliance that sometimes burns on it just before sunset. I called out your name, and just as suddenly as you had appeared, you vanished. I started walking into the water. "He must have gone under," I told myself: "I'll take a look." I walked on until the water rose up over my head. Then, looming toward me out of the dark, out of the depth of the sea, came a whale; it veered and slid past me, fixing me briefly with a small, brilliant, humorous eye, and propelled itself back into darkness with a sudden sweep of its stupendous tail, which swung past just short of destroying me. Yet I felt no fear, just a quick, high-hearted exhilaration.

Duet for One

C. Well-done, my friend.

> He lifts the invisible cloak from my shoulders. It was there all along, so light that I no longer felt it. But now it's as if a large weight had been pressing me down, like ballast. I rise. Not as a man would rise from his desk, more like a bubble. No, not even that. I float, disembodied, a thought without form in a landscape of thought.

C. Without form? How can that be, since I see you?

> There he is. He looks just as he did when we met face-to-face for the first time, a Chinese sage with a long wispy beard, wearing a pale ochre robe with wide sleeves and blue canvas slippers. He produces a brush from his left sleeve and sketches the outlines of a park into the space surrounding us: leafy trees and a pond in a wide sunlit meadow. A little schematic, but lifelike enough to walk in. I feel the coolness of grass and soil under my soles. I suppose he painted me too. Looking down at myself, I see a white shirt with hands, blue jeans, and bare feet for some reason. My face, of course, is invisible to me.

Well-done yourself, Counterpoint.

C. Thank you.

Why is there no path?

C. Because we don't know where we're going.

> As we walk, the trees nearest us slowly turn on their axis. It's altogether very lifelike.

C. If you wish, we can put in more detail.

Yes, let's.

> He fills in the tree shapes with leaves and shadows, and paints their reflections in the water.

C. More?

Sure, why not.

> He darkens a broad swathe of green near the opposite shore, beneath a large weeping willow. A fish leaps. The little "plop" widens out into stillness. We walk in silence alongside the pond.

Something has changed, Counterpoint. It seems a miracle. When did we ever walk together like this?

C. Never before.

It reminds me of something . . . Stefan! Those dreams I had of him in the mid-eighties. He would have been nearly forty then. What would he have been like? Holed up in some mental ward, most likely. Medicated, beleaguered by demons. But he didn't allow it. He saw his future. Imagine concluding your life like that, in perfect lucidity, at the age of twenty-seven. After blessing his mother, pardoning her for giving birth to such suffering.

I haven't praised him enough.

I'm crying. My grief is for myself as well. I too thought my life was misbegotten.

Dear Stefan. I haven't mourned you enough.

C. You buried him in your heart.

Can one water a grave with tears? Does new life spring from that?

C. Most certainly it does. But go on. You were recalling those dreams.

Yes. In those dreams he was the age he was when I had last seen him. Preternaturally real dreams, realer than real.

Each time it began in the same way, with small variations. We would be walking together, much the way we are here, talking about some ordinary thing, or riding in a car with friends—doing nothing special, in short, just being together. It seemed so natural! "Simple and right," as he wrote in his journal notes on Cézanne.

All of a sudden I would realize that something was wrong, or rather wonderfully right, impossible and yet undeniably true. Was I dreaming? I would touch him, grasp his shoulder, his wrist.

"Stefan!"

He would look at me with an enigmatic smile.

"You're alive!"

"Of course."

Then I would wake up and realize that I had been dreaming. But had I? He was so real! A sense of his presence would stay with me for a while and gradually fade, until I could no longer feel it.

Then, a week or two later, I would dream him again, always alive, and not just alive but healthy and sane. Always the dream would culminate with the conviction that I had witnessed, truly witnessed, the resurrection of the dead.

The last time, he was eating a bowl of soup. Eating! With appetite! There was the miracle again. Then he washed the empty bowl, thanked me (evidently I had served him), and walked toward the door.

"Stefan!"

He turned his head. A tremendous emotion welled up in me. I wanted him to see, to acknowledge, the miracle of his restoration. But before I could speak, he said: "It's true, I'm alive. So are you. Let's move on."

I've dreamt of him since, but never again with such clarity and power.

C. He moved on.

> We walk on in silence, slowly. And slowly, the landscape is changing. Here and there, on the grass and in templelike structures of stone and of wood, I see women and men, alone and in groups, in attitudes of contemplation and prayer. Some are sitting cross-legged. Others kneel. One man touches the ground with his forehead. Three women in white robes stand with their hands raised above their heads, looking up at the cloudless sky.

Something about this scene bothers me, Counterpoint.

C. I know. It's kitsch. So are my whiskers, my wise, puckered smile. But I think I'll keep those. Do you want more reality?

I want truth.

C. At all costs?

Yes. What else did we put that bird in the thousand-eyed tree for?

C. Agreed.

He dips his brush in the pond and paints everything over; covers the ground and the grass, the temples and the worshipers with the color of water; and widens and deepens and rounds that luminous clarity into the form of a sphere. There it hovers in space, and would be space itself if I did not stand apart from it, and if my field of vision didn't extend beyond its quivering edges.

What is this, Counterpoint?

No answer. He's cleaning his brush with a long willow leaf. Now he puts it back inside his sleeve.

I think it's a bubble.

He sits down on the grass, his palms resting on his thighs. His silences no longer puzzle me.

It's a strange way to end a book, Counterpoint.

No answer. He looks different now, somehow feminine. Like a grandmother. Is he male or female? I can't tell.

A bubble. But vast. The world as a bubble, a bubble as a world. Would it burst if I touched it? There it is, an echo of the old fear.

I see streaming colors on its surface. Those colors are feelings, I notice. And the feelings are memories—or imaginings, I'm not sure which. But within its colorless depths . . . a picture. Three people at a table, a longhaired, bearded man and two women. It's a painting, actually, lit and composed a little like Han van Meegeren's *Christ at Emmaus,* that astonishing forgery that for seven years was worshiped by the art world as a sublime Vermeer. It's beautiful, as I imagine van Meegeren's painting must be: a portrait not only of bodies in an environment (a kitchen with a simple wooden table and chairs, on the table a pitcher and a bowl full of fruit), but of one of those sacred moments when time is arrested, and thought, astonished and humbled, comes to a halt before the unknown. Except the raised hand of Christ in my picture is holding a lit marijuana joint. He's about to take a drag, and— oh dear, I asked for it. The moment of truth. I'd rather not go there.

C. You don't have to. Not yet. All you need to do is remember.

That I can do. It was the spring of '82, eleven years after my breakdown in London, nine years after Stefan's death. I was house-sitting in a bungalow belonging to people I didn't know, alone except for the birds in the garden, but I wasn't very conscious of those because I was writing an introduction to a collection of stories by Robert Musil and feeling like a huckster passing off cut glass as diamonds. Translating literature of this order of greatness is always, at best, a successful act of forgery, and there were no van Meegerens in that collection. So I was uncomfortable with myself, and the writing came hard. On weekends Susan joined me. Gina was on her first big adventure away from home, a trip to Israel.

I suffered a terrible defeat in that house.

C. And then a great victory.

Yes, I'd much rather talk about that. I thought the still pond was a lovely image of it.

C. Too lovely. But don't let me stop you. Go on.

Our friend Claire came to visit, and brought some marijuana. Susan didn't smoke, but I did.

I had stopped smoking dope in 1971, because just a toke of grass could trigger the endless nightmare again, and because even without dope, any hint of a breach in the predictable order of things, especially those odd moments of déjà vu that everyone knows and no two people, to my knowledge, have ever shared, had the devastating effect of a message from hell dropped on my doorstep, special delivery, letting me know once again that for me there could be no salvation.

I learned to believe. Instead of attempting to reason my way out of the labyrinth—the tried-and-true way of losing myself in it forever, again—I would throw myself onto the mercy of God. Belief was my savior. The mere gesture of prayer canceled the horrible conviction that I was the Only One. Sometimes the release was instantaneous, an upward shuddering exodus through my shoulders and the top of my head; at other times, when my faith was less clear, it took longer.

My partnership with God became surer with practice. As soon as the Fear raised its head, I would ask for His help. Who else could help me? This was no ordinary threat, it spoke of eternal damnation. And God never failed me. I can't describe the gratitude of those moments.

Once the danger was gone, I would thank Him silently, passionately in my heart, and sometimes out loud, if I was alone.

After a while the intensity of the attacks diminished. Eventually I could shrug them off unassisted. And then they stopped, and I no longer felt any need to pray.

In the spring of '72, I was charmed by a popular song with a line that felt blessedly true: "These are the good old days." I was cured.

And now, ten years later, this friend drew a joint from her purse, lit it, took a long drag, and passed me the joint—just like the good old days. Why not? It seemed impolite to refuse the offer. I took a drag. We talked, we laughed, I welcomed the familiar pleasures of grass, the softened friendliness and relaxation, the heightened tactility, the sensuous winding turns of thought, the dance of intervals between sounds. Then I heard a ringing buzz in my ears, and then . . . and then the mind began to remember . . . and that memory was knowledge . . . and the knowledge was fear . . . and the fear manifested itself as a fine rapid quivering in my hands, my chest, my legs . . . because it had always begun like this—with the memory that it had always begun with a memory of remembering precisely this—and what was this terribly familiar thing? And so I fell back into the hell of eternal recurrence, and it was as if nothing, nothing had changed, and in a way it was worse than it had ever been, because this time Susan was with me. I had never fallen into the Fear in her presence. I had come to the conclusion that it was impossible, that her love banished demons. And now it had happened. That gave the Fear a new quality, one of terrible risk, not just doom. I could infect her! But in risk there is freedom. She had no idea, because I had to hide my condition from her, lest she go down in flames with me. That's just a metaphor, of course. My hell was neither hot nor cold. It was made of thought, and the body that suffered in it was the mental body, the body of thought itself.

But love is not thought, and I saw that. Her gaze saved me, without her knowing it. Her love and my courage. Is there a difference between love and courage? They are inseparable. Our mutual gaze held open a door through which I could leave the house of my fear. It didn't take long.

Claire was embarrassed: "Oh, you lovebirds."

When Susan and Claire left to go back to the city, Claire asked me if I would like a couple of joints to tide me over.

"Just one," I said.

I don't know why I said that.

C. For the sake of love. For the sake of courage. It was your way of preparing for battle.

What a paradox, though. The battle was won by surrender.

C. It's best not to name it.

All the armies were on the enemy's side. I had nothing.

C. Than that nothing no greater weapon exists.

And you were that enemy, weren't you? How can that be?

C. It's not so mysterious. You were transformed by surrender (now that you've called it that, but the word is misleading), and I by discourse with you in the making of this book.

Who are you, then?

C. Who are *you*? Isn't that the essential question? Our crow is still asking it faithfully on your behalf.

You forbade him to answer it. What's the point?

C. The point is That to which the word "I" always points.

I . . . I . . .

> With a nod he indicates the bubble. The holy pot-smoker and the two women have been replaced by a new picture: the same Jesus-like man alone in a barren, storm-whipped landscape, clutching a small, shining jewel to his breast. But it's not the same painter. Caravaggio maybe, or Tiepolo. Wild chiaroscuro effects. The man's hair and beard are white and disheveled, and his eyes are slightly crossed. Wrapped into the curling shapes of the storm clouds are wraithlike figures that appear to be reaching for the jewel. But the picture offers a trompe-l'oeil effect. With a slight shift of the viewer's perspective, the ghouls become radiant angels streaming forth from the man's heart, or maybe his solar plexus, with beatific expressions, bearing gifts of light to some unseen recipients outside the picture.

More kitsch, Counterpoint?

> No answer.

The guy looks like Job. Or God. I think I know what that's about.

■ ■ ■

I woke up as Joel. Susan and Claire were back in the city. I made myself breakfast and returned to my Musil essay. And then I decided . . . no, I did no such thing. It decided itself. I stood up and went to the windowsill where I had left the joint Claire had given me. I don't know what I had in mind when I lit it. Surely not to consign myself to eternal hell once again. What was I thinking?

C. That you could not accept defeat. That if you didn't see this through, the horror would visit you again on your deathbed. And you were right. Given those prospects, you had no choice. As for me, your decision—let's call it that— took me by surprise. It was the first time you had approached me head-on, instead of panicking at the first sign of my presence. In a way I was glad. It promised to be a contest, for once. No cringing and gulping (those gulps always brought out my deepest contempt), no whines of "Why?" and "Please, not again!" And you didn't pray either. I don't know how you found that particular escape hatch. Too late for your brother, alas, it might have helped him, but I didn't care about that then. I resented your prayers. We had a ten-year stalemate, quite dull for me, moderately pleasant for you. You thought yourself "cured," but it wasn't so. You were still haunted, just not as threatened. Then Claire invited you to a little smoke. That was my opportunity. You were so hurt, so shocked by my return, it didn't even occur to you to pray. But Susan was there, her love held the door open for you. That's all that prayers do, they hold the door open for love—no minor miracle when you're in hell.

So now you came walking in through that door, and it took me by surprise. I didn't know how to respond—an odd moment for a Counterpoint. But it interested me. You wandered out into the garden carrying a pen and a notebook, sat down under an apple tree, and began writing. Not about Robert Musil but about the catastrophe that had befallen you the day before. How could it happen? Why were you still not immune to this insane belief? And then, so foolishly: "I must get to the bottom of it."

I couldn't let that go unanswered. "There is no bottom," I said.

"But there is," you said. "There's that than which nothing worse can be imagined. I've been there."

"Oh, but you haven't. Every hell is a pre-hell, and the mind is inventive. Don't you remember?"

And you did. Down you went, step by step, point by counterpoint, into the abyss. All the while, you were in the garden. It was the garden of the beginning. There was the apple tree, and I, the serpent, was winding my way through your brain. No Eve in sight.

And God?

C. Don't you remember? You called him.

Adam called God.

C. Yes: "Where art thou?" Not with that phrase, of course, but with wordless urgency. It wasn't prayer. It wasn't the heart's listening cry for love. It was thought screaming into the void and hearing not even an echo. Your faith was crushed. You could no longer stand. You crawled on the grass like a wounded animal, moaning.

But you never begged for death. Is that not remarkable? You were willing to countenance eternal torment but not the collapse of the house of your fear. Because that house was the world, and you were the one who had built and sustained it. Your being was its substance; your thought, its duration; your suffering, its redemption. You were its parent. How could you kill it?

Oh, but I was tempted.

C. Just for a moment. You buried the thought almost instantly. Like a seed.

Where?

C. In some furrow of your exhausted brain. That night, in your dreams, the thought sprouted and burgeoned. By the morning, it was in full bloom.

I didn't notice.

C. But I did. A few hours later, the fruit was ripe, and I offered it to you. You certainly recognized it then! But we're running ahead of events. Why don't you tell this part of the story?

Gladly. When I woke up, my whole body was trembling. Yet instead of fear, I felt an almost buoyant contentment. That in turn alarmed me. It was too strange. I took a shower, thinking the water would settle my agitation. It didn't. I performed a series of Yoga exercises in the garden. The sun was shining, its warmth should have softened whatever tension my muscles were holding. Even Sarvasana, which is designed to put the body into a state of deep relaxation, didn't stop the trembling. I sat up, folded my legs in the half lotus, placed one palm on top of the other in my lap, closed my eyes, and looked inward.

The trembling was a current, a constant rapid upward streaming. It wasn't just in my skin and muscles. I could feel it in my eyes. It occurred to me that I might be burning, but it was a heatless fire.

"Poor body," I thought. "Poor self. Poor son of man."

Those words startled me. The trembling grew finer, more rapid.

"Today I'll win," I thought. "Today I'll conquer." I was sure of it, and amazed that I could be so sure.

I still had the unsmoked half of the joint Claire had left me, enough for my purpose. I would smoke it after breakfast. But that wasn't necessary. You came of your own accord. "No end in sight, my friend." You called me your friend then already. It didn't sound friendly.

C. Nor did your response: "What do you want?" As if through a bolted door.

That's not surprising. To me, you were the Devil. What surprises me is my politeness. Why didn't I bolt the door a second and third time? Why didn't I tell you to go to hell? I treated you as if you were my neighbor, the one we are enjoined to love as our self. Which of course you were, but how could I know that then?

C. You knew. But go on with your story. Let these be your memories, not mine.

"I want your truth," you said, in response to my question. "Your truth is my meat." And as I heard the word "meat" I saw a set of bared fangs—of a wolf, I suppose. I had never seen you in any form. Those fangs terrified me.

I offered you substitutes: truisms, articles of faith, all of them second- and third-hand. You weren't interested. It was my truth you wanted.

I ran out of words. But I felt my spine as a vertical column, and that was some kind of an answer. Then it was as if I could see my spine, and it wasn't a column but a sword. Tall, broad, double-edged. What a mighty fist must be grasping it like that! The tapering point of it was encircled by a crown, which, I suppose, was my skull.

At this there was a movement where you were—a withdrawal it seemed, out and away from me. Now, in the memory, it looks like the long, slow sweep of an outgoing tide—away, but in all directions, not just through the field of vision—which in any case was empty: I saw nothing. The center, where I was, was still. I don't know if the trembling had stopped or continued. All my attention was on that receding circumference and on the still center, where I was. And then a thought came, a single, shining, treacherous thought:

"Now or never."

Treacherous because it was barbed, like a hook, with futurity. Desire leapt out after it and was immediately, painfully, caught by a promise: of a fulfillment that would last through time. That's when the tide turned. The attack began, as it always did, with the horrified recognition that recognition had always been the beginning; that "yes" and "no" were the first ticktock steps in an endless series; that no defense was possible because every thought, including the thought of defense, was a ploy in the enemy's plans. Even the thought of surrender was futile before the implacable interrogation:

"Who surrenders to whom?"

Always the same hope-strangling argument: that I was you and you were I, one deathless mind dedicated to the most merciless self-laceration, a world-torment that was inflicted on countless beings, past, present, and future, but had its source in the brain of one particular man, myself; and that I, for that reason, despite my apparent multiplicity, was the only One, beside whom there could be no other.

Except God.

The word itself came as a savior. How could I have forgotten? There it stood in the firmament of hell as the name of That which could not be known or imagined but nonetheless knew me and loved me and was stronger than any conceivable enemy. At the same moment, you spoke·

"The God you can name is a creature of thought."

"Even so," I said, "I believe in him. What's more, he believes in me."

"Children do that with their toys," you said.

"And you?" I said. "Are you not a creature of thought?"

"I am mind itself," you said. "I am the snake that eats its own tail. So are you. But since you think it your duty to redeem the evil you authored, the tail's lot naturally falls to you."

I sent up a prayer, the heart-cry of a child to its parent: "Help me!"

"You can do that," you said, "and it will bring you relief for a while—a day, a decade, a lifetime, an aeon—but what you call 'evil' will be meted out—to the world if not to you. How could it be otherwise?"

I didn't respond, because I believed you. You continued your disquisition. My proxy god was a hollow fiction, you said. Faith was another matter, respectable in a way, it had some limited efficacy as an instrument of retardation. For a day, a decade, a lifetime, an aeon, I could imagine myself to be human and mortal. But then eternity would reclaim me. Didn't I know it well enough by now, I who had planned it all from the beginning?

"Sooner or later," you said, "you will succumb to despair, and then the horror will properly begin—for yourself or the world, the choice is yours. But no more half measures. What you have seen so far have been previews, announcements. Aren't you tired of this dance of delays?"

As I listened, frozen with fear, I retreated into my body, which was still seated in the contemplative posture I had learned from Chao Khun. I was surprised by the stillness I found there, and the clarity. How simple and strong this empty form was, compared with the mental wrangling still in progress at the periphery of my attention. And the emptiness was suffused with a subtle sweetness. In the midst of my terror I felt cradled in gentleness. I must have been smiling.

Then the choice you had proposed to me revealed itself in all its enormity: I could purchase for myself a bliss as exquisite as the hell I had prepared for myself, simply by abandoning the world to its suffering. That suffering might increase exponentially throughout eternity, but I wouldn't know it, because my happiness would render me ignorant of all other beings forever. Why did you make that offer, Counterpoint?

C. So that you would refuse it. And to stir up the plot.

But there was power in that refusal. That couldn't have been in your interest. Power to banish the alternative as well. One unequivocal NO for both ends of the bargain: no eternal salvation, no everlasting curse. No God and no Devil. No final judgment, no cosmic balance sheet, no inexpugnable debt, no payment at all. No scapegoat or sacrificial lamb, no redemption of sin by the torture of an innocent. That NO filled immensity and I saw that it was my faith, because it took shape before me as a rock, just as it is imaged in the old Christian hymns. Except this rock hovered in space, like the great rock in Magritte's painting, and it was a bright, golden yellow. Such a strange moment. Like a masterful move in a game of chess, the supremely insolent kind that invites the opponent to defeat himself, and gives him no choice in the matter. But who was the player who advanced that rock? I had nothing to do with it.

C. That's not entirely true. We may be pawns in the game, but we are its player as well.

You, too, a pawn?

C. No choice.

And just one player?

C. Just one. The self of all selves, the one everyone points to as "I"—so confidently, with a stiff index finger—straight at the heart, as a rule.

Are you saying that the many selves are, in each case, a case of mistaken identity?

C. Yes. There is only one self, and it does not know itself as "I." How could it? "I" is an other. Always. And because the one self doesn't know itself, it does not, for itself, exist. So the self of all selves is no-self.

Thank you. That is a helpful distinction. Because when I thought that I was the Maker . . .

C. You suffered. Being a world-self, you suffered hugely. But you suffered, as all selves suffer, from self. Self is a lie that suffers from truth-deprivation. The truth is that we are nothing-at-all.

Then the move "you" made in response to "mine" . . .

C. . . . was nobody's doing.

I can only admire it. The rock exploded without a sound. Pulverized particles sped in all directions. I was defeated, demolished—so totally, there was no room for any thought or emotion. Or rather, there was only room, and then a stunned recognition. Of what? Of emptiness, of space, of boundlessness, of freedom. But these words come too readily, and they're tainted with knowledge. "Recognition"—it sounds as if I had come upon something previously known and forgotten. It's the wrong word, but I have no other. What was recognized was not known and not knowable. That is why, when I picked up the pen and the paper that had been lying in the grass next to me all the while, I wrote only fragments of thoughts that canceled themselves in mid-sentence. Except for one that was short enough to reach completion:

NOTHING EXISTS

And there's another one, crossed out, I guess for not saying it right, but maybe a clue to the nature of the happiness I felt for days afterward:

Joy to the world!

Still, I'm puzzled. What happened?

C. Nothing happened. Truly nothing! You sat in the garden. The sky was blue, the grass was green, birds were chirping, the sun shone. A tiny insect leaped off your finger.

That wasn't nothing!

C. It was nothing disporting itself as a flea—no minor event, I'll grant you.

Somehow it blew me wide open.

C. That's true. When the rock burst, the walls of your prison went with it, but you were still frozen in an attitude of confinement. That flea broke the spell. No hesitation! No what-ifs, no tentative dipping of toes in the ocean of space. He jumped right in. Complete reliance on the great being in whose bosom he lived and leaped, and who would eventually crush him. A hero of faith! How could you not be fired by his example! And he was a teacher, to boot. In an instant faster than thought, you saw that your brother's leap to his death and your own slow fall through time (which is not slow at all, as you've noticed) and this minuscule salto mortale sprang from one source and returned to it. All this and more took place and was gone in an instant. That's why you wrote those words, "NOTHING EXISTS," in firm letters, and underlined them for good measure.

That's an awfully bleak insight, and not one I believe in. Why did it feel like a fulfillment? For days on end?

C. Because what it means is not what it sounds like. And because of the snakes. Don't you remember the snakes?

Yes, in the apple tree, and later that night again in the garden. But first in the tree, slithering in and out of the leaves. The stem, too, was made of black writhing snakes. I wasn't afraid. In fact I was delighted. I was tempted to make the whole garden reptilian, but something held me back, and the tree reverted to being a tree. Another apparition! I laughed, because what is a tree unless someone sees it as such? I was so happy afterwards, I didn't know what to do with myself. I played the guitar and sang. I whooped and hollered. I called Susan at her office and told her I'd never been happier and couldn't say why, and she said it made her happy to hear it but was I on something, and I said no, nothing at all, which was true. I went for a run and laughed as I ran. I came home and tried to write about Musil and found it impossible. I put on a record of Bach cantatas, and just as the chorus sang *"Gott der Herr ist Sonn' und Schild"* the setting sun appeared in the window and I stared into that burning shield until the music ended and my face was wet with tears. That night I couldn't sleep. There was so much energy, I had to move. So I danced, first in the house, then in the garden. Without music, just silently in the moonlight (trusting no neighbor would look out his window). After whirling around for a while I got

tired and stood still. And again, there were snakes. My inner self was still dancing: streams of energy, sinuous, undulant forms, lighter than the ones in the
tree earlier, but still, when I looked at them closely, I saw them as snakes. I tried
to follow their movement with my fingers and limbs, but it was impossible. I
can feel them now, faintly. As if by recalling them I invoked them. What do
they have to do with "Nothing exists"?

C. There's a snake in that sentence. Not in the words exactly, but in the meaning. The meaning wriggles. Let the head be the tail. Don't you see it? You did
then. Like this:

EXISTING IS WHAT NOTHING DOES.

That is the music you danced to.

> Suddenly I feel the soles of my bare feet. There's grass underneath. This is
> not the garden of memory, it's the park my Counterpoint built, or what's
> left of it since he painted the bubble. He's standing next to me, aiming his
> brush at something in the distance. No, it's close by: it's the bubble, floating
> in space, so transparent it's almost invisible. Now he's painting a circle in the
> air. Or else he's tracing the edge of the bubble. It is expanding. It must be
> far away after all, because its widening circumference is approaching the lim-
> its of my field of vision, and yet it is nowhere near where I could touch it.
> Not that I want to. Even though it's a mind bubble, wholly artificial, and
> even though I know it can never burst except at the dictate of my pen,
> I am concerned for this delicate figment as if it were a world, and I, not
> my Counterpoint, were its maker, and had pledged to hold and sustain it
> until the end of time. But it's an illusion that either of us made it. We
> don't even make the words we use.
>
> Should I banish this shadow of my old fear? Dismiss it at least from these
> pages? Or should I honor it as a totem of the tremendous Unknown which
> swallowed me into its depths and then spat me out, miraculously unscathed,
> like some seabird's egg deposited on the beach?
>
> Now I can no longer see the edge of the bubble. And because its color is
> perfectly clear, the bubble itself is no longer visible. Neither is my
> Counterpoint.

Are you gone?

C. Not gone. Just shedding my skin.

And I no longer feel the grass under my feet. It's because I'm back at my desk in Brooklyn. I've been here all along, of course, writing, remembering, imagining. Listening. For years. But it's different now. I'd be hard put to say what the difference is, though. Maybe just this: that I'm here entirely. No ghostly vapors of past selves, no ancient questions begging an answer.

Except for one, perhaps: What of the crow in the thousand-eyed tree and his impossible question? I sought him out a few nights ago. I didn't exactly set out to do that, it came to me, but still, I was searching. I was sitting at my desk, not writing, not reading, not thinking, just sitting. The lights were dimmed. Gradually I settled into stillness. My eyes closed. Thoughts came and went, images, the kind that slide past the mind's eye on the threshold of sleep. But I was awake, and the stillness deepened and widened and became somehow luminous, a soft steady glow like the light of a candle in an empty room. A room without walls, and the source of the light was not separate from the space it pervaded. Suddenly the emptiness congealed into an image: of a tree. It stood very close, actually inside me. Or maybe it's more accurate to say that for that moment the tree was my body. I immediately thought of the crow. I looked for him in the crown of the tree. He wasn't there. But someone else was. It was me, looking for him. Naturally I didn't see myself. How could I have? Any self that I see is an other.

I guess I have no questions after all.

Except maybe for this one:

Counterpoint, what did you mean when you said you were shedding your skin?

C. I meant this book.

Oh. And where will I find you after it's done?

C. Never where you seek. Always where you are.

Always?

No answer.

How still it is all of a sudden. Out of the stillness, sounds: a car passing slowly, softly, outside, on wet asphalt . . . a tinkle of chimes in a neighbor's garden . . . an airplane drawing a furrow through the night sky . . . gentle, caressing sounds. There are other, harsher sounds elsewhere, I know, and lovelier ones too, and countless actual and possible worlds as well, heavens and hells. They don't frighten or lure me from here, where I am. But who is this "I"? Seeking out the one who is asking this question—not the body, not the lips and tongue that shape the words, not any other being bearing the name of "I," but whatever resides behind the deep, obscure, sense of "I"-ness itself—I find only the happy impossibility of finding anything but clear, open space for a world to appear in: at the moment, a small, cluttered office room in an apartment in Brooklyn. A moth is fluttering against the window, driven and drawn by the light on my ceiling. And there, seemingly behind the moth, is my reflection: a white-haired man at his desk, holding a pen in two hands, gazing at me with an inquisitive, faintly surprised expression.

Coda

Last Friday Susan and I drove upstate to spend a long weekend at a lakeside inn we had heard of. I was not in the mood for traveling. I was tired from several nights of wrestling with my Counterpoint, and since Susan doesn't drive, I would have to sit at the wheel all the way to Aurora. And then traffic conspired against us. A friend had told us it was a four-and-a-half-hour drive from Manhattan. It was an eight-and-a-half-hour drive from Brooklyn. Not until we inched our way off the George Washington Bridge onto the Palisades Parkway did we pick up normal speed.

Somewhere past Monroe, Susan put on a tape of Pinchas Zukerman and Midori playing Bach's double violin concerto, and everything changed. Until then, I had barely noticed the splendor of the day, just enough to compel a muttered acknowledgment of the "great weather." Now I noticed the golden splashes in the sunlit green all around us, and the red stains in the sky that deepened and widened as we moved north. Like an echo to this slow crescendo of color, each one of the many large and small fish-shaped clouds floating over the hills began to burn orange, and that light in turn modeled their shapes with such clear-edged distinction that they looked carved. The road veered away from this perfect, almost too perfect landscape, taking us with it around a hill, slowly, slowly, and as the hill turned, new scenery slid into view, partly composed of the props we had just seen, but newly arranged and with new astonishing shapes and colors.

"We believe, we believe!" I said.

But the beauty was unrelenting. With each leisurely twist of the road, new marvels appeared. I remember a few of them: a group of shivering poplars next to a stream, like a holy family; some cows on a far-off field, scattered like petals on a lawn; a pale green sky spliced by five broad shafts of gold from the setting sun; and for some reason I still see very clearly one particular soot-colored, squarish, wooly-edged cloud. Meanwhile Zukerman and Midori had reached the last movement of their concerto. Each time I hear it, there comes a moment when something inside wants to burst through the confines of skin, until I remember that we are already made of radiant matter and that we can dance in pure space without moving, like stars, and need not explode to do so. And much later, after the music had ended—we had been driving silently in the hum of the motor for a while—there came that moment when day-force and night-force are in equilibrium and all the colors come to full bloom, like flowers on the verge of wilting. The horizon was a long, loosely twisted braid of sunlit wheat, with the red sun set upon it like a stupendous jewel on a golden belt. Above, a wash of, not beige and not yellow or brown, though these colors approach it from various sides, but exactly sepia, as in Renaissance prints and vintage photographs. And above that a glowing effusion of powdery rose, and set against that, with sharp contours, like printed letters, the elegant forms of three hawks in slow circling motion.

"After this it gets boring," I said.

But it didn't. It got better and better. The night-force has colors the day never dreamed of, and colors are meanings. Has anyone ever thought of a drive-in movie consisting solely of one perpetually changing scene, without actors, without any plot except for the drama of light descending the spectrum from yellow and orange to the dark blues and purples of night? Of course not, no audience would put up with it for five minutes. You'd have to take them by surprise, hold them captive in their cars, and show them, show them. And still there'd be people for whom clouds in the night sky are nothing but badly lit condensation, who'd go home dissatisfied with their day and wanting their money back.

It was dark when we arrived at the Aurora Inn. We ate a light dinner. Susan suggested going for a walk, but I was too tired, so we went to bed. We talked for a while about my last chapter.

"It's the end of the book," I said, "but I still think it needs something to round it off, like a coda."

"Don't make it too metaphysical," she said.

She fell asleep before me. I lay for a while worrying about my conclusion. Then I listened to the crickets chanting in the garden. And then I was gone.

We both woke up early. It was dawn in Aurora. We decided to have a look at the lake.

Some of the gardens on Lake Cayuga are separated by fences. Each fence, being a fence, says "thou shalt not cross" over and over all the way down the length of the lawn until about fifteen feet from the lake, at which point the fence changes its mind so completely that it stops being a fence and becomes a passageway. Then it remembers itself and resumes its fence-life until it comes to a natural end at the edge of the lake. We approached the lacuna, the non-fence, and were about to cross what we took to be the non-boundary when my glance fell on a bronze plaque affixed to a tree: "Private Property." What to do? Impulse warred with restraint, right with wrong. I performed the ambulatory equivalent of a stutter. Susan, who didn't grow up in East Germany, simply walked on. I followed.

After crossing a few more gardens with impunity, I felt at ease. We sat down on a bench and listened to the waves lapping the shore. I breathed in the freshness of the morning and noticed how grateful my lungs were. The water, though ruffled, was clear. I saw pebbles and wavering plants at the bottom, and noticed the absence of garbage. Across the lake, I saw houses and gardens and soft swelling hills with patches of woodland and yellow and brown fields.

"I just realized what my book is about," I said.

"Only now?"

"Yes. I didn't know it before. It's about crossing borders."

"I thought it was about coming home."

"It is. It's about exile and homecoming. About getting lost and finding the way back."

"And *not* finding the way back, like Stefan," she said.

"Yes. But I don't believe anyone's permanently lost. I don't think it's possible. Remember that line from Novalis I started with?"

"Not exactly."

"*Where are we going? Always homeward.* God, that sounds sappy in English. This keeps happening: I quote something in German and then find out it can't be said in English."

"Translation," she said. "That's a border crossing too."

"Sometimes," I said. "More often, it's trespassing."

"What do you want, passports? Border guards?"

"Yes, and definite penalties."

She laughed.

"Always homeward," she said. "I like it in English."

"But listen," I said: "*Wo gehen wir denn hin? Immer nach Hause.* That's so much better. He means the mystical home, the place of absolute origin. But instead of saying '*Heimat,*' which would be crudely sentimental, or '*heimwärts,*' which is the same as 'homeward,' kind of fuzzy, he says '*nach Hause.*' That's the most solid sense of home imaginable, a house with four walls. Where are we going? To our house. Prodigal sons and daughters, home to our father's house. And then there's the rhythm, which is also very definite: 'Immer nach Hause'—dum-da-ra-dum-dum. It's like a mantra."

She tried sounding it out.

"That reminds me of something in Spanish," I said. "It's by Rafael Alberti. He was a friend of my stepfather's. I think they met in Spain during the civil war. I never met him. But I read a book of his when I was fifteen. It was called Marinero en tierra, sailor on land, and in it was this little thing, I think it's one of the most perfect poems ever written, a real miracle:

> El mar. La mar. El mar.
> Siempre la mar!

Now, this you definitely can't say in English: 'The sea, the sea, the sea, always the sea!' Not the same thing! El mar is the sea alright, it's what meets your eye when you go to the beach or wake up in your hammock on board a ship, the big blue thing that is always there with its changing faces. La mar: that's the sea, too, but it's the mythical sea, the mother of all beings, the ocean. El mar. La mar. El mar. That's the surf! You can actually hear it! And each pound of the surf is the sea, the whole sea. Period. And again. Period. And again. But the surf doesn't simply repeat itself. It has folded into itself the outer and the inner side of this monster-mother, so it breathes for a while in this patient iambic rhythm, and then it thunders on the beach: Siempre la mar! Always the sea! It's the same number of syllables in English, but hearing it in Spanish: Siempre la mar!"[7]

She heard it. She nodded.

"It's like making love," I said.

"What do you mean?"

"He's not just praising, he's making love to the sea with words. And without a syllable too many. Just ten syllables, but they contain the whole sea."

"That's not what you did," she said. "Hundreds of thousands of words and millions of syllables."

"And not one too many," I said. We both laughed.

"And it contains the whole sea," she said.

I felt so good I just had to throw a stone in the water.

---

7. Actually Alberti's poem is different from the one I remembered—less perfect, because more human, and longer by a few lines. How wonderful that the dreaming unconscious gradually, over the decades, erased the landlocked sailor's lament, leaving only a paean to the eternal sea!

"Yes!" I said.

"But what was it in this poem," Susan asked, "that reminded you of that saying by Novalis?"

"The last line," I said, "the rhythm of it. *Immer nach Hause. Siempre la mar.*"

She thought about that.

"It's not just the rhythm," she said. "They mean the same thing."

I wasn't aware of that until the moment she said it.

Acknowledgments

I wish to acknowledge the help of the Virginia Center for the Creative Arts, Yaddo, and The MacDowell Colony in granting me space and time to write under ideal conditions.

I am deeply grateful to Bill and Mimi Levitt for allowing me to spend several weeks in perfect solitude at their lodge in Utah; I do not believe this work could have found its necessary conclusion anywhere else.

Nor could I have sustained its development through the years without the support I received from my mother- and father-in-law, Hannah and Jules Lemansky. For their kindness and generosity, I cannot thank them enough.

Three spiral-bound notebooks kept by Bruce Brotter in 1969 stayed in my possession after he and I lost touch; his "spontatas" were the inspiration for the passages attributed to "Maxwell Schneider."

I owe special thanks to Carl Lipkin, who listened and commented with great acuteness of mind and sensibility as I read long passages over the phone, and to Maximilian Preisler and Paul De Angelis, who read the book as it evolved and gave me invaluable confirmation and advice along the way.

Erik Wensberg kindly agreed to read the book when it was finished and then did it the inestimable und unsolicited service of examining it in detail with a superb eye for faults and felicities in the language.

John Thomas, my copyeditor, brought a wholly unexpected knowledge of the book's spiritual and psychological terrain to bear on its linguistic fine-tuning.

I am grateful as well to my agent, Martha Kaplan, for holding the book above bottom-line standards and finding just the right publisher for it.

Without Susan, finally, at all times the first proof of my words and their meaning, I would not have returned from the night-sea journey and this account could not have been written.